BURT FRANKLIN: RESEARCH & SOURCE WORKS SERIES 684
American Classics in History and Social Science 181

THE DIARY AND LETTERS

OF

HIS EXCELLENCY

THOMAS HUTCHINSON, Esq.

THOMAS HUTCHINSON.
Governor of Massachusetts.

THE

DIARY AND LETTERS

OF

HIS EXCELLENCY

THOMAS HUTCHINSON, Esq.

CAPTAIN-GENERAL AND GOVERNOR-IN-CHIEF OF
HIS LATE MAJESTY'S PROVINCE OF MASSACHUSETTS BAY,
IN NORTH AMERICA

COMPILED FROM THE ORIGINAL DOCUMENTS STILL REMAINING IN
THE POSSESSION OF HIS DESCENDANTS.

BY

PETER ORLANDO HUTCHINSON

ONE OF HIS GREAT-GRANDSONS.

VOLUME II.

BURT FRANKLIN
NEW YORK

ERRATA.

Page 383, line 5 from the bottom, *for* " second " *read* " third."

" 383, " 3 " " " *for* " property handed " *read* " property probably handed."

Published by LENOX HILL Pub. & Dist. Co. (Burt Franklin)
235 East 44th St., New York, N.Y. 10017
Originally Published: 1884-86
Reprinted: 1971
Printed in the U.S.A.

S.B.N.: 8337-17839
Library of Congress Card Catalog No.: 73-132679
Burt Franklin: Research and Source Works Series 684
American Classics in History and Social Science 181

Reprinted from the original edition in the New York Public Library.

PREFACE.

At the time the first volume of this work was published, I did not think it likely that I should undertake another, and that is why "Vol. I." was not placed on the title-page. Favourable circumstances however have led to the compilation of a second, which absorbs the remainder of Governor Hutchinson's Diary and Letters; and what is equally valuable in a historical point of view, it gives opportunity for introducing portions of the Diary and Letters of the Chief Justice Peter Oliver, a prominent figure in those troublous times, and perhaps as much so as his elder brother the Lieutenant-Governor;—as also of those of his son, and of those of Thomas and Elisha Hutchinson. This work therefore, is the English account of the outbreak and course of the American Revolutionary war, in contradistinction to the American accounts, which have been legion, and which, for reasons not hard to discern, have been industriously and continuously introduced into the cheap popular literature of this country, and put off in Parts or Numbers by travellers or others, and carried to nearly every household for subscribers' names. It is time the English side of the story should be better known.

There is one matter I cannot avoid alluding to, however unwilling I may be to do so. At the foot of page 163 of the former volume, I was induced to throw out a challenge to one or other of the three gentlemen whose names were connected with the discovery in America of part of Governor Hutchinson's Diary, the existence of which copy had never been known or suspected by his descendants in England. In reply to that challenge Dr. Everett called attention to the subject at the annual meeting of the Historical Society at Boston in April 1884: he "commented somewhat on the ignorance of the lives and character of public men in America, displayed in such a charge of surreptitious use of Governor Hutchinson's Diary," and he produced letters to shew that the first volume of the Diary had been freely lent by the Rev. J. Hutchinson to Mr. Everett, the United States Minister in England, whom he met at the dinner table of the Duke of Sutherland at Trentham, with permission "to read," but there is no permission to copy. I am obliged to Dr. Everett for producing at that meeting the two letters of the Rev. J. Hutchinson, and the one by Mr. Everett, because they supply me with the very evidence I stood in need of. They shew that the volume was freely lent and honourably received, which gives me the pleasure of withdrawing all imputation of unfairness on that head, done only in ignorance, and of apologising to Dr. Everett, and to any one else who may have been annoyed thereby. Upon being better informed, I explained myself as shewn in the following letter to Dr. F. E. Oliver, and I hope there can be no offence in quoting it here:—

Old Chancel, Sidmouth, Devon, England, Dec. 5, 1884.

My Dear Sir,

According to promise, and having heard from my cousins, I now proceed to make a few remarks. They join with me in surprise that the Rev. John Hutchinson should have allowed the manuscript to go out of his custody, as he had always enjoined upon us the most jealous care over these papers. I can only account for it by concluding that he reposed the fullest confidence in the honour of a gentleman who held the high position of an Ambassador and representative of a great nation like yours, whom he met at the dinner table of the Duke of Sutherland at Trentham Hall, and that he would not go beyond the permission given him along with the loan. Mr. Everett, in conversation with him, took occasion to express a wish to see some portion of Governor Hutchinson's Diary, to which my cousin assented, and the next day forwarded to him what must have been the first volume, as it is that volume which contains the conversation between George III. and the Governor, a portion, about which Americans had manifested some curiosity. It is a relief to know who gave up the MS., because, for many years past different members of my family have suspected two or three of their friends, as possibly having made use of the opportunities which intimacy afforded, and to have incautiously lent it. Your Ambassador obtained it fairly and honourably, and as far as that goes, I have much pleasure in withdrawing any appearance of unfair implication against any of the three gentlemen before named, and of offering them every apology in my power, if I have aggrieved them by any such appearance. In the Diary and Letters just published, I know I have, at the foot of page 163, thrown out a challenge to the said three gentlemen, begging them, for their own sakes, to grant some explanation, because none of the Governor's family in England had ever known or suspected, that anything had, or could have been copied; nor would they have permitted such a thing, for the simple reason that they intended to reserve it for the pages of a printed book themselves.

My first stay at Blurton, a parish adjoining Trentham on the east, then a Perpetual Curacy, now a Vicarage, extended for several weeks, so long ago as in the autumn of 1833, and I was also much there during the two following years. After my cousin became Canon of Lichfield, and resided there three or four months out of the twelve, I sojourned with him in the Close on several occasions for weeks, if not months at a time, and the subject of the "Hutchinson Papers," or the "American Papers," as they were indifferently called, frequently became a topic of conversation. He often regretted his inability to find leisure to work up a volume out of the materials in his custody, and time went on. He was in residence again during the last quarter of 1864, and I was with him the greater part of the time, his children, and occasionally some of my other cousins, being there also. I then made a proposition, to the effect that I would do the manual labour if he would do the head-work, or in other words, I would be his Secretary or Amanuensis, under his guidance and dictation, if he would resolve to attack the subject in earnest. He was not in good health at the time, and said he had decided on going to Bath about the beginning of May in the next year, to drink the waters and recruit his health, and that if he took the papers with him to that place, which was in a direct line to Sidmouth, and near two-thirds of the way, would I come up the other third and join him, and then go boldly into it? I readily fell in with this plan, and leaving him on the 21st of November, I went S. by W. about 150 miles to Sidmouth, and he soon returned N.W. 20 or 30 to Blurton.

Just before the first of May, 1865, however, I received a summons to come to his funeral, and I attended it at Blurton on the 2nd of that month. Before his death he had expressed a wish that the papers should be handed over to me, so I took them home. Owing to sundry occupations of my own, and the common vice of procrastination, I delayed writing; but during several years, at odd times, I amused myself with unfolding, reading, ironing flat, repairing, arranging according to date, and binding into volumes, the letters and other documents, which were absolutely unintelligible until this was done. All this work had the effect of familiarising me with the materials, so that when I began in earnest, I wrote the volume in fifteen months, and spent two more in going over it a second time, and re-writing several portions, and even skimming it a third time, and felt that if I went over it six times, I could alter with advantage.

Such being the facts, how is it possible that my late cousin knew or suspected that any portion of his prized manuscript book had been, or could have been, copied? or that he would have suffered it, seeing that he was preserving everything to enrich the pages of his own proposed book?

As to the challenge above alluded to, the obliging answer to it as given in the Proceedings of the Massachusetts Historical Society for April to June, 1884, clears up many obscurities, but not all. The lending of the volume was fair and open, but there is a point beyond this which invites attention. There is every permission *to read*, but no permission *to copy*. And my cousin, in his letter of January 7, 1843, (which accompanied the book,) when alluding principally to the pages containing the conversation with the King, uses the words—"*to read them;*" and further down he says—"and therefore am proud to forward *for your perusal* the enclosed." Surely there is no permission here to make any copy, but only to read; and so the Ambassador evidently understood it, for when writing to Mrs. Everett, January 8, he says—"He has sent me to-day, *to read*, a part of his grandfather's private Journal, which has never seen the light." Mr. Rives, his Secretary of Legation, having transcribed so much as was desired, he stamped the act with his approval on the first of February, by appending thereto his sign manual.

Beyond an expression of surprise, I will refrain from making any remark on these facts, preferring to leave them to the judgment of others.

I readily excuse Mr. Rives for his share in the transaction, on the ground that as Secretary, he was merely carrying out the instructions of his superior in office. *Qui facit per alium facit per se*, is an old maxim that well suits the present case. I also have pleasure in exonerating Mr. Bancroft from blame, on the ground that he was in America when the other parties were in England, and could not know what they were doing; and I beg to offer to those two gentlemen every expression of regret for any annoyance I may have caused them.

You are at liberty, of course, to shew this letter to any person you please, and as it is a reply to what has appeared in the Proceedings, I should only be too glad to see it find a place in a future number.

I cannot conclude these remarks without expressing my gratification at the friendly and courteous tone of most of the notices and Reviews of my book in the American Journals, fearing, as I did, that in handling a controversial subject, there might be much to offend, however unwilling I might be to give offence.

I beg to remain, Dear Sir,

Yours faithfully,

Dr. F. E. Oliver. P. O. HUTCHINSON.

Some little time afterwards I received an intimation, as coming from the Officers of the Massachusetts Historical Society—"that Mr. Everett, although he had no written permission to have a copy taken of that portion of the Diary loaned him, it is more than probable that he had a verbal one, or to that effect."

I had not thought of this, and in my rejoinder I said—"I made no remarks on a probable verbal permission to copy, because there is nothing in the printed letters of my late cousin and of Mr. Everett that could lead me to do so, and for this reason the idea did not come across my mind. I simply adjudicated upon the evidence that was before me, and there I left it."

I am sorry I have been so long upon this subject, but having thrown out the challenge, I have been obliged to follow the incidents to their end. After an interval of 42 years, I have traced the mystery to the fountain head. What Mr. Bancroft may have done in America with what was copied in England, does not concern me. Mr. Bancroft has been pretty severely taken to task by me in the first volume, (p. 118,) for his shameful slanders on Governor Hutchinson; but though I blame him freely where I think he deserves it, I love fair play and justice so well, that I will defend him to the utmost of my power where I think he does not.

I beg again to express my full sense of the kind and valuable assistance rendered to me by Dr. F. E. Oliver, during the time this second volume has been in preparation; and I have also to thank Mr. C. G. Hutchinson, ("Hutchinson of Charlestown," p. 386,) for having forwarded to me many useful extracts from the Boston Registers, which have enabled me to fill in gaps, and verify dates in genealogical tables towards the end of the book.

DIARY AND LETTERS

OF

THOMAS HUTCHINSON.

CHAPTER I.

At the end of the former volume we left Governor Hutchinson at Tylney Hall, about five miles from Basingstoke in Hampshire, where, in company with his youngest daughter Margaret, commonly called Peggy, he was enjoying the hospitality of Mr. and Mrs. Welbore Ellis, of Pope's Villa, Twickenham. He had asked, and had obtained, the King's leave to come to England "for six or nine months," flattering himself that by the expiration of the shorter, or at all events of the longer of those two periods, all matters in dispute between the Mother Country and her Colonies would be so far accommodated, as that he should be able to return in peace to his government of Massachusetts, there to enjoy in all time to come, the prosperity and the happiness of the country he loved so well. Double the longest of those periods however had elapsed; yet so far from a settlement, the plot had rather thickened than otherwise: all attempts at conciliation had failed: several fierce and bloody battles by the beginning of 1776 had been fought: Boston was blockaded by a force of from ten to 17,000 Provincials, and every day only seemed to add to the bitterness, and put the possibility of accommodation still further off: yet he persisted in clinging to a forlorn hope of better times—of a happy chance, or a favourable turn—with a simplicity that may now almost surprise us. The motive for his coming to England is not very clearly stated; but the general tenor of his remarks to those members of the government with whom he chiefly came in contact when discussing the probable effects of the Boston Port Bill, the Declaratory, and some other Bills, may suggest that his chief object was to try and get those Acts either repealed or mitigated: but if he had cherished the feeling that he should be able to accomplish either of those ends by personal interviews with the Ministers, it is certain that he had been sadly disappointed. The King, the members of the Cabinet—aye, I may add, the great majority of the English nation, surveyed the position of affairs with an amount of equanimity that shewed how little they realised the gravity of the case. Absent just then from London, the centre of political activity, and staying at a friend's house, the graver topics of conversation in a great measure gave place to such as were of a lighter and more varied character. The story of Sir Robert Walpole and the Princess, here following, is sufficiently pronounced in its accents to startle most readers:—

January 1st. 1776.—The fine weather in the forenoon induced us to walk out; but the afternoon was dull, and the evening rainy. I meet here with Baretti's Travells, and Kempfer's History of Japan, with one or other of which I fill up gaps.

2nd.—After breakfast Mr Ellis gave us a more particular account of Sir Robt Walpole on the death of Geo. I. than I ever heard before, wch he says he had from Sr Robt's own mouth. Everybody considered Spencer Compton as the Minister, and paid their Court to him as such. Sir Robt himself supposed he had no chance, tho' it appeared Compton had no talents for it, but was a meer [*sic*] formal man, governed all by precedents; and when the Queen's dower was proposed, searched to find the most wch had been settled on a Dowager, and found it 30,000£, and proposed it accordingly. Some about the Court hapned [*sic*] to ask Sr Rob. Walpole what his opinion was? He said he had not considered much about it, but he was clear that a less sum than 50,000£ ought not to be mentioned for a Queen. This was carried to her; for very soon after Lady Sandon [? indistinct] of the Queen's family, sent him a card to aquaint him that—"The fat bitch forgave Mr Walpole, or Sir Robert, if he was then Kn^t."* He was

* The addition of £20,000 to her dower, proposed by the man whom she thought had spoken disrespectfully of her, might be calculated to soften her feelings towards him. This Princess was Wilhelmina Charlotte Caroline, daughter of John Frederick, Marquis of Brandenburgh-Anspach. She was married in Germany, Sep. 2, 1705, to Prince George of Hanover, Queen Anne being on the throne of England. On the death of Anne in 1714, the Elector

amazed; but concluded the Queen had been told he [had so] expressed himself while she was Princess. This caused him to seek an opportunity of throwing himself at the Queen's feet and declaring his innocence.

The Queen's prejudice being removed, other matters were soon settled. Compton was made Earl of Wilmington and Presid^t of the Council, wth a pension for life of 3,000£, and Walpole retained his posts and powers.

A cloudy dull day, and except ½ an hour's walk on the Terrace, kept house.

3rd.—[Mr. Jenkinson and his son arrived.]

4th.—[Rain] . . .

5th.—Left Mr Ellis's house after a most polite and courteous entertainment of 10 days, and returned to London. Find, to my surprise, Mr Richd Clarke arrived from N. England.

6th.—At Lord G. Germaine's: comunicated the intelligence I had rec^d from Boston. I never saw him more dull. Condemed Lord S. [Sandwich ?] for appointing such an Adm.* and supporting him when everybody else gave him up: said he did not know much of his successor: wondered at his being suffered to remain here so long after he ought to have sailed, &c.

7th.—At the Old Jewry: Mr White, &c.

In the evening Mr Mauduit called, and gives an account of

---

of Hanover came to the English throne as George I., when she and her husband took the position of Prince and Princess of Wales; and in 1727, when she was about forty, and he forty-three, they became King George II. and Queen Caroline, as she was usually called: and here we come to the point where, in some cases, the forgiveness of a Queen may be bought for £20,000 a year.

The taunt was rather severe:—"Mr. Walpole, or Sir Robert, if he was then Knight"—as if she did not know!

The following low and impertinent doggerel attempt at verses, taken from one of the Editions of Hume's History, is only tolerated here as going to support the idea of a portly figure in a lady. The impertinence runs thus—

"You may strut dapper George, but 'twill all be in vain,
We know 'tis Queen Caroline, not you, that reign,
You govern no more than Don Philip of Spain;
Then if you would have us fall down and adore you,
Lock up your fat spouse, as your dad did before you."

And yet, did not her great-grandson George the Fourth proclaim that "fat, fair, and forty" was perfection in a woman?

* Lord Sandwich was First Lord of the Admiralty. The Adm. probably refers to Admiral Graves, who in time was succeeded by Adm. Shuldham, sometimes written Shuldam in the Diary.

one of the N. England privateers being brought in by a Man-of-War. She had 70 men aboard. He says the rebels had taken the Island of St. John's and 25 sail of vessels belonging to Pool, who were at Canso.

Very stormy, and snow.

8th.—The snow lay all day to-day in the squares and parts of the streets, tho' not very cold. It was the *Tartar* wch arrived yesterday : left Boston the 16 Dec. : sent express to bring the crew of a rebel brig comissioned by Congress, and taken by Geo. Montagu. They seem not to know what to do with the prisoners here, being afraid to punish them as rebels, as the rebels threaten the like to their prisoners. Several store ships taken, and they are afraid of suffering for want of provisions as well as fuel at Boston. The story of St. Johns seems to be only two or three Beverly scooners, [*sic*] having plundered Mr Calbeck the Collector, and taken him and Mr Wright prisoners. They took vessels also in the Gut of Canso, but it does not appear what they were.

Called upon Mr Clarke at Mr Copley's in the evening.

9th.—At Lord Hardwicke's. Mr Nath. Coffin came to town, being a passenger in the *Tartar*, from Boston. The snow, &c. . . .

10th.—I walked to Devonshire Square and back. We have an account to-day, by the N. York packet, that Lord Dunmore had set up the Royal Standard, and a printed Proclamation invites all Whites and Blacks to come in : and the letters from Philad. say 2000 had joined him. Doctor Chandler says the people of N. York, or the major part, will join the K.'s troops, if any arrive, but it is certain the rebels are in possession of Mreal, [Montreal] and that Quebec is in danger.

11th.—Called on the Bishop of London . . . [Letter from Boston, &c.]

12th.—I paid James a quarter's wages, due Octr 4th. Report from Virginia of Lord Dunmore, said to be confirmed by way of Ireland : but it is added that Lee, one of the Delegates, was at the head of a body of men to oppose him.

13th.—Walked to the city again, and back. Dr Chandler, Flucker, and S. Oliver, dined with us. A letter bro't me to-day, I suppose by a passenger in the *Tarter* from Judge

Oliver of 15 December, [not saved] very discouraging, L[d] Hardwicke, in a note says, 9 or 10 Battalions are ready in Ireland, and are to embark in the course of the next month.

14th.—Snow storm continues, and I continued at home all day.

15th.—A fair sky, but N.E. wind, moderate. There is now so much snow on the ground, that fresh butter is advanced from 9[d] to 14[d] the pound, and all vegetables in proportion. In the evening at M[r] Sewall's.

16th.—Cold, and N.E. wind, continues. There is so much ice in the Thames as to obstruct business, and some say there has not been more since the winter after 1739, and they begin to fear a very hard winter. I went with M[r] Sewall to Lincoln's Inn Hall, and introduced him to M[r] Thurlow and [M[r]] Wedderburne, and afterwards to M[r] Jackson, at Southampton Buildings.

M[r] Ellis called—returned with M[rs] Ellis, M[r] and M[rs] Doyley to town yesterday.

Billy ill with his bilious disorder all day.

There is something yet remains to be settled concerning the Hessian troops, as M[r] Ellis says he finds, since he came to town.

In his Letter Book, at this period, he entered his opinions on the amount of forces destined for America, more fully than in his Diary. The name of his correspondent is not retained, but he was apparently residing in Boston. I have an objection to degrading Governor Hutchinson's letters to the level of Foot Notes. Having been written by him, they are as authentic as his Diary, and often more valuable, as containing more information. An intermediate place was suggested to me by a practical printer, and in certain cases it has its merits, making it worthy of adoption. And where is the reader that does not look with dismay at the sight of a long Foot Note—his spontaneous feeling being a desire to avoid and skip it altogether? And if he has courage to go through with it, he is likely to lose his equanimity at having the trouble to hark back in order to find his place in the text to go on. He writes to his American friend—

"I thank you for your two last letters of Nov. 28, and Dec. 15, and for so particular a state of affairs. I have not subject for so circumstantial a letter, and if I had so far as relates to publick measures, I am under restraint; besides—conveyances from hence are more liable to accidents than they are from you. In general it is agreed that the force for America is as great as has been desired by the Commanders there, and as certain of being obtained as the state of human affairs, always liable to disappointments, will admit of. I believe there is no doubt that eighty thousand tons of transports, besides what are in America, are actually taken into the service. Their destination I had rather should be known from the Bearer, and from other accounts than from my conjectures. It is supposed the first embarkation of 7 Regiments from Corke have been sailed some days. In addition to what had been before determined, Lord Loudoun on the 24th, at an Audience after the King's Levée, informed him that 1500 of the Guards were very ready for service in America, if His Majesty thought fit. One thousand I hear are ordered. I am always wishing, and yet always afraid, to hear from Boston. I count the days, and absurd as it is so near the close of life, I can hardly help wishing to sleep away the time between this and the spring, that I may escape the succession of unfortunate events which I am always in fear of. God is above all, a consideration which ought to keep the spirit from failing."

The Diary continues—

17th.—Called upon Mr Ellis and M^r^ D'oyly. Met the people returning from the execution of Daniel and Robert Perreau, twin brothers: as they came into the world, so they are gone out on the same day. Daniel was a Merchant, and great dealer in the Alley: lived with the wife of a Lieutenant, or some other officer in the Army named Rudd, as his own wife, and had several children by her. Robert is said to have had as fair a character as any man, and to have been greatly beloved by all his acquaintance in business, as an Apothecary of 12 or 1400£ a year profit. There was no evidence against Robert of any part in the forgery; but it was certain he published a forged bond, and there were strong presumptions that he knew it to be forged, for it being offered as a bond of Mr Adair's [?] to Mr Drummond, was scrupled; but Robert affirmed it to be Mr Adair's writing, and the next morning told Drummond he had seen Mr Adair, and that he acknowledged his hand, and though he had not seen him, yet went with Drummond to Adair to ascertain whether it was or not. Everybody agrees that Mrs Rudd ought to have been hanged, as being the most guilty; but the Jury had not evidence before them to convict her.

Lady Frankland, Cromwell, Waldo, Gray and wife, dined with us.

18th.—At Court: the Queen's Birthday. Very cold yet, but no snow to-day.

19th.—Still the cold continues. I called at a shop by Charing Cross where are sold thermometers and other glasses, and inquired how low the mercury had been in Farenheit's, and was informed that out of doors it had been as low as 19, but in the house just below freezing. This would be called moderate winter weather in America.

Mr Clarke and son spent the evening.

At Lord Dartmouth's in the morning. I left with him a printed Vindication* of my conduct, which at my desire, he promised to shew to the King. I desired him to renew his motion to Lord North for my son. He lamented G——'s misfortune, but said he did not see how Govt could do otherwise than it did.† . . .

20th.—At Lord North's, but could not see him. At Sir Gilbert Eliot's. He thinks Quebec is gone: says we have been deceived in supposing the Quebec Bill was agreeable to the French people. I thought infinite pains had been taken to make it disagreeable since it passed. He can't account for Carlton's scattering his forces about the country, and so leaving no part defended: intimated being disappointed in him. G——, he said, was known, when appointed, not to be a fit person: blames his not following instructions to suppress all riots, &c., by his troops. I expressed my doubts of a Governor's directing the military in the Plantations, in a case where the K. would not do it in England, but observed that G. had no doubt.

* This must be the Vindication alluded to at p. 575 of the former volume. There is no printed copy among the H. papers.

† This is doubtless the "G. G." mentioned at p. 586 of the other volume, who tried to sit upon two stools, and fell between both.

I called upon Mr Mackenzy, Hill Street, who was abroad.

In the evening at Mr Knox's, Soho. He says six of the seven Reg^ts at Corke were embarked, and he concludes the whole have been sailed some days: that they are to go first to Cape Fear: that Govr Martin has given strong assurance that many thousands in the back counties will take arms and join them he said further, that 4000 men had been in arms in S^th Carolina in favor of Governm^t, which I had not heard before. Eight battalions more, in Ireland, are to sail for Quebec the first of March: one regiment is going immediately, in order to be at Isle Coudre before the ice above breaks up. The four thousand Brunswickers are also to go to Quebec: twelve thousand Hessians and Frazer's Highlanders are for New York, and the remaining force, to compleat [*sic*] 35000 rank and file, including those now in America, are to join Howe, where he may order. Rhode Island is at present thought on. Eighty thousand tons of Transports are taken up.

21st.—At the Old Jewry: a stranger preached.

Dined at Lord Hardwicke's with Peggy, Mr Mauduit, and Auchmuty. In the evening at Dr Heberden's. Glasses in open air at 19. Wind changed to S.W., but a cold frozen air like some winter north winds in N. England.

22nd.—More moderate in the morning. At Mr Ellis's near an hour. Dined at the Attorney General's, with the Sollicitor Gen. [Thurlow and Wedderburn,] and Mr Jackson, and Sewall.

Cold again, afternoon. Wind northerly again.

The Americans, by their agents in England, were made fully acquainted with the amount of forces collected in various parts of the British dominions, with the times of their sailing, and even in some degree, with the points of destination to which they were directed. The forces mentioned above may seem sufficiently formidable for the purposes intended. Relief in any form that might afford deliverance to the half-starved and half-frozen inhabitants of Boston, naturally enough, was eagerly looked for. There is an original letter from the beleaguered city, written by Dr. Peter Oliver at the period to which we have arrived, couched in his usual excited and amusing style, wherein he first discourses on the fate of nations, and closes with a prayer for a new tobacco box. He sends his letter by the obliging hand of Sir William Pepperell, Baronet, the second of that title who, like so many other loyal men, was retiring back into the serener atmosphere of the Mother Country, where, though he got quiet and security, he suffered the pain of knowing that his vast estates were seized and sold to strangers, and his character traduced to justify it. There will be some account of the Pepperell family further on—modern and original, by one of the representatives of it.

Hear Governor Hutchinson's lamentation, poured out on the 8th of December, 1775—" Mr. Hatch called upon me, as he s^d^, by y^o^ direction, and asked if I had no letter to send to Amer[ica]? I never think of it but wth distress. My children suffering the calam. of war—my property taken possess. of by my enemies, and sold or destroyed—as elegant a house and appendages as I ever desired to enjoy, turned into Barracks—and my most priv. lett^s^ and papers put into the hands of malevolent men, and such scraps published to the world as they suppose will hurt my character; and possibly they may answer their purpose wth some of my countrymen; but here they fail of their end, for even those who are in opposition to Gov^t^ wonder at their folly, nothing having appeared out of character; and after one or two extracts had been reprinted in the anti-Gov^t^ papers, no further notice has been taken of them. But the wickedness lyes in giving, by their comments and remarks, a sense and meaning diff^t^ from what they know in their consciences, to be true. I never concealed my principles. I have repeatedly declared against violent opposition to the authority of Parliament; the measures used by tarring and feathering, and other injuries to such persons as thought they had a right to act according to their own judgment; and have freely spoke my opinion of the necessity of Parl^ts^ exerting its authority, by incapacitating persons guilty of such acts, and their abettors, for publick posts, and by laying other penalties, according to the nature and degree of offences wch I believe in early times would have been effectual." &c.

The Doctor's letter runs as follows:—

" Boston, Jany 23rd 1776.

" Dear Brother Elisha,

" I take this opportunity by Sr Wm Pepperell to inform you I received y^r^ last of Sep^r^—

" At last the Old North Meeting House is pull'd down by order of the General [Howe] for fuell for the Associators. Dr Cooper's

Meeting House is Barracks for the troops, and so is Howard's Meeting House..

"We have lately receiv'd good intelligence from your side of the water, such as seiz'd money for the Rebells:* a large number of troops for America. I hope we shall come to rights next summer.

"Last Saturday† Gen[l] Clinton sailed for Virginia with a few of the Light Infantry, to join Lord Dunmore. We have just receiv'd an acc[t] of a defeat of the Rebells at Quebec: 300 killed: it comes from the Rebells. Last ev[g] was acted at the Theatre the tragedy of Tamerlane, and *The Blockade of Boston.* I did not attend for want of money.

"We are threatned [*sic*] daily of being attack't by the Rebells. For my part I wish our Wife's and children were out of the way. I shall stand it to the last: if I can but live to see the Rebells disarm'd, and 10 Acts of Parliament where we have one now, will I believe secure our posterity from any further rebellions. Cruel hard life I lead upon expense, and in no business; but I believe, when matters are settled, I shall have business enough.

"I wish you would send me by a safe private hand, who may be coming in an arm'd vessell that you are acquainted with, a cheap Tobacco Box of iron Japann'd, in imitation of Turtle shell, ab[t] two inches and ½ diameter, round and flat; as I have left off snuff, I have began upon tobacco. However, I leave it to your judgment, not more that 2/- charge.

"My love to all. "I am Y[rs] Affectionately,

"PETER OLIVER, Jun[r]."

23rd.—At Lord Suffolk's. He promised to mention to the King my sufferings by taking my estate in America out of my hands, and that I would have desired an audience, if I had not wished to avoided giving His Majesty trouble. I saw M[r] Wedderburn there, who thinks Boston will not be abandoned by the troops.

Cold continues. Evening at L[d] Gage's.

24th.—Dined with M[r] Agar. S[r] Charles Thompson, S[r] Grey Cooper, S[r] Geo. Hay, M[r] Hely Hutchinson, and M[r] Courtenay, an Irish gentleman, formed the company. . .

* He appears to mean—that money had been seized which had been intended for the use of the rebels.

† It was now Wednesday.

25th.—At Lord George G——'s Levée. Very little passed, Mr Pownall being present. In the city at Mr Smith's, Aldermanbury, to settle what stores to send to friends in Boston.

Cold, and E. wind continue.

In a letter of the present period to some friend whose name is not recorded, the Governor has an entry in his Letter Book bearing date January 27, 1776, in which he speaks highly of the capabilities and the fitness of the nobleman whose Levée he had just been attending. He writes—

"It would have been impossible, on Ld Dartmouth's going out, to have found a successor who would have escaped abuse. I don't know of any person more to general satisfaction than Ld George Germaine. He has the character of a great man, and I verily believe is a true friend to both countries, and would have no inducement but a regard to the publick interest, to accept of a post attended with so many difficulties."

In the same Book the day after, that is to say, on the 28th of January, writing from St. James's Street to his brother Foster, who was shut up in Boston, he says—

"I have been much dispirited for many weeks past, more from the distresses of my family and friends, than from the loss of my property, the greatest part whereof I find is taken from me. It will be a great relief to me if I can hear you have lived tho' the winter.

"The force gone and going to America is greater that I ever expected, owing much to Lord G. G.'s zeal for the service of his country. God grant it may produce peace and tranquility to the most infatuated people upon the globe.

"You wrote me in one of yr letts to know the state of Mr Hall's money. I think I wrote you an answer; but from being so full of anxiety I am not certain, and had rath. repeat than neglect informing you.

"It is so uncertain into whose hands letters may fall, that I do not think it advisable to write you more particularly. It's natural for you to believe that disappointms and anxiety will cause age to advance faster than otherwise, in my regular way of living, it would do. I am however, in tolerable health, and do not despair of seeing before I die, my dear friends, to all of whom I desire to be remembered."

On the same day he addresses a letter to his son Thomas, also in Boston, which he begins thus—

"My Dear Son,

"I am never free from anxiety and distress for my friends in Boston, but never felt a greater degree than at this time.

"The *Tartar* arrived 3 w^{s} ago, wch brings the lett^{s} as late as the 16 of Dec^{r}: the E. winds ever since have kept out all the transports wch sailed wth her, one excepted, the news of whose arrival came yesterday. I have y^{r} lett^{r} also by the vessels wch sailed 10 days before the *T.*, and Mr Clarke and Mr Coffin, both tell me they saw you just before they sailed. I hope some of the ships wth supplies might arrive; but as this and other like events are out of our power to direct, or even to know here, I know of no relief but a patient acquiescence in, and submission to, the will of God.

"The weather is more severe than has been felt since 1739/40, and it would be accounted rather cold in N.E., the thermometer being about 19; it puts by all business, and prevents an armed vessel for sailing wth the produce of the subscript. money for the army. Aboard this vessel I have procured a promise for some necessaries for you, w^{ch} [will] be ready as soon as the sea will admit of it.

"It is uncertain what state you will be in when they arrive, but I thought it better to ship them if there was but a small chance for relieving you, than that you should have the ship arrive without them, tho' they should be of no service.

"All you say about my estate does not affect my spirits. It is a greater loss of goods at Milton than I expected. Perhaps I may not live to have it restored to me, or to receive a compensation, but I hope my children will." [Aside—They haven't yet. Patience! patience!]

The winter of 1775–6 seems to have been very severe; and yet an equally low degree of temperature has not unfrequently been observed in England within living memory—at all events for short periods. Addressing himself to Mr. Winslow on the 30th of January he says in his Letter Book—

"It will be to no purpose for any of us who have lost our estates for our fidelity to seek relief at present. We must exercise patience, and hope that in some way, and at some time or other, we shall, in a greater or less degree be relieved. It has been a very cold season in Eng^{d} for 3 weeks past. I would fain hope that there is no reason to infer it is proportionably cold with you."

I would wish to make a remark on the last sentence. The winter I was in America was accounted mild, the frost in Boston and in New York being lenient in its pressure. At the latter city there was a good deal of floating ice in the North River, and great heaps on the banks; but as the waters continued open, several persons who were engaged in the coasting trade, who had unrigged and laid up their small craft for the winter, rigged them again in January, and sent them to sea. If there was but little winter in America, I concluded there was none in England, basing my conviction upon the general prevalence of milder seasons in the latter country: my surprise was great therefore, on nearing England, when I beheld the hills in the Isle of Wight, towards the latter part of the month of March, all covered with snow. On expressing my astonishment, one of the sailors told me that the degree of temperature was generally just contrary on the two sides of the Atlantic, and that having been a mild winter in America, it had been a cold one in England. Whether there is any real truth in this assertion, I must leave to meteorologists to determine. In commenting on the cold in England, the Governor expresses a hope that it is not proportionably colder or more cold in America, so that this notion, or whatever it be, was not known to him.

26th.—Colder than it has been since the frost began: clear E. wind—has all the feeling of NNW. in America. In the city again—at Mauduit's, Palmer's, and Gines's. Called also upon Mr Taylor, Bread Street, and Mr Amory, College Hill.

27th.—Two of the Transports which came out with the *Tarter*, we have the news of to-day: other three not yet in.

Flucker, Quincy, D. Greene, and T. Clarke dined with us.

I called on Mr Cornwall—from home: on Mr D'Oyley. This, I think the coldest air I have yet felt in England, but the Thames is not quite close. With this degree of cold I think that Cambridge river, as low as Boston Neck, would be froze over. The weather stops all shipping in the river from business.

28th.—The cold continues: clear sun, and thaws only out of the wind, and on the south side of the great streets.

A vertiginous turn [swimming in the head] yesterday, discouraged me from sitting in a cold Church or Meeting House.

29th.—The cold and clear weather still continues, which must retard the American expeditions. Mr Keene called, and seems to have more spirits than when affairs were in a much better state. Yesterday I was at Mr Cornwall's. He says everything goes on with respect to troops as he could wish. The House of Commons met the 26th, but no motion has been yet made respecting America, and they have hardly been able to make 100 Members, to proceed on controverted Elections.

30th.—I went into the city to Mr Strahan's, New Street. He is very sanguine in his expectation that Government will succeed in America, and a report prevails that Lord Howe will go out in command of the naval force. It is said in the city that a transport is arrived which left Boston the 2nd Jan., and that Shuldham, and several transports from England were arrived, but no letters yet, and some doubt the news. Cold—Glass 19. Mauduit says his has been at 13: in some parts out of town it has been 11. The Thames in some places closed, but nobody ventures across. The current is swift, and the rapidity increased since 1739, by the obstruction from three or four new bridges below Fulham bridge, otherwise I think it would have been passable.*

31st.—Mr Curwen has a letter from Salem from Mr Pynchon, who writes that John Adams is appointed Chief Justice: Willm Cushing, Willm Read, and N. Peasler [? indistinct] Sergeant Judges of the Superior Court.

Feby 1st.—Cold rather abates. Mr Lyell has a letter from Plimouth which says a ship is arrived in 25 days from Boston; and the people say they met Admiral Shuldham going in; and on Lloyd's Books the Olive Branch, Frampton, is entered as arrived, but it is thought there must be some mistake.

Smith, Oxnard, and Whitworth dined with us.

2nd.—No further account of the Boston ship. At Lord North's Levée. He had heard nothing but the common report. Saw Guy Johnson there, of New York, arrived from Quebec.

Called upon Mr Watson at Garlick Hill: find him much

* The evils of the ancient and unscientific practice of obstructing and damming back the upper waters of a river by a number of clumsy stone piers, are fully recognised in the present day. The clearing away of old London Bridge, with its multitude of piers, had the effect of lowering the upper waters, by giving them a free run down stream. The fewer obstructions the better. The modern London Bridges are noble examples of scientific construction.

dissatisfied with American measures: still laments the Quebec and the American Fishery Bills, both which he blamed the Ministry for when they were passing. Mr Smith has letters from his father and other correspondents in Salem, dated in November, and representing the determined state of the people to die rather than submit, and yet urging an accommodation.*

More moderate to-day than for 3 weeks past, and some rain, but the Thames is froze over at Richmond, and the streets of London are covered with a body of ice 6 or 8 inches thick in some places, and as hard as the pavement.

3rd.—The frost seems to be over, and a general thaw to be began. It is now agreed that Lord Howe is going to America to command at sea.

4th.—At the Old Jewry. Mr White, &c.

A little while at Court, and in the evening at Dr Heberben's. The observers settle it that Farenheit's thermometer has been as low as 12 or 11½ at Greenwich, and that, one morning only: the general state for about 3 weeks has been about 20. Dr Herbeden, upon mention of some of the New River pipes being stop'd, remarked upon the great benefit to the city from that river, which not only a supply of more healthy water than it was ever furnished with before, but by the overflow of the cisterns, purified the streets and vaults; and he verily believed was the principal cause for the last 100 years there had been no plague, and other malignant distempers proceeding from nastiness and corruption, which formerly were common, and seldom seven years passed without.

5th.—The weather is now moderate—the thermometer at 47—the wind west—and we may expect vessels from America.

6th.—A vessel from Boston—another from Halifax. Letters by the latter of 2nd Jany say they have an account that Quebec was in the enemy's hands: from Boston December 28: four transports had arrived after the 16th, and one was taken. I have no letters.

7th.—At the King's Levée, which was fuller than I had known it. I observed a great number of officers kissed the

* Only the accommodation was to be according to their own fashion.

King's hand, I suppose on promotions. They have nothing relating to Quebec at Court. General Burgoyne told me he should go to Canada.

The determination of the Americans to invade Canada was a very bold measure, and it was prosecuted with untiring energy and perseverance under extraordinary difficulties, and in the midst of great severities of climate. Not awed by the arrival of successive bodies of fresh troops from England, but feeling that they were fully able to cope with them, they determined to undertake something more, and according to the grandiloquent style and phraseology of the older historians, "they resolved on carrying the war into the enemy's country;"—wherefore they told off bodies of men, who proceeded to attack Canada vigorously.

8th.—A vessel from New York. Col. Dalrymple and other passengers came out Jan. 10. They had no news of the taking of Quebec. The Congress rose higher and higher. One of Dr. Chandler's letters says they had fitted out 5 sail from 32 to 14 guns, and it was thought were going against Wallace at R. Island, and had ordered the several Colonies to build 30 sail of Men-of-War. They heard that Lord Dunmore had retired aboard the ships. I have a letter from my son to-day at Boston, dated the 21 December: * had all got well through the small-pox, and had a considerable supply of provisions and fuel.

9th.—[Dinner party. Conversation.]

10th.—At Mr Ellis's. This morning he says he now knows that 50,000 men, on paper, are to be in America this sumer; and he knows so much of raising them, that he depends on at least 40,000 effective men.

Mr Robie of Marblehead arrived from Halifax. . . .

11th. 12th. [At Church. Took a walk.]

13th.—The *Somerset* Man-of-War arrived from Halifax: sailed the 14th of January. Report at first that Quebec had surrendered, but contradicted. It seems agreed that Shuld[h]am was arrived at Boston, and that he had made new arrangements which pleased the people. It is said they had begun to throw

* This letter unfortunately has not been preserved. All letters from the interior of Boston at this particular time would be welcome.

ANDREW OLIVER.
Lieut. Governor of Massachusetts.

shells from the enemy, and one had fallen between the Chapel and the house that formerly was Col. Wendell's: this was on Xmas Day. The Conanicut people killed Wallace's Boatswain. He ordered a party ashore which killed 5 men, burnt 13 houses, one belonging to me, and brought off 50 head of cattle. Sir F. Bernard called. I could not lodge him.

14th.—Letters from Boston by the *Julius Cæsar*, a returned store-ship, at Plymouth: came out 19 Jan. Mrs Oliver, the Lt Gov^'s^ lady, wth her family, arrived in her,* and Mrs Wentworth. They [in Boston] began to pull down the Old North Meeting House for fuel the 18. Lt Gov. writes he thought they would annoy the town from Phips's farm as soon as the frost would admit of their working at their batteries. My son, the 15, rec^d^ my letter of the 24th Sept.,† which he says embarrassed him, it being difficult to remove, and yet it would be necessary if the troops removed. What is said yesterday of shells, is now said to have been cannon balls.

15th.—Mr Troutbeck came to town, having arrived in the *Somerset* from Halifax after an exceeding difficult passage.

M^r^ D'Oyley called and spent an hour. He thinks the troops will still go forward from Ireland to the southern Colonies, tho' it is so late. The Hospital Ship had got into Crook Haven: the rest of the fleet at Cork.

E., [Elisha] P., [Peggy] and I dined at Mr Watson's, Garlick Hill.

Mr. Troutbeck, like other Stormy Petrels in troubled waters, was one of the many birds of passage now crossing the Atlantic, and if we may judge from the Letter Book, which contains information as authentic as the Diary, and generally more copious, we perceive that the Americans were dropping in thick and fast upon the English shores. In the second volume there is a Letter to Mr. Paxton of February the 16th, begun by the Governor himself, but finished by the hand of Peggy. Speaking of the new arrivals, it says—

"The passengers in the *Julius Cæsar* are not yet come to town. Mr Troutbeck arrived the day before yesterday—had a very

* It has before been observed that Thomas Oliver, the present Lieut. Governor, was no relative of Andrew Oliver his predecessor.

† It is printed at p. 538, vol. i.

stormy passage, and is much emaciated, but will soon recruit. Boutineau and M[rs] Borland have been in town, but are fixed at Bristol. Lady Frankland has made a visit too, but is gone home to Chichester, near the three Flag Officers she knew at Boston. Admiral Montagu called on me to-day—grows fat with prosperity. M[r] Jo. Green and his wife keep house altogether, except when forced out. He has dined with me about half a dozen times, which I believe is as much as he has done at all other places besides his own room. Flucker can't like this country as well as his own, and everything goes cross with Auchmuty. They have been a little funny with his wife in the newspaper, and brought her a-bed with twins: he guesses what quarter it comes from. Sewall was very ill, but is now well. He, Gray, and Waldo, and Robinson have taken houses about half a mile from Hyde Park Turnpike towards Brompton, where there is a row of 50 or 60 houses built since you were here, but is not a clever situation, and they are growing tired of it.

"I did very well the first winter, but have had a bad cold for the last five or six months, except with short intervals of relief. I hope as spring comes on to recruit, but am much enfeebled, though I have not been so bad as to keep house for any considerable time together."

16th.—A motion yesterday in the H. of Com[s] by T. Townshend, to censure the K.'s declaration to the Parliam[t] of Ireland, assuring them that the troops from thence to America should be at the charge of this kingdom—w[ch] assurance could not be given without the authority of Parliam[t]. Lost:—224 against 104 or 6.* This seems to be the last effort.

I have been much indisposed to-day, and tried walking up and down the Park, and round Piccadilly.

I paid my stable man for horses to 5th January.

Admiral Montagu called upon me.

17th.—No news of Sir P. Parker wth the ships and Lord Cornwallis, the land force there sailing from Ireland. After several days W. wind, it changes to E. to-day, and rain.

Flucker, Waldo, R. Clarke, Gray, and T. Bernard dined [with him.] Sir F. B. promised, but went out of town a little before dinner to M[r] Scrope's.

* Adolphus, 2nd Edit., ii. 308, discusses the question more fully, and gives the Division on the Debate as 224 against 106.

18th.—At the Old Jewry—Mr White.

In the evening at Dr Heberden's—Bp. Bath and Wells, Dean Tucker, Dr Ross, General Parslow, &c.

19th.—Breakfasted at Dean Tucker's lodgings: Dr Chandler and Cooper there. The Dean is writing an answer to Mr Locke upon Government. He says, properly enough, all the talk about an original compact, is idle; but he adds that Man is gregarious, and not only associate, but [men] take their first notions of Gov^t from instinct. I thought he had better consider well the latter part before he threw it out in print. I rather thought feeling the want of Government, first puts into men the thought of submitting to it. He said he would think more upon it.

20th.—At Mr Cornwall's. Lord Hardwicke sent me a note to tell me Ld Cornwallis sailed from Corke the 13th, and was certainly bound to the southward from Virginia to S. Carolina.

21st.—At the King's Chapel, being Ash-Wednesday, to hear the Bishop of London, who preaches as Dean of the Chapel on this day. The King not present. From the character of Abram, that he would command his household, &c., he recommended care of children and servants—lamented the dissipation of the present age, &c.—and delivered his sermon, considering his age, with unusual fervor and vivacity.

Two Sewalls, and Clarke jun^r dined with us.

22nd.—Account of Admiral Graves's arrival from Boston in 18 days at Portsmouth. My letter from T. Oliver 22nd January, but it is said that there is advice of later date,—that Montgomery and 70 men were killed before Quebec, and that Arnold and 300 were taken prisoners. This gives some spirits to Administration, who had given up Quebec.

23rd.—We hear to-day that the *Trident* came out with the *Preston*, Admiral Graves, and that Sir Wm Pepperell is aboard, and other passengers.

24th.—At Mr Ellis's this morning. He has a letter from Paxton dated the 2nd of February, with a more particular account about Quebec than any other. He says an express was arrived at Boston from Rhode Island, which gave an account of an express from Schuyler from Ticonderoga to the Governor

of Connecticut, advising that Montgomery with 1500 men had attempted to take Quebec by escalade on the 1st of January: that they entred the town, wch must mean the lower town: that 70 men were killed, and Montgomery among the rest, and a Basset and many other officers: that Arnold was wounded, and a Major Green of Rhd Island, and 300 made prisoners: that the rest of the army were routed: that Schuyler had prėssed a strong reinforcement for the army in Canada: that they had brought mortars, cañon, &c., from Ticonderoga to the Rebel army before Boston, wch consisted of 12000 men: that the Rebels were building 30 odd ships in different parts to be ready in April—and many other articles of news: so that now there seems to be no doubt of the truth of the substance of the Canadian intelligence.

Sr W. Pepperell sent a letter from Boston to E. H.*

According to the arithmetical principles of the Rule of Three, and the corollary of a well constructed syllogism, the word "Rebel" used above, ought now to be withdrawn. Dr. Peter Oliver uses it in some of his letters freely enough to shock our sensibilities; but then that young man seems to have had a rather excitable temperament, (judging by the tone of his phraseology,) and then he was shut up in the beleaguered city, stewing, or freezing, or starving, according to the change of time or season, and was suffering persecution and the loss of property, and then he might say in his heat that all men are liars, or some men are Rebels. But the time is past. We have not forgotten those good old lines, where American treason has prospered so well—

> "Treason doth never prosper—what's the reason?
> Why, when it prospers, none dare call it treason."

25th.—At the Temple: a stranger preached, tho' Dr Thurlow, the Master, was present. At the Drawing-Room: the King more inquisitive about my being here, and what business I came on when I was here before, † than usual. In the evening at Dr Heberden's—a small company.

26th.—Went into the city, and found I had recovered my

* This is the letter of Dr. Peter Oliver already given.

† The visit of Mr. Hutchinson to England in 1741, being 35 years before the period to which we have arrived, has been alluded to in vol. i. p. 51.

strength, and walked there and back without weariness. Entered Guildhall with Wilkes's mob, who breakfasted at the Mansion House, and were as great blackguards as can well be conceived, and seemed ripe for a riot. The contest is between Wilkes and Hopkins, for the Chamberlain's place, who is elected by the Livery. Never was so near Wilkes, to have so full a view since I have been in England.

In the evening at Mrs Ellis's rout, where there was a vast assembly of nobility and gentry, equal to any I have seen in England.

27th.—Wilkes lost his election for Chamberlain; Hopkins exceeding near 200 votes, in between 5 and 6000, the number of voters. It is said the whole Livery would not exceed 7000. . . .

28th.—Mrs Oliver* sent a note to acquaint me of her being in Titchfield Street, and my daughter and I called upon her. Sir William Pepperell, and his brother Sparhawk called upon me. S^r W^m is more discouraged about the event of American affairs than anybody. His spirits are very low from the loss of his Lady.

Called on Sr H. Houghton and Mr Mackenzie, but neither at home. Three or four days past the weather has been mild, like the beginning of April in New England, and the trees are as forward here as at that season there.

29th.—At Lord G. Germaine's, and afterwards at Lord North's Levée. The latter intimated the probability of the troops leaving Boston. I said what I could in behalf of the inhabitants, &c., and of the Council's leaving the Province, which was like giving up the government. He said it was much the same thing to have no power, or room to exercise the powers of government.

March 1st.—A day without rain, &c. . . Wilkes made a speech to the Livery to-day, charging them with being as corrupt as the House of Co̅mons, which has lost him friends; and being down, it is hoped he will never rise again.

2nd.—By appointment at Ld George Germaine's. Presented

* Probably the Lieut.-Governor's wife, recently arrived.

to him Mr Apthorpe's Petition, in behalf of Mr Eliakim Hutchinson's family.* Mentioned Flucker's hard case, but chiefly dwelt on the inexpediency of removing the troops from Boston. He said he never was more astonished than when he came into office to find—which he did by accident—that a peremtory [*sic*] order had come from Lord Dartmouth, at all events to remove them. This must be done in November or December. He immediately applied to the King, who said the order was conditional; but he assured his Majesty it was absolute; and not only wrote a publick, but private letter to General Howe; though his great confidence was in the impossibility of carrying the order into execution. How it would be now, he could not determine—whether, if the Rebels were weak, Howe would not strike a blow; or whether he would keep a garrison in Boston; or whether he would not take post in the neighbourhood. I suppose he referred to a proposal for fortifying Nantasket. I mentioned the neglect of performing the promises made to me. He condemned it: attributed it to Lord North's indolence: said Lord Dartmouth could prevail on him if he would: he should dine with him: promised to speak to him, and would let me know how it stands.

Mr Binney, one of the Council for Nova Scotia, dined with us, and Flucker.

3rd.—At the Temple, Peggy with me. By a ship from Virginia, an account of the burning of the town of Norfolk. The circumstances not agreed: some say the rebels fired on the ships, and the fire was returned upon the town, which set some houses on fire, and the rebels burnd [*sic*] the rest.

4th.—Called on Sr W. Pepperrell.† Mr Ellis called. At Mr Knox's in the evening with Flucker. Mr Knox says a scooner from Virginia has orders, if troops are going out, to

* Mrs. Eliakim H. had a daughter Kate, and a son William.

The Refugees from America, scared from their ruined homes, had taken flight across the Atlantic, and were pitching down upon England by sixes and sevens, like rooks upon a corn field, to see what grain they could pick up; but so numerous were the flocks becoming, that the custodians of the granaries in the old country had great difficulty in finding a few grains each for all the hungry mouths.

† The two letters r in the middle of the Baronet's name, do not appear to be the approved spelling, though so written sometimes.

return with goods. There are no letters to the Secr[y] of State. Private letters relate the affair of Norfolk, as mentioned yesterday. He blames L[d] Dunmore for a very ill-judged attempt upon the rebels. He is now sure the *Liverpool* and two sloops-of-war being there, and Cap. Hammond and General Clinton near at hand when these advices came away.

5th.—At M[r] D'Oyley's. He says things now go on to his mind, and he hopes to see America in order before another year. He complimented me with an opinion, that I ought to go out soon.

6th.—A steady moderate rain all day, which tho' scarce any day is without rain at this season, is not common in London. We all dined at M[r] Burch's in Chesterfield Street, wth M[r] Flucker and R. Clarke. A vessel is said to be arrived at Corke, which left New York 5 days after the last, and a letter is published as from Albany of Jan. 10, which says Arnold was drawn into a snare by a correspondence with one Grant, a Connecticut man in Quebeck, who opened a gate and let him and his Company into the lower town, where they found they were betrayed, &c.

7th.—M[r] Clarke and Auchmuty called on me, and were anxious to do something to shew the sense of the Americans in London, of the removal of the troops from Boston, and particularly the difficulties to which the inhabitants would be exposed.* I went to L[d] Suffolk, and let him know how uneasy we were. He gave me more encouragement than I have had before, that they would not be removed. His Lordship told me at the same time, that he had said to the King that I proposed desiring an audience, to represent to him my losses in New England, and the distresses of my family, but was unwilling to give him the trouble. The King answered—"I hope the time of retribution is not far off."

8th.—A rumor to-day that the news from Boston of the repulse at Quebec was not well founded, and that letters

* This must refer to the loyal Americans and Refugees, who were anxious for the safety of their friends in the beleaguered city, now under protection of the English forces, as, if the troops were removed, as the Duke of Richmond, Lord Chatham, and some others proposed, they would be exposed to the tender mercies of Washington's army.

from N. York of Jany 18, by way of Ireland, took no notice of it.

9th.—Mr Douglas this morning met me and said Lord Mahon had told him there was a letter from N. York of 8th Feb^y, and no mention of Quebec, and that at Almon's shop they were all in spirits, supposing the news without foundation; and soon after Mr J. Clarke came in and acquainted me a vessel was arrived from N. York in 27 days, and he could not learn in the city that the news was confirmed; but upon going to Lord G. G.'s office I found all the former accounts confirmed by a Philadelphia publication; and Gov. Tryon's letter supposes Government to have gained greater advantages.

An account of Lee's being at N. York with 3000 men, and having disarmed the Long Islanders, which shews they are not all of a mind. It was feared New York would be burnt by one side or the other.

10th.—At the Old Jewry. Sir H. Houghton feared the accounts from Boston were false, but was much pleased with the account I gave him of the York news, which he had not heard before. Mr Knox called and gave me a full account of what they had from York—copy of a letter from Skene at Hartford to Tryon, tho' anonymous to prevent discovery, which mentions the accounts they had from the Express: that Carleton had sallied out after the repulse and killed 200: that he had hanged up 22 Canadians as Rebels: that Worster had left Montreal and retreated to St Johns. Skene is wild, and his accounts always doubtful. Tryon hoped he should prevail on the Indians to destroy the batteaux and craft on the Lake.

11th.—Lord Hardwicke, having presented Miss H. with two tickets, I went with her this evening to the Pantheon, being the first time I had seen it; and though it is thought as magnificent a show as any in Europe, or rather, as grand and elegant a room, yet I have no inclination to go a second time. Mr Burch and his family were with us.

12th.—So many vessels of Lord Cornwallis' fleet have put back, being separated in a gale of wind, that it is said a vessel is gone to overtake the squadron if possible, and to order them direct to Boston. The wind has been northerly yesterday and to-day, and probably the outward bound may sail.

13th.—In the morning at Mr Jenkinson's: afterwards Lord Hardwicke's, who read part of a letter from Sir Jos. Yorke of 2nd March, that the Hessians were stopped in the Hanover^n^ dominions by order from Lord Suffolk, the transports not being ready, but were again on their march: that they were greatly concerned lest they should not embark; and only one officer had resigned.

Mr Ellis, and afterwards Lord Hillsborough called: The latter staid more than an hour: says D. of Grafton will move to-morrow to bring in a Bill to repeal the Act for altering Massachusetts Charter.

14th.—The Duke of Grafton's motion in the House of Lords did not prove to be what Lord Hillsborough expected, but a motion that if any representation should be made by the Americans to the General or to Commissioners setting forth their claims, there might be an immediate suspension of arms, and that His Majesty should be assured by Lords and Commons, that such claims should be taken into consideration. A long debate ensued, but the motion was rejected by about 90 to 30.*

15th.—A fine soft day, the wind about SW, and remarkably pleasant. Dalrymple says a servant of Deane,† one of the Congress, had been prevailed on by Tryon secretly to obtain or copy his master's papers, but being suspected, had fled, and was come to England. From his account they conjecture New York will be destroyed. This I suppose causes a report that it actually is destroyed.

16th.—Peggy and I dined at General Gage's. Mrs Oliver, Sr Wm Pepperell, Mr Burch and wife, and Mr Sparhawk, made the company.

The General is rather dissatisfied—dislikes P., and thinks Lord G. too set in his opinions, &c.

To-day the wind at N., and I think the outward bound vessels must sail for America. The Hessian officers, several of

* Adolphus, 2nd. Edit. v. ii. p. 325, says 91 to 31.

† The second letter in the word is not clear, but the name seems to be Deane.

them, are in town. The report is that the troops would embark the 20th, must touch in England. This will take much time.

17th.—At the Temple with Peggy.

At Court, but not in the Drawing-Room. In the evening wth Sir F. B., who came to town yesterday, at Lord Mansfield's, and Lord Chancellor's. The latter gives no credit to the acct of a salley made by Carleton, and his killing 200 of the Rebels. Saw Lord Coventry the first time at the Chancellor's. Afterwards at Dr Heberden's. Sir John Cope, at whose house in Hampshire, I was with Mr Ellis, was there.

A vessel one day last week from Halifax, brings advice that to the 10th of February nothing had hapned at Boston remarkable.

18th.—A fresh rumor of a second battle at Quebec, and that the Rebels had left the Province; but no credit given to it.

19th.—Met Mr Rivington to-day in the Park, the Printer lately arrived from N. York, who I had never seen before. He thinks that a letter which mentions some of the Canadians, who had left the city and gone to the Isle of Orleans, wishing to return after the repulse of the Rebels, and being refused by Carleton, is genuine and may be depended on.—The days are so much lengthened that we took an airing to-day after dinner, the first time this season.

20th.—Mr Jackson called and let me know Gen. Conway had found the manuscript I sent Mr Jackson at the time of the Repeal of the Stamp Act, and would let me have it.* Sir S. Gideon called. At Mr Knox's in the evening.

21st.—Monsr Garnier, lately arrived from France, called on me. I enquired whether all was quiet? Disputes with the Parliament wch Garnier thought might as well not have been recalled. Two Edicts have given some trouble. The roads used to be repaired by statute labour. This fell out of proportion on the lower people. By a late Edict the former has been repealed, and it is provided that the charge shall be levied in proportion to estates, &c. By another Edict all the Companies of *Metiers* or Tradesmen are broke and abolished. Both these

* No such manuscript now appears among the family papers.

Edicts the Parliament refused to register. The King held a Bed of Justice, that is, went in person to Parliament: called for the Edict: directed the Question to be put to each Member: and the Edicts are registered. The Parliament afterwards protest against these Edicts as unduly obtained, and therefore null, the Members having been under awe from the presence of the King. This lays a foundation for the people to refuse to submit, and tumults and disorders follow.

22nd.—At the King's Levée. After the Levée the Lord Mayor and C. Council d^d [? delivered] their Address to the King upon the Throne, praying for an alteration of American measures. The King's answer was short but expressive, and well delivered:—That he deplored the unhappy state of his American subjects, into which they had brought themselves by a resistance to the constitutional authority of the Kingdom: that upon their return to their obedience, he should be ready to every act of mercy and lenity: that in the mean time it was his resolution to pursue those measures which were necessary to reduce them to such a state—or to this purpose.

At the Levée Lord Barrington informed me of the news of the loss of Sir F. Bernard's son W^m, a young Lieut. in the troops gone to Canada. He, with one officer more, an Ensign, and 30 men, were on board one of the Transports or Provision ships, bound to Quebec, in company wth 7 sail more off Charmouth in the Channel. The ship Bernard was in took fire: he, and the other officer, and 5 or 6 soldiers, took to a boat wch overset, and they were all drowned. The rest of the soldiers, and the ship's company were saved, and afterwards the ship blew up. Sir Francis is in town in poor health: was yesterday very anxious for this son, so as even to appear like a *pressentiment*.

We have now arrived at a date when Boston, having been kept in close blockade on the land side for the space of eleven months, though inconveniently circumscribed for nearly eighteen, and having sustained an intermittent bombardment for nearly a fortnight, was being given up and evacuated by the English troops, together with a considerable number of civilians who were hurrying on board such ships and transports as were able to find accommodation for them. The news of this momentous event, which may almost be looked upon as one of the great turning points of the war, could not be known in England for several weeks. Meanwhile the Members of both Houses of Parliament were hotly debating new measures, molifying or otherwise, that bore more or less directly upon the critical position of affairs. Little that was really new could now be brought forward; but amongst active persons, the most stirring was Edmund Burke, who attempted a Bill of a conciliatory nature, which was either supported or resisted, as party feeling or party conviction suggested. "The chief opponent to Burke," says Adolphus, ii. 292, "whose arguments are preserved, was Governor Pownall." After having encouraged the Americans in the early part of his life, by the favourable way in which he had countenanced their theories of liberty, Mr. Pownall at last found that, having sown the wind, he was reaping the whirlwind—that, like Lord Chatham, he was getting alarmed at the growing rebellion which he had heedlessly befriended, wherefore, he "veered his main sheet," and steered into the House of Commons at the last General Election under new colours, and as a supporter of the Tory Prime Minister against his ancient protegés, and the division shewed that Burke's motion was lost by 210 against 105. The Duke of Grafton sailed in the opposite direction. He hauled down his old Tory blue, and hoisting the yellow flag of the Opposition, moved for a return of the number of the land and sea forces, together with a variety of particulars which, if published, would be likely to prove injurious to the public service, upon which it was negatived by consent. Mr. Hartley made another attempt of a pacifying kind, but this also, being inapplicable to the situation, was rejected by the large majority of 122 to 21. But few subjects drew forth stronger language in debate than the project for employing foreign troops. Several divisions arising out of it had taken place in both Houses, with results however, in support of those who had argued in its favour. History shews that throughout the middle ages, when there were no standing armies available for sudden emergencies, it was the usual custom of the European monarchs to take Auxiliaries into their service—a very rough and undisciplined element; but by the advanced period of George III. the feeling on this practice had somewhat changed, or it was convenient for the Opposition to say so. The Duke of Richmond moved to arrest the march of the foreign troops before they should embark from the Continental ports, and alleged that it would cost a million and a half to hire 17,300 men. Lord Irnham taunted the foreign Princes who could let out their soldiers for such purposes. The Duke of Grafton, in opposing the motion, declared that the nation was taxed to the utmost already, and could not afford more expense. Lord Effingham exaggerated the numbers of the population in America, and alleged that their resources were truly formidable: argued that the Spaniards might join and assist them against us, or take the favourable moment to assail the shores of this country; and the French, no less awake to the opportunity, would fall upon Ireland. The Earl of Coventry foretold the separation between Great Britain and her Colonies; and other members in a similar strain, varied their attacks upon the same lines.

The Ministry, on the other hand, defended themselves and their measures with the usual arguments. Lord Temple reprobated the intemperance of the Opposition. Lord North, in the course of his reply, urged expediency as well as economy in accepting the services of the forces named, and assured the House that "men were thus obtained more easily and much cheaper than by the ordinary mode of recruiting;" and—"Mr Cornwall corroborated the Minister's assertion, that the pecuniary terms of the treaties were more advantageous and lower than had ever before been obtained."*

Thus do men contradict one another across the floor of the House. Those who take delight in studying human nature, or in looking beneath the surface of every day men, or in scrutinising the motives and incentives that prompt most people to adopt the peculiar set of opinions which they may choose to hold, will soon perceive that the majority of men are more swayed by passion than they are by sober reason. They argue, not so much to display their common sense, as to please their fancy, or they will wantonly bend their tongues to dally with their mental vices. When I use the hard words mental vices, I only mean mental peculiarities—whims and fancies, not always either wise or correct: and these mental vices—if I may venture to repeat the words—are not confined to the unrestrained sphere of social life, or to the familiar domain of the domestic circle, but find free entrance into the discussions of political strife. Mr. Speaker has a difficult task to perform sometimes, when he would keep the tone of political debate within the limits of Parliamentary decorum.

But the Governor wrote a letter to his son Thomas on the 26th of February, who was now in the tenth month of his imprisonment, wishing to send him what scraps of information he could, that would cheer his spirits with the hopes of a speedy deliverance, and

* Adolph. ii. 312.

what scraps of material stores he could supply him with, for they were reduced to short commons, and though they had unroofed churches, and pulled down houses and sheds for firewood, they had none too much to make the pot boil, or to warm their finger ends.

The letter was entered in the Letter Book by the writer, and with some haste, as several of the words are considerably abbreviated. I prefer retaining the abbreviations, though I know that opinions differ as to the expediency of so doing.

"St. J. S., 26 Feb. 1776.

"My Dear Son,

"The storeship has been most unaccountably delayed, but the articles for y^u^ and for y^r^ sister's refreshm^t^ wch I hoped would have been in B. before this time, are at length on board, and y^r^ brother will send you a memo. of them. I hope your full relief is not far off: 11,000 of the Hess. and Bruns. troops had marched the 20 Feby in order to embark, and the transports are sailed with them on board; the remainder are expected to embark the middle of next month. A delay in these foreign troops was feared, but they are more expeditious than was expected. A bomb ketch and one of the transports met with dang^r^ in a gale of wind off Cape Clear, and are put into Plim^h^, but it is said will be repaired, and follow in a few days Sir P. Parker, to whose fleet they belonged. Recruits for the Regim^s^ in America are raised remarkably successfully both in Eng^d^ and Ireland, so that there seems to be no doubt that the great force planned will be completed in all their parts,"—and more on ordinary subjects, which have been repeated in other places.

23rd.—An airing with Flucker and R. Clarke to Battersea Bridge. They and Bliss, and S. O. dined with us.

A southerly wind and remarkably warm day.

24th.—At the Old Jewry with Peggy.

Flucker dined with us. A very warm day till towards evening.

25th.—Easterly wind and cold. The Brunswickers embarked the 19th, and are expected to sail to-day from Staads for Spithead.

26th.—The same wind, and it is the season for a spell of it.

27th.—Dr Jefferds called—was very sanguine that some proposals were arrived from the Congress—was rather angry when I made light of the report, and said he had good authority—it came from the Att. General—but Jefferds did not hear him say so—a Master in Chancery told Jefferds the Att. General said so. In this way reports spread every day through this town. Peggy and I dined at Mr Ellis's:—Gen. Johnson and Lady Cecilia, Mr Douglas and ux., and the famous Bruce, made the company.

28th.—Account of the arrival of the Brunswick troops at Spithead.

29th.—At a grand rout of Lady Gage's making this evening. I went a little before 9, and came aw[ay] at 10. Near 700 persons are computed to have been there of the nobility and gentry. No distinction of parties. Lord Mansfield and Lord Camden, Duke of Manchester, Ld Ashburnham, Hillsborough, &c., &c.

30th.—Walked a turn or two in the Park with Sr Jeffery Amherst, &c.

31st.—At the Temple Church with Peggy, where Dr Cooper of New York preached. . . .

April 1st.—The wind has been two days past at west: prevents vessels from sailing. Gen. Burgoyne, who commands the Brunswickers, is gone to Portsmouth to embark.

In the evening at Mrs Jenyns's company, for one room only. Ld Gage, Walpole, Mr Stratford.

2nd.—A fine soft day. Lord Hardwicke called in the morning: gave me the history of his being offered the Secry of State's place in Ld Rockingham's time, which he declined, and that the King, which is unusual, took him as one of the Cabinet, which continued but six weeks, when Ld Rockingham dropped, and all his Ministry wth him.

Dr Chandler and R. Clarke dined with us.

3rd.—As warm as June. Called on Mr Preston, and Mr Mackenzy, and left cards.

A vessel from Virginia. Gen. Clinton had been there, and sailed, it is supposed for Cape Fear. N. East wind.

4th.—Burgoyne was going aboard in order to sail from Portsmouth yesterday at one o'clock with the Brunswickers for Quebec.

5th.—The Men-of-War and 12 Transports with 2500 Brunswickers sailed yesterday morning from Portsmouth for Quebec. It is supposed the fleet from Corke are also sailed: the whole force intended to Quebec being 7000 men.

6th.—Lord Townshend called. . . .

7th.—At the Old Jewry.

No Court to-day, being Easter Sunday. Wind west again.

8th.—Went into the city to Mauduit, and Brook Watson, Garlick Hill. In the *Advertiser* (*Publick*) of this day, there are some extracts from an American pamphlet said to be wrote by John Adams. These extracts are to shew open declaration against all plans of reconciliation; but the book contains the most shocking abuses of the King—*Royal Brute,* &c. This a loyal subject, would not reprint.

9th.—[The Hessians expected.]

10th.—Intelligence to-day of a vessel at Bristol from Philadelphia with above 2000 bbls. of flour, and 15000 staves. She was fitted out by the Congress to go to Nantes, and return with ammunition. The cargo is said to have been shipped by Bayard & Co. The Master was to open his orders in a certain latitude. He communicated them to his Mate, who consulted with the men, and they agreed to displace the Master, and take the vessel into their own hands, and bring her to England. The Mate is come to town.

11th.—The town is full of yesterday's news. It is supposed government will endeavour that vessels be stopped in France: but it is reported and believed that a French Nobleman, or one who assumed that rank, had been in America, and was returning in one of the vessels of this fleet; for 6 or 7 more came out bound to different ports in France.

In the evening went with Peggy to see the *Alchymist* acted at Drury Lane. Garrick in Abel Drugger, it being the last time he ever intended to act in that character.

12th.—[Party at John Pownall's.]

13th.— . . . Lord Hardwicke sent me two tickets—one for the first, and one for the second day of the Duchess of Kingston's trial.

14th.—This forenoon, at half after ten by appointment, I

waited on Lord Howe, where I tarried till about twelve. Mr D'Oyley and Mr Strachey, Member of Parlt were there. We had much conversation upon America: the state of the several governments: the terms upon which they were to be suffered,* &c. He seems much unacquainted. He complimented me by wishing he had my knowledge. Matters don't seem to be yet settled. If he goes out, I think it is not possible it should be otherwise. Mr Strachey goes his Secretary. Mr D'Oyley asked him before [he] went to Lord Howe's, jocosely, whether he did not intend to go to America? He answered—He supposed he should go if Lord Howe goes. I don't know what to make of it.

Mr Waldo dined with us. Lord Howe said he wondered there was no news of the Hessians.

15th.—Dutchess of Kingston's trial began to-day. My daughter was at it from between 7 and 8 in the morning till 6 or 7 in the evening.

An account of the Regiments from Cork sailing Monday the 8th for Quebec. Burgoyne, the day before, is supposed to have left the Channel. It seems now the opinion that there has been a delay of the Hessians sailing because they were not all ready, and did not like going in two divisions.

16th.—Wind keeps westerly yesterday and to-day, but no news yet from America.

I was at the Dutchess of K.'s trial to-day from 8 till 4. Thurlow, Wedderburn, and Dunning took up all the time the Court was together, except a quarter of an hour a civilian had been speaking, when I came away. The Lords did not come in till eleven. It is strange so much time should be spent on a point which seems not to admit of a minute's debate, her plea being that in a case of jactitation of marriage, it was determined before her marriage to the D. of Kingston, that it did not appear she was the wife of Augustus Harvey. [Hervey rather.] Her Counsel urged that even if it should appear there was collusion between Hervey and her, the sentence in the Ecclesiastical Court would bar a criminal prosecution. It is said the D. sold a house for 15,000£, and it can be proved that money was paid to Hervey.

* Doubtful word, hurriedly written.

I think this assembly has an appearance so grand and respectable that it is scarcely to be equalled.

17th.—I met Mr D'Oyley to-day. He speaks with uncertainty yet of Ld Howe's going, and added—"If he goes, I hope you will go with him." I am at a loss what can be the meaning of this. His Lordship was coming to my house this morning, but seeing me abroad, was hindered.

At Lord Hardwicke's, who informed me the Hessians were stopped because the full number of transports were not ready, but that the last post brought advice all were embarked and would sail the first wind, which to-day has been at S., or to the E. of south.

Mr Miller, Ld Justice Clerk of Scotland, breakfasted with us.

18th.—Met Lord Hardwicke in the Park, who took two or three turns:—says the Hessians will make no tarry after their arrival at Spithead.

Wind at W. again: no arrival yet from America.

19th.—Calhahan called, and breakfasted wth us. Lord Hardwicke sent me a ticket, which I gave to E. H. who attended the trial to-day. In the evening we were all at Ranelagh with Mr Burch's family, Dr Tarpley and wife, Flucker.

20th.—I attended the trial to-day by the help of another ticket from Ld Hardwicke. It engages the attention of the town, and little is said of America. Wind still to the west, and no Hessians, nor no news from the Continent.

There has been a report that the Regulators, to the number of 3000 in N. Carolina, had declared for Government, and Dr Chandler says to-day that Hammond, of the Roebuck, has wrote it to his friend in Ireland: but it wants confirmation.

21st.—At the Temple Church. Dr. Cooper of N. York preached.

At Court. In the evening, at Dr Heberden's.

22nd.—At the Dutchess's trial, Ld Dartmouth having sent me two tickets, and Lord Hardwicke one, wth Elisha and Billy. After 5 days she was capable of no defence against the clearest evidence of both marriages, and unanimously pronounced Guilty. The Court, as a Peeress, ordered her discharge on paying costs, w[th]out burning in the hand, tho' the Att. Gen. took exception.*

23rd.—Called upon Lord Hardwicke, and thanked him for his tickets. Bishop of St. David's and Soame Jenyns there. Censure the Duke of Newcastle for saying "Guilty" erroneously, but not intentionally: and [they] say he ought, *as several other Lords did*, to have withdrawn if he had not been satisfied, or to have pronounced her not guilty. The Bishops all sat until the Lords came in to deliver their opinions, and then they did not return to the Hall, but absented with a *salvo jure;* ridiculous enough when it was not, nor could be, a case of blood.

Flucker, Clarke, Urquhart, Chandler, and Wilkins, the last of N. York, dined with us.

24th.—Called early at L[d] Dartmouth's, but had a few words only, as he was just going out. At M[r] Ellis's and Lord Hillsboro'. All of them spoke in favour of the pamphlet, "*Experience preferable to Theory,*" in answer to D[r] Price.

Lord Hillsborough said —— was the falsest man that ever lived. He gave me some acc[t] of the D. of G.'s amours with Nancy Parsons. He was so extravagantly fond of her

* Adolphus dismisses the beautiful but wayward Miss Chudleigh in a single sentence: Hume enters more largely into her case. In 1744 she was privately married to Lieutenant Hervey, R.N., who eventually became Earl of Bristol. Some time afterwards she instituted a suit in the Commons, and having made oath that she was not married, she obtained a sentence in the Ecclesiastical Court, which Court declared her free from all matrimonial engagements. She justified her questionable oath to her private friends by saying that "she could easily reconcile it to her conscience, as the ceremony was a scrambling, shabby business." In 1769 she accepted the hand of the Duke of Kingston; but on the death of his Grace in 1773, Lady Meadows, his sister and heir at law, filed a Bill in Chancery against her. The Lord Chancellor admitted the validity of the sentence in the Ecclesiastical Court; but on the other hand it was contended, that this sentence had been obtained by collusion of the parties. A criminal prosecution was therefore commenced; a true Bill was found against her: and the case was now removed to the Lords in Westminster Hall. She was found Guilty, but owing to her rank she escaped vulgar punishment, and was dismissed on payment of the costs. It is said in the Diary that the Attorney General took exception to the sentence—presumably to the leniency of the sentence. Perhaps he would have contended that she was not a Peeress at all, and therefore could not plead her Peerage in mitigation: and if her marriage with the Duke of Kingston was not valid, the learned Counsel had the strong side of the argument in his hands: but if he had pushed it to extremity, he would have been an ungallant brute. Better let her go.

that tho' she pretended to be in bad health, and that it was necessary she should go to the S. of France, and he had consented, yet she was no sooner gone, than he ordered his carriage in order to overtake her before she left Dover, and would [have] exposed himself when Prime Minister to the censure of the whole nation, if Bradshaw had not begged on his knees that he would not; but all would not do, until Bradshaw offered to go himself and undertake to bring her back: and he went and overtook her before she left Calais, and brought her to London.

The D. was so infatuated as to carry her with him once to the Opera, and sat near the K. and Queen. All this time she disliked the Duke, and gave her company to the Duke of Dorset privately.

The King told Ld Hillsborough of it, and he told Bradshaw, and of their meeting at a milliner's in St. James's Street. Bradshaw told the D. of G. what he had heard. The D. disguised himself and watched one evening, when he saw her go in, and the D. of Dorset follow her soon after; upon which the D. of G. dismissed her, and she has lived with the D. of Dorset ever since.

Went with Peggy and Dr Tarpley and wife to Covent Garden Play house in the evening, to see *The Conscious Lovers:* the boxes not a quarter filled. Masquerades, Ranelagh, Concerts and many other diversions take up the town. Never was a time when so great a part of the people spend so great a portion of their time and estates in amusements and dissipation.

Guns this morning for the Queen's delivery of a Princess.

This was the Princess Mary who, at the age of 40, namely, in the year 1816, married the Duke of Gloucester. Some authorities say she was born on the 25th, though the 24th, as here stated, seems consistent.

This was probably one of the Princesses who occupied apartments in the Cloisters, Windsor Castle, in or about the year 1814, or perhaps 1815. For some years my father had owned a large house (now two houses) at the top of Peter's Street, Tiverton, Devon, with a sloping garden below the Churchyard running down to the river Exe, and having let these for a time to a gentleman, he was lodging at the period mentioned, in the Cloisters at Windsor, with my mother and three or four young children. I was five years old, and I used to go through the Cloisters frequently either with my mother or with the nursemaid, and I can still remember the general appearance perfectly: but what perhaps best served to impress the place most strongly on my young mind was, the figure, either in plaster or white china, of an ugly pug or bull-dog with black eyes, in one of the windows, which in my mind's eye, was a leaded casement; and although it was inside the window, I was afraid of it. This passage I think led to the 100 steps. Out of this walk the Princesses had a private entry into their own apartments. Their entry consisted in a covered passage a few yards long, at the further extremity of which was the doorway; but as all these alleys were surrounded by buildings, they were rather dark, and especially that one which led to the Royal residence. On passing the outer end of this entry, reserved to members of the Royal family, and casually glancing up it, my mother fancied she saw festoons of cobwebs hanging from the sides and ceiling so low as scarcely to be clear of people's heads as they passed under. This idea seemed too monstrous to be entertained for a moment. Could it be possible that any servants should neglect their duty so much as to omit occasionally sweeping the walls and ceiling of a passage through which the Princesses passed almost daily, until the cobwebs should be visible to the public eye? Rather too much to believe. In speaking of it my mother used the expression—"festoons of cobwebs"—but she must have been mistaken. A woman's curiosity, however, was not so easily satisfied—she wanted to have another look. One day she was going through the Cloisters alone, and glancing up and down, and observing that there was nobody about, she thought she would peep into the Royal entry. Wherefore, almost on tiptoe, with her nose in the air, and her eyes wide open, she walked up the dingy passage, and when she got nearly to the top, all at once the door was thrown open wide, and there stood a footman in the Royal livery, ready to receive her commands. She was so confounded at this unexpected apparition, that she lost her presence of mind, and uttering an "Oh!" she turned about, and withdrew considerably humiliated. When she returned and related her adventure, my father laughed and enjoyed the joke amasingly. A few years after, when I was a little older, and better able to understand the points of the case, on hearing the story related again, I said—"But, Mamma, do you think they really were cobwebs?" She assured me that they certainly were: for though the footman unexpectedly cut short her survey, she had at all events seen enough to be sure that they were "festoons of cobwebs."

Well, where are we? It is hoped that the reader will forgive a few anecdotes that grow like offshoots out of the Diary, for if they serve no other purpose, they serve to break the monotony of it.

The Dr. Price alluded to above, was Richard Price, D.D., Scotch University, and F.R.S., born about 1723, and died 1791. He was a Dissenting Minister of some note—a political and a polemical writer, an admirer of John Wilkes, and a correspondent of Benjamin Franklin. His views were rather extreme, and his Pamphlet advocating the independency of America, was attracting a considerable amount of attention. Writing to Chief Justice Peter Oliver in Boston (Letter Book, Feb. 27), Governor Hutchinson says—"A Pamphlet is published within 2 or 3 days by Dr Price, a tool of F——'s, wch makes great noise. It is calculated to do mischief. His principles are not properly republican, but anti-governmental, if you can bear that word, and would soon put down all the governments existing, without setting up any other in their stead."

The following is an original note of Lord Hardwicke, expressing a desire to see the Pamphlet:—*

"Apl 18th —76.

"Lord Hardwicke wishes Mr Hutchinson cd procure a sight of a pamphlet, of wch he saw an extract in the papers, writ expressly to assert the Independency of America. Thinks Govt shd have had the Pamphlet more speedily, as it wd *revolt* everybody here, without exception, if acted up to."

There seems to be a play upon the word "revolt," which is underlined.

25th.—At Lord North's Levée. The Hessians in the Channel.

26th.—At Mr Jenkinson's. The Hessians, he says, by advices last night . . . [something apparently wanting]. I asked the difficulty about Lord Howe? and he says he makes difficulties for want of understanding.

Mr Jenkinson asked me if anything was done for Billy? said he had spoke to Mr Robinson.

At Blackburne's in Scotch Yard, he read me a letter from

* Original Letters, vol. i.

one of the Congress Commissaries at N. York, that he was there with 6,000 men, and in a month would have 10,000—powder, &c. in plenty. A letter full of bravery.

The merchants in the city have rec^d^ letters from their correspond^s^ at Montreal of Feby 7th, one of which calls the repulse at Quebec a total defeat, and adds that if the forces can be there by the middle of May, Quebec will be in no danger.

At the Exhibition of Paintings in Pall Mall, some of which, especially the landskips—one of the sea near the Isle of Lundy, and another of Cap^n^ Cooke's landing place in Otaheitee, were very fine.

27th.—At M^r^ D'Oyley's, where I saw Mr Stracher, preparing for his voyage, everything being settled, and Lord Howe to embark next week. The Hessians all at Spithead. Mouat, in the *Canso*, sailed the 24th from Spithead.

Greene and Clarke dined with us.

Lord Howe had postponed his departure from time to time, until his friends, and even some of the Ministry, were at a loss to comprehend the apparent mystery of his delay. Mr. Jenkinson seems to imply that he was desirous of understanding all the particulars of his duties before he entered upon them. On the other hand, those who consider his movements, might suspect that he would conduct the war upon the same principles as his brother the General appeared to do, and if so, the mystery hanging over his prolonged preparations, might be in some degree accounted for.

The following is another original note from Lord Hardwicke, in which, among other things, he shews his curiosity on the subject of Lord Howe.

"Ap^l^ the 27th Richm^d^ —76.

"Ld Hardwicke's complim^s^ to Mr Hutchinson, with thanks for his American intelligence: the accounts are so scanty and imperfect that as a *Political Conjurer*, he cannot cast a figure ab^t^ them.

"He believes Quebec safe, as succour sailed from Dover in Feb^y^, and it will get up as soon as the river is open.

"He wishes Genl Howe was not so sparing of his vessels of intelligence, and he heartily wishes y^t^ Ld Cornwallis's corps c^d^ find their way to Boston. As to the Hessians, all that Ld H. knows ab^t^ them is, y^t^ as they are sailed thro' the Downs, they must by this time be at Spithead.

"What is the mystery ab^{t} Ld Howe? and when will he go?

"Ld H. will be in town on Monday to Dinner, and begs his compt^{s} to Miss Hutchinson."

Throughout the winter there had been great activity in all the departments, for the purpose of drawing together a large armament and in dispatching troops, who should be ready to act as soon as the spring weather would allow. It was apparent that something on a large scale was intended. In the Letter Book, under date February 16, 1776, the Governor writes—

"It is certain that a prodigeous armament is preparing, and will be very soon sailing in one large body after another, until the whole is gone for America. The destination of the several parts, I am not able to tell you. As the command will be in the two brothers, one by sea the other by land, people are less inquisitive than otherwise they would be. I do not think a choice of men could have been made more generally satisfactory to the kingdom, and under Providence, I think we may found a reasonable hope for a more favourable summer than the last. We Americans are plenty here, and very cheap. Some of us at first coming, are apt to think ourselves of importance, but other people do not think so, and few, if any of us are much consulted, or enquired after."

In accordance with these last observations he requests his friends not to address him on their letters as "His Excellency." In a postscript to one of February 27 he says—"Pray leave off *His Excell^{y}* in y^{r} directions, for everybody laughs at such things here."

The opening of the campaign suggested many pangs of apprehension in the bosoms of sympathising friends, for most people now felt that the season for child's play had passed. Writing to Mr. Winslow Jan. 30, the Governor said—"I am never free from anxiety for my friends in Boston, and feel a great proportion of your distresses."

Feb. 16 to Mr. Paxton—"Whenever a ship arrives, and I don't hear that y^{r} distresses are increased, I call it good news."

Feb. 26 to General Brattle—"I desire no earthly good so much as that of seeing my country and friends again in peace."

In speaking of the change of Admirals, he observes to Mr. Winslow—"I am glad you are relieved from an Admiral so much complained of. I know his successor will give better satisfaction: but you will soon have a gent. wth you, Ld Howe, to take the com̄and of the navy, who seems to have the universal voice of all ranks of the people in his favor."

Walpole writes, Feb. 15, 1776—"We have no news but those of preparations against America."*

28th.—At the Old Jewry, &c.

29th.—At Lord G. Germaine's to desire his favour for Sylvester Oliver, who encourages me he will do something for him.†

30th.—Called at Sir H. Houghton's, Upper Brook Street, and left my name. . . .

May 1st.—[Billy and Flucker to Bristol.]

2nd.—Lord Hardwicke called.

About four o'clock I came in, and to my surprise found Col° Browne arrived from Boston, having left it the 26 March in the *Lord Hyde* packet, and arrived at Falmouth the 31st April. But I was more surprized when he told me he left my son and daughter and their children, and Miss Sanford aboard the packet, and that the troops had quitted Boston, and were embarked, and many of them sailed with the packet to Halifax, and the rest to sail the next day.

The rebels had erected a battery on Dorchester Neck—had been seen on Hog Island, and Genl Howe had embarked part of his troops, and the transports had fell [*sic*] down between the Castle, and Dorchester Neck, intending to land at midnight: but a southerly storm of wind and rain came on suddenly, and rendered the landing impracticable, and the next morning he determined to evacuate the town: and such of the inhabitants as desired to remove, were directed to give in their names. My son and daughter and their families were favoured with passages to England: all the rest are gone to Halifax. They met with no molestation from the rebels: left all the merchandize of the town, except woollen goods, behind. This is a distressing affair to the inhabitants and their friends. How it may affect Government is more problematical.

3rd.—I attended by order with Col° Browne last evening at Ld G. Germaine's Office, where there was a Cabinet, but we were not called nor any inquiries made.

4th.—Various constructions upon the retreat from Boston.

* His Letters, Edit. of 1857.

† Brinley Sylvester Oliver, a son of the late Lieut. Gov. A. Oliver, and his second wife Mary Sanford. He was born Sep. 6, 1755, married Sarah Louisa Barton, Ob. s. p.

Sr H. Houghton thinks it will tend to discourage the friends of Government: others say it is what they have long wished for.

This important piece of news had soon flown far and wide. It had reached Walpole at his retreat in the country, and on this day, May 4, he expresses himself thus—"They write to me from London, that the Provincial army, having been reinforced, had prepared to storm Boston, and had begun to cannonade it, and that General Howe, unable to maintain his post, had withdrawn with all his forces to Halifax. I had heard this on Thursday,* before I came out of town, but did not believe it, for the Americans have done nothing yet that has given me a high opinion of their generalship."

It may be inferred that Governor Hutchinson was among the first, if not the first person in London, who received the news. As Colonel Browne came over in the same ship with the Governor's eldest son Thomas with his family, and his eldest daughter Sarah, married to Dr. Peter Oliver, it was but natural he should go to him with his news first. It was about four in the afternoon that the Colonel imparted his intelligence; and though Lord Hardwicke had been to the house that very day, there is nothing to shew that his Lordship knew anything of the matter.

A few quotations have already been made from Dr. Peter Oliver's Diary. After alluding to the battles of Lexington and Bunker's Hill, [i. 479] he proceeds thus:

"We remained blocked up in Boston till the beginning of March 1776, when we were ordered to embark. Tommy Hutchinson's family and mine went aboard the *Hyde* Pacquet for England. (My mother died in Boston in March 25, 1775, and my children were inocculated for the small pox in Nov. or Dec. 1775.)

"March 25th 1776 we set sail for England. After a tedious passage of 35 days we arrived at Falmouth the last day of April follow^g^, where we staid till the 6th of May, when 15 of us set out from Falm^th^ in post chaises of a Sunday morn, and got to London the 12th of May, of a Saturday ev^g^ at St. James's Street, at the G——r's.

"Now, as to the voyage:—The day before we set sail from Nantasket, Tommy's wife was delivered of a boy,† which had not

* It was now Saturday.

† The boy was subsequently baptised Andrew, after its mother's father, Lieut. Gov. Andrew Oliver. It lived and grew up, married, left children, and after a life of fairly good health, died of an attack of bronchitis, Dec. 23, 1846, aged 70 years and nine months. He was my father.

a drop of milk during the whole passage: was much emaciated, and no one thought it wou'd have lived. The lady well. As to myself, I was sick 21 days without any support: reduced almost to a skeleton: 7 children on board ship, and the eldest not 6 years old."

The subjoined, which was entered in the Letter Book by the hand of Governor Hutchinson, shews his desire to thank General Howe for many kindnesses shewn to his son at a very trying time:—

"S[t] Jam. Street, 6 May 1776.

"Sir,—My son, in a letter from Falmouth, has expressed in such strong terms his obligations to you for your care of him and his family in the time of their distress, that I may not omit the first opportunity of rendering my thankful acknowledgments, and of assuring you that I shall ever retain a most grateful remembrance of the favour shewn them.

"I cannot but flatter myself that under the present direction of the affairs of government in America, the friends of government in general will be relieved from the tyranny they are under, for which event every good man must wish and pray.

"I have the honour, &c."

During the week that was occupied by the Refugees in travelling from Falmouth to London we will recur to the Diary as before:—

5th.—At the Old Jewry. A little while at Court. Saw Lord Dartmouth there. Acquainted the Duke of Northumberland my son at Falmouth had letters for him from Lord Percy. He said he had received none by the Packet.

In the evening at D[r] Heberden's. Soame Jenyns's book upon the internal evidence of the Christian Religion much applauded. He wrote formerly *The Origin of Evil*—was then an unbeliever. M[r] Mackenzy called on me after he had been at Court.

6th.—At M[r] Ellis's, who advised me to apply to Government, and did not doubt of my provision being enlarged.

Soame Jenyns called. I told him I would leave out the *almost*, and say—*thou persuadest me to be a Christian*, for I had read with much pleasure half his book before breakfast. He did not own the book, but said I did honour to the author.

The wind between N. and NW., and it is thought the Hessians would sail to-day.

Received a letter from my son at Falmouth of the 2nd Instant, who intended to take passage to Portsmouth, and come from thence in the stage.

7th.—Called on Mr Cornwall, and left card.

Sr W. P., [Pepperell] * Sparhawk, and Browne, dined with us.

The Gazette in the evening announces the sailing of Comodore Hotham with the transports from St Helens the 6, half after 4, and that they were out of sight before dark. A report that Hopkins in the Philadelphia vessels, had possessed himself of New Providence, or the Bahamas, and that 7 of the transports, going out of Nantasket were lost, but the passengers, &c., saved. This last is said to come in a letter of the 29 March, from Nantasket, by way of Ireland. In every paper there are more or less falsities to disturb the peace of Government, and it is impossible to distinguish them.

8th.—A letter from my son at Falmouth, that he intended, with all his train, to set out as on Sunday last by land, tho' at great expense, and he drew on me for £200 for passage, &c., to be paid out of money he had remitted me. Capn Loring called, having arrived with Mrs Loring last night. Mr Clarke with us in the evening as far as Battersea. Loring thinks the troops need not have left Boston; and yet supposes a battery on Noddle's Island, [500 yards east of the city,] would have forced the ships from their anchors; and it's generally agreed the rebels would have had one there.

There is no doubt Ld D. gave peremptory orders to quit Boston, which must arrive just before winter. As soon as Ld G. G. came into office he saw these orders, as he told me, and was surprized: went to the K., who said he took them to be discretionary, but was convinced they were not, and Ld G. G. wrote immediately to relax them and prevent the execution, and the measures since taken have been upon the presumption that the troops would remain until they should be strengthened from home, and be enabled to beat the Massachusetts forces

* Sir William Pepperell was born Sparhawk, but his grandfather's Baronetcy was revived by a new grant in him, and he assumed the name of Pepperell.

before Boston; but the orders never did arrive. I was surprized to see M^{r} P[ownall] and M^{r} K[nox] looking over the Letter Book to see by what vessels the orders went. In my business as a Merchant I never wrote a letter of consequence but I tracked the ship it went by from the hour she sailed, and was anxious to inquire by every opportunity after her arrival: but the way [here] is, to send letters from the office of Secr^{y} of State of the Admiralty, to go as soon as may be. Some little thing or other hinders the sailing of the ship, and the Admiralty do not consider, or perhaps know, the importance of the Secr^{y} of State's dispatches: the ship lies five or six weeks, and the dispatches answer no purpose. I sent a packet this winter to Lord G. G.'s office to go in Government's box, and after six weeks Mr Knox told me it was sent back to London, the ship not proceeding. This shews the want of one great director to keep every part of the operations of Government constantly in his head.

9th.—At Ld G. G.'s and Ld N.'s Levées to introduce Cap^{n} Loring.

A ship arrived from Philadelphia laden with flour, &c. The account is, that she paid a duty to the Congress at $33\frac{1}{3}$ ꝑ c^{t} for licence, and that others were coming. The truth is, that the produce is 50 ꝑ c^{t} under the usual price, so that the exporter makes a good profit at any foreign market by paying only $33\frac{1}{3}$. But it's a strange thing to bring goods from declared rebels on any terms, and everybody is waiting to know what will be done by Ministry. The wind has been fair since Monday, and it's thought the fleet has a good offing.

Letter from my son at Exeter, dated the 7th.

10th.—An account of the arrival of a vessel from Florida, and advice that Hopkins with his small squadron from Philadelphia, had landed 500 men at Providence in the Bahamas, and possessed himself of the Fort: but it is said the powder was sent off in a King's scooner the night before they landed. This is the general report: more particulars we are to expect.

Letter from my son at Salisbury, dated last night.

11th.—Mr Vardell tells me he has a letter from Mr Cruger at Bristol which gives an acc[t] of a vessel there from Georgia, with news of Hopkins's taking possession of the fortresses at Providence.

My children, &c., came in to town before seven. I sent my coach in the morning to Hounslow to meet them. All are in tolerable good health—*Deo dentur gratiæ.* My wife's sister, [Grizel Sanford] much altered in less than two years. The distress she has been in has accelerated age.

In bringing up our forces to the front, one battalion after another, it is now necessary to bring up a new Diary, which has hitherto been held in reserve. This is the Diary of Chief Justice Peter Oliver, which begins at the time of his leaving Boston. It is comprised in seven thin volumes in red leather wrappers. He was the younger brother of the late Lieutenant-Governor Oliver, as mentioned before; and as he had suffered much persecution and many wrongs, he dipped his pen in fire. He had toiled through life in an honourable profession, not to his personal emolument, for he was yearly out of pocket by the mean and miserable acknowledgment he got for his labours, where "even the Door-keeper had a larger stipend;" [i. p. 142.]—he had been driven from the Bench "for receiving his salary from the King"; his estate soon to be confiscated and his house burnt—his only crime being his fidelity to the King and to the laws he had sworn to obey. Lastly, he was now driven out of America, so he sought refuge in the land of his ancestors.

The Title on the first page runs thus:—

Journal of a Voyage to England in 1776, and of a Tour through part of England.

The extract must be rather long, but it is hoped that the interest attaching to it will plead excuses. It begins as follows:—

"1776.

"JOURNAL OF CHIEF JUSTICE PETER OLIVER.

"After having retired to Boston, under the protection of the King's troops, for the security of my person against the fury of the most unnatural, ungratefull, wanton, and cruel rebellion that ever existed, and after having been confined to the limits of that town for eighteen months, the rebels, who had for many months surrounded the town with strong entrenchments, began to bombard and cannonade it on the 2[d] of March 1776, which held for three nights successively, but with very little damage.*

"General Howe, the Commander-in-Chief, thought proper to abandon the town, and gave publick notice to the inhabitants, that such of them who inclined to quit the place, should have transports provided for them.

"March 10th.—Accordingly, on the tenth day of March I embarked on board the *Pacific*, Indiaman, Capt James Dun, which lay in King Road, it being a very commodious vessell, which General Howe was so polite as to appropriate to the accom̄odation of my friends and me.

"11th.—There was an hot cannonading to and from Boston and Dorchester Neck, as also to and from Castle William and Dorchester Neck, which continued from 8 o'clock at night untill the next morning.

"12th.—Some firing at Boston in the night.

"16th.—A hot firing at Boston abt 11 o'clock at night, till 9 o'clock next morning.

"17th.—The troops at Boston embarked, and about 20 sail fell down into King Road by 11 o'clock this morning.

"13th. †—The King's troops began to blow up the Castle William.

"19th.—I dined on board the *Chatham* with Admiral Shuldham. The south Blockhouse of the Castle was burnt at night, and some of the walls of it blown up.

"20th.—The blowing up of the Castle Walls continued: and at night all the combustible part of the Castle was fired. The conflagration was the most pleasingly dreadful that I ever beheld: sometimes it appeared like the eruption of Mount Etna; and then a deluge of fire opened to the view; that nothing could reconcile the horror to the mind, but the prevention of such a Fortress falling into the hands of rebels, who had already spread such a conflagration of diabolical fury throughout America, which scarce anything can quench but the—*metu tremefacit Olympum.*

* During the night of Mar. 4, there were fired into Boston 144 shot from 18 to 24 pounds, and 13 shells from 10 to 13 inches. On the 9th from both sides, "More than eight hundred shot were fired during the night." "General Howe's effective force, including seamen, was about 11,000 men. More than a thousand Refugees left Boston with the army." "The fleet dropped down to Nantasket Road, were it lingered ten days."—Frothingham's Hist. of Siege of Boston, 298, 305, 311.

† The figures are 13, but coming as they do between 17 and 19, it should seem that 18 was intended.

"21st.—The fleet fell down from King Road into Nantasket Harbour, which afforded a grand prospect, there being at least 150 sail of vessells at anchor.

"22nd.—A high N.W. wind.

"23rd.—D°.

"24th.—A high N.W. and very cold at night, so that the vessell's bows and cables were loaded with ice.

"25th.—The first Division sailed from Nantasket to Hallifax, [*sic*] as also the *Lord Hyde* Packet, Cap^n Jeffries for London, with Mr Thomas Hutchinson and my son Peter, and their families, as passengers.

"26th.—I dined on board the *Renown*, Commodore Banks.

"27th.—I sailed from Nantasket, ab^t 3 o'clock, afternoon, in the 2nd and last Division of the fleet, about 70 sail, for Hallifax, under convoy of the *Chatham*, Admiral Shuldham, and of the *Centurion*, Cap^n Braithwaite.

"Here I took my leave of that once happy country, where peace and plenty reigned uncontrouled, till that infernal Hydra Rebellion, with its hundred Heads, had devoured its happiness, spread desolation over its fertile fields, and ravaged the peacefull mansions of its inhabitants, to whom late, very late if ever, will return that security and repose which once surrounded them; and if in part restored, will be attended with the disagreeable recollection of the savage barbarities, and diabolical cruelties which had been perpetrated to support rebellion, and which were instigated by Leaders who were desperate in their fortunes, unbounded in their ambition and malice, and infernal in their dictates. Here I drop the filial tear into the Urn of my Country.

> "O fortunatos nimium, sua si bona norint—
> Nov-Anglicanos!

"And here I bid A Dieu to that shore, which I never wish to tread again till that greatest of social blessings, *a firm established British Government*, precedes or accompanies me thither.

"28th.—A good wind.

"29th.—Ditto. Were on Cape Sable Bank.

"30th.—Wind ab^t N.E. A tumbling sea, supposed to be occasioned by the indraught of the Bay of Fundy.

"31st.—Ditto.

"April 1st.—A tumbling sea : wind at N.E.

"2nd.—A southerly wind and smooth sea. Made land, on a north course, about 3 o'clock afternoon, and came to anchor before Hallifax at ½ an hour past 7 at night.

"The appearance of the first sight of land was thus :—

"3rd.—Landed at Hallifax. Edward Lyde Esq. invited me to his house, where I tarried till I embarqued for England. I was very happy in being at Mr Lyde's, as there was so great an addition to the inhabitants from the navy and army, and Refugees from Boston, which made the lodgings for them very scarce to be had, and many of them, when procured, quite intolerable. Provisions were here as dear as in London. The rents of houses were extravagant, and the owners of them took all advantages of the necessity of the times, so that I knew of three rooms in one house, wch house could not cost 500£ Sterl^{g}, let for £250* Sterl^{g} ꝑ year. Thus mankind prey upon each other. Not so the brute species.† I pitied the misfortunes of others, but I could only pity them : for myself, I was happily provided for, and was the more happy, as I had been very sea-sick during my $6\frac{1}{2}$ days' voyage, so that I could not enjoy to my wishes, the grand prospect of the ocean covered with ships in view, and some so near as to converse with our friends on board them.

"Hallifax is a very agreeable situation for prospects, and for trade: it is situated on a rising ground fronting the Harbour and ocean. There are 6 or 7 streets parallel to each other on the side of the hill, of about $1\frac{1}{2}$ or 2 miles in length, very strait, [straight] and of a good width. There are many others which ascend the hill, and intersect the long streets. On the top of the hill there is now a most delightful prospect of the harbour, Islands near the entrance of the harbor, and of the ocean, so that you may see vessells at a very great distance at sea: and when the woods are cleared off, there will be a most delightfull landscape, but at present there is not a great deal of cleared land.

"The soil about Hallifax is very strong, so that nature seems to have designed it for pasturage, although there are some spots improved by tillage to good advantage, but it was expensive to bring them into tilth. There are other parts of Nova Scotia, as Cumberland, Windsor, &c., which are formed for tillage, and which are well improved: but the coldness of the climate must lessen the

* The £ is placed indifferently before or after the figures.

† The Chief Justice was rather out of humour with human nature at that time; and as for the brute species, the big appear to devour the small all the world over.

profits of the farmer, as his cattle must consume in the winter great part of his summer's produce.

"The harbor of Hallifax is a most excellent one, capable of containing the whole English navy, where they may ride landlocked against any storms; at this time there are 200 sail before the town: and when Ld Loudoun was here in the year 1757, there were above 300 sail of vessells in the harbor. It is above a mile wide for 3 or 4 miles, and it is deep with good anchorage, and a bold shore. Above the harbor there is a Basin which empties into it; it is 5 or 6 miles broad, and 7 or 8 miles long; a good shore, and in some places 50 fathom deep. In this Basin Duke D'Anville retired out of observation in ye year 1745, and here he left one of his 70 gun ships, which is now at the bottom of this Basin.

"The houses of Hallifax seem to have been sowed like mushrooms in an hot-bed, and to have decayed as fast; for although they have been built but a few years, yet there are scarce any of them habitable, and perhaps a conflagration might occasion a Phœnix to rise out of its ashes.

"The air is very unpleasant and uncertain: you will feel many changes of it in a day: and if you would be safe in visiting your next neighbour, let your servant attend you with a cloak; for although you may set out in a cloudless sky, a hard shower may overtake you after a few steps. But notwithstanding of these sudden changes, it is agreed by all, that the place is healthy: but if any one chuses to live there, he is welcome to do so, provided he will not compel me to live there too. There is something peculiar in the soil, it being composed of slate and gravel; that although in one hour you may be over shoes in mud from the rains, yet the next hour will give you a clean street to walk in.

"As to the inhabitants, like all others who are absorbed in trade, they are detached from everything but their own interest. Many of them were low traders from New England, and happy will it be for them if they may escape the lava which issues from that Volcano of Rebellion, but the smoke hath already enveloped many of them. So much for Hallifax.

"During my stay at Hallifax, as well as during my residence in Boston, I was treated with ye utmost politeness, not to say friendship, by General Howe, who offered and urged me to every assistance I might wish for, and assured me, now at Hallifax, of being provided with a good ship for my passage to England; but the *Harriot* Pacquet, Capn Lee, being sent to carry home Govr Legge of Hallifax, Mr. Legge invited my niece Jenny Clarke and myself, to take passage with him; not suffering us to lay in any stores for ourselves, but to partake in his, of which he had made ample provision.

"May 12.—We accordingly embarked in the s^d^ Packet on ye 12th May, having as passengers in the cabin Govr Legge, James Monk Esq., Solicitor General of Hallifax, and his lady, Mr Birch, Chaplain of a Regiment, and Miss Clarke, and myself.

"We embarked at 8 o'clock in the morning, and came to sail at 3 o'clock in the afternoon. There were six sail more in company, convoyed by the Glasgow Man-of-War, Cap^n^ How.

"13th.—Cap^n^ Lee, having above 40 sailors on board, and 14 carriage guns, brought to a schooner, supposed to be an American Priveteer, but she proved a fishing vessell from Liverpool in Nova Scotia.

"14th.—At 12 o'clock at noon we were ab^t^ 70 leagues from Hallifax, wind S.S.W., and a fine gale. Cap^n^ Lee, thinking that he was of sufficient defence, left the Convoy and the other vessells. At night a fleet of 6 sail pass'd us from the southward, supposed from Antigua as storeships for Hallifax.

"15th.—Thick and misty weather.

"16th.—A fine gale: went 9 knots.

"17th.—Foggy and rain: wind S by E: were on the south Bank of Newf^d^land.

"18th.—A fog on the Bank: caught 8 cod fish. Had like to have been sunk early in the morning by a large island of Ice, which was grounded in fifty fathom water. The fog was so thick that we were within 2 ships' length of it before it was discovered, the vessell going 7 knots. It was very large, and as high again as our mainmast. There was another very large island about a league off. In the afternoon we saw another, at least 200 yards long, and 150 f^t^ high, about 3 leagues off; and when the sun shone upon it, and threw different shades upon the indents of it, it made a most grand and glorious appearance, that neither the eye or mind could ever be tired with viewing.

"19th.—Fair wind, but very tumbling sea.*

"20th.—Ditto . . . . Ditto.

"21st.—Fair wind.

"22nd.—D^o^.

"23rd.—D^o^.

"24th.—D^o^.

"25th.—Tumbling sea.

"26th.—D^o^.

* Probably "a short sea," or a "chopping sea."

"27th.—D°.

"28th.—D°.

"29th.—D°. These tumbling seas are vastly troublesome to sick or well. If you are well, they snatch the victuals out of your mouth if you can get it there; but 9 times out of 10 it will tantalize you by letting it approach your lips, and then make it retire before it reaches them: and if you are sick and bed-rid, and so prevent their spite by not eating, they will come at you by making you exert your feebleness in holding fast to keep yourself from being toss'd to the opposite side of the vessell, which is often the case, so that if you would be quite secure, you must, when the waves lash you, keep time with them, and lash yourself also.

"30th.—Made soundings about 8 o'clock at night, in 50 fathom water.

"31st.—Made Scilly at 6 o'clock in the morning.

"June 1st.—Arrived at Falmouth Harbour about midnight. Thus through a kind Providence which protected us from the ravages of Rebellion in Boston, and from storms and islands of ice on the ocean, after a passage of 20½ days, though very seasick during the passage, we harbored near that Island of Peace and Plenty where Government is, and can be supported, and where Rebellion hath formerly been check'd in its wanton career, and whose authority it is hoped, will suppress that American one, which exceeds in cruelty, malice, and infernal ingratitude, the united Rebellions recorded in history.

"Our passage was short, our Capn a good seaman, kind and obliging; our fellow passengers agreeable; our ship a fine sea boat; our crew of abt 45 sailors, peaceable and goodnatured; our vessell defensible by 14 carriage guns; our Steward extremely attentive to his department; our stores large in quantity, and good in quality, and of various sorts;—but what avail are all the superfluities of life in possession, without the power of enjoyment? Sea sickness disrelish'd all, till the view and effluviæ* of the land restored us to the taste of those pleasures, the loss of which we reflected upon with regret.

"It is worth remark that this was the 98th time that our Captain Lee had cross'd the Atlantick ocean since the year 1750: happy

* In reality the word is *effluvium*, a neuter noun, the plural being *effluvia*; but some persons write *effluvia* in the singular, as a feminine noun, and *effluviæ* in the plural. As time has gone on the signification of the word has become much altered. In the present day we should rather use such words as scent, or aroma.

for him if the old proverb—He that is born to be hanged will never be drowned—is not his protection.

"After an agreeable repose from a disagreeable voyage, I rose at 5 o'clock next morning. I looked abroad and found myself surrounded with great variety of the beauties of art and of nature; a populous town, a fine harbour, handsome well-built keys, [*sic*] stone and brick buildings, high and well cultivated lands all in verdure, and arranged like gardens with their allotments separated by hedges. It is impossible to convey to a mind which hath not already felt a similar entertainment, that most agreeable pleasure which diffuses itself upon a sudden transition to such agreeable scenes, from a situation whence, for 6 months past, I had beheld nothing but nature in its decay, and a wild and waste ocean.

"At 6 o'clock I went on shore at Falmouth, and put up at an inn nigh the water, Snoxall, a good house. Attended publick worship at church, Mr Allen, preacher, a worthy sensible gentleman. After noon I viewed the town with Mr Allen, and at the south part entered a beautiful vista of $\frac{1}{4}$ mile in length of two rows of tall trees, which formed an alcove, the tops inhabited by rooks who, unmolested, enjoyed their rural pleasures. We then went to view Pendennis Castle, or Pen Dinas, wch in old British signifies the End or Head of a city. It stands about a mile from the town of Falmouth, on a hill towards the English Channell: it is a regular strong fortification, difficult of access, and in vain did Oliver Cromwell attempt to storm it in the Civil Wars. Opposite to it is a platform of guns at St Mawes, and these two command the entrance of the harbour, which is an excellent one, and capable of containing the navy of England.

"Falmouth is well built, a place of great trade, the streets generally too narrow; the inhabitants very civil, and many of them very polite; a good market, and plenty of fish. It is supposed that the smuggling business is carried on here pretty freely, notwithstanding the great care of government to prevent it; for it is usual on the heights of the opposite shore to kindle fires at night to give notice to the smuggling vessells in the Channel of the King's Cutters being in the harbor: some of those lights we saw as we entered the harbor. Falmouth is the rendezvoux of the English Pacquets. Self interest is the grand Idol of mankind, and smugglers are such sincere votaries, that they will murder their fellow creatures, and expose themselves to the halter rather than be hindred in paying their devotions at its shrine. It was this smuggling trade that laid the Foundation Stone of the American Rebellion."

The Chief Justice and his niece Miss Jenny Clarke remained a few days in Falmouth, in order to recruit themselves after their voyage, and they pleasantly filled up the interval by visiting the tin, lead, and copper mines, and other places of interest in the neighbourhood, before they undertook their long and tedious journey to London. Leaving them a short time therefore, order and arrangement suggest that we should return to the Diary of Governor Hutchinson. The end of the thread was dropped at the 11th of May, when his son Thomas, together with a large accompaniment of relatives, arrived in London, also from Falmouth. From that point we proceed:—

May 12th.—At the Temple. Dr Thurlow preached.

We have but three rooms on a floor, and my daughter and I take two rooms, and my sister[-in-law] a third. In the other two lodging rooms we are forced to stow my son and daughter's families, consisting of 12, great and small: The maids in the upper storey.

13th.—[Sir Jeffery Amherst speculates on affairs.] . . .

I received 100 guineas of Gines & co. Gave nurse 10 guineas: Mrs Sanford 10 guineas: Mrs Oliver 10 guineas: and 2 guineas to Doctor Oliver.

14th.—In the evening with my eldest son at Northumberland House, where there was a very great appearance of nobility and gentry, upon the Dutchess's invitation, an old Lady just able to rise and receive the complim^ts^ of the company, leaning on her cane. Lord Hardwicke made us known to her. I have seen no house in London equal to this.* Its present elegance and grandeur are from the present Duke, who a few years ago was meer [*sic*] Sir Hugh Smithson. The answer of the Duke of Newcastle to him, when he desired a Blue Ribband, and after denial had said that he believed he was the first D. of Northumberland who had been denied a Garter, is in everybody's mouth, tho' the truth of it is doubtful. He was the first Sir Hugh Smithson that was made D. of Northumberland. Be that as it may, there are very few Commoners who would shew less arrogance than he does after rising to a Dukedom.

* This splendid mansion was entirely removed recently, and the site of it is now occupied by Northumberland Avenue, leading to the Thames Embankment, near Hungerford Bridge, and by the buildings on each side of it.

15th.—Advice has been received that General Burgoyne with the fleet, was seen on the 24th of April as far west as the Grand Bank; but the fears of the surrender of Quebeck before he can arrive, seem to increase. The wind has been favourable for five or six days, which probably has given a good offing to the Hessians, which passed by Plymouth the 10th.

16th.—A raw cold easterly wind. I spent an hour at Mr Cornwall's, who says he does not doubt of the final success of government in the American cause, but the burden which it brings upon the kingdom lyes with more weight on his mind than I ever discovered before; and he observed that though the reduction was not doubtful, yet there was something to follow which few people thought of the difficulty of maintaining government and order after it was reduced. It was impossible Connecticut and Rhode Island, he said, should remain under their present Charters. He wished nothing more had been done about the Massachusetts Charter than altering the Council. I told him I was in doubt of the expediency of that, and had wrote so to the Secretary of State. I knew the attachment of the people, and feared the convulsion it would occasion.

Peggy dined at Mr Knox's, and went with them to the play.

17th.—Two persons called on me to-day—John Lee and— Carter, from Philadelphia, which they left the 21st of March. Mr Lee brought a note from Richard Smith, with whom I was formerly concerned in trade, desiring him to come to me, and let me know he should have wrote, but durst not: that he had been forced to leave Philadelphia, and settle at Burlington, &c. He brought the votes of N. Jersey Assembly, a great number of newspapers, two pamphlets; all which I sent to Lord G. Germaine.

At Mr Knox's in the evening, and there first heard that Mr D'Oyly was appointed under Secry to Lord G. G., and that Mr P[ownal] was appointed Comiss. of Excise. Had conversation on the state of America. All N. England is probably in possession of all the authority and power of government on shore, but deprived of all trade by sea. Tryon is at New York, but on board ship, without being able to do any act as Governor.

Franklin in the Jerseys, has more of the form of government, and held his Assembly in December, with which he did not incline to differ.* Penn at Philadelphia, sits altogether still, and acquiesces in all that his own Assembly, as well as the Congress think proper. Maryland, of late, has been more quiet than usual. Ld Dunmore keeps on board ship in Virginia; as does Martin at N. Carolina, and Ld Wm Campbell in S. Carolina. Sir J. Wright was leaving Georgia to go to Boston. East and West Florida are yet in possession of Gov., as well as Nova Scotia, but Canada is doubtful. Insurances are made on property in Quebec at 20 ꝑ c^t^ in London. Burgoyne may possibly arrive, as on the 10th of May, but it's uncertain as it is, whether before that, it will not surrender.

18th.—Called in the morning to give M^r^ D'Oyly joy on his appointment. He does not seem over pleased, and I believe he aimed at as good an income, attended with less trouble. He and she are fond of the country in summer, and Mr Knox's health obliges him to be in the country; but in the present state of America, there must be one of the Secretaries in town. Mr Ellis not at home.

19th.—At the Old Jewry.

At Court. The King passed me without speaking to me, which he had never done before, but there were several other gentlemen in the same circumstances, and he went round the circle much quicker than usual. The christening of the Princess was at 7 o'clock, and the company was in the Ante-Chamber, the Drawing-Room being kept shut on acc^t^ of the Christening.

In the evening at Dr Heberden's. The wind still at NE.

20th.—Report of an English vessel taken by Portuguese, and carried into Lisbon:—calculated to lower Stocks, &c.

21st.—Another report to-day, that Sir P. Parker and his fleet were certainly arrived at New York, and that letters were in town giving an account of it—that Stocks were fallen, &c., —all without grounds.

I met Col. Leland in St. James's Park, who is fully of opinion that if any Government letters reached Howe before he left Nantasket, the troops are not gone to Halifax. It's now

* This was William Franklin, son of Dr. Franklin, and a loyal man.

ten days since the Hessians left the Channel, and the wind has been to North, and Eastward of North, and still continues.

22nd.—Mr Ellis and Mr Jenkinson called: the latter sets out to-morrow for France to spend the summer on the Continent. Mr Stanley goes with him. Mentioning to Mr Ellis my thoughts of living in the country to save charge, he advises against it, and says—"Remain *in oculis civium* if you have anything to hope, for yourself or family. You will be forgot in the country."

In the evening with Mr Mauduit at Ranelagh. Lord Townshend joined us. Speaking of the Licences to export to America, he called it a shabby business. Mauduit says one Merry, a broken Vintner, applied to Cooper and Robinson for leave to carry beef from Africa, where it was said to be extreme cheap, to America; but alleged it was necessary to export goods to purchase it, and that he was not able to advance the money. Leave was granted, and Cooper gave him some sort of Certificate that the Treasury would be responsible. This Merry shewed, to gain credit; but instead of 5 or 6,000£ in one ship only, £30,000 was insured. This alarmed the Merchants, as there was no doubt the goods were to go from Africa. Before the ships proceeded, the King of that part of Africa where they were to go, forbad the exportation of cattle, and one ship went with goods to America—others were stopped by the clamour of the Merchants. Mauduit says it looks as if C—— and R—— were sharers in the licences, and calls it a very exceptional affair, and it looks as if it would be taken up again next session.

23rd.—I called at Lord Lucas's, Lord—late M^r^—Onslow, and Lord Harrowby's, new created, and left my name. At Lord North's Levée, to introduce my son. Afterwards desired Lord Gower, and he took him into the House of Lords to hear the King's Speech at the Prorogation.

As cold this evening as in March.

24th.—At Sir George Hay's, to obtain administration for Genl Winslow's wages, on the request of P. Winslow to my son Elisha, who treated me very politely; and after settling the business I went upon, he entred upon American affairs. I said to him that I did not approve of the Stamp Act; but I never had seen an opportunity since the repeal of it when Government could have conceded to the claims of America, without admitting their principle of total independence. He seemed to join with me, but not to be satisfied with measures; and he said Mr Conway made an excellent speech, and in it observed that he had received from me in the time of the Stamp Act, such reasons against the passing of it as were irresistible. I told Sir George I ever thought the taxing America by Parliament not advisable, but as a servant of the Crown, I thought myself bound to discountenance the violent opposition made to the Act, as it led to the denial of its authority in all cases whatsoever, and in fact, had brought on the Rebellion.

These remarks are more to the purpose, and, for a short sentence, aim more directly at the origin of the struggle, and account for his reasons in resisting it, than any single paragraph that might be pointed out anywhere in the Diary or Letters. Though he sided with the Americans in disapproving of the Stamp Act, he resisted their riotous proceedings, simply because riot was against law. As long as he was a servant of the Crown, it was imperative that he should uphold its authority, be his private opinions what they might. If all the officials of an Empire were to act according to their various individual sentiments, regardless of their instructions from headquarters, the result may be imagined—or perhaps the result would be beyond the reach of imagination. The last sentence of the extract which we have made from the Diary of Chief Justice Oliver is not so near the mark. He says—"It was this smuggling trade that laid the foundation stone of the American Rebellion." Less direct, but related in a kindred degree, as an ingredient of the general lawlessness, the smuggling trade had its influence.

25th.—[Hessians supposed to have sailed.]

26th.—At the Temple. Dr Thurlow. I met Mr Brooks, the Chaplain at Quebec, and afterwards Sr Tho. Mills. They both seemed very sanguine that the place would not surrender. Court mourning for the Grand Dutchess of Russia.

27th.—[Lord Cranley called. Hot day. Hessians.]

28th.—Everybody seems anxious for news from America.

For two or three days the winds have been favorable: at south most of this day. We are not sure that Howe went to Halifax, and the fate of Quebec is doubtful. Thirteen New Englanders, of which I was one, met by accident to-day in St. James's Park. Two or three more were in the Park at a distance.

29th.—Mr Blackburne of the Marshalsea called. He says there is a total change to-day in the Prince's family. Ld Bruce instead of Ld Holderness; Bp. of Litchfield [*sic*] (Hurd), instead of Chester, (Markham); and the sub-preceptors changed.

At the King's Levée. He asked if I did not think the weather very pleasing after so much raw disagreeable weather? I said I was glad of the raw weather, as it was the effect of a fair wind. But, he said—"you like a little mixture?" "Not whilst so important a service depended on a fair wind." "That was generous," he said, "but now you wish to have a little news."

I promised Mr Mckenzie at the Levée to write to him in Scotland.

[Dined at the King's Head, &c.]

30th.—Lord Dartmouth called, &c.

31st.—Dined to-day with Sir H. Houghton in Upper Brook Street. Mauduit, Dr Finch, (a Rector in the city), Mr Raymond, who married Lady Houghton's sister, and my son E. were the company. Sir H. says that when Ld Holderness returned from the Continent, where he went for his health, he perceived a difference in the Prince's behaviour, wch he attributed to ill impressions made by people about the Prince; and that he has ever since been wishing to retire, and at length the King consented, but found difficulty to prevail on Lord Bruce to be his successor, until a letter wrote by the King, which is said to be a very good one, had the effect. In the letter Lord Bruce's expectation of the Earldom of Aylesbury is hinted at very genteelly, but Lord Bruce made a point of having the Bp. of Litchfield for Preceptor. It is said a difference between Lord Holderness and Mr Jackson, Sub-preceptor, accelerated this change, and caused just at this time what has been long preparing, but kept private. I saw the Bp. of Chester, the late Preceptor, at the King's Levée on Wednesday last, with all the appearance of being much hurt, tho' it is said he has the promise of the first of the rich Bishopricks which falls. He may fall first. Upon the whole, this affair is not pleasing. The K. has been observed to be very pensive some time past. Misunderstandings between the K. and the Prince* are to be dreaded. They have been more frequent, not to say general, in the English than any other history.

South wind but no arrival.

June 1st.—A rainy day. . . .

2nd.—At the Old Jewry. A sensible young man preached, whose name I could not learn. Lord Hume and Lord Harrowby, two of the new Lords, called as they went to Court.

3rd.—Went into the Borough to Battlebridge with my sons. On my return found news from N. York by express from Tryon, which came out the 28th of April—that Quebec had been a second time attacked by Worster [?] and Arnold, who were repulsed with the loss of 1500 men—that more troops were on their way from N. England, &c. to Quebec, but the Lakes began to break up—that Lee was taken prisoner by Clinton in N. Carolina with 170 of Rifle-men who were a guard to Lee, as he was going to take the coīnand of the southern rebels—that Hopkins and his fleet from Philad. were blocked up in New London harbour—that Washington had left his army, and was returned to the Congress—that Putnam and Schuyler commanded at N. York—and that many of the inhabitants there, were ready to take up arms. This is the only good news for some time, and everybody on the side of Government is in high spirits. Lord Cranley, in his phaeton, stopped me in Piccadilly, and seemed in an extasy.[*sic*] Wind E., but exceeding hot for this country all day.

4th.—At Court. The King's Birthday. Took M^r Jo. Greene

* Prince George, afterwards George IV., was born Aug. 12, 1762. He was now therefore within three months of fourteen, and beginning to discover that he had a will of his own. Some people find this out very early. And young Princes, who have large prospects before them, and too many flatterers around them, are brought up in a pleasant, but in a very dangerous school.

and Sparhawk in my coach. A vessel arrived from Halifax with letters from Gen. Howe, May 12th. One of the transports taken by the rebel privateers, said to have the merchandize which was taken from Boston. Howe had received all the dispatches from Gov. which could be arrived. The private letters not yet come up, and we know nothing yet of our friends at Halifax. He had sent a detachment from his army to Quebec, but had heard nothing from thence. My three daughters at the Ball in the Chamberlain's box.

5th.—We hear that two or three other vessels came out of Halifax with the vessel arrived at Falmouth, and that Lt Gov. Oliver and divers other passengers are on board. At Mr Robinson's, &c. . . .

6th.—Called upon the B^p^ of Oxford, and left my name. Afterwards upon the Abp. at Lambeth. Dr Chandler with me. Rec^d^ a letter from Judge Oliver at Halifax, dated Ap. 17. He arrived wth the last division of 70 sail, April 3rd. Mentions the death of Ch. Just. Belcher.

I called on Mr Knox at the Office, and took a list of the persons and families wch removed from Boston, which I make to be 938 souls.

Judge Oliver writes Col. Browne that Billy Jackson, (who has been a steady asserter of Gov^t^), was taken by the rebels, and carried in (I think) to Newbury; ill treated, insulted, and haltered about the neck, and from thence carried to Boston.

7th.—I met Col. Ewing in Pall Mall coming to St James's Street, and turned back with him. He arrived in town last night from Halifax with his family. In the same ship (*Hall*) came his brother George and family, Royall Treasurer Gray, his son Lewis and family, Col. Hatch and family, and Col. Murray and wife. The Lt Gov., Col. Vassall, Mr Lechmere and families, and Peter Johannot, are arrived at Dartmouth. The Chief Justice in the packet wth Gov. Legge at Falmouth. Cap. Gore, Paddock, Joy, Laughton, &c., in another vessel at Dover, wth Ned Lyde, Pelham, T. Brinley, &c. They had heard nothing at Halifax from Quebec; nor had they any circumstantial account of affairs at Boston. A newspaper of 8 of April has a pompous Address from the Select-men of Boston to his Excellency General Washington, and his Answer. There was a report that a number of vessels from England were seen in the Gulph of St Lawrence the 16 of April. A Regiment for Quebec sailed from Halifax the 22nd of April. The *Glasgow* arrived also with Sr James Wright from Halifax, Gov. of Georgia. It was reported at Halifax that the *Centurion*, which sailed from thence to the southward about the 15th of April, had destroyed Newport in Rhode Island; but it was by vessels spoke with at sea. The Mass. Newspapers say the vessel Jackson was taken in, was worth 35,000£ sterl.

Several of the Masters of transports wch had been taken, obtained leave to go from Salem to London. Stopping at Halifax, a letter was found from Dr Eliot to young Mr Smith, which the General and officers were very angry at. Smith had wrote to his friends in such a manner as gave him great credit with General Howe, who opened all letters. I think it probable that this came to the knowledge of the heads of the people, and that Doctor Eliot, to whom one of the letters I suppose to be wrote, tho't it necessary to write such an answer as should shew he disapproved Smith's principles. It is said that the letter was sent open from Boston to Salem.

8th.—Waiting for more news concerning Quebec. Mr Lyde called in the evening. Mauduit took his leave of us for a month to go to Hampshire, Joshua Ironmonger's near Andover. Wherwell.

9th.—At the Temple—Dr. Thurlow.

Dined at Vanburgh Fields with Soame Jenyns, Sr Tho. Mills, and their ladies, besides Mr Pownall's family, and Peggy. Find from Mr P. that Howe only awaited the arrival of the W. India Victuallers to proceed to New York, and that the Hessians are ordered direct to the scene of action, not improbably to Delaware, or it may be to join Howe at New York. It was also said that Sir P. Parker and about 30 sail were spoke with near the coast of America, but Sir T. M., who had it from Cunningham, of Lord G.'s family, could not ascertain the day.

Treasurer Gray, George Erving, Murray, J. Hatch, and their families, came ashore at Deptford to-day.

Naturally enough, the movements of General Howe at this juncture were watched by all orders of men, as the summer campaign had now opened, and great expectations were entertained in England that something of a very decisive nature would soon be effected. The large amount of forces going out favoured these expectations, and the appointment of Lord Howe to the fleet confirmed them. The name of Howe was popular with the Americans, for an elder brother of these two commanders fought side by side with Americans, against the French in the reduction of Canada, and was there killed; and the Americans, out of a kindly feeling, subsequently erected a monument to his memory. Bearing these things in mind, it was thought to be a stroke of supreme wisdom to send out the two surviving brothers on the present occasion. Never was there a greater mistake! If they had been sent out with an Olive Branch, instead of shot and powder, to settle an amicable arrangement, then the choice would have been judicious enough; but to send friends out to shoot friends, was about the silliest thing that ever was done—and so I shall be able to shew further on.

Mr. Hutchinson's remarks on some of these points, when writing to Lieutenant-Governor Thomas Oliver, on the 17th of February, 1776, are the following:—

"I hope you will hold out until reinforced. The vast armam^{t} must bring infinite distress on America this summer unless there shall be a submission to Gov^{t}. Ld H. com^{s} by sea, and Gen. H. by land. This, I am assured, is agree^{l} to the K.'s priv. as well as publ. inclinat^{s}, and it is at the same time the most popular meas. wch could be taken, and I hope Amer. will erect statues to the two younger broth^{s}, as it has done a monum^{t} to the elder. I know of no service wch deserves a statue more than restoring a country from a state of anarchy and confus^{n} to a state of gov. and order."

As to those who deserve statues, we must rather judge after the current of events, and not before. There is an original Note, written at this time by the hand of Lord Hardwicke—not the easiest of hands to read—which betrays hunger for news, and which may reasonably find a place here:—

"June 9th —76.

"Ld Hardwicke is much obliged to Govr Hutchinson for the extract of the N. York Letter wch he hopes will soon be confirmed. It is very amazing that the American office has not vouchsafed to inform the public with so much as that Genl Howe and his troops were arrived at Hallifax: hopes what the papers have asserted is not true,—that the Army got there in a sickly state. Wishes Mr Hutchinson w^d^ ask some of his Friends who are lately come, why, during the Winter, when the Rebels had but a small Force before Boston, nothing was done by way of attack on their Lines, or rather, by way of Diversion for support? Those who were up in Long Island from Master Todd's *Advertisement*, one sh^d^ suppose that Gov^t^ imagined, they sh^d^ be Masters soon of N. York. Ld H. has seen a very curious Braggadochio Letter from Mr Hutchinson's old *Friend* Dr Franklin. It is dated from N. York 29th of March. He says ye Colonists are prepared for every Thing y^t^ can happen; the whole Continent in arms, and at N. York, Young and Old, Rich and Poor, Males and Females, at work on the Fortifications.

"Ld H. desires Miss H. may be asked how she sh^d^ like to carry a Basket with earth, or a Bundle of Fascines?—probably with, and for a Friend, very well."

The question asked by his Lordship above, has been asked by others; and although General Howe might doubt whether he was strong enough with his twenty Regiments to make a sortie in force from the city, for the purpose of dislodging from ten to seventeen thousand Provincials from a series of fortified positions subtending a front of nearly ten miles, and at the same time to leave troops sufficient behind him to ensure the security of his base, yet, the known weakness of Washington's army, the rawness of his soldiers, and his want of ammunition, might have justified the English General in making the attempt. In his *History of the Siege of Boston*, p. 269, Mr. Frothingham writes—"Washington could account for the inactivity of the enemy only by supposing that he was meditating some important enterprise." And he quotes the American Commander-in-Chief, who wrote, November 28—"Our situation is truly alarming; and of this General Howe is well apprized," &c. Adolphus ii. 340, says—"The whole force under Washington, did not, at the close of the year, [1775] amount to ten thousand, but was shortly afterwards augmented to about seventeen thousand, by drafts from the militia." And again—"It afforded much reasonable ground of surprize, that Howe should remain pent up in Boston, and make no military effort to relieve the miseries of his own troops, and crush the hopes of the Americans. He was not ignorant of Washington's alarming distresses; and this want of enterprize enabled his opponent to boast of his own exertions and situation, as unparalleled in the annals of history: he had maintained his post for six months without powder; and at the same time had disbanded one army and recruited another, within musket shot of more than twenty British Regiments." Lord Hardwicke's question seems not without reason.

To resume—

10th.—At length the Governm[t] is relieved from its anxiety about Quebec. An Express arrived this morning with letters from Gen. Carleton, advising the arrival of the *Isis*, and one or two other vessels the 6th of May; and that, as soon as 20 men were landed, he marched out of the town: that the rebels retreated with such precipitation, as to leave their cannon and other stores behind: that before the date of this letter, he had heard of their arrival at M[t]real, which they were preparing to abandon also, and gave out they would make a stand at Sorel and Chamblée: that the whole of the 29th Reg[t], and also the 47th Reg. from Halifax, arrived soon after: that there had been no action after the repulse the 31 Dec., in which Carleton says the rebels lost 700 men, killed, wounded, and taken: that the garrison had only ab[t] of Navy,* and 4 men killed, and 13 wounded during the whole siege: that by batteries from Point Levi, they had made some attempt upon the ships, but to no purpose. In coming down the river the Express met Burgoyne's forces about 100 leagues from the city. She sailed the 16. of May. Burgoyne carried the frames of two vessels for the Lakes, and ironwork, &c. for batteaux, but not timber and plank frames, as was reported. I fear it will take much time to prepare for such an army to pass the Lakes, and if Quebec could have been preserved without, this force had better gone to other parts, but that could not be foreseen. Indeed, it's probable the rebel army had advice of a great force expected, or they would not so precipitately have retreated.

I wrote to M[r] Mackenzie in Scotland, to acquaint him with the news.

11th.—The *Isis* sailed the 11th of March from Portsmouth; made the island of S[t] Peter's the 11th of April; sailed 50 or 60 leagues thro' large fields of thick ice until the 21st, when

* Something wanting.

she was clear of it; made the island of Anticosty, and entered the river S[t] Laurence on the 30th; anchored in a snow storm near Pilgrim's Islands; observed smoaks [*sic*] from Cape to Cape towards Quebec; May 3 arrived near Coudre, where she was joined by the *Surprize* and *Martin* sloop, both which sailed the 20 March from Plymouth. Douglas, of the *Isis*, ordered the *Surprize* up to Quebec on the 5th, and the 6th in the morning she was in view of the town, and found her private signals answered.

M[r] Knox tells me D[r] Franklin, with his Romish priests, was at Montreal just time enough to hear of the arrival of the troops, and to scamper back. One Miller, a Custom House Officer, and — Thomson, obtained leave to come with a vessel from Newbury to England. They say they were in Boston the 4 of May; that some of the people left there were laid under some restraint; that Inventories were taken of all the household furniture and other goods, of those who had left the town; and that it was intended to retaliate upon the owners the loss any of the rebels had sustained, by the seizure of their goods.

Col[o] Murray and Judge Browne dined with us.

12th.—L[t] Gov. Oliver, Col[o] Hatch, and George Erving, M[r] Chipman, &c., called upon me: all from Halifax. Col[o] Jn[o] Vassall, Tho. Brinley and wife, Peter Johannot, came to town yesterday, and a day or two before. All depend upon Gov[t] to support them. Advertisement in a Watertown paper, notifying the sale of Tho. Oliver, Jun[r],* Sewall's, and other estates in Cambridge, at the house of Jn[o] Vassall; and if no purchasers for the fee, then to lease the estates to the highest

* This may be a son of the second Lieut.-Governor of the name of Oliver. The name Thomas, of the date here spoken of, does not synchronize with the names in the pedigree of Lieut.-Gov. Andrew Oliver. Frothingham, p. 194, says—"The house of Governor Oliver in Cambridge, known as the Gerry estate, was occupied as a hospital. Many of the soldiers who died of their wounds were buried in a field in front of this house." Also quoted vol. i. p. 496.

In the Pedigree of L.-Gov. Andrew Oliver, of his two grandsons by his second wife, the eldest eventually married my father's sister, but the younger one came to an untimely end. It is stated thus in the Pedigree—"A son, whose death in infancy was caused by the rebels in Boston." What act of violence killed this child is not recorded. It was probably only an instance of Edmund Burke's superlative degree of Liberty, or "extreme of Liberty," as he called it.

bidders. This is tyranny beyond any instance in time of the Rebellion in England.

Paid Housekeeper to 1st of June.

13th.—Went with L[t] Gov. Oliver to Lord Dartmouth's: not at home: the Treasury, M[r] Knox, and the Admiralty. . . .

Judge Oliver with Jenny Clarke came to town in the evening. Lodgings in Jermyn Street.

At this point we must take another glance into the Diary of the Judge, and make a note of a few remarks of his, suggested by the circumstances of his journey. We left him and his niece recruiting themselves after a trying voyage; but at the end of four days they commenced the still more trying undertaking in the long and wearisome carriage drive to London, which was not accomplished under nine days, though the same is now achieved in a less number of hours. They passed through Truro, Liskeard, Plymouth, Ashburton, Chudleigh, Exeter, Honiton, Axminster, Bridport, Dorchester, Blandford, Salisbury, Amesbury, Andover, Basingstoke, Staines, and lastly London. Only such parts can be extracted as seem to claim notice for some particular reason.

"June 5th.—I sot [*sic*] out from Falmouth this morning in a Postchaise: pass'd through Penryn, &c.

"We viewed the church [at Truro] which was built anno 1517. On each side of the altar window was a fine piece of painting—Moses and Aaron, which seemed quite animated. They were taken from a church in Vigo, when Vigo was taken many years since: they were most excellent paintings.

"6th.—Sot out towards Plymouth. . . .

"7th.—This morning visited Lord Edgcumbe's seat. . . . We then descended the walks around the sea shore, which were varied with taste, and yet seemed formed on the plan of nature, with seats to rest on, and with hermitages; promontories on one side, and the sea opening through trees on the other,—filled the mind with pleasure. But I was in one walk deprived of pleasure for a moment, it being so like a serpentine walk of mine on the banks of the river Namasket, which so lately had been wrenched from me by the Harpy claws of Rebellion, that I was snatched from where I now was to the loss of where I had so late been in the arms of contentment. . . .

"9th.—Sot out from Plymouth. . . .

"10th.—Sot out from Exeter to Honiton. . . . We then sot off for Dorchester. . . . The Downs were covered with sheep, attended with shepherds and their dogs. The sheep were drove into hurdles at night, where they were confined till morn, and where they enriched the land which they had lain on, paying the owner of it large interest by their manure, for the use of his lodging them. The hurdles are made of slender sticks interwove, about 3½ feet high, in separate lengths, so that after the sheep had sufficiently manured the space which one hurdle enclosed, it was soon removed for the same purpose. It was pleasing to see the behaviour of the dogs in collecting the stragglers of the flock : for as there are no inclosures on the downs where the sheep feed, some of them will be at a distance from the flock: the shepherd then tells the dog to gather them: the dog understands his master, and the sheep know what the dog is coming for, and then resort to the flock. To see the amazing number of sheep within a few miles of this place, made me almost look down with contempt on the Americans, who boast of clothing themselves with the produce of their own wool; whereas all the American Colonies have not wool enough of their own to furnish themselves with cloathing for their hands and feet; and within a few miles of this place there are more sheep feeding than there are in all the American Colonies. Besides, the American wool, even in the northern parts of the Continent, is of a coarse staple; but in the southern parts, it degenerates almost to hair, and is unserviceable for human clothing, unless for the Romish Mendicant Priests' shirts to do penance in, and to make whips for them to scourge their bodies for the good of their souls. Another consideration prevents their wool from being of very great advantage, which is —— That in the northern parts of America, where the wool can be of any service, the winter climate is generally so severe that the sheep must be foddered with hay at that season, which makes the profit of sheep small, whereas in England, the sheep keep abroad in the winter, the verdure being pretty constant. . . .

"Dorchester is a very pretty town . . . It is said that taking this town in the centre, and six miles around it every way, that 600,000 sheep are fed. . . .

"13th.—Sot out from Basingstoke. . . .

"Dined at Staines, and rode over Hounslow Heath, ab^t^ 10½ miles from London. This Heath is also as infamous for robbers and as famous for roads, as Bagshot, and is ab^t^ 3 miles over; and here our eyes were saluted with 3 or 4 Gibbets, the insignia of Highwaymen's exploits. They may possibly serve *in terrorem*, but they are disagreeable to travellers.

"Before I entered London, the first man whom I met, that I knew in England, was his Majesty riding to Kew with his Guards. Soon after I arrived in London, and took lodgings at Mr Wheland's, a sadler in Jermyn Street, where I had 3 rooms well furnished at 1½ guinea ꝑ week. . . .

"14th.—Dined at Governor Hutchinson's where I was regaled as usual with meeting many of my old friends."

Now we have landed the Chief Justice in London, it may be remarked that in future there will be but few occasions for quoting his Diary. Whilst he remained there, and was continually coming in contact with Refugees like himself, he made a few passing remarks on political events, but the greater portions of these seven memorandum books, are taken up with descriptions of some of the places of resort or amusement in the metropolis which he visited: with country journeys into the manufacturing districts, for the purpose of inspecting mills, factories, workshops, or foundries, having a great desire apparently to make himself better acquainted with the uses and efficiency of machinery: and with pleasure trips into different parts of Wales, where he took delight in the scenery. The Governor's Diary proceeds thus—

14th.—With Judge Oliver to wait on Lord George: left his name. . . .

15th.—Breakfasted at Mrs Howe's the General's lady, in Queen Street May Fair, with Judge Oliver, upon invitation. We went afterwards to visit General Legge at No 4 Great Marlborough Street, and from thence to the Queen's Palace * to see the apartments, &c.

Account of many, if not all, the last division of Hessians for America at Spithead. It's thought strange there should be no certain accounts yet of Sir P. Parker, and the troops under Lord Cornwallis, tho' they sailed the 13th of February.

16th.—At the Temple Church—Mrs Oliver [his daughter] with me. Doctor Morill preached from Solomon's Song—The singing of birds is come, &c.† A florid description of the beauties of the spring, observing that the perfection of Art was its approach to nature, the imitation of which was necessary; and among other instances, mentioned the foliage in capitals of pillars—the festoons—without which they appeared naked;

* Buckingham Palace, vol. i. pp. 425, 449. † Ch. II. v. 12.

and the beauties of the roof over his head were owing to its resemblance of [to ?] the branches of the trees of the forest; and he descended to the milkmaids, who would make no shew without a Garland. Less of religion could not well be in a Sermon, the touches upon the wisdom of the Creator being slight.

17th.—Called upon Mr Knox wth J[udge] Oliver. He says the Highlanders, 3200, were spoke with the 21 of May, within six days sail of Boston: they left Cork the 28th of April, the Hessians 10 days after. The *Glasgow* from Halifax spoke with the *Greyhound*, and 4 sail of victuallers from Cork. The *Experiment* had been at Nantasket, and was spoke with going to Halifax. She ought to have 19 sail of provision vessels with her. The Hessians were ordered to Newport. Sr James Wright, who arrived in the *Glasgo*, [*sic*] was on board the *Scarboro'* when at Newport. He says the Rh. Islanders sent an Express to Hopkins at New London to come to take the *Scarboro'*, and that he sent word he could not be ready in less than 48 hours, and thereupon the passengers on board were invited ashoar, and offer was made to send hostages aboard; but the wind coming fair, the *Scarborough* came to sail, but was saluted from a battery on a point, of three-pound shot, only one of which struck one of the *Scarboro's* masts.

The state of America is now very critical and very interesting. Such of us as are in England are in great suspense and uncertainty. Some hope that this summer may produce a restoration of Gov^t^; others think the war may continue several years, and some that the kingdom will be wearied out. The repulse at Quebec affords a more favourable prospect than many expected, and probably that the Canadians and Indians will engage with the King's troops, and join in invading the frontiers of N. York and N. England. Carleton is supposed to have 8,000 men in Canada; Howe at least 9,000 at Halifax, including those which were there before they left Boston; Cornwallis had 3,500 gone to Carolina; near 8,000 Hessians, and 1000 of the Guards sailed the beginning of May from Spithead; and 3200 Highlanders a few days before from Cork; 5,000 Hessians and 1,500 Brunswickers are now embarked, and part arrived at Spithead; and it is thought there are about 3,000 recruits raised and raising to complete the Reg^{ts} in America.

This makes an army of 42,000 men, besides the Marines in the fleet, which may be landed on any extraordinary occasion, and exceeds what the Leaders in America thought in the power of the kingdom to raise and transport.

18th.—At Mr Lane's to visit Mr Lechmere * and family, and Mr Symes's, to Col. Vassall and family. At Lloyd's there is an acc^{t} of two Jamaica ships chased off Bermudas; one arrived, the other they are afraid is taken by one of the American cruizers. A Jamaica ship spoke with one of the men-of-war which convoyed the Hessians, and was in company with 80 odd sail the 22nd May off the Western Islands.

My son [Thomas] being obliged to take a woman and her child for the sake of nursing his youngest child [Andrew] for a day or two, my family now consists of 25, besides my coachman at board wages. Happy that I can support them, when many Americans are in distress, who have only their own persons to take care of.

I went to-day to Mr Blackburne's in Scotch Yard, Bush Lane, to accommodate an affair between Captain Loring and Mr Flucker, who owes Loring 900£ sterl., besides large sums to others, and has no way of discharging them but by his American lands.

* I presume this is an ancestor of Sir Edmund Anthony Harley Lechmere, Bart., M.P. Three or four dimes of years ago the father of the present Baronet, Sir Anthony by name, with his young son, a saucy and mischievous lad, whom I both remember well, lived for a time in a house in the Fort Field Terrace, at the town of Sidmouth in Devonshire. One of the other houses in the same row was occupied by Admiral and Mrs. White. The Admiral was a dapper little sailor, of rather diminutive build, and with short legs to a short body; and as Sir Anthony Lechmere had a tall thin figure—I see him now in my mind's eye—the contrast between the two was sufficiently striking. On the outside of the Terrace road there was a grass slope, which Admiral White had a pride in seeing kept neat, whilst the boy, who I think was an only child, and pretty well indulged, was always running up and down it, digging in his toes, and making holes, to the grief of the old sailor. One day the latter ventured to admonish young Lechmere on the impropriety of injuring the grass, when the boy, nothing abashed, cried out—"And what's that to you, Little Short-legs!" My father either witnessed this or had it from Sir Anthony, whom he knew well. I heard him tell it when he came home.

19th.—Called upon Sir James Wright, Governor of Georgia. Afterwards at the King's Levée. Several Hanoverian officers and gentlemen just arrived. A letter received by Gov^t^ yesterday from Lord Cornwallis 360 leagues distant from Carolina, dated 18th April; 25 sail only, out of 40—the rest dispersed.

In the evening at Mr Knox's—Sir James Wright and family there. All but Elisha and Dr Oliver went to Ranelagh.

20th.—A vessel from Halifax wth letters to the 25th. The *Greyhound*, the *Donation*, ship, and several victuallers arrived, but not the West India fleet. Howe had rec^d^ advice of the reinforcement, but not of its destination to R. Island, and intended to wait for it at Halifax. There is a great appearance that the summer will be near spent before anything important is done.

At Lord Hardwicke's—complains, and comes to town to the Doctor. Neither wealth nor title can add much to human happiness.

21st.—Letter at the Admiralty from Commod[ore] Hotham, with 84 sail in Lat. 44.57, Long. 30, from the Lizard, the 5th June: had parted with one brig only the 26 May in a gale of wind. He was sorry the winds being westerly.

Sir James Wright called:—Cap. Newton from Halifax.

In the evening with Doct. Chandler to Fulham: drank tea at the Bishop's, who read a letter from Dr Caner, in great distress at Halifax.

22nd.—Doctor Caner, passenger in the *Adamant* from Halifax, came to town to-day, and I called on him at his lodgings in the Haymarket. The soldiers set to guard his house, plundered it of his books, furniture, &c., and so they did Mr Troutbeck's.

Sir F. Bernard, his son and daughter, with Treas. Gray, and M^r^ Jo. Green, dined with us.

I wrote to Mauduit, and Mr Mackenzie at Belmont Castle, by Edinburgh.

23rd.—At the Old Jewry with Mrs Oliver and Peggy, and three grandchildren. A stranger preached. In the evening I took Dr Caner in my carriage to the Bp. of London's at Fulham.

24th.—An Express from Quebec came away the 25th of May.

No more troops had then got up, the winds having been contrary: but the officer who came Express says the Irish Regiments arrived the 26, and Burgoyne, who was at Coudre two or three days after: that Burgoyne had gone up the river towards Montreal with the 29th and 47th Regs, and left orders for the rest to follow as they arrived, without disembarkation: that the rebels had retreated to Sorel: that a detachment of the 8th, which was posted at Detroit, under Cap. Foster, with some Canadians and Indians, had taken a Fort on St Lawrence, near La Galotte [?] called The Cedres, with 360 of the rebels, prisoners: and that the whole body of the Western Indians were on their march to join the King's troops: and that Carleton might command 10,000 of the Canadians into service if he wished it.

At Dr Tarpley's in the evening. He had seen a letter from Mr Alsop at Quebec wch mentions the fireship prepared by the rebels, as discovered by him from the ramparts, and fired upon with a 24-pounder from the Fort, which caused fire to be set to the train sooner than otherwise, and defeated their scheme: and he adds, that if the ships had taken fire, and the town been stormed at the same time, they must have perished. When Montgomery was killed they had a masked battery, the guns loaded with grape-shot, [so] that, when the rebels entered, the battery was opened, and Montgomery being at the head of his men, he was tore to pieces wth the shot.

25th.—The wind has been towards the west a week past, and the Hessians, &c. remain at Spithead. I wrote to my brother at Halifax, to go in a packet from [the] Admiralty, to be made up to night. The letters from Halifax mention a ship missing, with 1500 bbls. of powder, arms, &c., which it is feared has fell into the hands of the rebels.

Lord Hardwicke having sent me a side of fine venison, Lt Gov., Jud. Oliver, Flucker, Vassall, Lechmere, Hatch, two Ewings, and Paul Wentworth dined with me on the haunch.

26th.—The Hessians, &c., remain wind-bound at Spithead. In the evening I went to view houses in High Street for my son and daughter.

27th.—The wind this morning at NE.

Mr Ellis called, from Twickenham. I went with Doctor Caner to Lambeth, to introduce him to the Archbishop, who was very gracious to him, and gave him an order for One Hundred Pounds on the Treasurer of the moneys received for the Clergy in America.

28th.—An account of Sir P. Parker's arrival at Cape Fear, the 3rd May, and all his fleet, including those which put back, except one man-of-war and three transports. This comes from Georgia. It was not known at Cape Fear the 6. of May where the forces would act.

The Brunswickers sailed yesterday for Quebec.

Wrote to Mauduit.

29th.—In the city at the Navy Office, on business of Arthur Savage.

Wind has been east three days, but changed to-day to west: fear the ships will return. Cap. Wood, Master of one of the transports, taken and carried into Cape Ann, which he left the 13 May, called, and gave an account of the state of affairs. He was at Boston the 7th of May: says all was quiet, but no trade going on.

Sewall and Clarke dined with us.

30th.—At the Temple Church. Doctor Witts [?] of Chiswick, Turnham Green, preached. Called upon Dr Caner.

Chandler, Lyde, and Jenny Clarke dined.

July 1st.—An account to-day that all the troops were sailed from Portsmth, but the wind is contrary, and their passage probably will be long.

In the afternoon went over to Fulham with Mrs Sanford and my three daughters* to the Bishop's gardens to eat cherries, strawberries, &c.

2nd.—Showery, and westerly wind still.

Dined at Mr Ellis's at Twickenham. Carried Lt Gov. and Ch. Justice, and Dr Caner in the coach with me, who were highly entertained.

3rd.—To Oxford through Uxbridge with Judge Oliver. We

* He had not got three daughters living. Presumably he meant his daughters Sarah and Margaret, or Peggy, and the wife of his son Thomas, heretofore Sarah Oliver.

arrived about 5, and went to the Oratorio with Dr Jefferds, and after it was over made a visit to the Vice Chancellor Dr Fothergill, who had received a letter from Lord Hardwicke acquainting him with my intention to make visit there. He complimented us with the offer of a Doctor's degree.* We took lodgings at the Angel Inn.

4th.—Upon a message from the Vice Chancellor we attended at the publick schools at 11, and after putting on the Doctor's scarlet gown, band, and cap, were introduced by the Beadles into the Theatre, and received by Professor Vansittart who, after a Latin speech complimentary, presented separately to the Vice Chancellor, who conferred the Degree of Doctor, *in Jure Civili, honoris causa,* and thereupon were placed in the Doctor's seats at the side of the Vice Chancellor; after which a Latin speech in verse was delivered by one of the Students in praise of the Spring: another in prose, elegant and much applauded, by Mr Lowth, son to the Bishop of Oxford, upon Architecture: and then a long Latin comemoration of Benefactors by Mr Bandinelle, [?] in a low voice and lifeless, being his first performance as University Orator. The whole ceremony was not over until two. A gentleman by the name of Paradis, born in Thessalonia, who had studied many years at Oxford, was admitted at the same time, and one other gentleman whose name I have forgot, to Doctors' degrees. We dined with Doctor Jefferds, and spent the evening at the Queen's College with the Fellows. Went through several of the Colleges in the leisure intervals of the day.

5th.—In the morning went to the Observatory by invitation from Dr Ormesby, Professor of Astronomy, and from thence to the Anatomy room in Christ Church College, by invitation from Dr Parson, Anatomical Professor. At both places [we] were accompanied by a Persian lately arrived in an East India ship, who is a professed Physician, Mr. Eliot, son to Sir

* Judge Oliver, in his Diary, speaks of the Degree as "Doctor of Laws," *quasi* LL.D., but the Degree was D.C.L. There is a catalogue of Oxford Graduates from Oct. 10, 1659, to Dec. 10, 1850, from which Mr. Basil H. Soulsby of C.C.C. has sent me the following extract:—"Hutchinson, (Tho., Esq., Governor of the Province of Massachusetts Bay, in America) cr. D.C.L., July 3, 1776."

Gilbert, being his interpreter. Went thro' most of the other Colleges. Jesus College, where I dined and spent one or more evenings in 1741, was quite familiar to me. We dined with the V. Chancellor in Queen's College, and spent the evening with the Fellows. The Dean of Gloucester was of the company.

6th.—The morning being rainy prevented a visit to Blenheim House, as we intended. We dined with the Dean of Christ Church, (Bishop of Chester). Mr Jackson, late Sub-Preceptor to the Princes, was of the Company. After the K. and Q. the Bishop drank the Prince of Wales and Prince Frederick together. He looked like a man hurt, and Mr Jackson seems to be of his family, and closely attached; and if ever the Prince should, as all that have preceded have done, be in a separate interest from the King, I think he will be of the Prince's party.*

We saw a Spartan at Oxford who seems to be above sixty and quite gray,—went from his parents when a boy, and served two campaigns as one of Kouli Chan's Life Guards, but not liking the service, with 50 more deserted—fled to the Caspian Sea, and tho' pursued by great part of the army, gat to Russia, and from thence, after some time, this Spartan came to England and 'listed into the Guards here for a short time, but for a number of years—I think 18 or 20, has been a fencing master at Oxford, and acquired esteem by his prudent demeanour.

We went in the evening to Thame, where we missed post horses, and were obliged to go on with the hired ones we took at Oxford, and did not reach Aylesbury until near ten.

7th.—After church we made a visit to Sir Wm Lee at Hartwell. Sir F. Bernard was taken about 5 in the morning with one of his epileptick fits, so that we did not see him until the evening, and then he was not conversible, but fancied it to be morning, and as it grew dark supposed there was an Eclipse—called for breakfast, &c.

* This was not a desirable prospect. The Prince of Wales, eventually George IV., was now thirteen years old and eleven months; and Prince Frederick, Duke of York, was twelve and nearly eleven months.

8th.—We set out from Aylesbury soon after 7, breakfasted at Missenden, and arrived in St James's Street about one.

[Gen. Howe reported to have left Halifax for New York with 6000 men. A vessel taken by a Massachusetts privateer with 1500 brls. of flour in her.]

It would be hardly fair to omit Judge Oliver's account of the visit to Oxford as it appears in his Diary, since the degree of D.C.L. was also conferred upon him. It stands as follows:—

"July 3rd.—Set out for Oxford with Govr. Hutchinson, and arrived in the afternoon.

"4th.—This being the day for the Encænia at Oxford, Mr Hutchinson and I were invited to accept of Degrees, as Doctors of Laws. Such an honor from the first University in England could not be refused. We were accordingly, after being habited in scarlet gowns, introduced into the Theatre by one of the Proctors who, in an elegant Latin speech, offered us to the Vice-Chancellor, Dr Fothergill, as candidates for Degrees; after which the Vice-Chancellor, who was seated 4 or 5 steps above us, admitted us to a Degree, and invited us to take our seats near to him. The Theatre was crowded with above 2000 spectators, the Ladies seated by themselves in brilliant order: ye Theatre is a most noble building, the ceiling painted in elegance, exhibiting the Arts and Sciences, and supported geometrically: the galleries are supported by pillars painted: in one part of the Theatre was an Orchestra for vocal and instrumental music. Three Orations were delivered, two in Latin, and one in English: the latter Orator was Mr Lowth, the Bishop of Oxford's son, whose subject was Architecture; and the propriety of his action, the elegance of his diction, and the justness of his sentiments, drew the attention and met with the applause of the audience. After the Orations, a fine piece of music closed the ceremony. The Theatre, (which for elegance and convenience, for the use for which it is designed, is not exceeded by any buildings in the kingdom), this day's performance in it, together wth the crowd of respectable spectators, afforded a most agreeable entertainment.

"After the Encænia was over, we dined with Dr Jeffries,* Canon of Christ Church College, who was very polite in shewing us what curiosities the time would admit of.

"5th.—Viewed the Colleges. Dr Myles Cooper, President of New

* Jefferds in the other Diary.

York College, waiting upon us with great politeness. We dined with the Vice-Chancellor, a most agreeable goodnatured gentleman.

"6th.—We dined with Dr Markham, the Bishop of Chester, who is Dean of Christ Church College, and has apartments in it: he was very obliging in shewing us the Library, paintings, and ancient medals and coins in that College."

His further remarks are but cursory, and as they offer no fact or sentiment that may be called new, they can be dispensed with. He returned to London with the Governor, to whose Diary we again revert.

9th.—[Unfounded reports.]

10th.—Yesterday's report from Corke is not confirmed, and is not credited in the city. Dined with Mr John Lane, Judge Oliver, and my sons T. and E. Met Lord Amherst in the Park. He laments the capture of the Ordnance vessel: says her cargo amounted to 10,500£. The Board is censured for not putting such stores in a vessel of greater force.

11.—[The Hessians wind bound at Plymouth.] In the evening I went wth Lt Gov. Oliver, and several of the Council, to see Breslaw's deceptions, which, though surprising, I think too low an amusement ever to attend again, and this is the only thing of the sort I have seen since my being in England.*

12th.—At Lord Hardwicke's. From want of better employment, I spend some time in continuing my History of Masss Bay, having the advantage of the books of the General Court from the Secretary's office. . . .

At the foot of the Title page of the first volume of his History are the words—"BOSTON, NEW ENGLAND. Printed by THOMAS and JOHN FLEET, at the Heart and Crown in Cornhill. MDCCLXIV." The second volume, three years afterwards, was also issued from the press in America, as thus declared—"BOSTON, NEW ENGLAND. Printed by THOMAS and JOHN FLEET, in Cornhill, and sold in Union-Street, opposite to the Cornfield. MDCCLXVII." The third volume, on which he was now

* Judge Oliver was also there. If we may form an opinion of the conjuring tricks with cards, &c., as recorded in his Diary, he seems to have enjoyed the entertainment amazingly.

engaged, remained in MS. at his death, and for 48 years afterwards; but it was then edited and published by the Rev. J. Hutchinson, Canon of Lichfield, only surviving child of Elisha, as thus announced — "LONDON, JOHN MURRAY, ALBEMARLE STREET. MDCCCXXVIII."

In July 1776, the date at which we have now arrived in his Diary, he wrote a letter to some friend whose name unfortunately is not recorded, in which he touches upon two or three points of his government in Massachusetts that are worth transcribing. The letter has apparently been entered in his Letter Book by the hand of his second son Elisha. He says—

"I was appointed to the government of Massachusetts Bay when Lord Hillsborough was Secretary of State, and his Lordship has, I believe for that reason, taken more notice of me than otherwise he would have done. He advised me to mention to you the circumstances of my appointment, and said he would confirm them when he should see you. I had for many years been Lt Governor, when Sir F. Bernard was recalled and the command devolved on me. It was easy to forsee the troubles in which a Governor must be involved. My private fortune was sufficient to support me genteely in America: three of my children were settled and able to support themselves and families, and I wished to spend the remainder of my life in ease and quiet. When the intention of appointing me Governor was intimated to me, soon after Govr Bernard left the Province, I desired to be excused, and to resign my place of Lt Govr also, and I fully expected another Governor and Lt Governor would be appointed; but my Ld Hillsborough advised me to consider further, and wrote to me that he would keep the place of Governor untill [*sic*] my further answer. This mark of confidence with so much condescension, put it out of my power to hesitate.

"The loss of my own and my children's fortunes, is certainly owing to my acceptance of the Government; for I stood so well with the people, that I am very sure I could have lived quietly upon one or other of my estates in the country, without engaging on the side of Rebellion, and perhaps might have interfered so far as to stop or retard the progress of it. For the first three years of my administration it certainly lost ground, and if it had not been for the plot laid by Franklin and others here in England, and the sending over my private letters, and the false representation made of them, I doubt whether there would have been a Rebellion to this day.

"It was thought expedient to appoint another Governor in my stead upon my desiring leave of short absence. I had no intention then to resign my government, but I acquiesced in the King's pleasure, depending upon the assurances given me, that I sh^d be no sufferer by the discontinuance of the King's Commission, and that some distinguishing mark sh^d be shewn of His Majesty's approbation of my conduct. The former part I gratefully acknowledge has been complied with—the latter remains.

"If I could obtain this favor for my youngest son, it would free me from the allowance I am obliged to make him, and with frugality would enable me to spend a few weeks abroad without involvement, and perhaps may confirm my health. If I was more a stranger to you than I am, I should hope for your interest from your benevolent disposition.—I have the honor to be, &c."

Upon this letter it may be remarked that he makes one or two observations which, to modern students of the origin of the war, will probably be deemed erroneous. It may be true that his acceptance of the post of Governor cost him his fortune and the fortunes of his children, simply because he thereby held an office that was obnoxious to the Republican party, and as they prevailed his estates were seized. Some Americans in recent times, have cast blame upon him for having accepted it at all. It is hard to say upon what grounds that blame can rest. His refusal of it certainly could not have prevented the catastrophe, nor settled the dispute, nor closed the breach between the two countries, that was every day widening more and more, apart from any small amount of influence he could have exercised one way or the other: and indeed, it might on the other hand be argued, that his refusal of the Governorship in 1771, might have produced quite the contrary effect, and have brought out General Gage and his troops to Boston so much the sooner: and as regarded himself personally, his refusal of the post would have thrown him open to a charge of cowardice, as of a man running away from his duty at a very critical time. Such are the considerations that now suggest themselves from a retrospect of the past.

And he flatters himself that if he had chosen it, he could have retired into private life, and have lived in quiet on one or other of his estates, whilst the storm was blowing over his head, and even have interfered to stop or retard the progress of it. The experience of Lieutenant Moody shews how fallacious such arguments were. Nobody was allowed to be neutral, if violence or insult could drive him to join in the frenzy of the day. James

Moody, as he says in his *Narrative*, page 2, was "a happy farmer without a wish or an idea of any other enjoyment than that of making happy, and being happy with, a beloved wife and three promising children. He loved his neighbours, and hopes they were not wholly without regard for him. Clear of debt and at ease in his professions, he had seldom thought much of political or state questions; but he felt and knew he had every possible reason to be greatful for, and attached to, that glorious Constitution to which he owed his security. . . .

"He thinks it incumbent on him to declare that it [the Rebellion] did not originate with the *people* of America, properly so called. They felt no real grievances, and therefore could have no real inducement to risk substantial advantages in the pursuit of such as were only imaginary. In making this declaration he is confident he speaks the sentiments of a great majority of the peasantry of America. But in every country there are multitudes who, with little property, and perhaps still less principle, are always disposed, and always eager for a change. . .

"The general cry was, *Join or die!* . . .

"It was in vain that he [Moody] took every possible precaution, consistent with good conscience, not to give offence. . . . He was perpetually harrassed by these Committees; and a party employed by them once actually assaulted his person, having first flourished their tomahawks over his head."

Soon after this he had to fly for his life. Perceiving an armed party approaching his house, he endeavoured to withdraw, but three shots were fired after him, happily without taking affect. Through many hardships and difficulties he at last was able to take shelter behind the British lines. He adds that 73 of his neighbours, equally averse to join in the Rebellion, effected their escape about the same time. This shews how hard it was for the peaceable to remain neutral.

It is amusing to see that the Governor puts Dr. Franklin's agency in sending out his letters in a very prominent place, so much so, as to impute to that act the chief, if not the sole cause of the Rebellion.

As regards the distinguishing mark of His Majesty's favour, held in reserve for him, he seems to have been labouring under a false impression. It was not the provision for any member of his family, as a compensation for losses that was contemplated, but a title for himself. This is plain in Lord Dartmouth's letter to him of the 9th of April, 1774, and printed at the end of the Preface to the Third volume of his History. To resume—

13th.—Called upon Dr Caner, Dudley, Rome, &c. Mr Robinson, from Bristol called: says the Master of the vessel arrived there from Boston, affirms that Dr Lyde and many others are imprisoned for refusing to swear they will take up arms in defence of their new government. This seems hardly credible.* Flucker dined with us: depends on the truth of the report of his family's being arrived in Ireland: has 300£ allowed by Treasury: last [?] of the Council 200£.

14th.—At the Old Jewry: Mr White. Called at Hatton Garden on Mr Greene, as we returned home.

Westerly wind: every day for some time past more or less showers.

15th.—In the city to ascertain Mr Winslow's money in Gines's hands—560,,6,,6. Expected arrivals from America, but find none.

16th.—My son T. received 200£, deducting 5£, fees at the Treasury, as one of the Council of Mass^s Bay.

Mr Flucker, last evening, received a letter from his wife at Corke, advising her arrival with her daughter, in 22 days from Halifax.

Called upon Mr Jackson, Southampton Buildings, and spent an hour.

Wind S.; troops not sailed from Plymouth.

Dr Oliver and his family moved to a house taken by Judge Oliver in High Street, Marybone Parish, having been between 9 and 10 weeks in my house.

17th.—Gave Mr Richard Clarke an order on Gines and Atkinson for 560,,6,,6, the balance of Mr Isaac Winslow's money in their hands placed by me, for which transfer I have Mr Winslow's letter to Mr Clarke, and in a letter to me Mr Winslow refers to a former letter by Capt. Gardner, in which he had given directions; but this letter was not delivered.

18th.—At Court. The King said more to me upon America than ever before, it not being his custom to say anything of public affairs at Court. I mentioned to the Abp. the case of Dr Caner, which he rec^d favourably.

* Incredible though it be, it corroborates what Lieut. Moody says above.

A vessel from Halifax, left it the 22nd or 23rd of June. Fleet sailed the 11th for Sandy Hook: the last part of the Highlanders did not arrive at Halifax till the 18th: expected to sail after taking in water the 23rd to follow the fleet, which, by the winds at Halifax, it was supposed might arrive in 5 or 6 days.

In the evening at Mr Knox's, and after at Mr Cornwall's until near 10.

19th.—At Lord Loudoun's, who goes into Scotland in 3 or 4 days. Wrote to Mr Mackenzie, and Dr Murray.

Account of the vessel from Halifax, that the Comissioners and their under officers had taken a vessel, and were to sail from Halifax by the 1st of July.

20th.—With my two sons T. and E. and daughter to Highgate, to call upon the Americans T. Erving, Loring, Boylstone, Paddock, Gore, Joy. Judge Oliver and family dined with us. Wrote to Mauduit at Uppark by Midhurst, Sussex—Lady Fetherstone's.

Wind west, and the Hessians, &c., still lie at Plimouth.

21st.—At the Old Jewry—Mr White.

Lieutenant Gov. O. called to acquaint me with his intention to apply to Lord North for his salary. It seems, as I had it from Mr Knox, that when Gen. Gage was superceded in the command of the army, he was promised, the whole of his salary as Governor should be continued; otherwise I should have thought the Lt Gov. might have stood a chance for half, but now he can have no more than his 300£ as L. G.

Rain forenoon, and again towards evening. Wind eastward of south.

22nd.—A letter to Government yesterday from Lord Howe off Halifax the 23rd June: joined the 2nd Division of the Highlanders from [the] Clyde two days before; so that the account of their arrival the 18th could not be true. When Lord Howe sailed there was no advice of the General's sailing from Nantasket, and hearing nothing on the passage, Lord Howe thought it best to steer for Halifax for advice. He designed to follow his brother without delay.

23rd.—Went out with my two sons and daughter to

Twickenham, intending to return before dinner, and proposed through Richmond, but were pressed to stay and dine: Sr Richd Worsley and Lady, and M^{r} and M^{rs} D'Oyley.

There's a letter from Genl Clinton of 13 May from Cape Fear. He had not heard from Genl Howe. It's said there's no prospect of anything to purpose at N. Carolina. Mr Paine has wrote of the 15th and says a regiment was landed on Ball [?] Island.

24th.—Called upon Lord Hardwicke at St. James's Square. In the evening to drink tea at High Street—all the families together. When I came home, heard the news of Mr Lillie's death at Halifax. What numbers have been brought to poverty, sickness, and death by refusing to concur with the present measures of America!

25th.—In the forenoon at Ld Hillsborough's. He promises to speak to Robinson on behalf of my son, and advises me to write to him, and to make use of his (Ld Hillsboro's) name. I asked him if there was anything in the report of his going Ld Lieuten^{t} to Ireland? He said he had heard it mentioned, and seen it in the papers; and one day he asked Lord North whether he had ever heard his name mentioned? He answered, that he had mentioned him himself to the King.

"Why, then," says Ld Hillsborough, "I must be the man."

"That I don't know," says Lord North; "objections have been made, but they don't appear to me sufficient."

Lord Hillsborough says his estate in Ireland is the objection.

M^{r} D Oyley says there are letters from Clinton as late as the 16th. Nothing worth mentioning; but there seems something more than he chooses to speak of. The report is in the city that it is not agreeable.

26.—Went into the city. They have an account from Providence of 4 Jam^{a} ships—one with 30 thous^{d} doll^{s} besides her cargo, taken by a S. Carolina privateer, and 2 small vessels.

The Hessians were met by a vessel arrived at Liverpool in Long 59, Lat. 43, the 2^{d} of July.*

* This must have been the first division, for some of them were at Plymouth so late as July 20.

Mr Ben. Gridley, Dan. Oliver, Mrs Hutchinson* and daughters, John Powell and daughters, Col. Chandler, Abel Willard and wife, and young Mr Johannot, passengers from Halifax.

27th.—Advice from Quebec that 350 of the rebels with Thomas their General, were made prisoners: had burnt the forts at St. John, and Chamblée, and fled to Isle aux Noix, and not like [likely] to stay there. The rebels took one of the transports with 150 Highlanders. One of the Hessians arrived at Halifax, having lost the fleet: carried two prizes in with her.

Went to Wimbledon to-day—the hottest day this year.

28th.—At the Temple Church: a Clergyman preached the doctrine, in the manner, and with the air and delivery, of a country minister in New England. I could not learn his name.

We begin now to expect something of importance from New York. I wrote last night to Mauduit, and to Mr Mackenzie.

29th.—Daniel Oliver came to town, and brings me letters from my brother, Mr Walter, and Putnam.

Mr Prout and two of his sons had escaped from Boston. Mr Walter writes that my goods, and my sons', which had come to the hands of the rebels, were divided between Dr Cooper and Mr Lothrop, and that Lothrop lived in my house: that the Highland vessel beat off two or three privateers, and ran into Boston, and there was stop'd.

30th.—At the Admiralty. Mr Jackson read me a letter from Plymouth, giving the acc^t^ of the arrival of a brig, Spencer, Master, taken by the *Cerberus,* laden with oil, which spoke with Admiral Shuldham's fleet the 26th of June, about 17 miles E of Block Island, with a fair wind for N. York—

* She was Eliakim's widow, and a daughter of Governor Shirley. Governor H. petitioned the Government for relief for her, as he did indeed for several others, and applied to the Archbishop of Canterbury for Dr. Caner. She lived on to the year 1825, and was buried at Croydon. I presume she is the person alluded to in the following inscription, which I copied from a flag-stone in the floor :—" Also of Mrs. Frances Hutchinson, died 19 July, 1825, aged 84 years." She was buried nine days after her death, as the following entry shews, which I copied the same day from the Parish Register :—" Frances Hutchinson, Gloucester Pla. Portman Square, St. Mary le Bone. July 28.84."

spoke with the *Greyhound*, Gen. Howe on board the day before.

A great eclipse of the moon from 10 to 12, almost total: very clear fine evening. Wind N.

The Thomas, prisoner at Quebec, is said to be Thompson, of the Province of Pensilvania—a trader turned into a General, and Thomas is said to die of the small pox.

31st.—Yesterday and to-day the weather has been hot, the air stagnated, much like the Dog-days weather in America. I took notice of the thermometer yesterday at the Admiralty, in the house, when it was about 70. In the sun abroad it would have been much higher: if the sun had been clouded over head for a few minutes, it would have been lower. I have observed, ever since I have been in England, that the changes from sunshine to cloudy are not only more frequent, but the degrees of heat and cold vary more than I ever observed in America, and in going up and down the Park, you will have blasts of hot or cold air, just as the sun happens to be abroad or not, tho' you are not under the shine of it, but in the shade.

I dined in High Street at Judge Oliver's, in comp^y^ with Gov. Legg, and Lt Gov. Oliver. I think, tho' the complaints against Legg have not been supported, it looks, by his discourse, as if he had no expectations of going out Governor again. He has rank of Major only in the army, and Lord George, while there are so many superior, and General officers from time to time in his Province, will hardly send him to it again.

August 1st.—Called upon Mr Knox. I find six brigantines, flat bottoms, intended to carry 12 guns each, are sent to Quebec —one was arrived—and are intended to be buoyed and drawn over the shoals and rapids in the river Sorel, into Lake Champlain. The first scheme was to send out frames only, and to build them, which I believe would have taken up as little time.

A small privateer of 9 carriage guns, called the *Yankee*, is brought into Dover. After she had taken a sugar ship, and a vessel laden with rum, and sent them in to America with what hands could be spared, the prisoners on board the *Yankee* rose upon the crew, and stood for the Channel, and arrived in 24 days.

Hot day again, and faint air.

Treasury adjourned for 3 weeks.

2nd.—The weather still hotter. It's thought the glasses in the shade must be above 80. Col. John Chandler, a fresh exile, dined with me, together with Dr Chandler.

General Haldiman has a letter from Quebec, several days after Carleton's, which says, besides the killed and wounded in the late action, great numbers lost their way and perished in the woods, and it's thought the rebels in the whole lost 6 or 700.

3rd.—It seems, Henry Johnson, a person who served his time wth Epes Sargent of Glo'cester, is Captain, and a Doctor Downing, who has been a very troublesome person at Brooklyne, Surgeon of the *Yankee*, privateer. Mr Lyde was aboard to-day, and Lewis Gray yesterday. The vessel left Boston the 4th of June. The Master and Surgeon seem to be under no concern—depend upon security from the prisoners in the hands of the Congress. The Ministers are at a loss what to do with them.

I called at the Admiralty, and was told the mercury there was yesterday, in a close but warm room, at 85. I saw it there to-day when it was not so hot—about 75.

Mr Simpson, Amory, Gridley, and Danforth, dined with me.

4th.—At the Old Jewry—Mr. White.

Called on Mr Greene, Hatton Street. Judge Browne, and Lyde dined with us. The prisoners taken in the rebel vessel, sent aboard a Guard ship at Sheerness.

5th.—In the city at Blackburne's, Bush Lane, and afterwards at Lord George's office.

There are letters from Ld Dunmore, who is upon Gwin Island, and Knox says in a bad situation the 26 of June. Has a regiment of Blacks, very sickly. Hammond was there in the *Roebuck*—knew nothing of Clinton; from whence it is concluded he went from Cape Fear direct to N. York. Some think he may be gone to burn Charlestown.

6th.—Governor Eden of Maryland had left Annapolis in an armed vessel, and was at Gwin Island with Lord Dunmore, or on board the *Roebuck*, Cap^n Hammond. A journal of his is shewn as late as 1st of July, and there is much talk to-day of dissatisfaction among the town people of the lower counties of Pensilvania, and the Jersies, but they are loose accounts.

7th.—At the Levée to-day: carried Judge Oliver to kiss the King's hand.

At Lord George's office. Mr D'Oyly has a story from the city—that Salem and Marblehead were burnt, and he seems to credit it; but I believe nothing until I know how it comes.

8th.—A long letter published in the *Morning Post,* said to be from Halifax, dated July 5th, giving a circumstantial account of the defeat of General Howe on the first. Though there are many palpable absurdities or impossibilities in this letter, yet it gave alarm to many people. The law against spreading false news, even in such important or interesting cases, seems to have lost all force.

Wrote to Mr Mackenzie to tell him there were no accounts from America.

9th.—Dined at the Bishop of London's at Fulham: Dr Caner, Chandler, and T. H. with me in the coach. A very raw cold day for the season, with rain. Attended evening service in the Chapel with the family.

10th.—Lt Col. Blunt arrived this forenoon from Gen. Howe, who landed on Staten Island with the army the 3rd [of July]. No opposition. All the Island—about 400—came in and took the oaths. [Neither] Ld Howe nor the Hessians arrived. Gov. [William] Franklin carried to Connecticut. The Mayor of N. York tried and sentenced to dye for corresponding wth Tryon, but not executed. Sixty of the rebel army came over from Jerseys with their arms. The rebels very numerous on Long Island, and the main [army] should wait for the Hessians or Clinton, unless something extra.

A newspaper says Clinton was at Charlestown, S. Carolina. A 50-gun ship, several men-of-war, and 30 transports over the bar: one 50-gun ship lost, (it's said here there was but one)—had summoned the town—resolved to defend. Between 4 and 500 of the Highlanders prisoners at Boston.

Wrote to Ld Hardwicke, Mackenzie, and Burch.

Mr Mauduit called this evening: returned the 8th from the country.

11th.—At the Temple: Dr Morrill.

The Gazette of last night, or rather this morning, gives extracts from Howe's, Tryon's, and Shuldham's letters. Howe mentions Gov. Franklin as a prisoner in Connecticut, and that the Mayor of N. York was sentenced to death for his correspondence with Tryon;—says the enemy have a hundred cannon mounted;—shall attempt nothing until the Hessians or Clinton arrives, unless something new to occasion it. A 40 and 20 gun ship preparing to go up the North [or Hudson] River. Between 4 and 500 of the Highlanders prisoners at Boston, Mass. Menzies, &c., killed.

12th.—A vessel to-day from Quebec with an account of the arrival of the *Tartar* and her convoy, which had materials for the navigation. The letter dated July 7th. This was late, the troops having been six weeks there.

13th.—Col. Bruce, of the 65th came to town from Halifax—sailed the 18th July. The Commiss^rs of the Customs sailed with them, but they lost company to the east of Isle of Sables, and it's thought not free from danger of the rebel vessels. Hotham had been at Halifax: his squadron off the harbour: all sailed by the 6th of July. They will be late at N. York.

Wrote to Ld Hardwicke, Mackenzie, and Cornwall.

14th.—News of the arrival of the *Aston Hall*, Parker, at Dover, from Halifax, with the Comiss^rs of the Customs, &c. Wrote Mr Burch the news.

General Haldiman has a letter of the 10th from Staten Island, which says the N. Hampshire Delegates had left the Congress, on account of their declaring for Independency.

15th.—Spent great part of this day in looking for a house to remove to, the adjoining houses to that where I dwell in St. James's Street are pulling down, which makes mine to be scarcely habitable.

Mr Morris, comiss^r of the Customs, called and hinted the irregularity of the American Board in coming to England. I thought they had suffered so much, that if this step had not been perfectly according to rule, it might well be passed over.

Received a note from Mr Jackson containing the substance of what General Conway said in my favour in the House of Commons last Session.*

16th.—M^r^ D'Oyley tells me they have now a certain account of Hotham's fleet; that a part sailed from Halifax the 2nd July, and the rest the 7th.

Mr Coffin called, and afterwards Mr Hutton: both arrived with the Board of Comiss^rs^. I took from Coffin's memorandum these minutes—

"The Highlanders sailed the 3rd of July for N. York—17 sail.

12 Hessians came in to Halifax the 5th: went out again the 6th.

Hotham being off the harbour.

The horse did not sail till the 12th or 13th."

17th.—A fair but cool day, not unlike the middle of September in America. Col. Leonard appears to-day. Paxton and Halloway not come to town. The Board came away without orders, but think the necessity of the thing will justify it.

18th.—At the Temple,—Doctor Morrill.

Halloway and his wife came to town to-day: called upon them in Suffolk Street. A message from Paxton at Clapham, where Col. Hatch lodges.

19th.—Waiting for news from America. Mr Mather arrived last night in town from Halifax, and called on me this morning.†

20th.—Paxton came to town, and called on me with letters from Mr J. Winslow. Mr Ben. Faneuil and wife, S. Waterhouse and family, Arth. Savage, &c., &c., so that Americans continue to thicken.

21st.—Mr Reeves, Secretary to General Clinton, arrived today with despatches from S. Carolina, wch he left the 15 July, the ships having been repulsed wth loss at Sullivan's Island, and the army intending to sail in 2 or 3 days for N. York.

Wrote to Ld H., Mr Mackenzie, and Mr Cornwall.

22nd.—Removed to a house in New Bond Street, No. 147,

* This note containing a report of what Gen. Conway said, is not forthcoming.

† The Rev. Samuel Mather married Hannah, a sister of Gov. Hutchinson.

being so much annoyed by pulling down houses, as to render my house in St. James's Street scarcely habitable.

23rd.—Received from Mr Paine a letter of 11 July, dd [delivered?] by Mr Reeves, with a circumstantial acct of the action at Cape Fear, the *Experiment* and *Bristol* having lost above 100 men each, killed and wounded, and Cap. Morris of the *Bristol* dead of his wounds.

24th.—Change of habitation is not pleasing, and I pine after my old lodgings; and besides, have a house less roomy and comodious, but hope to be reconciled to it.

Hutton, Paxton, Robinson, Dr Caner, and young Simpson dined.

25th.—At Princes Street—Dr Kippis.

A show of Americans:—Treasurer Gray, Flucker, Clarke, Willard, Danforth, &c.

26th.—Mauduit called upon me. He had seen the Gazette, but had heard nothing further. From that he collects that there must have been a misunderstanding and difference between the land and sea Commanders at Carolina, which has been the cause of that unsuccessful attempt.

27th.—Went with S. and P. to Clapham to visit Mr W. Vassall, and Hatch, and George Erving.

A cool day, like the autumn weather in N. England. Wind NE., but not high.

28th.—Mr D'Oyly does not suppose there is any breach between Clinton and Sir P. Parker, but supposes both engaged in this expedition because they had the chief command here, and hoped to obtain a Laurel before they went to serve under Lord Howe and Gen. Howe.

29th.—A rainy night and morning, after a great deal of fair and fine weather most of the month, tho' rather cold for a New England man. Afternoon fine soft weather.

Met General Harvey, who thinks we may hear very soon from New York, but it's more probable not these ten days.

Called upon Tommy and his wife and children, and with Peggy, took an airing to Chelsea.

30th.—In the city: called upon Mr Blackburne, Bush Lane. No arrivals. Settled with Gines and Atkinson, Bankers.

Judge Oliver and Mr Lyde returned from a tour of 16 or 18 days, to Birmingham, Dudley, Woodstock, &c.

31st.—At Wimbledon, Mr Morriss, with E. and P., at dinner. Mon^r^. Garnier and another Frenchman there, Frondé, with Hooton the American Inspector, and an old Dowager, Mrs Fowler. Went over Battersea Bridge, and through Wandsworth: came home thro' Fulham.

September 1st.—At the Old Jewry. The weather cool to-day, like the last of the month in Boston. In the evening at High Street.

2nd.—Called upon Mr Reeve, who gave me a particular account of the Carolina business. Clinton had wrote the 23 of May to Lord G. G. that he intended to embark at Cape Fear and go to the northw^d^, but on the 16th a frigate and small vessel had been sent the 16th [*sic*] to reconnoitre the bar and harbour of Charlestown. They returned the 26, and brought such an account that determined the sea and land commanders to go to the southward. Troops it seems were landed on Long Island, without the bar. The island is about a mile and half from Sullivan's Island, but the space between, at low water, is dry sands, except that next Sullivan's Island, which is 7 feet deep. They had been informed they were all fordable. He says Clinton knew nothing of the Forts being silenced, but supposed the contrary. Parker, with his ships, was over the bar, and the fort attacked was at a distant part of Sullivan's Island, and no comunication between the General and Admiral but by sailing 4 or 5 leagues, and Parker had no reason to expect aid from Clinton, for he knew the creek was not fordable, and they could not land in boats at once, more than 500 men. It looks as if Parker thought his ships sufficient to take the fort without the army, not considering, or not knowing, that he could not bring his ships within 900 yards of it. The men-of-war had not got back over the bar. It is said to be much easier to go in than [to] go out. The troops were not re-embarked, so that we are in painful expectation, &c.

Sir Egerton Leigh seems to fear whether the 50 gun ships will get over the bar.

3rd.—Rainy great part of the day by showers. Mauduit in

the evening:—laments his loss of money by Woolridge, the new Alderman and Sheriff, who has stopped payment, having spent his creditors' money in Elections, his principal recommendation being, that he is a busy man against Government. He was in America, and at my house in Milton while I was Governor.

4th.—Col. Maclean to-day comes to town from Quebec, and Gov. Eden from Virginia. Nothing very remarkable from either place. They did not expect to get down the Lake (from Quebec) till the middle of this month. Ld Dunmore was obliged to quit the shore, and retire to his ship. His conduct, upon the whole, is not much approved.

5th.—It is said to-day that Ld Dunmore had sent to Clinton to urge him to stop with the army in Virginia, and that the officer had returned with advice that the fleet and army left Carolina the 21 July, bound to New York; but it is added that one frigate remained behind, not being able to get over the bar, or for some other reason which does not yet transpire.

Rainy again all day by showers.

6th.—At the King's Levée: the smallest attendance I ever saw there, everybody being out of town. Saw Gov. Eden there. He says an officer which left Clinton's fleet about the 27th of July, came in to Virginia. The frigate supposed to be left, was the *Glasgow* transport with a company of Col^o Maclean's Highlanders, which ran aground and could not be got off. Saw Maclean also at the Levée, and Gov. O'Hara, and the new General of the Leeward Islands: Monk also, Sollicitor General of Quebec, and Sir Clifford Willingham, who it seems is his patron. Lord George.

7th.—In the city, and paid Excise 5£ for my coach, commencing 10 of July last. Paid off Public Advertiser 2,,7/-.

Chandler and son, Waterhouse, Doblois, Laughton, T. Greene, and Mr Boucher, a Clergyman Refugee from Maryland, dined with us. Mr Boucher tells me that when I made my speech to the Assembly, which brought on their long Answer, they sent to Mr Dulany of Maryland, to desire him to answer it. I think it must be a mistake, and that it could be only a desire to answer it in print.

8th.—At Prince's Street—Dr Kippis.

In the evening drank tea at High Street. Mauduit went yesterday to Wherwell, [?] Andover, for the remainder of the month.

9th.—Mr Vassall and family, Hutton, Paxton, Hallowell, Powell and daughters, all called upon me. Two vessels from Quebeck—returned transports. Nothing transpires.

10th.—The finest day since the month began. Three more vessels from Quebeck. Mr Knox says the brigantines are taken down to the timbers ends, so that it must be long before they are over the Lake.

11th.—Dr Nath. Perkins* called upon me. He has been about ten days in town: endeavoured, before he left Boston, to prevail on the Select-men to enquire, by a Flag which was going out, to the besiegers whether, if he would remain quiet, and mind nothing but the business of his profession, he might be secure from insult? but they declined doing it; and he was told they did not believe any gentleman would ill-treat him, but they could not answer for the low people. This was enough to determine him to remove, tho' with a most tender constitution: and after all the hardship of Halifax, he has been from thence to Ireland in company with Fitch, and from thence to Bristol, and so to London, having left even his plate in Boston.

12th.—In the afternoon with Peggy, my son T. and wife, and two children, went to Fulham, and spent some time upon the banks of the river, and returned before dinner.

We are now every moment expecting important news, which keeps me from taking a tour in the country, where I must be anxious more than in town, because reports are propagated there, of which it will be more difficult to form a judgment.

13th.—A fine soft and pleasant day. Judge Browne drank tea and spent the evening with us.

14th.—Still the weather holds moderate, and rather warm, without showers. I walked into the city below the Bridge, and

* Sabine informs us that Dr. Nathaniel Perkins was a Physician of Boston. He graduated at Harvard in 1734: he treated for smallpox by inoculation in 1764 when hospitals were established in Boston Harbour: went with the army to Halifax in 1776, on the evacuation of Boston: was proscribed and banished in 1778: and died in 1799.

back—near 7 miles from N. Bond Street. Called on Mr Blackburne. He cannot account for Carleton's dismissing the Indians from Quebec until he should call upon them. It is said the Congress refused to comply with the exchange of prisoners, for those taken at Les Cédres, and that Carleton would send home the officers who remained, as hostages for the security of performance.

Browne and son, Powell, Hallowell, and Boylston, Perkins, Faneuil, and Dr Cooper, dined with us. Report of an express from Howe comes to nothing.

15th.—At the Temple—Dr Morrill. Saw the Connecticut Colonel Hall, who gave me an account after service of news which Mr Rindge told him came by way of France, of a repulse at New York. I called upon Mr Rindge, who a week ago mentioned to him a report from Marseilles, to which he gave no credit. The anxiety for news raises reports of expresses and intelligence by other means every day, which die away before the next day, and make room for successors.

A cold rain this afternoon.

Royall, at Brighthelmstone, grows worse, and Doctor Perkins is gone down to him again to-day.

16th.—I don't remember ever to have seen the town so thin of people since I have been in London. My own anxiety, from the state of my country, keeps me in town. The two last days the wind has been at east, so that we hardly expect an arrival until it has blown two or three days at west again, which quarter it is in to-day. My children from Brompton Row, [Thomas's], dined with me to-day, and the High Street family, [Dr P. Oliver's], came to drink tea. This is some alleviation—to have my children and grand-children; but we are all in a state of exile from a country, which of all others is most dear to me, notwithstanding the unjust cruel treatment I have received from it.

17th.—A great deal of rain falls to-day. Mr Hallowell and Reeve call upon me. Reeve brings his Journal and Plan of the S. Carolina Expedition. A strange fatality attends this affair in every stage of it. The forces were intended to be there early in February, and by one cause of delay after another, did not arrive till May. Orders were sent after them not to go upon action there without some extraordinary circumstances should induce, but to join Howe. The *Ranger* sloop with these orders did not arrive till they sailed from Cape Fear. Duplicates of these orders were sent to Howe, and he sent after Clinton, but his letters were prevented by the engagement the *Glasgow* had with Hawkins's squadron, so that Clinton had gone on with his first orders, until he had sailed from Cape Fear. Even while under the first orders, he had determined to join Howe, until the vessels Sir P. Parker sent to reconnoitre, brought such encouragement as caused him to change his mind.

My son E. set out for Brighthelmstone and France.

18th.—Dined with my daughter P. at Mr Vassall's at Clapham. Paxton and Hatch and his wife. A cold northerly wind, but clear sky. It's now 70 days since the last letters from New York, and people make conjectures. Many are ready to suppose the British troops have met with discouragement, but there really is no probability that all the force which was intended, could be at New York before the 4th or 5th of August, and we may allow ten days after that to prepare for an action of any importance.

19th.—As cool this morning with a N. wind, as the middle of October in America. A letter last night from my son W. at Brighthelmstone, says Royall was given over by his Physicians. I called upon Hallowell. Mr Simpson and his nephew called on me, and Lechmere, Paddock, &c. Rain before noon.

Mr Geyer, who married Duncan Ingram's daughter, recd a letter from Ingram at Nantucket dated June 25, by way of Holland, to acquaint him, that feeling things [were] growing worse and worse at Boston, and that if he remained he should be obliged to take an active part, he was going to Surinam to spend 12 or 18 months: that he should have 6 or 7 vessels consigned him: and that several gentlemen were going passengers with him. This I have from Mr Lyde, to whom Geyer read the letter. They could not have heard of General Howe at York, nor of Lord Howe and the Hessians, what their destination was.

20th.—Paid my Coachman's board wages, &c., to the 14th Instant.

At Lord George Germaine's. He says Lord Stormont wrote, that the people arrived from Philadelphia at Dunkirk, say that on the 8. of August, when they sailed, there was no account of any action at New York, and they speak of no important news. On the other hand, fishing vessels at Dartmouth and Plymouth, both say they spoke with vessels at sea which reported that Howe was in possession of New York the same day the 8. of August.*

I stated the case of the Council and Putnan at Halifax, and he promised his aid in recomending it to Lord North—or rather, he said, Mr Robinson.

In the afternoon an account is recd at Lloyd's Coffee House of the arrival of a vessel from Virginia at Glasgow—spoke the *Boreas* man-of-war Aug. 16, off Delaware, and was informed that Lord Howe and all the troops were arrived at New York; and the 8th or 9th he left New York.

Mr Green, Mather and wife, Clarke, and Lyde, dines with us.

21st.—Dined at Croydon at Mr Apthorpe's:—Judge Oliver, Sally and Peggy, and Miss Fanny Hutchinson, all in the coach. A young gentleman—Ives, now Trecothick, and heir to Alderman Trecothick, dined there also. A very pleasant day, but still cool for the season, and east wind. Mr Apthorpe is much altered in his principles since the Declaration of Independence, and says now America must be subdued before there can be any concessions made.

22nd.—At the Old Jewry—Mr White.

In the evening drank tea at Mr D'Oyly's—Peggy with me. General Howe's lady, Mr and Mrs Agar. It has been reported some days past that Johnson, the Chaplain of the privateer bro't into Dover, had made his escape from the Guard-ship at Sheerness, and was gone to France, but Mr D'Oyly knows nothing of it, and does not believe a word of it. Mrs Howe discovers great anxiety, which is not to be wondered at.

23rd.—Mrs Howe received this forenoon, by a transport returned from Staten Island to Cork, a letter from General Howe, dated the 30th of July, which being by a precarious

* The battle on Long Island took place on the 27th of August, and Gen. Howe took possession of New York on the 21st of September.

conveyance, he only writes that L[d] Howe arrived the 12th: that the Highlanders, the Light Horse, and part of the Guards and Hessians were arrived: the rest within two days' sail. But the Agent for the Victualling Contractor writes that the transport sailed the 12th of August, before which time the rest of the Guards and Hessians, and all Clinton's army were arrived, and that they expected an attempt upon N. York in 2 or 3 days: that Washington was at Kingsbridge,* and Putnam commanded in New York: that Howe was 35000 strong, but this cannot be, unless he has been joined by more Provincials than there is any reason to expect. No letters yet to Government, but it is thought there must be, and that the Agent's Express has made more haste than the Government's [Express]. The Court and public officers are in great anxiety.

A privateer of New England, Simon Forester, has taken six prizes off Cape St. Vincent. I wrote to Lord Hardwicke, M[r] Cornwall, Mauduit, and Burch.

24th.—The wind shifts to the westward, and we may soon expect vessels. Billy returned yesterday from Brighthelmstone: says his brother E. sailed for Dieppe with a good wind Wednesday evening the 18th from Brighthelmstone.†

25th.—The papers to-day have Lord Howe's Declaration as a Comissioner, dated 20th June, off Massachusets Bay, in which he offers pardon to all who return to their allegiance. After he arrived at N. York it was sent to Washington, but refused because directed to "George Washington Esq.," and not in his publick character. The Congress approved this refusal. They have also the settlement of a new Government in Virginia. Patrick Henry Jun[r] their Governor, with Senators, &c.

Many people seem much struck with this progress in settling Governments in so many Colonies; but it is become necessary, there being no retreat without a total destruction of the power which the Congress have assumed; they must therefore push on, that being their only chance.

* At the north end of Manhatten Island; the city of New York being at the south end.

† It was now Tuesday.

26th.—[No news yet. The French and Dutch suspected of favouring the Americans.]

27th.—A fine warm day: S.W. wind. Report to-day that 7000 Provincials had joined Howe's army.

28th.—[A letter saying that the Hessians and Guards arrived at Staten Island the 12th of August.]

29th.—At the Temple wth Judge Oliver. A Dr Weekes preached a Michaelmas Day sermon—"Are they not all ministering spirits?" &c.*

An Express arrived last night from Staten Island: six weeks passage: all the forces arrived except the Highlanders carried into Boston, and one company to Virginia. . . .

30th.—[Sir P. Parker had arrived with Lord Dunmore and Lord Wm. Campbell.] In the *Publick Ledger* some mischievous person had published a card as from Mauditicus to Gov. Pownall, advising him not to brush fight wth Mr Hutchinson, but to enter into an open contest, &c. In the evening he sent a person with a letter, to let me know he had never published any anonymous letter or paper concerning me, much less against me. If I was the author of that paper, he was ready to enter into any personal or publick contest with me. Rediculous as this was, I thought it best to take no other notice than to tell him I was glad he had given me an opportunity of assuring him that I never directly nor indirectly was concerned in any publication respecting him, nor did I know or suspect the authors of them, but believed they were malevolent persons, friends neither to him nor me, but probably equally inimical to both of us; that I had never seen the card he refer'd to until I opened his letter, and I verily believed Mr Mauduit knew no more of it than I did.—Fresh east wind.

October 1st.—A vessel yesterday from Halifax. . . .

2nd.—[Provincial army said to want clothes. He had two teeth drawn by Dumergue.]

3rd.—[A young man returned from America brings general news.]

4th.—Mr Putnam writes to Judge Sewall from Halifax, Aug. 9, that upon rec^t^ of the Declaration of Independence, it

* Paul to the Heb. i. 14.

was proclaimed from the balcony of the Council Chamber to a vast concourse of people with great rejoicings; and that every sign with a Crown in or upon it, was demolished. *Quæ vox dementia cœpit.* The wind west. . . .

5th.—John Malcolm came to me some time ago, and acquainted me he would prefer a Petition to the Treasury against Mr Waldo, Collector at Falmouth, Casco Bay, for irregularly clearing a vessel which, Malcolm being a Preventive Officer, had afterwards seized, and wch had been condemned. I asked what induced him, or he informed me, it was because Waldo did not pay his salary. I asked him what need he do more than complain of that? He said Waldo had hurt him, and he would have the whole story told. I advised him to apply to the Cōmiss^r^, but he resolved to petition, and said he must appeal to me in his Petition. I discouraged him still, and he said I refused to do him justice. I told him I should be ready when called upon to answer any questions asked me. After repeatedly troubling me I saw Mr Flucker, and told him of Malcolm's design, and that it was pity to have any stir, and that Malcolm had mentioned my name in his Petition, but I knew nothing of Waldo's proceedings except in general. I had a remembrance he was charged with some irregularity. Flucker to-day told Malcolm I said I knew nothing of the affair, which bro't Malcolm to my house to enquire whether I had said so? I told him I might say so, but did not remember the words, for I knew nothing but by common fame, which was knowing nothing to his purpose, for I should not be allowed to mention it. He abused me for refusing to say what he knew, and charged me with refusing to do him justice when in my power. I told him he was a very ignorant and very abusive man, and I should give myself no trouble about him. In the evening he sent me an abusive letter saying that he put my name in his Petition by my express order, and if I did not let him know by Monday* what I intended to say, he would make the world as well acquainted with my real character as he is himself.—West wind.

6th.—At the Old Jewry. . . .

* It was now Saturday.

7th.—I wrote to Malcolm that a letter had been left at my house signed with his name, for the letter was not of his hand writing, nor is he capable of writing a letter which can be understood: that I should take no more notice of it *at present* [underlined] than to let him know I had always advised him not to petition the Treasury, but he persisted in it, and said he should appeal to me, and he hoped I would not refuse to do him justice: that I told him I should not refuse to answer any questions their Lordships thought proper to ask me: that I had told him I knew nothing but by report, and that their Lordships would not think hearsay to be evidence.

This man, John Malcolm, had been shamefully treated in America. He is incidentally mentioned in some of the Diaries and Letters; but however much he may have unjustly suffered persecution, or merited sympathy, the Governor does not now appear to be desirous of giving him encouragement. Judge Oliver, in his "Origin and Progress of the American Rebellion to the year 1776," speaks thus of Malcolm's case:—"In the winter of this year [1772] the ruling Powers seized upon a Custom House officer for execution: they stripped him, tarred, feathered, and haltered him; carried him to the Gallows, and whipped him with great barbarity in the presence of thousands, and some of them members of the General Court. Like the Negro drivers in the West Indies, if you grumbled at so wholesome of discipline, you had iniquity added to transgression, and lash succeeded lash; and there was but one way of escaping, which was, to feign yourself dead, if you was not already so; for in that case, you would be left to yourself to come to life again as well as you could, they being afraid of such dead men, lest they theirselves should die after them, sooner or later:—one Custom-House officer they left for dead, but some persons of humanity stepped in to his relief and saved him."

8th.—An airing as far as Brentford, &c.

9th.—Lent Wilmot a guinea: all before repaid. Account published to-day of Genl Howe's defeat at N. York, wth the loss of two General officers and 6000 men, taken from the Amsterdam and Utrecht Gazettes; said to be on 16 of August.* The last packet left the Hook the 20th of August, and brought letters of the 17th from Staten Island.

* It is needless to say that there was no foundation for this statement.

10th.—Mr D'Oyly sent me a note this morning, and soon after called. An express arrived with letters from Genl Howe, advising that he landed the 22nd of August, under cover of Commodore Hotham's guns, with the British troops and some of the Hessians, at New Utrecht on Long Island, with little opposition from a few flying parties: that it took until the 26th to form and advance with proper precaution to that part where the enemy was intrenched: that on the 27th he stormed their works, and possessed himself of the first intrenchments, with the loss of 53 men killed, and about 200 wounded. Among the first, Lt Colo Grant, Capts Logan and Nelson, and Lieutt ——: among the wounded Colo Monckton, shot thro' the body, but may recover—in general lightly wounded: that, of the rebels, about 3300 killed and taken prisoners—about 1000 prisoners—among them their Major General Sullivan, the lawyer, Lord Sterling, so called, and Udell, of whom I never heard before: that the Long Island people came in and were ready to take the oath.

The express says they were in a most distressed state at N. York, 4000 sick, and it was thought there would be no great difficulty in reducing it. It was doubtful what was become of the army that was in the second intrenchment, which Howe had prepared to storm, and made advances, but on the 30th in the morning, they were evacuated, and Howe took possession of them, and his posts were against the city. They left their cannon and other stores.

This first and crude account of the important Battle of Brooklyn on Long Island, which led to the capture of New York, tallies however in its salient points with the more perfect narrative as given in the sixth Chapter of Stedman's History, assisted as it there is with a plan of the country and disposition of the troops. It is there stated that 15,000 Americans crossed the East River from New York to Brooklyn, and posted themselves behind several redoubts connected by curtains extending from Wallabout Bay on their left, to some marshy inlets on their right: that Putnam was put forward with 10,000 men to occupy the ridges of a curved line of hills extending in a half moon four or five miles in front of them towards the south, from which direction the English were expected. Washington was present and directed these arrangements. On advancing from the Redoubts, and taking post on the hills, the American right was commanded by Lord Sterling "so called," the centre by General Sullivan, and the left was not extended far enough, as the event proved. On the south or English side, Sir William Howe had 9,000 men, but the opportune arrival of his brother Lord Howe with additional forces, raised the grand total, according to some, to near 30,000. Stedman however, uses the expression "near twenty thousand." In speaking of the disposition of the two armies now opposite each other, he says, page 197—"In their [the American] front, was an encampment of near twenty thousand men." On the side of the English, General Grant was opposed to Lord Sterling; General De Heister with his Hessians, to General Sullivan in the centre; and Sir Henry Clinton, and Sir William Erskine, having reconnoitred and reported the unprotected state of the enemy's left wing, General Howe directed those officers, with Lord Percy, to make a circuit to the east and out-flank them. Upon this they executed a movement in that direction, and penetrating the defiles, crossed the ridge, and began the attack with vigour. After some hard fighting, the Americans were thrown into confusion, and retired precipitately upon their base at New York. Stedman further adds—"The loss of the Americans was great. Two thousand were either killed on the field, drowned [in crossing a morass,] or taken prisoners: and among the latter, Generals Sullivan, Udell, and Lord Sterling." And he observes further down—"The loss on the part of the English did not exceed three hundred in killed and wounded, of which number between sixty and seventy were killed. Among the killed was Lieutenant-Colonel Grant, of the fortieth Regiment; among the wounded, Lieutenant-Colonel Monkton."

General Washington soon found New York to be untenable, and thereupon he made preparations to evacuate the city.

It was a little before this time that the leaden statue of George III., which had stood in New York, but which had been pulled down and cast into bullets, was returned to the British by the American soldiers, as mentioned, Vol. i. p. 520.

The Diary, on the 11th of October, proceeds to say—

11th.—Mr Jackson of the Admiralty, read to me part of a letter from Sir George Collier, Cap. of the *Rainbow* at sea, on his passage from N. York to Halifax,—that he left N. York the 8 Sept., and the packet wch sailed with him, being a heavy sailer, it was possible the ship he wrote by might get to

England before her, and advised of the defeat of the rebels the 27th Aug.,—that some preparations had been making for landing the troops from the East River, some ships having gone up to cover them, and 80 flat bottomed boats,—that when he was coming out on the 8th he heard cañonading from 9 o'clock to 11, when he had lost the sound of the cannon by the distance he had run. He adds, that this must be a very important action, on which much depends—that there were so many sick in New York as to induce him to think, from humanity to them, the city would not be fired, as was intended, it being not practicable to remove them. It seems by a letter said to be intercepted from Washington to Sullivan, that great dependance was put on annoying and defeating the King's troops by attacking them from the woods in their march; but this dependance failed. Their General Woodall was taken under a hay rick. He is a New York Representative. Sullivan (one of the Congress), was in a house, and it is said was surprised to see Rogers with the King's troops, supposing he was in the Rebel service. Lord Sterling, so called, was taken alone, and is prisoner on board a ship, where he was loth to go; but it was intimated to him that he would be in danger from the soldiers, who were much enraged from a report that he was the man who cut off the head of the King's statue at New York.

Perkins and Flucker, and their families, dined [with us.]

12th.—Paxton brought me a letter he has received from Lord Percy, dated 1 September, from Newtown, Long Island, which is 3 or 4 miles up the river, opposite the N. York shore. Among other things he says—"Take my word for it, they never will dare to stand before us again. Our men have found out the use of their bayonets, and I promise you they gave the rebels enough of them on the 27th., for the moment the rebels fired they rushed on them, and never gave them time to load again."

Wrote to Auchmuty, Mr Ellis, Mackenzie, and Lord Hardwicke.

13th.—At the Temple: Doctor Morrill. Captain Dunn, of one of the transports, has wrote of the 8th of Sept., the day the packet sailed. We are not yet in possession of New York, but I hope we shall be before night.

It is not necessary to amplify by giving details here, which may be found in the pages of most of our historians. Suffice it to say that the English crossed the East River on the 15th of September, and as Washington withdrew his troops from New York, the city was taken possession of at once. Several actions succeeded one another within a few weeks from this time, in all which the English were victorious,—as at White Plains, Fort Washington, Fort Lee, &c., but as on Long Island the Americans were allowed to retreat without molestation, so in these cases no pursuit was allowed; and when Washington was making his way to get beyond the Delaware river, after his forces had precipitately abandoned Fort Lee, followed by the English, he was allowed a fair start in every day's march, arriving at Princetown, and then twelve miles further to the river, unovertaken, at Trenton. Then came the English on his heels. "Yet the British troops," says McCormic's Continuation of Hume, "were detained for seventeen hours at Princetown, and marching thence at nine o'clock next morning, got to Trenton at four in the afternoon, just when the last boat of Washington's embarkation crossed the river, as if General Howe had calculated with the nicest accuracy, the exact time necessary for his enemy to make his escape." As this sort of thing had happened more than once, it began to attract attention, and it is duly commented on to Sir William Howe's prejudice by most of those who have written on the subject of this war.

At this place several pages of the Diary can be advantageously omitted. On the 14th of October Mr. Hutchinson left London for a fortnight's tour, during which time America is scarcely alluded to except in one place, where he expresses a desire to go to the town of Boston in Lincolnshire. He says—"My chief inducement to turn aside to Boston, was from its having been the mother of American Boston." He was accompanied by his daughter Margaret or Peggy, Judge Oliver, and his niece Miss Clarke, and Mr. Paxton, with his servant. They proceeded *via* Waltham Cross, to Cambridge, then through a small village called Milton, on which he writes—"thro' Milton, a small parish of thatched, but pretty good houses, not so pleasing as my own Milton would have been," and so on to Ely and Wisbeach by the Ouse, of which river he says—"not wider than Milton river in N.E., the country settled in the N.E. way, not in villages, but farm houses a little distant," and thence to Spalding and Boston. Of this latter he writes—

"21st.—Called upon the Vicar of Boston Mr or Dr Calthorpe, who received us with great civility, he being an acquaintance of

Sr F. Bernard, who had spoke of me in his hearing, much in my favour. Took a view of the church, which exceeded my expectation, both for the magnificence and elegance, and also for the extreme good condition in which it is kept. He shewed me the Parish Register: observed the marriage of John Cotton, Clarke,* to Sarah Story, in 1632: saw a very elegant monument of one of my family, Samuel Hutchinson, a wine merchant in 1696: went to visit his son's widow, an old lady of 85, in perfect health with all her teeth and her intellectual powers, with her daughter, an old maiden: found her husband had often mentioned his relations going to Ireland, and Mrs. Jenyns being of the family. She is widow to a clergyman, and lives in a very decent house. Some of their family, she said, lived at Alford, where a Mr Walker at present has the living, and I purpose to write to him to make some extracts from the Register," &c.

It appears to me, (the Editor), somewhat strange that he did not go on a short matter of twenty-three miles to Alford, the place where his ancestor William was born in August 1586, and examine the Register for himself. From Boston he turned away to Sleaford and Grantham, but as he was accompanied by friends, perhaps he was not master of his own movements. There is nothing like being entirely alone when there is work to be done. In 1857 I went into Lincolnshire for these purposes, and I was wise enough to go alone. No member of the family had been to Alford since they went to America, and when I arrived there it was after an absence of 223 years. I first stopped at Boston, and from the Register of that place I copied everything relating to the names of Hutchinson and of Coddington, from October 28, 1566, to June 30, 1629. I enquired for the tablet or monument of Samuel Hutchinson, and found it in fragments on the floor of the room over the south porch. It was of white marble, and had been a slab of about three feet long by two wide, and three inches thick, bearing an inscription referring to the said Samuel, twice Mayor, and to some of his children. It had formerly been fixed against the south wall inside, and a little to the east of the south door; and with the usual principles of church restorers, I gathered that by some carelessness it got detached and broken at the time the church was renovated about 1850. The Verger, who shewed it to me, did not think that any descendant of the defunct was then living in Boston. Proceeding to Alford and the parish Register there, I

* That is, Clerk in Holy Orders.

extracted everything relating to the names of Hutchinson and Sanforde, beginning with William, who with his wife Anne went to America, who was baptised August 14, 1586, and coming down to February 4, 1641, and these lists have been useful in family genealogy.

The Chief Justice, being one of the party, enriched his Diary with many racy entries, and a few sly hits at the Americans, which last it is to be hoped will now be forgiven. At Cambridge he writes—

"The farmers raise great quantities of wheat and other grain, and send to market vast quantities of butter, Cambridgeshire butter being of a good quality and taste. Here I cannot but remark the method in their Inns, of serving their butter at table in small rolls of ab^t an inch in diameter, so that it may be said, that butter is sold here by the inch, foot, or yard, as in Quebec in America, they really, in the winter season, sell their milk by the pound, and send it to market in bags."

They went to Cressingham in Norfolk, where, he says—

"We arrived safe, and were most cerdially received by my old New England worthy friend Wm Burch Esq., and his agreeable family.

"To meet with a valuable friend, of so worthy a character, who had been persecuted by a wanton rebellion for seven years successively, and who after having escaped its harpy claws, to see him and his family sot down in quiet, free from the tyranny of anarchy, and under the umbrage of domestic happiness, gave me great pleasure, and I enjoyed his satisfaction without envy, as being conscious that the joy which I received from this participation, did not lessen, but rather added to his stock."

When travelling over the Lincolnshire Fens, he becomes too severe—

"The lands seemed to be covered with sheep as far as the eye could reach over the Fens: and here I could not help reflecting on the proud boasts of the northern Americans, who amused themselves with raising wool for their own manufactures, whereas they did not possess sheep enough to make their own stockings; and here I am persuaded that at one view I saw more sheep feeding than the whole Province of the Massachusetts Bay, the most sheepish of all the Colonies, is stocked with. On these roads they raise amazing quantities of turnips for the use of their cattle, and I have seen double the quantities of land sowed with turnips, than I ever saw sowed with any sort of grain in America. An American farmer who is swelled with his own importance, would be surprised to see the progress of agriculture in England, with the other improvements of the land, and would shrink even out of his own sight."

The Chief Justice had not yet recovered his equanimity, and in drawing his comparisons, it must be borne in mind that America was a young country. Since then she has astonished the world by her progress. Of Boston he writes—

"Before we reached Boston we rode over a long and wide causway, which was thrown up out of the Fen, in order to make a turnpike, and the approach to the town had some resemblance to the entrance of Boston in America, viz.—over this neck of land, in view of a Gibbet, and of a windmill: may it never resemble it in its disaffection to government, and its fondness for anarchy.

"We put up at the White Hart Inn at Boston, a good house.

"Boston is a seaport: the tide flows to the town, and meets the river Witham. . . Mr John Cotton, who was ye first Minister of Boston in Massachusets Bay, was Vicar of this church, and from him the American Boston derived its name."

The party proceeded by way of Nottingham, Derby, Lichfield, Birmingham, Stratford-on-Avon, Woodstock, and so returned to London, where they arrived on the 28th of October. The 29th was rainy, but on the 30th the Diary continues thus—

30th.—At the King's Levée: as full as I remember to have seen it at any time.

31st.—At the House of Lords to hear the King's Speech. Introduced by Lord Polworth, and Judge Oliver with me; but I had no desire to go through the fatigue of standing 5 or 6 hours to hear the debates. The Opposition were 26 to 92, which is less in the Lords than formerly; but in the Commons it was much the same—242 of the majority, against 87.* It is pretty certain that the disproportion would have been much less if the subject of debate had been meerly [*sic*] a controversy between Court and Country parties, the independent country gentleman being generally against the Americans.

* These numbers tally with those given by Adolphus and the Continuator of Hume.

The account given by Judge Oliver, as written in his Diary, can scarcely be omitted. It runs as follows:—

"31st.—This day I went to the House of Lords to hear the King deliver his speech to the Parliament. The procession was grand, his Majesty being in the elegant state coach, which is glazed all around, and the body elegantly gilt, with a gilt crown on the top, with other decorations, drawn by 8 dun horses, the finest I ever saw, and kept in such order that their skin and hair appeared like a rich velvet. The amazing string of coaches, and the vast crowd of spectators in the streets and in the windows of the houses, of ladies richly dressed, and the groupe of figures from the first gentleman to the lowest link-boy was very picturesque, and was a true representation of the chequered state of mankind: but the whole, united with the apparent joy of countenances, exhibited an idea of the grandeur and importance of a British Monarch.

"I entered the House of Lords under the umbrage* of Lord Polworth. Without the Bar of the House it was much crowded, but within was a grand appearance of the nobility, and of ladies richly dressed. His Majesty was seated on his throne in the robes of royalty, with his rich crown upon his head. He then directed the attendance of the House of Commons, some of whom came, preceded by their Speaker, who also was preceded by his Mace Bearer, and followed by his Train Bearer: he was richly dressed in his gold-laced robes, and made a magnificent appearance. His Majesty then delivered his Speech, and with that dignity, propriety of accent and pronunciation, w[ch] commanded attention and created esteem.

"The passages to the House of Lords are a perfect labyrinth, and when a stranger, whose expectation hath formed an idea of the grandeur of an apartment for so august a body of senators, enters it, his ideas sink at the approach of so much inelegance; but it is a general observation, that even the Palace of the greatest Monarch is derogatory to the dignity of a petty prince: and the remark is too general, that the horse stables of the French Monarque are more elegant than the Palace of a British King. It seems to be a paradox, that a nation which riots in luxury, and whose coffers are bursting with riches, whose elegance of taste in architecture, and in every polite science, whose seats, both of nobility and gentry, vie with Asiatick pomp, and some of whose nobility, and even

* Umbra, a shadow; under the shadow of his wing. Compare the signification of the word 100 years ago with what it is now. If all words are liable to the same changes as this one, what becomes of the stability of the English language?

commonalty, can purchase 2 or 3 German Principalities,—I say, that it seems a paradox that their Sovereign should be suffered to wear more slender insignia of Royalty than many other Princes whom even his own private estate could purchase their whole dominions. I can assign no other principle for it but the national enthusiastick fondness for Liberty, which ever aims to reduce all to a level, and which overpowers the national principle of pride.

"His Majesty, after delivering his Speech, returned to his palace in grand procession, the populace hanging upon his chariot wheels, and filling the air with their acclimations. And here, one could scarce refrain from pitying the versatility of human nature, when they reflected upon the different behaviour of this populace not long since, to this most amiable of Princes, whom they almost cursed to his face, whilst at the same time they Hosanna'd a man who was known to be infamous in all vices, unharnassing the horses of his carriage, and dragging it with their own strength, this mock patriot sitting in it in triumph, pluming himself with pleasure, in seeing his triumphal car drawn in imitation of some eastern Monarch by Asses, rather [than] the more noble animal an horse. *Sic mutat gloria mundi.*" *

Mr. Hutchinson's Diary continues as follows :—

November 1st.—In the city: called upon Blackburne: no arrivals, the wind having been towards east for 8 or 10 days. Lord Gage called. Doctor Cooper, who brought copy of the Master of the Galatæa's letter, with the account of Gen. Howe's landing the 15th, and of an action the 16th, with the slaughter of 7 or 8,000 Provincials, but this copy made no mention of the loss on the part of the King's troops.

2nd.—Capn Balfour arrived in the evening from New York. He is Aide-du-camp to Gen. Howe. Lord Townshend sent me copy of a letter he had recd from Cap. Montresor wch was brought me after 11 o'clock, just as I was going to bed, dated Sepr 26. The troops made good their landing the 15th at Keps Bay, being expected at another place, met with no

* These allusions are doubtless addressed to the case of John Wilkes in 1768, who was committed to prison, when the mob waylaid the vehicle in which he was being carried, and taking out the horses, drew him away in another direction. To turn round and hurl low abuse at the person of His Majesty, was only to be consistent. In the History of this period by Adolphus, these stirring events are detailed in Chapter XV.

opposition, but took 200 prisoners who were flying from the town. The 16th at the heights of Harlem, had a skirmish between some of the light infantry, and about 3,000 of the enemy, 300 of whom killed and wounded, and 14 only of the King's army killed, and [blank] wounded. The 21st some concealed rebels set fire in the night to N. York, and about $\frac{1}{4}$ of the town destroyed, St. Paul's and Trinity churches being part. Six of the incendiaries were killed by the soldiers, 14 taken and to be tried. The 23rd the ships drove the enemy from the Battery at Powles Hook, and the King's troops took possession. The 25th General Prescot exchanged for the General Sullivan. It is said that Washington has about 30,000 men at King's-Bridge, &c., and that there is a flying camp of 10,000 in the Jerseys.

3rd.—At the Temple.

4th.—A vessel from Boston bought by Captains who had been taken, and obtained leave to come to England. Fenton's wife and family, and a son of Col° Hatch, passengers. The rest seem to be people who had been taken: said to be 70 in all. . . .

5th.—Mr Jonathan Down, son to Mr Jos. Down of Salem arrived in the Boston vessel, came and dined with us, and gave a more particular account of affairs than we have had for some time. He says no business goes on but privateering. He thinks there are 100 from the several parts of the continent. The Assembly have 112 at the publick charge. He says Indian corn is 5/- ꝑ bushel in paper money, which is near double what it used to be in silver and gold; so that their bills are sunk near $\frac{1}{2}$. He saw Dr. Pemberton, and does not remember any of note lately dead.

6th.—Dined with Peggy at Mr Ellis's. A sudden motion in the House of Commons made by Lord Jn° Cavendish, to address the King to revise instruction, &c., agreeable to Lord Howe's, and General Howe's declaration, kept part of our company, and Mr Ellis himself, in the House of Commons, and I dined with only three or four ladies without them. Burke spoke an hour, and among other things said the proclamation for a fast was little better than a blasphemy. Lord North sent out for all his troops, but mustered only 109; the minority were 47.

In the evening the Bishops of London and Chester, and ladies, Lord Buckinghamsh[ire's] Lady, Lord Harrowby, Sir Grey Cooper, Mr Jenkinson, Mr Cornwall, Mr Hunter, &c., with several ladies. I rec^d^ two letters from Mr Jon. Clarke at Montreal, the last 15 Sept. which I sent to Lord George.

7th.—At Lord North's Levée, who, among other things said he had rec^d^ a very good Pamphlet under a cover which he took to be my hand writing. Asked if I wrote it, &c. . . .

8th.—This and the three last days have been remarkably foggy. . . .

9th.—Lord Mayor's Day, which the Americans say, is not equal to our Election or Commencement Parades. . . .

10th.—At the Temple church. . . .

11th.—[Remarks about the change of Lord Mayors.]

12th.—Two or three transports arriving from New York caused a report that there was fresh news. . . .

Nobody seems to doubt that the fleet and army with Carleton and Burgoyne embarked on the Lakes the 2^d^ and third of October. The fleet consists of a 20-gun ship, a Rideau or floating battery of six 12-pounders, and six 24-pound^s^; a gondola of 10 guns; 2 scooners 16 guns each, and a great number of boats with a cannon in each: so that, though the rebels have more in number, the King's force seems to exceed in weight. . . .

13th.—Called upon Mr Ellis. By his advice I wrote the following, to accompany the letter to a noble Lord, &c.

"Governor Hutchinson, being prompted by zeal for your Majesty's service, and a desire to expose, and as far as may be to frustrate, the very criminal designs of the leaders of your Majesty's deluded unhappy American subjects, has wrote, and caused to be printed a small Pamphlet, which he begs leave to lay at your Majesty's feet, humbly entreating your Majesty's forgiveness of this presumption."

14th.—I sent the letter, &c. under cover, with direction, To the King, by a servant out of livery, to the Queen's Palace, to be delivered to the porter, with my desire that he would give it to the Page in waiting. The porter asked the servant if he was to wait for an answer? and upon being told he was not to wait, promised immediately to deliver it.*

A large fleet from Jamaica, above 100 sail, came out under convoy of two men-of-war, which saw them thro' the Gulf, and then one returned to Jamaica: the other, the *Pallas*, soon after left the fleet, or the fleet left her, and it is said, carried one ship only into Newfoundland. One of the fleet arrived to-day, above 13 weeks out, and gives an account of many vessels taken by the American privateers. It is said that one half the fleet are missing. One Jamaica house had 3 ships taken, and have stop'd payment for 400,000£, as the report is. My broker tells me to-day, several more must go, and many will suffer greatly by this great failure. The West India merchants, Jamaica especially, have encouraged the American revolt, and pay very dearly for it.

15th.—[More captures by the privateers. Mr Geo. Apthorpe in England receives a letter from America, sent by R. Temple. Details of no moment.]

16th.—[Letter from New York of Oct. 10, saying the last division of the Hessians had arrived out.]

17th.—At the Old Jewry. . . .

18th.—Mrs Murray, &c., Robinson and wife, Dudley and Rome, dined with us. . . . The papers say Cap. Cornwallis in the *Pallas*, is arrived at Portsm^h. His conduct as Convoy to the Jamaica fleet is censured, but he has not been heard. . . .

19th.—A very dark foggy drizzling forenoon again. . . . Lord Hardwicke called. . . . Lord Oxford . . . who, Lord H. says, is a very worthy good man. . . .

20th.—The wind shifted to west. . . . Peggy and I dined at Mr Robinson's . . . Navy Bills. . . .

21st.—At Court: a very full Drawing Room, Ladies especially. The old Dutchess of Bedford I had not seen before, since my being this time in England. The Duke of Montagu —I never observed so much of his person and demeanor. A Russian lady was there with a Red Ribband, which she wore

* This pamphlet seems to have been put forth without the author's name. No such pamphlet is found among the family papers, and it is unknown to the Editor.

over her shoulder, as the Knt[s] of the Bath do theirs; had her son with her, a very pretty boy about the age of the Prince of Wales [Fourteen.] She was the chief adviser and actress in the late revolution—brought the Czarina the Badge of the Order which the Czar wore, with the news of his death, when the Czarina delivered her the Badge which she had on herself. It is said that this Lady gave the Czar the doze [dose] which put him asleep. It's thought the present Czarina encourages her travelling, being rather troublesome, if not dangerous, at home. She has been in England before. She now desired to see the Queen, not in publick and at Court, but it was not thought proper, and submitted to come to the King to-day. I think she is called the Princess Deskau.*

The Queen never spoke with more freedom and condescension at any time of my being at Court; lamented the burning of the city of New York, &c.

Lord Talbot was very polite; said he hoped Ministry consulted me, but it is certain they do not. Saw Admiral Montagu at Court, the first time since his return from Newfoundland. Dined at M[r] Jenkinson's, &c.

Lord Buckinghamshire's appointment to be L[d] L[t] of Ireland made publick, and to-morrow he is to kiss the King's hand, L[ds] Hillsborough, Rochfort, and Dartmouth, all talked of. From L[d] H.'s conversation with me, he does not like being passed over. L[d] D. I doubt not might have gone if he would. Now the L[ds] Lieut. are obliged to reside for 4 or 5 years, the post is not so much coveted as it used to be. It is worth 16,000£ a year, and 3,000£ is allowed to fix out, but the expense of living is great. Lord Harcourt I never saw. His two predecessors L[d] Townshend and L[d] Hertford do not seem to have been appointed from anything very shining in their

* The Czarina Catherine II., was the daughter of Christian Augustus of Anhalt-Zerbst. At the age of fourteen she was married to the Duke of Holstein, afterwards Peter III. He was dethroned by a rapid course of events, in which the Empress was the principal mover, and she assumed the government alone June 28, O.S. 1762. He died a prisoner a few days afterwards, "by an hemorrhoidal accident," as the manifesto of July 7, issued by the Empress, made it known to the world. She was then 33, of a fine person, and great vigour of mind. The Princess who is said to have given the sleeping dose, was the talk of all Europe.

characters. It is said much depends on their Secretaries. The two last, Maccartney and Blaquiere, were made Knt[s] of the Bath upon their return.* The latter seems but a moderate genius, and the former not much superior. He is son-in-law to L[d] Bute, and lately made an Irish peer.

22nd.—Two vessells from Quebec, which they left the 25th of October. M[r] Mauduit has a letter of the 17th from M[r] Clarke at Montreal, and a postsc[t] I think of the 20th, with advice of the defeat of all the rebel force on the Lake, the 13th, 14th, and 15th of the month, and the King's troops landing at Crown Point, w[ch] had been set on fire and deserted, and proceeding to Ticonderoga, but no account of the state of that place. Other accounts say that Carleton had dismissed and sent home all the prisoners, which nobody here attempts to account for. One of the gun-boats with one of the King's officers and a number of men, was blown up in the action. Carleton had a prodigious force. Some blame him for taking up so much time in preparing it, while others think it was right to make success as sure as human skill can do. Dined at D[r] Huck's. . . .

The letter mentioned above, as having been sent by Mr. Clarke from Montreal, has not been preserved; but there is an original letter of Lord George Germain, in which he thanks Mr. Hutchinson for having given him a sight of it, or what was apparently the same, though there is some little looseness in handling the dates. It runs as follows, in a large hand, not very clear, and somewhat blotted, having been folded whilst it was wet:—

"Lord George Germain returns Governor Hutchinson many thanks for communicating to him the enclos'd letters: that from M[r] Clarke of the 27th of Septemb[r] gives a more unfavourable account of our preparations for passing the Lakes than any that has been yet received. Lord George begins to doubt whether the season will not be too far advanced for making any progress this campaign.

"Pall Mall, Nov[r] [date obscure] 1776."

23rd.—I find nothing to-day of blowing up the gunboat, and it may be a mistake. Lieut[t] Dacres arrived with letters from General Carleton and Cap[n] Douglass.

* Mentioned at p. 204, vol. i.

24th.—At the Temple. . . . The Gazette gives Carlton's letter: short, and as it is generally said, wrote as if he was out of humour. . . . In the evening went with Dr Douglass to Lord Mansfield's, and Lord Chancellor's *couchées*, where were Lord Cassilis, the new Scotch Peer in Parliament, Ld Barrington, Sr Charles Whitworth, Soame Jenyns, Mr Norton, Ord, Neville, Day, going to Bengal Advocate General, Gilbert, Wilmot, Bishop of Litchfield, Sir Sampson Gideon, &c.

Coming home Doctor Douglass mentioned Doctor Franklin's charging Dean Tucker with saying he had applied for the place of Stamp Master, as a falsehood. It's true, says the Doctor, he did not apply for the Stamp Master's place, but he applied to the Commissioners of the Stamp Office that he might have the stamping of all the paper, which would have been more profitable to him than the place of Stamp Master. This, the Doctor added, was told me by [blank] but he was living then, and I had no authority from him to make public what he told me.

25th.—The news from New York of an action, which has been rumoured for two or three days, seems to gain a degree of belief to-day. Mauduit shewed me copy of a letter one of his friends has rec^d^ from Whitehaven, dated the 19th Inst.,—that two vessels were come in from Corke, with intelligence that six transports which sailed from N. York the 18th of October were arrived at Corke: that on the 15th, 16th, and 17th, the King's forces attacked the rebels at King'sbridge, &c., dislodged Washington, killed, wounded and made prisoners 7,000, with the loss of 14 or 1500 of the King's forces.

Lord Townshend sent me a letter he had received from Cap^n^ Blomefield, dated Crown Point, 16th October; the account of the action on the Lake much the same wth the Gazette, only he says Arnold fought bravely, and that if they had all done as well, they would have overpowered the gunboats, and Carleton's scooner, before the other vessels could have joined them; but the rest of the rebel vessels thought of nothing but an escape.*

* Serjeant Lamb, in his *Journal of the American War*, speaks in high terms of the bravery of Arnold on this occasion, page 111. Gen. Carleton

He says Carlton had received such intelligence of the naval force on the Lake, that he thought it a risque to take the army with him in batteaux until that force was subdued, which part of his conduct is much approved of in England: but then Blomefield disapproves of the intention to take post at Crown Point, and says they have a moral certainty of success at Ticonderoga, where they were expected, the army there lying every night upon their arms. A small part only of the army was ordered to Crown Point when Blomefield's letter was dated.

Carleton is spoke of as a man of strong resentment,* as prejudiced against Lord George, and dissatisfied at not having a general command, Howe being his junior in the army; and some suppose he will not do any more than keep his own government clear of the rebels. It is also generally known that Burgoyne and he do not agree. Burgoyne, it is said, is coming home.

Dined at Master Holford's. . . .

26th.—At Lord Hardwicke's. . . . Ld H. made me a present of his collection of Sir D. Carleton's Letters, in Quarto.† . . . At Lord Gage's, where I saw the General, and Parson Mitchel of Brighthelmstone. Ld G. says Ld Derby told him he had a letter from Burgoyne Oct. 16th at Crown Pnt.

27th.—Further reports by other transports, &c. [Only reports.] Dined with Peggy at Mr Ellis's:—Mr Dunbar, who Mr Ellis calls his brother-in-law, Mr Harris of Salisbury, Mr Hooper of the Customs, Mr Halsell, Clerk of the H. of Commons, and Paxton. I have seldom dined where there has been a

was on board the *Maria*, Cap. Pringle. The English fleet chased the Americans, who were making for Crown Point, and after seven hours the *Maria* with two others came up with them and began the action. The *Washington* galley struck; Arnold in the *Congress* galley, and five gondolas, ran on shore and blew up the vessels. "The killed and wounded in our fleet did not amount to forty." Out of fifteen American armed vessels which engaged our fleet in the morning, only three escaped. Upon this the Americans burnt all the buildings at Crown Point, and then retired to Ticonderoga, when Carleton landed at Crown Point, and was there joined by the English army.

* Carleton was good at bottom. Anburey, i. 72, speaks of him as having "a good-natured, affable disposition."

† These are not forthcoming now.

more sensible conversation. A fact mentioned by Halsell I never heard before—that Burke, when he was at the Temple and about 22, wrote a then famous pamphlet to shew that a state of nature was to be preferred to a state of society,—a well wrote piece to imitate Lord Bolinbroke, and which I remember was believed in America to be wrote by him, but was afterwards said to be the performance of a Templar.

A cold day. At Kensington before dinner, Mr Heald's, and at Brompton.

28th.—In the city. . . . Dined with Gen. Gage. . . .

29th.—[Rumours unconfirmed.]

30th.—In Parliament Street I met Lord Amherst. [Talk about Carleton.]

Mr Strahan, and afterwards Soame Jenyns called upon me. Strahan says he has under Franklin's hand, extract of his letter which he wrote to Boston, to accompany the letters to Whately, which Franklin sent there, and Strahan promises to send it to me.

December 1st.—At the Old Jewry. . . .

2nd.—Called upon Mr Ellis. . . .

3rd.—Mr Nicolls, Lieutenant in the navy, who says he dined several times with me at Boston, called, being lately returned from the West Indies. . . . At Hardwicke's. . . .

4th.—In the coach with Mr Greene to Highgate. . . .

5th.—Reports . . . groundless. At Lord Huntingdon's. . . .

6th.—At the King's Levée. Court in mourning one week for a German Princess. . . .

Just as I was going to bed a sollicitor brought me a letter from Mr Robinson of the Treasury, desiring I would assist the sollicitor in procuring evidence to facts to be proved in a cause against some printers of the account of the affair at Lexington, wch is to be had at 9 o'clock to-morrow morning. The sollicitor wanted one to swear that Lexington and Concord are in Mass^s Bay. I wrote to Flucker to desire him to attend, and gave the letter to a servant, with a charge to go to Flucker's and call him up before 8 o'clock, which in these dark foggy days is as soon as anybody inclines to rise.

7th.—The printers found guilty after a very short trial. . .

8th.—At the Temple. In the evening I hear it said that an express is come from Portsmouth with an account of a fire in the Dock-yard there.

9th.—News of the fire at Portsmouth proves too true. It began in the Store-house for hemp and cordage, which house is said to be wholly burnt, being a very long building; but what value of stores is consumed is not mentioned.

An account in the papers taken from the Philadelphia papers, of the proceedings of the Howes through Lord Drummond, and afterwards through Sullivan, with the Conference held with the Howes and Franklin, John Adams, and Rutledge from the Congress, all printed by the Congress, causes great speculation. Lord Townshend called in a perfect rage, and hints that they may make what agreement they will, but Parliament must finally approve it. I supposed it to be true that there has been such a Conference, but doubt not Lord Howe will deny some part of what the Congress publish.

Met Mr Fitch, King's Advocate for Massachusets Bay, who arrived Saturday evening from Ireland. Lt Governor Oliver called. Called upon Sir Robert Eden in Queen Street—from home.

10th.—A Man-of-War from Quebec, sailed about a week in November.* General Burgoyne and his Aide-du-camp come in her: left Carleton at Crown Point, but expected soon at Quebec. Burgoyne, it is said, went out with a resolution to return before winter. . . .

11th.—Mr W. Palmer, son of my old friend Eliakim Palmer, long since deceased, dined with me, Col. Phips, Vassall, Lt Gov., and Paxton. In the evening at Lord Hardwicke's, where was Sir Francis Clerke, Aide-du-camp to Burgoyne. . . .

Under this same date the following entry is found in the Diary of Judge Oliver—

"December 11.—This day I attended the Levée of Lord George Germain, his Majesty's Secretary of State for America, where, in private audience, his Lordship treated me with great politeness, affability, and friendship. His character in private life is amiable,

* Anburey, writing from Quebec, Oct. 30, says,—"General Carleton and General Burgoyne are both here, the latter of whom sails for England in a few days."

his good sense qualifies him from his department, and his firmness of mind renders him equal to the subdual of an American Rebellion."

12th.—At M[r] Jenkinson's. . . .

13th.—A Fast on account of the American war, observed with strictness and great external devotion, the churches crowded more than ever known on Sundays,* and shops everywhere shut, and few people to be seen in the streets. . . .

14th.—In the city. . . .

15th.—At the Old Jewry.—M[r] White. Dined with Peggy at Lord Hardwicke's. M[r] Crinsley [?] from Quebec called. He says he saw an officer there who left Crown Point Nov. 2nd in the morning, and Carleton with the last of the forces, was to leave in the afternoon. Carleton's nephew, with a party of Indians, bro't off 100 head of cattle from within a mile of Ticonderoga. . . .

16th.—At Brompton Row.† . . .

17th.—A letter to the Admiralty. [Nothing definite.]

18.—No news yet. . . . Brook Watson arrived from Quebec. . . .

19th.—The despatches by the *Fowey*, and Lord Dunmore who was passenger, come to town. No letter from Gen[l] Howe, but one from Lord Howe to the Admiralty. It is agreed that part of the troops crossed over to West Chester from the East River, and attacked the rebels in their entrenchments, and drove them to the main body at Kingsbridge. It is said near 200 of the K.'s troops are killed. Col[o] Carr, Cap[n] Creagh, [?] and other officers; that the rebels a day or two after, retreated from Kingsbridge to the Manor of Courtland, leaving about 2000 in Fort Washington at Kingsbridge, and that Howe with the body of the army, was pursuing the enemy.

In the evening Lord Townshend sent me a long letter he had received from Major Dilkes, dated Nov. 3rd, with a particular account of the action. A detachment or brigade landed first, the 11th, and had some skirmishes: then the 17th

* According to Augustus De Morgan's *Book of Almanacs*, it was now Friday.

† Where his son Thomas, with his wife and children, was then living.

—25th, and at last the 28th October, when was the principal action. He speaks very contemptuously of the enemy: calls them Rascals, Cowards, &c., and they seemed to be well fortified; but it is certain they killed near 200; and though the King's troops had the advantage of pursuing them, yet it does not appear that the loss was much different.

Wrote to my brother [Foster] at Halifax by Mr Selkrigg.

20th.—Dined at Mr Masere's. . . .

21st.—Wrote this evening to Mr Ellis a very particular account of the proceedings at New York, from the 11th to the 28th of October. . . .

22nd.—At the Temple. . . .

23rd.—Gilbert Deblois arrived in one of the transports from New York. More letters appear which encourage hopes of reconciliation. I think the Machine too unwieldy for the Congress to manage, and keep the several parts together. In the evening at Mr Copley's. . . .

24th.—Doctor Chandler read part of a letter from his correspond^t^ Ingolls at New York, which gives an acc^t^ of the negotiations:—says that Lord Howe thought it necessary upon his arrival, his powers should be known: sent a message by a flagg to "G. Washington Esq.," which was sent back unopened, Washington saying he knew no such person: that Col^o^ Paterson was sent a second time, under pretence of demanding the discharge* of the regiment taken at St John's, who were to be exchanged for the men taken at the Cedars. What passed then he does not say, but a flag afterwards came from Washington by — Reed, his secretary, who married De Berdt's daughter, and who flourished away upon the oppressions and tyrannies which had made it necessary for the Colonists to take up arms. He was cut short by Lord Howe, who demanded what message he had, or whether any? "He came to be informed upon what terms his L^d^ship proposed to treat." Lord Howe said he did not propose to treat while they continued in arms: that upon their laying down their arms and

* The word "discharge" has been subsequently underlined, and the word "release" has been written over it, thus giving the reader his choice of the two words. It is in the same handwriting as the Diary.

submitting to Government, he was authorised to give them assurances of everything they could in reason desire: if they refused and chose fighting rather than submission, he would give them assurances they should have enough of it.

Lord Howe also sent copies of his Declaration to Amboy to be d[d] [delivered?] to the Commander of the rebel forces there, with letters or copies of the Declaration, under covers directed to several of the Congress, which were forwarded to them, but treated with neglect.

After the battle on Brookland, [Brooklyn] when Sullivan was taken prisoner, he informed the two brothers that he did not doubt if he might have liberty to go to the Congress, he should be able to convince them of the expedience of appointing persons to hear what his Lordship had to offer, and that it would be attended with success, &c. Sullivan was allowed to go upon his parole, and returned in 8 days. Soon after a flagg came from the Congress to desire safe conduct for Franklin, Jn[o] Adams, and Rutledge, which was granted, and they came in, and upon the first meeting Lord Howe desired to know in what character they considered themselves? John Adams answered—"As Delegates from the Free and Independent States of North America." Upon which Lord Howe said that he had nothing to offer them, and withdrew. Whether this be a full account, or whether what the Congress has published passed at this time, or whether they have heard what Lord Howe may have said at other times, and in other companies, and made it part of this conversation, time may discover.

Dined with Sergeant Ambler, &c.

25th.—At the Temple. . . .

26th.—Set out with Peggy in [a] postchaise ¼ past nine, and arrived at Tylney Hall by three. M[r] S[t] John and wife, and a Clergyman M[r] Courtenay, dined there: no company besides the Chaplain M[r] Jones, in the family.

27th.—An uncomfortable day: cold, especially in this vast large house: squalls of snow: probably rain in London. The Duke and Dutchess of Bolton dined at M[r] Ellis's, with Miss Lowther, sister to the Dutchess, and to Sir James Lowther, and a Clergyman, M[r] Pawlet, a natural son to the last Duke of Bolton but one, by the famous Polly Pecham, her name, from the part she acted in the *Beggar's Opera*, but her real name [was] Fenton. The Duke had three or four children by her while his Dutchess lived, and as soon as she was dead married her, but had no child afterwards, and the title went to a collateral Pawlet, brother to the present Duke, who died without issue, and so the title came to this brother.

This Clergyman's mother was an ordinary girl on the stage, employed on some occasions, and in a starving condition, just before M[r] Gay wrote his *Beggar's Opera*: taking the part of Polly, she charmed the town; but the D. of Bolton was the man who took her off the stage. She did many kind things while she was the Duke's mistress, and behaved extremely well while she was his Dutchess; and at his death was supposed to have had 50 or 60 thous[d] pounds of his fortune, but then married a tall Irishman, Kelly, spent her fortune, turned sot, and died miserably, and neglected providing for her children. This son has said she was the most unnatural mother that ever man had. The present Duke is no genius, but is an affable easy talking man, and neither his Dutchess nor he are any way haughty or assuming.*

28th.—With M[r] Ellis and M[r] Jones to Odiam, &c.

29th.—I kept house, the weather being cold; and a cold which I brought from London not decreasing.

The post brings M[r] Ellis, in writing, I suppose from M[r] D'Oyly, as it is from Whitehall, intelligence brought from Linn [Lynn] in Mass. Bay, November 26th, that the day before an express came from Gen. Lee, advising the taking Fort Washington on the 16th by storm, with 3000 men killed and made prisoners: that orders came to Linn from Boston to send

* John Gay was born in 1688, and the *Beggar's Opera* appeared in 1727, some fifty years prior to the date in the Diary to which we have arrived. Polly Pecham was in her theatrical glory as long as the Opera was popular. Her silly second marriage produced the results that might have been expected. She would have been a wise woman had she maintained her widowhood as the unfettered Duchess of Bolton. As to one of her sons speaking of her as an unnatural mother and neglecting her children, perhaps, being now linked to a sot and a spendthrift, she may have lost her control over her resources, and no longer able to do the thing she would.

every 4th man to supply the place of every 5th who were to be discharged the 31 Dec.; but many said they would not go: that Washington was at Kips * Kill, and Lee at an advanced post between Kipskill and Kingsbridge.

This account is very probable. The intelligence is further, that the people in Mass^s said, upon the taking of Fort Washington, it was all over with them, and wished they had hearkened to the proposals made them. This may have been the sentiment of some, but I fear is not yet the general sentiment.

30th.—Mr Ellis and lady, Mr Agar, my daughter and I, dined at the Duke of Bolton's at Hackwood, where we found Sir Philip Jennings, Cust, [or Clerk], Mr Corbet and his wife, Lady Augusta, daughter of Lord Bute, Mr Lane, who I can learn nothing of, and the Duke's family.

In the evening came in from London Sir James Lowther, and Sir Mich. Fleming, neither of whom I had ever seen before, and a Clergyman of the name of Watson. They reported that Cap^n Gardner was arrived from N. York: confirmed the taking Fort Washington, and also Fort Constitution, with the loss of 700 of the King's troops, which latter circumstance I hope is not true. . . .

31st.—I must do penance to-day for the fault of yesterday, and not go abroad tho' the weather is very fine. Mr Jenkinson and his young son were a-bed when we came home last night, and breakfasted with us this morning, coming yesterday from Sherborn. Mr Ellis receives a Gazette extraordinary of yesterday from M^r D'oyly with intelligence to Nov. 30, when Fort Washington, with 2700 men, and Fort Lee, with between 1 and 200 had surrendered, the last on the Jersey side, from whence, or the environs, 2000 men narrowly escaped. Genl Howe says he did not think it necessary to follow Washington, or to that effect, which occasions speculation in this family.

Lord Cornwallis was in pursuit of the rebels, who were retreating towards Brunswick. How far he was likely to follow is not said. As he had 7 or 8000 men, it is the opinion here he would run no risk if he marched to Philadelphia.

* Should be Peek's. This foot-note is in the Diary, and added subsequently by Gov. H.

I wrote to Mr Winslow. . . .

Thus goes out the year 1776, at which period the fortunes of the Americans were very low. The series of disasters that they had suffered immediately following the battle of Brooklyn, had reduced and demoralised their army, and had created an alarm bordering on despair amongst all orders of men who had cast their lot into the cause of open rebellion. If the Howes had followed up the advantages gained on Long Island, and had prosecuted them rapidly and vigorously through all the transactions that took place at the subsequent battles, and the retreat to Philadelphia, it is not too much to suppose that they would have brought the war to a speedy close. Most of the historians who have followed these events have commented on the unaccountable tactics of General Howe, and it appears that his conduct did not now escape the notice of Mr. Ellis's party at Tylney Hall, as mentioned above.

CHAPTER II.

CONTINUATION OF THE DIARY,

BEGINNING WITH THE YEAR 1777.

January 1st.—A letter from my son [Thomas] at Brompton, enclosing the Gazette, all being as well as I left them.

Mr Ellis's letters from London say that Ld Cornwallis, Winchelsea, and Shuldam are now on their passage for England. This puts an end to all expectation of further service this campaign, and affords another subject for Newspaper animadversions, the plan of American measures, and the execution of it.

2nd.—Mr Jenkinson with his son left . . . [Bad cold.]

3rd.—[Confined with his cold.]

4th.—Upon the whole, I feel better . . . [Mr Paxton and Adm^l^ Montagu arrived.]

5th.—[Cold still bad.] The post brings me a letter and N. York newspapers from Mr Mauduit. A Proclamation of L^d^ and Gen. Howe, promising pardon to all without exception, who shall within 60 days come in and subscribe a declaration to remain in peaceable obedience to the King, and not to take up arms against his authority, nor excite or encourage others to do it. Mauduit says it is easier to obtain pardon for rebelling than not rebelling: for at S. Carolina they have hung a Scotch Presbyter[ian] Minister for being inimical to the liberties of America. Mr Ellis disapproves of a promise of pardon without exception. It looks as if they intended to keep possession of the Jerseys, and to take possession of Rhode Island, Clinton having sailed the 1st of December.

Returned the papers by post in letters to Mr Mauduit.

6th.—A cold day. . . .

7th.—A very cold day: the water freezes fast in my chamber. . . . [Speculations about the future of America.]

8th.—The cold increases . . . set out at 10, and was in London 10 minutes after 3*. . .

9th.—Kept house . . .

10th.—I walked as far as High Street. . . .

11th.—In the city to visit Mrs Grant . . . from Newport, Rhode Island. She thinks the town of Newport will be burnt . . . I asked if she saw my tenant Pierce . . . she answered No. . . .

12th.—A wet damp day . . .

13th.—A warm fair day . . .

14th.—Lieutenant Brenton, returned from Halifax, called upon me. . . Dined at Mr Jackson's, South^n^ Buildings, my two sons E. and W. Found Gov. Pownall of the company, who was civil.† . . .

Gov. Pownall said that a son of Sir Gilbert Eliot, coming through France, stopped at a house of Madame—I forget the name—where he saw Ben. Franklin, Silas Deane, and the Duke de Choiseul.

15th.—Called upon Mr Ellis. At the King's Levée. Dined at Sr James Wright's . . .

16th.—Mr Ellis called and spent half an hour. . . .

* An original letter of Jan. 8, from Mr. Jonathan Binney at Halifax, informs us that he had sent the Gov. two quintals of fish. Mr. Binney thinks that the American game is nearly played out. "The American game I hope is near over," he says, "as I make no doubt long before this, General Howe is at Philadelphia, and General Clinton at Boston, as he had got possession of Rhode Island long since."

† This is faint praise. Pownall and the Governor were not exactly in accord when in America, on their principles of government. The latter was strictly a constitutional man, and perhaps he knew the Americans well enough to know, that where the spirit of liberty was disposed to run into the superlative, that spirit, for prudential reasons, rather needed the curb; whilst the former, not dreaming of danger, sought popularity and won it, by not discouraging the growing fashion. The relations between them were therefore a little strained. And when Pownall came to England, he supported the aspirations of the Americans in Parliament, until he saw that they were advancing from liberty into open rebellion. He had sown the Dragon's tooth, and now the monster was rampant in the land; so he turned about, and making overtures to Lord North, he entered the House this time to support the Tory Ministry, and he resisted the pretentions of the very people whom he had once encouraged. If he was out of humour with Mr. Hutchinson, he was probably as much out of humour with himself.

17th.—An exceeding thick fog. . . .

18th.—Celebrated as the Queen's birthday. At Court: Peggy also, with Mrs Ellis. . . .

To the Chief Justice Peter Oliver the scene at Court was a novelty, and the following description of it may be extracted from his Diary:—

"January 18th.—This day is celebrated as the Queen's Birthday. She was born on 19th May 1744, but it coming so near to the King's Birthday, who was born on 4th June 1738, and some inconveniences arising on the days happening so near to each other, the Queen's is always celebrated Jan. 18th.

"I went to Court, and here appeared brilliancy in its splendor. Before their Majesties appeared, 3 or 4 of the young Princes were introduced. The Prince of Wales exhibited an open, sensible, and active temper: Prince Frederick, the Bishop of Osnaburgh, is a fine youth with a manly, sensible behavior: one of the young Princes, ab^t^ 5 or 6 years old, behaved very genteelly, and chatted a great deal wth the foreign Ambassadors and others. Virgil's—*Jam nova progenies*, recurred to the mind.

"Their Majesties soon entered: the King was richly dressed in honor to the Queen, and was very polite and affable to the company: the Queen appeared in the *simplex munditiis*, for she is not in high dress on her Birthday, but on the King's Birthday she shines with brilliance. Her Majesty walk'd round and conversed with every lady; and tho' she is not a perfect beauty as a meer object, yet her sweet temper, her royal condescension, and her engaging affability, rivalled the charms of Venus. She is of so amiably a good temper, and adorned with so much virtue, and meddles so little with public affairs, that whenever Scandal herself recollects her Majesty, she at the same time recollects the—*digito compresse labellum.*

"But amidst this parade of Royalty, which is necessary, I could not help pitying those who were obliged to encounter the fatigues of it; but every species of roses hath its disagreeable prickles."

19th.—At the Old Jewry.

Mauduit called in the evening. The Gazette of last night offers pardon to all but the principal offender for discovery of the persons concerned in setting fire to two ships, and attempting to set fire to several houses, whereby the whole city with its vast wealth, was in danger of being destroyed; and subscriptions had been made for a reward to the amount of 500£ or upwards.

Drizzling weather.

20th.—My son E., my daughter, and I, dined with M[r] Paul Wentworth. S[r] Charles Douglass, M[r] Duke, of Barbadoes, Col[o] Phips, and Vassall,* Perkins and wife, and Gov[r] Wentworth's lady. Paul Wentworth says Lee, who is called *Junius Americanus,* is in France with Franklin, and that Deane and Lee are joined with Franklin by the Congress. Strange if Lee should return to England, and no notice be taken of it.

S[r] Cha. Douglass was Commander of the *Iris* at Quebec, and upon his return was made a Bart.;—a plain open man without ostentation or vanity: drinks no wine, and he says scarce any other drink but tea twice a day.

The city of Bristol said to be on fire, when an express came away the 19th at 8 o'clock in the morning.

21st.—Account from Bristol that the fire was suppressed on the 19th after burning down a row of warehouses, but combustible matter discovered to be laid with design in divers parts of the city, which keeps the inhabitants in terror. . . .

A ship which had been taken by the Americans bro't into Plimouth by the crew, which rose upon their captors. A report on 'Change that Clinton had possessed himself of R[d] Island without opposition.

A master of a ship named Hill, who had been taken and carried into Plimouth, N. England, bro't a letter to my son E. from his wife, dated the 20th Nov. He came away the 22nd to Nantz, and from France to England. They had not heard of Washington's leaving Kingsbridge, and talked as if they expected Government would be tired: were full of business made by the privateers. The paper money sank fast. My daughter

* "Col. Phips, the High Sheriff of Middlesex, [America], was obliged to promise not to serve any Processes of Courts, and retired to Boston for protection."

"William Vassall, Esq., a man of fortune and quite inoffensive in his publick conduct, tho' a Loyalist, was travelling with his Lady from Boston to his seat at Bristol in Rhode Island Government, about 60 miles from Boston, were pelted by the mob in Bristol, to the endangering of their lives." —Notes by Ch. Just. Oliver.

[in-law] says, if you have anything to part with, you may buy as much money with it as you please.

22nd.—The *Mercury*, James Montagu, arrived yesterday at Portsmouth, and an express to-day with letters from Clinton and Sr P. Parker Dec. 8, from Rhode Island, which they took possession of the 7th, without any opposition, the rebels retreating to Bristol Ferry, which they crossed, about 3000: three of Hopkins's squadron, and three or four smaller privateers running up to Providence, where Sr P. P. writes, he should give a good account of them. Clinton was sending forces to take possession of Conanicut and Prudence.

A ship with large quantity of cloathing taken by one of Hopkins's squadron. . . .

23rd.—At Lord North's Levée to introduce Mr Fitch.

Mr Hutchinson* of Q. Anne Street, who formerly was Gov. of St. Helena, dying last week, the papers published the death of William Hutchinson Esq., late Gov. of Mass. Bay. This occasioned many complim^ts to me from the Bp. of Oxford, Sr Cha. Wentworth, Col. Egerton, Mr Bacon, &c., &c., on seeing me alive.

24th.—Reduced to writing the account which Cap^n Hill gave of the state of Boston, Plimouth,—and sent it in a letter to Lord George Germain. Scraps of divers of my letters printed to-day with Remarks in the *Publick Leger*, most of which had been printed in other papers.

25th.— . . . My son E., Dr Oliver, and Dan. Oliver, went as mourners to Croydon to the funeral of Miss Katy Hutchinson, one of the daughters of the late Eliakim H. Esq.

26th.—At the Temple church. . . .

27th.—At Lord Hardwicke's. . . .

28th.—In the city, and called on Mr Palmer, Devonshire Square, but missed him. At Dr Caner's. I spake to the Bishop of London at Court in the Doctor's behalf, and to-day the Bishop called, and brought an order on Messrs Drummond for 100£, pay^t to me for the use of Doctor Caner.

It is said to-day that Clinton found 4000 hhds. of sugar in Newport, 1900 in possession of one man, all which he had laid

* I am not informed who this Mr. Hutchinson may have been.

hands on. Account of an American privateer of 10 guns and 90 men, bro't in to Plimouth, taken off Cape Finisterre.

29th.—Called on M^r^ D'Oyley. He says the Howes have explained the Proclamation in their letters: have intimated that at the expiration of the 60 days, other measures will be proper for such as stand out.

Mr Mason called. He has been 11 years in England upon the business of the Mohegan Indians: came to ask information about Laconia: supposes Jno Mason to whom it was granted was his ancestor, and has petitioned to have the grant confirmed, or such part as has not been since granted or possessed. I told him Mason was not his ancestor, and that if he had been, it was a naked grant, which had been neglected 150 years, and nobody could set up a claim under it.

Lord Hardwicke called and sat near an hour: had much of the history of his father the late Chancellor—told his son, not long before the Chancellor's death, he feared this would be a reign full of troubles. When asked what he thought of Mr Grenville's scheme for taxing America, said—They had not been used to taxes: told Abp. Secker, when he proposed sending a Bishop, that the Americans left England to avoid Bishops. The Chancellor was a Churchman, but a very moderate one.

I received 100 by the Archbishop of Canterbury's order, from Drummond's, for Dr Caner; the Bp. of London in a note desires I would not pay it all in one payment:—I suppose because none have had more than 50£ at once. I paid him 50£, and have the other for another time.

30th.—Letters to Mr Lane from Corke, a Master of his being arrived in a transport from Rhode Island, which sailed the 20 of December—says the troops had embarked, and were within 6 miles of Providence: that Clinton had let them know, if they burnt the town or the ships, he would give no quarter.

31st.—[Reports—unconfirmed.] News of a ship with 412 hhds. of tobacco from Maryland, on acc^t^ of the Congress, bound to France, brought in to Liverpool. The ship's company consisted of eight seamen, Americans, and eight Europeans, four of whom had been in American service before, a Master and

Supercargo. The four Europeans, who had never been before employed, laid the plot and sounded the other four, who promised to be neuter. The first four took an opportunity to secure the Master and Supercargo when in the cabin together, and then the other four joined and subdued the rest of the company:—secured a great number of letters and papers, which are brought to the Admiralty. The ship was a large transport, which had been taken with Highlanders, and must go to the owners. The cargo, supposed worth 18 or 20,000£, can have no legal owner or claimer, and must be the King's, but its thought will be given to the eight sailors.

I met Mr Watts of the Council of New York. . . .

February 1st.—Mr De Grey, of Chandos Street, Cavendish Square, called while I was at Sr James Wright's, who gives up all his intelligence from Georgia of a turn in favour of Gt, as ill founded. Francklin,* who was Lt Gov. of Nova Scotia, and put out to make way for Arbuthnot, a man said to be very unfit, has a new office made for him—Curator or Guardian of Nova Scotia Indians, with 300£ a year. They are so few in number, that it must be a meer nominal place without business.

[The intelligence in Lane's letters not confirmed.]

2nd.—Old Jewry. . . . The tobacco ship was taken by four sailors only; the other four Europeans being sick in their cabins. . . .

3rd.—A fine sunshiny morning. . . .

Mr Lane's Master [of his ship] is come to town from Ireland: says he saw Clinton within 5 miles of Providence, who enquired the state of the country—any stone walls, &c.? and the Master answered None; and now says the army might have marched into town without opposition, but were waiting for artillery, &c. He thinks they dare not burn the ships for fear Clinton should destroy the town: says, not an eighth of the people of Newport had left the town, and the rest in quiet possession of their houses. . . .

4th.—In the city at my Banker's. Mauduit and Lane and Fraser. Fraser says their Master left Newport the 17 Decemb.,

* Not of the family of Benjamin Franklin. The name differently spelt.

and Clinton had only embarked that day, which differs from the former account of the time of his sailing, and the place. When he left Clinton, a ship [was] bro't in by a man-of-war, bound with fish from Newbury Port to Bilboa, Tilestone, Master, one of Dr Pemberton's Meeting, who is come to town. It is said he was in Boston December 2nd.

Lord Huntingdon called. . . .

5th.—At Mr Palmer's in the Temple, and left my name. Capn Goodwin was sent to my house by Messrs Lane and Fraser. He says the Master of the transport had orders the day before he sailed to be ready at an hour's warning, and that it was generally supposed they would go up to Patuxet, but the weather was very cold when he sailed, and the wind continued at NW 12 days, and they ran to the E of the Western Islands. He says he knew of nobody of any note who left Rhode Island upon the troops landing, except one John Collings, and those who had been concerned in privateers, and that the day before he sailed Judge Bowles, a great rebel, sent in his name to the General, to take the benefit of the Proclamation.

I called on Mr Rome.

6th.—Called on Mr D'Oyley, where saw the famous planner of grounds—Browne. . . .

This day Judge Oliver went to pay his respects to Lord North. The following is taken from his Diary:—

"6th.—Having never seen Ld North, I attended his Levée at the Treasury, where were many of the first characters, and where I was politely received by his Lordship. I pitied him for the fatigue which he suffered in speaking to each person, it bringing to mind those two lines of Cowley the Poet, wch though they were designed for the Attender, yet may be very justly applied to the person waited upon, viz.—

'Were I to curse the man I hate,
Let attendance and dependance be his fate.'

"But such parade is quite necessary in political life: it keeps up distinctions, without which, as there is so little publick virtue, goverment would verge too much towards anarchy—perhaps it leans already beyond the centre of gravity; but unhappy they who hold the scale of Empire, subject to those forms, which every wise man despises, and only endures the fatigues from the sole consideration of their tendency to support the dignity and welfare of the common weal."

7th.—Dined at Mauduit's . . .

8th.—At Lambeth with Chandler to thank the Archbp. for the 100£ to Dr. Caner . . .

Account in the paper to-day of Lady Faulkner's death, wife to Gov. Pownall.*

Wrote to my tenant Pierce at Conanicut,† under cover to Gov. Wanton, and both under cover to Mr Walter, or in his absence to Mr Isaac Winslow, New York.

An astonishing account of a forgery. Dr Dod, Preacher at the Magdalen, having lived vainly much beyond his income, went to a Broker to raise 4200£ on a bond of Lord Chesterfield's, who, it was pretended, desired privacy. The Broker procured the money, and the person to whom the bond was made pay^l^, gave an order on Sr Charles Raymond and co. Bankers, and the money was paid to Dod. The Broker observing there was but one witness, signed as another witness himself. By accident, in transacting the affair, ink was spilt on Ld Chesterfield's name, and upon observing it, either the Broker or the Obliger, tho't it best to have a fair bond, and went to Lord C. to desire him to take it back, and execute another. Ld C. said he never gave a bond to any man in his life. This caused immediate inquiry after Dod, who was called out of his room from a large company just going to dinner. He sent in to desire his wife to go to dinner with the company, and he was carried to Sr John Fielding, who committed him to the Counter. Last night and to-day he was carried before the Ld Mayor, and committed to Newgate. The parties complaining were loth to be bound over to prosecute, but it was insisted on. Dod was Ld Chesterfield's Tutor, who came of age about a

* She was Harriet, daughter of Lieut. Gen. Churchill, and had been widow of Sir Everard Faulkner. She died Feb. 6.

† Conanicut is an island in Rhode Island bay. Mr. H. inherited an estate on it in right of his wife Margaret, daughter and co-heiress of William Sanford. It was confiscated with the others, but part of its value recovered.

year ago, and gave him a living of 300£ ℘ an., and it is said that for several years he has lived at the rate of 1200. Three thousand pounds of the money Dod returned, and gave an order for the rest, except 4 or 500£.

This is the strangest infatuation, so soon after Perreau's* detection that ever was:—*Quos Deus vult perdere, &c.* Dod has wrote several pieces in high strains of devotion. I once heard a very pathetic Address from him to the Magdalens; but his character has been very suspicious some time. The enemies of religion will be apt to take the advantage, and triumph.

Peggy blooded by Dr Heberden's advice, having a bad cough, and pain in her side.†

9th.—At the Temple: Dean of Rochester. At Court, and in the Presence Chamber. Lord Ravensworth, who I had never seen before, spake to me. . . .

10th.—[Easterly winds.]

11th.—The Bill for suspend. Hab. Corp. carried last night in H. of C. by 190 odd to 40 odd.‡ The Opposition loses its weight. [Speculations about Howe, Clinton, &c.]

12th.—A wet cold day: I kept at home. Lord Hardwicke called to tell me Wallis was arrived: left Rh^d Island 7th or 8th of Jany. No attempt on Providence: no other news. He says the N. York paper has been produced, which mentions the removal of the Congress from Philadelphia. He says the Master of the vessel wch brought it, received it from the Master of a vessel bound to the W. Indies, who reported that Howe was within 5 miles of Philadelphia. Ld H. adds, that he has it divers ways, that Dr Franklin is down in the mouth, and much neglected.

12th.§—Cap. Wallace, in the *Experiment*, came to town from Rh^d Island, which he left the 8th Jan^y.

Clinton had done nothing: its said he is coming home. The

* See back Feb. 17, 1776.

† Peggy was now beginning to go down hill.

‡ Adolphus and the Continuator of Hume both say 112 to 35. The object of this Bill was "to detain and secure persons charged with, or suspected of high treason, committed in North America, or on the high seas, or the crime of piracy." The numbers are corrected further on—the 18th.

§ The "12th" occurs twice over in the Diary.

taking the Hessians is confirmed. It's said the Americans had cloathed themselves with the regimentals they had taken, and the Hessians took them for part of the British forces. They had a report at Newport, that Lesley had marched and recovered the Hessians, but they say it was report only. They further say that Lee was taken prisoner by Col° Harcourt, who went out with 20 or 30 light horse to reconnoitre, and meeting a countryman, they compelled him by threats, and he informed of Lee's being in a farm house, at a few miles distance. The light horse went immediately: were fired on by the Guard, which fled. Lee fired two pistols from the house, and struck Col° Harcourt's helmet; but being threatened with certain death if they did not surrender, Lee threw open the doors, and claimed the benefit of the Proclamation, but was told it was too late. Other reports say that he told Col° Harcourt that he had just reached the summit of his wishes, and was going to take the command of the American army wch Washington had resigned to him.

13th.—At Lord Huntingdon's. He read me a letter from a natural son, a young officer in Clinton's army: mentions the affair of the Hessians, and of Lee: he laments that this stroke upon the Hessians had hapned at the close of the campaign: says things will never go well here while we have no Minister. If Lord N. had any spirit, he would take the direction of everything: and if Lord Sandwich, in his department, did not appoint proper Admirals, or did not order the cloathing, ordnance stores, &c., in such ships as that there should be not danger of their falling into the enemy's hands, he should turn him out: but now perhaps Shuldham will say—"If I can have the command, and you will get me an Irish Peerage, I will give you five thous^d^ pounds:" and so Shuldham, tho' superannuated, or without understanding, he must be the man. The K. says he thinks he is his own Minister. Matters are talked on $^3/_4$^ths^ of an hour in the Cabinet, and the K. says—"Well, you will take care of this, and you of that," and then an hour or two is spent in scandal — Lord such-an-one keeps such a mistress, and Lady such-an-one has such a gallant: the Ministers go and dine together, and late in the evening the Clerks are set to work, and may be write all night, &c. From this state of the affairs at home, he feels what some people call a misgiving as to the success of affairs abroad.

14th.—[Billy and his hoped for appointment.]

15th.—[Reports and rumours unconfirmed.]

16th.—At the Old Jewry . . .

17th.—Lord Gage called . . .

18th.—[Regrets at the capture of the Hessians.] Charles Fox said yesterday in the House of Com^s that in France, (where he has been), people thought very diff^y of the success in America, from what we do here; that they had no doubt the Americans could support their independence; and if it should prove that they could not without help, France and Spain would declare for them. This was on the debate upon the Bill for securing persons guilty, or suspected of treason in America, which on a third reading was carried, 112 to 35, about the proportion, or rather greater minority than at the second reading.

19th.—[Dr Heberden refuses his fees for Peggy.] Several Americans—Flucker, Hallowell, Sewall, Phips, Dudley, Rome, together wth Mauduit, dined with me to-day. The uncertain state of the news from America furnished sufficient subject for conversation.

20th.—Called on Mr Jenkinson . . .

21st.—A snowy night . . .

I am tempted to quote one page of the Diary of Elisha Huchinson at this place, not that it contains anything very noteable, but from the singularity of the order or sequence, or arrangement, in which the entries have been made. The page comprises seven days, namely, from the 23rd of Febuary, 1777 to the 1st of March inclusive; only the dates run upwards, or contrariwise, instead of downwards:—

"Saturday, March 1st.—At Brompton: called on Col^o Chandler and the rest; Mr Gray, and Blowers. Afterwards walked in the Park, where I met Mr Brown who, the day before arrived from Paris. Asked him to dine with Judge Oliver, and the Dr's family, and Mr Green.—Oranges, &c. 6d. Honey 1/.—1,,6.

"Friday, 28th.—Dined at Mr Vassall's, the company being the Govr, Genl and Mrs Gage, Mr Sheriff, Lt Govr Oliver and lady,

Judge Oliver, and Mr Paxton. Peggy to stay a few days at High Street.

"Thursday, 27th.—Mr Paxton and Mr Oliver dined with us. Drank tea at Brompton. Mrs Oliver lodged with Peggy.

"Wednesday, 26th.—Walked in the Park, where I was told a letter in N. E. Coffee H. for me. Took a boat, and found it was a letter from Mr P. W. Boat—1,,6.

"Tuesday, 25th.—Bought a p^r^ new silk hose . . . . 6,,0.

"Monday, 24th.—At the House of Lord's. No debate.

"Sunday 23rd, Feb^y^.—Walked to Old Jewry: in the [*sic*] again in the city. Called on Mr Bliss: went with him to Mr Perrin's to tea. Company."

In the absence of explanation, it is difficult to account for so singular a whim. The same thing occurs in one other place, but the rest of the memorandums are entered normally, according to consecutive date. This latter portion of the Diary is all in loose leaves, fragments, and is very imperfect. It has been written on sheets of different size note paper, either single or in fasciculi that have never been sown together, so that they have become very much confused. As the date of the year, and the name of the month are only sparingly given, as some parts have gone to pieces by damp, and others lost, and as the whole had been utterly disarranged, it has been impossible to restore what remains to a satisfactory state of chronological order. Comparison with other Diaries has assisted in some places. But as Elisha's records are generally of a very commonplace nature, rarely alluding to the great events of the day, these deficiences need not cause much regret. The record of the greatest value is the account of the death of his father the Governor, at which he was present, along with his brother-in-law Dr. Peter Oliver.

Now taking up the thread of the Governor's Diary at the 23rd of February, the days run on concurrently with the extract above, only in reverse order.

23rd.—At the Temple church: Doctor Wicks of Chiswick: a good sermon.

At Court—in the drawing room—the Queen not there. Saw and spoke with Sr Cha. Bromley, who, I had not seen since he was in Boston in 1747: surprisingly altered, which is owing to infirmity as much as age, tho' he says he is 73. He has been back [?] about two years from Russia, where he had been several years superintending the Czarina's naval affairs.

Doctor Dod convicted yesterday at the Old Bailey. In his speech he implicitly confessed his guilt, declaring that he was instructed by his Counsel that it was necessary there should be an intention of fraud, but he appealed to God, it was his full intention to have discharged the bond, and that Lord Chesterfield should never be called on for any part of it. His Counsel excepted to an irregular proceeding in examining Robinson as a witness, and finding a Bill upon his evidence, while he stood charged as an accomplice; and it seems the Court thought fit to refer it to the twelve Judges for their opinion, which probably must take some time before it can be determined.

24th.—The *Bristol*, Lord Shuldham, arrived yesterday at Portsmouth from New York, which she left the 8th of January.* Col° Dalrymple a passenger: confirms the defeat of the Hessians at Trenton the 26th December, and the loss of 2 or 300 of British troops from a large body of the enemy a day or two after. This is all owing to Howe's extending his posts as far as Burlington, after he had made an attempt to cross the Delaware 13 miles above Trenton, and failed for want of boats. Some letters say he might have passed,—whether they mean forded or by rafts does not appear,—and that he would have been in possession of Philadelphia without opposition. After that everything was unfortunate. The enemy took fresh spirits: drove the Hessians from Burlington by boats with cannon in the river: attacked, and killed, and took prisoners the Hessians at Trenton, and interrupted the regiments on their march from one post to another, and killed and took 200 of them. This has given a great turn to people's opinions here, and a prospect of protracting the war, and lessened the opinion of the abilities of the commanders of the British army.

The Congress had removed to Reading, where it was said only 13 remained. The *Orpheus* Man-of-war, brought in to

* Lord Shuldham! It was only on the 13th instant, some eleven days ago, that we read some rather mysterious remarks about Irish Peerages and how to get them. How much of joke, or of scandal, or of innuendo may lurk in those dark passages, I must not tell if I know. Happily I know nothing about it.

York 13 prizes, some taken off Delaware, most of them bound to France, on acc^{t} of the Congress. Called on Sr Charles Knowles.

25th.—[Dined with Canon Douglas, D.D.]

26th.—Peggy so well as to take an airing . . .

27th.—At Lord George Germain's Levée . . . The newspapers are filled with the bad condition of the King's troops, and the good condition of the Americans. Their privateers have taken a packet from Falmouth to Lisbon, and carried her into France; and it is certain that great quantities of cloathing, some say for 60,000 men, arms, &c., are gone from France to the American ports. What the issue will be God only knows. It looks more doubtful than it did a few months ago. It is the duty of all concerned to acquiesce in the disposal of Divine Providence, which governs all, and controuls and changes in the most unexpected way and manner.

28th.—[Dined with Col. Vassall, &c.]

March 1st.— . . . Mr J^{o} Green and Col^{o} Browne just returned from France. He says when he first went there in October, there was much talk of assisting America: that upon the news of the poor defence, then all subsided, and America was never mentioned in conversation.

2nd.—At the Old Jewry. Sr H. Houghton came . . .

3rd.— . . . The *Harriet* packet said to be arrived . . .

4th.— . . . Upon talking with Col^{o} Browne to-day I find Silas Deane to be a person at whose house Mr Tryon lodged in Weathersfield when I was in Hartford in 1773, and that my daughter and I made a visit there. He married a daughter of G——(?) Saltonstall.

6th.— . . . Lord Shuldham returned a visit I made on his arrival: thinks all will go well in America, though the war may be protracted by the little successes of the Americans in the Jerseys. Talk of a war wth France, principally founded on advice of a French man-of-war having sunk one of the King's sloops—the *Pomona*, in the West Indies . . .

7th.—The talk of the French war wholly ceases, and the stocks recover their former rate. John the Painter tried yesterday at Winchester Assizes: the evidence so full that the

Jury gave their verdict without going from their seats: the substance of his trial published in the papers: and among the rest of the evidence, that of his communicating his design to Silas Deane, &c.

8th.—Sr Francis Bernard and Lady came to town last evening, and dined with us to-day, with Paxton, Dr Caner, Chandler, and Boucher.

9th.—At the Temple with Sr F. B. Dr Thurlow. Gallipont, one of the Benchers, asked me why I did not sit with them? I told him I had no pretence. "Why, you are older at the Bar than we." I told him I had not been called to the Bar. "Why, are you not of our house?" No. I was an American Judge.

At Court and the Drawing-room. Lord President gave me an account of John the Convict's confession. He is a Scotchman about 25 years of age—his name John Aitkin: left Edinburgh about 5 years ago, and went to Virginia: has 'listed and deserted two or three times: has been in Europe about two years: confesses 8 or 9 thefts and robberies: denies that Dean gave him a Bill for 300£, but owns he communicated his design, and that he encouraged it: recommended him to Dr Bancroft in Downing Street: gave him 12 six-livre pieces: told him this was eno' to carry him to England: and promised his reward when he had performed the service.

It is said by Flucker that General Gage has a letter from N. York, advising the imprisonment of Dickenson by the Congress, for what he had wrote to his brother in a letter which was intercepted.

When Mr Boucher was at my house yesterday, I asked him how he knew that Delany was sent to, and desired to answer my speech to the Assembly? He said Delany told him so, and he thought it was a letter from Cushing, sent by a messenger express; but Delany gave for answer that he had met with so much trouble from the consideration, that he would never write any more. If he refused, the messenger was to apply to Dickenson. It is certain that tho' my speech was the 6. of Jan^y^, their answer was delayed till the 26th.

Lord North continues ill tho' said to be growing better. A *bon-mot* is often mentioned. He has been bled, blistered, &c.,

and is emasciated. He said to Dr Warren he was much obliged to him for introducing a number of his old acquaintance, which he had not known these 20 years. The Doctor was a little surprised, and suspected a delirium. I mean my ribs, Doctor, for I have not [been] able to feel them any time for 20 years past till now.

10th.—Col. Skeene, who arrived in the packet, called on me...

11th.—Ground froze hard . . . Burgoyne goes out in the *Apollo.* John the Painter was executed yesterday at Portsmouth.

The career, the villanies, and the trial of this man, are all given in the journals of the day. The following heads are from the Continuator of Hume's History of England:—

"A fire which had broke out in the Rope-house at Portsmouth on the seventh of December, was then ascribed to accident; but some six weeks after, the discovery of a machine in the hemp-house, designed for the same purpose, led first to suspicions, and afterwards by a train of circumstances to the final conviction of the incendiary, commonly known by the appellation of John-the-Painter, but whose real name was James Aitken . . . The restlessness of his mind, or the dread of punishment, made him ship himself off for America in the year 1773, and he continued there for about two years . . . He came back to England with the most deadly antipathy to the government and nation, and soon after formed a scheme to destroy the maritime force of the country . . . In the autumn of the year 1776 he went to France, and communicated his intentions to M[r] Silas Deane, the American Plenipotentiary to that Court, who told him, according to his own story,—'when the work was done, he should be rewarded.' . . . He took wonderful pains in the construction of fireworks, machines, and combustibles. . . . It was owing to this failure in his machines that the nation was saved from receiving some dreadful, if not irretrievable shock. One of them extinguished of itself . . . others, which he had placed in the Rope-house, took effect. . . . His next attempt was to burn the shipping that lay along side the quay at Bristol. . . . Soon after his departure from Bristol, he was taken up in Hampstead for a burglary. . . One Baldwin. . . found means . . . to obtain his confidence in prison, until he drew from him the whole history of his crimes. Upon his trial at Winchester . . his pretended friend . . . the acknowledged baseness of the witness, and he received sentence of death with the most perfect indifference. He was removed from Winchester gaol on the tenth of March, and executed on a gallows sixty feet high before Portsmouth dock gate, the principal scene of his guilt."

Adolphus says—"His confession proved his being employed by Silas Deane." Near three months after the execution of this man Judge Oliver was engaged in making a tour, and found himself in Portsmouth on the 27th of May. He wrote as follows in his Diary:—

"I waited upon Commissioner Gambier, who was so polite as to order his Clerk to shew me the Dockyards, &c. The yards, stores, and other works are expressive indications of the grandeur of the British nation, but I think are exceeded by those of Plymouth. The ruins and devastations by fire perpetrated by John the Painter, by the instigation of Silas Dean and other American patriots of rebellion, must raise an indignation in every loyal breast. This villain had attempted to burn the shipping in several places in England, as Bristol, &c., by the instigation of Silas Dean, now in France, and several other American incendiaries, but had failed in his various attempts, 'till he had perpetrated his designs by burning the Rope-walk here in December last, but failed in burning the Dockyards. He was detected and executed, and hangs now in Irons, on the opposite side, at the entrance of Portsmouth Harbour, on a Gibbet 60 feet high, as a warning to other villains of the like cast; tho' there are so many of those beacons stuck about England, that they rather serve as Mercuries to point out roads to travellers than to warn against the like crimes. This John [blank] ye Painter was a most finished villain in almost all crimes, as he confessed himself, and the Congress and their adherents could not have pitched upon a more proper person to have executed their diabolical purposes, than upon this fellow, but alas! how often are halters misplaced! Had they been tightened about the necks of some of his employers, neither the conflagration at Portsmouth or in America had committed such horrid ravages as have wasted the lives and habitations of so many thousands."

After an interval of 107 years, John the Painter has turned up again. The public press informs us as follows:—"While some sappers were making excavations at Fort Blockhouse, near Gosport, on Thursday, they came upon some remains which are believed to be those of 'Jack the Painter,' a notorious criminal, who more than a century ago set fire to Portsmouth Dockyard, and destroyed nearly the whole of the establishment. He was gibbeted, and his body, after hanging in chains several years, was buried at the spot where the remains were found."—*Exeter and Plymouth Gazette*, Sat. Nov. 22, 1884.

But, to resume—

12th.—Governor Pownall having lately buried his wife, Lady Faulkner, I called upon him to-day. There has been no visits passed for two years, which I think has not been my fault.

At Mr Keene's . . .

13th.—The raw cold east wind still continues . . .

14th.—Wind at NW, and Peggy takes an airing. I met Paul Wentworth in Pall Mall. He is angry that anybody should suppose Doctor Bancroft any way capable, and says he has not only Ld Suffolk's opinion, but is allowed by Lord Mansfield to say from him, that there was nothing improper in his conduct. He added, that Bancroft had told 20 of his friends what John the Painter said to him, and he supposed him to be a spy employed by government.

15th.—[Reports unauthenticated.]

16th.—At the Old Jewry with Judge Oliver.

At Court—and the Drawing-room, on the King's side only. In the evening with Sir F. B. at Ld Chancellor's, and Ld Mansfield's, and afterwards at Dr Heberden's. Ld Marchmont, Ld Willoughby of Parham, &c., at the Chancellor's: D. of Northum., Ld Dudley, Ld Panmure, &c., at Ld Mansfield's. Mention made of Bancroft, and of its being incumbent on him, when John-the-Painter was apprehended, to have imformed Govt of John's having been with him. Ld Mansfield said he had seen a Vindication of Bancroft in a newspaper, wch no doubt, by the appearance of it, was his own doing, but said nothing in his favour.

Ld Marchmont recommends strong souchong tea as the wholesomest breakfast can be eat.

Peggy's illness increases: bled again to-day.

Seeing Mr Garrick at Court, and the Archbishop of Cant., D. of Ancaster, Lord Chesterfield, and many more of the Nobility, Gentry, and Clergy cordially greeting him, I could not help thinking that he comes the nearest to the character of

Roscius of any player since his time; for as we meet with none of his fellow actors with whom Cæsar, Cicero, Pompey, &c., would make themselves familiar, no more is there any in England besides Garrick who are thought proper for the notice of people of distinction here. Garrick's private character being good, and his fortune great, and no unfairness in attaining to it, causes this distinction.

17th.—The *Hellespont*, Lister, arrived from New York: sailed the first week in February. Nothing of news except that the Congress have appointed Washington Protector of the United States, and established a Military Order of Independence, of which he is to be Sovereign; and 2700 of the troops had returned from Rh[d] Island to New York. No action anywhere.

In the evening I went for about half an hour to Lady Gideon's: Sir Eardley Wilmot, M[r] Trevor, M[r] Blair, the principal persons I knew, or had any conversation with.

18th.—Wrote to Col[o] Jos. Wanton at Newport, concerning my farm on Conanicut, sent by Colburn Barrett, to be forwarded to New York. Just as I was going to bed S[r] H. Houghton sent me a note, that he had heard the French fleet of 8 line of battle ships, and 11 frigates, had sailed from Brest, which disturbed my rest.

The movements of the French were beginning to attract considerable attention in England, not to say apprehension.

The letter for Col. Wanton, mentioned above, was entered in his Letter Book by the Governor himself, and as it may contain one or two facts worth preserving, I will extract it entire:—

"Lond. New Bond S. 18 March, 1777.

"Sir,—I have been informed that my estate upon Conanicut has, by force of an act or order of certain persons in Newport, been taken from the possession of my tenant Isaac Pierce, to whom I had given a lease of it, and that it has been possessed the last year by other persons, and that waste and spoil have been made there.

"M[r] Chesebro', who used to inform me very kindly of anything that occurred relative to my own and my [wife's] sister's affairs, has ceased corresponding with me since I left New England.

"Allow me to ask the favour of you to afford me y[r] assistance in obtaining satisfaction for the injury done me, and in securing my property from further injury.

"I left my Government just before Lord Percy arrived, and have not the honour of being personally known to him; but I think his Lordship must know that my sufferings have been occasioned mainly by my having been a servant of the Crown, and I doubt not he will be ready to favour an application in my behalf, so far as may be proper for him to interpose.

"It would be most agreeable that my tenant, or his son under him, should return to the possession of his leasehold. How that may be,—whether he wishes it, or whether he has it in his power, it is not possible for me to know. I think it probable that he desires it. He was at 130£ quit [?] rent, besides some duties of planting, &c., and making stone walls, and the two last years of his lease are at 150£ sterl.

"If the estate cannot come into his hands, I wish to have it under improvement the pres^t^ year, on as good terms as may be; and I most willingly convey to you for that purpose all the powers I could have myself if I was on the spot, as also to obtain for me any compensation for damages, sustained since the estate was taken out of my hands.

"I have heard that the man who dispossessed Lt Brenton has been compelled to ample compensation for his loss and damage. Whither other persons are able to obtain the like compensation, can be known upon enquiry. Generally, like justice should be done in like cases.

"My [wife's] sister Grizell Sanford, is owner of a farm at Blackpoint, which for several years has been let at the low rent of 100 or 120 dollars a year. Mr Cheseborough used to receive the rent. To what time it was paid can be ascertained by the receipts to the tenant. I could wish what is due might be received and sent to me for my sister, who has occasion enough for it.

"She has another farm on what is called Slocum's Island, let for 60£ sterling to Richd Sanford and John Robinson. Sanford is since dead, and Robinson in Boston, and the Island not being reduced, I suppose no rent can be recovered there, though two or three years are due.

"You will be surprised at my long narrative, &c., without any previous apology, but when I began my letter I had not seen my friend Col^o^ Browne, and unless I could be satisfied that you would not take amiss my applying to you, I would have applied to some other gentleman at Newport. The assurance he gives me that you will be ready to oblige me, has determined me to make my application to you, and to hope for the favour of an answer, and for your advice to any steps on my part, if you judge any to be necessary. "I am, &c."

"Hon. Joseph Wanton Esq., Newport."

It need scarcely be added, that no redress or compensation could be obtained, or any satisfactory information, owing to the confusion of the times; and it resulted by the progress of the war, that these estates were seized along with the others.

There is an original letter of March 18, written by Mr. Pelham Winslow in a small neat hand from New York, and addressed to Elisha Hutchinson, of which letter Captain Archdeacon was the bearer. It contains nothing material.

In the volume containing Elisha's letters to his wife during their long enforced separation, he continues to harp upon the likelihood of his return to America; and the accounts arriving in England of the succession of victories obtained by the British troops at Brooklyn, White Plains, through the Jerseys, and their pursuit after Washington until he reached Philadelphia, all raised such a feeling in the Mother Country that the war was virtually over—and so it probably would have been had General Howe only followed up his advantages with promptitude—that the Refugees in England began to talk of their preparations for returning. Elisha alludes to this:—

"New Bond Street, Mar. 2, 1777.

"My Dear Polly,

"About a month ago I gave a letter to Captⁿ Coffin, who was bound to Nantucket, by way of the West Indies.

"At that time our accounts from the army were very promising. Genl Howe advancing post-haste to Philadelphia. Genl Clinton in possession of Rhode Island, and in his way to Providence. Many of the poor American Refugees imagined they could see the end of their exile, and began to count the months of their punishment. A New York gentleman told me, if I did not mean to be hurried, it was time to begin to pack up.

"Later advices do not come up to our expectations . . . Genl C., instead of visiting Providence, is now on a visit in London; and by letters from N. York, we find Genl H. has not quite reached Philadelphia, there being unluckily, a river in the way."

The health of the Governor's youngest daughter Margaret, commonly called Peggy, had become so seriously impaired of late, that her father resolved to take her to the Hot Wells at Bristol, at that time a Sanitarium in considerable repute. All the symptoms of rapid pulmonary consumption had set in. They left London on the 20th of March, together with the eldest daughter Sarah, the wife of Dr. Peter Oliver, and were absent nearly two months. Though every page of his Diary at this period is filled with lamentations over the state of his child, there occurs here and there a short entry that may be worth extracting. Thus, he writes—

Mar. 31st.— . . . The Dean of Glo'cester came to my lodgings; shewed me a letter he had received from Turgot, the late Comptroller of the Finances in France, approving of the measures of the Americans, and wishing them success, and of the Dean's plan for setting them free. He rec[d] it from London under a frank from Lord Shelburne.

Ap. 27th.— . . . A little fishing scooner arrived the night before last from Salem with 4 men only, being brought by the mate of a ship, to bring him home: came out the 10 of March. I saw him, but he knew nothing.

Ap. 30th.— . . . My son writes, that by a vessel from York, they hear that Washington died of the camp fever.

May 8th.— . . . Yesterday took a full view of Bristol from Brandon Hill, where they say Cromwell erected his batteries, and beat down their houses. I think, take in all circumstances, and I should prefer living there to any place in England. The manners and customs of the people are very like those of the people of New England, and you might pick out a set of Boston Selectmen from any of their churches.

May 9th.— . . . Account from Plim[o] of the arrival of a packet from N. York, and of the destruction of the magazines at Peeks Kill.

May 13th.—Winchester Cathedral entertained us.* The monuments of W[m] Rufus, Card. Beaufort, W[m] of Wickham, Wainfleet, Bp. Gardiner, being all, except the last, extremely well preserved. We lodged at the George Inn, and about 11 set out for Southampton, the entrance to which is charming, and the town itself very agreeable. I went to the harbour, and viewed with pleasure the place from whence Winthrop, Dudley, &c., the first Magistrates of Mass. Bay in America embarked, from whence they dated their Declaration of affection to the Church and State of Eng[d]. . .

* On their return journey to London.

May 17th.— . . . we had a pleasant day's journey to London.

22nd.— . . . We took lodgings at the Dial House in Little Chelsea at 3 Guineas ℘ week, four weeks certain, to begin to-morrow.

30th.— . . . A strong desire to see and hear Lord Chatham carried me to the H. of Lords, where, after a long speech to inflame the kingdom, and to encourage France to cherish the rebellion, he moved for an Address to the K. to put an end to this unnatural ruinous war, to heal and redress grievances, &c., and to assure him that [the] House would do everything proper on their part, &c.

June 4th.— . . . This is the first Birthday I have absented myself from Court, but I had no heart to go from home.

5th.— . . . Lord Percy arrived in a packet from Newport. It is rumoured that he was not satisfied, and thought more due to him from Genl Howe than he received. Nothing done of importance the beginning of May. The packet left Newport the 5th.

7th.— . . . A vessel from N. York with news as late as the middle of May. Tyron, Browne, &c., with about 1800 men, had destroyed a large magazine of stores at Danbury, &c., with the loss of about 14 or 15 killed, and 60 or 70 wounded. In the march back [they] were harrassed as in the Lexington affair. It is said Worcester the rebel General, is killed, and Arnold wounded: above 100 privates killed, and 50 or 60 prisoners.

9th.— . . . I went to town: called at Mr Ellis's to congratulate him on his new place of Treasurer of the Navy, but found that he was gone to Weymouth to sollicit his re-election.

This day Judge Oliver and some friends went to Greenwich to see the King hold a review. In his Diary he writes thus:—

"June 9th.—Dr Chandler, Parson Boucher, Richard Clarke Esq., Mr Waterhouse, and myself, took coach for Blackheath, to see his Majesty review the Light Horse, where were at least 20,000 spectators outside of an area of several miles in compass. It was a grand shew and well worth seeing in the course of a man's life. After it was over we took a view of the late Sir Gregory Page's seat on the edge of the heath, which is a grand and elegant building, said to be begun and covered in the space of 11 months. Sir

Gregory's father was a rich brewer; and as mony [*sic*] answers all things, so it will also accomplish in a short time what mediocrity would be tedious in effecting. The house stands on two low a scite to correspond with its grandeur.

"Not far distant is the Hospital built by Sr John Morden. . . It was upon this Heath that Wat Tyler mustered his 100,000 men in rebellion in the reign of Richard 2nd . . . We then walked a little below the Gun Warren or Park, down to the river Thames, where the convicts work at ballast heaving . . . among whom was the infamous Dignum, who lately rendered himself so by gross cheats, impositions, and thefts. He was a man of liberal education, and had published some Observations which had merit, but by a dissolute way of life had brought himself to the condition of raising ballast for the publick, instead of raising a reputation for himself."

The Refugee Judge, being now out of work, had taken a short trip for the purpose of examining the beauties of Windsor Castle, Hampton Court, with some gentlemen's seats by the way, and under the date of June 16 he writes:—

"After leaving Hampton Court, we pass'd thro' Bushy Park, $1\frac{1}{4}$ mile, where Lord North hath a seat. We passed by a circular piece of water, with a statue in the middle: then to Teddington, $\frac{1}{2}$ mile: to Twickenham, $1\frac{3}{4}$ miles, a pretty village with a number of fine seats upon the Thames, particularly the late Mr Pope's, now in the possession of the R^t^ Honorable Welbore Ellis Esq." &c.

18th.— . . . At Mauduit's. Saw Mr Lethieulier, who fears a Treaty. M. says a friend of his had seen a letter from an officer in America, in which is an expression of this import—You must not be surprized if you should see me very soon in England, for I believe affairs are upon the very point of settlement.

His friend says he looks upon this intelligence much the same as if it came from Howe himself, and added that something was to come from Washington, but this was not explained.

24th.—[The blanks in the date are almost entirely filled up with lamentations over Peggy's increasing illness.] . . . I went to town: saw at Mr Knox's office a Carolinian just arrived: left N. York 25 May. Howe still at N.Y.: Cornwallis in camp in N. Jersey. There had been a small brush with his picket and a body of rebels. Washington still at Morristown: thinks not more than 700 strong: people divided whether the army goes to Philad. or to the n-ward: part of Carleton's force at Crown Point: the rest expected the beginning of June: Hotham and a squadron off Henlopen, and in Delaware Bay and river. Howe sends to Gov. a particular acc[t] of Danbury affair under Tryon.*

27th.— . . . D[r] Dodd executed this morning at Tyburn, after the strongest efforts by his friends: a Petition from the Corporation of London: another from the Jury who convicted him: and others from different parishes—it is said above 20,000 hands to them for a pardon. It is observable that Wolridge and other Aldermen, &c., in the city, in opposition to Gov[t], were the promoters of these applications. The King's refusal passes without reproach. If he had complied, the petitioners themselves would have promoted a clamour against him in some secret way or other.†

July 2nd.— . . . I went to town. Accounts from Quebec of Burgoyne's arrival the 6th of May, but no advice of the troops having moved the 4th of June, when the ship sailed.

* Governor Tryon, promoted to the rank of Major-General, led 2000 troops to Danbury, and on the 26th of April destroyed a large quantity of stores deposited there. The English force got back with difficulty, having two encounters with the Americans on the way, in which they lost 172 in killed, wounded, and missing.

† Dr. Dodd was born in 1729 at Bourne in the county of Lincoln, and was of Clare Hall, Cambridge. He entered into Holy Orders in 1753, and became a popular preacher in London. He published several volumes of sermons, and was a most prolific writer on religious and moral subjects. In 1766 he received the degree of LL.D., and soon after published a volume of poems. In 1769 he translated Massilion's Sermons, inscribed to the Prince of Wales. In 1771 appeared his three volumes of sermons to young men, which he dedicated to his pupils Charles and Philip Stanhope, afterwards Earl of Chesterfield. He had the living of Hockliffe, Bucks, was Lecturer at the Magdalen, received £100 a year as Editor of the Christian's Magazine, was Prebendary of Brecon, and Chaplain to the Bishop of St. Davids. These sources of emolument, together with some others, were not enough to satisfy his worldly vanity and profuse extravagance. He wrote an anonymous letter to Lady Apsley, offering a bribe of £3,000, if she would use her influence to get him appointed to the living of St. George's, Hanover Square. The secret was detected; he was struck from the list of Chaplains, and he withdrew to the city of Geneva. His friend Lord Chesterfield then gave him the living of Winge, in Bucks, when he returned again to England. Failing, however, to learn wisdom by experience, he went from bad to worse, and ended his career as related above.

In the London Magazine for 1773, p. 48, Jan. 19, we read:—" Same day the following convicts were executed at Tyburn, viz., Benjamin Bird, for forging an indorsement on a Bill of Exchange, [also several others] and William Griffiths, for robbing the Rev. Dr. Dodd on the highway, near Pancras."

7th.—No alteration, [in Peggy.] Sir Jn° Eliot called in his way to Sussex to visit Ld G. Germain's child. He recommends [Peggy] three of the Hemlock pills going to bed, and to eat freely of cucumbers. Thinks she does not lose.

11th.—An exceeding pleasant summer day, most of which she spent in the garden instead of the coach, but her fever exceeding high in the even^g. S^r Jn° ordered bleeding wch I consented to with reluctance; but the blundering Apothecary made one attempt in her foot, and two in her arm, without opening a vein, and I would not suffer him to go on.

I was at the Levée: the first time since I went out of town to the Hot Wells. Very few persons there.

12th.—A more quiet night than I feared, after the ruffle, attempting to bleed. I sent for Mr Atkinson of Chelsea, another Apothecary, who bled her very dexterously. Took 6 ounces. Spent all day in the garden. No abatement of her fever.

13th.— . . . A packet yesterday from N. York. The army not moved the 9th of June. It is generally said the Provincials are much distressed, their army small, and ill provided. The delay is now on the part of Howe, attributed to want of camp equipage—which were all arrived.

19th.—A more calm night but no strength gained. I went to London, [from Chelsea]. Called on Sr James Wright. He mentions a short note wth a pencil from Gen. Vaughan to his brother Lord Lisburne, of June 11, when skirmishes had begun: Grant's horse's head shot off by a cannon ball, the 12th. This should prepare for a general attack on the 13th.

22nd.— . . . I went to London: heard confirmation of the news of the *Fox* frigate being taken by M^cneal Manly, and some say another of the Provincial vessels near Nf^dland, and that great havoc was made among the fisheries. Admiral Montagu thinking he had not force enough to go out. I suspect he will be censured when enquiry is made.

31st.— . . . I went to London to the Secr^y of State his office. From M^r D'Oyly I am satisfied that Howe did not intend Philadelphia. Possibly if Washington had been willing to meet him in the Jerseys, there would have been a general action there, but I suppose he is gone with great part of the army and fleet to New England, having drawn what forces the Colonels could collect to the west of Hudson's River. If he had taken Philadelphia, he must have destroyed, [it ?] or have left too great part of his army there and in the Jerseys, to keep possession. I fear the fate of my own country, [Massachusetts] and that the principle town will be sacrificed.

At this place the Fourth volume of the Diary terminates. Most people who follow the course of the war, must agree "that Howe did not intend Philadelphia." At this date the full particulars attendant on the rapid and brilliant succession of victories achieved by the English army after the Battle of Long Island, were not sufficiently known in England, nor had there been time yet to comprehend the fact that America was then virtually conquered and won; nor did she, nor could she then perceive, that if the then present advantages were relaxed, and not followed up, they would be all lost, and never to be secured again.

CHAPTER III.

BEGINNING OF VOL. V. OF THE DIARY.

THE Fifth Volume begins with the month of August, but as the first three days are occupied with Mr. Hutchinson's anxieties on the subject of his daughter's declining health, whose lungs were greatly impaired, and whose strength was visibly decreasing, those days, and some others in other places, may be omitted. On the 4th there is an allusion to the reported capture of Ticonderoga. In commencing the attack on this important and strongly fortified place, the English troops under General Burgoyne, secured Mount Hope, and after this by great exertion, they possessed themselves of Sugar Hill, an advantageous post that commanded the works both at Ticonderoga, and at a neighbouring intrenched position called Fort Independence. These preliminaries having been accomplished by the 5th of June, the assault was intended for the next day. At dawn on the following morning however, it was discovered that the Americans had abandoned their works and withdrawn during the night. Lieutenant Anburey, who was present, tells us, [i. p. 323], that four men had been left behind, who were to have fired off the guns of a large battery that commanded the approach, and then to have made their escape as quickly as possible. The matches lay lighted beside the cannon. Great mischief and loss of life would have resulted if this proceeding had been carried out, but when the English entered, they found the four men dead drunk beside a cask of Madeira.

We read in the Diary as follows :—

4th.—A vessel arrived from Quebec, and yesterday an officer came to town, who says Ticonderoga was besieged by Burgoyne, and that the day he came away, June 6th, it was generally reported and believed that it was taken . . .

5th.—I wrote by Mr Blowers to my kinsman Ed Hn* at

* I have no record who this Edward Hutchinson was. All the Governor's immediate relatives had followed him to England, and his only brother

Boston, to thank him for his letter, and account of my friends: to tell him I tho't Mrs Merchant, as next of kin, the properest person to administer on Sally Rogers's estate:* to approve his remaining in the country, as I would have done in a private character: to express my wish to convince that in public character I had ever aimed at the true interest, &c., wch I had the comfort of feeling every day, and time would discover who judged right: to mention my distress: to Mr Walter and Mr Murray at N. York, acknowl^g their letters: to the former, that I would take care of his business, as well as Mr Winslow's of Braintree: and to the latter, that I tho't it best he should stay in America: to both the case of my daughter, who in the morning was lower than usual.

6th.— . . . There is an Address of Burgoyne's in the papers to-day to the people, dated at Putnam Creek, June 29th last—flowery, but upon the whole, well adapted.

8th.—We made a long journey in the coach to Hampton Court, which Peggy bore beyond expectation, and happily, just at the gate of the Palace we met M^rs D'oyly, who has apartments there, and who kindly took my daughter into a gentleman's house, of her (M^rs D'oyly's) acquaintance, where she rested on a sophy, while Mrs Sanford [Grizell Sanford, spinster, his sister-in-law], and my daughter Oliver, went over the Palace. We left my son E. at Richmond, who provided a good but extravagantly dear dinner for us at the Star-and-Garter, where we stayed to tea, and came back to our lodgings just after sunset. A better day than I feared. As warm a day as any this year, but no hotter than what we call moderate in America.

10th.— . . . To-day Mr Newton and his wife, just arrived from Halifax, where he is Collector . . .

15th.—Treasurer Gray called upon me. He had made an

Foster had withdrawn to Halifax in Nova Scotia. There is an Edward Hutchinson in the Pedigree, brother of Elizabeth, who married the Rev. Nathaniel Robbins. The Governor and he were first cousins, except that their grandmothers were different people, because their grandfather Elisha married twice. This Edward is the only one I can think of, if he were alive in 1777. He is marked as having died single, but in what year is not stated.

* Sally or Sarah Rogers was daughter of George Rogers, who married the Governor's younger sister Lydia. Sally died in 1776.

extract from a Sermon preached in 1759 at Boston by Doctor Cooper before Gov. Pownall and the Court, with his remarks. I had not heard of the most material facts he charged upon Cooper: several he altered: the only one remaining which I had any doubt about his printing was—a meeting with Warren and the rest in Service time on a Sunday afternoon, until sermon was near over, and he came to baptize a child: but this, Gray affirmed to be notorious in the town, and that it was but a short time before the famous 19th of April . . .

16th.—Sensibly more feeble, and had a bad day. In this kind of life the days and nights pass incredibly swift, and I am six months older and nearer to my own death, than when my daughter's illness began; and it appears like the dream of a night.

18th.—Easterly wind and raw, and no airing. Removed what furniture we had in London to Little Chelsea . . .

Cap^n^ Loring, son of Com^o^ Loring arrived from New York, wch he left the 16 July, when Lord and Gen. Howe were both there. So much of the summer gone, and nothing done. There had been an attack upon a redout in the Jerseys, when Cap. Finch and 14 others were killed, the place being carried. Prescot, who commanded at Newport, surprised at a house out of town, and carried off.* Loring reports that Ticonderoga and Fort Wm Henry were in possession of Burgoyne, and that the garrison of Ticonderoga were made prisoners. The packet and a man-of-war with transports sailed at the same time. Loring has no publick letters, nor any private wch mention his news, and many doubt the truth.

19th.—It is said to-day that an officer who came in [with?] Loring, gives the same account he does . . .

20th.— . . . It is said everybody believes the news of Ticonderoga, and that New England would now be the object. I fear the destruction of poor Boston. What have those men to answer for who have brought on this destructive war!

* This gallant exploit was planned and executed by the American Colonel Barton, who, with a party of officers and men, surprised General Prescot in bed, and carried him off to the headquarters at Providence. This was a good set-off against the capture of General Lee.

21st.—I settled with Wm Atwick: paid him in full of rent, and delivered up my house in New Bond Street. Where, or whether I shall take another house in London, God only knows. Nothing can be more uncertain than my present state. My daughter continues to decline. What will be the state of America?

Mauduit called in the evening: says the *Fox* is retaken by Sr G. Collier, and carried into Halifax.

22nd.— . . . The *Flora* frigate, going to Halifax to repair, fell in with the *Boston* [and] the *Hancock*, two of the best rebel vessels they have, and the *Fox*. While they were looking at one another Sr G. Collier in the *Rainbow*, who had not been out of Halifax 3 hours, hove in sight and came up to them as fast as he could, but could not tell what to make of them. The *Flora* threw out false colours, being at a loss what to make of the *Rainbow*. As soon as they were known to the rebels' vessels, they made the best way they could. The *Flora* followed the *Fox*, and took her, and carried her into Halifax. The *Boston* and *Hancock* steered different courses, and the *Rainbow* followed the *Hancock* 36 hours, when she came up with her, and she struck without firing a gun. The *Boston* steered towards the Bay of Fundy, where the *Diamond* was cruising.*

23rd.— . . . An express arrived from Quebec, with an account from Burgoyne, of his being in possession of Ticonderoga: 500 of the garrison killed; 500 prisoners; and 7000 escaped into the words, the Indians pursuing them.†

25th.— . . . The *Gazette* to-day gives a particular account of the action at Ticonderoga. The rebels left the Fort and were followed: lost 2 or 300 killed, and more wounded and taken prisoners, but fought better than their enemies expected. About 60 of the K.'s troops killed—more wounded. Burgoyne was at Skeensborough the 28th of July: the rebel army at Fort Edward.

26th.— . . . A vessel from N. York: sailed July 29.

* This account came by the packet from New York, in letters which left that city July 18.

† Lieutenant Anburey was present, as stated above; yet his account of the occupation of Ticonderoga is a very peaceful affair compared with this. But see the next entry.

M[r] Hutchinson,* Secr[y] to Gov. Shirley at Dominica, and son to Eliakim H., late deceased, came passenger. He was taken in his passage from Dom. to London, and carried to N. England, where he was prisoner on his parole many months. He says news came the 22nd that Burgoyne was as far as Fort Edward, upon which the fleet and army sailed—destination not known. They spoke with a vessel which informed them they saw the fleet off Cape Henlopen. Washington having left part of his force in the Jerseys, was gone with the rest towards Albany. Matters were now at a crisis.

28th.—Mauduit called last evening, and urged me against my inclination to go to Court to-day. The Queen asked where I had been? I told her I had been six months in the country with my sick daughter. "What, she that used to be here? Why, she looked fine and healthy. I hope she will get well again."

A vessel from Quebec, and it is said brings news that Schuyler wth 1500 men at Fort Edward, had laid down their arms . . .

29th— . . . Sir James Wright came over to see me. He disapproves much of the fleet and army their going to Delaware and Chesapeak, as is now believed, and wishes they had gone northward.†

September 1st.— . . . At Lord George's office. M[r] Knox says Howe certainly intended to go to Philadelphia when he left New York, and that Hotham writes to Lord George that Clinton had sent an express after him, to inform him of Washington's return with his army to Morris-town.

3rd.—An autumn day, which would admit of going abroad for sick persons in a coach only. My son E. received a letter from his wife,‡ dated Aug. 23rd at Cove [of Cork], being just

* His name was William. He was descended from the sixth son of Richard, a younger brother of the first William. His widowed mother, and his sister were now Refugees in London. They were eventually interred in the Apthorpe vault in Croydon church. I find no record of what became of him—whether he married, or left offspring, or died single.

† It was this very removal of General Howe's forces southward, instead of marching north to support Gen. Burgoyne as expected, that led to the surrender of Burgoyne and his army at Saratoga, as will be noticed further on.

‡ There is an original letter of hers in the Letter Book to her friend "Ophelia," giving some account of the voyage. Is it unfinished and not signed.

arrived after 24 days passage in the *Albion* frigate from Rhode Island. She intended the next day to Corke, and by first opportunity to England.

7th.— . . . In the Evening the most remarkable northern light I have seen since my being in England, and seldom exceeded in America.

15th.—My son E.'s wife came to London from Dublin yesterday at one o'clock,* but finding we had moved from N. Bond Street, sent a Porter to Little Chelsea, who returned that he could not find us. She then went to the New England Coffee House, and could get no intelligence there, nor find where Judge Oliver lived. At length she found Col° Browne in the evening, who conducted her to Judge Oliver, her grandfather, and a messenger came to my son after he was in bed, who rose and went to town, and to-day they came over and dined with us, but a distressing day it has been, my sick daughter having sunk visibly; and being left alone with her, I was not without fears of her change before her sister [Sarah], who went to London, could return. In the evening some revival.†

21st.— . . . Her breath grew shorter. The last words she said were to Dr Oliver—"I am dying,"—and continued speechless, and but little, if at all, sensible, until about half after ten [at night], when she expired . . .

22nd.— . . . I desired my two eldest sons to go to Croydon, and provide a grave for her near Miss Katy Hutchinson lately buried there.‡

General Haldiman set out yesterday from town for Quebec. I sent a card to him to wish a happy arrival, and recommended Jon^n and Edw. Clarke as two Consignees of E. India tea, and sufferers, &c. . .

25th.—The dear remains of my daughter deposited in a brick

* There is an original letter from Pelham Winslow, dated Newport, Rhode Island, June 23, 1777, mentioning her endeavours and difficulties in securing a passage to England.

† Elisha had been separated from his wife, owing to the state of the times, from the first of June, 1774, when he left America with his father, until the 21st of September, 1777, being a space of three years, three months, and 21 days.

‡ Peggy's death is mentioned in Dr. Peter Oliver's Diary. He says—"Sep. 21 or 22. Peggy Hutchinson, Mrs. Oliver's sister, died at Chelsea of a consumption: 23rd year of her age."

grave built in the church at Croydon near Mr Apthorpe's tomb, and that of Mrs Katy H. Her brother-in-law Dr Oliver, her cousins Daniel and Silvester O., with Mr Lefontaine, the young gentleman of the house where we are, followed the herse in a mourning coach as relations. My daughter [Sarah] and I went early to High Street, [Judge Oliver's], and returned at 12 o'clock. This is the custom here, when the near relatives don't leave the house as soon as death comes into it. A distressing day to me, especially at leaving the house with the body of my dear daughter, and returning to the place again after its removal.

October 1st.—In town again, and closed my agreement for the house in Sackville Street, the rent at 110£ a year unfurnished, the rent to commence on Michaelmas Day.

7th.—A letter came to-day from Brook Watson at Margate to Mr Knox, dated yesterday, giving an account of a transport, Cap. Blackburne, arrived from N. York, an hour or two before that he sailed Aug. 30: that the 28 an express came from Ld Howe, advising that the 16 part of the army landed at Baltimore; the rest at the head of Elk river, within 40 miles of Philadelphia; that Washington had marched his army to Philadel.; that Burgoyne was below Albany; that Clinton was preparing an expedition, supposed to meet him; that Sullivan had landed 4000 men on Staten Island in the night, and had been drove off the next day with the loss of 900; that an attempt had been made the same night at Huntingdon on S. Island, and another at Kingsbridge; and the rebels repulsed with loss at both.

A New York paper of Aug. 22 says there had been risings of the people at Boston, and the merchants had been compelled to promise to sell their goods at the old price for paper money . . .

8th.—At the King's Levée: very thin. The Bishop of Lichfield, and Sr Robt Eden, all I had any conversation with. The K. seldom says anything of American, or any publick affairs at his Levée, but he asked me to-day if I did not think it strange there were no letters yet? "Surely we may expect them every hour." I said—"There are private letters Sir." "Yes, but no publick accounts."

11th.—The Edinburgh news paper of the 6th says that a vessel at Clyde from Quebec, sailed the 24th Aug., and letters say that Arnold wth 12,000 men, had surrendered, and that upon this news, several gentlemen had set out from Quebec for New York. This is only corroborating former reports.* But the state of Howe's army, and the time spent this summer without effecting anything material, gives the most concern . . .

16th.—Lent sister [-in-law] G. Sanford 5 Guineas. Began a journey into Norfolk with Mr Paxton in a post-chaise . . .

19th.—This being the D. of Grafton's day for receiving his friends when he is at Euston, [in Suffolk], Mr Burch had intended a visit before we came, and tho' with reluctance, upon his urging, I accompanied him, his son, and Mr Paxton. We found Mr Holt, Member for the county, and his brother [-in-law?] Genl Parker, brother to Ld Macclesfield, Mr Stone, head Comiss. of Excise, Mr Metcalf, and Grigsby, Norfolk gentlemen, the Minister of the parish, Mr Host, [?] Lady Dutchess, and Lord Euston. The dinner not more grand than at Mr Ellis's . . .

22nd.—Went on to Lord Townshend's at Raynham † . . .

24th.—Lord Townshend carried us through a great part of his estate, which is immense, and in admirable order, about 12,000£ a year, besides eleven livings in his gift . . . I rode a mule Ld T. brought from Portugal, and found her much easier than any horse I have rode in England.

Nov. 1st.—On horseback to visit Mr De Grey, elder brother to the Ch. Justice . . . The evening paper gives an acct of the arrival of the *Swallow* Packet, 7 ws and 3 days passage from Elk in Chesapeak Bay. Howe had landed and was about to march. Washington encamped between Howe and the rebel magazines.

* It is needless to say that these reports were without foundation.

† Bless the gossips, how they talk! Is there no way of stopping their mouths? Read the following absurdity,—"London, May 23. A treaty of marriage is said to be on foot between the Hon. Mr. Hutchinson, late Lt. Gov. of Boston, N.E., and the Rt. Hon. Lady Dowager Townshend, mother to the present Viscount Townshend of Portman Square."—*Essex Gazette*, 27 July, 1775.

This is quoted by Whitmore, in his 'H. and O. Genealogies,' p. 22.

3rd.—Began our journey between nine and ten to London, after receiving the *Gazette* from Mr D'Oyly, with the account of Genl Burgoyne's discouraging situation.* At Newmarket met with news that an express was gone from London to Lord Weymouth at Chippenham, with an account of Washington's defeat, and Howe's being in possession of Philadelphia, and in the evening Lord March came in to Chesterford, where we lodged, from Lord Weymouth's, and read to us the account sent from London.

4th.—Dined in Sackville Street about three o' clock, after travelling 45 miles, most of the time in the rain . . .

6th.—To Fulham: the Bishop received me very courteously. Dined with my son E.[lisha.]

In the evening at Brompton, at the baptism of my son's [Thomas's] youngest son Andrew,† by Dr Kippis. The ceremony differs from that in New England. Before the first prayer the Minister makes a long discourse upon the nature of the ordinance: after the words of baptism, he speaks of fighting under Christ's banner, or to that effect: then addresses to the parent, [and] tells him his obligation: then concludes with a short prayer.

7th.—In the city. Called upon Blackburne, Mauduit, &c. Afterwards at the King's Levée, and at the Queen's Caudle. Met Dr Poyntz, who I had seen at Lord Townshend's, Mr Cornwall, &c. No official news yet. I mentioned to the King a letter Blackburne shewed me, which was kept open until the ship was ready to sail, and which says certain advice was just then received of great success of Howe, which might be depended on as certain. This was the fullest account the King said he had received.

Letters, (Mr Knox writes one), were recd to-day from Ld Lt of Ireland, wch mention letters dated N. York 23 Sep., 8 o'clock in the evening, and that advice just then came in from Howe.

* This does not refer to the surrender at Saratoga. The news of that disaster did not reach England until the beginning of December.

† This was my father, born on board ship in Nantasket Roads, March 24, 1776, as before mentioned. There was another son William, born after this, *i.e.* June 14, 1778.

8th.— . . . Paul Wentworth called: makes no doubt of Washington's defeat,—his authority, what he hears from Franklin's friends in the city; talks like a friend to the cause of Gov^t, and urges the necessity of the measures they have taken.

9th.—At the Old Jewry. In the evening at Dr Heberden's. Called with Mauduit a few minutes at St. James's, where the Queen's apartm^ts were filled with Nobility, &c. . .

10th.—Lord Mayor's show,* which I had not curiosity enough to go out to see, but sat at home mournfully reflecting on being at the like show last year with my dear child, where she probably took a cold, which laid the foundation of her fatal distemper . . .

11th.—I called upon Lt Gov. Bull, lately arrived with his family from South Carolina, in Hart Street, Bloomsb. He had seen me in Boston many years ago, but I have no remembrance of him.

Dined with Mr Jenkinson :—Mr Cornwall, Dean of Norwich, and their wives, and a Winchester gentleman, with Mr Jeffrys, an Irish gen. lately from Paris, where he saw Franklin about a fortnight ago—says Deane is more noticed there than Franklin —heard the news of Washington's defeat before he came away. Not a word more yet arrived here.

13th.—At Mr Ellis's. He gives me more news by the *Bienfaisant:* mentions that Howe took possession of Philad. the 24th Sept.: says nothing of any action, but that of the 11th: Congress at Trenton: city fired in 3 places, but extinguished: shipping all burnt: Washington's army crossed the Schuylkill: Howe's gone after them: Clinton said to be gone to Burgoyne, who was entrenched at Saratoga.

Dined with Judge Oliver.

The evening at Lord Hardwicke's.

Wrote to Lord Townshend, Burch, and Paxton.

15th.—Mr Boucher, Addison, two Maryland Clergymen, Dr Chandler, Auchmuty, and J. Green, dined with me. Boucher said Delany himself told him of the application made by

* Surely the Governor is mistaken in his day. This may be explained by the fact that the 9th was Sunday, and the show therefore held on Monday.

Boston House of Rep. to answer my Speech.* Boucher lived ten years near Washington, and was very intimate: thought his capacity below mediocrity: by no means equal to such a post: civil and polite.

18th.— . . . Mr Jackson called, and left with me two small tools, from among many, wch he had of the same sort, and which were ploughed up from under the surface of a piece of grass ground, wch he supposes never to have been turned up for 1700 years or more, being a long divisional strip between tilled grounds, where they lay open, but having lately been inclosed, ceased to be of use for that purpose. One seems to have been a chizzel, the other a gouge, and are of copper, or a mixed metal, partly copper, and he thinks belonged to the ancient Britons, rather than the Romans. They were found in his own grounds in Norfolk.†

Dined with M^r and Mrs Ellis without any other company. He gives a character of the Duke of Norfolk, who has just succeeded to his title, as the most despicable, and even sordid man in the kingdom. His son, the Earl of Surrey, to whom the late Duke left 7,000£ ꝑ ann., and about 11,000£ ꝑ an. to the father, is a great gambler, devoted to dissipation. They are both Catholics: the Lady of Ld Surrey a Protestant. But M^r

* Perhaps this refers to some speech made before the Governor left America.

† The simplicity of the above remarks may be excused on the ground that at that period of our history, the knowledge of Celts and Palstaves "of copper or mixed metal" had made but slender progress. In the "Costume of the Original Inhabitants of the British Isles," by Sir Samuel Meyrick, and C. H. Smith, Esq., the subject of this mixed metal is alluded to. Describing the Plate representing the ancient Briton clothed in the skin of the brindled cow, with the circular shield, and spear tipped with bone, the experiments on the composition of ancient bronze implements by Dr. Pearson, and published in the 'Philosophical Transactions' for 1796, p. 395, are duly mentioned. From a series of analyses it resulted that different implements yielded different proportions of metal in the alloys of tin and copper. Though the average proportion for this species of object is generally about one of the former to nine or ten of the latter, he found them vary from 1 to 6, 1 to 7½, 1 to 10, &c.

The long strips alternately of grass and tilled ground, running across the large enclosures, a practice still lingering in the midland counties, although of date anterior to the Norman Conquest, were doubtless specimens of the open-field system, thus scored by balks, furlongs, or linches, so called. Mr. Seebohm, F.S.A., gave an interesting account of this system before the Society of Antiquaries in 1879 and 1880, as recorded in the pages of the Proceedings, 2nd S. VIII. 88, 355.

Ellis says it would not be matter of wonder if the D., the first day of Parliament, should take the oaths and his seat in the H. of Lords.

20th.—The Parliament met. I felt no inclination to go to the House of Lords, though Lord Chatham was to go down and make an angry speech. Once hearing him was enough for me. My son E.'s wife found means to get in. I sent the Bp. of Rochester a set of my History and the Collection to-day, as I had done to the Bp. of London yesterday, and from both rec^d very polite cards. In the evening at Watson's.

Only the Bishop of Rochester's "Card" has been preserved. A set of his History must mean the two first volumes of his History of Massachusetts Bay, and the "Collection," I take it, the Collection of his Speeches to the House of Representatives. The Bishop's "Card" runs thus:—

"The Bishop of Rochester presents his complim^ts to Govr Hutchinson, with his best thanks for his obliging present, wch will do honour to his Libary, and give both instruction and amusement to him. The Bp. makes no long stay in town, but will take the first opportunity of paying his respects to the Governor on his return.

"Deanery House, Westm^r."
"Nov. 20th 1777."

Lord Chatham had not won the Governor's heart, and he had no desire to go and hear him speak. How indeed should he have won it, seeing that his Lordship had frequently uttered expressions calculated to encourage insubordination, and embroil the two countries? and in spite of the many proofs that the Americans had given, all tending to shew that they intended, if possible, to break away from the Mother Country, yet the Noble Lord, together with a few others of equally limited vision, could not see it. "The assertion that America aspired at independence, was treated as an unfounded calumny, calculated only for purposes of delusion." Hence, his refusal to believe a patent fact, acted as an incentive to further excesses. To declare that the Americans were justified in their resistance, was encouragement enough to teach them that they had a powerful friend in a place where he could do them much service in promoting their views, which was a premium to go on. But his Lordship was not alone in his indiscretion, there being several Peers in the one House, and several Commoners in the other, who were equally unpatriotic and un-English in their principles and in their teaching, and who were thereby aiding and abetting the very war, and the very dismemberment of the Empire, which they pretended to deprecate. If they really believed that the Americans had a right to complain, why did they not say how far they might go, and where they ought to stop? Vague declamations about ill-defined wrongs, act as encouragements to unbridled licence; and the Continuator of Hume writes—"that the leaders of the minority in both Houses were not only the encouragers, but in a great degree, the authors of the American rebellion." The ill-advised zeal of these declaimers had fed the aspirations of those who were now striking for total independence, and had led them to a confident hope that they would soon get everything for them; but these encouragements were hollow and illusory, for in criticising the famous speech of November 20, 1776, Adolphus says—"Lord Chatham then explicitly stated his repugnance to the independence of America." The contradictions uttered by some of these great men were sometimes so palpable, that it was not always easy to understand what they really meant in the conduct of American affairs, and it is a question whether they knew themselves. Certain it is, that they fanned the flame into fiercer fires; so that it was the opinion of some men, that the rebellion in America should really have been first stifled in the Parliament of England: and it may be assumed, that if half-a-dozen Members out of each Chamber had been hanged, a very sedative effect would have been produced in the Colonies.

Return we to the Diary:—

21st.—Called on Mr Cornwall, who gave me a full account of the debates in both Houses. The Opposition in both agreed on the same measure—to propose an amendment in the Answer to the King's Speech, to pray him to order an immediate cessation of arms, and then to proceed to treat wth them. Strange as such a notion is, such men as the D. of Grafton, Ld Chatham, Shelburne, Camden, &c., spoke in favour of it in the Lords, and Burke, Barré, Fox, Wilkes, &c., in the Commons. Let what motion will, be made, in opposition, the number is much the same:—in the Lords 28 to 86: in the

Commons 86 to 243: and the last year it was near the same proportion.*

22nd.—At Lord Townshend's, Portman Square. Lady Townshend asked me if I had a mind to see an instance of American loyalty? and going to the sopha, uncovered a large gilt head, which at once appeared to be that of the King, which it seems the rebels at N. York, after the Declaration of Independence, [July 4, 1776], cut off from the statue which had been erected there, and sent to Fort Washington, in order to fix it on a pole or pike: but by some means or other it was buried, and after the surrender of the Fort, Montresor [?] took it into his possession, and sent it to Lord T., which he rec[d] last night. The nose is wounded and defaced, but the gilding remains fair; and as it was well executed, it retains a striking likeness . . .

In the first volume, page 520, I have said that during one of my visits to New York, I was one day shewn the spot where the statue of George III. had stood, and was told that at the out-break of hostilities it was taken down and cast into bullets, because it was well known in the city that it was made of lead. The American who told me this did not say it was gilt, or whether it was an equestrian group or a single figure, and perhaps he did not know, nor did I think of asking such questions. It is probable that the lead was given to the British and Hessian troops at the Battle of Brooklyn on Long Island, and close to New York, fought on the 27th of August, 1776; and possibly the head was carried away northward a few days after, when the Americans withdrew from the city and marched towards Fort Washington. If it was put on a pole or pike at that place, for the diversion or the derision of the Republican soldiary, it may have been buried within the works when the Fort was assaulted and captured on the 16th of November following.

In the Diary, at one or two places—October 10, 1776, for instance—the Governor observes that amongst the prisoners taken at the Battle of Brooklyn, was a Lord Sterling "so called." It has been said that when this officer, who commanded the American right wing, fell into the hands of the English soldiers, there was some

* In Adolphus, vol. iii. p. 13, the numbers in the Lords are 28 to 84, and in the Commons 86 to 243, he, however, placing the higher numbers first. The Continuator of Hume says 97 to 28 in the Upper, and 243 to 86 in the Lower House.

apprehension that he would be roughly handled, as it was understood that it was he who had sawn off or cut off the head of the King's statue. As to the mysterious expression "so called," some light is thrown upon it in a foot-note on page 123 of Serjeant Lamb's *Journal of Occurrences during the late American War.* The note says—

"His father, Mr. Alexander, (for that was his real name), went to America many years ago, where he acquired a considerable estate. Upon the death of Lord Sterling, a Scotch Peer, whose name was Alexander, either the late or present Mr Alexander, came over to England and laid claim to the title. When the cause was tried by the House of Lords, and the claim rejected, the Lords forbade him to assume the title on pain of being led round Westminister Hall, labelled as an imposter; but ever since, by the courtesy of his countrymen, he has been distinguished by the title of Lord Sterling. The first Lord Sterling obtained a grant of Long Island, and was the first that settled it with British inhabitants. He died in 1640."

This little concatenation of circumstances may serve to awaken an excusable curiosity into the history of the statue. It is not likely that it had been made in the Colony, but was probably a present from a friendly King to a loyal city. His Majesty came to the throne in 1760, and the catastrophe happened in 1776—a space of sixteen years; so that we have a limited range during which the work had been done. Mr. Hutchinson had seen the King, and had talked with him often enough to know his features well, and we have his testimony that the likeness was good. The modeling—the casting—and the gilding—could scarcely have been done by an inexperienced hand. We would willingly know who had been the sculptor: whether the work had been a single figure or an equestrian group: when it was executed: and though we know all about the distribution of the body, we should like to be informed as to what has become of the head.

It is time to hark back. Rumours of coming events in America had found their way to England at intervals for some weeks past, causing a considerable amount of uneasiness, as they implied some want of capacity in Sir William Howe, and some reverse of fortune to General Burgoyne; but nothing of a tangible nature was received until the beginning of December.

December 1st.—Almon tells me this morning, a vessel is arrived at Nantz from Charlestown: sailed 19 October: advises the total loss of Burgoyne's army, and the distressed state of Howe's. I think Almon wishes it may prove true, as do too many, out [of] opposition to Administration.

Major Cayler arrived before noon, with letters from S[r] W. Howe. M[r] Knox mentions his being in possession of Philad. the 26 Sep[r], having had a subseq[t] action with Washington after that, and beat him: that Clinton had taken the Forts in the Highlands: and that it is said Burgoyne had retreated. This is all I hear with certainty; only, it is agreed, that the *Augusta*, a 64-gun ship, ran aground; and being stripped, was burnt: and that the *Merton* [?] sloop is lost. Affairs look less favorable than Ministry expected they would. Howe's going round to Chesapeak instead of going to join Burgoyne, is censured much; and it begins now to be said, that he has not capacity for the place he is in.

2nd.—The *Gazette* in the evening gives a full account of yesterday's intelligence. Howe had met with more obstruction that was imagined he would, and lost, in the whole, three or four hundred besides wounded and missing. The *Augusta* ship of 64 guns, burnt by accident in Delaware River. The rebels still kept possession of Mud Island, about 5 miles below Philad., which our ships were preparing to attack. The obstinate resistance made at one place and another, is astonishing to all parties here. Clinton had taken several Forts: destroyed the booms: one of which, he says, the rebels pretend cost 70,000 pounds: and Wallace, the 17th October, was off Esopus, which Gen. Vaughan had laid in ashes; but not a word said of Burgoyne; and everything is in the dark, except we credit the rebel newspapers, which are very unfavorable.

3rd.—Going into the city, I met M[r] Watson, who gave me the first account of a ship from Quebec, with advice of the surrender of Burgoyne and all his army.—At M[r] Ellis's.

4th.—The papers this morning all agree in the arrival of the *Warwick* man-of-war, which sailed the 28 of October from Quebec, and that Burgoyne's army laid down their arms, after having been some days without provisions. It is said they are to be sent home: that Fraser is killed, with 800 men, out of a thousand, with which he attempted to make way thro' an infinite number of Provincials.

Where the blame will lay [lie] seems undetermined. Howe's leaving Burgoyne after he knew he was on his way to Albany, and going upon the southern expedition, is not at present accounted for. Stocks sunk at once 2 or 3 pt . Ministry however had the same majority or near it in a debate last night in the H. of Commons. Sir Wm Meredith returned to the min. side [?]* and Governor Pownall . . .

5th.—Into the city—universal dejection: opinion that Howe will not keep Philadelphia. Dined at General Gage's wth two sons, E. and W. Lt Gov. Oliver and wife, and Judge Oliver, and Major Cuyler, lately arrived express. He is aide-du-camp to Howe, but connected wth Mrs Gage's family: gives but an indifferent account of the prospect for the winter: does not pretend that Howe can have any assistance from the navy: is drawing lines of redoubts. The possession of Philadelphia is really, in my opinion, a disadvantage, and his army would be better in New York, in the state it was last winter.

6th.—Mr Ellis called. He says the kingdom must subdue the Colonies, or the Colonies will subdue the kingdom. The fishery will be gone; the islands gone, &c. The Opposition themselves are confounded when they come to the consequence of their own motion for a cessation of arms. Various reports of Howe's being shot; Vaughan taken prisoner, &c., which do not appear to have any foundation.

7th.—At the Old Jewry. [Some unknown gentleman bowed coming out.] Sir James Wright called after church. He speaks freely of past measures, and as freely of the necessity of a more vigorous exertion than ever. Happy would it be if the consideration of the terrible consequences of another year's campaign might dispose to reasonable terms of accommodation, but there seems little prospect.

10th.—Mr Paxton came to town last evening: dined and spent this evening with me. A newspaper from Boston wth the particulars of Burgoyne's surrender to Gates the 17th of October.

* Blotted and indistinct. Query—ministerial side.

11th.—At Lord Huntingdon's where I saw General Conway the first time. He was very conversible, but attached to his old system: asked me whether I thought the Americans would hearken to any proposals of accom̄odation? and seemed to refer to a plan. I said I imagined they were so determined, that nothing short of a separation would satisfy them. After I left him I found Lord North had informed the House, that as soon as the holidays were over, he would lay some plan of accommodation before them, but would make no proposals to the Colonies during the recess.

12th.—At Mr Ellis's, who laments the state of affairs, and the dispirited Administration: says things are very difficult, but not desperate.

At Lord Hillsborough's, and left my name: the Bp. of London's the same.

At Lord Hardwicke's, who says there will be a change—in the American command certainly,—if not further.

At Dr Kippis's, who has all the air, the house, the wife, &c., of one of our clergymen in a country town.

At Col° Vassall's, Berner's Street, and left my name. At Sr W. Pepperrell's, Queen Anne Street, West.

Everybody in a gloom: most of us expect to lay our bones here. We have reason to say the battle is not to the strong, &c.

15th.—Kept house, my cold increasing. Paxton, with E. and his wife, dined. Reports of more ill success:—that Vaughan had surrendered on Hudson's river—that Burgoyne had shot himself. Goverment, it is certain, was never more distressed. Loth to concede to American Independence, they seem to despair of being able to prevent it: and yet it is the prevailing voice—We cannot stop—America must be checked, or they will not admit of English Independence.

The proposal made by Ld North of laying before the House the 20 Jan., to wch time Parlt is adjourned, a plan of governmt for America, a compliance with wch he hoped to enforce, discovers the feeble state of Govt. Ld Chatham is too old to come in. He certainly wishes to enforce the authority of Parliamt in general: but to save his own views of opposition to all administration but his own, has adopted notions of a partial constitutional dependence of a colony, which, upon just the same reason, infers a total independence. We are to expect further accounts from America, still unpleasing.

The clamour increases against the Howes, who ought to be heard before they are condemned.

19th.—My cold continues bad. Accounts from N. York, by way of Ireland say, that Mud Island was taken, and the river Delaware cleared. The question some people ask is—What good will Philad. do us now we have got it?

20th.— . . . A little time every day I generally take for continuing my History, and a little more in reading; both which give me relief.

23rd.—Find my pulse very quick this morning: stay at home and keep to barley drink, and avoid animal food: my cough not worse: try, in the evening, a large dose of brimstone and molasses my daughter Oliver prepared for me. Lord and Lady Gage sent to invite me to dinner to-morrow, but am obliged to excuse myself.

31st.—A cold NE. wind . . . Mr Eliakim Hutchinson's widow, daughter, and son, dined with me upon a fine haunch of venison, a present from Ld Hardwicke, with Judge Oliver's and son E.'s families.

At the end of another year, it may be permitted to make a short pause. The fortunes of war had oscillated from one side to the other, and back again, but the actual advance to either party, had not been very perceptible. England however, was in the ascendant in August 1776. The Battle of Brooklyn virtually laid the Colonies at the feet of the Mother Country, and the successes that followed confirmed the accuracy of this assertion. It was said that Sir William Howe wanted a little more dash. "But General Howe," says the Continuator of Hume, "was much more blamable for not pursuing the advantages gained on his side. With cold and dilatory caution he checked his brave men in the career of success." He occupied New York—beat the Americans at White Plains, at Forts Washington and Lee, and then followed them leisurely to the waters of Philadelphia, where he arrived, writes Stedman—"just when the last boat of General Washington's embarkation crossed the river, as if he had calculated, it was observed, with great accuracy, the exact time necessary for his enemy to make his escape." Says the Continuator—"But nothing of the vast, the vigorous, or decisive, appeared in the plans or conduct of General Howe, who, from so often stopping the progress, chilling the ardour, and benumbing, as it were, the faculties of his victorious troops, acquired the disgraceful nickname of the Military Torpedo." This should seem to have been a play upon the word *torpid.* A resolute hand would then have terminated the war, for the fate of the Colonies was in the grasp of the General.

As to the affair of Saratoga, it may be observed, that if England had been struck with surprise on receiving news of the Battle of Bunker's Hill, the recent account of the surrender of General Burgoyne and his army at Saratoga, had intensified surprise into a stronger word. Various excuses were offered by different people according to the tendency of their sympathies; but we gather from the Diary, that from the first rumour of disaster in that quarter, there was a feeling among the Ministers, or among those who were closely associated with them, that Sir William Howe was to blame for going south to Philadelphia, instead of going north to support General Burgoyne. That Howe was expected, and that a sort of belief to that effect was prevalent among Burgoyne's troops is certain, because Lieutenant Anburey, who was with them, distinctly says so. He writes, Vol. ii. p. 6,—"It was universally understood throughout the army, that the object of our expedition was to effect a junction with that under General Howe, and by such means become masters of the Hudson's river, dividing the northern from the southern provinces. You can easily conceive the astonishment it occasioned, when we were informed that General Howe's army had gone to Philadelphia, and it was the more increased, as we could not form to ourselves any idea how such a step would facilitate or effect a junction."

It is late in the day however, to discuss these military movements, and it is only done so as far as may apply to the remarks made in the Diary. At a subsequent date, when these officers returned to England, they lost no time in meeting their accusers, and fought bravely to overcome the slanders that had been heaped up against them. The adverse accounts which had crossed the Atlantic of late had seriously impaired the popularity of the two brothers Howe; but with an amount of fairness and love of justice, to friends, foes, and all orders of men, Governor Hutchinson writes under December 15th—"The clamour increases against the Howes, who ought to be heard before they are condemned."

But the unexpected intelligence had struck a heavy blow to the hopes of the Loyalists and Refugees, who were getting impatient to return home in peace. Even the Governor, who had hitherto so fondly and so persistently clung to this hope, at last begins to betray signs of despair. On the 25th of May, 1775, he wrote—"I see my contemporaries dying away so fast, that I am more anxious than ever to hasten home, lest I should die here, which I dread above all things:" but now, on the 12th of December, 1777, he writes—"Most of us expect to lay our bones here."

CHAPTER IV.

BEGINNING OF THE YEAR 1778.

Jany 1st.—I called upon Ld Huntingdon. He was very open in condemning Howe's conduct: at a loss where to find a successor: inclines to Sir H. Clinton: mentioned the talk of Murray: doubted whether Lord Amherst would go. In the evening I sent him a letter I rec^{d} from Dr Gardiner at N. York, and extract of a letter to Dr Chandler from Mr Wetherhead. Mr Thomas, one of the Massachusetts Council, arrived last night from N. York, last from Ireland, called on me.

2nd.—Col^{o} Scott of Boston, who arrived at the same time with Mr Thomas, called with Mr Timmins. Affairs never looked so dark. Mauduit spent an hour in the evening—very gloomy.

Ld Huntingdon returned me the letters. He sent [to] me, informing me his son, (natural), Mr Hastings, came to town last night, and confirms everything in those letters. I suppose he came in the Irish fleet.

4th.— . . . Dined with Mr Ellis, his wife only, and his nephews. I was surprised to hear him say that he did not believe there was any thought of a change in the American command by land. He had heard talk of a division, or separate com̄and of part of [the] naval force: he added he had not had much opportunity of informing himself, coming to town the day before . . .

5th.—A report this morning that the D. of Manchester has a letter from France, which says they had entered into a treaty with the Americans for 31 years . . .

7th.—In the city at Mr Palmer's, Devonshire Square, upon my affair with Dupuis' Executor. Talk prevails there of a French war. Lord Mansfield is gone suddenly to Paris. Stocks fall: Bank st. at 120, was at 141 when I bought for Mr Winslow.

Wrote by the packet to Dr Gardiner, in answer to a letter rec^d^ from him to Jos. Wanton Jr., Esq., at Newport, respecting my estate and my sister's, which I inclosed to Mr Colburn Barratt at N. York, and prayed him to forward.

8th.— . . . At Court. Dr Ross, new Bp. of Exeter, kissed hands: first time of seeing the Queen since my daughter died . . .

9th.—A *Gazette* extraordinary gives letters from Ld Howe, and Gen. Howe, as late as 29 Nov., but nothing very material. The enemy's shipping was either burnt by them, or escaped up the river, and they have lost nothing but their old cannon, and a quantity of shot.

The General writes that he was just upon moving to go after Washington, who, it is thought, was also just upon moving, to keep at such distance from him as he should think fit.

10th.—At Brompton, at my son's, [Thomas's], where I had not been since the death of his child.*

11th.—At Prince's Street—Dr Kippis. Called on Bliss, who is as yellow as saffron with the jaundice . . .

12th.—Into the city with my son T. in the coach. I called on Blackburne: he says Murray is sent for from Minorca: that Howe had determined to burn German-town, and the environs of Philadelphia . . .

13th.—Called on Lord Huntingdon: shewed him Putnam's letter. He says Ld George's Lady is dying with the measles; otherwise he would have talked with him on the subject: he hears, he says, orders are gone to recall Howe: added that Clinton, Sr Wm Erskine, Grey, Leslie, had all wrote to be recalled if Howe remained, and the officers were universally discontented: that Clinton had said he wished old Robertson was chief, that he might take all the care of the army, except fighting, and that he was his second: but this could not be,

* There is no mention of this child in the Pedigree or any family record. It comes in between Andrew and William. Andrew was born March 24, 1776, and William June 14, 1778, a space of two years, two months, and 21 days, and considering the interval of time, this boy or girl, whichever it may have been, could only have been a few months old.

because R. was a younger officer. This connexion makes probable what it is reported R. said when he heard H. was gone to the southward instead of N. England—"By G—— he deserves to be hanged!"

Ld Huntingdon apologised for Clinton's conduct at S. Carolina: said he had been constantly sea-sick for a month or two, and all his spirits wasted: that there was a Lt Coffin who Parker wished to make a Captain: that he sent this Coffin to Charlestown to reconnoitre: that he made return that Sullivan's Island Fort was unfinished: that there was a ford of not more than 18 inches from Long Island to Sullivan's Island: that Clinton was persuaded by Parker to attempt Charlestown: that when he landed at Long Island and found not less than 6 or 7 feet water, he advised Parker of it, and sent Gen. Vaughan, to offer, with three or four battalions, to go up with the fleet to Charlestown: that he proposed to go up by a creek in boats: that there was a point called Hedeson's Point, or some such name, where were two or three heavy cannon, which raked this creek, and therefore it was necessary they should be silenced by the ships: that to his surprize, before he had any answer, Parker began to fire upon the Fort at 800 yards distance: that he stood like a beast upon deck, receiving their fire from the Fort, not regarding how many of his men were killed for many hours, doing no execution: that Lee had no apprehension the Fort would stand the fire of the ships, and ordered the garrison to make the best retreat they could, and even to leave Charlestown; but when he saw the ships anchor 800 yards off, he led the garrison, knowing they were secure: that Clinton was hurt [offended] because Lord George did not publish all his letter, but that the clauses not published were kept back out of sincere kindness to Clinton; and though Clinton resented it and came home on that account, yet he returned satisfied; and Lord Huntingdon, when Clinton shewed him the paragraphs, observed to him that, with persons who knew Clinton's character, they could do him no hurt, yet, with the world in general, a construction would have been made to his disadvantage: that Lord Rawdon had made up the difference between Clinton and Sir P. Parker, but Parker was brought to acknowledge he had not done justice to Clinton in the account which he gave in his letters to Lord George. . .

14th.—A storm of rain all day, and easterly wind. Staid all day at home: wrote five or six folio pages of the History of my own administration. This has been my diversion at times ever since I came from the Hot Wells. [Jan. 1775, I. 345.] Sometimes for a week together I write more or less every day, and then neglect it some days together, and fill the time with reading. If I had not found such employment for my thoughts, my troubles would have preyed upon me much more than they have, and I believe been too powerful. I thank God I have never quitted books, and so, I have not lost the relish of them. My friend Mr Ellis cautioned me against it, and mentioned his going into the country with Sir R. Walpole after he was out of place: that he would take up a book, and in two or three minutes throw it down and say—"How happy should I be if I could but relish a book as once I did."

Lord Hardwicke called notwithstanding the bad weather, and sat half an hour. I shewed him Putnam's letter. He did not approve of it.

15th.—At Lincolns Inn Hall to see Dupuis' Executor. Full of Americans—Paxton, Lechmere, Paddock, Fitch, Pickman. The new Bishop of Exeter called also.

16th.— . . . Dr Chandler, Paxton, Leonard, Fitch, Danforth, Scott, and Jackson, Americans, dined with me.

17th.—At Mr Ellis's, Hanover Square. Carried Dr Chandler in my coach to Lambeth, and dined with the A-Bishop, Mrs Cornwallis, Bp. of Rochester, Dr Wynn, a civilian, Mr [blank] Dr Wise, and Dr Backhouse, [?] Chaplains. Generally he has a full table on Saturdays, but it was remarkably thin to-day.

It was said Murray is coming from Minorca.

An article of news seems to gain credit, and is said to come from private letters, as well as newspapers:—that upon debate, the Congress were equally divided upon a question whether they should relinquish their claim, or rescind their vote for independency, and treat with the Commissioners, and that a fresh member was called in, and turned the vote against rescinding,

&c.,—and the distress of the people is said to be intolerable, being destitute of necessaries.

18th.—At Prince's Street: D[r] Kippis.

Just before dinner L[d] Townshend came in, and mentioned the arrival of Lord Cornwallis, who was not then come from the King: had heard nothing remarkable: both armies gone to winter quarters: fleet to Newport: 7 regiments to New York: talk that there was a division in the Congress, and that Washington was for peace.

Dined at Lord Hardwicke's: General Paoli and Mauduit, besides the family. In the evening M[rs] Yorke, who I had not seen before, widow of Charles Yorke, and her daughter. Lady Mary, I suspect, must have something imperceptible in a general acquaintance, which has been an impediment to a match, her person and behaviour being engaging.* Lady Polwarth, with her Lord at Nice, for his health.

19th.—Yesterday being Sunday, the Q.'s birthday was observed to-day. I intended to stay at home, but being invited to dine at L[d] Huntingdon's, and obliged to dress, I went for a little while to Court, and luckily was the 2nd person the King spoke to; immediately after which I left the Drawing-room, and was at home soon after 3 o'clock.

A gloomy day it was to me, from the recollection that this day twelvemonth my daughter took the cold which laid the foundation of her illness.

Found less company at L[d] H.'s than expected:—young Lord Fielding, Col[o] Hastings, and M[r] Hastings, his n. son, (L[d] Huntingdon's). L[d] H. discovered that he had no expectation of a change in the Amer. command, and despaired of success.

* Tastes and preferences are infinite, and they are unaccountable. There are many agreeable, accomplished, and estimable old Maids in the world. They may have become so from choice, or disappointment, owing to some of the hundred-and-one impediments which are too often to be encountered in bringing these matters to a happy conclusion. We have heard of a staid old Maid who one day gave vent in very strong language, in speaking of a number of fast young ladies of her acquaintance, who were rapidly picking up husbands all round her, by their irresistible arts and flirtations, which put her out of patience with them, and then she wound up her impassioned diatribe by exclaiming—"Ah! it is the trash that is picked up, whilst the best are always left!"

He was to have dined himself wth Lord G., but the death of Lady G. prevented.* . .

20th.—Parliament meets, but no business. . .

23rd.—At Lord Hardwicke's, and the Bishop of London's: the rest of the day upon my history: in the evening Mauduit called.

25th.—A severe N. East storm: did not stir out all day. Lord Gage dropped in in the midst of it, without cloak or great coat, of which it's probable he has neither, the polite part of the kingdom affecting to wear neither, but to walk about in the rain: and women particularly, of middle rank, often walking with their silk hats and silk cloaks, designed as a part of their dress in fair weather.

27th.— . . . At D[r] Lee Parkins's. Young Gould from Boston, 28 of August. He speaks of great distress in the town: all government at an end: their paper money sunk to almost nothing, &c.

29th.—Lord Percy called, after a long time since my visit upon his arrival. Spent an hour—Paxton with him: good natured, easy, and pleasant, as well as free in conversation: plainly discovers his opinion of wrong measures this year: related very circumstantially Sullivan's artful manner of persuading Gen. Howe to let him go out, to send persons in to treat: the manner of Franklin, Adams, and Rutledge's treatment of Lord Howe, &c.

I received a letter two days ago from M[r] Wanton about my estate at Conanicut. Lord Percy brought a message from him to acquaint me with the ruinous state of it; but my letter dated March 19 † did not get to hand till 22[d] Oct[r].—At Lord North's Levée. Lord Amherst left his card when I was abroad.

30th.—At Lord Huntingdon's. He says L[d] Amherst has declined going out: that Clinton has wrote to him that he will

* Dr. Peter Oliver speaks in his Diary of going to the "Queen's Ball Room," on January the 18th, which was Sunday. Perhaps, like the Queen's Drawing Room, the affair came off on the Monday. He writes thus—"Jan. 18, 1778. —I went to the Queen's Ball Room with Wm. Hutchinson, son of Eliakim Hutchinson." The next entry is this—"In Apl. following my father and J. Clarke went to live at Birmingham."

What induced the Chief Justice to settle down at Birmingham is nowhere stated.

† See back, Mar. 18, 1777.

not serve under Howe: that he should not like to command the *débris* of Howe's army: and that he (L[d] H.) believes that as soon as the East River is free of ice, Clinton will come home. While that is froze, he says N. York is so exposed, Clinton will not leave it. Upon the whole, L[d] H. supposes Howe will keep the command.

31st.—Spent good part of an hour with M[r] Cornwall, w[ch] he desired might be in confidence. He says L[d] North had suddenly engaged to the House what it is now very difficult to perform—some plan of conciliation: that if he had committed an error himself, he should think it the best way frankly to acknowledge it: he did not suppose that would be the case now: he owned he saw nothing could be offered but what would make the case worse than at present, or without it: he mentioned three or four diff[t] schemes thought of—the least exceptionable, a proposal, that if the colonies [would return] to the same subjection they were under in 1763, all the Acts passed since should be repealed, (Lord Chatham's proposal was only "suspended,") and already should then commence for the future governm[t] of the Colonies. But to whom is this proposal to be made, or what security can be given for any compliance with it?*

Called on Lord Amherst wth Paxton: left cards. At M[r] Jackson's.

1st February.—At the Old Jewry.

At Court, on the Queen's side of the Drawing Room only. In the evening at L[d] Mansfield's, and the Chancellor's: never saw them so full—D. of Devonshire, L[d] Dartmouth, Macklesfield, Percy, Abercorn, Marchmont, Falconberg, Beaulieu, Lewisham, A-Bp. of York, Bp. of Llandaff, M[r] Oswald, D[r] Courtenay, *cum multis aliis,* unknown to me. At D[r] Heberden's. A raw foggy disagreeable day. D[r] Watson says that Clarendon House stood in Piccadilly, and ran back up Albemarle Street, where 5 or 6 houses now stand: that the Duke of Ormond lived in that house when Blood seized him.

* Since the surrender of Burgoyne the aspect of affairs between the two countries had assumed a very serious complexion. The tenor of these discussions shews that both Houses were at their wits' end to devise some scheme for accommodation. Had they not discovered by this time that the Americans did not want accommodation?

2nd.—At Lord Hillsborough's: his son [blot] Lord Fairford at breakfast with him. Talked with great freedom: said he and I had always thought exactly alike: asked what those members of Parl[t] could do at such a time, when they did not approve of particular measures, and yet in general approved the design of Ministry, in restoring America to the Empire?—the present Ministry, tho' feeble and irresolute, was better than what would come in their room if there should be a change: and yet it was difficult to vote for what was directly against their judgment: asked whether L[d] North ever consulted me? I told him No. He said he was a good man, but apt suddenly to resolve on a thing, which upon second thoughts he repented of, and intimated that to be the case when he promised to lay some plan, which he now found more difficult than he expected. There is talk of a letter from Gates to Lord Thanet, w[ch] Lord Fairford said he heard Lord Petersham say he brought, [having been assured] upon Gates' word, that there was no politicks in it. Lord Loudoun asked me yesterday at Court if I knew Gates? and said, when he was in America, he was the laughing stock of the army, as an ignorant nonsensical fellow.

A raw, unpleasant dark day.

3rd.—At Lord Hardwicke's, where I met Soame Jenyns, who gave an account of yesterday's debate in the H. of Commons. A motion was made by Charles Fox, that no part of the troops now in Great Britain and Ireland should be sent to America, [even] tho' new levies of raw men should be placed in their stead. He spoke more than two hours in support of the motion: nobody said one word, so that it can't be called strictly a debate. The Question was called for, and carried—259 against, to 165: a larger minority than has lately been known. Both L[d] H. and S. Jenyns thought it impolitic to make no answer, and that the Ministry lost hands by it. In the Lords the same motion was made, and 91 or 2 Lords were against 31 or 2.*

* The Continuator of Hume speaks of the "contemptuous silence" with which the speech was received. He says the motion was rejected by 259 to 165 in the Lower House, and 93 to 31 in the Upper.

4th.—My cough returning last night I kept house, being a raw day.

There has been much talk for two or three days of L[d] Chatham's coming in—some say in L[d] Dartmouth's place. M[r] Howard, brother to Lord Hingham, mentioned a day or two ago, that Lord Chatham had wrote to the M. of Rockingham, that he could not bear to see the Kingdom ruined, and intimated his not being able to go all lengths, &c. Administration must undoubtedly be distressed, and seem afraid to take the measures which all agree ought to be taken, by changing the American commands.

5th.— . . . The report of Lord Chatham's separating from the Opposition gains ground.

6th.—At M[r] D'Oyly's. He says the papers laid before the House show that there was no thought of Howe's joining Burgoyne until he heard of his being at Albany: and now the clamour seems to be reserved either for Burgoyne or the Ministry. I met L[d] Onslow, and asked him whether there could be all this smoak [*sic*] about Lord Chatham, and no fire? He says No: that L[d] Chatham has certainly left the Opposition.

7th.—At M[r] Ellis's. He has removed all my apprehensions of L[d] Chatham: says there is nothing more than that he did not like the motion of the Opposition, to make the enquiry now before Parliament, and would not come down: does not like the state of things: particularly fears difficulties from the plan which Lord North has promised: thinks, himself, a declaration might be made of Parliament's being ready to admit Members from the Colonies.*

* If Mr. Ellis talked in that way, he must have quite forgotten that the Americans did not want to be represented in the English Parliament, the distance, and the length of time in those days, of imparting and receiving intelligence, being insuperable objections to an unwilling people. In "The Declaration by the Representatives of the United Colonies of North America," &c., a copy dated 1775 being before me, the pleasure of complaining richly adorns every page, and at page 11 Representation in Parliament is alluded to, as thus:—"After the most valuable right of legislation was infringed, when the powers assumed by your Parliament, *in which we are not represented, and from our local, and other circumstances, cannot properly be represented*," &c., &c. This passage is quite enough to shew that at this time they did not desire representation, although at one period the want of it was said to have originated the quarrel.

It is said D'Oyly is removed from Lord George's office.

10th.—Called on M^r D'Oyly. He has put himself out, but it is because he sees he does not please Lord George. He shews his attachment to the Howes more than ever: Lady Howe and M^rs D'Oyly always together. He speaks freely of Lord George's taking Thomson into his family. Some points look strange. Lord Hardwicke said to me yesterday, he had heard, and believed it, that Gen. H. is recalled. This affair of D'Oyly's looks like it. D'Oyly says no orders are gone to call Gen. Murray to England.—Judge Browne dined and spent the evening. Called on Mr Agar.

11th.—At home all day upon my History, except a short walk to Pall Mall and back. I am in danger of too much confinement for my health, and often go out wth reluctance.

Reports that Burgoyne's men are stopped at Boston.*

12th.— . . . The Howes lose ground every day. It is now said that upon information of Ministry's not being satisfied, they desired leave to come home, and that it has been granted, and Clinton is to take the command: but some think he will be come away, before the leave arrives.

Mauduit in the evening—is very low-spirited at the state of affairs.

13th.—My family all dined with J[udge] Oliver, High Street.

It is now past all doubt that the Howes are recalled. I called on Mr Keene: talked upon Ld North's conciliatory plan. He intimates proposing to ascertain the proportion of a tax to be made by America—suppose 2/- a head. I told him all would be scouted and ridiculed. He said something must be done: the Country Party was going off: they had lost 50 members: they should not have a majority of 20 if something was not done: spoke of the danger of a fresh war, and sinking stocks.

14th.—Never were men more universally condemned than

* The march of General Burgoyne's army to the neighbourhood of Boston, the severity of the winter, with the bad accommodation, the brutal conduct of Colonel Henley towards the English prisoners, the prosecution of him for his cruelties, with Burgoyne's masterly pleading, and skilful forensic management of the trial, are given in the second volume of Anburey's Travels.

the Howes. It is now said, two men of less capacity were not to be found. Tuesday the 17th is appointed for L[d] North's plan to come before the House. He never was so much perplexed before, and his friends think he is making bad worse.

16th.—Called upon M[r] Ellis. Wondered, considering his caution, to hear him speak so freely of the present state of Government. He says there will be 400 Members at two or three o'clock in the House, and let what will be before them, soon after four they are reduced to little more than 100; the absentees at Coffee Houses, taverns round Parliam[t] House, rooms above or below, or on the ground floors, eating, drinking, &c. By 7 or 8 the House is full again, and presently, after the "Question! Question!" many flustered—constant contention, who is up, and ought to speak: and in this strange irregularity, somehow or other, affairs go on, and Government holds together.

Dined at M[r] Ellis's: Douglas, Paymaster of the Navy there.

17th.—At Lord Hardwicke's. He opened Lord North's plan, as it had been communicated to him. He seems willing to give up all, but is confused in his notions of government, as every man must be when he departs from the fundamental principles, and admits governed to be governors. It is agreed on all hands that Commissioners are to go out. It follows that the whole powers they are to be entrusted with cannot be communicated to Parliament, or, in other words, made publick.

The K. therefore, must be impowered to instruct them, as he may constitutionally do, in treating upon peace or war, with any who are not subjects, &c.*

18th.—Last night Lord North communicated his plan—the substance [being] to relinquish taxing, if the Colonies will engage to contribute by their Assemblies, an adequate proportion to the charge of the Empire: to appoint five Commissioners, fully impowered to treat with any body corporate or individual, for the restoration of peace upon those

* This implies a difficulty on the very threshold. If the King is to treat with the Americans not as subjects, this would be a confession that they are free and independent, which is the very thing they were contending for, and which England denied.

terms, the Commission to continue till June 1779. Upon this plan, as all is to be done by Act of Parliament, the King may instruct the Commissioners to give up any further points he thinks proper.

It is said the French have actually entered into a Treaty of Commerce with them as Independent States. It is difficult to judge what effect this concession will have upon the minds of the people. At present they are much divided: so are the friends of the Minister, though they vote with him. We Americans are silent.

Plectuntur Achivi. [The Loyalists are plucked!]

At Lord Townshend's. He is in great wrath: condemns the pusillanimity of Lord North: has been down into Norfolk: encouraged subscriptions: subscribed 500£ himself, though involved and straitened beyond bearing. His poor Lady looks distressed also. When I see so much uneasiness of mind in persons of that high rank, it ought to make me more sensible of the goodness of God to me. I am less unhappy under all the troubles brought upon me by his Providence, than they appear to be in what the world calls affluence and prosperity: for though he is so involved, yet with prudence and [*sic*] oeconomy, his estate and income are so great, he might soon extricate himself.

19th.—Two Bills bro't into the H. of Commons: one for renouncing the right of taxation; the other to enable the K. to impower Co͞missioners, &c. Nothing said.

20th.—At M^r D'Oyly's in the morning. He raves! The nation is ruined! but the recall of the Howes is the cause (with him) of the ruin. Everybody, however, it must be acknowledged, is struck with this motion. Lord Hillsborough called and spent an hour. When he persuaded me to take the Gov^t he thought he was doing public service, and serving me; now he saw what I suffered, he wished, for my sake, he had not urged me.

I said there was no judging what effect this turn would have: still the country might be saved, and much would depend on the Commissioners. I thought there seemed to be a ort of amazement in people's countenances. He said it was a sullen silence. He agreed [that] all the best men in the kingdom were voting in Parliam^{t} for a measure they disapproved of. But one of the Cabinet was in it—that was Lord Dartmouth. He did not know but Ld Weymouth might think less unfavourably than Ld President, Ld Chancellor, Ld Suffolk, and Lord Sandwich, who were utterly against it. I asked if the King did not countenance it? He thought the K. would never thwart his Minister, and would rather, when dissatisfied, change him. I was yesterday at Ld Huntingdon's. He says the K. is for it: he does not like the dismembering his Empire, but he wants to be quiet, and to enjoy his small circle of happiness in Buckingham House.

It is certainly a cricis.

Some great turn in affairs seems approaching.

Mr Perry from Boston, by way of Halifax, and Mr Messerous [?] from New York, called on me. The former left Boston Jan. 3^{d}. No such want of provisions as has been reported. Cloathing and many other articles extreme scarce. The paper money makes great confusion in all dealing.

21st.—At Mr Jenkinson's, who is very silent, cold, and reserved: asked a question or two: he answered he had no hand in what was doing. It not being one of the *mollia tempora,* I withdrew. Everybody where I go is out of temper. What can be more unpleasant than to be obliged to vote for what they utterly disapprove?

22nd.—At Marybone Chapel with Judge Oliver, &c. Afterwards at Court. Lord Talbot said a great deal upon the plan: thought we had better withdraw all our troops, and make a naval war: said he did not know how to join the Opposition.

In the evening at Dr Heberden's. Not one word of government matters.

23rd.—I obtained, after long solicitation, £300 for two years' salary for Mr Putnam, Att^{y} Gen. of Mass^{s} Bay, by an order on the Bank, paying Mr Rowe 7. 10/ for his fees.

Whilst there is so much fault found with the Minister's plan, I keep more at home than usual, to be out of the way of giving offence. I am sure I can do no good by finding fault with it.

24th.—At Mr Ellis's. He says the House sat till one, upon motions for amending the Bills: one—that the Massachusetts Charter Bill should be suspended, and he says Mr Wedderburn was for a total repeal, and that he is to bring in a Bill to-morrow, but Mr Ellis disapproves, and so he does of the whole measure, and yet says he is forced to go with the torrent. I told him—If the torrent was left to its natural course, it would run the other way. He did not know but it might. I said—At Lloyd's I heard everybody declared against the proceedings. "Why," says he, "don't they pour in their petitions?" I told him it would not do for me to concern myself. "No," says he, "by no means. Keep as much out of sight as you can: there is scarce a day but somebody or other has a fling at you in the House. Don't offend the Ministry who are friendly to you; but your friend Mauduit might do a great deal."

Afterwards at Lord Hardwicke's, where I saw Soame Jenyns. They are for the Bills, though they say they are as ill-timed as is possible.

I was at Paxton's lodgings. Lord Percy was there just before. He says there is great confusion. He won't go to the H. of Lords till the affair is over. He does not like Lord Carlisle's being at the head of the Commission.

25th.—Went into the city, and called upon Mr Strahan, who says all is given up: after that upon Blackburn and Mauduit.

26th.—At Lord Huntingdon's. Americans dined with me:—Lt Gov. Oliver, Sr Wm Pepperell, Flucker, Waldo, Hatch, Paxton, Hallowell, Vassall, with Mr John Lane.

27th.—Dined at Lord Townshend's: only Paxton, and L^d^ and Lady T., daughter, and governess. Countess Dowager of Egmont, a most agreeable Lady, in the evening. Ld T. says there is a breach with the Chancellor, and that he is going out. He talks like a man in a frenzy about the proposed measures: told his Secry. to bring him the names of two people that wanted some little provision: Lord North would be out, and he could expect nothing from Lord Rockingham, &c.

Adm. Gambier called on me. He came from Mr Robinson's, Secry. to the Treasury. He says Robinson said enough to convince him Lord N. wishes he had not gone so far as he has, &c.—Publick fast.

March 1st.—At the Old Jowry with my children as usual. At home the rest of the day and evening.

2nd.—Called on Sir James Wright, and left my name. A letter from Mr Walter, New York, Jan. 5. News to Feb. 2^d^. It's now agreed Clinton will stay and take the command of the army, and Sir Wm Howe return.

Affairs go on yet in the H. of Commons. The measure is that of the minority, to whom the Minister gives way: the majority do not like the measure, but they follow the Minister. Montesquieu says, the English Constitution will perish when the legislative part shall become more corrupt than the executive. I have found it difficult to conceive what he intended, seeing the executive must be the corruptors, who must be as corrupt as the corrupted. I don't know whether the present state of things may not be nearly his idea.

3rd.—Called on Mr Preston, Charles Street. In the city to Devonshire Square, and back a-foot. I think there will be an acquiescence in measures more than I expected. Ld Percy said to Paxton—Ld North will not be Minister a month hence; but I believe he does not guess right, for it is—a guess.

4th.—Called on my friend M^r^——. He is generally reserved, but opened himself to-day. He would have died before he would have taken the part Lord —— has done. He is sure that if he had been in his place, and the K. had proposed such a measure to him, he should have given up all his places rather than have complied with it. So strange a measure is not to be paralleled in history. He had spoke to the Sollicitor General to shew him the repealing the Boston Charter Bill could answer no end now. If reserved to the Commissioners, it might be one of the terms conceded to induce them to submit. The Sollicitor answered—"Let them have it if they will." In short, he despaired of the Commonwealth.

What an astonishing state of affairs is this! The first men condemn measures as most absurd and fatal. They do not vote for them, but have not resolution to vote against them.

Everything which is a contradiction is now carried by the Opposition. The measure is theirs—they vote for it—three fourths of the House don't like it—but when the Speaker says—"The Ayes have it," nobody will say—"The Noes have it," because they will not divide against it. Things being thus carried without dividing in Parliament, the people seem at present to be easy. . .

5th.—The Bills passed the Lords—arguments from necessity—humiliating, but no help for it—no division upon the question. Mr Knox called upon me. He says all will end in some sort of known established government over America. I tell him all is conjecture: there's no saying what is the probable consequence next week, or more than next year; people everywhere being struck out of their senses, and when, and to what degree they will recover, is uncertain.

6th.—At Lord Hillsborough's, where were Mr Ellis and B. Gascoigne. All agreed in sentiment—all condemned the proceedings in Parliament—and all declined opposing them.

Left my name at Lord Temple's.

Advertisement published in the Publick Leger of this day, charges Gov. H. with bringing a nurse and maid from America, and then deserting them: that the maid run mad: had been in Bedlam: and had recovered; but was an object of charity, and subscriptions were proposed for her at St. James's Coffee-House, &c. Signed [blank] Williams, Attorney. In every part, as to me, an infamous lie, and is occasioned by my son's bringing a maid who proved a common prostitute and thief, and behaved so badly that he turned her off, and had provided a passage for her to Halifax as she proposed, but afterwards refused to go, and went into service, and stole from her master, and he turned her off, and she either run mad or counterfeited madness, and was sent to Bedlam.

7th.—Upon inquiry into the publication of yesterday, it seems to be a trick of an Attorney to draw money from the public. My sons saw him and he promises to unsay in the next newspaper what he has said yesterday and to-day. . .

9th.—This morning at Lord Temple's by appointment. He laments the state of the nation—is at a loss whether it is owing to the weak ministry, or to the Opposition. I thought the principles of the Opposition gave them more encouragement. He asked my age, and mentioned his own: find they are very near alike. He was born on 7th October, and I the 20 September, the same year.*

10th.—In the city at Palmer's. At Mr Jackson's: had much conversation on his errand to America. Lord Carlisle, Mr Jackson, and Mr Eden, of the Board of Trade, being the men. Mr Jackson says there must be peace, at all events—the war cannot go on. Eden has always been in Lord Suffolk's office, and perhaps is not so thorough an American. Lord Carlisle is a young man; was a good scholar at Eaton [*sic*] or Westminster; has spoke once in the H. of Lords; has involved a great estate in a great debt by dissipation. The choice is found fault with. Jackson thought Lord North should have pitched upon one or more of the Opposition to be more agreeable to the Americans.

11th.—A raw cold day. I kept at home and amused myself with correcting my History, &c.

12th.—At Mr Ellis's: more open than ever: speaks of confusion in government: the most preposterous motion that ever was: to lay a tax of 1/4 on all salaries, pensions, &c., above 200£ a year, carried in the Committee, and recovered in the House by 147 against 141, which was all the majority Lord N. could make by summoning from all quarters:—Min[isters] run about the House as if they did not know which side to go. He added—"There's no going back—it must be pushed through."

At Lt Gov. Oliver's.

13th.—Called on Mr Jackson again. Carried him extract of a letter from Mr Wethered of N. York to Dr Chandler, wch mentions a disposition in the Congress and people to treat, which I found to be pleasing to Jackson, who said—"It's well, if one half of it is true." I mentioned no names.

* In Vol. i. p. 41, the extracts from his mother's Memorandum book give particulars. He was born Sep. 9, 1711, and his wet-nurse was hired, or at all events came, on the day following. The change of style explains the seeming contradiction.

Dined at Mr Ellis's. General Paoli,* and Judge Oliver. Not a word of English politicks. Routs, Concerts, Operas, &c., in which I took no part.

14th.—Lt Gov. Oliver called. I shewed him a private letter from Lord Hillsborough in 1770, in which he says he is extremely glad that I have departed from those apprehensions which induced me to decline accepting the government; and he assured me he had never heard I had declined it, and seemed surprized: asked the reasons? I gave them,—the prospect of increasing difficulties, and a desire to apply myself to the most agreeable office I ever sustained—that of Chief Justice, in which I thought I had done good, and had been very little abused for it. He complimented me by saying nobody ever gave more general satisfaction; said it was impossible, after being thus drawn into the government, I should ever be left to suffer.

Judge Oliver's family, E. and wife, Browne, Dr Chandler, Boucher, and Addams [?] dined with me. Politicks enough! It was thought Boucher would go chaplain to the Ambassadors, says it has been objected, that he has been active in opposing the American measures, and no such persons are to have any part in this Embassy.

Gov. Wentworth arrived last night from Philadelphia—24 days passage: The report [is] that the country is open 30 miles round: many deserters from Howe's army: ice in the river Delaware: nothing very important.

15th.—At Dr Kippis's. . .

16th.—The papers to-day announce a French war, and say the F. Ambassador has acquainted Lord Weymouth the F. King had entered into a Treaty with the Colonies as Independ^t

* General Pascal Paoli, was the son of Hyacinth Paoli, one of the chief Magistrates of Corsica. Pascal distinguished himself in the cause of Corsican freedom, when the Genoese and the French were threatening her independence, but the French were too strong for him and his army. When all was lost he fled to England, where he lived and died. What can a small and weak state do against a large and a strong one? It may be a serious question,—which is the best course for a true Patriot to take for the greatest good to his country?—To fight and be conquered, and succumb to an exasperated enemy; or meet him half way in peace, submit to the inevitable, and make the best terms possible?

States. It is said Lord Stormont has given the same intelligence. Mr Morris, of the Customs called, and says Adm^l Hill informed him Ld Sandwich had ordered all the Captains in the navy to their ships immediately.

17th.—Everybody is struck dumb!

The declarations from France, that they have entered into a Treaty with the Colonies as Independent States, seems to make a war inevitable. I met Genl Monkton. He is in pain for Howe's fleet in the Delaware: thinks the French force gone out may be too strong for them. The message from the King is to be comunicated to-day. An address must follow—whether for an immediate declaration of war doubtful.

The sudden agreement of France seems to be the effect of the new measures here. Franklin's act * probably carried him to require an immediate answer; otherwise the Colonies would close wth England; but this is conjecture.

18th.—In the city to Blackburne's, Bush Lane. He says the subscribers to the new loan complain of Lord N. If he saw a French war was so near, he ought to have let them know it: if he did not know it himself, he was not fit for a Minister, &c.

An Address voted yesterday, but nobody knows yet what are the determinations of Government. America seems to be lost.

Paxton, and young Hatch, Jo. Burch, and Mr Hare dined with me.

19th.—Called on Mr Ellis. Laments the universal despondency: should not wonder if this afternoon the Americans were acknowledged Independent—a term they always avoided as a Religious distinction, but will always boast of as a Civil character. After all, I shall never see that there were just grounds for this revolt. I see that the ways of Providence are mysterious, but I abhor the least thought that all is not perfectly right, and ordered by infinite rectitude and wisdom.

20th.—The H. of Commons sat last night till 4 o'clock debating whether the Ministry had ill planned the measures of last year; and after all, it went off without a division. I

* The word is of doubtful reading. It may be 'act' or it may be 'art.'

met Mr D'Oyly: he says he did not get home till 5 this morning. Everything stands still. The season will be lost. Never was a Government in such a state.—Gov. Wentworth called.

22nd.—At Dr Kippis's.

At Court. Small Drawing-room. King advised to walk much, &c.

Browne and son, and Dr Chandler, dined with me. In the evening at Dr Heberden's—Dean of Glocester, Bp. of Chester, and Exeter, Mr Pelham, *cum multis aliis.*

Mauduit declares for Independence of America, and wishes Parliament to acknowledge it. Never was such an instantaneous conversion of a whole kingdom. There is the strangest cessation of measures that ever was known: nobody knows what is to take place next. Lord Chancellor told me the Comission for the American Commissioners had not yet come to him. He added—"I suppose that will be one of the last things."

23rd.—[Speculations upon the same subjects.]

24th.—Everything still indecisive. The debates yesterday in the H. of Lords shew more than ever a disposition to concede to the revolt of the Colonies, the minority gaining ground. A change of Ministry in whole or in part looks probable. Some say Lord Chatham will come in, while others say his infirmities from age will not admit of it.

To my surprize Dr Robertson of Edinburgh came in about noon.* I had corresponded with him in America, but never saw him before. An hour's converse was very pleasing. He has laid aside his History of the English Colonies. He gave this reason—that there was no knowing what would be the future condition of them. I told him I thought, be it what it may, it need make no odds in writing the History of what is past, and I thought a true state of them ought to be handed down to posterity.

* Dr. William Robertson was born in 1721, and educated at Edinburgh University. He was the author of a History of Charles V., a History of Scotland, a History of America, which, as indicated in the text, was never finished, and some other works. He was made Principal of the University of Edinburgh, Historiographer to the King in Scotland, and Minister of the Old Gray Friars. He died much esteemed in June, 1793.

He said, upon Dr Franklin's recommendation, he had procured Diplomas for several of the New England Clergy, who he had reason to believe became active in promoting the revolt, and mentioned Channing; and upon my naming Cooper, remembered him also,—and Winthrop, tho' not of the Clergy.

He gave me an anecdote, which he had from David Hume. When Dr Franklin had been at the Board of Trade, upon his first coming to England 20 years ago, Hume said to Mr Oswald, then one of the Lords of Trade, that there had been with them a friend of Hume's, an American, the greatest literary character he had ever known from that part of the world. Oswald said he could not tell what his literary character was, but he was much deceived if he had not enough of the spirit of Faction in him to put a whole Empire into confusion.

25th.—At Lord Huntingdon's. He says there certainly has been a Message from the King to Ld Chatham. What the answer was is not certain. Some say that he was willing to come in, and take the guidance if only two or three of his friends might be with him: others, that he declined unless there was a new Ministry. The first, Ld H. thinks most probable, and he believes Ld Shelburne expects the Seals in Ld George's place, who is to be made a Peer; and he supposes Barré will be Secretary at War, Lord Barrington for some time wishing to resign. A strange world in which we live. It's certain the political clock stands still.

Sir Eardley Wilmot called, and spent half an hour in a pleasing conversation. I mentioned Dr Robertson's anecdote of Hume and Oswald. He observed that it struck him, because he knew Oswald well, and that he had the greatest talent of discerning men, of any person he ever met with.

Account by the French mail of stopping all English vessels in the French ports, except smugglers.

26th—Into the city and back before 12 o'clock, a-foot.

At Lord North's Levée with Sir F. Bernard. But few people there. I never saw him appear more oppressed with business. Had an opportunity of speaking to Mr Robinson, and procuring an order for my brother's salary from Jan.

1776, but am further solliciting that it may commence July preceding.*

Sir F. Bernard has seen Mr Jackson: he sees no prospect of advantage in going Commissioner: doubts whether he shall go. Lord Carlisle, at Lord North's Levée, appeared to be much engaged. In the city Mr Rashleigh told me people were much disturbed—English ships stopped in the ports of France—Spain also, declared to support a trade with America as Independent States. All tending to confusion. Called on Dr Robertson.

27th.—At Sir H. Houghton's, but did not see him. Lt Gov. Oliver's, Dr Robertson's lodgings, who was just come from Court. Lord Stormont kissed the King's hands on his return from Paris. Uncertainty still remains. Everything stands still. Dr Robertson says some great genius must rise and save the nation.

Mauduit brought me in the evening a printed sheet of his own composing, in favour of declaring the Colonies independent. He appears to me to be employed by Ministry.† It is difficult to say how the people will receive it. If he has done the thing against his own judgment, it is something very different from his general character. Gen. Harvey, who has always taken kind notice of me, died to-day.

28th.—Calling upon Mr Ellis this morning, he assures me there is no truth in any of the reports of Lord Chatham, Shelburne, or Camden's coming in; and he does not believe any hint has been given to any of them. I shewed him the sheet Mauduit gave me. He does not believe Lord North knows anything of it: does not seem to have a high opinion of M.'s judgment: believes him to be an honest man.

Sir F. B. and son, Greene, Thomas, and Sewall dined with me, and Jud. Oliver.

29th.—At Paddington church . . . Mr Boucher says Mr

* Foster Hutchinson, the Governor's younger, and only brother, removed to Halifax, Nova Scotia, on the evacuation of Boston, where the English government did what they could to help a faithful servant.

† Could Mauduit have been employed by the Ministry to do the very thing they were trying to prevent? This is a strange idea, though there may have been something in the background, better known to him than to us.

Eden seemed to think last week the Commission was at an end, but for two days past it has been settled that it is to go on with all speed; and he thinks the Commissioners will go out with all speed. He said there had been a demur about Lord Carlisle: he certainly discovers more fondness for the employment than the other two.

31st.—Still silent. Motions in each house of Parliament by [the] Opposition upon particular parts of the conduct of Administration, which take up all the time of Parliament. Everybody discontented—the general language. This cannot last. Mauduit in the evening; his spirits gone—reserved—seems to be for giving all up, and yet hardly thinks it right.

April 1st.—Went over to my dreadful lodgings at Little Chelsea. Strange it should be so, and yet I felt an inclination to see the place where I went through such a scene of distress; —where I saw and heard the last of my dear child . . .

3rd.— . . . The three Comiss^rs^ kissed the King's hand—Lord Carlisle, Mr Eden, and Gov. Johnstone, in the room of Mr Jackson. . .

4th.—Called upon Mr Cornwall who, I saw by his countenance, to be engaged, and had only two or three words. I said I had no concern for myself, but I had no prospect for my children. He bid me not be concerned: government would never let them suffer. America, he said, was lost. Unnecessarily, I thought, given up. Most shamefully, he added. Gov. Johnstone he seemed surprized at: asked what Mr Ellis said?

At Sir James Wright's: shewed him Mauduit's sheet. He had not seen it, but had heard that language for ten days past, and he had no doubt it was thrown out with the knowledge of government.

Mr Fitch, Clarke, Johannot, and Dr Perkins dined with me.

7th.—Walked into the city to Lime Street, Mauduit's Counting House. I can't tell what to make of him, but rather believe he has been persuaded by Ministry to publish the sheet for Independence of the Colonies.* It is now the current talk that the motion will be made this week. Fresh talk to-

* No copy of this sheet has been found amongst the Governor's papers.

day of a treaty on foot between the Howes and Congress in America. Everybody now wishes it may be true, as there is no degree of spirit left in Administration.

8th.—In the House of Lords last evening the D. of Richmond moved for an Address to withdraw the force from America. The motion, Ld Loudoun says, made a small book, as it contained all the reasons wch had been assigned for removing Ministry, &c. This was answered by Lord Weymouth, and then Ld Chatham declared against American Independence, in a speech of about $\frac{1}{4}$ of an hour. The D. of Richmond replied, chiefly to Ld Chatham, and reflected upon him with some severity. As Ld Chatham was rising again, he made some difficulty,—pulled up his breeches, and sunk down in his place, and fell back with his mouth open, and insensible. Ld Shelburne, and Ld Mahon, who was behind the throne, ran to him, and Ld Dunmore assisting, thus carried him out of the House. He soon had his Physicians, and came to himself, but is not well enough to be sent home this morning. This accident broke off the debate, which is to come on again to-day.

We have arrived at a cricis. Well indeed, might he exclaim—"What an astonishing state of things is this!" and—"Never was Government in such a state!" Mr. D'Oyly raved, and declared that the country was ruined; whilst Lord Townshend talked "like a man in a frenzy." The perplexity of Administration, and the alarm among all orders of men, seem to have shewn themselves immediately after hearing of General Burgoyne's disaster at Saratoga. At last the Governor writes—"America seems to be lost." The two Bills introduced at this time by Lord North are denounced by Franklin. In a letter from Passy of February the 26th 1778 to David Hartley, M.P., he says—"I received yours of the 18th and 19th of this month, with Lord North's proposed Bills," and then he tears them to threads. But matters have suddenly culminated in a startling event, and the Earl of Chatham has hastened his death by declaiming against the prospect of American Independence, which he had done so much all his life to encourage, but now, when he sees it has come to the point, he characterises as a dismemberment of the Empire. So long ago as January the 14th 1766 he declared that Parliament had no right to tax the Colonies, to which Mr. Grenville replied—"That this Kingdom has the sovereign, the supreme legislative power over America is granted —it cannot be denied; and taxation is a part of that sovereign power. It is one branch of legislation." But it was required that this branch should be lopped off, and the Constitution mutilated. And he would not believe that the Americans, in the midst of all their excesses, contemplated Independency, or a separation from the parent state, although for a series of years it had been notorious that their aspirations had tended in that direction. In the debate on the 1st of February 1775, [Adolph. ii. 186.] the subject was alluded to, when he exclaimed—"But were he once persuaded that they entertained the most distant intention of rejecting the legislative supremacy, and the general, constitutional, superintending authority and control of the British legislature, he would be the first and most zealous mover for exerting the whole force of Britain in securing and enforcing that power." And in November of the same year the Duke of Richmond, with Lords Shelburne and Camden, denied that there existed any intention of the sort. "The assertion that America aspired at independence, was treated as an unfounded calumny, calculated only for purposes of delusion." [ib. ii. 280.] With these views, and in order to quiet the country, they frequently urged the advisability of withdrawing the fleet and the troops from the Colonies. To have done this would have been something like removing the Police from London, in order to promote the peace and the security of the inhabitants. In their case it would have been tantamount to relinquishing America quietly to the Americans. Hence the Governor wrote, on the 6th of December 1777—"The Opposition themselves are confounded when they come to the consequence of their own motion for a cessation of arms." No doubt, if their motion had been carried, they would have been very much perplexed to know how to carry it out.

What could be more encouraging to the Sons of Liberty across the Atlantic, than to hear such words uttered as the following, in the House of Lords?—"Resistance to your acts was necessary, as it was just," by Lord Chatham, on the 20th of January 1775; or another assertion, which has been quoted in amazement before, as spoken by the Duke of Richmond, and seconded by Lord Camden —"I think the Americans have good right to resist. I hope they will resist; and that they will succeed." Succeed in what? In dismembering the Empire? This was something like exclaiming —"Fight on boys—we'll back you up!" How is it that they escaped impeachment, as traitors to their country?

But to put the most tender construction upon these utterances, to say the least of them, they were highly indiscreet and injudicious, because anything spoken in the House of Lords would have great effect out of doors; and it was well known that Mr. De Berdt, or Dr. Franklin, or *Junius Americanus* Lee, or Mr. Quincy, or twenty other Americans, who were at different times in London, were eagerly on the look out for any favourable remark so spoken, which was immediately hurried off to the Congress, or to other leaders of Burke's "extreme of Liberty," there to be made use of by Samuel Adams's "Independent we are, and independent we will be!"

But what says the discursive, versatile, and industrious chronicler Walpole, on the momentous signs of the times, in the atmosphere and aroma of which he lived? On the 1st of September 1777 he wrote,—"In one thing alone all that come from America agree, that the alienation from this country is incredible and universal." And on the 20th of February 1778 he writes,—"All that remains certain is, that America is not only lost, but given up."

He does not omit to notice the catastrophe in the House, and he notes down as follows, on the 8th of April,—"Though my fellow labourers of this morning will give you a minute account of the great event of yesterday, I should be a very negligent gazetteer if I took no notice of it. Lord Chatham fell in the Senate—not by daggers, nor by the thunder of Lord Suffolk's eloquence. He had spoken with every symptom of debility, repeated his own phrases, could not recollect his own ideas, and, which is no new practice, persisting in our asserting sovereignty over America, *though he could not tell by what means.* It was only new, to confess his ignorance. The Duke of Richmond answered him with much decency and temper, though Lord Chatham had called *pursuit without means* timid and pusillanimous conduct. The Earl was rising to reply, but fell down in a second fit of apoplexy, with strong convulsions and slabbering at the mouth."

As soon as he could be removed he was conveyed to his villa at Hayes in Kent, where he died on the 11th of May following, being in the 70th year of his age.

Copley's well known picture in the National Gallery represents him leaning back in a moribund state,—pale, and with closed eyes, the Duke of Cumberland, in a light blue coat with breeches and stockings, balanced in colour by the Earl's crimson robes, holds his left arm—a little awkwardly; Lord Viscount Mahon, on one knee, in dark blue, supports his feet and legs; whilst the Hon. James Pitt, in black, and his relative in dull green, stand close on the further side of the dying nobleman.

9th.—Last night in the H. of Lords, the D. of Richmond's motion was rejected by 50 only, against 33,—the largest minority at any time, tho' the greatest question in favour of Americans, and tho' L[d] Shelburne had left the minority upon this question. This question was in a Committee, where no Proxies are received.

Dined at D[r] Heberden's: M[r] Harris of Salisbury, Soame Jenyns and wife, Daniel Wray and wife, and Mauduit.

At L[d] North's Levée, and a little while at Court.

13th.—At Lord Hillsborough's, who kept me above an hour, giving me the history of his whole political life. Called upon Chandler. He read to me the heads of what he drew up for Governor Johnstone, one of the Commissioners. They left town in order to embark on board the *Trident* at Portsmouth. Mauduit says it's pity they dont go in three different ships, for they will quarrel before they get to America. In my passage from England to America, [in 1741,] I could not help observing how much a company shut up 6 or 8 weeks in a cabin is disposed to form little parties—to take sides, and to grow tired, and to be alienated one from another.*

14th.—It seems to be an opinion gaining ground, that Howe will not come home, notwithstanding his leave. Some think he will strike a bold stroke to retrieve his credit; others, that he will come to an accommodation; all—a sudden start. In the Commission Lord Howe and Sir William Howe are named, and not the Commanders-in-chief for the time being. Lord Cornwallis is gone with the Comiss[rs]. This, it is supposed, is to

* Always the case! I went out for a frolic, and started on the first of January in a fine sailing ship of something under a thousand tons, not pressed for time, having had a friend go out in the same ship the year before. We were seven weeks beating against westerly gales, and could scarcely get up New York harbour for ice. I observed the same cliques and parties and back-biting and tittle-tattling, and I was told that in every voyage there was always one disagreeable passenger who made mischief. The return voyage, made the year after, was accomplished in eighteen days, by favour of the same westerly wind. I remarked on this difference to one of the sailors one day. He said—"I understand, sir, that it is up hill going to America, but down hill coming home." He said it gravely, but whether he believed it or whether he was at his fun, I cannot say. I prefer a sailing ship. There is a something delightful in the art and the science of trimming, and steering, and managing, a fine ship under canvas. The rapid passages of the present day give no time for the evils mentioned above.

prevent the command falling to Kniphausen, in case of Howe and Clinton both being absent.

Dined at Col° Vassall's, Berners Street.

15th.—Advice yesterday, confirmed to-day, of a frigate at Bourdeaux from Boston, with John Adams on board, which it is said has taken a ship bound to N. York with 30,000£ on board. Adams, it is supposed relieves Deane.

18th.—A letter to Dr Chandler, Philad. 10 Feb.. says a vote of the Congress had been printed, in which they decline ratifying the Convention of Saratoga, until it should be ratified by the Court of Great Britain. J. Clarke also, went from Boston to Philad., writes Mauduit 24 Feb., that he wishes there was a prospect of Burgoyne's men leaving Boston. No letters yet from Howe.

20th.— . . . Sir H. Houghton called. He wonders at Mauduit's publication—was at Mr Jenkinson's when the thing was talked of. I did not think Jenkinson would have run to that extreme. Sir H. H. says he told Mauduit that he wondered at his handing about such a paper: and told him though Gorr H. might have done such a thing with better grace, yet he should have thought it officious in him to have dictated such a measure.

Paul Wentworth called.

23rd.—Advice that the Commissioners in the *Trident* sailed for America from Portsmouth the 21st about 12 o'clock. The wind has been fair ever since. Mauduit says the main-stay of the *Trident* was discovered to be cut almost through—no doubt with a bad intent.

24th.—Wind still to the northward, but there seems to be no expectations whether the Commissioners arrive sooner or later. I met Bridgen indeed, who says, the Americans have been so cheated by the French, as to be sick of their alliance.

26th.—At the Queen's Drawing-Room. It was said that appearing at such a time would be deemed more respectful,* but it was a thin Court. Dukes of Chandos, Montagu, and Gordon; Lords Abercorn, and Pelham, and Lord G. Germain, Lord Harrowby, and some Bishops: the Duke of Buccleugh also, and Duke of Beaufort, who I had never seen before:

* The King being absent. He was at Chatham.

Lord Loudoun, and Ladies plenty—among them old Lady Say and Sele, said to [be] four score and four, with a high head like a young girl: never was a more rediculous figure . . . Lord Delaware arrived to-day from Philadelphia: supposed to come from Corke in a ship of the last fleet.

27th.— . . . Judge Oliver and Jenny Clarke [his niece] set out to-day for Birmingham. He talks of fixing in the country near that town, never to come to London again. He has left his son's family of wife and three children here in town: promises to contribute 100£ a year to their support. I told my daughter [Sarah] I would allow the like sum so long as I am enabled by Gov^t to do it, and make the first quarterly payment the beginning of June.

29th.—Account received yesterday of the sailing of 12 sail of French ships of the line from Toulon, under the Count D'Estaigne, alarms all Americans: and everybody is amazed that 40 sail of like ships are lying at Spithead. The King returned in two or three days from Chatham, but it is said is going with the Queen to Portsmouth.

May 2nd.— . . . Dined at the Arch-Bp.'s at Lambeth . . .

3rd.—At the Old Jewry with my daughter. Mr Brinley and Johannot dined with me . . .

5th.— . . . Called on Mauduit at his Compting-house in Lime Street. Never saw him in such distress: opened himself with freedom: professed that when H. arrives he shall be prosecuted for the Pamphlet he has published: has heard nothing suggested. I told him his nerves were affected: every mole-hill was a mountain: mentioned to him my lying awake whole nights in America, fearing I should be called to account in England for neglect of duty to the King at the time of the Confederacies—at least, I concluded I should suffer much in my character for yielding to the demands of the people when my sons were in danger. He seemed relieved. The Bishop of Exeter asked me at Lambeth what ailed Mauduit? I had no suspicion this was his trouble.

It is said an Ambassador is coming over from Spain, where the Treaty of France is utterly disapproved, and that he is to come through France, and to mediate.

7th.—Strong south wind still. A vessel yesterday from N. York, Mar. 24. Gov. Cleveland arrived: was told of the repeal of the Acts: said they had better have sent 10 thousand men. Many French and other prizes taken. Several frigates and transports said to be lost in the Sound between N. York and Rhode Island.

Account of Massachusetts Resolves:—That no Mandamus Counsellor, &c., should be at liberty to return: but if he should, [he] shall be sent out of the Province: and returning a second time, shall be put to death.

8th.— . . . Mauduit left alone, was in the horrors about his book. Dr Apthorpe said he had read Mr Mauduit's book with great pleasure. "My book?" [Mauduit loquitur] "I don't own it: I beg you would say I disown it: how cruel is it——" &c.

I—when the company was gone—told him he would put people upon making criminal what was not so, if he discovered such concern. "Oh! I did not know—would give 1000£ he had had nothing to do with it. What, if he should be called upon—must accept a challenge, or may be, be sued in large damages." It is the strangest conduct I ever saw in him. He attacked Mr Pitt with ten times the acrimony. Nobody besides himself sees anything exceptionable.—Wind still S.W.

9th.—The K. and Q. returned to-day from Portsmouth.

Wind still unfavourable.

Mr Mather came to town from Hillersdon, (?) where he lives, and dined with us. Mauduit in the evening, in a strange disturbed state of mind. I did what I could to quiet him, and endeavoured to dissuade him from a measure very prejudicial to him, and which, if he was less disturbed, he would not have thought lawful.

10th.—At Bow church, Dr Apthorpe's new living, where he officiated. This is the gift of the A.-Bp. for a book which he has published in answer to Gibbon's attack upon the religion of Jesus.

I wrote to Mauduit. He called in the evening and thanked me. Wind still contrary.

13th.—The House of Commons yesterday voted to be at the expense of Lord Chatham's funeral, who died on Monday last, (the 11th,) and of a Monument in Westminster Abbey.

It seems now agreed that the French fleet went through the Strait's mouth for America without stopping at Cadiz.—Wind still S. west, and strong.

14th.—Gen[l] Burgoyne arrived last night, leaving his army behind. News of M[r] Boutineau's death at Bristol, of the gout in his stomach.* General Burgoyne forbid going to Court. A Board of Enquiry appointed. It is said he is come home upon his parole.

M—— called in the evening. My letter on Sunday stopped him from doing what would have hurt him exceedingly. He said to me again, it was a good letter. I assured him if any man had offered me 500£ to suffer him to have done what he proposed, I would not have taken it.

16th.—At Lord Huntingdon's, who was more free than ever in speaking of the ——, which, considering my obligations, I wondered at. He was 14 years in office, until he voted contrary to the King's mind in Wilkes' affair, and was dismissed from being Master of the Horse, which he called 3000 a year.

Greene, Timmins, Quincy, and Scott dined with me.

At Lloyd's. There is an account of the *Ariadne's* taking the *Randolph* frigate of 36 guns, after 5 hours engagement; and Cap. Pringle of the *Ariadne* killed. And that a 64 gun ship had sunk two other frigates—one of 32, the other 20 odd guns.

17th.—At D[r] Kippis's.

At Court. The King said little, except about the weather. The Queen, supposing I had a place in the country, asked where? I told her I had none of my own, but sometimes I visited my friends. I had been at M[r] Ellis's. "He is a very good man," she said. .

23rd.—An hour or near it at Lord Hillsborough's, where I had a fuller account of the present unsettled state of affairs than I have heard from any other person. Whether he will come into office or not is doubtful. He does not seem to be altogether without expectations. . .

Lord H. said that Thurlow, all agreed, would be Lord

* Mr. James Boutineau, Attorney-at-law, Mandamus Counsellor, banished, proscribed, and his estates confiscated. He withdrew to England, where he died.

Chancellor, and a Peer. Wedderburne was intended for Att^y General, but he would not touch it, and insisted to be a Peer, and rather submitted to take the place of Ch. Justice of the Common Pleas, and he had the promise of them, without considering that De Grey could not be turned out. When he was talked with, he discovered no inclination; was infirm, but could attend: besides, every day a place was expected to fall, worth 7000£, wch he intended for his son. Whenever he quitted he should expect a Peerage, and a pension equivalent to his salary. Well, it must be done, and all was promised him. Sir Fletcher Norton, hearing this, attacks Lord North: charges him with the indignity offered him in giving a Scotchman, who did not know an ounce of law, the preference to an old servant who took the Chair upon being pressed to it, upon the strongest assurances of being first provided for. He insisted upon his Peerage, and would wait for De Grey's place. He had the place of Ch. Justice in Eyre with 3000£ for life, which he was willing to throw up when Ch. Justice. Lord N. said it was gone too far to be altered. Sir F. threatened an Impeachment for a waste of public money; that he would throw his Speaker's robes over the Chair; take his seat, and be the first to move for an Impeachment. Thus the matter now stands. Lord H. says Wedderburne will carry it. Sir F. possibly may be satisfied by another large provision out of the general store. . .

27th.—Called this morning on Mr Cornwall: promises to bring on my brother's petition lying at the Treasury: speaks lightly of Burgoyne's speech in the H. of Commons yesterday, and condemns his saying the men who had deserted from him after the capitulation, had done it wth a view to get to Clinton or Howe. This may be made use of to bad purposes.*

Strange confusion in the House, upon high words between

* General Burgoyne was allowed to go to England on his parole. Lieutenant Anburey, ii. 20, thus writes:—"In the beginning of this letter I mentioned that General Burgoyne is sailed for England. No doubt, on his arrival, his enemies will be attacking him in all quarters. Do not be led away with the general voice, and follow a misled faction: the General, in every situation of danger and difficulty, ever had the confidence of the army," &c.; and the writer goes on and devotes a whole page in hearty praises of the General, as a good officer and a thorough gentleman.

Lord George and Temple Lutterell, and all order seems to be lost there. . .

29th.—Dined in the city with Mauduit. Nobody but Mr Parry, a Prebend[ary] of Worcester. He says Mrs Ann Pitt, eldest sister of Lord Chatham, has wrote to Mr Daines Barrington from Florence, that being at the Opera, the Grand Dutchess spoke to her, and said that, as she was an English woman, she would be pleased to know that the G. Dutchs father, the King of Spain, had wrote to her [that] he utterly disapproved of the Independency of America.*

30th.—At Lord Huntingdon's, where I met with Mr Vane, who told me he was descended from Sir Henry Vane, once Governor of N. England. Just as I was going out Colo Barré came in,—the first time I met him anywhere since I came to England. I said I had been unfortunate—having endeavoured —— He made a rather awkward apology—discovered no inclination to say much of our acquaintance in New England, where I had shewn him, when Lt Governor in 1759, more respect than he received from the Governor, which he then took notice of.

Here I first heard of [illegible]val of the *Andromeda* at N. York; that Clinton was to sail for Philadelphia the 25th of April; and that Howe had taken his passage in the *Grayhound* frigate; therefore may be every day expected.

Mr Ellis called. Speaking of Burg. [Burgoyne's] imprudence in saying the men had deserted with a view to join Clinton, he explained himself, that he would not be understood, that he approved of their deserting, but on the contrary, if he had known of it, he would have hindered it. This was the next day after his speech.

31st.—To Twickenham in coach with Mrs Ellis. Gen. Paoli and Mr Ellis went on horseback.

June 1st.—With Mrs Ellis to Richmond. She called on Genl Williamson's lady: I went to Lord Hardwicke's. I wrote to Col. Browne under Mr Ellis's Frank, at Cowbridge.

2nd.—Returned from Twickenham.

* Very sincere! It was well known that at this very time the King of Spain was intriguing with France to assist America against England.

Lady Bernard died last week, the 26th, at Aylesbury. Paxton was there on a visit. She had been in poor health several months, but took an airing the day before the night in which she died, or rather towards morning.

The letters from N. York lament the conciliatory measures, as they are called; fearing they will make the Americans more tenacious of their Independence: speak of a treaty as a matter uncertain, but rather believe they will not come into it.

3rd. — Parliament prorogued — which most people seem pleased at; no good being expected from its sitting. Lord Chancellor [ ] resigned the Seals; Mr Thurlow succeeds, and Wedderburne Attorney Gen.; Wallace, Sollicitor [General;] Lords Rochford, Suffolk, and Weymouth Garters.

An old parrot, which has been in the family 16 or 18 years, died.

4th.—At Court—the Birth Day.

5th.—Intelligence to-day that the Toulon fleet sailed the 16 of May thro' the Straits, and stood to the westward.

6th.—A vessel from New York. Lord Huntingdon met me and informed me Lord Rawdon's brother, who lost his leg, was arrived; and that Clinton left New York, which he did the 5 May, to take the command at Philadelphia. He added that Clinton had large orders—to remain at Philad.—to evacuate it —or take what steps he thought fit: that there were great rejoicings upon Clinton's having the command: that some liked, but more disliked the conciliatory Bills, &c.

8th.—I finished my brother's business at the Treasury: received 341·5/ his salary to 5th of April last, and lodged it with Gines & Atkinson, Bankers,* and at the same time lodged Mr Putnam's money there, being £365 12 6. . .

* Foster Hutchinson, a lawyer of eminence, removed to Halifax in Nova Scotia on the evacuation of Boston in March 1776. He married a dau. of Gen. Jean Paul Mascarene, and was the father of twelve children:—Margaret, d. young; Sarah, ob. cœl.; Elizabeth, ob. cœl.; Lydia, m. Slater, s. p.; Abigail, d. young; Joanna, ob. cœl.; Hannah, m. Snelling; Foster, ob. cœl.; Thomas, d. young; Grizel, ob. cœl.; Margaret, m. Sabatier; s. p.; Abigail, ob. cœl. Hannah and Mr. Snelling had Eliza, d. young; and William, who is said to have burnt all Foster Hutchinson's letters and papers. Said William married, and had William, ob. cœl.; Foster, ob. cœl.; Jonathan, and Frederick, d. young, and Eliza Snelling, who m. Mr. Stirling, and had William John, the last and sole representative.

9th.—The wind still continues contrary. A large French fleet sailed 3 or 4 weeks, and no ships followed. Everybody complains of the languor and inactivity in publick affairs. This detention is the hand of Heaven.

10th.—Paxton brought me to-day a letter from Lord Townshend's, wch was taken out of a prize, and carried into Glasgow. It is from a French officer in Washington's army, De Portail, a Brigadier General, dated Dec. 11th. Howe had not then taken Mud Island, but it was thought he would. The writer attributes the American success, not to their strength, but to the astonishing conduct of the British forces. He condemns the sending Burgoyne with such an army thro' a horrid wilderness, where the Americans could harrass and distress them, and could fight in the only way advantageous to them. He says [that] after the victory at Brandywine, and another I forget, little or no advantage was made for want of cavalry, but expresses astonishment *á la lenteur et la timidité* of the General. He says there are different opinions upon the final success of the Rebellion. He doubts it. If the English can keep 30,000 men in America, it must be subdued. If Washington's army had been destroyed last year, it would have finished the war. He says the Americans are in want of warlike stores, linens, woollens, and most of the comforts of life: they have been used to idleness, to drinking tea, rum, to smoaking, &c.: they will not hold out in war. It will not do to think of sending a French force to act in concert with them: they have a violent antipathy to the French: they would sooner go over to the British army than fight with the French. There was a proposal for a French force, aided by the Americans, to recover Quebec: he doubts whether any possessions on the Continent can be a benefit to France. If there should be war wth England, he thinks it better to take Jamaica, and those islands which cannot maintain independence. It appeared to him the best scheme [would be] to keep the English from sending troops to America. If they can be deprived of their Colonies, he supposes their trade must be in a great measure lost; their naval force ruined; and they will become of little consideration in Europe.

As a circumstance to prevent the Americans from succeeding,

he supposes that they cannot attain to a naval force under a long course of years: and if England should give them up, they never would unite, but quarrel one State with another, of which there are already some buds, (*germes.*)*

22nd.—A remarkably hot, sun-shiny American day. . . Much talk of Burgoyne's publication. Some say he has ruined himself by it. A report that he is ordered back to America. . .

At Lord Townshend's. It is said that when Burg[oyne] arrived, Charles F. asked him his plan?—To charge Howe with leaving him to be sacrificed. "If that's y^r plan we must forsake you: we are determined to support H." The next news—that Ministry is chargeable; and his speech in the H., and his new publication, are conformable to this account.

25th.—Began a journey in a post-chaise with Mr Paxton, and lodged at the Blue Posts Inn in Witham. I lodged there in September 1775, and left on the table when I washed, a ring with my wife's hair, which the Landlady had taken care of, and now returned to me.†

27th.—We sailed up one of the most pleasant rivers in the world from Harwich to Ipswich, about 12 miles, in a well accommodated passage boat, which goes every day at six pence a passenger. My servant carelessly left my wig in a box in the boat, which he did not discover until the evening.

30th.— . . . The post brings advice of the return of Keppel to Portsmouth, after taking two French frigates, and suffering the French merchant ships to sail through his fleet. There is a mystery in this conduct.

The French had for some time been playing a double game, and so had the Spaniards, despite the soft accents of the Grand Duchess at the Opera. Dr. Cormick writes—"The conduct of France and Spain had for some time been an object of just suspicion. In the midst of all their assurances of friendship for Great Britain,

* The above is probably a free translation of the Frenchman's letter. The States held together pretty well until the internal rebellion in Lincoln's time, at which stormy season they were spoken of in England as "The Disunited States," and the boasted national motto *E pluribus Unum*, became *E pluribus plurimum.*

† This was a pattern Landlady. This excursion into the Eastern Counties and other districts will not contain much that need be quoted, and space must be economised.

a fraudful intercourse with America was carried on." Adolphus says—"The public regarded, with due indignation, the treacherous interference of France." At this time Franklin wrote from Passy—"The English and French fleets, of nearly equal force, are now both at sea. It is not doubted but that if they meet there will be a battle." As a preliminary to such a battle, Admiral Keppel left Portsmouth on the 13th of June, and steered his fleet to the waters of Brest and the Bay of Biscay. On the 17th he observed two frigates, the *Licorne* and the *Belle Poule*, reconnoitring his force. On bringing these to a parley, the *Licorne* suddenly fired a broadside into the *America*, and then struck her colours. The *Belle Poule* had a smart action with the *Arethusa*, and escaped by running into shallow water, when the *Pallas*, another frigate of the enemy, having cruised sufficiently near the English ships to make observations, was taken and secured. It was with these that Keppel returned to Spithead. It could not be expected that Walpole would have been silent on this occasion, wherefore he writes—"Well, the signal is fired! Admiral Keppel has had a smart skirmish with three frigates of the Brest squadron, and has sent one [two] of them in. They fired first, and yet seemed to have provoked him, that they may plead we began the war."

These remarks are inserted at this place, because it was from this date that the war with France began.

July 2nd.—The London papers of Tuesday evening * mention Keppel's having sailed again from Portsmouth, upon Ld Sandwich's arrival there. . . M^r De Grey called upon us.

6th.—Paxton left us this morning, and went to Ld Townshend's at Raynham. The post brings us Gen. Howe's arrival—being at Court, &c. Philadelphia to be evacuated, and if we may guess, America to be admitted Independent. Great rejoicings in Washington's army upon news of the Treaty with France. Long live the K. of France! the general shout, (*Vive le Roi!*)

9th.—A letter from my son T. He says Philadelphia [is to be?] evacuated, as a preliminary to a Treaty: but I can't make a Treaty consist with the proceedings of the Colonies in their Treaty with France, &c.

24th.—We went to Cowbridge [in South Wales], 12 miles;

* It was now Thursday.

where we found Mr Browne and Mr Murray, our two countrymen, and their females, as we had found Dr Caner and Mr Apthorpe, and their families, at Cardiff, all waiting the state of the present contest, if it may any longer be said to be a contest, with America.

31st.—We set out early for London . . . I arrived at eight.

August 1st.—The calm among all sorts of people is astonishing. It looks just the same as one might expect it would, if the English and French fleets were parading in the Channel upon friendly terms; and yet every minute some decisive stroke, some say, may be expected. The British forces in America are mouldering away—the Commissioners treated with neglect—and all considered as a matter of indifference. Why don't Government withdraw its forces, and leave the Americans to that Independence which the Ministry seem to expect they will attain to?

2nd.—Walked down to the Old Jewry and back. . . Account last night of an action in which four or five of Keppel's fleet were engaged with the Brest squadron, which had gone into harbour. No ships taken; and it is said the *Victory*, [Keppel's ship,] lost many men,—but it occasions triumph. Bells ringing at 12 o'clock at night.

6th.—At Court. Keppel's Captain Faulkner introduced to the Queen.

8th.—Colo Chandler, Mr Clarke, and Mr Powell, with my son T., and Dr Oliver and wife, dined with me. All lament at the prospect of being debarred from the country which gave them birth, and deprived of the estates which they left there.

9th.—At Prince's Street. After service called on Daniel Leonard, beyond Buckingham Gate. He has been very dangerously sick while I was in the country, but is now recovered. His wife and children came last night from Halifax.*

11th.—Wrote by Packet to Putnam at New York, that I

* Daniel Leonard was the same with *Massachusettensis,* the writer of a series of loyal Letters at the commencement of the contest. He has been frequently quoted in the first volume.

heard the March and April mails miscarried, by wch I informed him of the receipt of his salary. The letters from the Commiss[ioners] to the Congress—the answer—a private letter of Johnstone to Laurence—and his answer—with the Resolve of Congress—all appear in the *General Advertiser*. Never was there an instance of such mortifying appearances in the publick prints. The design undoubtedly is—to bring Parliament to give them up. What the event will be, God only knows.

Lord Hardwicke having sent me a side of fine venison, Gen. Gage, Sr J. Wright, Gov. Wentworth, Lt Gov. Oliver, Mr Gray, Lechmere, Flucker, Leonard, Paul Wentworth, J. Newton, dined with me.

13th.—My son and grandson Tommy H. dined with me. Everybody despairs of being able to return. A report that Mr Lee, who has remained hitherto at Cambridge, has sold his estate, and is about to leave the country.

19th.—The same weather continues.* It is now two months since the last date from Clinton's army. There is a most unaccountable unconcern and indifference about publick affairs, wch never were in so bad a state since the days of Charles the First.

22nd.—As I was at dinner a porter came from Lord Townshend to desire me to call at his house, and he would tell me some news—the fellow said *good* news: and to give the porter sixpence. After I had gone part of the way, I had no doubt it must be a trick to get sixpence, as Lord T. had so many servants, and was inclined to return—but went on.

When I came, I found he had met a porter in the street. Instead of good news, he informed me of the arrival of Major Crew and General Paterson from N. York, the latter, who had the dispatches, not in town, but every minute expected:—that Lord Howe was blocked up in the harbour of N. York—that Clinton had been attacked passing thro' the Jerseys—some officers killed—knew no more particulars, only that he had not above a fortnight's provisions. This last article, if true, is more than all the rest.

* Frequent entries concerning the long continuance of great heat. The summer of 1778 appears to have been one of the hottest on record in England.

23rd.—At Dr Kippis's.

Lord T. sent me a précis—summary of the intelligence:—Clinton lost 375, killed, wounded, and missing: arrived the 4th July at N. York. D'Estaigne's* fleet arrived at the Hook the 11th: had been into Chesapeak and Delaware, and missed Ld Howe and the transports but a few days. This is a kind providence, as all the provisions and stores of the army must have fell into their hands. Ld Howe had 6 of the line, 3 of 50, 2 of 40, and many frigates, and lay within the Hook in line of battle. The morning Paterson came away, D'Estaigne was preparing to come to sail—supposed to be intended to Rh. Island. No account of Byron.

25th.—Account of a prize arrived, taken by Byron, who was left with 3 sail—it was at first said with 10, in long. 55, lat. 41, the 28 July, so that it may be long before he reaches N. York. —A very hot noon.

27th.—For want of better employ, spent most of the day upon my History. . .

With the end of the month the Fifth volume of the Diary terminates. If we may judge by the entry on the first of August —especially by the latter portion of it—and a few others following that date, we might infer that the game was nearly played out, and that we were coming to "the beginning of the end."

The unaccountable lull in public affairs so often alluded to, though more especially of late, as the gravity of the situation was becoming more intensified, and the strange inactivity of Administration, may have resulted from the fact, that Ministers had tried all plans in vain, and were now at a loss to know what step to take next. The number of conciliatory Bills that had been introduced into Parliament, both by the Constitutional party, and also by the most ardent favourers of American liberty, had shewn at least, that there had been no lack of willingness on the side of England, to come to a peaceful accommodation if possible. This may be made still more apparent, by referring to the friendly advances several times carried out by Commissioners specially sent for the purpose; yet, in all cases, their proposals had been met either by indifference, by evasion, or—as with the Commissioners now in America—by

* Stedman and Adolphus write the French Admiral's name D'Estaing; Hume's Continuator spells it D'Estaigne.

positive insult. The difficult nature of a war in a thinly settled, and partially cleared country, amid the forests and fastnesses of wild nature, had not been sufficiently taken into account. If we look back and take a survey of the fortunes of war, as they have presented themselves from the materials used in this book, we shall see that America was virtually won to England immediately after the success that followed the occupation of New York in August 1776, and virtually lost in October 1777 by the disaster to General Burgoyne at Saratoga. The entries in the Diary subsequent to that event, plainly show that the Refugees in England were well-nigh convinced that there was little chance of their ever returning to America again. In a melancholy strain of wit the following words, by the Governor's hand, were written on the fly-leaf at the end of vol. vi. of his Diary—"*Vincit qui patitur*—Motto for Refugees." And yet, if we may judge by an extract from a letter from Grotius to his father of April 16, 1621, after he had escaped from prison, and which he had quoted on another fly-leaf of his Diary, he continued to cling to the country that had ruined him in fortune, and had never ceased to try and ruin him in fame:—"*Ego non desino omnibus mihi recté voluntatibus Patriam commendare, cujus amorem, mihi nullæ unquam injuriæ extorquebant.*"

CHAPTER V.

BEGINNING OF VOL. IV. OF THE DIARY.

September 1st.—The changes in the last four or five years of my life make the whole scene, when I look back upon it, appear like a dream or other delusion. From the possession of one of the best houses in Boston, the pleasantest house and farm at Milton of almost any in the world, and one of the best estates in the Colony of Rhode Island—free from debt, an affluent income, and a prospect of being able to make a handsome provision for each of my children at my death—I have not a foot of land at my command, and personal estate of about 7.000£ only; depending on the bounty of Government for a pension, which, though it affords a present ample provision for myself, and enables me to distribute 500£ a year among my children, yet is precarious, and I cannot avoid anxiety. But I am still distinguished by a kind providence from my suffering relations, friends, and countrymen in America, as well as from many of them in England, and have great reason to be thankful that so much mercy is yet continued to me.

3rd.—A New England man—Nutting, of Cambridge—goes in the Packet. He is to be employed as overseer of carpenters, who are to rebuild the Fort at Penobscot. This he gives out. What Ministry propose is matter of conjecture only, but this measure looks as if they expected to continue some hold of the Colonies.

10th.—At Court. The Drawing-Room being very thin, the King said more to me than usual. After something upon books, and my being acquainted with them when young, and finding the benefit of it now I am old, he asked what sort of reading

I found most entertaining, or, I spent most of my time in? "None more pleasing than History. It gave me pain however, to compare the present times [with those] which had preceded." "I believe so—none were more wicked. I fancy," he added, "some of the wickedness of the times went from hence to America." "I knew it well," I answered. Turning from me, he looked back again—"They are a sad nest." "I hope Sir, they'll be broke up in time," was my return.

13th.—At Dr Kippis's.

The *Montreal*, with Gov. Carleton on board, from Quebec, spoke the 8th with a Packet from N. York. D'Estaigne could not water there, and was gone, as supposed, to the Delaware. Ld Howe had sailed after him with 7 ships of the line and a store ship, armed of the same force as a line of battle ship, five 55 guns, and two 44, and frigates. Two of the 50 guns found their way in, notw^th^stand[ing] D'Estaigne's squadron; and the *Cornwall*, one of Byron's ships, was arrived. The French had destroyed and taken 30 sail of one sort and another.

14th.—The accounts open more to-day. No victuallers among the prizes taken by D'Estaigne. The Cornwall arrived but the 31 July: the *Raisonable*, a 60 gun ship, had also joined, so that Howe had 8 line of battle ships, and no store ship, she being designed only for a battery in harbour.

15th.—The packet wch came out wth the armed vessel also arrived. Howe not sailed the 1st Aug., but was to sail the next day. D'Estaigne was seen the 28 July, steering, as supposed, for Rhode Island. Gov. Arbuthnot arrived from Halifax: sailed about the 20 Aug. One of the three ships wch were with Byron, arrived there the 16th. I have a letter from my brother of the 18th: complains much of his dark prospects.

19th.—I called to-day upon Mr Knox at the office. He said he had at last accomplished what he had been endeavouring, and had brought "them" to take possession of Penobscot; and shewed me a letter to Sir H. Clinton from Ld George, directing him to send a sufficient body of the troops to Penobscot, as soon as they could be spared, to cover the workmen, who were to be employed in building a Fort, Mr Nutting being tho't proper for overseer of the workmen, &c. It seems it is to be placed where Castine's Fort was built; and this is to be erected into a new Province, and to be given to the Refugees, upon the same quitrents as the N. Hampshire and other Grantees, as a recompence for their sufferings, and to ease Government of the expense it is now at for their support. It put me in mind of Mr Locke's story of Ld Shaftesbury's friend, who, after he was privately married, sent for his Ldship and another friend, to ask their advice: and I observed the same rule so far as to find no fault with the most preposterous measure, because already carrying into execution, Nutting having sailed in the last packet. However, I intend to make Mr Knox acquainted, in the most prudent manner I can, with my sentiments.

Called on Sir Guy Carleton.

22nd.—I finished the revisal of my History, to the end of my Administration, and laid it by.*

The wind at east, but the sun very hot. Mr Rome, Paxton, my son T., and wife, and daughter Oliver, with young Spooner, and little Tommy H.—dined.

23rd.—Set out in [a] postchaise with S. ½ after 9, and arrived at Ld Hardwicke's at Wimple Hall, ½ after 4, while they were at dinner. . .

29th.— . . . A goose for dinner on Mich[aelmas] Day, occasioned an observation—that otherwise, money would be wanted before the year was out.

October 1st.—Returned to town. . . Nothing can be more obliging than their treatment of company while they stay. One custom they keep up, which is laid down almost everywhere else—they allow their servts to take vails. This is no small tax, and I believe they have fewer visitors on that account. I left two guineas, besides 4/- to the groom. My servant says Lady Grey calls for all the money that has been left while in the country, and distributes it among the servants in proportion to their rank. They are very numerous—must exceed thirty men and women.

5th.—Nothing remarkable to-day except the news of the capture of two French East India ships, which make four out of

* This then must have been the day on which he completed the third volume of his History of Massachusetts Bay, which was published in 1828.

five, which were expected, there having been advice of two taken before. . .

13th.—Express from Halifax, Sep. 8, that Byron had got in there, and sailed the 4 Sep. with the *Culloden* to join Howe: another from N. York with advice of blocking up Rhode Island—L[d] Howe's sailing—D'Estaigne's going out to meet him—two days without engaging. At length Howe, having got the weather gage, and expecting in half an hour to begin a general action, a storm rose which scattered the fleets—dismasted some—D'Estaigne's squadron gone to Boston—Howe said to have followed, and to have got back to Rhode Island. Sir H. Clinton went from N. York to Rhode Island with 4000 men, which caused the Provincials to withdraw. Parker, with Byron's ships, arrived Aug. 28 at N. York. All the store-ships but one were arrived at York.

14th.—At M[r] Knox's office: confirms the account of yesterday. . .

16th.—A letter by packet from M[r] Walter at N. York of Sep. 6, mentions Johnstone, one of the Commissioners, resigning. He had wrote to some of the Congress, and taken other methods to gain them, which they pretended to be an affront: and upon the Commissioners' demand of the delivering up Burgoyne's men, according to the Articles of Surrender, the Congress declared they would not treat with Johnstone.* He has exposed himself shamefully, and the nation debases itself more than if they left the Americans to enjoy their independence.

17th.— . . . Six of Byron's fleet lay at New York the 6 September. . .

19th.—In the city. Procured freight from M[r] Rashleigh for two barrels of beef, and two firkins of butter, a present to my brother at Halifax, and sent them by a waterman, on board the *Adamant*, Cha. Wyatt, at Blackwall.

Returning, met the King in his charriot, and the Queen with him, with the Guards and Attendants in Cheapside, going to review the troops on Warley Common. The crowd not being great, I observed, as I had my hat off, and nobody else [in the

* This may make us smile, as it is the reward he got for the countenance he had hitherto given to the Sons of Liberty.

way], they each took notice of it; but whether they thought me there by accident, or to see the show—can't say.

21st.—Dined with Mr Lane in the city, where I found Admiral Gayton, who I knew in America about the time of the Louisburgh expedition, and who married Mrs Rawlins' daughter, who kept a small shop just by my house. Mrs Gayton died since I came to England. It is said he has saved 30 or 40.000£ by his command in Jamaica, from whence he lately returned. He was poor before. Swears like a fool at 67 years of age.

Upon 'Change: they talked of war with Spain, and stocks fell 1 or 2 ℘ ct. I asked what grounds? They knew none, except that England was sending half a dozen ships to the Mediterranean to protect her trade.

22nd.—Mr La Fontaine, my old landlord at Chelsea, called, and dined with me. Mr Clarke and Quincy in the evening. They both agreed in an anecdote, which I never heard before— That when the dispute between the Kingdom and the Colonies began to grow serious, John Adams said to Sewall that he was at a loss which side to take, but it was time to determine. Sewall advised to the side of Government, and proposed to Governor Bernard to make Adams a Justice of Peace, as the first step to importance. Bernard made a difficulty on account of something personal between him and Adams, but Sewall urged him to consider of it a week, or some short time, and acquainted Adams the Governor had it under consideration, but Adams disliked the delay, and observed, that it must be from some prejudice against him, and resolved to take the other side. Sewall was superior to Adams, and soon became Attorney-General, and one of the Superior Judges of Admiralty. Adams is now Ambassador from the United States to the Court of France, and Sewall a Refugee in England, and dependent upon Government for temporary support. Such is the instability of all human affairs.

26th.—Lord Howe* and Gov. Johnstone arrived. Many people had great expectations of something being done by Lord H. before he quitted his command, and the disappointment must

* Lord Howe was succeeded by Adm. Gambier, and in April 1779 to him succeeded Com. Sir G. Collier.

be in proportion. Much of the news has not yet transpired. Affairs have a dark aspect.

27th.—Lord Howe, in the *Eagle*, was very near being taken by two or three French line of battle ships off Scilly. This Mr Watts tells me, from Col^l^ Sherriff, who was on board. He says that Billy Smith, as he is commonly named, one of the Council of N. York, who has been supposed to side with the Americans, lately came in to New York. Bedford harbour destroyed, and Martha's Vineyard put to ransom. All the damage is not equal to 5 frigates, 2 sloops, and 30 or 40 transports burnt and sunk at Rhode Island, to avoid their falling into the hands of the Americans or French.

Dined with M^r^ and Mrs Ellis.

28th.—The *Gazette* to-day sets affairs in no promising light in America. The French fleets indeed, have been in good measure disappointed, but they are secure in Nantasket, and our fleet can be of no great use, but upon the defensive. Provisions will be difficult to obtain for them, unless some of the English transports should fall into their hands, and this there is great reason to fear.—Mr Rome dined with me.

31st.—It is said to-day that four French frigates have attacked Dominica: that they have carried two of the Forts, &c. It is added that the French have published a Declaration of War.

Flucker, Greene, Dr Chandler, Bliss, Gridley, and Dr Oliver,—dined. Some of the company mentioned at dinner a circumstance of Genl Brattle's death at Halifax. He was always a great feeder, and being at dinner at a gentleman's table, having his plate filled with fish, one who was at table took notice of his countenance, and said to him—"You are not well, General,"—but he went on eating, until it was observed that his mouth was drawn on one side, and he was advised to get up, or something to that purpose, which he agreed to, and had just time to say to the servant—"Set the plate by for supper." These were the last words he spake. An instance of the ruling passion continuing to the last, and agrees with Pope's—"Bring the jowl!"

November 1st.—At the Old Jewry. . .

2nd.—The Stocks are fallen 2 or 3 ℘ c^t. from the Dominica news: report of Declaration of War by France: disappointment in the expectations of Lord Howe's following D'Estaigne a little closer. When Ld H. knew two of D'Estaigne's capital ships were dismasted,—his own fleet not weakened, except by springing a bowsprit in one ship, and a topmast in another,—he should remain at Sandy Hook a whole week,—take no step to interrupt D'Estaigne at Rhode Island,—but when he had reason to suppose he had sailed for Boston,—then to follow,—and as soon as he found he was in Nantasket, to give over all further thoughts of annoying him, and return immediately to England.*

3rd.—In the city with my son T. and sister [in-law] G. S., [Grizel Sanford], in the coach. More captures of the French W. India ships. It is said that the account of a fray at Boston is confirmed from Halifax. It looks as if Howe and Johnstone would not agree well when Parliament meets, the latter being very free in charging the loss of America to the fault of the former.

5th.— . . . It seems agreed that D'Estaigne's Lieutenant was killed in a fray between some Privateer's men, as it is said, and the French seamen about bread, there being two sorts, and the best given to the Frenchmen.

6th.—At the Levée, St. James's. A great string of sea officers—Sir George Rodney, Admiral Keppel, Lord Howe, Sir Robert Harland, Sir Hugh Palliser, Admiral Campbell, besides Sir John Lindsay, and other Captains. Many land officers. A publication of Sr H. Palliser's in the *P. Advertiser* of to-day, shews that there is not a perfect understanding with Keppel, and probably must bring on a dispute.

In the evening at my son's, Brompton Row, at the Baptism of his youngest child William,† by Dr Kippis.

7th.—The account of the surrender of Dominica, taken from the French acc^t by authority, appears in the papers of this day.

8th.—At Prince's Street—Dr Kippis.

* This is something like the American tactics of his brother.

† My father's younger brother.

10th.—Took Drs Chandler and Cooper in my coach to Fulham, where found the Bp. of London at home, and very courteous. He thinks Lord Howe had never seen the King since his arrival until Friday last, and that he is much of a grumbler. Governor Johnstone complains as much of Lord and General Howe. There is no knowing who and who will be together when Parliament meets.

Lord Townshend having sent me a hare and two pheasants, I asked Mr Watts, Chandler, Cooper, Mauduit, Sewall, Major Small, Fitch, Hallowell, and Lane, to partake of them.

13th.—Dined with Mr Watson, Garlick Hill:—Admiral Arbuthnot, Hallowell, Clarke, Brattle, Cap. Arbuthnot, son to the Admiral, has lost a leg, and a Mr Mure—I suppose Hutchinson Mure.

14th.—Mr Combe, a Clergyman, came passenger in one of the vessels from N. York to Ireland. He had been imprisoned, and at length was banished from Philadelphia for refusing the oaths. He says he expects to return next year—that the Americans are so averse to the French, that they will break among themselves. This is his opinion, but I don't find it a general opinion.

18th.—Auchmuty, Brinley, and N. Coffin, called on me and spent half an hour.

I bought 3 vol. in one of the *Reliquiæ Romanæ* at Hayes's, and the Views in Venice, at two Guineas, I think cheap. Pridden asked the same price for the *Reliquiæ* only—imperfect —9 or 10 prints wanting.

There is a man in town who left Boston the 22nd of September, arrived 8 or 10 days ago from Halifax. He says he saw the funeral of D'Estaigne's Lieut^t. He brought a newspaper which mentions the death of Dr Eliot, about the middle of September: also of Ezek. Lewis. Dr Eliot was long my friend. One of my last letters from Dr Pemberton, said his sentiments were the same they used to be. After Howe left the town, he wrote two letters to England which were intercepted, and carried to Halifax, and copies given. They were very strong in favour of American proceedings. Some thought he expected they would be intercepted, and that he desired to have it known at Boston that he publickly owned the cause. He said to my son at Boston he was afraid, or had reason to think his continuing in Boston had made him obnoxious to the people without the town. Great allowance must be made for the difficulty of his circumstances: but after all, as no man is without infirmity, perhaps his might be a disposition to temporize, always, I trust, having satisfied himself he was to be justified:—but this must be left. Some of the Americans speak lightly upon the news of his death. I heard the news with grief, and wished to see him again in this world. Dr Pemberton and he, for many years, were the best neighbours I had.

Dr Chandler dined with me to-day, and read his letters from Dr Ingols, as late as the 26th of September, who thinks the new alliance with the French will break the alliance which the Americans have formed among themselves. . .

19th.—I called upon Sewall, at his lodgings, and asked him to dine with me. After dinner, some mention being made of Dr E.—"I have not the least doubt," says S., "that man is gone to h—ll." "Oh!" says I, "that's going a great length," or something to that effect. "If there is such a place as h—," he repeats it, "I have not the least doubt he is gone there." The reason he gave for his declaration was, his opinion of the Dr's duplicity; and the instance he gave was his frequent meeting S., and joining him in conversation, and appearing to disapprove of the measures taken before the 19th of April,* and of his avoiding him after that, and never saying any more upon the subject. I excused him—his dependance being on his people, who were now, or after that day, warmly engaged; and Mr S. being peculiarly obnoxious to them, being seen with him, would make the Dr obnoxious also. This was rash beyond anything I ever observed in S. before. He is in poor health, which occasions, or increases discontent and uneasiness of temper—the best excuse I can make for him. God forbid that he or I should have our infirmities so strictly marked against us. We should not be able to stand.

* The Battle of Lexington, the first Battle of the war. It was to Dr. Eliot that the Governor sent his books and fossils for Harvard University, as mentioned, I. 450.

23rd.—Visited Lord Huntingdon: very civil and communicative: had not seen L[d] G. Germaine, but had seen L[d] North: seems less unfavorably disposed to the Ministry than when I last saw him: condemns some of the Opposition, who wished the nation's misfortune, for the sake of a change of Ministry: says the first motion in the H. of Commons will be to declare the seats of the American Commissioners vacant.

At Gov. Shirley's—left my name, and Sir W. P. [Pepperell ?]

Rain, and much wind.

Lord H. thinks Pigot might have done more in obstructing Sullivan at quitting R. Island; and I thought he had heard Clinton was of the same opinion.

25th.—Several transports arrived to-day from N. York; said to leave it the 19th of October. Clinton returned: nothing said more than that he had foraged successfully. Byron gone towards Boston.

26th.—Paxton came to town last evening with L[d] Townshend, who at my request took Sewall in to the H. of Lords to hear the K.'s Speech, which recommends vig. [vigorous ?] exertions. The Addresses of the two Houses opposed, as usual. Gov. Johnstone supposed 28,000 men enough to conquer America: harped upon the old string under another Ministry, and finally divided with the Ministry, being 207 against 106. In the House of Lords the majority was 177 to 31. After Lord Shelburne had spoke, there was a stroke of canes as a mark of applause, which gave such offence that the House was immediately ordered to be cleared.

28th.—Lord Galloway stopped me in the street, and informed me of the arrival of M[r] Drummond, S[r] H. Clinton's Aide-du-camp, who left New York the 29th Oct[r]. Grant sailed with 5000 troops, and three line-of-battle ships for the W. Indies the 27th. Pigot is also arrived. It is said a body of troops were gone to the southward. Byron was at sea, but rather as a security to the smaller squadron, than from any prospect of annoying D'Estaigne.

December 3rd.—Left cards at M[r] D'Oyly's and Jenkinson's. At Lord North's Levée: mentioned Boylstone's arrival, and tho't he might give intelligence. Ld North said—"If he will." Arch-Bp. of York, Bps. of London and Chichester, Lord Shuldham, Palliser, Young, several of the Nobility, and many Members of Parliament. Rather a full Levée.

Met T. Boylstone in the street: was at a loss how to greet him: said I was glad to see him well, or—hoped I saw him well: added—I little expected to see him here. He answered—he little thought I should remain so long here. I thereupon said—"Since you are here, I should be glad you would call on me,"—or to that effect.

At the Levée Gen. Monkton, tho' Governor of Portsmouth, and now gratified by Administration, seemed discontented with American measures, and said, if they tried another year to reduce them, it would be in vain. Sir Henry Houghton seemed to be for giving up the charges—not being to be borne. Strahan said—"You must go forward—you can't go back if you would." Sir Henry said—"See what will be the effect of to-morrow, when Burke's motion comes on."

4th.—In the House of Commons a motion to consider that part of the Manifesto of the Commissioners, which threatens the Americans with prosecuting the war with severity, supported with great vehemence by the minority,* who made 126 against 207. Governor Johnstone supported the Manifesto.

5th.—Dined with M[r] Jackson, Southampton Buildings. There I saw Galloway for the first time . . .

7th.—Called on D[r] Gardiner . . .

Visit to M[r] Galloway also, where I found M[r] Delany. Galloway is of opinion the middle Colonies are tired of the war, and says, if the army had not moved from Philad., all Pensylvania and New Jersey would have returned: and he says, if the war be properly prosecuted, they will do it yet. He condemns all past measures, there having been no system. I asked him about W. Smith. He supposed I knew him to be a sensible man, and who loved his interest. I said—"Yes." "It's natural

* It was only a short time ago that the minority were crying out for more concessions to the Americans, and abusing the Ministry for not withdrawing all the troops from America!

then," he added, "to infer that the American cause was in a very declining way, or he would not have left it."

Galloway says it can be demonstrated that 50,000 Americans have been slain or died in Hospitals by sickness. He says they have been often excessively straitened for provisions, when the country has been full, and he will have it to be owing to the disaffection of the inhabitants, who were not willing to supply the army. I told him I supposed it must be the bad state of their paper currency, but he would not concede to it Dr Gardiner thinks their crops have been very short this year, but Galloway says they have not been remarkably so. I thought it strange, if there was so great a disaffection, that bodies of men had not petitioned the Congress to treat when such liberal terms were offered. The reason, he says is, they are afraid of being put to the bayonet. I think this must be exaggerated.

Mr Galloway was of the first Congress. I do not know the special occasion of his quitting that cause. His friends say he never intended Independence; and that when he found that was resolved upon, he left them.

Mr Galloway says the Members of the Congress for Pensylvania, and all the Members for the Assembly for the Province, were elected by 157 votes only, though there are 30,000 qualified to vote in the Province.

8th.—At Lord Hardwicke's, who desired me to bring Mr Galloway to see him on Thursday the 10th. The H. of Lords last night divided upon the motion to address the King upon the subject of the Comissrs Manifesto—37 for the Address, 71 against it; but this is a great minority upon so strange a motion.

A rainy day, and very high S.W. wind.

9th.—At Kensington Square to call on Mr. Lechmere and Newton, but both from home. In the evening with Paxton at Mr Copley's.

10th.—At Lord Hardwicke's, where I saw Sir Charles Cocks:—much conversation. Ld H. saw no way how the war could be carried on with France and America both.

Ld Gage called. He says Colo Gray, Dickens, and 6 or 7

officers of the Guards, are ordered to embark for America in the fleet now at Portsmouth, and supposes an additional force to be going out.

Admiral Palliser has lodged a charge against Admiral Keppel, which must bring on a Court Martial.

Mr Jenkinson, Secretary at War, in the room of Lord Barrington.

11th.— . . . A.[dmiral] Palliser, having exhibited a charge of not doing his utmost, &c., against Ad. Keppel, Temple Lutterell moved in the House of Commons to address His Majesty to order an enquiry into Palliser's conduct in not observing signals. It seemed chiefly designed to give room for debate, the motion being dropped. Shuldham and Pigot, both blamed Palliser for appearing in the Newspapers, and others blamed the Admiralty for ordering a Court Martial without hearing Keppel. It's an affair which threatens a good deal of trouble . . .

12th.—Dr Chandler has a letter from Wilkins of Octr 9th, who writes in hopes of seeing peace another year. He adds—he hopes to hear H—— is hanged.

In the city. Mr Frazer says that some of Byron's squadron have taken on board the *Rawleigh,* and a vessel he was sending to Martinico, D'Estaigne's papers, which give an account of his designs, and that they will be of great use to Byron. Letters from France say a vessel is arrived from Boston, which sailed the 4 of November, and that D'Estaigne sailed at the same time, but this is not credited.

14th.—Richard Silvester, a Custom-House officer, who used to be often applying to me for one purpose or another at Boston, called on me this morning. He came from N. York in one of the transports—left Boston in June. He married the mother of Will More, who was imprisoned with others for the riot at destroying my house in 1765. Silvester says More was Captain of the men who destroyed the tea. I asked him how he knew it? He said his wife, More's mother, told him so.

Took Mr Galloway in my carriage to Lord Hardwicke's, who was very inquisitive into his whole history, which was plausible enough. Mr G. went into Congress at the earnest sollicitations of his friends, in hopes to moderate matters. He proposed a fair or equivalent state of the claims of the Colonies in the first Petition, but a very different one was carried against his opinion, by means of Adams and his adherents, so that of all the Colonies there was a majority of members in each for the Petition, but Galloway still says there was nothing precise in it as to the expectation of the Colonies, and some things very exceptionable: that he then desired to know of Adams whether he did not intend Independence? and he declared he did not: but as soon as the affair was over, owned in company he intended nothing short of it: that it had been his object 17 years: that he had made it his business whenever it was in his power, to inculcate the principle upon the minds of every youth likely to be of any significance.

When this design was thus made apparent, G. determined to quit. He was chosen by the Assembly of Phil. when he was absent, but excused himself; and tho' another was not chosen in his stead for three or four months, yet he never met with the new Congress. He says Mr Adams was so enraged with him, and enraged the people so much against him, that he was afraid of assassination. The vote for Independence, he says, was carried by 7 Colonies to 6. The 4 New England Colonies, [with] Virginia, Pensilvania, and New Jersey, made the seven: that, on the first trial, Pensilvania members were against it; but after three or four days Dickenson was brought over, and made the majority of that Colony in favour of it, and also the major vote of the Colonies. This man, in his *Farmer's Letters*, disclaimed any such intention. G. says he is of an unsteady mind. He soon after lost the confidence of his constituents, and has had no share in the Congress nor Assembly ever since.

Debate in the H. upon the army. Mr Jenkinson opened the state of it, Lord Barrington having resigned as Secry at War: 160,000 men voted for the army next year. It is said, in army and navy in Britain, Ireland and the dependencies, together with the Militia in pay, will amount to 300,000.

15th.—At Mr Ellis's.

Mr Weekes, Missionary at Marblehead called on me. He

arrived in one of the transports at Corke: left Boston in July, pretending to be going to Bedford, in a small vessel which found the way to Rhode Island, where he staid during the siege, and then went to York. He says he was tried six different times for offences against the State: has left his wife and 8 children at Marblehead.

Mr Thompson of Yorkshire called.

16th.—Dined with Mr Wray, in Dean Street, Soho—Lord Hardwicke, and Lady Grey, Lady Bet. Polworth, Miss Gregory, Bp. of St. Davids, and Lady.

17th.—At Court—the Queen not there—confined with a cold. The King said somewhat about the weather. [I] observed that I was more affected by the state of America than by the weather. I hoped they looked more favorably than they had done a year or two past. He thought so too, and particularly in New England. I did not know but they might in Connecticut, but in Massachusetts I thought the leaders had as much sway as ever. He asked if they had not changed their leaders? No: they had the same men as at first, particularly Hancock and Adams. Hancock, he said, was but a weak man: Adams, he had heard, was very able. I agreed with him, and gave him my opinion of their different characters, &c.

Col^o^ Stewart arrived: left N. York the 18th Nov. D'Estaigne sailed the 4th. Bryon saw part of the ships, but in a storm and thick weather lost them. Took a brig soon after, which came out with them, and Bryon's ships suffering in the storm, put into Newport. This was very unfortunate, and people are in pain for the W. Indies, or other parts where that fleet may be gone.

Col^o^ Stewart bro't a copy of a letter wrote by Mr Ethan Allen, in behalf of the Green Mountain Men, who refuse to acknowledge the Congress, to whom the letter was wrote.

Mr Jackson, John Pownall, Galloway, Dr Chandler, Sir Francis and T. Bernard, Sir W. Pepperell, and Col. Leonard, dined with me.

18th.—I received two copies of an Act of the State of Massachusetts Bay, passed the 10th of October. Each came from France under a blank cover; one, by the superscription, I suspect to have been sent from Boston, the other to be covered in France. This Act prescribes above 300 persons, of which I am first named: then Gov. Bernard, Lt Gov. Oliver, Timothy Ruggles, after which they are generally named in alphabetical order. They, and all others, though not named, who have absented themselves from the State, and been inimical to it, upon their return to the State, are to be forthwith committed to prison, and as soon after as may be, sent out of the State; and if they return a second time, without leave of the General Court, they are to suffer the pains of death, without benefit of Clergy.*

Five hundred copies were to be sent to the Ministers at the Court of France, to be published, &c.

Col^o Stewart brought another Act, which orders the estates of all these persons to be sold; but this, it was not thought necessary to send to me.

20th.— . . . An account is said to be received, and is credited, that the *Somerset*, a 64 gun ship, was lost off Cape Cod. Where D'Estaigne was bound, is not yet ascertained . . .

21st.—The account of the loss of the *Somerset* is from a tender of D'Estaigne, taken by the *Culloden* 25 men were said to be lost on Cape Cod—the rest made prisoners. The report is, that the French designed for Toulon, but the fears are that they are gone to the West Indies.

22nd.—The *Roebuck* arrived, and another ship from N. York;—Ld Carlisle, and Mr Eden, Commissioners; Ld Cornwallis and Gen. Grey of the army. No news of the *Cornwall*. The *Somerset*, and *Zebra*, sloop, are certainly lost in the storm.

23rd.—A visible concern in people's countenances—except some of the Opposition. Mr Knox called. He says transports are preparing for the first embarkation of 3000 men to sail by the 20th of February.

* "I have read the histories of most of the civil dissentions of which we in the present age of the world have any knowledge; but I have not met with an instance equally arbitrary, revengeful, and severe, with the Acts of the new State of Mass. Bay. They put my patience to the test, but you don't think them worth notice."—The Governor to J. Putnam, Aug. 3, 1779, in Letter Book.

In the city. They say D'Estaigne went to the W. Indies. Byron was not sailed from Rhode Island the 22nd of November: had sent for the *Monmouth* from N. York to join him —which made 13 sail.

24th.—Mr Abel Willard called this morning. He says his brother Rogers has a letter from Jos. Taylor at New York, acquainting him that Mr Blowers* went from Rhode Island to Boston: that he was immediately apprehended and committed close prisoner, according to the late Act of Massachusetts State, and that he was to be sent away, agreeable to the provisions in the Act.

Dr Gardiner called: has a letter from his son, who obtained leave to visit his father at N. York, but he was sailed when he came there. He writes that he was present when the Act of Attainder passed in Boston, and in the Gallery, heard the debates: says the persons named in it were much abused. The Act however, met with opposition, and was finally carried by 61 to 33. Another Bill for sale of the estates passed the House, but the Council refused the consideration to December, when it is supposed it will pass.

25th.—A feverish disorder, which gave me a poor night, prevented my going abroad to Church or Meeting; for Christmas is observed in both, and the streets are more orderly than they are on Sundays.

Mr Weekes, Green, and Bliss, dined with me, with my son T. and wife, and Dr Oliver.

Mr Weekes says that when the plan of Government recommended by the House to the towns for consideration, came before the town of Boston, Otis appeared, and spake so well against it, that he prevented its passing, as otherwise it would have done; and it was put off to another day, when they chose Otis Moderator, and he spake so well on introducing the subject, that it was rejected by a great majority. He dressed himself very decently on that occasion, but soon after returned to his sordid dress and demeanor about [the] streets.

26th.—At Lord Hardwicke's. He is much affected with the state of things in America, lest D'Estaigne should sweep all

* Some account of Mr. Blowers is given in vol. i. p. 341.

before him, which may cause, he said, such a crash as we never felt before. "And yet, my Lord," said I, "there are many people among us who wish for it." "There always are," he said, "some who had rather command the wreck of the Constitution, than that it should be preserved entire under the guidance of other persons."

Warm weather still, like September and October in America: and it's often as cold in May or June in England.

27th.—At the Old Jewry.

Dined with Mr Ellis. Sir Robt Smith only. Balfour, Captain of the *Culloden*, thinks it probable D'Est. is gone to Toulon: others, from the same circumstances, think to the West Indies. The fleets which have lain four or five weeks, and part much longer, in all 300 sail, sailed from Plimouth to the westward, the morning of the 25th, under a strong convoy.

The execution of Roberts and Carlisle, two Quakers, at Philadelphia, for aiding and assisting General Howe, is made certain. Roberts is said to have been worth 20,000£ sterling, which is all confiscated. He is also said to have left surviving a widow and ten children.

29th.—Dined with Mr Knox, where I met for the first time, Doctor Ferguson, Secretary to the Commissioners. He is very agreeable in conversation, and as unreserved as a prudent man can be. I asked where he lodged? Without informing me, he let me know he designed to wait on me.

30th.—But a dull day, first meeting Mr Keene, who soon discovered to me the apprehensions of Ministry, from the state of Byron's and D'Estaigne's fleets, and the hazard Grant's forces, and the West India Islands were in, for he supposes it 100 to one that D'Estaigne went to the W. Indies; and I found everybody else in the Park, &c., going the same way, though there is no fresh advices. The prospect is indeed very dark for this Kingdom. Wind last night was very high at W. to NW.

31st.—Lt Gov. Oliver, Lechmere, Vassall, Rome, Watson, Galloway, and Mauduit, dined with me. G. speaks his mind very freely of the often repeated neglect of Gen. H. to pursue the advantages gained over the enemy; declares he is utterly at a loss for his conduct in going round to Chesapeak; that he

(G.) gave his opinion against it; and that Gen. H. asked if he thought it a dangerous navigation? and upon his saying "No," the General made no reply.

Wind very high all day at S.W. People in pain for the fleet lately sailed. Advice that the *Russell*, a 74 gun ship, ran down an outward bound Indiaman in the Channel, which sunk, and about 40 only of the crew saved. The Master of the Man-of-war is blamed; the *Russell* damaged so as to go into dock.

In the night the wind changed to north, and blew with as much violence as anybody remembers—but it is common to say so.

End of 1778.

England at this period, was in a very critical position, not only as regarded the impending loss of the largest and the most wealthy of her dependencies, but a war with France begun, and a war with Spain in expectation: and yet, how entirely these great national events, and anxious struggles against increasing taxation, are forgotten and swept out of memory. When I was in America, I found that the subject of England, "the British," and the provincial successes in the Revolutionary war, were the constantly recurring topics of conversation. I ascribed this in some degree to their knowing that I was an Englishman. A lady asked me one day whether we were not always talking about America in England? I was injudicious enough to smile, and say, we never thought about it: or we might casually allude to America as we might to France or Spain, or any other country, if the subject under review suggested it. I was much to be condemned for my want of good breeding. I should have pleased her more if I had said that we had never ceased repenting the loss of the Colonies, and that we took all the blame upon ourselves.

It may be seen by the Diary, that though Mr. Hutchinson had many repeated opportunities of conversing with the King at Court, the current politics of the day were rarely alluded to, leaving his Majesty to lead the conversation, and if they were touched upon, a passing remark sufficed, as it would be evidently inopportune to discuss such subjects in a mixed company.

The crafty and underhand proceedings of France, in respect to their secret Treaty with the revolted Colonies, raised a feeling of great indignation in England when it became known. So long ago as fifteen months before the period at which we have arrived, namely, on the 17th of July, 1777, Walpole wrote—" The open protection and countenance given by France to the Americans, is come to a crying height." That an ancient Monarchy, proud of its long and unbroken succession of Kings, and jealous of its monarchical institutions, should so far forget its consistency and sound judgment, and be so imprudent as to encourage the people to rise in rebellion against their lawful rulers in a neighbouring state, and thereby to popularise republicanism, with all the excesses of unbridled liberty, was an anomaly that did not escape observation. But a terrible retribution soon recoiled upon France. Her citizens, thus encouraged, followed the example and applied the experiment on their own soil; and by the use of the Guillotine, swept away all traces of the ancient regime in deluges of blood. It did not end there; for the force of evil example is great, and the Irish Rebellion, with all its barbarities, broke out immediately upon it.

The three Commissioners had now returned from America—pretty well snubbed and crest-fallen. Young Thomas Hutchinson, writing to his brother Elisha, August 20, 1778,* makes the following remarks :—

" Although I have done with the expectation of returning to America, yet cannot help being more inquisitive after accounts from thence, than from any other quarter. I don't find Government have rec^d any despatches from the Commissioners as yet: those by the way of France are enough to shew the matter of negotiation will end much as was expected. The very few Americans that are left in and about London wear pretty long faces. Billy is at Yarmouth: he writes me his health is better than usual. Daniel and Sylvester [Oliver] are both in the country, and it is now become a rare thing to meet a Yankee even in the Park. The Govr has been very well since his journey, and I think is more reconciled to the thoughts of ending his days in England than I have ever observed him to be. Necessity has no law."

Governor Johnstone is another instance, among some notable cases already aluded to, of a person who, at the commencement encouraged the thirst for liberty by his speeches against the Ministry and their repressive measures, only to turn round when the monster was becoming too strong, and then recommended the

* Orig. Letters, vol. i.

application of the bullet and the bayonet, and thought that America could be conquered with a force of 28,000 men. Governor Hutchinson went upon a different principle. At the commencement he used all legal and constitutional repressive measures to check the growing fever, but by the 1st of August, 1778, thinking there had been contention enough, he wrote—"Why don't Government withdraw its forces, and leave the Americans to that Independence which the Ministry seem to expect they will attain to?" Look on that picture and on this.

There is printed at page 13 in "Senate—No. 187," among the laws of the General Court—"An Act to confiscate the estates of certain notorious conspirators against the government and liberties of the inhabitants of the late province, now State, of Massachusetts Bay;" and there is there given, a list of the names of those who are specially marked out for early manipulation.

The Keppel and Palliser affair, which caused a great fuss over a small matter, had scarcely yet developed itself, but it was soon destined to amuse the community a good deal. On the 25th of August, 1778, Walpole wrote—"The papers say that Keppel and Palliser have fought a duel: I do not know how truly."

CHAPTER VI.

BEGINNING OF THE YEAR 1779.

January 1, 1779.—The new year begins with a dark prospect for this poor kingdom. A vessel express in 33 days from Jamaica brings advice of their expecting a great French force to invade them.

Many houses hurt by the wind last night.

6th.—To Richmond to Lord Hardwicke's—Mr Galloway in the coach with me. Among other things he says,—when Dr Franklyn first arrived from England in America, after the revolt was begun, he came to Galloway, they having been long friends; that Galloway opened his mind to him, and hoped he was come to promote a reconciliation: that the Doctor was reserved, and kept upon his guard: that the next morning they met again, and the D^r said—" Well Mr Galloway, you are really of the mind that I ought to promote a reconciliation?" Galloway said " Yes"—and no more passed: that for five or six weeks Franklyn kept much at home, [and] people seemed at a loss what part he would take. S. Adams opened against him as a suspicious person, designing to betray the cause. At length a more full conversation was proposed between F. & G., and the D^r read to him three fourths of his Journal while he was in England, but company interrupted: that the Doctor's natural son, the Govr of New Jersey, had told Galloway that his father had avoided any conversation with him upon the subject of the colonies; but suspecting his father's intention, the son said to him, he hoped, if he designed to set the Colonies in a flame, he would take care to run away by the light of it: that soon after, Galloway and the two Franklyns met together, and the glass having gone about freely, the Doctor, at a late hour, opened himself, and declared in favour of measures for attaining to Independence :—exclaimed against the corruption and dissipation of the Kingdom, and signified his opinion, that from the strength of Opposition, the want of union in the Ministry, the great resources in the Colonies, they would finally prevail. He urged Galloway to come into the Congress again; and from that time, united in the closest connection with Adams, broke off from Galloway, who lost the remaining part of his Journal, which probably was the most interesting. Galloway remembers Franklyn told him a plan was laid for stopping him in England, which a friend of great character in the law gave him notice of, and that he gave out he should sail in a fortnight by the packet, but went off suddenly by another opportunity.

In the late storm one of the back chimnies in Lord Hardwicke's house, St. James's Square, was blown down,—went through the roof and floors, and the chamber where Lady Mary or Miss Gregory would have slept, if the family had not removed two or three days before to Richmond. Two maids lodged in the chamber, and one of them, not inclining to sleep so near the fire as Miss Gregory's bed was placed, removed it to another part of the room, and escaped without hurt.

9th.—Called on Col° Montresor, and left name. On Martin Howard, where Paul Wentworth came. He says Gov. Johnstone made a point of it that Mr Temple should go out with the Comiss.—that his passage and all his expenses were paid by Government, and his salary paid him from the time he was dismissed: besides all this, eighteen hundred pounds of his account as Surv^r General was never allowed, and will never be demanded. This seems incredible: but the whole plan of the appointment of Comissioners was infatuation. Howard says Temple arrived with carriages, and thirty or forty packages, he and his family taking up the cabin, and Lord Bute's son, and other officers of rank in the steerage: that he talked of nothing but Carlisle and Eden: that he had wrote to Washington: and after vapouring a few days, set out, to the astonishment of all the poor Refugees, for Boston,—perhaps to take possession of some of their estates.

10th.—At the Old Jewry: collection for poor Dissenting

Ministers. I told Mauduit I came to put in my mite. He said they deserved nothing from me. They had behaved exceeding ill. He was a subscriber, and did not think it worth while to withdraw his name; but if it was not there, he would not now put it there. The Dissenters were favourers of the American revolt, without entering into the merits of it. As by far the greater part of the Americans were Dissenters themselves, the Dissenters in England seem for that reason to wish well to their civil dissensions also.

12th.—A well wrote but severe letter to Sir W. Howe in the P. Advertiser, undoubtedly by M——t. He desired me some time ago, if I saw anything in the paper, and anybody suggested it to be his, to say I knew nothing of it. Indeed, I do not know anything of this, but from the style and sentiment.

18th.—At Court, being the Queen's Birthday—or rather, observed as such. She was not out, expecting soon to be brought to bed. I saw more of the countenance, air, and manner of the Prince and the Bishop than I had ever done. Two more amiable persons have rarely been seen. "A cold day,"—as the King observed; for considering the multitude of persons he has to speak to, it's very excusable to make the weather the subject of some of them.

21st.—At Lord North's Levée.

Dr Berkenhout, who I had never seen before, called on me. He introduced himself saying Lord North was meditating provision for the Americans by grants of lands, and was desirious of knowing how far it would be agreeable to them. I said I did not imagine Ld North desired him to apply to me. He answered No, but he himself tho't I was most likely to know. I replied, I could not judge unless I knew where and in what manner the provision was intended. If in that part where I was Governor, it was difficult to find people to go upon new lands if given to them. The American Refugees were in general persons of liberal education, not brought up to labour, and many of them too far advanced in life to begin the world. He did not think New England a proper place, as it was so full of people, but talked of part of N. Jersey. I thought such a proposal might better be deferred to another year. He went over in the same ship, and under the same encouragement with Temple. He spake as if there had been a misunderstanding between them. He seems to be a busy inquisitive forward man.

22nd.—Ministry, its plain, have some hopes from the Carolina expedition. They have sent to some persons of S. Carolina to go out in the next packet. The state of the West Indies yet but precarious.

Garrick's death and character in the papers of yesterday and to-day. No actor upon the stage ever attained to so general esteem, and he is everywhere considered as the English Roscius.

24th.—At the Chapel St James's. The King attended without the Queen. Dr Kaye, Sub-Almoner, preached.

In the evening at Dr Heberden's—Bps. of Carlisle and Exeter, &c. Much said of the deceased Garrick, and the universal esteem had of him, the great notice taken of him by the nobility and first commoners, and the great pleasure it gave him: but some of the physicians present thought it shortened his days, as he was very indulgent to his appetite; a lover of high eating, and though not intemperate, fond of rich wines: had been long subject to disorders in his kidneys and bladder, a stone being found in the neck of the latter, and one of the former having wholly perished. From nothing, when he came upon the stage in '39 or '40, he accumulated above 100,000£, of which he died possessed, besides living all the time in an expensive style. It is not probable that Roscius or any player between him and Garrick ever raised the like fortune from the stage.

26th.—[Mr Paxton unwell.] . . . Paxton* seemed much affected with the thought of being buried in London. He had seen them take the bones up after they had been buried a few years, and cast them into a common heap. I said to him, I could not help an inclination to have my bones mixed with, or near to those who had been nearest to me in my life; but I asked him if he should have a bad leg or arm, not to say a bad tooth, whether, after it was separated, he would care much what became of it? and what reason there was to be concerned

* The name of Charles Paxton, late Commissioner of the Customs in America, occurs in the list of persons mentioned in the Confiscation Act.

about the other bones, more than about those? Very true, he said: however, he would give 100 guineas to be laid by his father and mother under the Chapel in Boston.

27th.—A drizzling day. There seems no doubt of Hotham's arrival, some say at Antigua, others Barbadoes.

I received letters of Nov. 4 from Col° Wanton at Rhode Island. He had not been able to find any tenant for my estate, but should make something of the grass sold to the army.

February 1st.—Mr Garrick's remains were buried in Westminster Abbey, the procession going by Charing Cross, between one and two o'clock. The streets were more crowded than when the King goes to Parliament. I called upon Mr Galloway at his lodgings while the people were collecting. We both of us chose to go into the city through Holborne, rather than remain in such a crowd, and so we saw nothing of the show . . .

5th.— . . . Advice of the taking of a French frigate of a new construction, of 36 guns, by the *Apollo* frigate Cap. Pownal, of 32 guns, after a smart engagement: the French—40 men killed, the English—8—many wounded—brought into Portsmouth.

7th.—Old Jewry: Mr . . .

Sir H. Houghton, coming from Meeting in my coach, told me he thought he had it from good authority, that some such offer had been made of mediation on the part of Spain: and afterwards at Court, Mr Burrell of the Excise, said he thought it probable. He had been assured the Prince of Asturias was favorably disposed. What length affairs have gone in Spain, is not agreed, but there seems to have been too much smoak [*sic*] to be no fire; and it is thought the Prince has taken a great share in the government, if the King is not wholly laid aside. It has been common in that family for the apparent successors to the Crown to be impatient, and for the Princes to become unwilling or unfit to continue to reign.

Blowers, Upham, &c., are desirous of a Court of Admiralty at R. Island. I wrote to Lord Sandwich desiring a hearing upon the subject.

8th.—A packet from New York . . . General Lee, a duel with young Laurence . . .

9th.—I called this forenoon upon Govr Johnstone at Kensington Gore. I was desired to deliver him a letter from Mr Upham from N. York. I was well inclined to it, having never seen him, except in the H. of Commons, where I was much abused by him. I found him very civil, polite, and obliging; and as he has altered his sentiments on American affairs, I hope he will alter his opinion of me, his only charge against me being misrepresentation to the Ministry, of the intention of Adams, &c., to stir up the people to revolt . . .

10th.—The news papers of this day mention the death of a M^r De Groote, in the Charter House, a grandson of the famous Grotius, who died about 1645. I think he must be more remote than a grandson, though Thomas Dudley, Gov. of Mass^ts died in 1651, and his grand-daughter Mrs Miller, died but last year. But Dudley's son, the father of Mrs Miller, was born but a short time before his father, the first Dudley, died, and this Mrs Miller lived to ninety . . .

Upon reinspecting the newspaper, I find that Isaac De Groote is said to be great-grandson of Grotius, and probably last of his name. My great-grandfather died in 1675.

12th.— . . . The city illuminated, and great disorders last night, to celebrate Keppel's acquittal. Sir H. Palliser's house in Pall Mall much damaged by the mob. Lord George G—— opposite, windows broke, and door burst open, and the mob dispersed by the Guards. Lord North's house surrounded, and the Admiralty insulted. Windows broke where there were no lights. My housekeeper waked me after 12 to tell me she must put candles in the windows, or they would be broke to pieces, Dr Parker's windows just by, being all broke. I gave my consent, and she stuck up a few in the drawing-room.

13th.—Several of the mob carried before Fielding yesterday, who committed them; but this did not discourage a general illumination last night. Mauduit never remembered any so universal. Every house must have something, but a little matter satisfied. I put only 3 candles in each window of my drawing-room. There was no mischief, and the streets were quiet sooner than the night before. What made it more difficult to restrain the mob, was the general concurrence of all orders in the imprudence of Palliser in the prosecution, as those who stood out would have been charged as approvers of it. Even Lord North, Lord George G——, Lord Dartmouth, Hardwicke, the Bp. of London, &c., &c., put up lights. I went up to Mr Ellis's about 9 and saw he had none, and I was vexed with myself for my own, but soon after his flambeaux were lit.

Sober people have said that if they were sure of being always obliged to conform to such caprices of the people, they would chuse to live in Paris, rather than London. Some say there must be a third illumination to-night.

14th.—Quiet last night . . .

17th.—Illumination again last night upon Keppel's coming to town. Almost everybody conformed: Lord George's house fuller than before. I kept my windows dark—had one square broke after I went to bed. The whole is extravagance. Sir Hugh Palliser, from personal resentment, without consulting anybody, brings a charge against the Admiral. The Lords of the Admiralty, it seems agreed, could not avoid a Court Martial. The Admiral is honourably acquitted. Palliser sinks into disgrace.

The Opposition triumph as if it was a victory gained over Administration, who have had no concern in the prosecution. The thanks of both Houses given to Keppel in just such terms as the Opposition chose, whereas no victory was obtained; and if no charge had been brought against him his conduct would have remained very doubtful. But the Ministry vail to every measure to humour the people, and unless they shew more spirit, it looks as if the disorders would increase.

As warm to-day as it is commonly in May.

18th.—At Lord North's Levée . . .

21st.—At Prince's Street: a young man preached—his gown and his hair à la mode of the young Episcopal clergy.

Keppel dining yesterday in the city with a Committee, who presented him with his freedom in an heart of oak box, was dragged by the rabble from Charing Cross to the London Tavern, Bishops-Gate Street; the horses being taken out, the coachman removed from the box, and a sailor with a blue flag put in his place. In the evening the houses in the city were generally illuminated, but not to the west of Temple Bar. The mob which followed him to his own house in Audley Square made great slaughter of the windows in their route. I hapned not to fall within it, and escaped. Mr Ellis had his windows broke, and even Charles Fox, which one of the newspapers intimated was a contrivance to lessen the clamour, which the friends of Government would make more loudly if they were alone.

22nd.—A prize sent in to Falmouth, taken by Cap. Eden in a privateer, brother to Sir Robert, &c., bound from Guadaloupe to France. It is said that Hotham and Grant had taken St Lucy . . .

24th.—Lord North began to open the Budget, which took so much time that he referred part until to-morrow. Fifteen millions must be raised. Seven millions he had agreed to borrow. He hinted his hopes of France's relinquishing the American connexions, &c.

25th.—I called on Mr Eden, who seems to approve of the Court of Admiralty at Rhode Island . . .

26th.—At Lord Carlisle's, to acquaint him with the application for a Court of Admiralty at Newport, which he approves of.

At Lord Hardwicke's, where was Stewart the Architect, or Planner of grounds, who dined at Sir Samp. Gideon's, and Dr Douglas. I went with the latter to St. James's, to enquire of Lady Egremont, in Waiting, how the Queen and Prince [blot] did? Much company in the Caudle Room.

At Lord Huntingdon's, where was his nephew Capt. Rawdon. I suppose he who lost his leg, tho' he is so well fitted with another that no difference appears.

At Mr Ellis's, who has been confined 10 days with a boil.

Called on Mrs Burnet and Col^o Leland—which is doing a great deal for me in the visiting way.

Often colder in June.

28th.—At Dr Kippis's. At Court. Much talk of Byron's arrival in W. Indies, but nothing authentick. Peace between the Emperor and K. of Prussia past doubt. Q—— whether England gains or loses?

In the evening at Dr Herberden's. Mr Frampton, a country gentleman I don't remember there before. Dr H. says his thermometer was at 63 this day at noon: that the mean of the mercury for the whole month of February has been 48½: that for 10 years past the mean the whole month of April has not exceeded 48: that the two last months of January and February only ½ an inch of rain has fallen: that usually in Jany and February there falls 4 inches of water. It is remarkable that in America and Italy, as far as we have yet heard, the cold has been more severe than for many years past.

March 1st.—The fine weather still continues, and W. wind. The cry now is for an E. wind, to bring the troops expected from Scotland, and some I suppose from the Continent.

3rd.—Dined at Lord Dartmouth's—Lord and L. Clarendon, and L. Charlotte Hyde, Mr Ord and wife, Mr Hopkins, Sir G Carleton, and Gov. Legge.

Wrote to Putnam, Waller, Blowers, and Wanton.

4th.—Certain advice of Byron's arrival at Barbadoes Jany 12th—one ship not arrived . . .

6th.—Green, Thomas Reeve, Weekes, dined with me, and Mr Clark, Missionary at Dedham, lately arrived from New York. He was confined on board a Guard ship at Boston two months . . . hard of hearing . . . His father was Minister of Salem village . . . this son was a preacher among the Congregationalists . . . he thought fit to conform, and go to England for Orders . . . He applied to me for a Certificate of his character, which I gave him.

8th.—The newpapers mention the death Lord Suffolk at Bath. He took great notice of me when I first came to England, but I have never yet met with any person who, when I asked anything for any of my family or friends, would make use of their influence in my behalf, which I attribute to a fear lest it should be considered as a favour which, if granted at their request, would lessen their claims for themselves, or some of their connexions. He has left no children. The Countess is said to be with child. He has an uncle, his presumptive heir, who has only daughters; and after him the title would go to a very remote relation . . .

11th.—The private letters from N. York say there are more

than 100 privateers at N. York fitted and fitting, to cruise against the French and the Americans. A letter from Blowers to Bliss says the Refugees are in high spirits from an expectation that the Rebellion will soon be over. Both kingdom and Colonies are so much exhausted by it, that it is difficult to say which will, of necessity, give way soonest . . .

12th.—Dr Chandler called and read a letter from Dr Ingolls of New York, of Feb. 5th. He says a letter from Silas Deane to France has been intercepted, in which he says, unless they can be assisted with several millions in specie, they shall not be able to go on with the war another year; and Ingolls adds, that he had seen several other letters to the same purpose. He says the people in the Colonies are in a consternation with a tax of 15 millions of dollars, which they are to pay next year, and so every year for 18 years to come: and it is certain either that their paper must continue at its depreciated rate, or if it should rise in value, that the burden of so great a tax must be insupportable. He thinks, with a little aid from England, the Rebellion will be over this summer. Speaking of the measures in England, he calls the speech made by Lord North the last year—that *miserable* speech.

16th.—Accounts received this forenoon of the taking of Pondicherry, &c., from the French. This is a great affair; but as on the one hand, by distressing the French, we may hope to incline them to reasonable terms of accommodation, so, on the other, we are in danger of drawing the Spaniards into the war, in order to the relief of their ally.

18th.—At Lord North's Levée . . .

19th.—The papers say John Adams is gone back from Paris to Boston. It does not appear that he sustained a public character. It seems agreed Franklin is now sole Minister from the revolted Colonies. Mr Strahan, the King's Printer, and now Member of Parliament for [blank] told me what I did not know before—that soon after Franklin was of age, he procured by his labour, money enough to pay his passage from Philadelphia to London, where he supported himself 18 months by working as a Press-man in a Printing house in Wild Court, near Lincolns Inn Fields. After Franklin came over Agent for Pensylvania, he proposed several times to Strahan, to go and make a visit to his old master Watts, who was then living, but something or other was always in the way.

21st.—At the Chapel, S[t] James's;—Bishop of Exeter. He was much awed, and delivered his discourse much more gracefully when I heard him at the Rolls.

At Court. I mentioned to the King what I heard yesterday from Halifax, which he had not heard.

Spoke to M[r] Hele-Hutchinson at Court.

In the evening at D[r] Heberden's.

I never was more disordered in speaking to the King than to-day; and by his sudden turning and speaking to the next person, I think he discovered it.

24th.—In the city. An airing with M[r] Galloway to Camberwell and Peckham, and home by the Greenwich road. He says, while the army was at Philadelphia, some pieces taken from the English papers, had been republished in the Philad. papers, against the Minority: that Howe sent his Secr[y] Mackenzie to Galloway, who was a sort of Town Governor, to put a stop to all publications of that sort. Soon after, something wrote in Philadelphia against the Minority or Opposition was published, which occasioned the sending Mackenzie a second time, to know whether the orders had been given. Galloway said he hardly thought Mackenzie was in earnest. No orders were given not to publish anything against the Ministry. The printers were sent for, or sent to, by Howe, and required to publish nothing against the Minority.

He says further, that General Howe advised him to make his peace with the Revolters, when the King's troops were about to evacuate Philadelphia, and to apply to Clinton for a flag of truce. Galloway said there was no chance of his obtaining a pardon; but Howe continuing to urge it, Galloway applied to General Clinton, who utterly refused to shew any countenance to the proposal. He does not scruple to say, there was never a week when Howe had it not in his power to reduce America, and that he does not believe he ever intended it.*

* These are remarkable words, and not a little damaging: they are, however, in accordance with a few stray remarks made elsewhere. It may be

26th.—Sir George Rodney met me in the Park, and having never spoke to me before, asked if I had heard the news? No. Lord Stormont had just told him, from Mr Penn, that not only Philadelphia, but the whole Province of Pensilvania, had declared for Government . . .

27th.—Sir G. Rodney's news is come to nothing . . .

28th.—At Prince's Street. Dined with Strahan, where Galloway was to have been, but not well. General Peckham there, who had served under Prince Ferdinand, and afterwards was made a Colonel and Major-General by the K. of Prussia.

Strahan shewed me the original Advertisement in Franklin's hand writing, about his sending the Letters to America, wch F. sent to Strahan to be printed in the *London Chronicle:* an extract also from the letter which F. sent to America, accompanying the Letters. Of this he promised me a copy: the extract is in F.'s hand writing.*

31st.—A letter from Putnam from N. York, 17 Feby which I sent Lord North for perusal. Colo Vassall says he knows that young Laurens, son to the late Congress President, has wrote to his wife from Philadelphia, that he doubts not matters will be accommodated this summer. This is the young Laurens who fought a duel with Lee. It is one of the young fellows who lodged in the same house with me at Bath, the first year I came to England. He married a W. India Merchant's daughter in the city, and left her here when he went to America.

April 1st.— . . . General Robertson's being appointed Governor of N. York occasions much talk. Gage tells me Tryon is superseded, not with his consent. Robertson is not only old, but has had one, if not more apoplectic strokes, and is not popular.

2nd.—Good Friday . . .

4th.—Easter Sunday. At the Old Jewry. A stranger preached, &c. Remarkably warm southerly day. Dr Chand[ler]

---

sound policy to send out a mutual friend to conciliate, or to try and negociate for a peaceful solution of a dispute; but if the quarrel has past friendly negociation, and if the sword must be drawn, then, in that case, a General who is a sympathiser with Revolters, only goes out to assist them. He draws the sword to play with his duties, and designedly cheats his Sovereign.

* These promised extracts are not found among the Governor's papers.

and son, Bliss, E. H. and his wife at dinner. Mr Ellis called. I observed to him Lord G.'s declaration in the House —that Govt, after the Americans had refused the offers, was not held to them. He said it was very well, but such a declaration was ill timed. The Opposition sought for it to make an ill use of it, and Lord North, he said, always gave in to Opposition upon these points.

5th.—A warm south wind. With Mr Keene and Colo Townshend in the Park. The latter had the care of shipping off the recruits from the river Medway. He says there are 15 or 1600, and with the Guards make about 2,000; and the Scotch troops being 2500, the embarkation will not be 5,000 without foreign troops, which Keene said would not be good for much.

7th.—In the city. Report from France yesterday; unfavorable from Ireland; favorable of W. India affairs—all vague. I wrote to Judge Browne at Cowbridge, in answer to a letter from him, to send his son to town; my taylor should make his uniform; I would give him 10 gs, which would be eno' at present for other purposes; and he should breakfast and dine with me while I staid in town.

8th.—An accident last night furnishes subject for conversation in a dearth of foreign news. Mrs Ray, who has lived as a concubine with Ld Sandwich for many years, and who has several children by him, some well grown, has been at Covent Garden Playhouse; and just as she had got in, or was getting in to her charriot, a Clergyman, who it is said, had made his suit to her to be his wife, and had been refused, came close to her with a pistol, and shot her through the head. He immediately fired another pistol, with intent to blow his own brains out, but failed, and was thereupon secured. It is said he had been an officer, and had left the Army or Navy, and that his name is Hackman. Lord Sandwich, it is said, was waiting supper for her return, when the shocking news was brought him.

Captain Bruce, who had been an officer in the Train in America and at Boston, murdered himself this morning, after several attempts by stabbing, cutting, &c., in a cruel, bloody manner.

Walpole—the accomplished and indefatigable—was not likely to allow such a sensational story to pass unnoticed. It is hoped that the reader will forgive the insertion of his version of it here, which is sufficiently valuable, as coming from his pen. Writing to the Countess of Ossory April 8, 1779, he says—

"I was interrupted by the strangest story I ever heard, and which I cannot yet believe, though it is certainly true. Last night, as Miss Ray was getting into her coach in Covent Garden from the play, a Clergyman shot her through the head, and then himself. She is dead, but he is alive to be hanged—in the room of Sir Hugh Palliser. Now Madam, can one believe such a tale? How could poor Miss Ray have offended a divine? She was no enemy to the Church Militant or Naval, to the Church of England, or the Church of Paphos. I do not doubt but it will be found, that the assassin was a Dissenter, and instigated by the Americans to give such a blow to the State. My servants have heard that the murderer was the victim's husband:—methinks his jealousy was very long-suffering! *Tantæne animis celestibus iræ!* and that he should not have compounded for a Deanery! What trials Lord Sandwich goes through! He had better have one for all . . .

"The assassin's name is Hackman: he is a brother to a reputable tradesman in Cheapside, and is of a very pleasing figure himself, and most engaging behaviour. About five years ago he was an officer in the 66th Regiment, and being quartered at Huntingdon, pleased so much as to be invited to the Oratorios at Hinchinbrook, and was much caressed there. Struck with Miss Ray's charms, he proposed marriage; but she told him she did not choose to carry a knapsack. He went to Ireland, and there changed the colour of his cloth, and at his return, I think not long ago, renewed his suit, hoping a cassock would be more tempting than a gorget—but in vain. Miss Ray, it seems, has been out of order, and abroad [in public] but twice all the winter. She went to the play on Wednesday night, for the second time, with Galli, the singer. During the play the desperate lover was at the Bedford Coffee House, and behaved with great calmness, and drank a glass of capillaire. Towards the conclusion he sallied into the Piazza, waiting till he saw his victim, handed by Mr. Macnamara. He came behind her, pulled her by the gown, and on her turning round, clapped the pistol to her forehead, and shot her through the head. With another pistol, he then attempted to shoot himself, but the ball only grazing his brow, he tried to dash out his own brains with the pistol, and is more wounded by those blows than by the ball.

"Lord Sandwich was at home, expecting her to supper at half an hour after ten. On her not returning an hour later, he said something must have happened: however, being tired, he went to bed at half an hour after eleven, and was scarce in bed before one of his servants came in, and said Miss Ray was shot. He stared, and could not comprehend what the fellow meant: nay, lay still, which is full as odd a part of the story as any. At twelve came a letter from the Surgeon to confirm the account,—and then he was extremely afflicted.

"Now, upon the whole, Madam, is not the story full as strange as ever it was? Miss Ray has six children; the eldest son is fifteen; and she was at least three times as much. To bear a hopeless passion for five years, and then murder one's mistress—I don't understand it. If the story clears up at all, your Ladyship shall have a sequel. These circumstances I received from Lord Hertford, who heard them at Court yesterday from the Lords of the Admiralty. I forgot that the Galli swooned away on the spot."—Vol. vii. p. 190.

Again, April 17, he writes as follows—

"For the last week all conversation has been engrossed by a shocking murder committed on the person of a poor woman connected with a most material personage now on the great stage. You will have seen some mention of it in the papers. I mean the assassination of Miss Ray, Lord Sandwich's mistress, by a Clergyman, who had been an officer, and was desperately in love with her, though she between thirty and forty, and has had nine children. She was allowed to be most engaging; and so was the wretched lover, who had fixed his hopes of happiness on marrying her, and had been refused after some encouragement—I know not how much. On his trial yesterday he behaved very unlike a madman, and wishes not to live. He is to suffer on Monday . . . I shall reserve the rest of my paper till Tuesday."

Accordingly, on Tuesday he writes—

"The poor assassin was executed yesterday. The same day Charles Fox moved for the removal of Lord Sandwich, but was beaten by a large majority; for in parliament, the Ministers can still gain victories. Adieu!"—vii. 193.

At this day also, the proceedings in the matter of the second Court Martial were dividing the attention of all London, and on this he remarks—

"Though Sir Hugh Palliser's trial has been begun this week, the public does not honour it with the same attention as Keppel's. It does not brighten for the Vice-Admiral."

Again, May 9—

"Palliser's trial has ended shamefully. He is acquitted *with honour*, of not having obeyed his Admiral's signals,—which is termed blameable, for not having given the reason why he did not, —and that reason was, the rottenness of his mast, with which he returned to Portsmouth, without its being repaired yet."—vii. 199.

10th.—With Judge Oliver, Howard, and Col° Leonard to the Bp. of London, at Fulham, to whom I introduced them, and he received us with great politeness.

We came home to dinner, where Dr Chandler, Thomas, and my son E. joined us. Chandler, after dinner, mentioned an anecdote of Dr Franklin. When Morris resigned the Government, and Denny succeeded, at an entertainment, Franklin sat on one side of Denny, and Morris the other. Franklin expressed his wishes to be able to contribute to the success of Denny's administration. Morris, in a very audible voice observed, that no man was more able than Franklin to promote such success, but you will find he has a heart as black as H——. This brought to my mind the revenge Franklin took after Morris was dead, for in the History of Pensilvania, he remarks upon Morris's going out, and Denny's succeeding, that according to the Scotch proverb, change of Devils is blithesome.

11th.—Yesterday at dinner I recollected I had not seen Captain Poynton, one of the Massachusetts Refugees, for a long time, and enquired of the company what was become of him, but nobody knew anything particular, and supposed he was at lodgings near London. This morning a man came to me to know if I had heard anything of Capn Poynton: said his own name was Poynton: that he is a peruke-maker, Leicester Fields, Orange Court: that they are brothers' children: that the Captn used to be often at his house, but sometimes would stay away months at a time, but being absent longer that ever before, since his being in England, for some time past he had been enquiring, but could get no intelligence since the latter part of July last, when he left his lodgings at Eltham, and carried his baggage, &c. to Charing Cross, which he went with from thence in a Hackney coach.

It is odd such an enquiry of me, so immediately after my accidental enquiry, without any suspicion of anything amiss. There is reason to fear something bad has hapned,—that he has been destroyed for the sake of his baggage, or at least, that he died, and his death has been concealed for the sake of what he left.

At S[t] James's, K. and Q. . . .

12th.—In the city, and rec[d] a year's interest of Bank Stock. In the evening Johannot* being at my house to drink coffee, I asked him about his message to Washington when the troops left Boston. He says the Select-men, all but Austen, applied to Howe for leave to send out a Flag to Washington, to let him know, that if the King's troops should be molested in their embarkation, Howe would certainly set fire to the town, &c. Johannot says Howe made a difficulty, but finally consented. Austen, the Selectman said in Johannot's hearing, he never would be concerned in such a message: there was no need of it: the troops would not be molested: the town would not be fired. Being asked how he knew? he answered "*Very well*," but did not say how. The two Generals understood one another: but whether he discovered this by his sagacity, or had any evidence of a communication, he did not say.

Johannot and another went out, and after waiting a long time in a snow storm, before the Flag was answered, Col[o] Leonard and some others appeared, and after receiving the message, co͞municated it to the officer in command at Roxbury, but Washington being at Cambridge, Johannot and the other returned without any answer at that time; but soon after, whether on that day or the next, or what day I did not enquire, an answer was given—that General Washington would take no

* Mr. Danforth, writing from London, Nov. 8, 1779, to Elisha Hutchinson, then in Birmingham, says—"Probably you saw in the papers an account of the death of Peter Johannot. The funeral was attended by Mr. Gray and myself. Has been blind about 5 years." The following occurs in the Diary of Dr. P. Oliver:—"1809, Aug.—Peter Johannot dyed this month in London aged 79." Perhaps this latter was a son of the former.

notice of such an application. But Johannot says everybody was easy, and looked upon themselves as secure from any attack upon the troops, and from firing the town, as if a Treaty had been made in form.

By the letters from New York, it appears that Livingstone, the New Jersey Governor, had a narrow escape at Elizabeth Town, the bed where he lay being warm, when the King's troops entered his house. Two of his daughters had not left the house: one of them was extremely frightened, and ran to the top of the house, but recovered herself upon polite assurances from Lord Cathcart, of protection. But it looks as if the skirmishes made at different places had been of no service, and that the Americans will boast of their bravery in repelling the King's troops.

13th.—Mr Galloway, who returned yesterday from the country, brought me his letters from New York. In one of them it is said Govr Hutchinson had wrote confidentially to a friend, that Government was disposed to give up its claim to America, if it could be secured against the injuries from America, when inimically disposed—or to that effect, which he blames the person who rec^d^ the letter, for mentioning. I have not the least remembrance of giving the least pretence for such a report, and rather think some other person may have written to that purpose; and upon a suggestion that such a letter was received, it might be reported I was the writer.

14.—I wrote to day by Major Small to Mr Walter and Putnam to inform them of the letter I had seen yesterday;—that I had given no foundation for such a report; that I had wrote to no persons except them in New York; and I desired them to vindicate me, and to enquire how such a report took its rise.

19th.—Cap^n^ Hyde Parker and Col^o^ Campbell arrived in town from Georgia: confirm the account of a second battle there, which they call a smart one—1000 said to be killed, wounded, and taken—most of their officers included in this number, and one General. Nine vessels taken with provisions: the communication with S. Carolina said to be cut off, which I don't well understand. Another account says there is great desertion from the rebel army in S. Carolina.

20th.—No *Gazette* yet to explain the news of yesterday. The action is said to have been between about 1000 of the King's troops, under Sir James Beard, and 1500 Provincials: the provision vessels bound to D'Estaigne at Martinico.

Dined at Lord Hardwicke's—Galloway, Auchmuty, and his nephew.

21st.—The *Gazette* of last evening, though it is more favorable with respect to the loss of the English than was feared—only 5 privates and no officers being killed—yet it makes the American loss less than reported—about 350 only, killed and taken prisoners, and an uncertain number drove into the river and drowned; but it gives no intimation of any further progress expected.

22nd.—At Lord North's Levée . . .

29th.—After long waiting compleated taking out the Commissions for a Court of Admiralty at Rhode Island, and left them with Mr Stephens, desiring him to forward them under cover directed to Sampson Salter Blowers Esq. at New York.

30th.—Wind changed to the eastward, and it is expected the fleet will sail, but Lord Cornwallis was in town last night waiting the result of Gen. Howe's motion for an Enquiry, which was rejected by the House of Commons; Lord Hardwicke, in a note to me says—in an awkward and undignified manner.

May 1st.—No account of the fleets sailing . . .

2nd.—Old Jewry . . . Adm. Gambier says that about 10 days before he sailed, Gen. Clinton proposed an attempt upon Providence to destroy the shipping, and Clinton went to the E. end of Long Island, and Gambier went in his own ship to Newport, from whence he was to advise Clinton of the state of Providence; that in a dark night one of Gambier's boats rowed up to Providence: saw there were only two hulks, which had been designed for fire-ships to burn the *Raisonable*, and an old brig hauled up; all the rest of their shipping having got out when D'Estaigne was at Rhode Island. Not content with this, he hired several Refugees who, in disguise, went to Providence and returned, confirming the other account; upon which he gave advice to Clinton, and went back himself in his ship to New York.

3rd.—An Express arrived about noon from Adm. Arbuthnot, who sailed from Portsmouth, Saturday the 1st Ins^t^ with the fleet for America, and the next morning met an Express boat from Jersey with intelligence that on Friday 5 men of war and 50 transports had made a descent on that Island, and he thereupon determined to sail immediately thither for its defence. It's unlucky the fleet to America should be diverted; but I don't hear Arbuthnot blamed for going there without orders.

4th.—Called on Mr Jackson, Southampton Buildings, who I found very friendly and obliging. Last night the House of Commons resolved to go into an enquiry upon Howe's motion. Lord North spake against it, but there was no division. This affair causes a great jumble. I think it probable Howe himself who made the motion was content it should rest; but Charles Fox, hoping to bring Lord George into trouble, would not suffer it. On the other hand Mr Rigby and some others, expect to set Howe in a bad light, and fell off from Lord North; or possibly Lord North himself did not care much if an enquiry should be made, provided it does not come from him.

Nothing more from Jersey.

Dined at General Gage's, with a great number of Americans.

5th.—A rainy day: I don't recollect so much in a day since Christmas. It is said Arbuthnot did not reach Jersey until Monday afternoon: success still uncertain.

Sir Hugh Palliser honourably acquitted.

6th.—Nothing yet from Jersey except the first letter, Saturday the 1st in the afternoon, advising that the French had attempted to land, and been repulsed; but as several ships were in the offing, supposed to be a reinforcement, it was expected a fresh attempt with a reinforcement. General Conway, Govr of Jersey, went out of town Monday night at eleven o'clock for Portsmouth, and sailed next day for Jersey.

7th.—Everybody anxious for news . . . Sir Hugh Palliser's acquittal published in the newspapers. No publick rejoicing.

The sentence does not leave him without an imputation of negligence in not acquainting the Admiral with the state of his ship.

8th.— . . . Advice of the French being repulsed from Jersey before Arbuthnot appeared, and that he was gone to join his ships, which went to Torbay.

9th.—At Dr Kippis's. Called on Mr Galloway, who dined with me. He says that upon Ld Cornwallis and General Grey giving their opinion that the reduction of America was impracticable, a Cabinet Council was called yesterday, and it was moved to let the enquiry before the House rest where it is: that Ld Cornwallis called Mr Eden out of the Council Chamber, and advised to it: that the Council are to meet again to-morrow.

10th.—It is said Arbuthnot joined the merchant vessels at Torbay.

A rumour at the Treasury that there is an insurrection in Ireland.

I was an hour and more with Lord Hillsborough. He is strong in favour of an Union with Ireland, upon the plan of the Scotch Union . . .

15th.—Doctor Gardiner and Col^o Pickman called on me from Bristol, and dined—with two Auchmutys, Col^o Chandler, and Treas^r Gray. They are all anxious to return to America, except Gray. He and Ch. Just. Oliver, and Secretary Flucker, wish to have some provision in England, and never much think of America. I can see reasons which are personal for each of them. I have more of the old Athenians in me; and though I know not how to reason upon it, I feel a fondness to lay my bones in my native soil, and to carry those of my dear daughter with me.

19th.—Installation of Knights of the Bath. I had no curiosity even to see the procession, and went into the city. General H. was one. The evening before, the enquiry into his conduct was going on in the H. of Commons, and to-day he appears with his Star—a mark of approbation for his signal conduct at Long Island, which is now one principal part for which, by the public voice, he is censured.

20th.—At Lord G. Germaine's Levée. I thanked him for his patronage and publick avowal of the cause of the American Refugees in the House of Commons. He seemed pleased with it, and said it was no more than they were justly entitled to.

I expressed my concern lest the Opposition should spin out the time in examining Howe's and Burgoyne's witnesses. He did not doubt he should have three or four days left to examine others.

While I was waiting, Cumberland, Secr^y to the Board of Trade, said he was astonished the Americans could bear the abuse offered them by Gen. Grey at his examination in the H. of Commons, when he declared the Americans were disloyal almost to a man. He wondered they did not join in an Address to the King, and a declaration of their motives to leave* their country estates, friends, &c. When he was gone, some who sat by me asked what I thought of the proposal? I said I never chose to give an opinion suddenly upon a matter of that importance.

June 2nd.—Talk of a rupture with Spain: disturbance in Ireland, &c., &c., and Bank Stock falls 2 ꝑ. c^t;—about a month ago was at 118; has gradually sunk to 110.

3rd.—At Lord North's, and Lord George's Levées . . .

4th.—The King's Birthday. I have attended every Birthday, except when my dear daughter was in her last illness; but I had no spirits to-day.

Dined with Col^o Vassall, in a company of Americans. Galloway shewed me a long letter from New York, from Mr Cox, a Pensilvania Counsellor, whose wife remains at Philad., and corresponds with him. He says the Indians are come down on the back of the Colonies. He expects Gov. Franklin will soon go into New Jersey, and assume his Governm^t, and has flattering expectations that peace will be restored this summer. Burgoyne's witnesses finished yesterday in the H. of Commons. It is expected Lord George will call his Tuesday next the 8th Instant.

5th.—At Lord Townshend's. Sr Jno Blaquiere was there—

* Instead of "to leave," the sense of the passage seems to suggest that the words "for having left" would make a hurriedly written sentence clearer.

just come from Ireland. He says La Mothe Piquet returned to Brest, and that he is not sailed again; but that four frigates, Jones Comm^r [Commodore?] sailed the middle of May, or sooner, with troops—some say 600, some 2000: that there had been no account of them since. He adds that upon a recommendation of the Congress to France, that if they could not be supplied with 500,000£ sterl. they must submit. Application was made to Spain, France not being able to advance the money, and that Spain had advanced it, the money having been actually paid on a day he named, to one Spence [?] for the use of the Americans. Whether Spain lends it to America, or France borrows it of Spain, and lends to America, he does not know.

7th.—Dined at Sir Richard Sutton's: Mauduit, Galloway, and Knox. Galloway said that at the desire, and in behalf of the Magistrates of Philadelphia, as well as for himself, he applied, as soon as he heard the city was to be evacuated, to Sr Wm Howe, to know what was to become of them? He advised them to make their terms with Washington, and to apply to Gen. Clinton for a Flag of Truce. This was grievous advice. Galloway found access, and communicated it to Clinton, who did not refuse a Flag, but advised them not to ask it, assuring them they had no reason to despair: he did not doubt America would be reduced, and encouraged them their salaries should be continued,—and they remained with the army.

Another affair was mentioned which hapned in the Jerseys. Galloway had proposed to the General, (Howe), with a troop of Light Horse, Americans, to surprize Livingstone and his Council, and the Assembly of New Jersey, all convened at Trenton, and Howe approved of it, only, some of the Regulars were to be joined. All at once, just as the business was to have been executed, the General sent Balfour, his Aide-du-camp, to Galloway, to let him know the General had altered his mind: that as there would be a cartel in a few days, it would only make a few more prisoners to exchange.

Both these matters, Sr Richard doubted whether it would not be best to ask no questions upon. The first, he said, if proved, would amount to Treason, and Ministry would be abused for concealing it, and not bringing Howe to trial. The second, Howe would find some way to evade, and say he had other reasons he did not think proper to give to Galloway.

Besides, Sir Rich. Sutton added, that it was not the design of Ministry to bring an accusation against Howe, but merely to vindicate themselves from a charge of not having made sufficient provision, or not given proper orders for the reduction of America.

9th.—General Robertson was examined yesterday in the House. The minority endeavoured to prevent it . . .

10th.—Robertson again in the House last night, and further examination ordered to-day . . .

11th.—Robertson still under cross-examination by the minority, most, evidently, for the sake of taking up the time and preventing, if possible, Galloway and others from being heard; and the further examination of him was put off to Monday. Robertson was asked—not when at the Bar, but by some of the members in a circle, and I suppose not in the House,—whether he thought it practicable to attempt the works on Long Island? He said—If, upon a chase, anybody had been stopped by them, he should have thought him a very bad huntsman.—Rain all day—scarce any cessation.

12th.—Darby returned yesterday with the ten ships which accompanied Arbuthnot. It is said the Brest fleet are out, 25 sail of the line, and that orders are gone to Sr Cha. Hardy to sail immediately. Sr Wm Meredith made a motion last night to address the King to grant a new Commission for treaty with the Americans, which was rejected without a division.

14th.—Called on Sir Richard Sutton.

Prince William* set out this morn^g^ at 4 o'clock for Portsmouth, to embark on board *Admiral Digby*, without any servant—his tutor accompanied him—he is about 14.

16th.—The Spanish Ambassador this morning before the Levée, was at Lord Weymouth's, and presented a Rescript from his Master, which is called a Manifesto, and is said to amount to a Declaration of War. This was communicated in

* Afterwards King William IV.

substance, in the afternoon, by Ld Weymouth to the Lords, and by Lord North to the Commons. In the latter, great abuse of the Ministry, but the consideration referred until to-morrow, when it is said the Manifesto will be translated and brought before Parliament. A great consternation.

Mr Galloway at the Bar of the House of Commons, examined from 7 o'clock to between 11 and 12, and not finished.

17th.—The Grand Fleet under Sir Charles Hardy sailed yesterday from St Helens: the E. India ships which had sailed were recalled, and are gone out under one convoy of the Grand Fleet.

Stocks not so much affected to-day as was expected. It's thought the French fleet is gone to Cadiz to join the Spaniards.

18th.—The Opposition are in a sad hobble. They forwarded an enquiry into Howe's conduct, but intended to produce such witnesses only as would vindicate him. After they had been heard, and Lord George G. proposed to call witnesses, they would have stopped; and I have it from such authority as satisfies me, offered to forbear moving for a vote of thanks or exculpation, but Lord G. insisted on going on. They tried to perplex old General Robertson, but he was too cunning for them, and sometimes turned the laugh upon them by his answers. Last night, when Sir Ric^d Sutton was putting questions to Galloway, Burke stood up and asked if he was not a Member of the Congress? Galloway answered—"Yes;" then followed—"Have you had your pardon?"—the answer—"No;" and as Galloway was giving a reason, viz., that he had been guilty of no offence but for his loyalty, was pronounced by the Congress a capital offender against the new States, there was a cry—"Withdraw! withdraw!" and by means thereof two hours of the short remains of the session were spent, and all the charge which would have been bro't against Howe in that time avoided; and then Galloway was called to the Bar again.

Cool, or west wind.

19th.—The Bishop of London called and spent some time. He laments the deplorable state of the nation. He says all is owing to the Opposition, and the Opposition is owing to Lord

Bute in the beginning of this reign, whose imprudence in turning so many out of office, and his timidity of conduct afterwards, put all into confusion. I observed that I had a curiosity to see him, but had never been able. He surprized me by saying he had never seen him in his life; which is very extraordinary, as the Bishop has been so many years in the House of Lords, and so often at Court . . .

21st.—A gentleman who knew me, and asked how I had been since he last saw me, informed me Saturday morning as I was taking my walk, that he went to Aylesbury a day or two before, and that Sir Francis Bernard died Wednesday night the 16th, which has been since confirmed.

22nd.—A warm debate last night in the House of Commons. Lord North proposed a Bill to enable the King to encrease the Militia, not exceeding a number equal to those already established. This was generally agreed to, but it occasioned bitter reflections on the Ministry, and Lord North in particular, who was reproached with the places he had provided for himself and family. He vindicated his conduct, but shed tears, and declared he had long wished to resign, but had been prevented.

An express from New York—letters to 25 May. An expedition to Chesapeak, it is said had succeeded as well as could be expected: many vessels destroyed wth great quantities of tobacco, also magazines of provisions, and military stores laid up for Washington's army: two towns burnt, &c. Query, as to the last article?

23rd.—At Lord George's office. Mentioned to Mr Knox what I heard from Dr Chandler,—that one of the American privateers, under British colours, had brought to—a Spanish despatch boat,—broke open the packets, and passed for one of King George's subjects, and came into Boston, and bragged of the exploit. This [story] John Gray, son to the Treasurer,* brings from Boston. Knox seems to be much pleased with the accounts from New York.

24th.—At Court, where I had not been for near two months.

* Harrison Gray the Treasurer, is mentioned in the Confiscation Act, as among the "notorious conspirators," whose estates in America were to be seized. A biographical notice of him in Sabine's 'Loyalists,' vol. i. p. 488.

The K. took notice of the favorable appearance in America, particularly the dissatisfaction of many parts with the Congress: asked about Laurence, who I said was now out: he asked who was in his room? I told him Jay. Who was he? A lawyer—he had a brother in England. "What," says the K., "a Doctor—where is he?"

"Somewhere in England," I said.

"Not doing any good, I believe."

"No, I believe not."

He mentioned the wickedness of Opposition. I answered—"I detest them."

"I am sure you do," was his reply.

The Queen all goodness, asked how I had my health?

"As well as the times will admit. I use exercise, temperance, and try to keep my mind in an easy state."

"Ah," she replied, "there is no happiness without tranquility of mind. The health of the body depends much upon the mind."

26th.—I enquired of John Gray, who informed me that when he was in Boston, several of the Privateers which came in there were reported to have stopped Spanish vessels and plundered them, informing them they were under the King's Commission, and that two Masters that came from Boston with him in a carteel [?] ship, were on board the *Bunker's Hill*, an American privateer, when she met with a Spaniard, which they boarded and plundered. The privateer carried English colours at that time, and informed the Spaniards she was fitted out at Bristol, but he says nothing of opening packets. One of those Masters, he says, was named Storer, and is since arrived at Whitehaven . . .

27th.—At Dr Kippis's. Danforth and Bliss dined. A cold north wind like March. It is said Sr Cha. Hardy was left in the lat. of 48, but he had heard nothing of the French or Spaniards.

There are great endeavours speedily to man more English ships. An Act passed suddenly to invalidate all protections against a Press—to look back to the 16th. A stratagem was made use of the 23rd in the evening. No seamen appearing anywhere, the Tower was lighted up, and a report was spread that the King had removed Lord North—that he was in custody, and that he was bringing down to the Tower.* Many thousands collected upon Tower Hill, expecting him. Care was taken to block up the avenues with sufficient guards. Ten or a dozen different Press-gangs came on suddenly and secured several hundred, among whom were many masters and mates of colliers and other vessels, who were sent immediately down to the Nore. Some have proposed pressing the crews of all privateers, in which service it is computed 70,000 men are employed.

30th.—Judge Sewall came on a visit from Bristol last evening, and dined with me to-day, wth Danforth and Bliss. Expected Paxton from Pangbourne, that we might begin our journey to-morrow, but he has failed. Galloway and Mauduit in the evening: the former very angry with Lord Howe, for comparing him to the Apothecary in Romeo, whose poverty had driven him to say what he did not think: desires to publish his own examination.

July 1st.—People seem alarmed to-day with the debate of yesterday in the House of Lords. Upon the Militia Bill the minority proposed an amendment, and Lord Weymouth, with Lord Gower, voted and argued with them: Lord Chancellor and Lord Sandwich against them: and the amendment was carried by three quarters of the Lords. I met Mr Keene of the Board of Trade in the Park, much dejected. Lord T. told Paxton Lord North must go out.

2nd.—Left the town with affairs in great uncertainty; but I have no concern with them in town more than in the country. About two began a journey with Paxton, and about 8 reached Guilford, thro' Fulham.

4th.—Poor lodgings at a poor Inn. [at Wickham.] Went to church and heard Mr Rashleigh . . . A monument of the Earl and Countess of Carlisle . . . Dined 6 or 7 miles from

* It is hard to imagine how persons in authority could have lent themselves to the perpetration of such a disgraceful trick. Soldiers and sailors will voluntarily enter the services if they are fairly paid, fairly looked to, and fairly provided for in case of injury in their country's defence.

Wickham with Admiral Montague at Widley . . . Went on 5 miles to Portsmouth . . .

5th.—Called on Sir Sam[l] Hood . . . Sir Thomas Pye, Admiral of the Port . . .

6th.— . . . Went through the dockyard. The *Saint George*, a 90 gun ship, having all her timbers in, from bottom to top, I went into her hold, which struck me more than I imagined with the grandeur of it . . .

7th.— . . . We came to Rumsey, about 30 miles from Portsmouth. This is a considerable market town: a large old church. An apple tree grows out of the tower, which came up by accident, and a supply of earth has been afforded it, so that it bears fruit, which is carried about as a curiosity . . .

9th.—We went from Poole to Wareham . . . The Roman Amphitheatre, [near Dorchester,] and especially the Roman Camp, are the most curious works of antiquity I have seen in England . . .

10th.—We rode 8 miles to Weymouth . . . In the afternoon we went to Bridport . . .

11th.—In the forenoon we went to the Presbyterian Meeting. . . . In the afternoon at the parish church . . .

12th.—Set out early on horseback and rode to Lime [Lyme] to breakfast—a watering place where a few families were collected. An old man upon the beach shewed us where the Duke of Monmouth landed, and told us his uncle was hanged for being one of the men who rowed him ashore. At the George Inn, where he lodged, they have a room which they yet call Monmouth's room.

We went up a very long bad hill from Lime town, and went down one as bad into Sidmouth. From the top of the last hill, [Salcombe Hill] Paxton descryed the fleet lying in Torbay, but I could not then see them, but afterwards with a glass, had a view of the ships, but imperfect, from the top of the house where we lodged; and in the afternoon saw very plain, a long ship, which we made no doubt was the *Terrible*, going to join the fleet.

My principal design in going two or three miles out of my way to Sidmouth, was to shew my regard to M[r] Smith the

Presbyterian Minister lately settled there, but unfortunately he had gone from home this morning to see the fleet at Torbay. I found unexpectedly, Sam[l] Sewall from Bristol.

Sidmouth is a town convenient for smugglers. One Cap. Follet, one of M[r] Smith's congregation, who long used the Newf[d]land trade, was very polite to us.

It may be remarked in a note here, but not in so degraded a place as a Foot-note, that Mr. Isaac Smith, the Minister of the Presbyterian or Unitarian Chapel at Sidmouth, was an American Refugee who had struggled through many trials till he found a rest in a remote country town in England, where we should scarcely have expected to have found him. The Chapel was founded in 1710 at the top of High Street, and in the angle formed by Mill Lane, now called All Saints Road. He was appointed in 1778, and continued until 1784. Writing to Dr. Eliot Sep. 14, 1778, the Governor says in his Letter Book—"I took pleasure in the acquaintance and frequent visits of your friend M[r] Smith, while he continued in London. He has been for more than five years preaching to a Dissenting Church at Sidmouth, and was ordained last summer, and is unusually esteemed."

Salcombe Hill, that rises on the east side of the valley of the little river Sid, is about 500 feet high where the road passes over its brow; and though it is twenty miles from this spot to Torbay, it is possible that good eyes on a clear day could discern large ships lying there. The house where the Governor and his friend lodged was probably the London Hotel, the York not having been built till the commencement of the present century. Some old people have said that the Hotel once stood across the street, where there is now an open space of ground; but this assertion requires further proof. The Follet family, now wholly faded from sight, long flourished here as merchants and shipowners. The ground occupied by York Terrace was then covered with dockyards. The ships built there, and destined for the Newfoundland cod fishing trade, were launched over the open beach in calm weather, and taken to Exmouth to be completed for sea. The south coast of England lying extended opposite the coast of France, was so favourably situated, that the smuggling of French brandy was carried on to an enormous extent; but the lowering of the duties has rendered this illicit trade now unprofitable, so that it has almost died a natural death.

The Governor's eldest son Thomas, with his wife Sarah (Oliver) settled down at Heavitree near Exeter, and there they rest; and one of their sons, Andrew, with his wife Anne (Parker) in the later years of his life, bought a small property at Sidmouth, which I now have.

13th.—Left Sidmouth at ten o'clock and went to Exeter . . .

14th.—I viewed the Cathedral . . . A large Library behind the Altar I think must have some books of value. I took down a thick folio Concordance, printed in 1650, the author Samuel Newman, Teacher of a church at Rehoboth, N. England. With some improvement, this laborious work has been reprinted from time to time, and the name of Newman is now lost, and it is called the Cambridge Concordance . . .

After dinner we went about 20 miles to lodge at Ashburton, a large old town with but indifferent buildings, the streets full of people. About 250 French were then there,—Masters and officers of vessels, which had been taken, and who were sent to this town from Plimouth, and were at large, only not to walk more than a mile from the town.

A man came to us by the name of Dolbear, a brazier, to enquire after his relations of that name. Dolbear, who was many years partner with Jackson in Boston, went from Ashburton in the last century, and settled at Boston.

15th.—Excessive hot. We travelled very slow, and reached Plimouth . . . My father spent some time in Plimouth in the year 1696, and had been many weeks before in Portsmouth, waiting for convoy to New England . . .

16th.—In the forenoon waited on Lord Shuldham, the Admiral of the Port, who rec^d^ us with great civility; and as he was to dine with Cap. Hartwell, made us his guests. We saw two Captains and some other officers of two Swedish men-of-war which put in to Plimouth for water, as pretended, but his Lordship suspects them to be spies for the French. One is a two-decker of 44 guns; the other a frigate of 28. The *Apollo* frigate, of 28 guns, looks as if she was a match for the largest of them. The officers' uniform was fantastick—a white sash round the arm, a short blue coat, a cap with a white feather on one side. At dinner, Sir Hyde Parker, and Cap^n^ Gambier, we had known in America; Col^o^ Parker, Member for the county, and Col° of a Devonsh. Regiment, said to have 14,000£ a year, but rather reserved, and gave Lord Howe for his toast; a Mr Barter, [?] with Capn Oury, [?] the Comissioner, Capn Garnier, and Capn Harvey, besides Lord Shuldham, Capn Hartwell, Paxton, and T. H.

In this county I observe pack horses employed for carrying hay, faggots, stones, coals, wood, water, earthen ware, and many other articles usually carried in carriages with wheels, in other parts of England: scarce anything carried on trucks, except barrels, hogsheads and such things as cannot be divided into quantities small enough for horse burdens.*

17th.—Walked round the Catwater, and had a view of the Sound, Harbour, &c. Dined at a sumptuous entertainment with Lord Shuldham. Mr Bastard said to me to-day, that Hartley the Member, told him that when he was not† last in France, he thought from what he observed, if Franklin's schemes should succeed ill, he would be made a sacrifice [of], and in a note to F. he advised him to take care of himself. Franklin sent him an answer, that the caution brought to his mind the common language of a mercer—"It's only a remnant, and therefore of little value."‡

18th.—Lord Edgcumbe arriving yesterday from London, we made a visit to Mount Edgcumbe . . .

19th.—Having been most politely entertained by Lord Shuldham, &c., at Plimouth, we took leave of it this forenoon, and dined and lodged at Ashburton, on our return to London.

20th.— . . . Enquired at Exeter for our countryman Curwen, who had been in town from Exmouth that day. I left a card at his lodgings. At Exeter met with the London Evening of 18th, with the Act of Massachusetts Bay for confiscating the Estates of Gov. Bernard, Hutchinson, the Mandamus Counsellors, and the Crown officers, declaring them aliens, &c.

From Exeter went on and lodged at Collumpton.

* Except the main arteries, the roads in the remote and hilly counties of Devon and Cornwall were rough, stoney, narrow, and steep; but the great improvement in them during the last fifty years, has rendered the employment of pack horses wholly obsolete.

† The "not" is in the original, but it appears to be unnecessary to the sense of the passage.

‡ This occurs in Franklin's Correspondence, ii. 25.

22nd.—We had most of the way rain to Bridgwater . . . The rain ceasing, we went on to Glastonbury. . . Soon after I arrived I went up the Mount to the Tower, but the ground being wet and clayey, and the hill sharp as the roofs of most houses, it was a most fatiguing walk for a man so near 70. I went into the Tower, which has suffered but little injury. I have scarce ever seen so grand a prospect, certainly in no part of England I have been in.

23rd.—[To Wells and Bath.]

24th.—Left our own carriage and servants at Bath, and took a post chaise to Bristol. Called on Lt G. Bull, Oliver, Lechmere, Sewall, Simpson, Waldo, Barnes, Faneuil.

Dined with Simpson and Waldo, and returned late to Bath, near ten o'clock.

29th.— . . . At two o'clock the 29th came to my house in Sackville Street, and in the evening had the satisfaction of seeing all my children well, to drink tea with me . . .

August 1st.—At the Old Jewry . . .

2nd.— . . . William Apthorpe, who I saw with his wife last year at Cardiffe, went soon after to New York, and from thence to Boston. He arrived there the day Mr Timmins left Boston, and as soon as he landed was apprehended and sent to prison. He, and most of his connexions have always favoured the American cause.

3rd.—Went into the city: many long faces: account at Lloyd's of the taking the island St. Vincent by the French . . .

5th.—At Court. The K., enquiring about my journey, asked who went with me? I said Paxton, an American, one of the Commiss^rs of the Customs. He said I should be very careful who I took with me. There was one lately come over, I answered, I should not chuse to have trusted. "Who's that, T.? what's he come for?" I did not know: I fancied he was willing to secure both sides. "That's bad," he said, and turned to somebody else.

Lord Hillsborough kissed the Queen's hand on his going to Ireland. He told me Lord North desired him, when he was going to take leave last week, desired him* to defer it, he

* The repetition of the words "desired him" seems to have been unintentional.

having mentioned him to the K. for Secr[y] of State, but as the K. had said nothing to him, he took leave of him yesterday at the Levée. He said he could not account for the K.'s backwardness. I said I supposed some were solliciting who he did not chuse to offend. Lord H. said to me it was not a thing to be desired—the Ministry never was so disunited. They would not speak to one another upon publick affairs.

10th.—Advice of the arrival of a vessel at Glasgow—sailed from N. York the 12th or 13th of July. And. Pepperell, M[r] Cutler, and a young Simpson, passengers. They had advice of Prevost's retreat to James Island; that he thought himself secure until he could be reinforced. On the other hand, the enemies to Government boast that there are accounts arrived in France of his having been attacked on this Island, and as they say—*Burgoyned.* It is astonishing there should be Englishmen suffered publickly to express a pleasure in the defeat of the King's forces.

11th.— . . . There seems to be no authority for the report of a vessel at Glasgow from New York the 12th July. Cutler left it the 6th, at the same time with S[r] W[m] Erskine, and he says the advice from Prevost was rec[d] the night before.

12th.—S[r] W[m] Erskine, who was said to come with Gen. Jones in a vessel to Milford Haven, is not arrived, but went in a vessel bound to Cork, where some of the fleet are said to be arrived. It is reported to-day that Prevost has retreated to Beaufort, and that letters from Greenock mention it as part of the intelligence from N. York . . . P. of Wales 17 years old: day observed at Windsor.

13th.—No kind of news. M[r] Abel Willard* informed me that somebody, and he thought M[r] Gore, had a letter from Boston, in which the writer mentions the Acts passed in Mass. Bay for sale of delinquents' estates, in w[ch] it is said that though they passed, yet nobody professes to approve of them.

14th.— . . . Besides Temple, three other Americans are come to London—Jos. Cordis, Oliver Smith, and W[m] Greene, son of

* He was one of the Barristers who signed the farewell Address to Governor Hutchinson, and an obnoxious Loyalist. He left America in 1776, was proscribed and banished, and died in England in 1781.—Sabine's 'Loyalists.'

Rufus Greene, all from Boston, and professed subjects of the new State. They appear publickly, avow their principles, and no notice is taken of them, when the estates of all such as have left America and taken shelter in England are confiscated by Acts of Government, and their persons are liable to be imprisoned, and perhaps worse treated if they return.

16th.—A Boston woman, Mrs Johnson, came with a Petition to me, recommended by Lane & co., Cap^n^ Scott, &c., to put her in a way for relief. Her husband, a ship Master, came with his family to Bristol in 1775; has since sailed out of England; was taken and carried into Boston 16 months ago. I advised her not to think of applying to the Treasury.

In a Boston newspaper my estate is advertised to be sold. I have not yet seen an account of the sale. It is said the Massachusetts new State claims all the territory within the N. and south lines of the Charter, between the western settlements of New York, and the south sea. I hope the ingratitude, as well as the extravagant cruelty of this act will appear hereafter for the benefit of my posterity. It is entirely owing to me that any claim remains to this territory; for when the Comissioners from the two Colonies met at Hartford in 1773, those on the part of Massachusetts would have consented to relinquish all claim to it, and declared to me their willingness, but I prevented them, and encouraged them to risk the breaking off the Treaty, which the N. York Commiss^rs^ pretended would be the consequence of a refusal being signified, the N. York Comiss^rs^ no longer insisted on their demand.

17th.—An express to-day from the *Marlboro'* of 74 guns, bound out to join Sir Ch. Hardy; that she met the French and Spanish fleet in the Chops of the Channel; that he was chased, together with the *Isis, Southampton*, and *Cormorant*, within 4 leagues of Plimouth, when they gave over chase, and the *Marlborough* sent the *Cormorant* into Plimouth. They counted 63 sail. The *Ramillies* sailed before the *Marlborough*, and it is feared may be taken. The fleets were seen Saturday the 14th.

18th.—Another express to-day from Falmouth, that the combined fleet was seen from thence on Monday morning the 16th. It is said at the Treasury, there is advice of the arrival of 11 East India ships at Cork, and that Sir Cha. Hardy met them, and carried them in. This will account for the two fleets not seeing one another. The *Marlboro'* said to have gone into Falmouth. Great anxiety. Wind fresh easterly.

19th.—The report of the E. India ships come to nothing. No news of Sir Cha. Hardy. Alarmed all day with expresses, without being informed of the intelligence they bring. Agreed—that the fleets are seen off Plymouth; said to be off the Rame Head—63* sail of the line—100 in all. Upon 'Change. Bridgen told me they were in an half moon, and 100 sail of transports within them; and he did not seem pleased at my doubting it. The anxiety is great in many: I wonder it is not in more. I wrote to Lord Hardwicke, and to Mauduit at Cowdray—Lord Montague's.

A letter from D[r] Murray. A young man there from Providence, Rh. Island, tells him the people abuse me as much as ever. This is my misfortune, as I wished for the esteem of none so much as of my own countrymen. I think it is not bias which satisfies me that what Tacitus observes was natural in his day is the cause—*Odisse quem læseris.*†

East w—fresh.

20th.—No other intelligence than that the fleet on Wednesday the 18th had not advanced. The wind probably prevented. It is said the English fleet was off Mounts Bay, but no certainty. The dock at Plimouth is thought to be the object of the enemy, and that they intend to land a little below the Rame Head, and to cross over and burn the dockyard, &c. The wind here continues fresh, near N. East. It is generally believed the *Ardent* of 64 guns, mistaking the enemy for the English fleet, is taken.

21st.—East wind continues. Accounts, if any, received by Government, not made publick. A letter of the 18th from Plimouth says the *Ardent* is taken, but a postscript to it says that she is since got in much shattered. Many think notwith-

* Adolphus says 66.—iii. 193.

† To hate the person whom you have injured.

‡ The uncertainty about the fate of the *Ardent* is set at rest by Hume's Continuator and others writing some time afterwards, who say she was taken.

standing, that she is taken. She was a very swift sailing ship.

Jabez Fisher says a friend of his has rec[d] a letter of July 7, from Carolina, which says Prevost had retreated 80 miles towards Beaufort. The reports from Holland are that he had surrendered. . . .

22nd.—At D[r] Kippis's.

An express last night says the French fleet was out of sight on Thursday. It's thought they are gone to Brest, and will bring the forces which, it is said, in a great number of transports, are to embark there. Wind still E. The *Ardent* seems to be given up, as the express says nothing of her being in Plimouth.

23rd.—Not one word to-day from the fleets, nothing having been seen or heard of them at Plymouth. Letter from Lord Hardwicke, and another from Mauduit, both of which I answered. Mentioned the difference between 1588 and the present time. Everybody then alive and active in every part of the kingdom; supine and motionless now, though we have as much to fear as they had then.*

24th.—Admiral Gambier called. He says the market women went off in boats from Falmouth with vegetables, &c., supposing the fleet to be English: that they were on board the French Admiral who, after many questions about the fleet, the forces, &c., sent them ashore to bring more refreshments.

No advice of any sort, the wind still between east and north, and something rather inclining to W. of north. I went into the city and expressed my astonishment to several, that the merchants did not fit out every ship capable of assisting the British fleet. It is said ten or a dozen East India ships now lye in port which may be made equally strong as 36 or 40 gun men-of-war, and upon an emergency might be of infinite service.

Blackburne told me to-day, that meeting M[r] Temple in the street, he said to him—"Why, I have not seen you for a long time." Temple answered—"Six weeks ago I dined with General Washington."

* This of course refers to the expected attack from the Spanish Armada.

25th.—The wind at east again. Not a word of Sir Charles Hardy which can be depended upon. It is said the combined fleets were seen on Saturday from Falmouth, but no official accounts.

Besides Sir D. Lindsay, Gen[l] Grey and Col[o] Roy are at Plimouth, the latter, I hear in the Park, has wrote that they can stand a siege of two months from 20,000 men.

26th.—The Captain of the *Thetis* frigate from Lisbon, came to town—saw Sir Cha. Hardy's fleet Wednesday the 18th, [blank] leagues SW. of Scilly. The *Hector*, one of the fleet, spake with the *Thetis;* mentioned Ramillies and Marlboro' having joined; and Cap[n] Gell of the *Thetis* saw a ship going to join, which it's thought was the *Jupiter;* to avoid the enemy Cap. Gell stood for the Bristol Channel. It is doubted whether the enemy's fleet is not yet in the Channel.

The wind fresh at east, but fine weather.

27th.—Called upon M[r] Strahan. He says M[rs] Blunt, who I took to be M[rs] Stevenson's daughter, or Stevens, the woman at whose house D[r] Franklin lodged many years, received about two months ago a letter from him, in which he says he hopes to see her at her hut in Kensington. Preparations were then making in France for an invasion, and his hopes must be founded upon the success of it.

M[r] Ellis called. I told him my estate was sold to a rich Sears.* He says he hopes I shall have it again.

29th.—At D[r] Kippis's.

Dined at Lord Mansfield's at Caen Wood: only Lord Rob. Manners besides the family. My Lord, at 74 or 5, has all the vivacity of 50. Lord Rob[t] is only brother to the Duke of Rutland, and is now Lieutenant of the *Alcide.* My Lord predicts he will be one day Admiral and Commander-in-Chief of the British Navy: bad him make a minute that he foretold it. He gave me a particular acc[t] of his releasing two Blacks from slavery, since his being Chief Justice. A ship belonging to Bristol was upon the coast of Guinea. The two nations of

* The word looks like Sears. At Nov. 14, 1775, however, he speaks of his Milton property as reported to be sold at Vendue; and at Sept. 30, 1779, that "one Brown of New York" had purchased it.

North and South Callibar had a controversy—I don't recollect what it was about, but they agreed to leave it to the English Captain, and they came aboard his ship to the number of 250. He made them all slaves—carried, or sent them to Martinico, where they were sold. By some means or other these two were sent to Virginia, being brothers, and sons to the chief man of one of the nations, and called by Lord M. Princes. After having been 6 or 7 years in Virginia, they absconded from their master—hid themselves in the hold of a ship bound to Bristol, and were not discovered until the ship was upon her voyage. Upon her arrival at Bristol, they found a way to make their case known, and to apply to Lord Mansfield for an *Habeas corpus.* Upon enquiry, there was full evidence of the fact, the Master of the Bristol ship being in England, and witnessess who were in Guinea at the time; but there was a fair purchase by the Virginia planter, and the Master of the ship in which they had escaped, kept them confined in order to return them, and to avoid the penalty to which he would be liable by the laws of the Colony, for bringing them away. His Lordship thought the case was not without difficulty. However, the Writ issued, and I think they were brought up to London. They acknowledged the two nations were at war, and that captives were made on both sides with design to sell them for slaves; and if they had been taken and sold, they would have disdained seeking relief. The whole transaction was beyond sea, and they had never been ashoar [*sic*] until he brought them ashoar by the Writ of *Habeas corpus.* Under all these difficulties, he says he would have found a way to deliver them. After waiting some considerable time, the Master of the ship who had thus kidnapped them, with others, at Bristol, thought it advisable to make up the matter, and to engage to send the two Princes home to Guinea. How the Virginia planter was satisfied his Lordship did not say, but he seemed much pleased at having obtained their relief. The rest of the 250 probably are dead in slavery, and the villain who captivated them* has escaped the judgment of man.

* Took them captive. Another instance of the change in signification of a word in the space of one short century.

Dr Franklin being mentioned, my Lord said that he carried his grandson* to Voltaire, who said to the boy—"*Love God and Liberty.*" I observed to his Lordship that it was difficult to say which of those words had been most used to bad purposes. He seemed pleased with my remark.

Lady Mansfield must be about 80—has the powers of her mind still firm, without marks of decay: her dress perfectly simple and becoming her age—is said to be benevolent and charitable to the poor. Lady Say, of the same age, I saw at Court with her head as high dressed as the young Dutchesses, &c. What a carricature she looked like! How pleasing, because natural, Lady Mansfield's appearance!

A Black came in after dinner and sat with the ladies, and after coffee, walked with the company in the gardens, one of the young ladies having her arm within the other. She had a very high cap, and her wool was much frizzled in her neck, but not enough to answer the large curls now in fashion. She is neither handsome nor genteel—pert enough. I knew her history before, but my Lord mentioned it again. Sir Jno Lindsay having taken her mother prisoner in a Spanish vessel, brought her to England, where she was delivered of this girl, of which she was then with child, and which was taken care of by Lord M., and has been educated by his family. He calls her Dido, which I suppose is all the name she has. He knows he has been reproached for shewing a fondness for her—I dare say not criminal.

A few years ago there was a cause before his Lordship bro't by a Black for recovery of his liberty. A Jamaica planter being asked what judgment his Ldship would give? "No doubt," he answered, "he will be set free, for Lord Mansfield keeps a Black in his house which governs him and the whole family." She is a sort of Superintendent over the dairy, poultry yard, &c., which we visited, and she was called upon by my Lord every minute for this thing and that, and shewed the greatest attention to everything he said.

I took occasion to mention that all the Americans who had

* The Editor has here omitted a few words in a parenthesis. They concern genealogy rather than history.

brought Blacks had, as far as I knew, relinquished their property in them, and rather agreed to give them wages, or suffered them to go free. His L[d]ship remarked that there had been no determination that they were free, the judgment (meaning the case of Somerset) went no further than to determine the Master had no right to compel the slave to go into a foreign country, &c. I wished to have entered into a free colloquium, and to have discovered, if I am capable of it, the nice distinctions he must have had in his mind, and which would not make it equally reasonable to restrain the Master from exercising any power whatever, as the power of sending the servant abroad; but I imagined such an altercation would rather be disliked, and forbore.

I observed the report, that Lord Hillsborough had left to go to Ireland, and been sent for back, and that he was to be appointed Secr[y] of State. My Lord said he knew nothing of it: he thought however, nothing more likely. At parting he hoped next time we met, it would be in better times.

30th.—The hottest day at noon I have felt this year, and it would have been thought very hot in Boston. Wind about SSE.—very little of it. It's not improbable the fleets may be in sight of each other, and too little wind to meet: but for 12 days past we know nothing of them.

31st.—At M[r] Ellis's, Twickenham—dined with—no company. Returning—just on this side Turnham Green, between sundown and dark, I thought the wheel of the coach on the opposite side to that on which I sat, went over a round log or stone, but finding no consequence, and the road full of carriages passing both ways, I did not stop the coachman. Soon after, I saw people run by the coach, and some one cryed—"A man is run over!" The coachman then looking back, missed the footman, and stopping, said to me—"Patrick is not behind," and immediately turned the coach, and after driving a few rods, perceived the footman held up by several people. As soon as I came up I desired them to carry him into an Inn or ale-house a few steps distant, where a country fellow at my desire, put a lance into his arm, and took away 8 or 10 ounces of blood, but I had little hopes of his life, and he himself said it was not possible he should live. I had him carried into the coach, and brought him home. The wheel, of not a light coach, went over his shoulders and breast, but having a strong chest no bone broke: the flesh was much bruised, and the most favorable circumstance of all, there are no symptons of internal hurt. If he recovers, it is one of the most merciful escapes I have known. Perhaps there is no part of his body where he could have received so little hurt. If he had fell with his face downwards, the wheel would have gone over the upper part of the spine, or back bone, which was the case of a Negro servant belonging to me above 20 years ago at Milton, driving a cart. He fell under the wheel on his face, and passing over his shoulders, he never had any feeling afterwards in any part of his body, and died after a few days languishing. He can give no account of his falling, and it is difficult to account for his falling before the wheels. As both legs are scraped, it is probable he fell asleep, and pitching forward, might be entangled, and come to the ground before the wheel.*

Mr Ellis came from Mr Robinson's of the Treasury, at Sion Hill, and says Government advices stand thus:—The 17th Sir Cha. Hardy was about 6 or 8 leagues SW. of Scilly. He had rec^d^ advice of the combined fleets being in the Channel by the Southampton frigate, which he dispatched immediately to give intelligence, ordering the Captain to send a cutter into port, and to cruise in the frigate off the land. The Southampton beat [about] till the 26th and then sent ashoar. The east wind blowing strong, the two fleets probably lost ground, and a Dutch ship on the 24th sailed through the combined fleets, and the Skipper was examined by the French or Spanish Admiral, concerning the English fleet, of which he could give no account: but what is remarkable—the combined fleets, on the 24th, were just in the same station or cruising ground, which the English fleet was in the 17th, and all the intervening time both of the fleets were cruising at a small distance,

* Notwithstanding this attempted explanation, it seems hard to imagine how a footman up behind a carriage, could fall so far forward as to get before the wheel. In spite of his injuries, in due time he recovered. This man Patrick Ryley, or Reily, as he wrote it, came with the family from America; and when the Governor swooned and died, it was he who caught him in his arms and supported him.

without the one seeing, or being able to gain intelligence, of the other. . . .

September 1st.—Autumn begins with one of the hottest days this year. It is said the thermometers in the hottest part of such days are at 81, 82, 83, in the shade. . . .

M[r] Flucker tells me he saw a Boston newspaper dated in November, with an article, that Gov. Hutchinson, in August before, had wrote to D[r] Franklin in Paris, for leave to go to Boston to settle his estate, and when that was done, to return to England. And it was added—that his estate was settled to his hand. I suppose this to be wit. I wrote to D[r] Lloyd in August, and sent him a Power of Attorney, &c.

2nd.—Produced no other intelligence than Sir Cha. Hardy's being seen off Scilly.

3rd.—Alarming news! Sir Charles's Secretary arriving in town at one or two o'clock in the morning. He left the English fleet off Plymouth the first, the enemy then off Ushant, and said to be above 60 sail line of battle, the English but about 40. Whether they will go up to S[t] Helen's, or wait to fight the enemy, is made a question upon which there are different opinions. We are in a more critical state than anybody living has ever known.

4th.—Intelligence of the arrival of Sir Charles Hardy's fleet at S[t] Helen's, or, as others say, at Spithead. Where we shall first hear of the enemy's fleet is extreme doubtful and uncertain, but we have scarce any room to hope for any favorable account. Wind fresh, but not violent, at about S. to SSW. I wonder at the small degree of perturbation in so great a part of the people at a time of such imminent danger.

5th.—Fleet at Spithead certain. Lord Sandwich gone to Portsmouth. Various opinions: prevailing opinion that Sir Charles has done right: begin to open more freely against Keppel for suffering the French to escape him last year, when he had them in his power. Some say K——l and P——r both deserve to be h——*

6th.—No account yet of the enemy's fleet. In a letter from

* The intelligent reader must try to fill up the blanks. I had rather let it alone.

Mauduit of yesterday from Midhurst, he seems to think they will block up the Channel between Dover and Calais, and land in Essex and Kent. The fleet from the Downs near Midhurst could be seen at Spithead. He says a large ship was then standing in, which I suppose is the *Blenheim* from Plymouth. I think it more likely for the combined fleet to go with the transports to Ireland.

Alarmed to-day with Byron's being worsted by D'Estaigne—said to come from Holland; and, as if that was not enough, sombody has inserted a plausible account of the taking of Halifax. This is a deplorable state.

7th.—More bad news. Barrington come home in the *Ariadne* frigate from the W. Indies—supposed dissatisfied and complaining. The Granadas taken by the French. D'Estaigne's fleet much superior to Byron's: the latter came off, as the vulgar saying is, second best, in an action between the two fleets, the particulars not yet abroad. Not a word yet of the combined fleet. Wind strong SW. last night and to-day. My Banker said to me in the city, that he nor I had never seen such a day. Strange that stocks were hardly anything affected —not more than ½ p c^t^.

8th.—No official accounts from the West Indies. The arrival of eight E. India ships at Limerick is some alleviation; but all the W. India islands are considered as in the most imminent hazard. Possibly the advantages in the east may bear such a proportion to the disadvantages in the west, as to bring about an accommodation. But man proposes, God disposes, and the events which time is to bring forth we are to wait for, and cannot conjecture what they will be. Never was the state of the British dominions more changed in so short a time, and all contrary to all human appearances.

9th.—Mr White of the Old Jewry dined with us. His mother was a near relation to Lord Barrington. Nothing further of Admiral Barr^n^.

10th.—Admiral Barrington arrived yesterday evening. His business here does not transpire. It is said he lays no blame to Byron: that the French fought badly: that their whole fleet of 26 sail was engaged with 7 of our ships: that Byron, with 16 ships, was becalmed two or three miles to leeward, and could afford no assistance: that in the 7 ships 138 men were killed, and 243 wounded—among the latter Cap^{n} Fanshawe of the *Monmouth*, and two Lieutenants: that the French had 900 men killed, and 1500 wounded, many of whom were officers. Probably this account is exaggerated, but it has raised the spirits of the people.

My son Billy went to Margate about 2 o'clock. Yesterday he spat blood, which alarms us all and him exceedingly, he having long been troubled with a cough which threatens his lungs.*

Wind at N. People now begin to think the invasion over.

And so they began to breathe somewhat more freely. Such a scare had not spread so much consternation in England since the days of the Spanish Armada. Its true magnitude is little dwelt upon by our historians—first, because the period of greatest alarm did not last long; and secondly, because the writers coolly recorded the circumstances of it after the danger was over: but the Governor was writing at the dark moment, with a sort of sword of Damocles hanging over his head, and in continued expectation of hearing that slaughter and death had stepped ashore upon some unprotected part of the coast, and that England would then be in the hands of France and Spain. Stedman, ii. 161, writes as follows:—

"The British fleet, under Sir Charles Hardy, who was appointed to the command upon the resignation of Admiral Keppel, was by this time also at sea. It consisted of thirty-eight ships of the line, with something less than its due proportion of frigates, and cruised in that part of the sea which in nautical phraseology, is called the chops, or mouth, of the Channel. The great superiority of the combined fleet in the number of ships, guns, and men, seemed to justify the forebodings of those who prognosticated the ruin of the British Empire; and to add to the dangers of the present moment, preparations were made on the French coast, and an invasion of Great Britain, was threatened under cover of the combined fleet. On the other hand, every precaution was taken by the British Government which prudence suggested, for defeating the expected attack. A Proclamation was issued, ordering the cattle and draught horses to be driven from those parts of the sea coast on which a

* Billy was going down hill very fast, and destined soon to follow his sister.

landing should be effected; the Militia was embodied; and numerous cruisers were stationed in the narrow seas to watch the enemy's motions. All these efforts of the Government were nobly seconded by those of private individuals; for such energy had the national spirit acquired under the prospect of the difficulties that surrounded, and the dangers that threatened, that meetings were held in most of the principal towns, and voluntary contributions made to raise men for the defence of the nation.

"About the middle of August, Count D'Orvilliers, with the combined fleet, passed the British fleet under Sir Charles Hardy, in the mouth of the Channel, without either fleet having discovered the other, and proceeded on as far as Plymouth, taking in the way the *Ardent*, a British ship of war, on her passage to join Sir Charles Hardy. The Count D'Orvilliers made no attempt to land, but continued for several days parading with the combined fleet in sight of Plymouth, until a strong easterly wind set in, and compelled him to quit the Channel. As soon as this abated, he returned to the coast of England, and cruised off the Land's End. The same easterly wind had also driven the British fleet to sea; but on the last day of August Sir Charles Hardy regained his former station, and entered the Channel in full view of the enemy, who did not attempt to molest him. He now endeavoured to entice them into the narrower part of the Channel, where their greater superiority in number would have less availed them; and they followed him as high as Plymouth, but chose to proceed no farther. Their crews were said to be sickly: their ships to be in bad condition: and the season for equinoctial gales was fast approaching. They therefore soon afterwards quitted the English Channel, and entered the harbour of Brest. Thus, all the apprehensions which had been raised were quickly dissipated."

In those days it was considered a duty in an English sailor to hate a Frenchman, and by an inevitable corollary, to treat him accordingly; and as next-door neighbours proverbially disagree, the narrowness of the Channel will explain causes and effects. As for Spain, it was not forgotten that Philip had married Queen Mary, and that he had not succeeded in gaining the affections of his adopted subjects—and perhaps he never tried, and after he had returned to his own country, there had been no love lost on either side. Hence, as Adolphus says:—"A Spanish war was never unpopular." Speaking of the fleets, iii. 158, he remarks:—"The enemy insulted the Channel with an irresistible force." Dr Cormick informs us:—"The two fleets amounted to more than sixty sail of the line, with nearly an equal number of frigates and smaller vessels." In his Private Correspondence, i. 446, Franklin, writing from Passy, near Paris, October 4, 1779, betrays disappointment:—"We had reason to expect some great events from the action of the fleets this summer in the Channel, but they are all now in port without having effected anything." From a remark on the next page we learn that the military forces are congregated on the opposite shores of France, ready to be transported across for the hostile landing. It runs thus:—"The sword ordered by Congress for the Marquis de la Fayette, being at length finished, I sent it down to him at Havre, where he was with the troops intended for the invasion."

Considering on the one hand the comparatively destitute condition of England, from the fact that the greater part of her navy was distributed on foreign stations, and on the other, the overwhelming power of the combined fleets, supplemented by the troops and transports congregated on the coast of Normandy, at a period too, when there were still some weeks of summer weather to run, it may indeed seem strange that the whole affair ended in nothing. The summer rarely breaks up on the south coast of England, to be succeeded by the first signs of autumn, or the equinoctial gales to make themselves felt, until some little time after Michaelmas Day. An energetic Admiral would not have allowed such an opportunity, favoured by two or three fortunate circumstances, to slip through his fingers as the French Admiral did.

The Diary next gives the account of an unhappy accident to Lord Temple—

13th.— . . . The Newspapers give an account of Lord Temple's death, Saturday the 8 at Stowe, having been thrown out of a phaeton, and his skull fractured. He has held out to 68, with a crazy frame, and for a year or two past seemed rather less feeble than formerly, and is come to his end by a sudden violent stroke.

14th.—Rain until 4 o'clock, except a short time in the morning. For a month or two past my catarrh seems to have abated. I have been very regular in my diet and exercise; have drank very little, and some days no wine; have eat no milk; and for near a year past have constantly eat about two ounces of honey with my breakfast of Soushóng tea, and but little butter. At dinner sometimes drink porter, and sometimes toast and water.

15th.—Robinson the new appointed Governor of New York, left town yesterday or to-day to embark at Plimouth. Dr Jeffries and young Willard go in the same fleet, which is to be made up at Cork. It is again asserted that the *Ariadne* spake with Arbuthnot. She sailed some time in July from St Kitts, and might be off Bermudas the 5 of August. Wind W. to-day, and we may soon expect news from America.

16th.—About nine set out with Reily* in a post chaise for Furle. Stopped at Mr Apthorpe's, Croydon; went into the church and looked upon the grave of my dear child; enquired whether there was room for me, and was informed there was.

The time spent here, and post horses one of the stages, kept us from reaching Furle before sunset.

17th.—At Lord Gage's; found no company except Capn Kemble, brother to Genl Gage's lady, and Mr Wilmot, a lawyer, Comissr of Bankruptcy, and relation of Sr Eardly W. Paxton came in this forenoon from East Grinsted, where he lodged last night, coming to town yesterday morning from Pangbourne, an hour or two after I set out.

We walked about among Lord Gage's tenants.

18th.—Went to Lewes; saw Count Bruhl, Lady Amelia Carpenter, &c., from Brighthelmstone. A very high west wind. Sir Jno Lockhart Ross, and a small squadron gone over to St Maloes; it is said are expected back to-night to Portsmouth.

A letter from my son Billy at Margate; had a return of his spitting blood, but was better when he wrote.

19th.—Paxton and I were at church. Lord and Lady Gage to Lewes. Firle [hitherto Furle] affords but a poor congregation. The Clergyman not much esteemed. They have been quarrelling about singing† ever since I was here 4 years ago.

20th.—At Simson [?] a little village three or four miles from Furle, where there was a fair, chiefly for cattle and sheep, but booths for haberdashery, and variety of other wares. We

* This is the man that was run over, and thought to have been fatally injured. He must have recovered very rapidly, for the accident took place only seventeen days ago.

† Delightful! That is just what they do in the present day. Truly, history repeats itself, and there is nothing new under the sun.

went to the house of a wealthy young farmer—Caldicut, or a name like it—and were entertained with wine, tea, and coffee.

I am now entering my 69th year.*

21st.—Dined at Coneyborough with Mr D'Oyley, a young Clergyman—married a Yorkshire lady wth 40,000£, and has livings of 1000£ a year. He lives in a house of Mr Medley, Ld Gage's colleague for Seaforth: has a park, and could well afford us a haunch of venison and elegant dishes besides, with a dessert of excellent fruit: five or six ladies in company, with Mr Fuller, of Lewes, Member of the last Parliamt, besides Lord Gage's family. Fuller seems to have been a dissatisfied man when in Parliament, and not content now with Opposition. We made it near ten before we came home. Coneyborough is about 3 miles from Lewes towards London, but the house not seen from the road, tho' at a small distance.

This day was one of the darkest I had seen—1777.†

22nd.—General Paoli and Comte Genteli came from Brighthelmstone and dined with us, and returned in the evening.

23rd.— . . . In the evening the whole family went to an assembly at Lewes, and returned soon after eleven. Lord Pelham's and Lord Gage's families were the most respectable, tho' there were many other very fashionable people. My relish for such meetings is intirely over, and I went merely to avoid being singular. Paxton, who is three or four years older than I am is still highly delighted with them.

24th.—On horseback thro' Glynde into the London road, and so home by a corner of Lewes.

Sir Sampson and Lady Gideon came from London: bro't this day's Extra. *Gazette.* It seems the project of Penobscot had been prosecuted, and a Lt Colo Maclean wth 600 men, had taken possession; but before they could compleat any works, they were followed by a naval and land force from Boston, of which Sr G. Collier at New York, having intelligence, he

* He made the same remark March 9, 1778. He entered it on the 9th, O.S. In most families children have their birthdays impressed on their minds at an early age, by the yearly recurring plum cake, or a juvenile tea-party.

† Second anniversary of Peggy's death.

sailed wth the *Raisonable*, and four or five more,—arrived above a fortnight after,—just as they were about to attempt to storm the imperfect fortifications; and destroyed, or obliged the rebels to destroy, their whole naval force which had been drawn up the river Penobscot; and the landmen and seamen marched thro' the woods towards Boston.

At New York a fort on Hudson's River had been surprised and carried, and the garrison made prisoners, but was soon after recovered. On the other hand Tryon, with above 2000 men, under convoy of a number of small men-of-war, which Colyer [Collier?] commanded, had landed in the Sound—destroyed the vessels and stores in N-haven harbour, and burnt the towns of Fairfield and Norwalk, and a small town of Greenfield,—and returned to New York.

Arbuthnot said to be arrived. The *Greyhound* w[ch] carried L[d] Cornwallis, bro't the dispatches from Penobscot.

It must be a heavy stroke upon the Americans the loss of so much of their navigation; but it appears that the attempt to settle Penobscot was very hazardous, and the arrival of Collier was critical, and a delay of a day or two might have been fatal to the Penobscot settlement. Besides, it is difficult to conceive any advantage we can reap from it.

25th.—A solitary walk to the Windmill, to take a view of the Channel.

In the evening a letter from my son W. at Margate: his complaint of shortness of breath is new to me, and gives me great concern.

26th.—Wrote to my son, and to Mr. Clarke at Margate. No church—breakfast being delayed until some time after service began. In the evening service at home as usual, M[r] Wilmot read the church service: Lady Gage the sermon.

27th.—All dined at Lewes with M[r] Fuller, Member for [blank] the last Parliam[t]. In the evening I returned wth Lord Gage to Firle. Sir Sampson Gideon, Paxton, Wilmot, and Kemble, went to Brighthelmstone.

An account at Lewes that Paul Jones, an Irishman in the French service, had taken a 40 gun and a 20 gun ship, off the

Humber, with a number of colliers—Jones in a 50 gun ship with a frigate or two.*

28th.—I took my leave of the family last night, and set out early this morning for London. My own horses met me at East Grinsted, and I came to town about 5 o'clock: found my son at home from Margate before me, his ill state of health increasing.

29th.—A vessel from Boston, which had been carried in there, but claimed as belonging to Bermuda, and the owners not enemies to the American States; and upon that claim discharged, and suffered to come to England. This is a very odd state of things. It seems she left Boston but about 25 days ago. Seven or eight Jamaica ships taken and carried in there. Goes a great way towards retrieving the loss of their fleet at Penobscot.

30th.—Mr Blowers writes to Mr Bliss of June 30, that one Brown of New York had purchased my estate at Milton for 38,000£ lawful paper money.

Lord Sandwich asked me in the Park whether I heard anything from America? said there was a report, but he hoped it was not true, that D'Estaigne, with 16 sail, was gone to New York.

[Wrote] to Lord Gage and Lord Hardwicke.

October 1st.—Called on Lt Gov. Ball, and Mr Livius. The ship the latter was going in to Canada, laden with stores, military, &c., on account of Gov^t, is taken by Paul Jones, and sent in to France.

* Briefly—a fleet of merchant vessels, returning from the Baltic, convoyed by the *Serapis*, 44, Cap. Pierson, and the *Countess of Scarborough*, 20, Cap. Piercy, fell in with a squadron under the command of Paul Jones. This person was a native of Galloway, though, by association, sometimes accounted an Irishman. "*Non ubi nascor, sed ubi pascor.*" Being off the coast of Yorkshire, Cap. Pierson signalled to his merchant vessels to escape, and run for the nearest ports, whilst he commenced an action against a greatly superior force, which consisted of the *Bon Homme Richard*, 40, a frigate called the *Pallas*, 32, another called the *Alliance*, 36, the *Vengeance* brig, and a cutter. The *Countess of Scarborough* had 4 killed and 20 wounded, and the *Serapis* 49 killed and 68 wounded, when they succumbed. The *Richard* lost 336 in killed and wounded, according to Adolphus, whilst Stedman says 306, but it may be suspected that the middle figure has slipped out; and she was so shattered that she sunk two days afterwards. Paul Jones was in the service of the hostile allies, for he was decorated by the King of France for this battle, and thanked and promoted by the Congress of America.

2nd.—A severe Edict of the new Governor of Granada, discharging the estates there of all debts due to British subjects, and even to the Dutch, because they suppose British subjects are a collateral security to the Dutch.

Galloway, Dr Chandler, Leonard, Hallowell, Bliss [dined with him].

3rd.—Old Jewry. Livius and Bliss.

Very cold day—began our fires.

4th.—Arrival of General Grey from New York, and a fleet of transports at Cork. Arbuthnot's fleet arrived Aug. 24th after 13 weeks from Portsmouth, said to be all well. No remarkable occurrence yet transpires.

5th.—A letter by way of Cork from Mr Walter, of Aug. 23. No news then of the fleet. He says Sr H. C. [Clinton] was preparing for an expedition, and it was whispered eastward, as soon as Arbuthnot arrived, and if true, I might probably hear from him next from another quarter.

6th.—Dined at Amen Corner, Dr Douglas's:—Mr Knox, Sr Jno Eliot, and Strahan. Sr John upon a merry pin. Q—whether Strahan or he most of an Infidel? Both, especially the first, rather too free with religion to consist with politeness at the table of a Divine, and who appears to have a sense of religion himself.

From Mr Knot, things look but indifferently in Georgia, and Sr James Wright is in poor spirits. Clinton's going to Boston was intimated; and Ethan Allen and the Green Mountain men said to have entered into alliance with Clinton, and Brandt to have been within a few miles of Sullivan's Magazines. But the great concern is the destination of the French fleet, said to have sailed from Martineco, and to have been seen off Crooked Island the latter end of August.

11th.—From London to Lord Hardwicke's, Wimpole Hall: set out ½ after 8, arrived rather before three.*

12th.—Find no company but the family, and none expected until the last of the week. A long walk in the Park and Gardens, and the rest of the day in the Library.

* "The Gov. set out this morning on a visit to Ld. Hardwicke at Wimpole Hall, Cambridge Shire."—Elisha's Diary.

13th.—On horseback to a little village about 5 miles off, called Great Eversden . . .

14th.—A ride again—to Caxton and back. This is my Lord's publick day, but only D[r] Plumtree and family, and M[r] Baynes, a Clergyman who was 12 years in the East Indies, and lately returning, is forced to take up with about 60£ a year, and to do the duty of three Curacies in this neighbourhood.

A letter from my son T. with no favorable account of B.'s case, and discouraging account of D'Estaigne going to America.

15th.—My ride to-day was to a small village of Bourne . . .

16th.—A rainy windy night and cloudy day w[ch] kept me from riding.

17th.—The family at church. D[r] Plumtree, Master of Queen's, has the living, and preached from—"Evil communications corrupt good manners."*

18th.—I rode to Bassingdown, a more considerable village than most in this neighbourhood, about 4 miles from Wimpole: a large church, but poor living—about four score pounds: about a mile beyond to Lithington, a larger, but worse built village, and excessive dirty roads.

Soon after I returned, Lord Polwarth and his Lady came to make some stay, and M[r] Charles Yorke with his son, being expected to-morrow, I purpose to decamp in the morning, know it must be most pleasing to the family to be without strangers.

Lord H., speaking of L[d] Rockingham said—"He owes my brother Charles and me above four score thousand pounds, the interest of which is paid out of his Irish estate."

Lord P., speaking of † who lives at L[d] G. G.'s, called him "That scoundrell:"—wondered at L[d] G., that he would give such cause for the world to insinuate such things of him. I was astonished at the freedom with which he spake of what it's shocking to think of.

19th.—Left Wimpole at ¼ past 8, and was at home, having p[d] for 48 miles post chaise, ¼ before three.‡

* 1 Corinthians xv. 33.

† Indistinct—possibly on purpose.

‡ "19th.—After dinner walked to Sackville Street, where I found the Gov., who had arrived a few hours before from Ld. Hardwicke's."—Elisha's Diary.

Nothing can be more polite than my entertainment has been. The oeconomy is too steady, or has too much sameness, to please for a long time together. The Library is always open to everybody. The first appearance of my Lord and Lady is in the breakfast room exactly at ten. Breakfast is over about eleven: everyone takes care of himself, and does just what he pleases until half after three, when all meet at dinner: between five and six the ladies withdraw: the gentlemen generally go into the Library—some chat, others take up books; at eight a call to one of the drawing-rooms to tea or coffee; which over, if there is company disposed to cards, any who don't like them converse, or take their books: exact at ten the sideboard is laid with a few light things upon it, that anybody disposed to supper may take it: and exact at eleven, as many servants as there are of gentlemen and ladies, come in with each of them two wax candles, and in procession we follow to the Gallery at the head of the great staircase, and file off to different rooms. This is high life: but I would not have parted with my humble cottage at Milton for the sake of it.

20th.—In the city: received dividend at the Bank—at Gines's, &c. Rec[d] my brother's salary, $\frac{1}{4}$, to 5 of July last, from M[r] Rowe.

In the evening at Brompton to visit the late L[t] Gov. Oliver's daughter Louisa, arrived from Halifax, where she had been ever since the evacuation of Boston by Howe.*

Called at Lord George's office. M[r] Knox said I was the only man to go Governor of a new Colony at Penobscot, and that D[r] Caner should be the Bishop. I shewed him a letter I had received from M[r] Weekes, which speaks in pompous

* Under date Oct. 15, we read the following in Elisha's Diary.—" Walked out with M[rs] H. and called on M[rs] Willard. I walked to Sackville Street: met M[r] H. Gray, who acquainted me that our cousin Louisa Oliver was arrived from Halifax. I afterwards met my b[rother] Tommy and his wife, going to bring her from the city, where she arrived last evening, having slept at M[r] Watson's, in whose vessel she came, having had a passage of 5 weeks."

She was the Lt. Governor's youngest child, by his second wife Mary Sanford, born June 16, 1759, but I have no record as to whether she married, or when she died. At this period she was 20 years and four months old. Elisha's Diary shews that she lived occasionally with her uncle the Ch. Justice Oliver at Birmingham.

terms of the benefits from the possession of this country. He was much pleased, as it is his own scheme, and few people here think well of it. I said to him I thought we had better stay until we heard more of D'Estaignc before we thought any further on measures for restoring peace to America.

21st.—At Court: remarkably thin Drawing-Room—about 18 ladies, including the Queen, and two or three of the Bed-Chamber. The Prince of Anspach, and the new Russian Minister were there. The King inquisitive where I had been. I mentioned Lord Hardwicke's. He asked whether he was in spirits? thought he generally failed: then enquired after Lord Polwarth: mentioned Lord Marchmont as weakly. I thought he had done pretty well, being above seventy. The Queen made enquiry also, &c.

Rainy from noon.

22nd.—East wind. It is said the fleet are ordered to sail from Portsmouth.

I am astonished at seeing so little concern upon the minds of so great a part of the people—I might almost say all, when it appears to me that the nation is in such imminent hazard of some grand convulsion. The enemy's naval force threatens destruction: then—Ireland seems upon the verge of revolt: the French and Spanish fleets are much superior to the British in Europe: the enormous National Debt must stop in a short time the raising any further sums, or a general bankruptcy must destroy the public credit. The latter may happen: and tho' individuals in vast numbers be ruined, the nation may, by means of part only of the present taxes, raise enough every year for a defensive naval war against all Europe.

25th.—Account of the fleets sailing from Portsmouth, Friday the 22nd. It is said the Danes have restored a ship bound to Quebec with Gov^{t} stores of great value, and another ship—both taken and carried into Denmark by one of Paul Jones's squadron.

26th.—I have a bad cold, with a cough, and nurse at home to-day.

A very kind letter in the evening from Ld Hardwicke:—says I may lodge in a more magnificent house, but in none where I can be more welcome. He is not very free with compliments.

28th.—A heavy gale at about SW., and rain most of the day, but the wind abates at afternoon. In some pain for the fleet, which passed by Plim[th] Sunday night. News of the arrival of a fleet from Quebec, but nothing yet of D'Estaigne.

Lord Stormont kissed hands yesterday—Sec[y] instead of Lord Suffolk.*

29th.—Wind NW and fair day. Nothing from sea. M[r] Clarke's letters from Quebec of 16th Sept. say their last acc[t] from Butler not favorable: had been worsted in several skirmishes, and retreated to Niagara: had sent for more men: Sir J. Johnson gone with 500 troops, and ordered to collect all the Indians he could. Sullivan said to have 7000 men.

31st.—At D[r] Kippis's. Col[o] Chandler and Bliss d. [dined.]

A fire in the evening began in a hop warehouse by London Bridge: burnt the Water Works, which I heard the Collector of the tax say, would cost about 5000£ to repair—but he added, they were insured.

November 1st.—A dull heavy air, natural to November. Colds have been epidemic last week, and some time before. I have had a share, but have not confined myself, except when it rained.

The East and West India ships which were in Ireland, are all heard of in the Downs. India stock one ꝑ c[t] only advance: others stand. My Broker says they fall upon good news, and rise upon bad—contrary to all sense and reason.

2nd.—Danforth d., Johannot in the evening. Mauduit called, and took in writing from Johannot the particulars of the message with which he went from the Selectmen to Washington, to let him know that Gen[l] Howe had declared he would set fire to the town if the troops were molested in embarking; and to intreat that Washington, to satisfy the minds of the inhabitants, would engage not to molest the troops. The form of the message was shewn to Howe by Cap. Balfour

* Walpole writes Oct. 31.—"Lord Stormont has got the late Lord Suffolk's Seals of Secretary."—vii. 266.

his Aid-du-Camp, and approved of, and Johannot went out with it under Howe's Flags.

3rd.—In the city. Mr Campbell, Broker, sold my Bank stock, 2300£ at 110¾, to be transferred this day fortnight . . .

4th.—The news of the day, that Jamaica is taken . . .

5th.— . . . The Jamaica news questioned. Some however believe it.

7th.—At the Old Jewry.

Dr Chandler, E. H. and ux. [uxor ?] d.

An article in yesterday's *Morning Post,* conjectured to be put in by Temple:—"Boston—not Hely Hutchinson, upon report that Governor Dalling would quit his Government of Jamaica, has *modestly* hinted that he would not refuse that appointment. Dean Tucker is his friend, and will endeavour to engage the interest of the laudable Society for Propagating the Gospel. This may account also for a late visit to the Bishop of London."

8th.—In the city. Met the new Lord Mayor, Aldermen, &c., in procession from Guild Hall, where the Mayor had been sworn.

9th.—No curiosity for seeing the pageantry of Lord Mayor's Day, though the pleasantest weather of any I had seen upon this day since I have been in England.

This day three years my dear daughter took the cold which held her until the Qu. Birthday, and which she then so increased, as to fix upon her lungs, and prove fatal to her.

In the evening Mauduit mentioned what he had heard of Genl Grey. Some of his friends enquired whether the papers gave a true account of his examination before the H. of Commons, and in particular, whether he was really of opinion the Americans could not be subdued? he was backward in giving an answer; but at length being pressed, he gave this answer—"Let us see a change of Ministry, and then we will shew you what can be done with them."

12th.—Bliss has a letter from Van Shaack * at Bristol, who

* Peter Van Schaack, of Kinderbrook, New York, an eminent lawyer and estimable man. Banished, and driven from America during the war he returned afterwards, and died in 1832.—Sabine's Loyalists.

says a man is arrived there from America, who came in a neutral vessel, and was put ashoar at Weymouth, and spake with, or was on board, an American privateer which left Salem the 1st of October, when an express had arrived from Washington with an account of the arrival of the French fleet at Sandy Hook.

Dined at Mauduit's with Mr Ironmonger, his son, and Mr Lethieulier, and Galloway.

15th.—Met Lord Barrington in Hanover Square. He says D'Estaigne was not before New York the 2nd of October: that Ministry has this advice from Halifax: and that he had seen the Circular Letter to the several offices with this account.

Rain most of the day.

16th.—In the city. Called upon Mr Watson. He says the ship, (speaks of but one,) left Halifax the 18 October: that a vessel arrived there from N. York the 8th: that the troops for an expedition to the southward had embarked; but upon news of the French fleet being bound there, disembarked: that it was said in Halifax, D'Estaigne, with 9 ships, arrived in Boston Sep. 28.

17th.—Dined with Mr Ellis—Lord Hillsborough and Lady, Lord Fairford, Lord and Lady Cranborne, Ld Barrington, Mr Stanhope, Bamber Gascoyne, and Mr Agar.

Much weight on Ld H.'s brow. He is come back from Ireland—been to the Levée. Nothing seems settled.

18th.—At Court: very cold. As soon as the King spake to me, I came home. Lord and Lady Shelburne presented on account of their marriage many months ago. He looked not very pleasant. The Dutchess of Bedford was at Court. Lady Shelburne is her niece. In 1740 I was at the Foundling Hospital, at the first Christening, when the Dutchess, with the Duke of Bedford, was there, but I see no remains of the person I saw then.

19th.—At Lord Hillsborough's. He does not know what he is to be. When he went to Ireland he was to be, he says, Secretary of State: he was surprised to see Lord Stormont's appointment. He esteemed Ld S. very much, but did not know what to make of it. However, he was content:—he had got rid of a great deal of trouble. Now he is returned he finds a vacancy is to be in the Secretary's department (Lord Weymouth), and in the place of Lord President;—this intimated as if it remained to be settled which he was to fill: complains, no elasticity. I hoped there would be more when he comes in. I asked how the affair with Ireland could be settled? "No way but by Union." Much was said about the terms of union: differs from Scotland. He proposes 44 Members in all, to be added to the H. of Commons: a number —16, 20, or what shall be agreed, and the King shall appoint, of the Irish Peers to be created Peers of G. Britain: the remainder to enjoy all the honour and privileges they now enjoy, and no new Irish Peers to be created.

He says the major voice is for it in Ireland. Lord North wishes it of all things: no plan laid for effecting it. L[d] North cried when he talked upon it. This caused L[d] H. to say there was no elasticity.

28th.—Only my two sons E. and W. [At dinner probably.]

In the evening a letter from Sir Sam. Hood,* advising that

* Afterwards Admiral Lord Hood, who gained glory as a brave and a skilful sailor. He had a very large nose. At the period of the Diary to which we have arrived, his name had scarcely come forward, but he was a rising man: so was Nelson then a rising man: so was Sir John Jervis: so was Captain William Parker of the *Audacious* at the affair of the first of June, '94, after which he was made an Admiral, and being in command of five sail of the line in February, 1797, he was so fortunate as to join them just before the action to Sir John Jervis's fleet, and after the Battle of St. Vincent he was made a Baronet, and Sir John was elevated to the Peerage. He was Parker of Harburn: and though there were three Baronets of this name then afloat, (Sir Peter, Sir Hyde, and Sir William,) and all Admirals, they were not related to each other. Sir William had a house on Ham Common, where he lived with his wife, (*née* Jane Collingwood,) and his family, when he was on shore, and one day Lord Hood was expected to call on some business connected with their profession. Hereupon the mother admonished one of her children, (Jane, in due time the wife of Captain Roberton, R.A., and secondly Captain Cocks, R.N.,) and warned her that a gentleman was going to call who had a very large nose, and that if she should happen to be in the room at the time, she must remember not to look at it, because that would be very rude and unlady-like, and she should be angry with her if she did. Not long after this Lord Hood was announced. Sir William and Lady Parker were in the drawing-room, and the little girl, having received her lesson, took good care to be in the room too, to see what was to be seen. The *enfant terrible* is an object much to be dreaded in most houses, and philosophers have never told us whether it is better to instruct a child what it ought or ought not to do before strangers, or leave things alone and hope for the best. During a rather prolonged visit, the mother was

the fleet sailed from Torbay the 16th: does not believe they will meet the combined fleet, tho' he wishes it.

24th.—At Lord Huntingdon's upon his return from the country. He is quite altered in his opinion of Sir H. Clinton: says he is utterly uneaqual to his post: unsteady, capricious, regardless of discipline, &c. Lord Rawdon, he says, resigned his post of Adjut^t General merely because he would avoid all share in the blame which by and by must be charged somewhere. There seems to be a perfect dearth of men fit for service by sea or land. Gov^t has failed in all its measures, merely for want of fit officers to carry them into execution.

25th.—Parliament meets. Some say Lord Shelburne is Secretary in the room of Lord Weymouth, some, Lord Hillsborough. At Lord H.'s yesterday: it seemed to be a doubt whether Lord N. would carry his votes. This the Opposition have often boasted at the first of the Session. No Session has opened when the public affairs have been in a more distressed state.

Two or three vessels are arrived from Halifax, which came out the 26th of October. They bring vague reports of D'Estaigne's fleet being scattered in a storm, but nothing to be depended on. It was said yesterday at Lord H.'s, that Lord Stormont was of opinion that they were very much afraid in France, some disaster had befallen him.

26th.—Before the King went to the House of Lords yesterday, Lord Bathurst, (if not before), kissed the King's hand as President of the Council, and Lord Hillsborough, as Secretary of State, instead of Lord Gower.

Lord Gower was in Parliament, but did not speak. Lord Weymouth went into the country. Whether one or both will join the Opposition, remains to be determined. In the Lords 41 opposed the Address, and proposed an amendment: 90, including 8 Proxies for it. In the Commons 233 for the

---

horrified at seeing the child's eyes constantly fixed upon Lord Hood's nose; and as soon as his Lordship had left, she took her severely to task for her impropriety, but the only answer she got was—"La, ma, I couldn't help it."

I have often heard my mother, (who was another daughter of Sir W. P.) tell this story with great glee.

Address, 134 for Amending.* L[d] Hardwicke would have made 91 in the Lords, if he had not come off after 11 o'clock. The Lords sat until between one and two, which is longer than usual.

Card from W. Palmer, that he had paid in £1000 to Gines and co.

While I was at Lord Hardwicke's this forenoon M[r] Yorke came in, a young gentleman who is son to M[r] Charles Yorke, the late Lord Chancellor for two or three days, and is now Presumptive Heir to Lord Hardwicke.

27th.—Letters to the Admiralty yesterday of Oct[r] 8th by a packet from N. York, that D'Estaigne arrived upon the coast of S. Carolina Sept. 2nd: that he sent ashore letters to the Congress: that being at anchor off the bar of Charleston, a storm came on the 4th at night, and the whole fleet slipped their cables and put to sea: and that they had no intelligence of them at N. York since. It is said, but how the intelligence comes is not known, that a number of the ships arrived at Porto Rico.†

Livius, Hallowell, Fitch, Leonard, Paddock, Gore,—dined. Rain all day.

28th.—At D[r] Kippis's.

I hear from Galloway that Rhode Island is to be evacuated: that 2500 men were going from New York under L[d] Cornwallis, and 5000 under Clinton: the first said to be intended for the W. Indies, the other for S. Carolina; but the certain destination was not known, nor is it probable they will sail until they hear more of D'Estaigne.

Lord Littleton, a man of great parts, but of a most profligate publick, as well as private life, after dining yesterday in gay company, went home and died last night about 11. It is said, in a fit.

* Adolphus says there were 41 for the amendment, and 82 for the Address, not noticing the 8 Proxies, which would bring the sum up to 90, as above. In the Commons, he has the same figures as the Diary.

† Nov. 28 Walpole writes—"Fortune has shewn us some partiality. D'Estaigne's fleet of twenty-two ships has been dispersed, and probably suffered considerably, by a terrible tempest that lasted for three days off Carolina."

29th.—A duel this morning between Charles Fox and Mr Adam, both Members of the House, for words in debate. Fox slightly wounded. Adam, it is said, fired a second pistol; and some say there will be a second combat.

Sir George Collier arrived from New York, passenger in the *Daphne* frigate, sailed the first of November. No further news of D'Estaigne. Some here doubt whether he ever intended to go to New York. It's very difficult to account for the uncertainty what is become of him. All the intelligence of his being off Carolina is from a letter in a rebel newspaper. I have letters by the packet from Mr Walter, Putman, John Prout, T. Goldthwait, lately arrived at N. York from Penobscot, and Tho. Oxnard. Mr Walter mentions the death of Major, or Jo. Goldthwait, and of Willm Apthorpe. Three Regiments, one British, and two Hessian, bound from N. York to Quebec, met with a violent storm: most of the transports dismasted: the *Renown* man-of-war, the convoy, and five transports returned; one taken and carried into Delaware—the rest missing.

Brook Watson has a letter from Joshua Winslow at Halifax. He was one of the tea Consignees, and made his peace, and remained quiet at Marshfield ever since -74, but lately left them; the 30th of September he was at Boston, and says they were then in a deplorable state, but I do not understand what that means.

Dined at Lord Huntingdon's, where I saw General Vaughan the first time, and had much conversation with him upon American affairs:* think he will go out again. Mr Lovel

* General Vaughan was brother to Lord Lisburne of Mamhead near Dawlish in the county of Devon, whom the Governor occasionally met in London. Among the papers I see a memorandum of October 22, 1793, to the effect that Thomas Hutchinson the younger, who by this date had settled down at East Wonford House, in the parish of Heavitree near Exeter, lent Lord Lisburne the sum of £5,000 for the residue of two terms of 500 and 1,000 years, by way of mortgage, secured with interest, on lands in Cardigan, and reciting previous instruments, in which appear the names of the Rev. Nutcombe Nutcombe, John, Andrew, and Jane Quicke, Andrew Jelf, Messrs. Leigh and Stokes, and Stephen Hawtry.

Twenty-two years after this, however, namely, in October 1815, the three sons of the lender, who had deceased in 1811, joined in an application to the Court of Chancery in order that the mortgage money should be paid off.

Mamhead passed through the hands of several owners, and now belongs to Sir Lydstone Newman, Bart. It was in the picturesque grounds of this place

Stanhope, Stanley, Sir Harry East, Col. Hastings,—of the company.

31st.— . . . The duel of yesterday was from Almon's having printed in Charles Fox's speech expressions reflecting on Mr Adam, who thereupon demanded of Fox whether he had used those expressions? He denied having named, or had reference to Mr Adam in particular in any part of his speech. But Mr Adam applied a second time, and required Mr Fox to sign a paper, charging Almon with falsehood. He gave his reasons against it, renewing his declaration that he did not intend Mr Adam, who again appeared content. But upon further consideration he applied a third time, and declared that Mr Fox must either sign such a paper, or meet him. They accordingly met yesterday—both fired—Fox was scratched by the ball in one side of his body. Mr Fitz Patrick, Fox's Second, then asked or said to Adam he hoped he was satisfied? He said—"No, not unless Mr Fox would sign the paper he required," and fired a second time—missed Fox, who thereupon fired his pistol into the air.

Those who are most acquainted with the absurd notions of honour which now govern great part of the world, blame Adam's conduct.

December 1st.—Called upon General Vaughan: afterwards Sir Richd Sutton. I wondered at the freedom before Mr Hayes of the Customs, an old Gent. who seemed to be a citizen, and myself, of Sir Richard in saying that he heard Admiral Keppel's Secr^y^ died some time since, and left one Mr Minifie, a Clergyman, his Executor, who found among the Secretary's papers, his Journal, in which he has minuted the day before the action with the French, that the Admiral said —"I think we may beat the French fleet, but if we should, it will be the rivetting of this damned Ministry." Sir Richard said he would go to the bottom of the story, and endeavour to make it publick, let the consequence be what it would.

---

that Mrs. Nightingale met her death, and was caught by her husband, as represented in white marble in Westminster Abbey by Roubilliac, in his strange, but beautiful monument, wherein Death, in the lineaments of a skeleton, is striking at her with a dart.

3rd.—The wind continued violent all night. I called upon Mr Knox, imagining Collier had brought more news than Ministry chose to publish; but he will own nothing except that Rhode Island was evacuated, and the troops, &c., all arrived at N. York. He wondered he had no private letters brought to him from some of the Americans. I told him I could not find that any had been received. He says there are no accounts of D'Estaigne since his being put from his anchors in the storm, or none upon which dependance can be had.

Strahan told me yesterday—and believes it—that one of our Surgeons, who had been prisoner at Brest, and is now in London, reports that 123 Surgeons, who attended the French seamen in their sickness, and all the nurses died, as did 23,000 of the fleet. This must be exaggerated; but all agree that the mortality has been so great as to be rarely paralleled.

4th.—Chandler received a letter last night of the 27th Octr from N. York by the *Daphne,* which says—the *Perseus* arrived last night from Georgia, where all was well. They had heard nothing of D'Estaigne since the storm. As nothing is said of Sir James Wallace it is feared he was not arrived. It is strange there should be no accounts of D'Estaigne. Genl Vaughan is ordered out immediately to the West Indies. He and Sir Richd Sutton, Sir W. Pepperell, Livius, Galloway, and Dr Chandler, dined with me.

Young Goldthwaite, son of T. Goldthwaite,* now at New York, called on me. He tells me Epes Sargent of Glocester, and his wife, are both dead the last year: that he was firmly attached to the old government: that his son was largely concerned in privateers, and had made a great fortune, which caused such an alienation of the son from the father, that he once said to young G., he should not be sorry to see their two fathers in the cart together.

Wrote by packet to T. Goldthwaite.

* Thomas Goldthwaite of Chelsea, Mass., had a grant on the Penobscot, which was confiscated: was a Judge of the Court of Common Pleas, and Colonel of Militia. Early in the war he embarked for Nova Scotia, was shipwrecked and drowned.—Sabine's Loyalists.

As we shall have but few opportunities of again seeing the name of Sir William Pepperell in these pages, it will not be inappropriate to introduce here a few remarks relative to his family. Several writers have given full accounts of the early members of it, from whom we learn that William Pepperell, of Tavistock in the county of Devon, removed to America in or about the year 1675, and settled at Kittery Point in Massachusetts, where, by industry and good management he realised great wealth, which was cherished and added to by his son of the same name. This son, as Colonel of the local Militia, proved himself to have been possessed of superior military genius, inasmuch as by his skill in conducting the siege of the strongly fortified city of Louisburg, which the French had built at the north-east point of Cape Breton, that place surrendered itself to his forces in the month of June 1745, upon which event he was created a Baronet by his Majesty King George the Second. His only son predeceased him, but his honours were revived in 1774 in favour of William, the son of his daughter Elizabeth, who had married Colonel Nathaniel Sparkawk. He assumed the name of Pepperell. It was this second Baronet who, like many other Refugees, was now living in London, anxiously watching the signs of the times, and speculating on the fortunes of war. Lorenzo Sabine, in his Sketches of Loyalists of the American Revolution, at page 170, thus speaks of his wealth and of his immense losses:—

"In 1778 he was proscribed and banished, and the year following was included in the Conspiracy Act. In May 1779, the Committee on confiscated estates offered for sale his 'large and elegant house, with the out-houses, gardens, and other accomodations,' &c., 'pleasantly situated in Summer Street, Boston, a little below Trinity Church.' His vast domain in Maine, though entailed upon his heirs, was confiscated. This estate extended from Kittery to Saco on the coast, [some 30 miles,] and many miles back from the shore; and, for the purposes of farming and lumbering, was of great value; and the water power and mill privileges, rendered it, even at the time of the sequestration, a princely fortune."

For the following particulars of the later branches of the family, I am indebted to Edward Walford, Esq., M.A., one of the representatives of it in the female line. The second Sir William Pepperell, having lost his only son in his lifetime, unmarried, died at his house in London in December 1816, when the title again became extinct. He left three surviving daughters—

I. ELIZABETH ROYALL, of whom presently.

II. Harriet, m. in 1802, Sir Charles Hudson, afterwards Palmer, Bart., of Wanlip Hall, Leicestershire.—See Burke's Peerage.

III. Mary Hirst, m. William Congreve Esq., of Congreve Hall, co. Stafford, and of Aldermaston Park, Berks. Ob. s. p.

ELIZABETH ROYALL, (as above), m. about 1792, the Rev. Henry Hutton, D.D., Rector of Beaumont, Essex, who died in 1832. She died 1856, leaving issue,—

I. Charles Henry, D.D., Fellow of Magdalen College, Oxford, and afterwards Rector of Great Houghton, co. Northampton. Born 1794, ob. cœl. Feb. 12, 1862.—(See Gentleman's Magazine for May 1862 for particulars as to the Huttons and Pepperells.)

II. Henry, M.A. Rector of Filleigh, North Devon, m. 1823, Elizabeth Sophia Beevor, and left issue—

1. Caroline Sophia, born in May 1824, m. August 1845, the Rev. Abraham William Bullen, Rector of Great Baddow, Chelmsford, Essex.
2. Henry, born in May 1825, m. in Nov. 1848, Caroline, d. of Dr. Atherstone, of Table Farm, Grahamstown, South Africa, and has, with other issue, PEREGRINE WILLIAM PEPPERELL, Lieut. R.N., eldest male representative of Sir William Pepperell, m. 1885 his cousin, the eldest dau. of the Rev. A. W. Bullen, (see above).
3. Charles William, born July 1826, m. in March 1852, Elizabeth, Maria Henrietta, eldest d. of Sir Andries Stockenström, Bart., of Maaström, near Grahamstown.
4. Emily, born Nov. 1827.
5. Julia, born Aug. 1829, m. Nov. 1864, Carl Frederick Joubert Watermeyer Esq., of Wynberg, near Cape Town.
6. Louisa, born in April 1831, ob. cœl.
7. Frederick, born Sep. 1832, died an infant.
8. Sophia, born July 1834.
9. Anne, born March 1836. Ob. cœl.
10. Augustus Fortescue, born June 1838, m. April 1872, Ellen, d. of Captain Preston, R.N. (retired.)
11. William Pepperell, born Jan. 1840, m. Jan. 1885, Margaret Maria, d. of Frederick Damant Esq., of Humansdorp, Cape of Good Hope.
12. Elizabeth Fortescue, born April 1843, m. March 1867 William Henry Brewer Esq.

III. William Palmer, M.A., of Trinity College, Dublin, and Incumbent of St. Peter's, Chester; m. but ob. s. p. 1856.

IV. Thomas Palmer, M.A., of Magdalen College, Oxford, late Vicar of Sompting, Sussex, born 1805, m. firstly, Mary, d. of James Drummond Esq. of Strageath, co. Perth; and secondly, 1853, Maria Elizabeth, d. of Edward Wingfield Dickenson Esq. of Dosthill House, Warwickshire, and had issue by his first marriage—

1. Henry Edward, M.A., of Balliol College, Oxford, and Assistant Master at Harrow, born 1838, m. firstly, Edith Maria, d. of George Harris Esq., of Harrow, who d. 1867, and secondly, 1869, Lucie Adele, d. of Mons. Th. Piquet, of Geneva, and of Millières, Bourbon Lancy, France.
2. Edmund Forster, born 1832, late Rector of Aylmerton and Runcton, co. Norfolk, m. Maria, d. of the Rev. Cremer Cremer of Aylmerton, and has issue.
3. Thomas Palmer, born 1832, formerly in the Carabineers, ob. cœl. 1857.
4. Mary Beatrice, born Dec. 16, 1836, m. 1858 Colonel A. Piquet of Geneva, and had issue Mary, Edmund, Beatrice, and Frank. The Rev. Thomas Palmer has, by his second marriage, Stewart Yates, Ralph Thicknesse, Reginald Ernest, and Herbert Royall Pepperell.

V. Elizabeth, m. 1818, the Rev. William Moreton-Moreton, of Moreton Hall, Cheshire, who d. about 1837, having had issue two sons who died young, and two daughters, Frances Annabella, who m. John Craigie Esq. of Jedburgh, N.B., (Residence, Moreton House, Pau, Les Basses Pyrénées,) and Elizabeth, a Sister of Mercy at Clewer, near Windsor.

VI. Mary Anne, b. April 1796, m. 1822, the Rev. William Walford, M.A., of Oriel College, Oxford, of Hatfield Place, Essex. He d. 1856, and she d. 1872. They had issue—

1. Edward, M.A., formerly scholar of Balliol College, Oxford: b. 1823, m. firstly, 1847, Mary Holmes, younger daughter of John Gray Esq. of Clifton, near Bristol. She d. 1851, leaving a daughter Mary, who m. Colin Campbell Wyllie Esq.: and secondly, 1852, Julia, daughter of the late Hon. Sir John Talbot, Admiral, and G.C.B., and has issue—
   Edward Arundell Talbot, b. 1860.
   Moreton Philip, b. 1861.
   Julia, m. P. H. Conron Esq.
   Edith, m. F. Waddy Esq.
   Ethel Mary.
2. Henry, M.A., of Wadham College, Oxford; Rector of Ewelme, Oxon; b. 1824.

3. John Thomas, M.A., of King's College, Cambridge; late an Assistant Master at Eton, now a Jesuit Priest; b. 1834.
4. Charles, M.A., of Brazenose College, Oxford; b. 1835, a Chaplain at Bombay, m. Miss Moberly, niece of the Bishop of Salisbury.
5. Frederick, b. 1836.
6. Mary Anne, died an infant.
7. Jane, m. the Rev. Daniel Trinder, Vicar of Highgate, Middlesex.
8. Frances Mary.
9. Caroline, died an infant.
10. Emma, d. 1844, aged 14.

VII. Louisa, m. in 1824, the Rev. Thomas Parry, Archdeacon of Antigua, and afterwards Bishop of Barbadoes, who d. about 1870. They had issue—

1. Edward St. John, M.A., Balliol College, Oxford, and formerly Principal of Leamington College; b. 1825, m. a sister of Sir Henry Tyler, M.P., and has a large family: his son Reginald St. John, b. 1861, is Fellow of Trinity College, Cambridge.
2. Henry Hutton, D.D., Bishop of Perth, Western Australia, b. 1829, m. firstly, Miss Bessie Thomas: secondly, a widow lady, and has 2 sons and a daughter.
3. Reginald, Colonel in the army, retired; m. Miss Morant, and is a widower with 2 children.
4. Herbert, died young.
5. Louisa, m. Gen. Nicols, and is dead, leaving 4 sons, and 2 daughters.
6. Charlotte, m. Gen. Chamberlain, and has one daughter, and 2 sons who d. young.
7. Amy, late a Sister Nurse in King's College Hospital.
8. Emily.
9. Caroline, m. Colonel Dalyell, and has a large family.
10. Beatrice, a Sister in the Protestant Sisterhood at Clewer, near Windsor.
11. Blanche, m. the Rev. Arthur Hardy, Chaplain in India, and has a large family.
12. Maude, m. in 1884, the Rev. Charles E. Freeman, Vicar of West Malvern.

VIII. Anne, died unmarried.

IX. Harriet, m. the Rev. D. T. K. Drummond, of Edinburgh: she survives as his widow: they had a son who d. an infant, and a daughter who married a Clergyman, and is now a widow.

X. Frances.

5th.—Old Jewry. Called on Mr. Green. He has a letter from T. Brattle* at N. York, who has petitioned the Assembly at Boston to admit him—which was to be considered in September.

Genl Vaughan said yesterday at dinner, the charge of the navy last year was seven millions. His brother Ld Lisburne is one of the Lords of the Admiralty.

Willard,† Bliss,‡ and Porter. [dined with him.]

6th.—Gov. Bull called: the Bishop of London. The latter says he has been in the neighbourhood of Lord Shelburne—I suppose at Bath; and that he knows that for a fortnight Lord S——'s friends and family depended on his being Secry of State. He intimated that they expected Lord Gower's difference with Lord North would terminate in bringing Lord Shelburne in. This looks as if Lord Shelb's alliance with the Bedford family would connect Ld Gower with him in political matters, though Ld Gower as yet has voted with the ministry.

The Hussar frigate has taken a rich Lima ship, and sent her in to Portugal. The *Tartar*, one of Gov. Johnstone's squadron, has taken a Span[ish] frigate, which took out part of the money

* Thomas Brattle, of Massachusetts. He was born at Cambridge in 1742, graduated at Harvard University in 1760, and received the degree of A.M. at Yale and at Nassau. In 1775 he went to England, and he was included in the Proscription and Banishment Act of 1778. While abroad, he travelled over various parts of Great Britain, and made a tour through Holland and France, and was noticed by personages of distinction. Returning to London, he zealously and successfully laboured to ameliorate the condition of his countrymen, who had been captured, and were in prison. In 1779 he came to America, and landed at Rhode Island. In 1784 the enactments against him in Massachusetts were repealed, and he took possession of his patrimony. He died Feb. 1801.—Sabine's Loyalists.

† Abijah Willard was appointed one of the Mandamus Counsellors in 1774: he was captured, and was on his way to prison, when he freed himself by signing a Declaration and asking forgiveness. He went to Halifax with the Royal Army in 1776, but eventually died in Massachusetts.

Abel Willard is described by Sabine, as having been one of the Barristers and Attorneys who were Addressers of Hutchinson; who withdrew to Halifax in 1776; was proscribed and banished; and died in England in 1781. There was also a Levi Willard, who retired temporarily to England, but Abel is probably the person mentioned in the Diary.

† Four gentlemen of the name of Bliss are mentioned by Sabine, of whom Daniel, born in 1740, a lawyer, and one of the Addressers of Hutchinson, on his leaving, is the one spoken of above, or Jonathan, born in 1742, a lawyer, a Member of the General Court, and proscribed in 1778. Revolutions make great havoc among families. A glance at Sabine's two volumes is enough to convince us of this.

of the Lima ship's cargo, and landed it at Ferrol; and coming out again, was taken by the *Tartar.* Nothing more of D'Estaigne. The prevailing opinion is that Wallace is taken.

The Bp. of London says Ld North has engaged all the money he wants, and that Ministry is determined to carry on the war in America with vigour.

7th.—Upon a motion last night by Lord Ossory in the House of Commons, to charge the Ministry with neglecting the affairs of Ireland, Mr Macdonald, who married Lord Gower's daughter, moved it might be *Minister* instead of *Ministry;* for that all was chargeable upon Lord North, and attacked him in very illiberal language—called him "whimperer," "whiner," &c.

Lord North excused his tears once when he had been blamed for his absence, which, for an excuse obliged him to mention the death of a child.

The motion was rejected by a majority of about 90.

Called upon Sir Geo. Collier.

My son T. H., wife, and Louisa [Oliver], Sylv.[ester Oliver], Flucker.

8th.—In the city with my son T., but learn no intelligence, except the arrival of many ships from different parts. The very few captures which have been made since the French war began keeps up the spirits of the merchants there—enables them to lend all the money Government wants, and the good terms upon which they lend it makes them more quiet under the amazing debt which is brought upon the kingdom in general.

9th.—The estimates for the present year passed last night in the H. of Commons. Lord George [Germaine], on being asked whether the American war was to be continued, answered, that the Ministry had no thoughts of withdrawing the forces from America. This would give great advantage to France and Spain, but he was not able to say in what manner the war would be carried on there, and if he knew he should not think it proper to mention it.

10th.—Yesterday Lord North opened to the House what he proposed [to do] to satisfy Ireland—to take off the restraint upon woollen manufactures; also upon glass; to allow a free trade to the British Colonies and Africa. Regulations would be necessary to be made by the Irish Parl^{t} in each of these articles. He thought this would be satisfactory to Ireland. Sir George Young asked whether he thought it would be satisfactory to England also?

11th.—In the city. Blackburne asked if I thought there would be a change of Ministry? I did not know where they would find a Premier. Lord Gower, he added, had expected it. He had it so that he was sure of it. Lord Carlisle sought one of the Secretary's places. This country is ruined by party.

In the House of Commons last night, the Minority moved the affair of Ld North refusing the Chiltern Hundreds to Mr Byng. Ld N. exculpated himself by saying he had said to Mr Byng that he had promised them to Col^{o} Tuffnel; but if he did not insist upon it, Mr Byng should have them. The motion obtained; and upon another motion, a Bill was ordered to be brought in to make the Member eligible to any vacant county or borough, notwithstanding their former election, which they are to be allowed to vacate.

Copley, Stanton, and my children. [presumably, at dinner.]

12th.—At Prince's Street. Mr Thompson, a middle aged man, said to have no congregation. Rainy all day. No account yet of D'Estaigne. Dr Chandler, Bliss.

Copley yesterday, (who spent a year in Italy), made a remark which occurred to him upon seeing the loaves of bread taken entire out of Pompeii. He says they are exactly the shape of our loaves, (not bricks); that the letters of the bakers' names are still plain. He wondered this practice of stamping their bread, never put them upon the same sort of stamps for letters and printing.

The surprise of Mr Copley may be shared by others. That they did not do so shews how people will sometimes stand for centuries on the brink of a great discovery without making it. Instead of saying a new discovery, we might in this case rather say, a new adaptation of old materials. The stamps they had: and why not stamp paper with ink, as well as loaves without?

The Copleys will not now be mentioned much more in the Governor's Diary, if mentioned at all. In the fragmentary Diary of his son Elisha they are several times spoken of; but as the recorded facts have only been written on sheets of note paper of different sizes, which have never been sewn together, and many of them lost, it is difficult to arrange them in chronological order; and the difficulty is increased by the absence of the year and the month, except at rare intervals. Though the entries contain no valuable information, perhaps it would be an omission to ignore them altogether; and it would be a slight to degrade them to the low level of a Foot Note, so they shall have an intermediate place, like the long extracts that have been given before.

From the Diary of Elisha Hutchinson.

"18th. [summer time, 1777 or 1778?] Fair, warm, and pleasant. Rain in evening. Walked to Brompton. Tommy and wife, Louisa, and 3 of the children dined with us. After dinner Mr. Clarke, Copley, and Mrs. Copley, and two of their children joined us at tea."

"25th.— . . . After dinner with Mrs. H. and Mr. Willard jun., to Mr. Copley, who with Mrs. Copley and two of the children, we walked to Buckingham House, and were two hours going through the rooms, and viewing the paintings, after which we returned and drank tea at Mr. Copley's."

"20th—[1778?] Called on Mr. Hallswell: with Mrs. H. to Copley's: afterwards to the Treasury, and received a quarter's allowance to the 10th."

"19th [April, 1779?] Fair, warm, and pleasant. Walked into the city and called on Mr. Mauduit, who seems to be as hearty and well as I have known him to be. Called on Mr. Lyde. Mrs. Esdaile dined with us. Mr. Clarke, Mr. and Mrs. and Betsy Copley at tea."

"14th. [May 1779.] Walked with Mrs. H. to Pall Mall, and spent about two hours very pleasantly at the Exhibition Rooms of the Royal Academy. Mr. Copley has not exhibited any piece this year. We drank tea at the Doctor's, [Dr. P. Oliver's,] with Mr. and Mrs. Copley, and Mr. Pelham."

"9. [July, 1779.] Walked to the Exchange and to Lombard Street. On my return stop'd at Mr. Copley's, where I met Mrs. Galloway and Mrs. H., who came to see Mr. Copley's picture of [blank]* and other pictures. We then went—Mr. and Mrs. Copley, and my brother Bill, with us—over to Sr Joshua Reynold's, where,

* Perhaps Lord Chatham's illness in the House of Lords.

among a multitude of fine paintings, I thought none better executed than one just taken, of Admiral Keppel. On our way home we called on Mr. West, whose rooms were principally filled with portraits of the King, Queen, and Royal Family: but what most engaged our attention was, a full length portrait of the King, which was not quite finished, and he told us was designed for the Queen's Palace—a most striking likeness, in the King's military dress, Lord Amherst, and Lord [blank] at a distance on horseback, and the prospect of the Camp, the King in his boots, as having just dismounted his horse."

"4. [1779?] Fair, early in morning: afterwards cloudy and rain. Went in coach with Mr. G. [Galloway] at 7 o'clock to Mr. Copley's, Leicest^r Fields, where, after waiting till nine o'clock for the coach, we walked to 3 Kings, Piccadilly, and finding the coach, after waiting an hour, (and not being able to find Mr. O., throu' mistake in the direction), had gone forward, Mr. O. took a post chaise, and with Mr. Clarke set out to overtake the coach, and I returned home to breakfast."

"2nd. April, [1781?] Fair, moderate, and pleasant. Walked out to Edward Street. Called on Mr. Willard, and on Mr. West."

"3rd. Walked with Mrs. H. to Leicester Fields, and left her at Mr. Copley's."

"3rd. May, [1781?] Fair morning—afterwards rain. Miss Galloway called and took Mrs. H. and Betsey an airing as far as Islington. I then walked to Spring Gardens with Mrs. H. to see Mr. Copley's Exhibition, and called at Mr. Copley's, Leicester Fields."

"14. [May, 1781?] Cloudy morning and some rain; afterwards fair and pleasant. In coach as far as St. Clement's Church, and met Mrs. H., who came in coach with Mrs. Galloway, at the Exhibition of pictures in Somerset House. After viewing the pictures we walked to Leicest^r Fields, and called on Mr Copley: from thence came home to dinner. We drank tea at Mr. Galloway's—Mr. Hale there."

"August 27. [1781?] Met Mr. Mather, who tells me he has a letter from his father, and another from a man who married his sister Hannah. His mother Mrs. M.* died about 2 years ago, of which he has but lately been made acquainted with. Col. Fry I likewise met with. I then walked to George Street, Hanover Sq., and dined at Mr. Copley's, who has changed houses to great

* She was one of the Governor's sisters named Hannah, born in 1714, and married to the Rev. Samuel Mather.

advantage, the rent being nearly the same; but the house is elegant and well finished, and well calculated for his living."

"August 29th.—Called on Mr. Copley, George Street."

"October 1st. [1781 ?] Fog in morning, afterwards warm and pleasant. My brother went to ride. I walked to George Street and called at Mr Copley's, who, with Mr. Clarke and Mrs. Copley [*née* Clarke,] were gone down to Gravesend to see Mr Startin set sail for Boston, on board of Cap. Callahan."

It is hoped that this long interpolation, dedicated to the Copleys, though fragmentary and of small historical account, may be allowed to pass without censure. The painter removed from Leicester Fields to George Street, Hanover Square,—to that house on the east side, in short, so long known as the residence of his son Lord Lyndhurst.

13th.—Steady warm rain, like an American day. Old Cap[n] Bruce who used to trade between London and Boston many years, called on me. He brought part of the tea which was destroyed: pretends he should be afraid to go to sea, for fear of being taken, and ill treated by the Americans, and is petitioning Government as a Refugee. John Rowe* owned a quarter of his ship. I believe, says Bruce, he knew very well the design to pull down your house. There's Doctor Chauncy and Doctor Cooper, I have heard M[r] Rowe say he knew they both used to write in Thomas's paper—*The Massachusetts Spy*.

14th.—A cold clear day. In the city. Dined at M[r] Ellis's, who is very anxious to hear of D'Estaigne: says the papers taken in the Spanish packet mention D'Estaigne intending first for the southern part of the Continent, then to New York, Rhode Island, and Halifax, but in what order I do not recollect: and he was to detach some ships in order to take in Bermuda.

M[r] Livius, Ch. Just. of Quebec, met me in the street. He had just seen one of his acquaintance who was in the fleet under D'Estaigne, the 25 or 26 of August, when off Long Island, one of the Bahamas, or near them, where the fleet divided, and part steered for France, where this person, I suppose a prisoner, went; the other part, under D'Estaigne, for America. Seven

* There is a kind and characteristic letter by John Row to the Consignees, printed in the first volume at page 97.

days after parting, a violent storm came on, and lasted three days, first at N. East, at last at S. East. This person thinks it probable that many of D'Estaigne's fleet must have been drove to the Straits of Bahama.

Strange, there is yet no account of them!

15th.—At Ld Hardwicke's, and then Ld Huntingdon's, where I saw his L^d^ship's nephew Cap^n^ Rawdon. He says the Americans have hanged the late Ch. Justice of Detroit, with whom he was well acquainted—his name Deshon—and that Col^o^ or Cap^n^ Hamilton, the officer made prisoner in the spring, is in a dungeon, and in irons. Many stories undoubtedly are false, and many facts exaggerated. I saw Galloway afterwards, and advised him to write to his friends, and collect the instances of capital and cruel punishments, which were fully authenticated, or so notorious as not to be denied, and he promised he would.

Dined at Dr Heberden's:—Mr Crofts, Member for Cambridge, and lady; M^r^ and Mrs Wray, Mr Bryant, a man of fortune and learning, Mauduit, and the Doctor's family.

16th.—Rainy day and evening, but still very moderate as to cold. Bliss d. The wind being east, it is expected the fleet under Rodney will sail. Genl Vaughan left town Sunday the 12th. He is to take the command of the land forces in the West Indies. Never was the kingdom in such a state. The cry is—There are no men fit to command the Army or the Navy; and it is certain that all the distresses of the nation are owing to the unfitness of officers both by sea and land.* Byron has retired, and is pitied. Poor man—he did what he thought best, but is a weak man. Keppel's enemies will not allow weakness to be his only failing, but say he did not wish to destroy the French fleet, lest he should establish the present Ministry. As for land Generals, Howe has no advocate to undertake his cause in print, and Clinton they say, has lain still all the summer, merely from indecision, and a fluctuating state of mind.

* When things come to the worst they begin to mend; and it is certain that within twenty or thirty years after this date, the glory of the Navy, at all events, had grown to such a pitch of brightness, as that, by the commencement of the present century, England had as good reason to be proud of her sailors, as her enemies had to be afraid of them. The period of Nelson and his compeers is now looked back upon as the bright spot in the annals of the British Navy.

17th.—In the city. The wind round again at S. West. No arrivals. Everybody wondering there is nothing certain yet of D'Estaigne. A vessel is arrived at Falmouth from Boston, which sailed as late as the 13th November. She was bought by some persons who had been taken prisoners, and obtained leave to come to England. The passengers say they had received no account of D'Estaigne.

18th.—The news to-day is—that Capn Moore, who was taken prisoner at Granada, and sailed in a merchtman of D'Estaigne's fleet, is arrived in town. He says they met with a violent storm Sept. 16: that he saw that day and the next, five sail of the French men-of-war sink, and 14 or 15 merchant-men, in lat. 38, and long. 60: that his own ship, or that he was in, was lost at Fayal in their way home. He gives no account of the rest.

Prickman, Van Schaack, Waterhouse,* Frye, E. H., Gardner, Perkins. [dined.]

19th.—At Gray's Inn Chapel, and heard Dr Stebbins—and an excellent preacher—sensible, serious, and christian.

In the evening at Lord Mansfield's, Chancellor's, and Dr Heberden's. The accounts of D'Estaigne thicken. Moore's account cannot be true, seeing Lieut. Atkinson came to France in one of the St Domingo ships, and the *Protecteur* was his convoy, and both arrived at Rochelle: but he agrees in the storm the 16, and thinks a 50 gun ship and a frigate, were lost: but he says D'Estaigne and all the men-of-war except five, parted from the fleet the 25 Aug., and steered for America, so that Moore must have supposed some of the large merchtmen to have been men-of-war. Lord North thinks the account of D'Estaigne's arrival in France is to be relied upon.

John Adams, with F. Dana for his Secretary, are coming from Boston to France in the characters of Ambassador and Secretary to the Court of Great Britain; but before they come over, Independence is to be allowed them.

20th.—Everything in American affairs happens contrary

* Samuel Waterhouse of Boston, Mass., described as "the most notorious scribbler, satirist, and libeller in the service of the conspirators against the liberties of America." He withdrew to Halifax, and then to England; was proscribed and banished; and was in London in 1779, a Loyalist Addresser of the King.—Sabine.

to probability. An officer arrived to-day from Clinton. D'Estaigne, who was supposed to be lost in a storm, and many of his ships, remained on the coast of Carolina till late in October. Wallace fell into his hands. D'Estaigne landed his troops, and joined Lincoln, and made an army of 8,000—enough to have swallowed up the British troops in Savanna, where they all retreated: but notwithstanding his numbers, and all that sea force, after two attempts he left the coast, and came with part of his ships for Europe: the rest he sent to the West Indies. It is said the French and rebels, between them, have lost 3000 men: the British not above 40. This I had from Sr Richd Sutton, who brought it to Mr Mazeres in the Temple, where I dined with Mauduit, Galloway, Mr Townsend, &c.

21.—An express to-day from Georgia confirms the account of yesterday, with many circumstances not then mentioned. The French fleet had left the coast, except three frigates, which remained at Charlestown, S. Carolina.

22nd.—The letters from New York by the packet mention advice from different quarters that Adm. Hyde Parker had taken a number of French men-of-war. It is reported here that several victuallers were taken, which seems to be the most that can be expected.*

23rd.—A dull day to me, from reflection upon the occurrence of yesterday, and perplexity what step to take.

24th.—My son W. had incautiously accepted a draught from Cap^n^ Douglas, an E. India Captain of his acquaintance, at two years sight, for more than 500£. He says the Captain was to secure him, and went away without doing it; but as it was not payable in less than two years, he has all along flattered himself the Cap^n^ would be home to discharge it himself. And now the time is up, and the demand of payment made. His illness adds to his and my distress. I hear this afternoon eight or nine ships from India are arrived, but am anxious lest Douglas should not be among them.

25th.—By my paper this morning Douglas is not among the ships, and I give up all hopes of relief from him, and

* Then follows some shorthand referring to an incautious act of his son Billy, who had accepted a Bill for £500, at two years, now come due.

expect to be obliged to pay the money. I went to my son [Thomas] at Brompton, where he is at lodgings. By his Newspaper Douglas is one. Which to believe, I am at a loss, and am still in suspense.

A very cold day, and this trouble kept me from church, as I intended.

All my children, S. O., Louisa O., and young Spooner, [at dinner?]

D'Estaigne is certainly arrived in France: no certainty of any other part of the fleet which was at Georgia.

26th.—At Dr Kippis's. Cold in the morning, but abates afternoon. Wind N.

27th.—In the city with my son T., who went to Lloyd's, where he is assured their list may be depended on, and if so, Douglas must be arrived, and I hope that will relieve me from the trouble which the imprudence of my son W. would have brought upon me, as well as upon himself, who is in a very feeble declining state, and unable to bear trouble.

The men-of-war for Gibraltar and the West Indies sailed yesterday. Fresh wind and fair all night and to-day, that it's probable they may be near the Landsend.

28th.—The wind continuing fair, it is expected the fleet under Sr G. Rodney are clear of the land.

Lord Hardwicke called. He says Sir Joseph writes him from the Hague, that Paul Jones in his own ship, lyes without any colours; that the *Serapis* and others, under French Commissions, ride with French colours, and none of them are moving. It's supposed our frigates are cruising for them.

Cold much abated yesterday and to-day, but drizzling rain and raw.

Wrote to Paxton at Pangbourne.

29th.—Mr Ellis called upon me. He observed that the arrival of Adams and Dana made a noise: people supposed they had powers to treat; but they could have no good design, as they came to France. If they had come to Holland or Hamburgh, and sent from thence to know how they would be received, something might come of it, but not so now.

I wrote Mr Sewall at Bristol, in answer to a long letter of his upon a demand made of him by T. Boylston* for rent at Boston.

Raw foggy day. Wind still E. My son Billy came to town, and dined with me and Bliss.

30th.—A strong opinion in the city yesterday and to-day that Adams and Dana are come to France with offers of accommodation, and that affairs with America will be soon settled, and stocks rise near 2 ℘ c^t: but the opinion dies away, and they were falling again before night.

31st.—Advice that a fleet of Dutch ships, being bound down Channel, six large ships with naval stores had joined, and thereupon a squadron of ships slipped their cables and sailed from Spithead in persuit of them, to search and stop the ships with naval stores, being for the French.

* Sabine tells us there was W. N. Boylston, son of B. Hallowell, but who took the name of Boylston; and Thomas, who is the one here spoken of. John Adams said of him in 1766—"Tom is a firebrand. Tom is a perfect viper, a Jew, a devil, but is orthodox in politics however." But he became a Loyalist, went to England, failed in business, and died in great poverty.

CHAPTER VII.

BEGINNING OF THE NEW YEAR 1780.

January 1st.—At Court: the first time I had been there on New Year's Day: remarkably full of Ladies, in particular. Cold, foggy, and dark. Lord Lisburne said a French letter had been intercepted which gives an account of Parker's taking the French ships.

I said to Lord Lisburne I was glad Cap^n Vaughan had so fine a time. He said he had a fair wind: he hoped he would do service: he had two good qualities—he could not bear inactivity, and I forget the other. I added a third—He is well principled.

Flucker, Rome, Willard, Danforth, Clarke, Startin, E. H. [at dinner, no doubt.] My son Billy lodged last night in town, after three months absence, or thereabouts.*

2nd.—At the Old Jewry without my children.

Mauduit tells me a Lima or Register ship is carried into Crookhaven with 3 millions of dollars on board. A privateer of Liverpool took her, which took the Carnatick Indiaman.

3rd.—In the city. Billy received a letter from Cap. Douglas at Portsmouth, in which he expresses his concern at my son's ill state of health, of which he had wrote to Douglas, and his surprise at the Banker's having made a demand on him for the Bill which he had accepted, and adds that he does not doubt,

* Whence came the final *s*? Such words as *thereabouts*, *whereabouts*, and *hereabouts*, are common, even in the pages of our best writers. *Thereabouts* simply means *about there*, or that place: *whereabouts*, is *about where*, or what place: and so also *hereabouts* is *about here*, or near this place. If we may say *thereabouts* why may we not say *abouts there?* The use of the final *s* is evidently of long standing; and however much we may condemn the practice, on the ground of impropriety or inaccuracy, we do nevertheless frequently see such words in the writings of many of our best modern authors.

now they know he is arrived, they will give my son no further trouble.

4th.—Express yesterday, with advice that Com^r^ Fielding had stopped two Dutch men of war—searched the ships under their convoy, and seized seven of them laden with naval stores for the French, and was returning with them to Portsmouth, and that the Dutch men of war were following them.

Daughter Oliver's family, and S. O.

5th.—In the city. The Dutch business has hardly any effect upon the stocks. It is not likely it should give them any real offence. They have been told, what we stop shall be paid for. This increases their export. What gets safe to France, they pay for: what is brought in here, we pay for. Government has been duped by its own subjects. Foreign states are now trying what they can do.

Lord Gage called—came in warm. "I have this minute parted," says he, "with a gentleman who said he wished D'Estaigne had taken Georgia and all the troops there, for then the war would have been at an end, and we should have been no more burdened with additional taxes."

"What can such men mean? Do they imagine the nation would submit to the humiliating terms which would have then been required?"

"No; that was not the reason of such a wish. A change of Ministry was the thing."

6th.—The stocks rather rise than fall. It is almost incredible, with such an immense debt, and prospect of still increasing it by several year's war.

7th.—In the city. At Watson and Rashleigh's. They say the capture of 5 French frigates and 14 transports by H. Parker's squadron, comes so many ways that there can be no doubt of it. It's strange that in more than three months there should be nothing from Parker himself.

Dined with Dr Parker at the Chaplain's table—Sir Egerton Leigh, and a clergyman, Rector of Hammersmith.

8th.—Called upon Mr Maseres.

Carried Mr Boucher and Addison in my coach to Lambeth, and dined with the Archbishop:—Lord Wellesley, son of Lord

Mornington; Lord Brome, a pretty boy of 6 or 7 years, or less, only son of Earl Cornwallis; D[r] Chertsey, of Ch. Church, Oxford; D[r] Lort, Abp's Chaplain; and a gentleman I did not know; M[rs] Cornwallis, and a little Miss, [being present.]

The Archbishop says he knew Sir F. Bernard at Cambridge, though some years after him. I thought he was of Christ Church, Oxford; but the Abp. was positive he could not be; and yet, for 9 or 10 years we lived together in Boston, and 4 or 5 years since, I have always understood it so.

The company went to the Chapel before dinner, which was exceeding cold, and I without a surtout. [It was Saturday.] D[r] Lort went through the Litany as fast as a Clerk would have gone through an instrument, which was mere matter of form in a court of law.

9th.—At D[r] Kippis's. [Sunday.]

Dined with M[r] Ellis:—D'Oiley and wife, M[r] Bateman, Brett, Le Cras, Falkingham, Stephens, of the Admin., Palmer. M[r] Stephens says two of D'Estaigne's ships were not arrived in France—the *Tonnant*, and *Sagittaire;* nor the *Experiment*, Wallace's ship. Wallace and his lady are aboard the *Sagittaire.* They hear from France that Sir P. Parker's squadron has taken the *Alcmena*, one of the frigates that D'Estaigne left with the French ships coming to Europe, besides 6 or 7 ships of that squadon, and that the *Fier*, a 50, of the same squadron, had got into Martinique.

10th.—Called on M[r] Livius, Devonshire Street, and crossed through the fields, back of Bedford and Montague Houses, to Percy Street, and so to High Street, Marybone. I endeavour to walk 3 or 4 miles every day if there is time enough in the day without rain: and altho' I must expect the infirmities of age to increase, yet, by joining temperance to moderate exercise, we have room to hope for a mitigation. (Two Chandlers and Bliss.)

11th.—Called this morning, as I walked into the city, upon M[r] Thom. Bernard, Lincoln's Inn, who gave me a more particular account of his father's last sickness and death than I had ever heard before. For near two months before he died, a dropsy had added itself to his other complaints, and for several of the last weeks the Physicians apprehended the water would rise to his lungs, and immediately stop the use of them.

He was best stocked with anecdotes of any man I knew, and fond of communicating them, which he could do with a good grace. When he had so little use of his reason as scarcely to distinguish his own children, he would tell one of his stories as he lay in bed, not forgetting any circumstance, with the same propriety of modulation of voice in the several parts, as he used to when well. About a week before he died he was seized with an epileptick fit, more violent and lasting than any he had had before, and being looked upon as near his end, his son Thom. was sent for from London. When he came down he endeavoured to rouze his father, and he had reason enough to say,—"Are you come? Well, I will get up and come down presently." A few minutes before he died, being bewildered, he fancied himself on the water, and in some dangerous place, and said with his usual tone of voice,—"Never fear: if you will but have patience, I don't doubt we shall get safe through; but take care how you ever get into such a scrape again." A convulsion presently came on, and his children were obliged to lay hold of him, to prevent his throwing himself out of bed, the water rose in his stomach as they apprehended, and he died in their arms.

Mauduit, in the evening, brings intelligence that the Jamaica packet is arrived: confirms Hyde Parker's having taken the French convoy, with which there were no men-of-war, but six large ships, with their lower deck guns in the hold, served as a convoy, and were intended, after unlading, to be completely fitted as ships of war. No news of the return of D'Estaigne's ships any*

Letters also, from the Commander of Cooke's ships at Kamskatka, dated in June, giving an account of Cooke's, and three or four more, being killed on a new discovered island in Lat. 22,—of their having attempted discovery northward without success,—but of their intention notw[th]standing, to make a further trial the past summer.

* The end of the sentence is wanting.

The singular account of the last moments of Sir Francis Bernard, as related above, can scarcely be allowed to pass without some remark; and the news of the death of Captain Cook, only just then arrived in England, cannot fail to arrest our attention for a moment. The boy James Cook, born in 1724, son of a poor cottager, followed the plough till he was thirteen years of age; was bound apprentice to a grocer when seventeen, but sighing for a sea life, he engaged with a ship owner at Whitby, and sailed in a collier in the year 1746. He continued in the coal trade until 1753, when he got appointed to the *Eagle*, and entered the Royal navy: he received a Lieutenant's commission in 1760,—applied his active mind to the study of mathematics and navigation,—was raised to the rank of Captain of the *Endeavour*, when an expedition was organised to proceed to Otaheite for the purpose of observing a transit of Venus in 1769, and he sailed down the river Thames accompanied by Sir Joseph Bankes, Dr. Solander, and Mr. Green: and after having accomplished this object, he proceeded to prosecute a series of explorations and discoveries in the Pacific Ocean, so that he did not return to England till June 1771. In April 1772, he embarked on board the *Resolution*, accompanied by the *Adventure*, Captain Furneaux, to try and penetrate the ice fields in the Antarctic regions, and returned to England in July 1774. In July 1776, he again set sail, at first attempting the often tried "North-west Passage," where, being foiled by the ice, he once more steered for the Pacific; and having an unfortunate altercation with the natives at Owyhee, he was there killed on the 14th of February, 1779. He was a remarkable instance of natural genius, improved by self-culture.

The minute particulars attending the death of Sir Francis Bernard, as given by his son to Governor Hutchinson, are sufficiently noteworthy by their authenticity, if not by their singularity, to make us pause at this place. Pardonably curious, (as I hope), to know more of the family so often mentioned in the Diary, I consider myself fortunate in being able to draft into these pages the following brief account of it; [for which account I am indebted to Mrs. Napier Higgins, sole surviving child of the last Baronet.]

"Sir Francis Bernard came of an ancient Northamptonshire family; his grandfather was first cousin of Sir Robert Bernard, the father of Sir John Bernard, M.P. for Huntingdon, in the Long Parliament, whose name is so often met with in the history of the Commonwealth. Sir Francis was born in 1712,—was educated at Christ Church, Oxford,* and was called to the Bar, where his position was good enough to procure him election as a Bencher of the Middle Temple. He married a niece of Lord Barrington.

"His original Colonial appointment was to the Government of New Jersey in 1758. The Earl of Halifax, then First Lord of Trade, appointed him at the request of Lord Barrington. In 1760, he was appointed to the government of Massachusetts Bay, which extended from the 42nd to the 46th degree of Latitude. Its inhabitants then numbered about 250,000. On arriving in the Colony, one of his earliest public acts was to extend the foundations and usefulness of Harvard College, in which he continued to take a great interest. He entered with great spirit on the duties of his office, and remained Governor for nine years, during the first five of which he was extremely popular. In February 1762, the House of Assembly unanimously passed a resolution for granting to him the island of Mount Desert, as an acknowledgment of his public services, and this was sanctioned by the Home government. However, in 1763, orders were addressed by Lord Egremont and the Lords of Trade to the Governors of the American Colonies, requiring them to carry into strict execution the laws of trade, and notifying that enlarged authority had been delegated to the Commanders of the King's ships stationed in America, to seize all vessels concerned in any prohibited commerce. The published letters of Governor Bernard, shew that he regarded the policy shown in these orders to be unwise and injurious, both to English and colonial interests. His expostulations were without effect.

"Before his return to England in 1769, George III. created him a Baronet, and ordered the expense of the Patent to be paid out of his Privy Purse. He arrived in England in August of that year, where he was extremely well received, not only by his Sovereign and the Government of the day, but by many of the leading public men of both the great parties in the State. Not long afterwards he had the good fortune to succeed to an estate in Buckinghamshire, called Nether Winchendon, which is sometimes referred to in the preceding pages.† While he was still Governor, he gave the name of Winchendon to a small town which is still known by the name in Massachusetts. His estates in the Province, which

* This may serve to recall the conversation that took place Jan. 8, 1780, between the Archbishop of Canterbury and the Governor, when the latter dined at Lambeth Palace. The Archbishop (Cornwallis) spoke of Sir F. Bernard positively as of Cambridge, but Mr. H. thought he was of Ch. Ch. Oxford. The Archbishop was labouring under a false impression.

† Vol. i. pp. 194, 249.

were large, were confiscated by the State of Massachusetts Ap. 30, 1779, and his son and immediate successor, Sir John Bernard, received as compensation, a grant from Parliament of a considerable sum of money. There used to be, and probably still is, at Christ Church, Oxford, a portrait of Sir Francis Bernard, by Copley.

"Owing to the state of his health he resided for the last few years of his life at the Prebendal, near Aylesbury, where he died. A Memoir of Sir Francis, and also his Letters, have been printed, but it is now difficult to procure them.

"Two of his sons were men of considerable mark. After the death of Sir John, Sir Thomas, the next son, succeeded to the title. He was very well known in the earlier part of the present century as a philanthropist, and many of the philanthropic movements of that time were originated or promoted by his efforts. He wrote many pamphlets on such subjects, and is mentioned in the *Memoirs* of Sidney Smith as the first person of consequence in London who took him by the hand, and to whom the witty Divine owed his appointment of Preacher at the Foundling Hospital. In his writings will be found numerous suggestions for improving the condition of working people, which have since been carried into effect. An interesting Life of this gentleman was published by Murray in 1819. On his death without issue, his brother Scrope, who on his marriage had assumed the name of Morland, succeeded to the Baronetcy. He sat as Member for Aylesbury and St. Mawes n several Parliaments, and for many years was Under-Secretary of State for the Home Department. The last member of the family who succeeded to the Baronetcy was Sir Thomas Tyringham Bernard, who continued the family name, and dropped the name of Morland. He was M.P. for Aylesbury in two Parliaments, and died in 1883, in his ninety-second year."

He left no son living, and therefore the Baronetcy became extinct; but the estate of Nether Winchendon passed to his only surviving daughter Mrs. Napier Higgins, who has recently published the first two volumes of a work called—*The Women of Europe in the* 15*th and* 16*th Centuries.* Two daughters of the Governor were successful authors. One of them, Mrs. King, (daughter Fanny), a contemporary of Hannah More, wrote a book called—*Female Scripture Characters*, which went through twelve Editions during the first quarter of the present century. It was mentioned in one of the Obituary Notices of the late Sir T. T. Bernard as a curious fact, that on the day of his death in May 1883, 154 years after his grandfather Governor Bernard was elected a Westminister student of Christ Church, Oxford, his own and only grandson, Mr. Francis Tyringham Higgins, obtained the same studentship at the same College.

The following extracts from the printed *Memoirs* of Sir Francis Bernard, page 39, will corroborate several of the remarks made above:—

"In February 1762, the Assembly passed a unanimous resolution —'That, in consideration of the extraordinary services of His Excellency Governor Bernard, there be granted to him, his heirs and assigns, the Island of Mount Desert, lying on the north-eastward of Penobscot Bay, and that a Grant thereof, to be laid before His Majesty for his approbation, be signed by the Secretary and Speaker, on behalf of the two Houses.'

"Of this, the Lords of Trade expressed their approbation in the following terms—'We can have no objection to your acceptance of this grant, as a testimony of the approbation and favor of that Province, in whose service, and in the conduct of whose affairs, you have manifested such zeal and capacity.'*

"The Island was of considerable value; and perhaps it may not be going too far to state, it was a mere voluntary expression of good will, it having been partly intended as a recompence for some expenses which the Governor had incurred in improving the provincial buildings at the Castle, and in some public commissions. But whether it was to be deemed a gift, or a compensation, made little difference: in every event, it marked distinctly and decisively the popularity that attended his administration.

"A title to unappropriated lands, derived originally from the people and their representatives, approved by Administration, and ultimately ratified by the Sovereign, appeared in itself sufficiently unimpeachable. It could hardly have occurred at that time to a speculating mind, that the subsequent events respecting that title, were possible; that the situation of Governor Bernard should oblige him to sacrifice his popularity, to his duty and his integrity; that eventually, the very people which had made the grant, should, by a special act of their newly created State, confiscate this with his other property; and that, when Britain, (in whose cause the sacrifice had been made,) had provided relief for the other sufferers by the American troubles, in most cases with liberality, this, by the decision of the Board of American Claims, and under a total oblivion of the cause of forfeiture, should be one of

* Letter from the Lords of Trade to Governor Bernard, dated May 21, 1763.

the few instances in which relief and compensation had been denied."

At page 42 we read :—

"Upon the death of Chief Justice Sewall in 1761, Lieutenant Governor Hutchinson had been the first who had applied to the Government for the appointment: the assurance of it was hardly given to Mr. Hutchinson, when Mr. Otis attended on behalf of his father,* (a lawyer of eminence and character, and one of the Board of Council, but not in general friendly to Government,) claiming a promise made by Governor Shirley, one of Governor Bernard's predecessors, that Mr. Otis, the father, should be appointed to the Bench on the first vacancy. Governor Bernard did not feel it to be either in his power or inclination to forego the word which he had given, and Mr. Hutchinson was appointed; whereupon Mr. Otis resigned his office of Advocate-General, and declared perpetual hostility to the Governor's administration; an hostility which he continued for several years, not only with talents, but so far as warmth of temper did not mislead, with candour and liberality."

12th.—I had a very cold walk this morning to Mr Strahan's in New Street, Fleet Market. He read me a copy of a letter he had wrote to Dr Franklin, advising, that he, Strahan, had it from undoubted authority, that John Adams had been vested with secret powers by Congress to treat upon terms of accommodation with Great Britain: that he hoped F. would upon this occasion think what a dishonour, &c., it would reflect upon him to have such a negotiation carried on by another than himself: that he might put the greatest confidence in Strahan in communicating what should occur as proper to be done upon such an occasion: that he hoped for an answer to this letter: that even that sacred regard which he had to his Majesty, &c., should not tempt him to make any use of what he, F., should write, so has to do him any prejudice.

There was a Moravian Clergyman in the room when Strahan read the letter. At once hearing, I could not retain the words, but I have minuted the substance. I accounted for the strong attachm^ts^ to Franklin's person, by supposing he might have a licence tacitly, at least, from [blank] but his imprudence in

* This subject is alluded to in vol. i. p. 65.

suffering anybody besides himself to know he had written such a letter is unaccountable.*

13th.—A very cold day. This weather affects my son Billy: his complaints increase, and the great discharge from his lungs enfeebles him, and he loses ground daily. [Here follow a few remarks in shorthand referring to money transactions.]

14th.—I called at Lord Hillsborough's, where I met Lord Cranborne. Long conversation upon the state of affairs in general, and American in particular. Lord Cranborne said little. Lord H. seemed apprehensive of trouble from the new Associations;—expected they would form Committees of Correspondence, and may-be furnish themselves with arms, as they had done in Ireland.

Strahan, Maseres, Mauduit, Galloway, Livius, T. Bernard, dined.

Mr. Stanley died suddenly on the 12th., at Lord Spencer's.

15th.—In the city. A West India Dutchman, said to be from St. Eustatia, informed Cap. Paisley that Hyde Parker had met with La Motte Piquet returning from Georgia, and had taken five or six of the men-of-war, besides transports. Some believe this, but most people do not.

My two sons, and families, [at dinner.]

16th.—At Dr Kippis's.

Dr Oliver, wife, Chandler, Danforth, Bliss.

It was said at dinner that the Dutchman's news gains ground. Stocks do not lose ground.

Rodney said to be spoke with the 6th Instt off Cape Finisterre.

17th.—In the city. Stocks still rather rising, though it is now the time for the first payment of the subscription to the Loan for the next year. The extraordinary success of the

* William Strahan served his time as a printer in his native town of Edinburgh, and afterwards removed to London. In 1770 he bought a share in the patent place of King's Printer. By good conduct he prospered, and sat in Parliament in 1775. He was the friend of literary men, with whom he had naturally been much associated. He was disposed to recommend Dr. Johnson to the good graces of Lord North, as a step to Parliament, but the whole project did not take effect. Strahan died in 1785, aged 70.

British ships in coming home safe from all parts causes money to be plenty beyond all expectation.

18th.—Observed as the Queen's Birthday. I was not at Court, being low in spirits.

Dined at M[r] Knox's, where I first heard, to my great surprise, that M[r] Stanley, after eating a hearty breakfast, having left upon his table at Lord Spencer's, letters to his servants to make provision for his reception at home a day or two after, took a solitary walk into the woods, and soon after was found with his throat cut by his penknife, lying upon the ground dead or dying. He might have lain some time undiscovered if his groans had not been heard by a person not very far from him. His father died in the same manner.

No man's general character was more unexceptional than M[r] Stanley's. Religion I don't bring into consideration, because the want of it is no blemish in the present day. His letters, when he was sent to France to negotiate the last peace, are said to do him honour, and his whole conduct was approved. He seldom spoke in Parliament. I am obliged to him for once censuring one of the Opposition for abusing me when it was not in my power to answer him, and make my defence. In private company he was rather reserved, and spake with caution, and always pertinent. I spent some days two or three years ago with him at M[r] Ellis's, Tylney Hall. He was exceeding regular and exact in his behaviour. I think he never laughed—don't remember he smiled; loved to talk of classical literature. It is said he was a very good scholar, and that he has left an elegant translation of Pindar in manuscript.

After all this, strange that such a man should be impatient to die! I think he would have been less likely if he had married and had a family he could reputably live with and delight in; but he chose to live a batchelor, occupied a large house in Privy Gardens, joining to Lord Loudoun's; a fine sight [site?] at Palton [?]; another at the Isle of Wight; and yet spent great part of his time from home; and when at home in town, commonly dined at an hotel: left one natural son at Winchester School: suffered his family to be extinct. But this is the vitiated detestable taste of the present age.

He had an estate of 1500£ ꝑ ann.,—the Manor of Chelsea, which he has given to Lord Cadogan, great-grandson of Sir Hans Sloane, by one of his daughters, Mr Stanley being grandson by another: the residue of his real estate, about 2500£ ꝑ annum, between his two sisters, Mrs Ellis and Mrs D'Oyly, and upon their death without children, each being too old to expect any, 500£ ꝑ ann. to each of their husbands for life, and the reversion of the whole to Mr Sloane: legacy of 3000£ to his natural son, besides other legacies.

Mr Knox observed that England never had been upon the eve of so many important events as at present. He referred I suppose to Rodney's fleet—to Clinton's attempt upon Virginia and Carolina—and to Hyde Parker in the West Indies.

19th.—In the city. Ordered my Broker to purchase 3000£ Navy Bills, a year old next month, at 4¾ discount, if paid in a year. This will give an interest of between 7 and 8 ꝑ ct.

20th.—Cold N. wind and sleet most of the day. I kept within. Mauduit called in the evening. Conversation upon Lee, one of the Aldermen, who has been near two years abroad, employed at different Courts, engaged in behalf of revolted America, and yet he has continued Alderman, until, a few days ago he sent his resignation. Another Alderman, Woolridge, is of so infamous a character, that when Maseres dined with the Aldermen, &c., being then Deputy Recorder, and hapned to sit next to Woolridge, one of the Common Council called out—"Mr Maseres! how can you sit by so infamous a fellow? He is one of the most notorious swindlers in all London. Besides having been two or three times bankrupt, and known to be insolvent when he was chosen Alderman, he has been guilty of the grossest frauds in a great number of instances; for any one of which, if he had been indicted, he would have been sentenced to labour on board the *Justitia Hulk!*"

Mauduit mentioned a number—but one very singular. When a bankrupt, he prevailed with the Assignees to suffer his furniture to remain, upon giving security it should be paid for, at the rate it was appraised. Soon after, he sent for a Broker, and desired him to make sale of it. The Broker thanked him, and came a day or two after to take the goods and prepare for the sale. Woolridge appointed a time at a short distance, not being able to attend it sooner, but observed to the Broker, that it would be a convenience if he could advance £300, which the goods would reimburse in two or three days. The Broker gave an order on his Banker for £300, wch Woolridge received immediately. When the Broker came to sell the goods they were all gone. Thus, not only the Broker was cheated of his 300£, but the Bondsmen to the Assignees were obliged to pay the 800£. The Broker bro't an action against him immediately. Soon after came on the Election of Recorder. Mr Adair applied to Woolridge for his vote. He did not deny it, nor absolutely promise it. Adair followed him close,—when he opened himself and said he was so harrassed with the suit of the Broker, that he could give no answer: he could not tell whether he should be at liberty to vote any way: but if he could be freed from that embarrassment, he would vote for Mr Adair. Two or three of Adair's friends, who knew how necessary Woolridge's vote would be, paid the 300£ to the Broker, and Adair was chose by a majority of one only, and Woolridge for that time was saved from the *Justitia*.

21st.—In the city. Made a purchase of 3000£ Navy Bills, dated in February last.

An account of Sir G. Rodney's having fallen in with a Spanish 64 gun ship, five frigates, and 19 store-ships and victuallers on the 7 Jan^y^, Lat. 42, and taking all but one of the store-ships or victuallers: that the store-ships he had ordered to England—the provision vessels he had taken with him. The account is not doubted, but it is not come officially; but a person who was in the action is said to have arrived, and being examined at the Admiralty.

A vessel from St. Kitts with letters to 21 Nov. confirms Parker's taking the victuallers, &c., but blasts the hopes of all who had any from the Dutch vessel. The fleet, however, was then upon a cruise.

Flucker seized with a bleeding at the nose on the 19th, and said to have lost a gallon of blood before it could be stop'd. Surg. Hunter told him if the vein had not burst as it did, he would soon have died. He is better, but weak with the loss of blood.

Wrote to Judge Browne at Cowbridge.

22nd.—A very cold day. At Brompton, called on Flucker, who lost more than a gallon of blood, and is feeble.

At Lord H——'s. I lent him my MS. History of Mass^{ts} Bay, which he has been reading in the holidays at Richmond. He flatters me upon the candour which he says he discovers in it, and excused his not returning it, Lady Grey desiring to go through it.

In conversation I mentioned my surprise at Mr Stanley's catastrophe, and dwelt some time upon it, and never thought, until I came home, of his brother Charles, who died just in the same way. I then recollected, or fancied, that he was in some degree of confusion, and was very sorry that I had said anything upon the subject.*

E. H. and wife, Dr O. and wife, Mr Clarke, and Startin.

23rd.—At Prince's Street;—Dr Kippis. Very cold and very raw.

Dined at Sir R. Sutton's;—Galloway and daughter, Mr Kay and wife, Knox, Mauduit, Maseres.

The Spaniards declared against England in June last. In the Spanish packet which was taken by a N. York privateer, and sent home to Government, there was a letter from the Govr of Guatimala to the Govr of Havana, in which he writes that pursuant to the orders he had rec^d from the King, dated in March, he should stop the Register ships from going to Spain: should endeavour to engage the Mosketo Indians, &c. Knox thinks this an instance of the perfidy of the Court of Spain, who at that time was a mediator between England and France: but it may perhaps be considered as no more than a necessary precaution, from the desperate state of that mediation, and the approaching breach with England, which Spain

* When you are in general society, never reflect on those who have been hanged, for you know not whose toes you may tread upon: and never speak of your Pedigree or your Coat-Armour, for there may be those within hearing who never had either.

foresaw their engagements with France would force upon them.*

24th.—Dr Chandler and Bliss.

People are in pain for Sr G. Rodney's prizes, one only, wch separated from the rest the 9th instant, having got in. Cold N. wind.

25th.—House of Commons met yesterday. Lord G. Gordon behaved like a madman.† He would read a pamphlet of more than 100 pages upon Irish affairs, the Opposition themselves condemning his behaviour. The Members, instead of turning him out or silencing him, left the House themselves. He divided the House upon his absurd motion—he only on one side, and 39, being just enough to make a House, on the other.

My catarrhish disorder and deflexion upon my breast, has been very troublesome last night and this forenoon. Very cold, but I took my walk in the morning.

26th.—A sleet in the air all day, and disagreeable cold. In the evening Mauduit from the city: says a letter from Plimouth takes notice of the arrival of the *Pearl,* and that the rest of Rodney's prizes are in the offing. A vessel from N. York on Lloyd's book. I recd a letter from Paxton at Reading, and answered it.

27th.—A black cold day. My son Billy laments the cold, which he thinks makes his distemper to increase with rapidity. He sinks daily, and is unable to go up to his chamber without resting.

Reports, but uncertain, about Rodney's ships. Some people are anxious at their not arriving.

There's an account in the *Morn. Chronicle* of an uncommon degree of cold at Edinburgh. On the 13th of this month Farenheit's thermometer at a high window to the north at one o'clock, was at 6 degrees above 0. In five hours after sunk to 0. Laid on the snow it sunk 14 deg. below 0. Thursday evening [the 20th.] in the first exposure it was at 0. Every

* The Governor was always ready to put the best construction upon doubtful appearances.

† Beginning of the "Gordon Riots."

two hours that night observations were made by two thermometers on the snow, and two in the open air. The two last sunk to 14 degrees, and the two first 23 degrees below 0.

28th.—A dull day. My youngest son sinks fast—not able to come down to-day, as he has done from the beginning of his illness.

29th.—Still easterly—moist, and yet very cold weather. Dined at Mr Strahan's, where were Lord Westcote, Sir G. Cooper, Mr Jackson of Admiralty, &c.—but a terrible cold drawing-room.

30th.—High east wind to-night—dry, and very cold this morning. My son a more easy night and day than for some time.

Chand., Bliss, E. H., Dr O., and wives, S. O. [Sylvester Oliver.]

31st.—My nerves much disordered last night: pulse quick, and I feared a fever begun. Kept house to-day, and am tolerably well.

Col^o^ Putnam called on me: arrived Saturday night, [it was now Monday], from N. York with his wife, and daughter of 11 y^rs^ old. He is in doubt whether Clinton sailed the day he came out,—Dec. 23rd. On the 25 at night, a storm at N.E.—wind W. the next morning. If Clinton was out, he says it would be a fair wind. They met wth no other damage than the loss of some of their stock upon deck.

The Sixth Volume of the Diary here ends—conterminous with the month of January 1780. The Governor had but four months more to live, so that the next and last volume contains but comparatively few entries—the greater portion of its pages being blank. The rapid progress of William's or Billy's chest complaint, which the sharp air of the winter season was accelerating, together with his death and burial in February, seemed to do much to complete the wreck of his father's constitution, which the troubles and anxieties of the times had already enfeebled.

The vagaries of Lord George Gordon, which were now beginning to display themselves before the astonished world, could scarcely do much mischief in Parliament—first, because he was only one individual amongst a great many better men than himself; and secondly, because he was too mad and outrageous to be listened to. To be listened to, an unreasonable demagogue must at all events put on the semblance of reason. In this case there was no attempt at anything of the sort. Hence the extraordinary division which he forced upon the House on the 24 of January—himself alone supporting the motion, and every one else against it. Whether such a division had ever taken place in the English House of Commons before, or whether it ever has since, deponent knoweth not, but it is sufficiently rare to make a note of. In that day the qualification for the exercise of the Franchise was very different from what it has been since; yet it may be asked with reason, whether the then Duke of Richmond was less mad than Lord George, seeing that, at the very time when a mob of roughs, amounting to a number, variously stated at from 40 to 100 thousand, were besieging the Houses of Parliament, insulting and endangering the lives of those members who tried to get either in or out, he was occupied in introducing a measure for promoting greater liberty for the subject, and was advising the House to "admit to a right of suffrage every man of full age, and not disqualified by law." But even as the "Liberty, Equality, and Fraternity," so warmly advocated by Egalité soon recoiled upon his own head by cutting it off, so "This wild scheme of popular reform," as Adolphus writes, iii. 256, "met with a practical rebuke in the moment of its projection. Before the sitting of the House, the mob, occupying all the passes to Palace Yard, rendered the approach difficult even to their favourities, but those who had not acquired this disgraceful distinction were robbed, beaten, and even threatened with the loss of their lives. The mob were prevented from rushing into the House by the activity and resolution of the doorkeepers alone: several Peers exhibited, on their entrance, incontestable proofs of the indignities they had sustained, and stated to the chair the danger of other members, while the Duke of Richmond, in the genuine zeal of reform, complained of the interruption of his harrangue, and seemed to consider his speech of more importance than the lives of Lord Boston and the Bishop of Lincoln, who were at that moment declared to be in the hands of the rabble."

Lord George Gordon was embroiled in religious controversy, but his Grace was descanting on political freedom. Universal suffrage may be a very fine theory to captivate the shallow, and is put forward upon the principle so strongly contended for in the American *Declaration of Independence*, where we are told that "all men are born equal," which they certainly are not, for no two men are alike either in physical frame or mental power: but even conceding that they are much alike at birth, simply as being the children of other men, they soon shew how different they are from one another when their faculties begin to develope themselves. If however, there is any person living who thinks that all men are alike, let him make the experiment by committing the management of his affairs to the care of the first so-called man of twenty-one whom he may chance to meet in the city of London on Lord Mayor's Day, (being careful to ask his age), or upon the Race Course on Derby Day, or Rag Fair, or the Rookery; and then he will find out that all men are not alike, either in temper, temperament, capacity, or moral principle: and yet, though no man in his senses would entrust his own little affairs to any except to those in whose knowledge, skill, or integrity he had some confidence, these theorists would hand over the more important affairs of the nation to the dangerous manipulation of all classes of men alike. But as the uneducated and the debased far outnumber the cultivated and the honest in every country, the principle of Universal Suffrage is the principle of putting the control of the national welfare into the hands of the most ignorant portion of the population; or, in other words, it is to outweigh the influence of the instructed and the best qualified, by the evil preponderance of those who are the least capable of being useful to the State. As the majority rule the whole community, it is the largest and the worst half that rules the best. Where the experiment has been tried, it has been found necessary, for the absolute safety of the kingdom, that a vigilant police espionage should be exercised, with a strong repressive power, lest the largest, strongest, and least competent half should run the Ship of the State upon the rocks, and wreck the others. If the Franchise could be extended upwards to the clearer waters of intelligence, where knowledge, the responsibilities of property, and intellectual culture chiefly prevail, the further it could be extended the better; but as the best men are already secured, it can only be extended by going downwards to the dregs. If the lower orders could be so far improved as that there could be an educational test instead of a property test applied to them, they could then be entrusted with a great privilege; but in the absence of this security, no statesman would proceed downwards without the greatest caution to a class, whose chief idea of the value of a Vote, consists in how many pints of beer they can sell it for. A crafty and an unprincipled Minister might do so: but I draw a strong line of demarcation between the Statesman and the Minister, for a man may be a Minister but no Statesman. An unprincipled Minister might do so to serve his own selfish ends, absorbed in securing the votes of the ignorant, knowing that the votes of "Beer-and-tobacco men," if they can be obtained, count up to him just as much as the votes of their betters, and can be more easily gained by specious arguments, which would not dupe higher-grade citizens. Such a Minister is no Statesman. He would sacrifice the common interests of his country and of his countrymen, so long as he could obtain the advantage of his own present emoluments.

On one of the fly-leaves at the end of the sixth volume of the Diary, which we have now just finished, the Governor has jotted down a number of extracts from Books that he had been reading: and amongst others the following from *Selden's Table Talk*, containing some remarks on parliamentary representation, apposite to the train of thought I have indulged in above. Selden says—

"All are involved in a Parliament. All men once had a voice in chusing Knights. In Hen. 6th time they found the inconvenience. One Parliament made a law that all under 40/. rent ꝑ ann. should be excluded from a voice. They made the law who had been chosen by all, as well under 40/. as above. All consent *civilly* in a Parliament:—

"Women are involved in the men:
Children in those of perfect age:
Those under 40/. in those above:
Those above in the Knights."

The Gordon Riots had not burst forth as yet, but they were looming at no great distance. The ebullitions that had hitherto manifested themselves were only the harbingers of a grander display, soon to set London in a flame.

CHAPTER VIII.

BEGINNING OF THE SEVENTH VOLUME OF THE DIARY.

February 1st, 1780.—The prospect of returning to America and laying my bones in the land of my forefathers for four preceding generations—and if I add the mother* of W. H. it will make five—is less than it has ever been. God grant me a composed mind, submissive to his will; and may I be thankful that I am not reduced to those straits, which many others who are banished are, and have been.

In the city to-day, but no fresh intelligence.

2nd.—Some abatement of a long spell of very cold weather, and the sun has shewn itself part of the day. Wind keeps still to the north. It is said that the whole of a fleet of near 100 sail to Ireland and England are arrived from New York.

3rd.—My Banker in the city says they have advice that the siege of Gibraltar is raised, and that the Spaniards have lost 3000 men by sickness. I don't find it to be depended on.

The Petitions and Associations forming by enterprising men in so many counties for reducing salaries and pensions have a threatening aspect, and some fear great coufusions from them. Stocks, under all discouragements, rise rather than fall. Bank Stock this time last year at 106, now 113.

* When William and Anne went to America in 1634, they took William's widowed mother with them. The Governor, in his writings, nowhere mentions her name, and probably did not know it. In the First Covenant of the First Church of Boston, however, there are lists of the Members admitted. After William and his wife, and most of his children, come the Wheelwrights, and his mother. The entry is this—"12th of 4th moneth. John Wheelwright, and Marie his wife. Susanne Hutchinson, widdowe." This Susanne appears to be the name for which I had been long looking, and is "the mother of W. H." mentioned above. The name is either Susanne or Susanna.

4th.—General National Fast:—a day which for several years has been observed in London more strictly by attendance on public worship, and forbear[ce] of all business than any other day set apart for the purposes of religion. It being the pleasantest day for some days past abroad, I was more afraid of the churches, where the dampness and cold within was more sensible than if the weather had continued cold.

My son Billy, just after he was in bed last night, coughed and spat much blood, which greatly alarmed and distressed him, and causes him wholly to despair of recovery.

5th.—Walked to Lambeth to call on D[r] Lort, the Abp.'s Chaplain, but lost my labour, he being from home.

Dined in the city to-day at Mauduit's—Sir R. Sutton, Maseres, D[r] Watson, Kay, and Galloway.

M[r] Mackenzie called on me in the forenoon—conversation about General Howe, who married Lord Strafford's niece; and I think M[r] Mackenzie's lady is of the same family. He condemns the Howes—says there is no accounting for their conduct. I thought they all along flattered themselves they should be able to effect a conciliation, and therefore never pursued the rebels to that length they otherwise would have done.* That they might fancy, he said, at first, but it was not possible after two y[rs] experience. They might prolong the war, he sometimes thought, for the sake of enriching themselves. The General, he said, certainly lived in a different state from what he had ever done before: his friends however, gave out that he had made nothing. Lord Strafford, he said, enquired of Byng, an high Opposition man, who married another of Lord Strafford's nieces. Byng said he had made very little—not above five thousand pounds. This, M[r] Mackenzie observed, was too insignificant a sum to enable him to change his state of living as he had done.

6th.—Old Jewry.

* Those who attentively consider the course of the war after the Battle of Brooklyn, or even after Bunker Hill, must feel that General Howe gave America to the Americans. There are two ways in which a General can deal with an opponent:—one is, to fight him: the other is, to pretend to fight him.

Peter Oliver, son to the late Lt Governor,* called on me:—just arrived in town from N. York: sailed with the fleet the 23rd December: storm came on the 25th: the 26th saw a ship they took to be the *Solebay*, having carried away her main and mizen top masts, and they judged the head of her mainmast. The *Solebay* is not yet arrived.

A newspaper from N. York, of Dec. 15th, contains an Act of the new State, confiscating the estates of a great number of persons, beginning with Lord Dunmore, their former Governor; Tryon, their last Governor; and goes on with Watts, and four or five more of the Council, and a great number of others; and concludes wth Sir Henry Clinton, and banishes them all upon pain of death.

Doctor Cooper, late Prest of the College at N. York, now an Episc. Clergyman at one of the Chapels in Edinburgh, called on me.

7th.—A prospect of more moderate weather: wind westerly, and sunshine without frost. My son seeing the sun pleasant, wished to go into the coach, but I discouraged him, the air not being warm, and his distemper has advanced too far to leave any room to hope for relief from any means now to be used.

8th.—Mr Thompson† (Lord George's,) called, and among other things mentioned that he had a great curiosity to shew me—but I was not to speak of it—all Gov. Pownall's and Doctor Franklin's correspondce with Dr Cooper of Boston, and then related the particulars. I shewed him the extract I had made from one of Franklin's letters, and mentioned another which he said he well remembered. He said he had copied them all over, and made a present of the originals to the King, who was vastly pleased with them.‡ I thanked him, and said

* By the second wife Mary Sanford; born Sep. 17, 1749. He married, but other particulars are wanting.

† This is the same person apparently with Count Rumford.

‡ On one of the fly-leaves at the end of the sixth volume of his Diary, the Governor has copied off part of one of Franklin's letters, and possibly from the batch alluded to above. It is dated July 7, 1773, and one passage which speaks of Mr. Hutchinson's missing letters, runs thus—

"The Letters might be shewn, even to some of the Governor's and Lieutenant-Governor's partizans, and spoken of to everybody, for there was no restraint proposed to talking of them, but only to copying. And possibly, as distant objects, seen only through a mist, appear larger, the same may

I should like to look over them, but I had seen them, and taken a cursory view of them. Dr Jeffries lent them to me upon a promise to return them. One of Franklin's letters in 1770, in which he declares his opinion upon the constitutional Independence of the Colonies, and another, in which he gives an account of my Letters, I copied, and returned all the originals.

I think Jeffries would have given them to me, if I had desired it, but as Dr Cooper had left them with Jeffries's father for security, and they came into the son's hands by some accident, the father not intending they should, I scrupled desiring the son to do a thing which I doubted whether he could justify, unless some important purposes for the public could be served by it. It is very extraordinary that he should afterwards give them to Thompson, if he did do it. I remember to have heard that T. was more intimately acquainted with Mrs Jeffries than with the Doctor. This is a curious anecdote. Franklin will not care who sees his letters, but Governor Pownall will think himself ill used if he should ever hear that his private correspondence with Cooper for many years, has been given to the King.

I thought when I sat down to make this minute, that Mr T. desired me not to mention anything about it, but I was under a mistake—he spake of it without any reserve. It was another matter he desired me not to mention. Speaking of the desperate measures of the Opposition, and of the backwardness of

---

happen from the mystery in this case. However this may be, the terms given with them could only be those with which they were received. There is still some chance of procuring more, and some still more abominable."

The following is the printed version of the same portion, as given in *Franklin's Private Correspondence*, vol. ii. p. 377, and the reader, if curious to compare them, may learn that the same thing is not always exactly the same. The printed version says—

"The letters might be shewn, even to some of the Governor's and Lieutenant-Governor's partizans, and spoken of to everybody; for there was no restraint proposed to talking of them, but only to copying. However, the terms given with them, could only be those with which they were received." The last sentence is omitted, as well as some other parts.

The Governor's conscientious scruples about taking the letters from young Jeffries, when he believed them to be within his reach, put his sense of honour in a very proper light.

the Ministry in prosecuting offences, and even in referring to the Attorney and Solicitor General the consideration of the Committees of Correspondence, he added, that the Head did not want spirit—the King had said to Lord George [Germaine], that if the people were determined to ruin the Constitution, it might not be in his power to help it, but they should never make him their prisoner.

"That expression," I observed, "would admit of diff^t constructions: the King might resolve to leave the Kingdom."

"No," says T., "he has said he would die a King."

If this be a true account, which I have no reason to doubt of, it shews that the King sees in a more serious light the present violence of Opposition than people generally imagine he does. It shews also that Lord G. is extremely incautious in trusting such an amount of his conversation with the King to a young man, especially as it is not possible they should have lived so long together without Lord G.'s having discovered that T. has not the faculty of retention. This brings to my mind the conversation I had with Ld Polworth at Wimpole, which I have minuted in October last.*

9th.—A mild air, which I have taken as much benefit of as I could, and hope we may expect a spell of moderate weather, that by the blessing of God invalids from age, and the severity of the weather, may recover some degree of health.

10th.—General Prescot in town: the *Solebay*, in which he was passenger, being arrived at Portsmouth dismasted.

A packet arrived from Lisbon. Letters mention a report of an engagement between Rodney and a squadron of Span. ships, several of which are said to be taken or destroyed. People very much differ upon the degree of credit it deserves.

11th.—Gen. Gage, Mr Burch, and son, Flucker, Putnam, Watts, and Chambellin of the Treasury, and Col^o Bruce, dined with me.

The acc^t of Rodney's action seems to gain ground. Mr Walpole has wrote to Lord Stormont that the Spanish Ambassador at Lisbon had rec^d an acc^t from Madrid that one of the Spanish ships had blown up, and one had got into Cadiz, but

* Oct. 18, 1779.

nothing said of any other. Other letters say that it was reported in Lisbon one ship had blown [up]. Rodney had taken six, and one escaped.

12th.—Account to-day of the arrival of the *America* and the *Pearl* with the remainder of Rodney's prizes, which he did not carry to Gibraltar. Sir James and Lady Wallace came to town from Paris. He says the account there was that eleven Spanish ships sailed from Ferol to join the rest at Cadiz: that three separated: that Rodney met the remaining eight near Cape St. Mary: that upon one of the Span. ships of 74 guns blowing up, the rest attempted to escape: that three did escape: five were taken, two of which, having lost their masts, and being in possession of the English, were so far in Cadiz bay, that a gale of wind coming on, they could not work out, and ran into the port to save their lives.

Some hope, as this is the French and Spanish account, we may expect something more.

I dined with Mr Mackenzie—the company Lord Loudoun, Lord Cassilis, Lord Drummond, Col. Charles Stuart, Frederick Stuart, Lord Bute's son, Mr Woodford, Tod, and Sam. Martin, besides Mr Mackenzie's lady, and Mrs Stuart.

13th.—Dr Kippis's. A raw, foggy, E. day.

The *Gazette* of last night gives Mr Fitzherbert, Resid^t^ at Brussels, his acc^t^ of Rodney's last action, as rec^d^ there, viz.—that on the 16th of January he met with the Span. ships, consisting of eight: three had separated in a storm some time before, and no account where they were gone: of the eight, one blew up, three were taken, viz., one of 80 guns, the other two 70: the four remaining gat into Cadiz in a shattered condition. Mr Fitzherbert gives the names of all the ships.

Dr Chandler, Bliss.

The particulars of Rodney's first captures, on the 9th [or 8th] Jany are in the *Gazette*, the *America* and *Pearl* being arrived.*

* The historians of the day say that Rodney was despatched first, to convoy transports to relieve Gibraltar, and then proceed to the West Indies: that Don Juan de Lungara, the Spanish Admiral, tried to intercept this supply with eleven men-of-war and two frigates: that three or four of his number separated from him in a storm: that on the 8th of January Rodney engaged and took a 64, four frigates, and two smaller armed vessels, with 15

14th.—It is said to-day that 5 sail of Spanish men-of-war were in Algerisa Bay, near Gibraltar, and that there is room to hope that Rodney may come up with them; but I think they will get on to Cadiz, or run thro' the Cut of Gibraltar.

15th.—A vessel from Atigua brings intellegence of H. Parker having taken 8 sail more of victuallers bound to Martinico. Several of the N. York ships arrived at Portsmouth—T. Goldthwait, Mr Domat and wife, &c., passengers.

16th.—My dear son declines faster than common in his distemper, sensibly sinking from day to day, and the symptoms of the last stage appear. At his desire Dr Chandler visited him to-day, to whom he opened his mind with great freedom, and the Doctor, who I trust has a serious sense of religion upon his own mind, expressed a satisfaction at seeing so much of it in my son, which he assured him that amidst the levities, follies, and sins of youth, he never wholly lost sight of, and from the beginning of his illness has kept in his mind.

To the mercy of God, the searcher of hearts, from whom no secrets are hid, I desire to commit him.

17th.—But little abroad. Doctor C. again visited my son, and prayers were made as for a person in extreme danger.

18th.—Still sinking . . .

My own catarrh and cough have been very troublesome to-day.

Mr Domat called—from New York. He and many others are arrived without any money, and in a most distressed state.

19th.—I sat by my son after his brothers and sister left him this evening, until between 11 and 12, all this time struggling for life, and longing for his dissolution . . . He soon after fell into a doze, and waking, said he never was in so sweet a sleep in his life . . .

20th.—Soon after I rose I enquired of one of the servants if

---

merchantmen: that on the 16th, in another engagement, he took the *Phœnix*, Flag-ship, 80, with Don Juan on board, and three other ships: that two struck, but were driven to leeward, and one lost: that the *San Domingo* blew up with all hands: and that, having relieved Gibraltar and Minorca, he proceeded to the West Indies. Admiral Digby brought the prizes to England, and took the *Prothée*, a French 64, and two store ships, on the way.

he had been up to my son. He said he had carried up his ass's milk, but that he was unable to take it, and while his watchers were holding him up he fell back. I asked in what manner? He said in a fainting fit. I went up to him and met one of his watchers at the door, who said he was dead. He sank back and died without a groan, and perhaps in as sweet a sleep as he had felt the evening before. I could not help taking a look at his dead countenance, which I wished I had not. The servant was ordered to conceal his death from me until I had been to breakfast, which caused such an answer from him.

This, my youngest son, was 27 years of age last August, born at Milton, where his mother, of all earthly objects ever known, deservedly the dearest, had retired to avoid the small pox in Boston.

21st.—Kept house—my cough increasing. Took Elix. asthmat. at night.

22nd.—Had a better night than expected, but my cough bad in the day, and fever increasing. Took two tea spoonfulls of the Elixer,—

23rd.—but had a very bad night: high fever and little sleep.

Sent to Dr Heberden, who thought my fever very high: ordered two draughts of Tartar Emetic, &c., to be taken before dinner, and in the evening, and a third at going to bed, with Thebaic Tincture, 8 drops, and I had a tolerable night, but &c. the next morn.

24th.—My pulse increased. However, as I held up, could read and write, which he wondered at, he only ordered the like draught, viz., one in the day, and one at going to bed, and one in the morn.

The funeral of my son this morning in the church at Croydon.

25th.—I had the worst night I have had for many years, and expected a fixed fever; but while I lay calm in the morning, I thought my fever abated, and when Dr Heberden came, he was of the same opinion, but ordered to take one draught more before noon, and the Thebaic tinct. draught at night. I have reason to be thankful for a much better day than I expected.

26th.—A bad night—some sleep, but not quiet after two o'clock. Keep about my room still. Pulse 105.*

27th.—My fever still the same: little appetite or rest.

28th.—Much the same night. Being a fine warm day, I took an airing in Hyde Park and to Chelsea, and was much refreshed.

29th.—A good night without medicine, but think my fever high: afraid my pulse is quicker, or which is most certain of all—I think so: but I find my nerves affected, and give way to every groundless apprehension. Only Mauduit's coming in and telling me my pulse was better than when he saw me last, gave me a calm evening.

March 1st.—I took my medicine last evening, by which means I had probably a more quiet night. Dr Heberden in the morning called, and finds my pulse still high—96. He was very particular in his enquiries as to any symptoms except my cough and high pulse, and upon the whole advised to continue my draught at night, and if I found any new occasion, to send to him: recommended light diet and moderate exercise, and hoped I should not have further call for a Physician. I took an airing, but my fever seemed to be high. In the evening tried repeatedly, by my watch, for 4 or 5 minutes together, and thought it did not exceed 80 in amount, and omitted my draught.

My cough troubled me in the night; my fever was high in the morning; but after lying an hour or two, I think my pulse was slower than for 8 or 10 days past.

2nd.—Much the same. I forbore my draught, but felt guilty for neglecting Dr Heberden's directions, it being doubtful whether my fever was abated so as to warrant me.

The confirmation of Sir G. Rodney's taking and destroying so many of the Span. ships in his way to Gibraltar gives spirits to those who wish well to the country. He has added 5 line-of-battle ships completely manned to the squadron at Gibr.

3rd.—I took my draught last night—proved diaphoretick,

* The shock of his son's death had probably its effects on his health.

but I had not much sleep. I hope however, I am not worse to-day. An airing to Peckham. Rain prevented my walking any part of the way. In the evening found no sensible abatement of my pulse: my appetite however, was better to-day than for ten days past.

Mauduit in the evening, says it is certain one of Clinton's transports, with 170 Hessians, was arrived at St. Ives. The officer wrote up to know what to do with the men, but nothing more is known of the cause of her coming to England, except that she fell foul of another vessel, and sustained great damage, and stood for Europe.

4th.—A good night followed by a poor day. Dr H. called and wondered to find my pulse so high, but said nothing discouraging besides. My imagination always takes the dark side. Fever I thought higher than at any time. Towards bed time supposed it more calm.

An airing to Clapham over London Bridge: walked a mile near Clapham, the air rather cold, and I feared I had taken cold.

5th.—I should have attended publ. worship if [I] had not feared taking cold, having had as good a night and morning as [I] could expect.

Mr Thompson, from Lord George's, called to tell me that Digby was come in, and had brought with him a French 64, and 3 E. Indiamen; Rodney with 4 or 5 ships gone to the W. Indies. With Digby came 5 Spanish and 1 French line-of-battle ships—the first completely fitted for our service.

6th.—Charles Fox's speech printed in the *Morn. Chronicle.* He hopes the Secr^y^ of State will no longer be continued for America—the salaries to the Governors cease—and above all, the pension to a late Governor, Mr Hutchinson, that firebrand and source of the American disputes.

Happy should I be if I could as well acquit myself for all other parts of my conduct thro' life, as for the part I have taken in this controversy.

Mr Ellis called, and informed me Lord North said much in my favour.

7th.—I had a very indifferent night; much of my cough, and pulse high, which continued all day until evening.

An airing with my daughter* to Newington Green, and Newington town.

A Flanders mail with advice that Gaston's squadron had met with a bad storm: one ship foundered, and five put into Ferrol dismasted.

The vessel at St. Ives left Clinton off the Capes of Virginia the 28th December. She has 30 Provincial troops on board besides Hessians.

8th.—I slept most of the night, and rose, hoping my distemper was going off, but my fever kept up its height, and

9th.—I had the most discouraging night since my first complaint, having scarce any sleep, and felt some pains and other symptoms which made me apprehend my distemper fixed. The greatest part of the night I was calm, and free from any kind of pain, except of mind, from want of sleep.

10th.—Slept last night beyond what I have done since my illness began.

11th.—Restless again, with but little, and that, confused sleep. An airing and moderate walk yesterday and to-day.

12th.—A restless night and gloomy day: an airing in the Park.

13th.—A third night with little or no sleep. In the morning desired to see Dr Heberden. He stayed till two o'clock before he came, and Lt Gov. Oliver, Paxton, and others coming in, in the mean time, and all encouraging me, I wished I had omitted it. I am not well, but by the goodness of God my cough is abated, and my pulse rather better than worse.

14th.—A tea spoonfull of Diascordium composed me last night, and I rested remarkably well, but my feverish pulse does not go off.

15th.—Walked near two miles, the coach by my side.

16th.—Set out with my son-in-law Doctor Oliver in a chariot, and lodged at Bagshot. An encouraging night.

17th.—Tried a horse a mile or two—the wind colder than I expected, and I think I took cold, and was fatigued in the

* Sarah, his eldest and only surviving daughter, and wife of Dr. Peter Oliver. She only outlived her father by 25 days, and his term of life was to be only three months longer.

evening. At the inn in Petersfield was seized with a violent cough, a pain crossing [my] breast, which bro't on a shortness of breath I never felt before.

18th.—My pain almost gone, but my weakness at my breast remains. Rained all day, and we were obliged to lie by at a wretched old inn.

19th.—Went on to Portsmouth: lodged at a private house: no amendment.

20th.—To Chichester.

21st.—To Petworth.

22nd.—To Brighthelmstone, where we remained until Monday the 27th,* for answers to our letters to London.

28th.—To Tunbridge Wells thro' Lewes.

29th.—To Bromley. Dr Oliver took the horse and went to London, the next morning the 30th, and I went in the chariot to Wandsworth, where I had desired him to meet me. He advised to lodging in the country.

30th.—We went to Richmond—my son and I, and Dr Oliver and his wife.

31st.—Remained looking for a house, or good lodging.

April 1st.—The landlord having engaged his rooms, we were forced to exchange our lodgings to an inn a mile distant in Twickenham Road.

2nd.—Went on with my son and daughter towards London, and by advice remained to the 4th with my daughter in High Street [Marylebone], when I went with her and her husband to lodgings at Brompton Park, after a very unsuccessful attempt of near 3 weeks. *Fiat voluntas Dei.*

18th.—For a fortnight past I can discover no abatement of my disorder. I think my general weakness increased. My children try to encourage me not to think so—say they see no signs of it—that my nerves are greatly affected, and my case appears more desperate to me than it ought—and that my countenance is better rather than worse.

May 3rd.—I still continue, as I think, declining; but abroad in [the] carriage every fair day, and have made trial so as to walk a horse.

* It was now Wednesday.

7th.—No apparent abatement of my weakness, unless my being able to do more yesterday and to-day than I expected is any evidence. I was near two hours on the horse to-day, and I think rode 7 or 8 miles, and near, if not quite half the way upon an easy trot—the rest walked. This is more than I was able to do at any time when on my journey, and I desire to be thankful for every favorable circumstance.

12th.—I still continue in much the same torpid state. Yesterday I was near two hours on my horse, walking and trotting gently, and as long to-day. My shortness of breath does not mend. The weather grows fine. Perseverance in keeping the air, on a horse and in the coach is pressed upon me.

15th.—My horse begins to be too fatiguing. My son still insists that my countenance is not that of a decayed man, and will not despair.

22nd.—A week passed and no abatement: last night almost sleepless.

Here the Diary ends abruptly—eleven days prior to his death.

Before I go any further I would pay my addresses to Charles Fox, and administer to him a mild opinion on his unwarrantable and untruthful slander uttered in the House of Commons, as mentioned in the Diary on the 6th of March, where he uses the words—"Mr. Hutchinson, that firebrand, and source of the American disputes." Mr. Hutchinson's meek observation upon this is not very firey—"Happy should I be if I could as well acquit myself for all other parts of my conduct thro' life, as for the part I have taken in this controversy." There is one consolation—the detractor will not be believed by those who learn, from the evidence contained in this work, what Mr. Hutchinson's real sentiments were on the great questions of the day—his conciliatory motives for coming to England, and his endeavours when there, to intercede with the Ministry for the mitigation of some of the repressive measures with which the Americans were offended—or his general disposition to put the most favourable construction on the conflicting points that were agitating the public mind—and even to make excuses for some of the excesses of those whom he thought had been misguided and misled. A score of instances might easily be pointed out, either in his writings or in his conduct, where he acted like a pacificator, but who can point out a single place where he acted like a firebrand? What would Mr. Fox have done, if he would have avoided those disputes of which he complained? Would he have avoided them by giving the Americans all that they asked for? for that was the only way in which those disputes could have been quieted. If he advised Mr. Hutchinson to have taken that course, he was advising him to become a rebel. And he was virtually advising him to become a traitor to his King and Mother Country, in breaking the oaths of fidelity and allegiance to which he had sworn when he was appointed Governor. It has before been shewn how sundry Noble Lords, in their places in the Upper House, defended the Americans in their violent proceedings, and refused to believe that they had a thought of separation, even at the very time when they openly proclaimed such a design at their public meetings, and were even in open hostilities in order to effect it. That this design was cherished long before the war commenced was evident in 1761—two years before the conquest of the French in Canada, four years before the passing of the Stamp Act, and fourteen years before the first shot was fired at Lexington: for Mr. Frothingham, in his History of the Siege of Boston, p. 4, alluding to a speech of James Otis in that year, says—"The idea was entertained at this period, that an American Empire was close at hand."—This was followed in 1769 by the before quoted exclamation of Samuel Adams—"Independent we are," &c. Yet a certain section of the Members in both Chambers of the Legislature could not or would not read the signs of the times, or what in most men's eyes was something plainer than mere signs. "Were he [Lord Chatham] once persuaded that they entertained the most distant intention of rejecting the legislative supremacy," &c., "he would be the first and most zealous mover for exerting the whole force of Britain in securing and enforcing that power."* He had already recommended the case of the revolters to the Cabinet Ministers by saying—"Resistance to your acts was necessary, as it was just," which was sufficiently encouraging; and the Duke of Richmond added his approval, and "hoped they would succeed." Who were the "firebrands" in the face of this evidence? Truly, as Governor Hutchinson says, in his letter to Mr. Walter, of May 19, 1779—"The Opposition—to whom the Rebellion must be attributed." And no wonder Lord Lyttleton told them to their faces that—"Those who defend rebellion, are themselves little better than rebels."† A cause cannot be a good one that can only be supported by misrepresentation. Let Charles Fox and his inaccuracies go.

* Adolph. ii. 186.

† *Ibid.*, ii. 300.

The fragmentary Diary of Elisha supplies some scraps of information relative to the Governor's declining state and last days, as well as the particulars of his death, to which occurrence he was an eye witness. At the time of the illness and death of Peggy, his health failed him in a way unknown to him before, for which he consulted Dr. Eliot, but the unusual symptoms passed off as he recovered from the strain that had so much tried his nerves; and then, at the loss of Billy his health gave way again. The anxieties which he had suffered ever since he had been in England, owing to the abnormal state of political affairs, the condition of his country, and the dark prospects that hung over the future of his children, had all served to undermine his constitution. The tremulousness of his handwriting towards the latter portion of his Diary may serve to indicate that his nervous system had become a good deal shattered. He sought a change by leaving Sackville Street for Brompton Park. As he did not give up his town house, the move was intended to have been temporary only,—but he never returned.

From the Diary of Elisha Hutchinson.

April 5th, 1780.—The trees and fields quite covered with snow this morning: afterwards, several flights of snow. Walked out and took a letter from the Postman to the Judge* from the Doctor, giving very dire accounts of the Govs health, and of Mrs Oliver's illness, attended with very alarming symptoms, which has determined me to set out in the morning. Walked into town to take a place in the diligence, but all were engaged.

6th.—Fair and cool, with some flights of snow and hail. Set out with [the] Judge in [a] postchaise at ½ past ten o'clock for London—our first stage at Coventry, when we took a cold morsel, (at the King's Head, Thomas Soden, next door to Peeping Tom,) and proceeded on our journey to Daventry: changed horses and got to Towcester, (51 miles,) at ½ past seven o'clock.

7th.—Cloudy morning, and cold; fair afternoon. Set out from Towcester a few minutes before 8 o'clock; changed horses at Stony Stratford—Brickill, Dunstable, and St. Albans, where

* Elisha and Judge Oliver were then in Birmingham. Dr. P. Oliver in London.

we stopped an hour, and took another cold repast; and changing horses at Barnet, reached High Street, [Marylebone] at ½ past five o'clock, (60 miles), when finding that the Govr had taken lodgings at Brompton, about ½ a mile from my brother's [Thomas's,] Brompton Row, immediately went in a Hackney coach to my brother's, who was gone to the Governor's, and to whom I sent a card, acquainting him with my being just arrived, and soon after went, and found him very low, but better than we had expected; and Mrs Oliver tells us, some of the symptoms, which had been very alarming, had abated. Indeed, the greatest danger seems lest the Gov., who is greatly reduced, should wear himself out with the continual worry of spirits produced by the very hypocondriac state in which he at present is.

After tea we returned to High Street, and slept at the Doctor's, there being only the children and servants, the Doctor and his wife constantly residing with the Governor.

8th.—Fair. Walked over to [the] Governor's and dined, and the Judge, and Tommy. The Govr seems in better spirits whilst he has us all about him. After tea walked to High Street with the Judge.

We called on M^rs^ and Miss K. Hutchinson.

11th.—Flying clouds and some rain. The Doctor came over to breakfast with us. The Governor a pretty good night, but gives all up this morning: wastes away—his life spent—thinks it best to go to Sackville Street and die . . . [faded out] . . . Thus the morning passes: at dinner—his friends about him—he recovers something of his spirits, and if [he] does not wear himself out, he may chance to others—those about him. He is taking the bark in small quantities. If he should be able to continue it, and the weather should prove favourable, we shall hope for good effects, notwithstanding he seems to have fully determined his own fate.

After breakfast walked over to Brompton: returned in coach with Gov. and Mrs Oliver to High Street: afterwards a few miles on the Kensington road. The Gov. seemed better, and we had less of gloomy conversation, as they tell me, than usual. The Judge dined with us. The Governor has been better this afternoon than at any time since I have been in town, and what is most extraordinary, is willing to own it himself.

12th.—Fair morning: afterwards cloudy and rain. The Judge set out this morning about seven o'clock to go to the diligence from Piccadilly to Birmingham . . .

17th.—Fair morn^{g}—sometimes showers—hail and snow. Walked to Brompton: came back in coach with Mrs Oliver: returned to Brompton with Govr: and back again to High Street . . . Called on Mr Galloway, Mrs H., Mr Dennison, and at Govr Shirley's, and Mr H. Walked to Strand: from thence thro' the Park to Mr Leonard, and to Brompton to dinner thro' Grosvenor Place. Tommy came to tea, after which I took leave . . . The Govr more cheerful, and much of his own countenance. May we have still further encouragement to hope for his recovery.

18th.—Fair and pleasant morning. In a Hackney coach soon after seven to the 3 Kings, Piccadilly, where I found the Birmingham coach, with one passenger only, whom I afterwards found to be a young woman going to her parents, who live near Birmingham, and who had lately been married to a [blank] who keeps the [blank] near Marybone Work-House. We left the 3 Ks at $\frac{1}{4}$ before 8 o'clock, changed horses at Brentford, again at Colnbrook, and at Maidenhead. Just before we reached Nettlebed, about 2 o'clock came on a most violent storm of wind, attended with as large hail and smart lightening and thunder as I have known since I have been in England. We stopped half an hour, and proceeded to Oxford, where we arrived at 5 o'clock . . .

19th.—Fair and cold morning: cloudy afternoon. Set out from the Angel Inn at $\frac{1}{2}$ past six o'clock, and in two hours reached Euston, 14 miles, where we breakfasted: changed horses at Shipton, and got to Stratford at one o'clock, where we dined: and changing horses at Henley, reached Colemore Row at $\frac{1}{2}$ past six o'clock, (having parted with my Diligence traveller at the Castle Inn,) where found my family and the rest of the company, M^{r} and Mrs Startin being there at tea, in good health.

26th.— . . . We dined at the Judge's, and at tea. After

dinner went with the Judge to M[r] Ballard's, our shoe-maker in High Street, and saw a man or lad from Ireland, known and exhibited by the name of [blank] Upon our entering the room, we asked him his height? He told us he was 7 feet 11 in. and ¾ without shoes. He is large and well proportioned to his stature, and has not an uncomely countenance. He has a pale and light complexion. He told us he was not quite 20 years of age: has grown gradually to this stature: none of his family of extraordinary size. His dress very decent: a coat and waistcoat of red or moreen cloth, the latter with a gold binding; a p[r] dark jean riding breeches, and silk stocks. He likewise told us that at his meals he did not eat more than men of a common size. He is [the] most extraordinary production of nature, and nearly, if not altogether equals the accounts we have of the Patagonian Race.

30th.— . . . M[r] O. has a letter from the Doctor, who writes discouragingly of M[rs] O., and says the Governor has not gained anything since we were in town, but refers to Tommy, who is to write me more particularly.

May 1st.—Fair and moderate. The *Gazette* of Saturday* night has a letter from Gen[l] Clinton of the 9th Mar. at Cha [blank]. He gives advice of his sailing from Sandy Hook the 26 December, arriving at Tybee the 1st Feb[y] [blank] and was preparing to attack Charlestown, which was well fortified and prepared for defence. He met with a series of bad weather—several transports lost, but men saved, and other damage, but hoped for success. Letters likewise from the Commanders.

7th.— . . . Wrote Tommy expressing my anxiety and concern that he had not wrote, it being more than a fortnight since I left London, and the only accounts of my sick father and sister, from M[r] Clarke and others, which only mention in general that they were no better, but express their dread of the event of their illness. May Heaven be kinder to us than our fears, and send us more favourable accounts.

11th.—Fair and pleasant. A letter was bro't to me this morning before breakfast from M[r] Oliver's, from my brother, bro't by M[r] Porter, who arrived this morning from London.

* It was now Monday.

My letter is dated the 6th. The Govr remained much in the state I left him. Mrs Oliver's symptoms continued very alarming.

I have before observed that Elisha's Diary is written on sheets of note paper, sometimes single and sometimes in fasciculi, which however, have never been sewn, though some of them appear to have been pinned together, judging by the empty pin holes; hence, they are mixed, confused and perplexing to arrange, as the dates of the year, and the name of the month are but very rarely given. From the last date above, namely, the 11th of May, to the Governor's death on the 3rd of June, being a space of three weeks, I find no remains of the Diary whatever. In the interval, however, Elisha was summoned up from Birmingham to London again.

Perhaps I had better explain here, if I have not sufficiently done so already, my reasons for inserting the account of the death in the first volume, at what is manifestly the wrong place. I had several reasons for so doing, which are the following—

1.—I had no expectation that the first volume would succeed well enough to furnish inducements to undertake another, so that there seemed no likelihood of a second chance, but in this I have been agreeably deceived.

2.—Although in good health, I was seventy-two, and that is a complaint from which no man ever recovers, so that if it were ever done at all, I did not think it would be accomplished by me.

3.—As there was no record of the event in existence, except in the two loose leaves of the son's Diary, which any accident might destroy, I was glad of an excuse to get the particulars into print, in order to secure them.

Having lived however, to compile this second and concluding volume, I insert the account here in its proper place, and on the first opportunity it must be struck out of the first, the portion to be struck out, beginning with the words, "But in spite of his desire," &c., at page 451, down to the full stop after the words, "fully come to hand in England," on page 453.

What remains of Elisha's narrative is the following:—

[G]overnor slept tolerably well, as he had done for several nights past; arose as usual at 8 o'clock, shaved himself, and eat his breakfast, and we all told him that his countenance [ha]d a more healthy appearance, and if he was not better, we had no reason to conclude that he had lost ground. He conversed well and freely upon the riot in London the day before, [Gordon riots], and upon different subjects, 'till the time for going out in the coach, at intervals however, expressing his expectations of dying very soon, repeating texts of Scripture, with short ejaculations to Heaven. He called for a shirt, telling Ryley his servant, that he must die clean. I usually walked down the stairs before him, but he got up suddenly from his chair, and walked out of the room, leaving the Doctor, [Peter Oliver, his son-in-law] and I behind. We went into the room next the road; saw him whilst he was walking from the steps of the door to the coach, (a few yds. distance), hold out his hands to Ryley, and caught hold of him, to whom he said "Help me!" and appeared to be fainting. I went down with the Doctor. The other servants had come to support him from falling, and had got him to the door of the house. They lifted him into a chair in the Servants' Hall or entrance into the house, but his head had fell, and his [end of the first page] hands and f[eet?], his eyes diste[nded?] rolled up. The Doctor could feel no pulse: he applied volatiles to his nostrils, which seemed to have little or no effect: a be[d?] in the mean time was bro't, and put on the floor, on which he was laid, after which, with one or two gaspes, he resigned his Soul to God who gave it. I was unhappy in being so near. The scene was too affecting, and I could scarce support myself from falling. I pray God it may having [have] a proper influence on my future conduct in life, and with great sincerity can say, that the summit of all my wishes and prayers to Heaven, is contained in one short petition—May I die like him! My brother came in soon after. We then consulted how we should communicate to M[rs] O. this distressing account, in her weak state and low condition. It was determined to send for D[r] Chandler, to whom the Doctor went, and returned with him, who made it known in the easiest and best manner possible, and then went to prayer with us. After dinner D[r] Ch. went home. I went with Tommy to his house, where we opened the Gov.'s Will, of which there was . . . [end of second page] . . . last A - - t - - ed [?] . . . after directing that - - s funeral charges should . . . [blank]

. . . gave his whole estate in the following manner* . . . [blank] . . . I came back to the house to tea, and wrote to M[rs] H., acquainting her with the melancholy event to us, but easy and happy departure of the Governor.

4th.

4th.†— I went to bed, but my nerves were so affected, and my thoughts disturbed, that I could get no sleep, or next to none, the whole night. At eight o'clock I took what papers, money, and small matters of value were in the house, and went in the coach to Tommy's, where I left them, and went to Charter House Square to acquaint D[r] Apthorpe with what had happened, the Governor having expressly desired him to reserve a place near my syster in the church at Croydon. He promised everything should be in proper order on [Fr]iday next, the day which we have proposed [for] the funeral. I then went [to] M[r] Lynn, Walb. . . [?] Street, and engaged him to provide and conduct the funeral: from thence to the Bull and Mouth Inn, in B. and M. Street, and paid for a place in the . . . t coach for Birmingham, which sets out [end of the third page] from thence at 5 o'clock in [the] evening. I returned to my brother's, where M[r] Ly[nn]came, and went with me to Brompton Park. M[rs] O. has bore the shock l[ess] than we feared: slept well with an opiate, but seems to be bewildered, her mind weak, and takes less notice of what happens than she did. Her disorder seems to be increasing, and in all human probability, must soon put a period to her life. Thus we are perhaps one [of] the most distressed families upon earth. Whilst earthly comforts are swiftly failing, may we desire solid comfort from Heavenly fountains which never can fail us. After dinner called in the coach on Tommy, and from thence to the Green Man and Still in Oxford Street, from whence about ½ past 5 o'clock I set [out] in [the] Post Coach for Birmingham, in company [with] a M[r] Taylor of Wolverhampton, and a M[r] Campbell going to Ireland, and a young G[ent] in a Clergyman's grey going to Oxford. [We] changed horses . . [blank] . . and

* A copy of his Will is given further on.

† Twice repeated. This date shews that his father died on the third. The fragment begins without date.

at Uxbridge, and got to Hywiecomb [High Wycombe] at ½ past nine, where the rest of the company went in t . . .

And thus ends the fourth page. Words, or parts of words that are worn out or lost, have been replaced within square brackets. Such portions of the Diary are missing as might have given some account of the funeral, but the Parish Register shews that he was interred on the 9th.

The riots in London to which the Governor alluded, almost at his last hour had, by the mistaken zeal of Lord George Gordon, been urged on to very serious proportions, so that by the time of the funeral, London was in several places in flames; the cortege however, probably took the route by way of Battersea and Streatham, by which it would avoid the city, which by this time was in the hands of the King's troops.

Horace Walpole wrote as follows on the day Mr. Hutchinson died:—"At eight I went to Gloucester House: the Duchess told me there had been a riot, and that Lord Mansfield's glasses had been broken. . . . About nine his Royal Highness and Colonel Heywood arrived, and then we heard a much more alarming account . . . About eight the Lords adjourned, and were suffered to go home, though the rioters declared that if the other House did not repeal the Bill, there would, at night, be terrible mischief . . . Lord George Gordon was running backwards and forwards, from the windows of the Speaker's Chamber, denouncing all that spoke against him to the mob in the Lobby . . . No saint was ever more diabolic than Lord George Gordon. Eleven wretches are in prison for the outrage at Cordon's, and will be hanged instead of their arch-incendiary."

"Nothing ever surpassed," he wrote on the 4th of June, "the abominable behaviour of the ruffian apostle that preached up this storm. I always, you know well, disliked and condemned the repeal of the Popish statutes, and am steadfast in that opinion: but I abhor such Protestantism as breathes the soul of Popery, and commences a reformation by attempting a massacre. The frantic incendiary ran backwards and forwards naming names for slaughter to the mob: fortunately his disciples were not expert at assassination, and nobody was murdered for the Gospel's sake. So blind was his zeal, and so untutored his outlaws, that though the Petition was addressed, and carried to the House of Commons, the chief fury fell on the Peers."

The next day he recurred to the subject—a subject which at that juncture excluded all others from conversation:—"The Jack of

Leyden of the age, Lord George Gordon, gave notice in the House, of Commons last week, that he would on Friday, bring in the Petition of the Protestant Association; and he openly declared to his disciples that he would not carry it unless a noble army of martyrs, not fewer than forty thousand, would accompany him. Forty thousand, led by such a lamb, were more likely to prove butchers than victims, and so, in good truth, they were very near being . . .

"Early on Friday the conservators of the church of England, assembled in St. George's Fields to encounter the old dragon, the old serpent, and marched in lines of six and six—about thirteen thousand only, as they were computed—with a petition as long as the procession, which the apostle himself presented: but though he has given out most Christian injunctions for peaceable behaviour, he did everything in his power to promote a massacre. He demanded immediate repeal of toleration, [to the Roman Catholics,] told Lord North he could have him torn to pieces, and running every minute to the door or windows, bawled to the populace that Lord North would give them no redress, and that now this member, now that, was speaking against them . . . You will be indignant that such a mad dog as Lord George, should not be knocked on the head."

On Thursday the 8th of June he wrote—"I came myself yesterday [to town,] and found a horrible scene. Lord Mansfield's house was just burnt down, and at night there were shocking disorders. London and Southwark were on fire in six places; but the regular troops quelled the sedition by daybreak, and everything now is quiet. A camp of ten thousand men is formed in Hyde Park, and regiments of horse and foot arrive every hour."

On Saturday the 10th—"I have this moment received two letters from town to tell me that Lord George Gordon was overtaken in his flight to Scotland, and was just brought prisoner to the Horse Guards. This is all I know yet, except that some say he was seized in the Park, and was not fled . . . Four convicts on the eve of execution, are let loose from Newgate, and Lord George Gordon is sent to the Tower."

"The Tower," he adds, "is much too dignified a prison for him —but he had left no other."

On February the 2nd we are told—"On Monday is to begin the trial of Lord George Gordon, which will at least occupy everybody for some days."

It would have been better if he had been shot in the tumult, for his captors did not know what to do with him when they had got him, and so he escaped hanging.

Unfortunately the portions of Elisha's Diary synchronising with the above events, are missing, so that we lose his description of them; but there is a loose leaf with the writing nearly all faded out, apparently belonging to the 16th of June, on which he speaks of going to Hyde Park, to see the soldiers encamped there. It is this—

"Mr Domett drank tea, and then we walked into the Park, which was crowded with great numbers of people, amongst the rest the Dutchess of Newcastle, [?] and some others of the nobility, the Park being every day crowded at evening since the Camp has been there.

Met Lord Townshend in Edward Street on horseback, just set out from his house. He stopped me and said, then Ld Hillsborough will interest himself in your favour. I said Ld H. was very polite. He said something of Mr Paxton. I asked his Ldship if he was in town? He said—"Yes, at my house." I had gone but a few yards: he called me back, and asked if there was anything in the military line in his department? he should be glad to serve me. I expressed my thoughts that there were places in the Ordnance Office. He replied, he had nothing in the civil line, and was then trying for something for Mr Haton. I had some little other conversation, and we parted.

On the other side of the leaf there are entries tending to shew that he and his brother were engaged in winding up their father's affairs. On this page there are dates:—

17.—Fair and pleasant—hot. Walked to Brompton: from thence with Tommy to the Treasury thro' the Park, and returned to Sackville St., and from thence to Brompton in a coach: after dinner to Sackville St. to settle something there, and back to tea: after tea to Brompton Park with Tommy and his wife. Wrote to Mrs H. Called on Mr Paxton.

18.—Cloudy—some rain. Went in a coach to Sackville St. with Tommy. Walked to Cockspur Street and to Craig's Court, to see Mr Cox about the house: returned to Sackville Street, to look after the books, &c.: to Brompton in coach to dinner: afterwards to Sackville St. in a coach with some packages to the Green Man and Still in Oxford Street. Called on Dr

Chandler, and on Mr G., where I met M^r [blank] from Virginia, who was returning in his carriage to Brompton, and I came home in it with him.

Franklin was at this time residing at Passy near Paris, and having heard of the riots, and having heard of the death of the Governor, he informs us that the one was ascribed to the other—not the riots to his death, but his death to the riots. In his Letter to Mr. Carmichael, of June 17, he writes—"Governor Hutchinson, it is said, died outright of the fright." Whatever happens, or whatever has happened, or whatever will happen, we are all of us fond of explaining how and why, and are quite sure we are right.

Sarah, the wife of Dr Peter Oliver, and the Governor's eldest daughter, followed him within four weeks. It was she who would not leave her father, when his house was attacked by the mob on the 26th of August, 1765, in the city of Boston, as mentioned in the third volume of his History, page 124:—"The Lieutenant-Governor [himself] had very short notice of the approach of the mob. He directed his children and the rest of his family, to leave the house immediately, determining to keep possession himself. His eldest daughter, after going a little way from the house returned, and refused to quit it, unless her father would do the like. This caused him to depart from his resolution, a few minutes before the mob entered."

This is alluded to by the Hon. Robert C. Winthrop, in his Introductory Address, delivered at the Lowell Institute, Boston, Jan. 5, 1869, where he says—"Hutchinson, as the mob approached, was engaged in bearing to a place of safety a beloved daughter who had refused to quit his side, and was thus compelled to abandon his precious papers to their fate. Everything was destroyed, or thrown out of the windows," &c.

Dr. Peter Oliver does not appear to have made the entries in his Diary day by day, as they occurred. From the way in which many of the statements flow one into another, it might be inferred that he wrote them at irregular intervals in groups or batches. Thus, the following extract summarises a variety of diverse subjects, to which our attention has been recently directed—

FROM THE DIARY OF DR. P. OLIVER.

Feby 2, 1780.—Willm Sanford Hutchinson, Mrs Oliver's youngest brother, died of a pulmonary consumption, aged 27^yrs and 6 m. Governor Hutchinson being unwell all winter, and this shock happening, almost overcame him. I went into Hampshire and Sussex for a fortnight with him in March: returned in Ap^{l}, and found Mrs Oliver exceedingly ill. The 4th of Ap^{l} the Gov., Sally, and I, took lodgings at Brompton Park, 1 mile from Hyde Park. She grew daily worse, as also her father.

May 18th.—Mrs Oliver delivered of a son: put to bed well, but in 3 days she faltered.

June 3rd.—The Govr died suddenly, in the 69th y^{r} of his age.

Mrs Oliver grew worse faster every day till she died, which was the 28th of June, past 3 o'clock in the morning. That day I completed my 39th year: she was 35 y^{rs} and 7 months old. She died perfectly resigned to the will of Heaven, but in great agony of body.

July 3rd.—She was buried at Croydon church, next to her father, myself, Mr Willard, Mr Blowers, and Mr Domett, mourners. She was one of the most virtuous, amiable, and kindest wives that ever man was blessed with. A greater loss I could not have sustained, but Heaven's will be done, and I acquiesce, knowing whatever is, is right. She is relieved from a deal of misery and distress: she had gone thro' more than any one who knew her could have imagined.

July 21st.—I set out with a wet nurse, and my 4 children for Oxford.

22nd.—From Oxford to Birmingham ab^{t} 7 o'clock.

24th.—I took a room in the Hotell.

25th.—I put my two eldest boys to School at Windsor Green, under the care of Mr Pickenige. I put my daughter to school at Mosely, under the care of Mrs Henrison, in Worcestershire, and the nurse and baby in New Hall Street. Thus I had disposed of my children in the best manner I possibly could. It appeared hard at first to part with them, but I have got reconciled at last to it; but the pleasing reflection I had of seeing them often, was soon turned into sorrow, for my dear little infant, who was very near my heart particularly, was drooping in a few weeks after I had got lodgings for it, and finally was seized with convulsions the 20th of Aug^{t}: lay in that state till the morning of the 27th, 3 o'clock, and then died in the greatest agony. I had it opened by Tomlinson: its lungs, heart, diaphragm, stomach, and intestines, and all its viscera, were in the soundest state. Whatever produced the fits was someth^{g} on the brain, which could not have been perceived if we had opened its head.

I moved the 29th of Augt to High Street, opposite New Street, at Ballard's, one bed-room only, at 3/6 p^{r} week, from the hotell.

30th.—I buried my little baby the north side of St Phillip's church, and near the vaults—6 feet deep: Mr James read prayers.

31st of Augt. I paid off and dismissed Nurse Dove, hoping never to see her again, &c.

On the fly leaves at the beginning and the end of the last volume of his Diary, the Governor has jotted down several memorandums, referring to the receipt and to various payments of money. The last dates in his own handwriting are of the first of June, he dying on the third; and these efforts are in a clearer and firmer hand than many of the entries in the body of the Diary made a few weeks before. There are some items referring to his Bankers' account with Gines and Atkinson; and on the other side, amongst the payments, it appears that he was not only contributing to the maintainance of his children and other relatives by quarterly advances, but also by gift or loan to quondam American friends who had withdrawn to England, and who were suffering the privations consequent on the troubles of the times. Among these latter may be mentioned Mr. Charles Paxton, who had been Commissioner of Customs at Boston, and who is abused and slandered in the account of him given by Lorenzo Sabine, with an amount of political spite and severity, such as we are almost ashamed to read in the present day. In January 1780, he has a balance of £6,387 15*s.* 3*d.* with his Banker. The following are payments—

Jan^{y}.	A Merchant	20 ,,	— ,,	.
10.	James Fisher	45 ,,	— ,,	.
17.	Peter Johannot. W. S. H.	70 ,,	— ,,	.
25.	Jno Campbell, for Navy Bills	2942 ,,	6 ,,	4
Feb. 9.	John Carter	27 ,,	10 ,,	.

	12.	T. Latham,. 3116. 16. 6	12 ,, — ,, .
	23.	Self, by E.	105 ,, — ,, .
Mar.	1.	S. Oliver	25 ,, — ,, .
	—	E. Hutchinson	25 ,, — ,, .
	—	T. H.	50 ,, — ,, .
		Jn° Campbell, for Navy Bills. 5816. 2. 4	2494 ,, 6 ,, .
April	16.	Bethell Cox	51 ,, 2 ,, .
	—	Lynde Funeral	48 ,, 11 ,, .
May	3.	John Carter. 5945. 9. 10	29 ,, 14 ,, 3
	13.	Self, by my son T.	52 ,, 10 ,, .
	—	A Merchant. 6017. 19. 10	20 ,, — ,, .
June	1.	T. H.	50 ,, — ,, .
		E. H.	25 ,, — ,, .
		S. O.	25 ,, — ,, .
		P. Reily	24 ,, — ,, .
		M. Greenup	10 ,, 10 ,, .

A few pages further on, bearing dates ranging through the first three months of the year 1780, there are two columns of entries under the heading "House Expenses." From these a few scattered items may be selected—

Feb.	7.	Handkerchiefs	1 ,, 1 ,, .
		1 Tea [one pound presumably]	10 ,, 9
	10.	Fruit for dessert	5 ,, .
	23.	Three women, for mourning [for Billy]	18 ,, 18 ,, .
March.		Tea	10 ,, 9
		Mr Mauduit's Wm. for Bandanoes *	1 ,, 10 ,, .
May	1.	Hairdresser	6 ,, 16 ,, 6

After these the Governor's memorandums cease, but a continuation of the entries by his son Thomas inosculate with them, and from these latter a few may be taken. They of course date subsequently to his father's death.

RECEIPTS.

1780.		
June.	Cash left in house, 45 Guineas	47 ,, 5 ,, .

* India silk handkerchiefs.

	Rec^{d} Widdows cloaths	3 „ 3 „ .
July.	Rec^{d} for d^{o}	1 „ 11 „ 6
	Rec^{d} Mr Tatterall, for coach	14 „ 19 „ .
	Rec^{d} Kemble and Venn.	16 „ 13 „ 2
Nov^{r}.	Rec^{d} Sam. Mather	20 „ — „ .
1781.		
Mar. 15.	Rec^{d} of Mr Paxton, money lent him, £60.	
	In^{t} on d^{o} £1 „ 17 .	61 „ 17 „ .
Ap^{l}.	Rec^{d} for old silver buckles	1 „ 13 „ 6
	Rec^{d} a p^{r} d^{o}, Billy's	1 „ 6 „ 10
	Rec^{d} Gold lace of suit cloaths . . .	5 „ 16 „ 2

Mem^{d} Mrs Sanford [Miss Grizzel Sanford] to Mrs Smithson. May 8th 1783. I am to pay Mrs Smithson at the rate of 40£ ꝑ ann. for Mrs Sanford, from this time, ꝑ agreement.

Balance	in my hands after the final division,	
	July 1781	18 „ 12 „ 1
	Rec^{d} for rem^{r} Billy's effects.	4 „ 4 „ .
	Rec^{d} Saml Mather his Note to the estate	32 „ 10 „ .
	Rec^{d} suit cloaths, lace taken of [off] .	18 „ .
Jany 1782.		
14.	Rec^{d} 1. dividend on Gines and Atkinson, bal^{a}	22 „ 16 „ .
	Rec^{d} 2 silver seals	12 „ .
Mar.	Rec^{d} 2 odd spurrs	16 „ 9
Oct.	Rec^{d} T. H.	20 „ — „ .
	Rec^{d} E. H., out of dividends	10 „ — „ .
	Rec^{d} P. O., Junr	10 „ — „ .
Ap^{l}. 1783.		
	Rec^{d} of the Treasury	20 „ — „ .
	Rec^{d} at d^{o}	10 „ — „ .

Here the record of the Receipts, in so far as they appear in this book, terminates; the items that follow are taken from among the Payments.

PAYMENTS.

June 1780.			
	14.	Pd probate Will	4 „ 13 „ .
		Pd 5 Mourning rings	4 „ 14 „ .
	20.	Pd Mr Rowe on £150 recd for Foster Hutchinson	3 „ 15 „ .
July.		Paid E. H. charges in coming to town, moving, &c.	5 „ 0 „ 8
		Paid Dr Oliver 10 Guineas	10 „ 10 „ .
	21.	Miss Sanford and Nurse, 2 Guineas	2 „ 2 „ .
Aug.	7.	Nurse Whitmore, mourning, 6 Guineas	6 „ 6 „ .
		Dr Oliver borrowed of her, 1 G.	1 „ 1 „ .
		Coach and cart, Mrs Sanford and Nurse moving	17 „ .
		Paid for Elisha's carpet to Berm[ingham]	3 „ 8
		Paid Water tax	15 „ .
Nov.	7.	Mrs Hales, a quarter's board, Mrs Sanford	10 „ — „ .
Dec.	20.	Paid Mr Carter advertising coach, omitted	2 „ 6
1781.			
Jany		Paid Mr Rowe for Fos. Hutchinson	2 „ 10 „ .
Mar.		Paid Sr Will Pepperell a debt of Billy's	20 „ — „ .
	15.	Paid Nurse Whitmore	10 „ — „ .
Apl.		Mrs Sanford, tea ½ lb.	4 „ .
		Paid appraising	10 „ .
1782.			
Aug.	8.	Mrs Smithson, a Qr	9 „ — „ .

The record of his burial stands as follows in the Parish Register at Croydon, in Surrey :—

"June 9, 1780. Thomas Hutchinson Esq., Late Governor of the Massachusetts, Aged 69."

Lorenzo Sabine tells us that Mr. Apthorp, (or Apthorpe) had married a niece of Governor Hutchinson, and this family connection will account for the friendly relations on which they stood. He writes :—

"Apthorp, East. An Episcopal Clergyman of Massachusetts. He was born in 1733, and was educated in England. In 1761 he was appointed a Missionary at Cambridge, by the Society for the Propagation of the Gospel in Foreign Parts; and during his labors there, was engaged in a warm theological controversy with Dr Mayhew. Retiring to England, he died there in 1816, aged eighty-three years. His wife was a niece of Governor Hutchinson, and a daughter of Eliakim Hutchinson. His only son was a Clergyman. One daughter married Dr Cary; one, Dr Butler; and a third, a son of Dr Poley [Paley];—the husbands of the two first were heads of Colleges. Mr Apthorp was a distinguished writer. In 1790 he lost his sight."

Let us glance at the Governor's Will. How different a Will from that of his father! Truly, says Mr W. H. Whitmore, page 18, in his account of the Genealogies of the Hutchinson and Oliver families—"Probably few men in the Province had so large an estate." And he gives the particulars of it, as extracted from the Probate Office in Boston, Massachusetts. The list of bequests is unusually long and generous, wherein are remembered, not only relatives, but a large number of personal friends: and it may be inferred that his table was handsomely furnished, since he not only gave his wife 600 ounces of silver plate, but he had enough afterwards to divide into seven portions, to be distributed among his children. It was he who, in the earlier part of his life, gave his large silver tankard to the North Church, to be used for the wine at the celebration of the Holy Communion, but which has been bought back into the family, as mentioned in vol. i., page 394, and he bequeathed £300 to the same church, besides £80 to the poorer members of the congregation; but since those days the Wheel of Fortune had taken a turn, so that riot, mob-law, and confiscation had left the Governor unable to name an article that he could call his own, wherefore he merely specifies a legacy of £300 for Elisha, and divides into four portions whatever his children might be able to scrape together afterwards, and these they are to share among themselves.

The original Will is preserved in the Will Office at Somerset House, Strand, London, from which place I procured the following office copy:—

"The last Will and Testament of Thomas Hutchinson, formerly Governor of Massachusetts Bay, now of Sackville Street, Westminster. My body I commit to the earth, to be buried at as small expense as can consist with decency; My Soul I commit to the mercy of God, through the Merits of Christ, humbly imploring the forgiveness of the innumerable sins of a long life. I make my two sons Thomas and Elisha my Executors. I give to my son Elisha Three hundred pounds, having giving him less than I intended in my life time. The residue of my Estate, of what kind soever, I give to my three children in the proportion following, viz.:—Two fourth parts, thereof to my eldest son Thomas Hutchinson; one fourth part to my son Elisha Hutchinson; and one fourth part to my daughter Sarah Oliver: and if either of my children shall die in my life time, it is my will that the part given to such child, shall go to his or her surviving children, to be equally divided. I revoke all former Wills, and declare this to be my last Will.

"In testimony whereof I hereunto set my hand and seal this tenth day of April, in the year of our Lord 1780.

Thos Hutchinson—— (L. S.)

"Signed, sealed, published, and declared by Thomas Hutchinson as his last Will, in the presence of us, who signed as Witnesses in his presence.

Peter Oliver.
Patrick Reilly.
Patrick Taaffe.

Besides his son-in-law, the two other witnesses were his Irish men-servants, the first of whom had accompanied him from America. The following memorandum is appended to the Will:—

"Proved at London 14th June 1780, before the Worshipful George Harris, Doctor of Laws and Surrogate, by the Oath of Thomas Hutchinson Esqre, the son of the Deceased, and one of the Executors named in the Will, to whom Admon was granted, having been first sworn, duly to administer. Power reserved to Elisha Hutchinson Esqre, the son also of the deceased, and the other Executor named in the said Will, when he shall apply for the same."

At his death, it appears that the Governor had no more to leave than between six and seven thousand pounds. In his Diary, under September 1, 1778, he speaks of £7000 as being all he then had in the world; and on the fly-leaf of the last volume, in account with his Bankers, there is this entry:—"1780, Jan. To Balance, ꝑ acc^t. . . 6387,,15,,3."

There are a few scattered entries in the different Diaries which, though they have lacked sufficient connection with the preceding course of events, yet, by favour, may be admitted here. The following is on a loose leaf of Elisha's Diary—is of uncertain date, but probably of about the period to which we have arrived:—

"19th.—Cloudy and moderate. Walked to Brompton, and returned to town with Tommy. After tea as far as Mr Galloway's. Mr Dillon called, and told us he is to return to Birming^m on Monday, the business he came to town about being at an end—his claim to the Ld High Chamberlain; that, as being descended from the same ancestor with Lord Percy, and most probably an elder branch of the same. The Judges however, determined the Statute of Limitations to be a Barr to the claim, having for more than 60 years be——." end of the page.

Although Elisha had taken up his residence at Birmingham, as had also the Chief Justice, and his son Dr. Peter Oliver, they occasionally visited London. The first being there, and calling on his friend Mr. Watson, apparently on the 25th of August, though in what year there is nothing to prove, made the following statement in his Diary:—

"Cool, and several heavy showers. Mr W. has a striking likeness of Dr Franklin by Mrs Wright in wax, and another which was designed for himself, but there is want of resemblance: they being dressed, and [in a] sitting posture in the room, would deceive the nicest discernment at first entrance, and every one at first is led to speak to them."

Presumably they were as large as life. Franklin had long known, and corresponded with this lady. There is a letter of his to her in his Correspondence, vol. i. p. 34, tending to dissuade her from coming from London to Paris, for the purpose of practising her art of modelling portraits in wax, alleging that two or three other artists already profess it there, and then adding—"but it is not the taste for persons of fashion to sit to these artists for their portraits."

The subjoined explanatory Note is appended to the letter:—

"Mrs Mehetabel Wright was altogether a very remarkable woman. She was the niece of the celebrated John Wesley, but was born at Philadelphia, in which city her parents settled at an early period. Mrs Wright was greatly distinguished as a modeller in wax, which art she turned to a remarkable account in the American war, by coming to England and exhibiting her performances. This enabled her to procure much intelligence of importance, which she communicated to Dr Franklin and others, with whom she corresponded during the whole war. As soon as a General was appointed, or a squadron begun to be fitted out, the old lady found means of access to some family where she could gain information, and thus without being at all suspected, she continued to transmit an account of the number of the troops, and the place of their destination to her political friends abroad. She at one time had frequent access to Buckingham-House, and used, it was said, to speak her sentiments very freely to their Majesties, who were amused with her originality. The great Lord Chatham honoured her with his visits, and she took his likeness, which appears in Westminster Abbey. Mrs Wright died very old in February 1786."

That curious collection of wax figures, representing Kings, Queens, and sundry great personages, kept in a mysterious and little known chamber in Westminster Abbey, is not so numerous as it used to be. It formed an interesting series, not only as portraits, but also as specimens of costume. Not one in a thousand of those who enter the Abbey are aware of the existence of such a chamber. But of late years a considerable portion of the collection has been improved out of existence, or removed elsewhere, for the ever increasing numbers were growing so great, that it was becoming difficult to know what to do with them. If they were sufficiently good as works of art, or true in their portraiture to the lineaments of the originals, they would be worth removing to a place where they would be more open to the public. Perhaps it might be added that the sons have been educated above their fathers, and that though the fathers held the wax figures in the highest admiration, the sons prefer resorting to the National Gallery.

CHAPTER IX.

THE Governor had been quietly laid in his grave, and his two sons now found themselves in a country moderately new to them, and thrown upon their own resources to make the best of things—to scrape together what was left for them, to watch the course of events, to see whether any varying phase in the fortunes of the war, which still dragged its slow length along, was likely to open a way for their return to the land of their birth, or, on the other hand, to settle them down where they were. It was beginning to be said on both sides of the water that people were getting tired of the war, and mutually desired peace. Thomas, when writing from Brompton, Nov. 23, 1780, to his brother Elisha in Birmingham, uses these expressions :—*

"American spirits begin again to rise upon the last acc^ts rec^d from thence. Col. Chandler has a letter from his wife, who says the cricis for American Independence is past. The people are sick of their new alliance.† Mr. Wilson writes from New York, that it was with difficulty carried at a town meeting, to make another attempt this autumn, many being for a composition with Great Britain. The best chance is from dissensions among themselves. A son of Col. Warren, who perhaps you know, arrived in town a few days ago: and another, of G—— Trumbull, is close in Newgate for carrying on a correspondence with Franklin for some time past, as the papers have told you."

Judge Oliver, in his usual joking style, addressing himself on the 9th of June, 1781, to Elisha, who was then in London, sends the following message to Mr. Joseph Galloway, late Speaker of the Assembly in Pennsylvania, but then a Refugee in England, couched in these facetious terms :—

* Original Letters, vol. ii., dated from 1780 to 1800, inclusive.
† With the French—which was true enough.

"Tell Mr. Galloway that he will have so much time upon hand that he may venture a visit to Birmingham, as Philadelphia will not be swept and garnished this—this—century. As to pretty Miss Galloway, if she will accept of my compliments, present them to her, and let her know that if she inclines to see the whole world, she will find it here in miniature; and miniatures are the most agreeable objects for vision, as their different parts do not crowd upon the eye. But if she refuses my compliments, do not tell her anything I say about this important matter."

Thomas writes to his brother on the 20th of July this same year:—

"Our accounts from America afford a good prospect of the reduction of that country; but we have already found it will not do to depend much upon prospects."

There is an original letter of August the 29th this year 1781, addressed by Mr. Galloway to Elisha, in which he gives him his opinion upon men and things at this period. He says:—

"You ask me what Chapter of politics we are in now? Indeed, my Dear Sir, this question would puzzle Solomon himself. Such is the folly or wickedness of the persons entrusted with carrying on the American war, that it is impossible to form even a distant conjecture when either of us shall cross the Attlantic with safety. We see Lord Cornwallis gaining victory after victory with but little fruits attending them. Like a bird he passes through the country, but conquers no part of it. Sir Henry [Clinton] with 13,000 British, and 7,500 Militia, is sleeping in New York, and dreaming about an expedition to Philadelphia, and I fear it will prove only a dream. When I see a General enter a Province—give the people assurances that he does not mean to desert them—cordially invite the Loyalists to take up arms, and to seize upon and bring us the disaffected, then, and not till then, will I pretend to presage an end to the rebellion. This policy one would imagine would be familiar to a school boy. Our Generals have had it repeatedly pointed out to them, and yet they go on their old wretched way, entering Provinces, and then deserting them, leaving the unhappy Loyalists the sacrifices to this folly. Under these circumstances we know no remedy but patience; stealing at the same time a little comfort, from a hope that the course of folly 'll have its end, and our prospects become more agreeable."

Thomas to Elisha, as follows:—

"Brompton, Aug[t] 30th, 1781.

"Dear Brother,

"It is so long since we have heard anything of the welfare of our Birmingham friends, that it was carried by a full vote, that I should sit down and make the enquiry. The Doctor told us that we should hear from him within a week; probably from new quarters, but nothing as yet appears. We have always had good news from America since you left us, but the prospect of a settlement seems to be little advanced by it; and the accounts of the dispositions of the southern people are rebellious beyond what could have been imagined,—many of property chusing rather to leave their estates and go to the northward, than submit to the protection of this Government. Such was the situation of Carolina, that Gov[r] Bull writes Mrs. H., he dared not venture to his country house, six miles from Charlestown, for fear of assassination; but such a state I think can't last long."

In the Diary of Dr. Peter Oliver we read:—

"1781. Nov.—Mr. Abel Willard died of a slow fever in London, the first week in Nov[r], 1781.

"Nov[r] 25.—News arrived in London of the capitulation of Lord Cornwallis and his brave army the 19th of Oct[r]."

Upon this astounding piece of news, Mr. Pelham Winslow writes from New York on the 1st of December, 1781, as follows, to Elisha:—

"You express great confidence, and reputation from Lord Cornwallis's bravery and good conduct, and from thence presage a happy termination to the present campaign. Great must be your mortification and disappointment, when you hear of his catastrophe; and further observe, by the Tenth Article of Capitulation, the Loyalists left exposed to the vindictive resentment of a set of people whose tender mercies are cruelty:— men whom he was sent to protect and defend—men whom he had encouraged and excited by repeated Proclamations and promises of protection, to take up arms and co-operate with him, and quit their families and fortunes, should be the only people left unprovided and unprotected by the capitulation, is surprising and alarming, and gives great uneasiness and apprehensions to the Refugees and friends to government here. Where the fault lies I will not pretend to say: time will evince, and I hope the hand of justice will inflict prop punishment upon the delinquents. But thus much I will pretend to say, (without the gift of prophecy)—That if Great Britain thus permits her friends to be sacrificed, she may bid adieu to America; for no government can expect subjection without protection, or at least, an equal participation of sufferings amongst its subjects. What has, or what will be the fate of those unhappy men, we have not yet heard, but in all probability a halter will be the only reward a great many of them will receive for their Loyalty. I will not dwell upon the subject—'tis too painful, but refer you to the bearer [Mr. Fowle, a nephew of Mr. Secretary Flucker], and many of your unfortunate countrymen, who are flocking home in this fleet, possibly to avoid a similar fate.

"The last intelligence I had from Plimouth, [Mass.], our friends there were all well.

"Compliments to all friends in England in general:—to the Judge, Mrs Hutchinson, the Doctor, &c., in particular, concludes me your sincere friend and oblig'd Hum^l^ Servt,

"PELHAM WINSLOW."

"Elisha Hutchinson, Esq., London."

Pelham Winslow was a son of General John Winslow. He graduated at the University of Harvard, and entered the office of James Otis to fit himself for the bar. On the outbreak of hostilities he preferred the Royalist side, and took refuge in Boston. On the evacuation of that city he removed to Halifax, and subsequently to New York. He was proscribed and banished, and in 1783 he died at Brooklyn, leaving a wife and an infant daughter. Sabine gives a long account of several members of the Winslow family. The shameful treatment of the Loyalists, as mentioned above, was severely commented on by the writers of the day.

The late Governor's eldest son, on the 8th of December, 1781, pours out his feelings to his brother Elisha, and I need scarcely add that all these extracts are taken from the original letters. He says:—

"The unhappy American news has quite stunned us all; and for one, I am determined not to allow myself to expect a visit to that country again, after so many opportunitys lost, and misfortunes hapning, whether from bad conduct in our Commanders or not, I leave every one to judge for himself. I think the prospect darker than it ever has before been, notwithstanding we are told twenty thousand troops are to be sent away as soon as possible, and the war carried on in quite a different manner, and that Government will by no means relinguish their object of conquering a country on which, in a manner, depends the salvation of this kingdom. The unhappy fate of the poor Loyalists in Lord Cornwallis's army is dreadful, and *his* agreeing to that Article of Capitulation, which gives them up to the mercy of Congress, is a matter that remains to be explained. After so many gallant actions he ought not to be condemed unheard."

Lord North, the Tory Premier, announced in the House on the 19th of March, 1782, that his Ministry had resigned; and the country party, generally consisting of the least cultured half of the community, whose simplicity enables them to believe anything, and taught by the harangues of the Opposition, rejoiced that there was going to be a change, as yet never having heard of the expression—"Peace with Honour." Writing to his brother on the 22nd of March, Thomas says:—

"The common people are much elated at the fall of the Ministry, and depend on a peace immediately with America, at least."

On the 11th of April the following paragraph occurs in his letter:—

"We are made to expect peace with America; and it will I think determine whether we are to be beggars the remainder of our days or not. I own I fear we have little to hope: however, I intend to give A. S.* a power to transact anything for us there. Miss Sanford will do the same. I must have a line from you before I can receive your money at the Treasury."

Again, on September the 12th, 1782, he writes:—

"We have had fine reports of a change in American politics, in more than one Province. A letter from Mr. Walter to Sr. William Pepperell has occasioned much talk, and many opinions respecting future events in that quarter. That great oppression by enormous taxes, and perhaps a fear of French slavery, had occasioned great uneasiness in some parts, even to opposition to the present government, I believe is true; but we must wait the arrival of the

* Andrew Spooner. He was shortly going to take ship for New York. His mother was Margaret Oliver, a daughter of Lieut.-Gov. Andrew Oliver, by his second wife.

next pacquet to know what, or whether any good consequence will result therefrom. I am, &c., Thos. Hutchinson."

The following original letter does not contain anything o importance, but who the Edward Hutchinson could be who directed it to Elisha, and signed it with his name, I was for some time considerably at a loss to decide. I had thought that all the late Governor's relatives of his family name had withdrawn from Massachusetts; but on examination I believe him to have been the son of Edward Hutchinson who married Lydia Foster. The writer of the letter is marked down in the Pedigree as having died unmarried. His sister Margaret however, married the Rev. Nathanial Robbins, whose descendants reside in Boston at the present day. The writer must have continued in America throughout the period of the war, and have accommodated himself to the change of times; and whatever ostensible sentiments he put outwards to the light of day, like an overcoat, it may be inferred by certain expressions in his letter, that he was not quite comfortable in the society by which he was surrounded. His father was half brother of Governor Hutchinson's father, and their two wives were the daughters of Colonel John Foster. The letter is the following:—

"Cambridge, [Mass.] 15th Sepr, 1783.

"My Dear Kinsman,

"Though I have never wrote to you as I can remember since your departure from hence, yet I have been far from forgetting you, especially since, by the disposition of Providence, your family has been made small. I was very glad to hear of your health and welfare by Mr. Spooner; and as his return to England gives me a fair opportunity of writing, I trust I shall not be troublesome in just letting you know that I am yet alive in a much altered country, very disagreeable to me in their conduct and manners, though many individuals are very worthy people, and I am happy in the friendship of some of them.

"I intended to have wrote you by Mrs. Belcher, but her going to England was always talk'd of as uncertain and at a distance, and when she concluded to go I was absent from hence, and knew nothing of it Pray make my compliments to her when next you see her, and if it be not too much trouble, pray favour me with a line when it shall be convenient to you. My kindest regards wait on Mrs. Hutchinson and my little cousins. Pray present my sincere duty and respects to the worthy Judge Oliver. I am glad to hear he yet lives, and hope his useful life will be lengthen'd out, as a comfort to you all. Remember me kindly to Doctor Oliver, and my poor little motherless cousins. I han't time now to write to him, or I would. Mrs. Fayerweather, at whose house I now am, desires me to give her best regards to you and Mrs. Hutchinson.

"Mr. Spooner having been on the spot, makes it needless for me to relate some particulars which otherwise I might.

"I am, My Dear Sir,

"Your Affectionate Kinsman

"ED[D] HUTCHINSON."

"Elisha Hutchinson, Esq."

During my sojourn of several months in Boston, I occasionally amused myself with visiting the Burial Grounds, and reading the inscriptions. I have before spoken of Copp's Hill, where the Governor's wife was laid. The Granary, at the north-east end of the Common, contains memorials of the names of Spooner, Oliver, and Hutchinson, not far from Franklin's Pyramid. I saw a brick tomb covered with a large slab of red sandstone, or something of that appearance. In form, shape, and nature, it was parallelopipoidal, or what is more commonly called, an altar tomb. Across the top of the slab were cut the words—"Doct[r] WILLIAM SPOONER. No. 112," and longitudinally the following, in Roman capitals :—

Here lyeth the Body of Cap. Peter Oliver
Aged 52 years, who lived much beloved,
And died much lamented on the 11th day of
Apriel, anno 1670.
Here lyeth interrd affection resolution
Religion pitty under dissolution.

And exploring further south, I came upon a large loose slab of grey stone, some four feet long, two wide, and three inches thick, with one long side, or upper edge, cut into a serpentine outline. It was leaning up against a brick altar tomb, as if its original place had been lost and forgotten. The surface was much corroded, and the inscription, in four lines, scarcely perceptible, but it began with "MARY HVTCHINSON," the same surname being discernible in two or three other places. The only dates legible were apparently 1669, and September 1671. I made sketches of these memorials, which I still have. If this slab referred to members of the Governor's branch of the family, the dates tally nearest with the births and deaths of some of the children of Elisha and his first wife Hannah Hawkins. He was born in 1641, having been a grandson of William and Anne, the first settlers; and it is on record that at the later date of 1717, he was himself interred in the Granary.

I am tempted in this place to explain that there were three heads of families of the name of Hutchinson who emigrated from England to Massachusetts between the years 1632 and 1635. They all probably emanated from the Great Yorkshire stock; but as that stock had been continually throwing off branches, it resulted that none of those heads of families who found themselves in close proximity in America, could point out the exact link of relationship that might exist between them. I wish to say a few words on each of these, and I will take them in the following order:—

1.—Richard Hutchinson and his first wife Alice, who, after their removal from England, chiefly identified themselves with Danvers or Salem, and consequently, for distinction sake, may be styled *Hutchinson of Salem.*

2.—George Hutchinson and his wife Margaret first lived at Charlestown near Boston, though their offspring cultivated their own estates in the conntry; but taking their early settlement as a handle, this branch may be termed *Hutchinson of Charlestown.*

3.—William Hutchinson and his wife Anne removed from Alford in the county of Lincoln—their son Edward with Mr. Cotton in 1633, and themselves with the rest of their family the year after; and as they had a principal residence in the city of Boston whilst the family continued in America, they may, at all events for that time, be called *Hutchinson of Boston.*

I. Enlarging upon these, and taking Number one first, it may be observed, that on arriving at Salem in 1635, Richard soon established for himself a highly respectable position. The year after his arrival the town authorities made him a grant of land in the neighbourhood, and twenty acres more in 1637. Other grants succeeded in 1654 and 1660, these latter being at Hathorn's Hill and Beaver Brook. Though his family maintained their hold on Salem, they were much occupied in the long and laborious process of subduing their lands to useful cultivation, which the succeeding generations continued to follow to their honour and profit, as steady members of the community, deserving the good opinion of their neighbours. At the outbreak of hostilities Colonel Israel Hutchinson commanded a regiment before Boston, but he was not at Bunker Hill.

They were sufficiently literary and cultivated in their ideas as to have kept scrupulous records of the genealogical accessions, changes, and losses, that had taken place within their domestic circle, so that they brought down a very circumstantial Pedigree, dating from the earliest members who set foot on American soil.

As I have two MS. copies of the Pedigree, written by themselves, one being as a register, and the other in tabular form, and given to me by the family more than twenty years ago, and which copies are now before me, I am able to speak with admiration of the care with which it appears to have been kept. From Richard to the present representatives there have been ten generations.

Col. Israel Hutchinson came of the youngest son of the fourth generation, and his great-grandson William Augustus, born in 1826, and married in 1856 to Esther Emery, is now his representative.

The sixth generation was carried on in the male line by two sons—Elisha and Joseph. Elisha had Andrew and Jesse. Andrew had Nathaniel and Stillman. Nathaniel had Everett and Ann Jane. Now this Everett, born in 1826, is the eldest representative of the family of Hutchinson of Salem. All others are junior to him. His father's younger brother Stillman had two sons, who come next; and his grandfather's younger brother Jesse had sixteen children, ten of whose sons married, and all had families. Jesse's descendants constitute the third offshoot or sub-branch. There is a memorandum attached to the Pedigree referring to him, which runs as follows :—"He was father of sixteen children: the greater part of them are widely known both in the United States and Great Britain as the celebrated Hutchinson singers. Jesse, the 9th son, was gifted with a talent for poetry, which he displayed in composing the greater part of the songs they sang. These songs were generally set to music by his brother. The brothers were staunch Abolitionists. They have gone out west lately [about 1860], and founded a town in Minnesota, to which they have given the name of Hutchinson."

I well remember when they were in England. During their tour they visited and sang at Exeter, sixteen miles from where I was living, and I have always regretted I did not go and hear them. I have one leaf of a quarto serial called "The People's Magazine," bearing date April 25, 1846, on page 225 of which is represented "The Hutchinson Family: A Sketch by Margaret Gillies," as they generally appeared before the public. There are three young men and their sister. The other side of the leaf is occupied with a glowing description of their talents and some account of their parentage. They did a great deal of work, and I hope they carried back a great deal of money. By a friend who had long lived at Boston I have been told that they established a residence near Lynn, until the swarm became too large for the hive, when they departed to seek new pastures.

Next we come to Joseph, the younger brother of Elisha, father of the prolific Jesse. This cadet had numerous descendants, his grandson Hiram leaving New England, and establishing a lucrative business in France, which he left to his eldest son Alcander, who married the daughter of a French Count, a scion of the old Noblesse, reduced low by Revolution and Republicanism; for those who know not how to raise themselves, generally strike a balance by pulling everything down to their own level.

Such is the respectable descent of this family in America; but some of its members desired to know something of their ancestry if possible prior to their having left England, and in order to effect this end, they called in the services of the late

Col. Chester, who was to search records and find out all he could. After a considerable amount of labour, of travelling, and of research, he produced a long Pedigree, basing the English portion of it upon the old Yorkshire genealogical tree, originally traced by Henry St. George, King-of-Arms, and given in the early quarto editions of the Life of Col. John Hutchinson. But though stamped with the authority of the Heralds' College, Col. Chester has taken one or two liberties with it which may be alluded to again; and in the commencement of his performance, which was printed in the *New England Historical and Genealogical Register* for July, 1868, he tells us that the founder of the family in England is reputed to have come from Normandy with William the Conqueror. This attribution is too stale now to pass unchallenged. If you want to pay a compliment to a family, and know nothing of its founder, the safest plan is to say—"he came over with the Conqueror." Well, no, this coin will not pass now-a-days. No one ever said this but Col. Chester. All tradition before him—for there is nothing but tradition to go by—has said that he came to England in the fleet of Harold Harfager, King of Norway, when that invader entered the Humber, and encountered the Saxons at Stanford Bridge, below York, a few weeks—or rather, to be more precise, some eight or ten days, before the Battle of Hastings. We do not touch firm ground until we come down to the commencement of Henry St. George's Pedigree in 1282.

The earliest recorded grant of coat armour was to the younger branch of Thomas Hutchinson, of Owthorpe, the eldest son William being of Cowlam, and both of them the sons of Anthony. This appears in the Visitations of Nottinghamshire in 1569 and 1614, and vol. iv. of the publications of the Harleian Society. It is described thus:—*Per pale Gules and Az., semé of Cross-crosslets or, a Lion rampant guardant Argent.* Crest—*a Cockatrice Azure, legged and combed or.* Col. Chester does not appear to have been aware of this grant—or, at all events he made no use of it where it was essential to the Pedigree he was engaged in compiling, and by neglecting it, he assigned a wrong coat of arms instead.

PEDIGREE OF HUTCHINSON OF SALEM, FROM DOCUMENTS IN THEIR POSSESSION,

in which the portions omitted by Col. Chester are restored in italics.

RICHARD HUTCHINSON = 1. Alice. 2. Susan. 3. Sarah.
The first in America, about 1635.

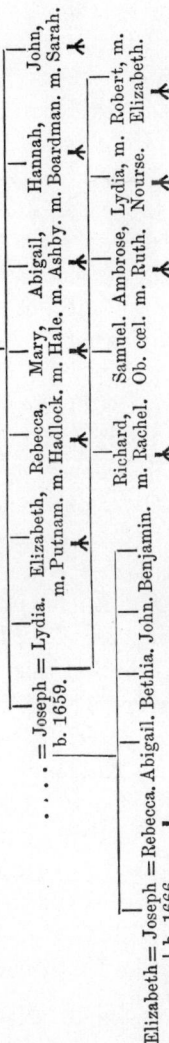

. . . . = Joseph = Lydia. Elizabeth, m. Putnam. Rebecca, m. Hadlock. Mary, m. Hale. Abigail, m. Ashby. Hannah, m. Boardman. John, m. Sarah.
b. 1659.

Elizabeth = Joseph = Rebecca. Abigail. Bethia. John. Benjamin. Richard, m. Rachel. Samuel. Ob. cœl. Ambrose, m. Ruth. Lydia, m. Nourse. Robert, m. Elizabeth.
b. 1666.

Joseph. = Abigail Goodall. Ruth, m. Huchinson. Bethia, m. Putnam. Ebenezer, m. Hannah. Three infants. Elisha = Ginger Porter.
b. 1690.

Col. Israel H. = m. twice.
Descendants still living.

Joseph = Hannah. 2. . . . . Ruth, m. Elliott. Abner, m. Elizabeth. Josiah, m. Sarah. Sarah. Elizabeth, m. Nichols. John, m. Lydia.
b. 1722.

Elizabeth, m. Goodale. Hannah, m. Elliott. Elisha = Sarah Buxton. Mary. Hannah = Joseph = Widow Goodale.

Andrew = *Martha Bayment.* *Jesse* = *Polly Learitt.*
b. 1775. *b.* 1778.

Elisha, m. Nancy. Joseph = Sarah Curtis. Archelaus, m. E. Hutchinson. Levi, m. Betsy.
b. 1782.

Nathaniel = *Lucinda Pearson.* *Stillman, m. Emiline.* *Sixteen children. The Singers. Ten of the sons married and had families They went to Minnesota.*
b. 1798.

Everett. *b.* 1825. *Ann Jane.* *b.* 1827. *Alvaro Oliver.* *Stillman Hubbard.*

Hiram. = Mary Ann Lufberry. Joseph. Mary, m. G. P. Hutchinson. Elisha, m. Ruth.
b. 1808.

Alcander = Henriette de Loyauté. Abraham Lufberry. Sarah. Mary. John. Charlotte. Hiram. Charles.
b. 1833.

Renée-Caroline. Marianne. Barnard. Hiram.
b. 1859.

The St. George Pedigree dignifies William Hutchinson of Wykome or Wykeham Abbey, as the eldest and principal representative of the whole and entire family; but as in 1581 a grant of arms, different and distinct from the preceding, was made to one Edward Hutchinson of Wickham in the county of York, son and heir of Richard, who was however believed to have gone to Ireland, the Colonel concludes this Richard, appearing in the Pedigree, to be the same Richard whose son had Wykeham and the grant. He writes thus:—"This sufficiently establishes the parentage of Edward Hutchinson, whose father was, I suspect, the Richard Hutchinson, son of Anthony, last named, whom St. George supposes to have gone to Ireland." This extensive shuffling of the cards, after St. George had arranged them, and accompanied by the words "I suspect," can scarcely be accepted by genealogists as conclusive or satisfactory, but at the same time, having a desire not to be unbecomingly dogmatical, I will not deny what I cannot disprove.

The Harleian MS. in the British Museum, 18,011, &c., gives a short Pedigree of four generations, immediately pertaining to the recipient of the 1581 grant, and this achievement is thus described in Heraldic language:—*Per pale Gules and Azure, a Lion rampant Argent, within an Orle of* 16 *Cross-crosslets or.* Crest.—*A demi Wyvern Argent, scaled Azure, beaked, crested, and wattled Gules, issuant from a Ducal Coronet Or. Literas patentes hor. armorum concessæ Edwardo Hutchinson, per T. Flower, Norroy, an°* 1581, 4 *July.** Col. Chester insists that this was a *confirmation,* and not an original *Grant.* His words are:—"The fact that this was a *confirmation,* and not a *grant,* of arms, of itself proves that the arms had been borne by the family from time immemorial." Where is the evidence that it was a confirmation? There is no evidence given but the bare assertion, and this assertion is made in the face of the word "*concessæ.*"

To the cadet branch of Thomas Hutchinson of Owthorpe, the St. George Pedigree gives but two sons—William and John, but Col. Chester asserts with confidence that he has discovered

* By an accidental misprint, the word is June instead of July, in the New Eng. copy.

a third called Lawrence, if not a fourth named Robert. And then of this third son he observes:—"As, in my opinion, the descendants of this third son are now the only living representatives of this ancient family"*—what! the only representatives now living? Thus, at one stroke, he sweeps out of existence the whole family. By so doing he gives great prominence to Lawrence, the said third son, from whom he deduces the House of Salem, for which he was working. This kills off all the descendants of Julius, the Editor of the Life of Col. Hutchinson; and yet I have a certain knowledge of a number of them now living, who have succeeded in right of birth, to sundry heirlooms and family property. The following letter from a grandson of Julius to me, will make all this very clear:—

"Tisbury Vicarage, Salisbury, Oct. 26, 1885.

"Dear Sir,

"I return you the Pedigree you have been good enough to send me, by the same post. The early part of it seems to be simply transcribed from that in the quarto Edition of Mrs. Lucy Hutchinson's Memoirs: but in the latter part of my branch of the family there are numerous errors; e.g.,—My grandfather [Julius, the Editor,] lived at Owthorpe some time, and sold it, though Col. C. says it had previously passed out of the family. I never heard of my grandfather being in the East India Co. service, and do not believe it. He was a Fellow of New College. His father had an estate at Mardock, in Herts., and on the death of his uncle unmarried, he came into possession of Owthorpe, the old Hutchinson property, Hatfield Woodhall, the ancient Boteler estate, and 4 other manors; but many were encumbered by his uncle, from whom he inherited them. He himself was very improvident and hasty, and sold his estates. He married Frances Goodwyn, sister of Gen. Gordon's great-grandfather, only daughter of Henry Goodwyn, of Maize Hill Castle, Kent. This gentleman was in early life, in the E. India Co. Service, which perhaps led to Col. Chester's statement, that Julius Hutchinson was in the E. I. Comp. Service.

"His second son Charles was my father; my mother was a Baldwin, of Lancashire, grand-daughter of the Duke of Chandos, some of whose property, handed down from the Princess Mary, and sister to Henry VIII., I inherit. I have no family: but my brother Pierrepont has 4 sons. The Elizabeth mentioned as daughter of

* New Eng. printed copy, p. 9.

Julius, was my annt Lady Dryden, of Canons Ashby, of whom there is a numerous progeny. Col. Chester has made strange errors in his Pedigree, as he knew my cousin Sir Henry Dryden, who is an excellent genealogist, and has gone to him for information. I shall at any time be happy to shew you various pictures and heirlooms of the family, and a silver gilt cup given by Q. Elizabeth to Sir Francis Boteler, including some of Lucy Hutchinson's manuscripts, and an old Boteler Pedigree, which my grandmother preserved, if you will give me a day or two's notice of your visit.

"Believe me,
"Yours truly,
"F. E. HUTCHINSON."

If Colonel Chester were alive I would give him my mind. Painful as it may be, the cause of truth requires that such errors should not be hushed up and concealed. The accuracy and the pride of literature consists in its trustworthiness. How is it that the historical and the genealogical writings from the country to which he belonged, should be too often received in Europe with mistrust? If that nation sees its interest, as well as its dignity, it will do its best in trying to stamp out this patent evil.

How sang the Swain to the Shepherdess?

He—"Where shall I go for Truth, my dear?
I've searched the world both far and near."
She— "Go here, go there,
Go any where,
But not to the Western Hemisphere."

As regards coat armour, Col. Chester makes no allusion to the first grant, in which the field was semé of Cross-crosslets, with a Lion guardant, and a Cockatrice on a Wreath, for a Crest, which is the bearing that strictly belongs to the Owthorpe branch; and he assigns the second grant, of 1581, to the son of Richard who was supposed to have gone to Ireland, which bore a Lion non-guardant, and surrounded with an Orle and a Crest of a demi Wyvern issuing out of a Coronet, which Richard was a younger brother of Laurence's father, so that Lawrence, not being descended from the recipient, could not in any way inherit it. An inspection of the Tabular Pedigree given in the early quarto Editions of Lucy Apsley's Life of her husband, makes all this very plain.* Yet the Colonel gives him an altered version of it, which, in fact, is a mixture of the two, for it has the field semé, and a Cockatrice of the first grant, and the Lion non-guardant, and the Coronet, of the second. And to this mixture is assigned a Motto. It is the motto of the Earl of Donoughmore—*Fortiter gerit Crucem,* transposed, not very classically, into—*Gerit Crucem fortiter.*

The descent from this Lawrence is carried on through Thomas, and Thomas, to Richard the great-grandson, who married Alice Bosworth; and this Richard is declared to have been the one who proceeded from England to Salem in or about the year 1635, taking with him this first wife and five children, The proof that the Richard in England and the Richard in America were one and the same person may be supported by the re-appearance or recurrence of the several names of the different members of the family in the Registers of both countries; but there is not so much stress laid upon this important mode of evidence in the Pedigree, as there might have been.

Supposing the continuity of the family from England, and so across the Atlantic to America, to have been satisfactorily established, the English portion may be put aside as done with: the more modern or American portion I have already reviewed, assisted as I have been by the copious particulars put into my hands by the family, some years before the services of Col. Chester were required.

The Colonel made out his American part from similar materials obtained from the family, but he took some trouble to search the American records as well. In this portion he has not killed off one branch after another with the same facile hand as in the English part, but he has done what is equally misleading—he has utterly ignored and passed by in silence the entire elder branch of Elisha, with his two sons, and his grandsons, and his great-grandson Everett, and the sixteen children of Jesse, and the ten sons who married and all had families.

* Let me remark that the arms engraved under the portrait in the quarto editions, are entirely wrong. Perhaps they did something to mislead Col. Chester.

This multitude, which belongs to, and represents the eldest branch of that stock in America, by being thus kept out of sight, would not be known or suspected to have an existence. In the printed Pedigree, where speaking of Elisha, page 29, we are told who he married, and then the notice of him ends by saying that he "died at Amherst, 12th of October, 1800." Not one word of his numerous descendants. The casual reader, or indeed the enquiring student into this genealogical tree, would be deceived into the belief that the younger branch alone comprised all that now remained of the family. In the light of truth this is not as it should be. I must protest against this mode of making Pedigrees. Some Pedigrees are dear and some are cheap; and if a case could be found where a Pedigree has cost upwards of £400 sterling, it would be rather hard if it should turn out to be not worth 400 pence.

II. *Hutchinson of Charlestown* is the next branch of the great parent stock that claims our notice. For upwards of 250 years its long succession of members have maintained a quiet and steady course of industry on their own estates, or in other ways to the good of their country, and to the advantage of themselves. Their domestic history seems to have been kept with care and fidelity, and their descent through nine generations from their early planting at Charlestown to the present time, bears the stamp of accuracy, from the number of the particulars and the regularity of the dates. It is not known with certainty where they had resided in England prior to their migration, but George Hutchinson, and his wife Margaret, appear in the records of the Colony as the first of their name in Massachusetts. To Mr. Calvin Gibbs Hutchinson of Dorchester and Boston, a worthy representative of this early stock, I am indebted for many particulars which I prize highly. Respecting this first couple he writes:—

"George Hutchinson and his wife Margaret were early settled in Charlestown, Mass. They were dismissed 14th 8th mo. 1632 from the Boston Church, and on Nov. 2d 1632, united with 33 others in forming the First Church in Charlestown. John Harvard, founder of Harvard College, was afterwards a pastor of this church.

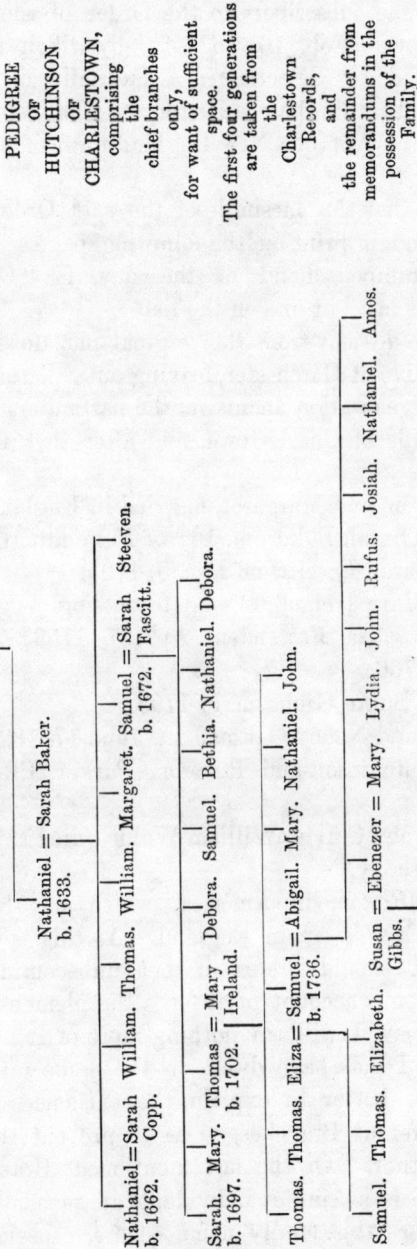

PEDIGREE OF HUTCHINSON OF CHARLESTOWN,
comprising the chief branches only, for want of sufficient space. The first four generations are taken from the Charlestown Records, and the remainder from memorandums in the possession of the Family.

GEORGE HUTCHINSON = Margaret.
Went to America about 1631.

Nathaniel = Sarah Baker.
b. 1633.

Nathaniel = Sarah Copp. b. 1662. | William. | Thomas. | William. | Margaret. | Samuel = Sarah Fascitt. b. 1672. | Steeven.

(children of Samuel and Sarah Fascitt:)
Sarah. b. 1697. | Mary. | Thomas = Mary Ireland. b. 1702. | Debora. | Samuel. | Bethia. | Nathaniel. | Debora.

(children of Thomas and Mary Ireland:)
Thomas. | Thomas. | Eliza = Samuel = Abigail. b. 1736. | Mary. | Nathaniel. | John.

(children of Samuel and Eliza:)
Samuel. | Thomas. | Elizabeth.

(children of Samuel and Abigail:)
Susan Gibbs. = Ebenezer = Mary. | Lydia. | John. | Rufus. | Josiah. | Nathaniel. | Amos.

(children of Ebenezer and Susan Gibbs:)
Susan. | Ebenezer. | Elija Gibbs = Nancy Oakman. b. 1798. | Silas Whitney. | Mary. | Abigail.

(children of Elija Gibbs and Nancy Oakman:)
Susan Gibbs. | Calvin Gibbs = Roxanna. b. 1836. | George Oakman = Leonora.

(children of Calvin Gibbs and Roxanna:)
John Calvin. b. 1857. | William Waldo. Ob. cœl. æt. 19. | Alice. | George Anthony.

"George is one of the subscribers to the Order of the inhabitants of Charlestown, (Feb. 10, 1634–5), by which they agreed to be governed by Selectmen: a facsimile of the document is given in Frothingham's History of Charlestown, and this is the beginning of our New England form of town government."

I may add to this, that the facsimile of the said Order is inserted at page 50, and in print on the following page. The signature, in the cramped hand of the day, is "Geag Huchinson," and is the last but one on the list.

The following is the descent from the original pair down to the present representative at Dorchester, leaving out collaterals. Down to the fourth generation inclusive, the particulars are taken from the Records of Charlestown, and after that from family papers:—

1. George Hutchinson, and Margaret, married in England.
2. Nathanial H. and Sarah Baker, m. 16th of 1st month 1659.
3. Samuel H. and Sarah Fascitt, m. Dec. 5, 1695.
4. Thomas H. and Mary Ireland, m.— date missing.
5. Samuel H. and Eliza Fessenden, Ap. 27, 1758: 2ndly Abigail Flagg, m. in 1766.
6. Ebenezer H. and Susan Gibbs, m. in 1793.
7. Elijah Gibbs H. and Nancy Oakman, m. June 17, 1825.
8. Calvin Gibbs Hutchinson and Roxanna Parker Hill, m. March 4, 1857.
9. Four children—John Calvin, William Waldo, (died 1879), Alice, and George Anthony.

III. *Hutchinson of Boston*, in America, which has been called *Hutchinson of Lincolnshire*, in England. As this is the Governor's Branch, I should prefer, if not unbecomingly obtrusive, to reserve some account of it for a Supplementary Chapter. With this view I will say nothing more of it here. I have a feeling that I may have dwelt on the name rather long, but I thought it better to explain the existence and particulars of the different Branches, so as to prevent their getting confused together. Of the last mentioned Branch, I do not think there is a single individual at present in America; so that where this family name occurs, especially in the northern portion of the Continent, it probably belongs to one or the other of the two first described above.

Before resuming the regular narrative of events, it may be permitted to quote a short passage from the Diary of Elisha, in which he mentions an event as occurring in Birmingham—an event worth giving, as exhibiting the debased morals and low sensibilities of the people at large, only a short century ago. It runs thus:—

"1782, Jan. 23.—Cloudy—rain in evening. Walked into town and found the High Street, from Cross to Cross, thronged with people, to see a woman carted and whipped. Public discipline being very unusual in this town, always brings the multitude together."

Public discipline and public opinion are now at variance. Happily we have advanced. Such a barbarism, and such an outrage on public decency would be hooted down in the present day by the lowest of the people.

The war was not yet over, but many persons thought that the game was nearly played out, or that they could espy at no great distance—the beginning of the end. The capitulation of Lord Cornwallis seemed to bring things to a crisis. In his Letter Book, writing to Mr. Edward Lyde on the 5th of May, 1782, Thomas Hutchinson says:—

"The great change which has recently taken place in the political world here, I dare say surprized you much. I hope and think the Loyalists of America will not be sufferers by it. The new Ministry are very popular: the voice of the nation seems to be for peace—more especially with America. Whether this can be effected without a general one, seems to be more doubted now than when the change hapned."

And again, to the same, on the 2nd of January, 1783:—

"We look upon the war as at an end in America, and hope to hear private animosities subside."

The situation of the Loyalists and Refugees was looked upon as critical and painful, and a general feeling of anxiety existed amongst them.

"Those Loyalists from Massachusetts," he writes to his brother, on the 31st of January, 1783, "who are in town, or some of them, met at Sir Willm Pepperell's last week, to debate on what was proper to be done in the present precarious situation of compensation for losses and sufferings. I have heard it hinted, two Noblemen at the head of the old Administration, had signified to Sir Willm the propriety of an application to Parliament at this time; but do not vouch for the truth of it. At the meeting they only desired Sir Willm to endeavour to find out the opinion of those Noblemen, and also of the present first L^{d} of the Treasury before the next meeting, which is to be to-morrow. This is all I have heard of the matter. The New Hampshire men have also enlisted under G. Wentworth, to consider what is proper for them to do." &c.

To some unnamed friend whom he addresses "Honble and Dear Sir," he writes, on the 20th of February, 1783:—

"The settlement of peace, and throwing the Loyalists on the mercy of their inveterate enemies, is truly deplorable; but we now have no remedy left, unless the humanity of the nation should interest itself in our behalf. I think this should, and I hope it will be tried: the present Administration discourage the attempt at present; and when the matter cools, it may be too late."

To his nephew Andrew Spooner, on the 22nd of the same month and year:—

"The conclusion of peace will undoubtedly make a great alteration in the circumstances of England and America. I hope both may be bettered by it; but I suppose much will depend upon the returning cordially [*sic*] of each to the other. We wait with impatience to hear what reception the peace met with on your side the water: the disposition here seems to be to bury the hatchet."

Upon the prospects of peace there arose among the Loyalists a very natural desire to know what chances there were of recovering any of their lost estates. Andrew Spooner was in America, and his uncle Thomas, in the following letter, requests him to make enquiry:—

"Brompton, 31st Mar., 1783.

"Dear Nephew,

"This being the first direct opportunity from hence to Boston, I embrace it to write you a few lines, tho' I am yet without any advice of your situation, and what your reception has been in your native country. I have before wrote you three letters, two of which I think went by the way of Halifax, but as possibly all may have miscarried, I will mention that in them I wished you to give me the most particular account you were able, of the state of what was my father's interest in America. I should like to know who are the present holders of it, and what each part sold for. I have lately been informed the farm at Conanicut had not been sold a short time ago. Mrs Sanford's farms I hope are in the same situation; nor can I think you will meet with much difficulty in procuring her rents for her, she never having rec^d^ a farthing from this government, and her quitting the country being a thing she could not avoid. I was very sorry to hear of the death of Mr Cheseborough, who I dare say, would have been friendly, had he lived. Both your grandfather Oliver and my father had a considerable interest in lands at the eastward, about York, at what was called Phillip's Town. There were many proprietors —Mr Cushing, Mr J. Adams, Dr Warren, and others who I do not recollect. I wish to be able to ascertain what the Oliver and Hutchinson interest was: perhaps you could get a particular acc^t^ of these affairs from Mr Oliver of Salem. We have heard nothing from America since the peace was concluded. If advices should be such from thence as I sincerely wish they may be, it's not unlikely you'l see many returning there before another winter. Mrs Grant died about two months ago, and Mr Flucker is also dead."

After so serious a quarrel the return to feelings of amity was slow. Those who expected to see England and America hurry to embrace one another with cordiality as soon as the sword had been laid aside, were disappointed. On the 7th of June, being nine weeks after the preceding, he says to the same person:—"I could hardly have thought it possible so long a time could have elapsed since the peace, with so little intelligence from America. What has transpired I own does not altogether please me, for I wished to see a mutual returning cordiality between the two countrys. May it yet take place!"

The attempts suggested above to try and ascertain the

situation, extent, and circumstances of the different lost estates, shew that no delays occurred in paving the way to their recovery if possible. This was a long and tedious process, extending over many years, and eventually succeeded only in part. Amongst the materials from which this work has been compiled, there is an old map of the New England Provinces in case, measuring 39 inches by 42, bearing date Nov. 19, 1774, by Thos Jefferys, Geographer to His Royal Highness the Prince of Wales, near Charing Cross. It is to the scale of seven miles to an inch. The long narrow island of Konanicut or Conanicut, stretching north and south about ten miles, appears in Narragansett Bay, opposite, and to the west of the city of Newport, in Rhode Island, where the Sanfords, originally of Boston in England, had settled down: and "the lands at the eastward, about York, at what was called Phillip's Town," I take to be at or near the York laid down in the old map, a place situated near ten miles north of the mouth of the Piskataqua river. In subsequent letters, and as long as the efforts for sale or recovery were pending, the expression "the Eastern Lands" is of general use; and I presume that by this expression the lands near York are intended.

The majority of the Refugees who had withdrawn to England whilst the storm was raging, desired to know on what terms they could return again to America now that the atmosphere was clearing. Some of them, however, discovered that the door was shut against their return. Colonel Benjamin Pickman was now in England, and was anxious to know in what odour he stood with the Congress, or with the more settled form of government in what was now being called the United States of America. Sabine informs us that this gentleman was born at Salem in 1740, and graduated at Harvard University in 1759. He was a merchant, a Representative to the General Court, and a Colonel in the Militia. And he quotes John Adams, who in 1772 said of him, that he was very upright, sensible, and entertaining: that he talked a great deal, told old stories in abundance about the witchcraft, paper money, &c. And Sabine proceeds to say:—"In 1774 Colonel Pickman was an Addresser of Gage. He went to England. In 1775 we find him a guest of Governor Hutchinson, and the next year a member of the Loyalist Club, London. In 1778 he was proscribed and banished. A year later his house was at Bristol. In 1783 he was in London, and saw M[rs] Siddons play Jane Shore at Drury Lane Theatre,"—and that brings us to the date at which we have now arrived. Being in London, he wrote to Elisha at Birmingham, what is now a brown and dilapidated-looking letter, in the following terms:—

"London, 18th June, 1783.

"D[r] Sir.

"Various are the reports circulated with respect to the dispositions of the inhabitants of the United States of America towards the Refugees. It is generally thought that all may return except those who have taken [up] arms against them. Cap[n] Tho. Napp [?] is arrived from Newbury Port, but brings no new intelligence. I have not received a line from America since my leaving Birmingham; unless I hear soon from my friends, I shall determine to remain in England untill next spring, and shall return to Birmingham, where we will pursue the pleasant walks you formerly mention'd. I hope you will not have explored all the country before my return: however, there is little danger, if the weather at the Five Ways is the same as it is in London—extremely rainy.

"I dined on Saturday last* with Sir William Pepperell, in company with M[r] Palmer, lately arrived from Surinam—looks very yellow, and is much emaciated.

"I send you the Franks, and think you had better use one before you know my determination about going to America. A vessel will sail in a fortnight for Boston.

"Pray remember me to M[rs] Hutchinson, the Judge, Miss Clarke, and the Doctor.

"I am Y[r] Friend and Ser[t]

"BENJ[N] PICKMAN.

"P.S.—I shall be obliged to you if you will send the enclosed to 27 Colemore Row."

And Sabine further adds—"He returned to Massachusetts, and in 1787 the Legislature restored citizenship, and a part of his confiscated estate. He died at Salem in 1819, aged seventy-

* He was writing on Wednesday.

nine. Gentlemen of his lineage are of great respectability in his native State at the present time."

Thomas Hutchinson the Governor's eldest son, or "the Judge," as he might be styled for distinction's sake, since he had been Judge of the Probate Court for the county of Suffolk in Massachusetts—was losing the robustness of his health—or he thought so, which was the same thing to his mind, and he had been advised to think of a milder climate in the winter; yet he was only 43 at this period, and he lived on for 28 years longer. The original letter here subjoined will reveal his sentiments on this point:—

"Brompton, 24th Sepr, 1783.

"Dear Brother,

"I returned here on Saturday last;* my health is better than it has been, but I cannot call myself well. Some friends advise me to go to France, or to one of the warm Islands. My own intention was to return to Brighthelmstone in ten days or a fortnight, as my coming up was of necessity. I am much at a loss what course to take, but could wish the application to the Commissioners might be made before I leave the town again. Silvester [Oliver] thinks his brother [Daniel] will be in town this week. I know not what the lands at the Eastward were, as to quantity or value. Perhaps you might think the affair deserved a journey, but you will judge for yourself.

"I am Yours Affectionately

"THOS HUTCHINSON."

The journey to France was decided on, and Elisha came up from Birmingham to join in the expedition. Dr. P. Oliver writes in his Diary:—

"1783. Octr 13.—Elisha and family set out for London, for France.

"Tuesday, Oct. 28.—Tommy and Elisha Hutchinson set out for France from Brompton.

"30th.—They arrived at Calais in 3½ Hs—all very sick."

Chief Justice Peter Oliver, on the 14th of October, wrote after Elisha before he had sailed, when he said—"I advise you to keep a Diary of your proceedings and expenses: much

* It was now Wednesday.

future satisfaction may be derived from it." I fear this good advice was not very rigidly attended to, as I cannot discover any evidence of it amongst the family papers. They proceeded to Nismes in the far south, and on the 7th of December the Chief Justice wrote such a letter to Elisha as nobody else could have written, and being the original, may perhaps be worth giving entire.

"Brummichameaux, Decr 7th, 1783.

"*Monsieur!*

"*Faites vos reflections la-dessus, et daignez me communiquer en reponse*—the dogs take your French,—it is so like the chattering of a monkey—you shall never have another line of it from me, and I hope never to have a word of it from you or yours. I only wrote the above to let you know what I could do if I would, and that inspiration hovers over Colemore Row at my command:— and now, my dear Sir, I come to the purpose.

"I received your kind letter from Calais some time since, and you would have received one from me long ago had I have known the direction. Yours of 7th Novr at Paris, and another at Nismes, of 22nd Nov^{r}, I received this day: but I was most pleased with your being fixed near Nismes in so good health, and satisfaction with your winter quarters: for your uninterrupted success, health, and spirits, be gratefull; and do not think, because you are now in the regions of romance, or in fairy land, that the bubble will never burst. Enjoy what you can without being unmindful of those whose affection follows you to your every situation. The itinerary you promise me from Polly: tell her that I ever have received her letters, upon any subject, with parental affection and pleasure, and that I shall think, whatever postage I may pay for so distant letters, will be money better laid out than in the funds, as I shall always have the interest of it at my command.

"I wish to hear of your brother's confirmed state of health: to him, to Sally, and to their children, I tender my kind regards. I enclose my love to Peggy, Betsy, Mary, and George: tell them to buy the biggest and lightest French box that they can buy at Nismes, and lock it up safely: let Peggy keep the key, and peep at it once per day: but I fear it will all evaporate from a French box; so that I believe that an English wicker basket will be more retentive.

"Now for ourselves—

"You boast of your day or two's cold weather: we have been so unhappy as not to have had one: a most uncommon November, without a gloom to hint at a suspension, immersion, or scarification: it is now pleasant and moderate. You rumble in the English papers with your balloons: we have ours too, which travel 50 miles in less than three hours:—nay, more,—we have had a machine made in Birmingham, and which is now on exhibition in London, in which a man can transport himself by wings to any distance, and steer himself through the air as a bird. It extends from the tip of the wings near forty feet. The man's name is Miller: I believe you have heard me speak of him. Donisthorpe, Whitmore, and Gill made the nice machinery. If it succeeds all the balloons will burst: but *cui bono?* no one yet says.

"Cousins Daniel and Louisa keep a true bachelor's and maiden hall at the Five Ways: none are permitted to visit but Mr Galton's and our family. Louisa is as well as usual, and would be better if she chose it: she can bear an evening's walk from Colemore Row. Kitty hath got a pretty tabby kitten for her company; but as it is not sufficient, she is now going to live in London on her mother's invitation.

"We have a trunk of diamonds and a bundle of letters left here for your wife by Andrew Spooner, which are so sealed that I shall let nothing leak out of them: he carried a letter for each of you to London, which I suppose you may have received. We have had a number of Americans in town lately, as Silas Deane, Geyer, &c.; four of them supped here two nights ago, viz.—Mr H. Bromfield, Prentice, Austin, and Brewster. I could ramble on; but enough to convince you that English paper is larger than French, and that a Birmingham man can crowd more into it than a Nismes inhabitant can into his: such as it is, you have it, and a remembrance of you from Colemore Row, Five Ways, &c., will leave no more space than to tell you that he who fills it is "Your affectionate friend,

"P. Oliver."

PETER OLIVER.
Chief Justice of Massachusetts.

The expenses of travelling were very serious. We must, however, bear in mind that the party so travelling was a numerous one. There is a Dr. and Cr. account, ranging from the time they started to January 1784, which will shew what could be done for how much money :—

Cash Account, T. and E. H. since Oct. 1783.

1783. Oct.	Cash pd. E. H. at Brompton . .	2 2 0		By the several payments on acc. E.H. to Messrs. Drummonds as settled at Dijon	688 2 4
	Do. pd. Charles, Servant . . .	3 3 0		Bal. on this acc.. .	145 8 2
	Do. travelling trunks	8 3 0			
	Do. Hire coaches to Dover . . .	12 12 0			
	Do. E.H. at Dover	8 18 6			
			34 18 6		
1784. Jan.	Bills brought with me . .		400 0 0		
	By Messrs. Danforth and Rashleigh, as settled at Dijon		398 12 0		
			£833 10 6		£833 10 6
	To Cash paid E. H. since 10th Dec. 1783. . . .		448 6 9	By account, several payments on acc. E. H.	688 2 4
	To ½ travelling expenses .		326 12 8	Bal.	86 17 1
			£774 19 5		£774 19 5

My chief satisfaction after looking at the above is this—that they were able to afford it.

At this date there is another original characteristic letter in the handwriting of the Chief Justice, and as it would be hard to separate and disentangle his jokes from the mention of a few political facts—and facts are always valuable—the whole may as well be taken together. As leading up to this point, there will be no harm in just mentioning a few occurrences that had then recently taken place. Lord North and his Ministry resigned March 19, 1782. Rockingham Ministry formed and met, after which Parliament was prorogued July 11, and assembled again December 5, in the same year, at which time the strange coalition between Lord North and Mr. Fox astonished the country. Disorganization of the Ministry, and interregnum in February, 1783. New Ministry met April 2, and close of the Session July 16. More shuffling of the cards in December of the same year:—And Chief Justice Oliver to the rescue in January 1784:—

"Birmingham, Jany 18, 1784.

"And I am glad, my Dear Sir that I have contributed one drop from the Heliconian fountain to quench your epistolary thirst; but perhaps, as the *gutta cavat lapidem*, by pouring draught after draught, I may possibly create a nausea, which your appetite may reluct* at.

"Your letter of the 27th Decr past, threw me into my former predicament when a boy of 4 years old; then I thought it the completion of happiness, when an uncle or aunt gave me a gilt figure on gingerbread; it then pleased my fancy and gratified my appetite; thus, between your cold water and my gingerbread, the account between us is balanced.

"I arrange my subjects under politicks, and domestick life;—the first being of the greatest importance, let me tell you that the Wheel again revolves: it stood still some time for want of greasing: at last the Coalition carried through the House an East India Bill by a great majority. The House of Lords thought it an infringement upon the prerogative of the Crown, and upon the rights of the people also, and it was there negatived by a small majority—upon which the King dismissed all his Ministers, and appointed Lord Temple to the first Commission in the Treasury, and Chancellor of the Exchequer, and Mr Pitt one of the Secretaries of State; Lord Gower President of the Council, and Lord Thurlow, High Chancellor. Ld Temple, after acceptance, resigned, and Mr Pitt is now in his place. After this Ld North made a bold speech, and declared Mr Fox to be his best friend, and that he would support him. Mr Pitt hath lost one vote, but he doth not flinch. How it will end time will tell. The city of London supports Mr Pitt.

"In the East Indies, in last June, there were two hot battles,—by sea, and by land: Sr Edward Hughes lost many hands, and

* Or feel a reluctance at. From the Latin *Reluctor, aris*; dep., to struggle, to wrestle against. In Bailey we have, To reluct, [*reluctare*, L.] To be averse to, strive against.

it was a drawn battle. Sr Eyre Coote was dead, and Col. Stuart fought a much superior force, and came off victorious. After these actions, the news of peace arrived.

"You ask about America. Congress is despised by all the Governments, and they are in that disorder which I suppose will occasion some convulsions. They had a great shock of an Earthquake at New York the latter end of November, after the troops had left them. Nova Scotia populates fast—60,000 already. When America is overstocked with English manufactures, they will be ready for another war with England. France hath protested Congress Bills, and the Congress Financier hath clipped all the English and foreign gold to pay their subsidies. Mr Clarke hath heard from sister Cabot, and that she was tolerably well. John Temple and his wife are arrived in London.

"Now for domestick news.—The Five Ways remain where you left them. Birmingham as busy as usual. Butter at 12^d^ ℘ pound. Gingerbread at the old price. Guinea coiners now in the dungeon. Your garden thrives amazingly; but what is of serious importance, Mr Pott desires to know of you what he shall do with the cow—she is dry: as also, what price to have, or what to do with the rails, and shall be glad of your directions: and what is of the greatest importance of all, Mrs Pott paid me a guinea some time since for you. I have wrapped it carefully in a paper for your orders: It distresses me so much in my custody, and burns in the paper when I think of it, that I fear its setting the house on fire. If you wish me to send it to Sr John Lambert, your orders will be obeyed; if not, a dose of laudanum every night will assuage my sleepless hours: and so Sir, with maids', wives', and batchelors' Hall compliments,

"I am Your Humble Servant,

"P. OLIVER."

"Dear Polly.

"If you will not write to me, I will to you: indeed, I have heard that there is a letter for me upon the road from Nismes. If I was very apt to be impatient, I should be so now, for I have expected it for some time past. Remember, that the post is the quickest and safest conveyance, and a few shillings for postage, I can save out of apples and oranges.

"I am much pleased to hear of your pleasant situation, and hope you will enjoy much health, and that the purpose of the journey will be answered, by a compleat restoration of Mr T. H.'s health. I have heard much of the antiquities of Nismes: you will certainly attend to them.

"While you enjoy your vernal sun, I have here enjoyed an American snow-storm, and an healthy cold air. Farenheit's thermometer hath been here at 20 degrees, and it was the first cold day which I have felt in England, but it was agreeably cold; and as you are not fond of such severity, I am glad that you did not suffer it.

"I shall expect that your Itinerary will give me the descriptions of places, and their distances, for I cannot yet learn how far you are from Birmingham: how soon or late you may return I have no conjecture, but whenever it may be, be sure, return unfrenchified in thought, word, and deed. I shall then expect to hear of the Alps, and that you had seen the passage which Hannibal made through them with his vinegar: and if you should take an airing to Rome, measure the height of the Tarpeian Rock, that I may know whether a man or woman may now break a neck by a leap from it. Mr Gimlet, who lately married Miss Barrs, died last week. Kitty is going to London to her brother.

"I have no more room but to add my sincere wishes that you may be under the protection of a kind Providence as to your health and conduct, and to assure you of the inviolable love and friendship of

"Your Affectionate Grandpapa

"P. OLIVER.

"Miss Peggy!

"I hope you are in good health, and that you have much improved in reading and needlework, and that you will have no more occasion to go to Mr and Mrs Korkland's school.

"Miss Betsy!

"I shall expect to see you come home a woman. There is a fine tabby kitten to play with: she will bite, scratch, and play without hurting you.

"Miss Poll!

"How do you do? There are more dogs than two now. Be a good girl, and then I shall be glad to see you.

"Mr George!

"Cart and horses enough: don't cry and make a noise, and then I will love you.

"All of you be good, and mind Pa and Ma."

Sir John Lambert, mentioned above, was residing in Paris, and the letters were sent to him, to be forwarded to Nismes.

The children, separately addressed, were those of Elisha and his wife; all of them died during their years of adolescence. The youngest child John, afterwards Editor of the third volume of Governor Hutchinson's History of Massachusetts, was not born for nearly ten years after this period. On one occasion, when I was staying with him at his Parsonage, (now Vicarage,) of Blurton, in Staffordshire, he said to me in the Library, laughing, that he had recently made a discovery—that in turning over some of his father's papers, he had found out that he was a seven months' child. The fact however, was of no consequence: he was a strong, active, and healthy man, both in mind and body, and attained to the age of seventy-two.

The Chief Justice went up to London on matters of business in February, and what he did or did not, and what he had to communicate, are best revealed in his own words. Just before starting, he despatched a missive, in which he speaks of the severity of the winter as follows:—"On Christmas Day our snow fell, and is not yet gone, but is snowing on to add to the heap: such a winter hath not been felt in England for eight years past. Freezing of many persons—the canal here hath been froze for two months past—at Gainsborough in Lincolnshire, a boxing match on the ice—drowned eighty-six persons out of ninety." Of political matters he writes:—"Our political wheel stands still. Ld N. and Mr F. still oppose the Prime Minister Mr Pitt, to prevent his carrying a vote; and what the consequence will be—whether a dissolution or a new coalition, is not determined; and all publick business stagnates. The House of Lords have addressed the King against the East

India Bill of the Commons, and on his dismission of the late Ministry, and where it may end, time will discover. There are also addresses from many parts of England and from Ireland on the subject." We next find Mr. W., whoever he may be, playing at the unpleasant game of hide-and-seek:—"Your friend Mr W—— is here incog.: he hath given all up in England, and whether that will do, I fear he is going to America in the spring. I pity him." He continues:—"Parson Walter is arrived from Nova Scotia: many other Refugees are come. America is in a bad plight—they will lose their whale and cod fishery, and Nova Scotia will ruin the four N.E. governments." Fortunately for the United States the rueful prognostications of the Chief Justice were not verified. "Mr Randolph," he says, "died last week, and Brigadier De Lancey is like to die by an apoplexy, if not dead." The Mr. Randolph here mentioned can be no other than John, who had been Attorney General for the Crown in Virginia, but retired to England, and died in London, January 31, 1784, which was "last week" to the writer of this letter to Elisha, bearing date February 9. Oliver De Lancey, the son of Stephen, a French Refugee, and Ann Van Courtlandt, of New York, was a stanch Loyalist, and held the rank of Brigadier General in the King's service. Lorenzo Sabine, in his valuable work of reference, mentions several of the name and family. This one, now "like to die by an apoplexy, if not dead," lived on however to another year, and, as Sabine says, "died at Beverley in 1785, at the age of sixty-eight."

And now being in London, his son the young Doctor, informs us in his Diary how and when they got there. He writes:—

"1784. Feb. 20.—On Friday my father and Miss Clarke went to London in the two-days coach, and on the evg of the same I went in the Swan post coach, [and] arriv'd on Saturday 1 o'clock.

"I saw Major Upham my old friend, Dr Jeffries, Mr Saunderson, &c. &c. &c. I stayed in London above three weeks, and returned heart sick of it, without effecting my business with the Commissioners of the American Department."

Very likely. All those who petition their Governments soon get wearied out by official delays, objections, difficulties, and any sort of excuses that can be laid hold of. And now, being in London, the father wrote to Elisha as follows:—

"London, March 5th, 1784.

"My Dear Sir,

"I have not received a line from you since the 27th Decr last, tho' I have impatiently expected one. It is true, I have just now heard that there is one for me at Birmingham, but do not expect to see it these ten days, so that you will not expect an answer to it.

"I have been here a fortnight, and have got into Chancery Road, and am where I was when I set out; but publick affairs are in confusion. The East India Bill drove off all the old Ministers; and Mr Pitt, the new one, cannot carry a vote. The Commons have addressed the King twice, to dismiss him, as having no confidence in him; and twice hath the King replied that, as no specific charge is against him, he could not do it, especially as the sense of the nation is for him, as expressed in very numerous addresses in his favor. Thus publick business stagnates, and it is very probable there will be a dissolution soon, for taking the united sense of the people. The city of London is stanch for Mr Pitt, and Westminster cool to Mr Fox. The former dined in the city last Saturday,* and was drawn by *asses* instead of horses, and on his return had his coach broke, and his life endangered. He is to go again next Saturday, and to take or give t'other knock: and so, fight D—— fight B——

"Mrs Startin sailed for Boston in *Callahan* last October: was 70 days out: met with a terrible storm: the fore mast lost: put into Halifax to refit and get provisions: sailed in a few days: and after being two days out, was lost in a storm on the back of Cape Cod, after having narrowly escaped with life, by being forced to be let down on a sailor's back, who went down by a rope from the vessell to the shore. They have heard from her in Boston: she was going to New York to meet her husband: the vessell lost, and the cargo much damaged. Unfortunate lady! I hope she will never part again from her husband untill their final dissolution.

"We have had the severest winter for nine years past: it sot in 25th Decr, and is but just quitting its hold. I left poor

* It was now Friday.

Mr E. W. at Birmingham, where he had been incog. about a fortnight. Many months are now open [fair weather]: he hath taken a passage from Liverpool for America in all this month: he seems to be hurried, and I am afraid *worse* than nothing. I am glad you have saved your debt.

"Mr B. Thompson [Count Rumford], the American Secretary, hath better luck: he is Adjutant-General and Aide-du-Camp to the Elector of Bavaria, and a rank of Colonel there. He was lately Knighted here, and is soon going to his post. There is one piece of good luck. Ingersol of Great Barrington, is lately married to a fortune in Norfolk of £500 ₽ year, and 5000£ in reversion:—there is another piece of luck; and those are all the pieces of good luck for Americans.

"Mr Mather's wife is like to die, and Mr Boucher hath lost his wife.

"I forgot Borland's good or bad luck. He is married to a lady at Bristol of £1500. His mother is married by this time to a Mr Knight of Rhode Island, who first courted her.

"I left your Birmingham friends well, except Louisa, who keeps house too much to be well.

"There are some letters in town for Polly by Capt. Murray from Halifax, to be delivered by himself, from Miss P. Winslow. If I can, I will forward them. Mr Winslow and family are there. Mr Walter is here, having left his family at Port Roseway. Col. Ruggles hath built him a large house near to Annopolis: they settle there very fast. The whalemen are leaving Nantucket for Nova Scotia, and the New Englanders will suffer extremely by overacting their importations, and English merchants suffer by them. Mrs Haley sails for Boston this month with 15 or 16 Bostonian passengers. Dr Cooper died lately, by which France, they say, hath got rid of one pensioner. S. Adams hath become insignificant, having quarrelled with Hancock. In short, there will be trouble enough among them soon, and if the Act of Navigation subsists, the 4 New England Governments are ruined.

"Miss Clarke says—

"My love to all,
Both great and small;

and if you can convey mine at the same time, it will save you trouble.

"Pray how is your brother? Tell my dear Polly and her little ones I want to hear from them and see them, as soon as possibly it will suit them.

"I am in great haste, as you may see, and so, lest the Bellman should pass by, I wish a good night.

"Y[rs] Affectionately

"P. OLIVER."

"Queen Anne Street, East, No. 78."

The political events, and the Parliamentary changes of the spring of 1784, constitute the most solid, and therefore the most generally useful portions of the letters of the Chief Justice at that rather critical period. The fact that his relatives were abroad, and were thirsting for English and American news, served him as a spur to action; and without such spur these letters, of which several original ones are preserved, would not have been written. His chief correspondent was Elisha—perhaps because Elisha had married his grand-daughter, of whom he was extremely fond. After a few humorous remarks, of no moment or relevancy, in a letter of May the 17th, he speaks as follows:—

"The Parliament hath been dissolved some time, and this week the new one meets. There had been so many Addresses for a new Ministry, that it was thought most prudent to have a new choice, and it is probable that M[r] Pitt will have a majority of about 120. M[r] Fox hath been chose for some part of Scotland, and I suppose will be for Westminster, unless a scrutiny prevents. It is surprising what arts have been used in his favor. The D[s] of D——re [Duchess of Devonshire?] and some other noble Ladies, have degraded themselves much in parading the streets for him; and if we may believe some of the papers, have lowered themselves by the ladder of indecency. Many riots have happened in Covent Garden, at the Election, and last week a Constable was killed; several are in custody; the Foot Guards were ordered out, and L[d] J. Sp——r had like to have lost his life by a bayonet. Many riots in different parts of the kingdom. L[d] Sheffield is ousted at

Coventry, and Sr Sampson Gideon and Mr Wilmot were Chaired there. Cruger for Bristol in the room of Daubeny. Ld North's chance at Banbury was critical. Col. North lost his election. Ld Lewisham lost his for Staffordshire. Ld John Cavendish his. Mr Bacon is out for Aylesbury.

"Among the Scotch Peers, L^{ds} Marchmont, Glencairn, Rosebury, and Lauderdale, are left out. Several new English Peers are created, as Sr James Lowther, L^{d} De Ferrars, son of Ld Townshend, created Earl of Leicester. Lord Paget, Earl of Uxbridge. Lord Bulkley, an English Baron. Noel Hill, Baron Berwick, with several others.

"As to American news, the Loyalists are used very ill: the State of Vermont in arms against New York. Mr Startin and wife have again met at New York, after having lost her baggage; but I hear that *he* hath recovered his lost household stuff at Philadelphia. Parson Appleton is dead, ÆT. 92.

"As for domestick news, we have little. I do not hear Louisa talk of leaving Hagley Row: she mends this warm weather. We have had winter till within this fortnight, but now the hills smile, the fields laugh, and the valleys sing for joy. The winter extended to or from America, for in March they sledded [slayed] across the Delaware, to and from Philadelphia. Your neighbor Mrs Galton, hath lately brought a daughter and son, and is well. Mr Pickman hath left Birmingham, to reside at Mr Lane's in London, in expectation either of going to his family, or receiving his wife in London. Manufactures full of hands. Mrs Taylor of Moseley, dead.

"Mr Watson, who had engaged his passage at Liverpool, I hear is in London; but Mr Green says he doth not know where.

"As you talk of a removal, I suppose that you are now on Classick ground, and therefore I have begun my letter in a Classic form, and I design to finish in the same manner, and so S^{r}, Miss Clarke salutes you all, and wants much to hear of the children. Salute your wife and children for me. Salute also your brother and his family, but not in the manner in which you salute your own, unless it should suit you. Farewell.

Dated at Birmingham, May 17th, 1784. *Memo*—We have no calends here.

More last words, to fill up.

"Mr Copley is not in the Exhibition this year. He now exhibits his Major Pearson, and again his Lord Chatham,* for what they call raræ show.

"Thirteen oxen, forty sheep, eleven calves, two and twenty cows, four peacocks, nineteen rabbits, a bunch of asparagus, head lettuce, salmon radishes, brilled shad, and a good fat hen"——

Here the page ends, and the next is missing. Surely the reign of George the Third was a very troubled one. Never did party contention run higher, or open violence more disgracefully assert itself. The attention of the nation was now fixed upon the proceedings of the new Parliament, which assembled in the spring of 1784, on which event the same writer, on the 2nd of June, thus informs us:—"The Parliament hath met, and Mr Pitt hath 160 or 170 majority, but the State arrangements not yet made. Mr Fox's elections for the Orkneys and Westminster are disputed; but if ousted of both, somebody will make room for him. The waggoner's store by me hath a barking dog to keep off mischief; and a barking fox, or even a cackling goose may save the Capitol. London hath celebrated Handel's Jubilee in Westminster Abbey with above 500 vocal and instrumental performers, and exhibited a scene of astonishment unequalled in history. The profits will be above £12,000 [or, it might read 14,000] for charitable uses."

Of the new impost called the Receipt Tax, he makes this remark on the 21st of June:—"Notwithstanding Addresses and other opposition, the Receipt Tax is confirmed in Parliament. It has sent in £12,000 already. One Member of the Commons says he hath paid above £400 since March. It will bring in £200,000 ꝑ year, tho' calculated at but £100,000."

On the 8th of July he writes:—"The St. Omer's hero [Burke] hath been hissed out of the House—Raynard is humble. New taxes on coals, hats, windows, gauzes, horses, and ribbonds, and what-not are issuing, and people generally say—'It must be so.'

* The painting of his Lordship's illness in the House is probably meant.

"Mrs Macauley Graham is gone to America to settle a code of laws for them; and a woman is like to be the only hero to save them. Mr Pickman's son is here in town [Birmingham] with his father, and the father is like to go to America soon, and take his chance. He saith he hath received your letter, and will answer it before he goes.

"Thank your brother for his kind letter, which I received in your packet of Decr, and which came to hand 2 or 3 days since: I design to answer it soon.

"The Prince of Wales had like to have lost his life, by riding his horse between two post-chaises. He hath been ill, but the papers say he is better.

"Tell Polly I am obliged to her for her Itinerary:* it hath given us all around great pleasure . . .

"Fox's scrutiny is going on: and at the present progress of it will take up 9 or 10 years, and cost £300,000, according to computation."

Pass we next from the father to the son, the young Doctor of Medicine, who, on the 27th of July in this year 1784, poured out a lengthy lamentation on the rudeness of the times, the ingratitude of supposed friends, and the curses that were going to fall upon the English nation if the loyal Refugees were not speedily indemnified for their sufferings and their losses: and all this he wraps up in a sheet of fools'-cap paper, and directs to his brother-in-law Elisha Hutchinson, at Dijon. Being at Birmingham, he says:—

"I live now in Newhall Street, No. 28: was oblig'd to take refuge here from Colemore Row, since the last week in December last, after having been robb'd of several articles, and my life in the utmost hazard from my drunken landlord; for we are obliged to put up with every insult from this ungrateful people the English, without any redress—as witness our cruel neglect from those who have publickly declar'd in our favour. What are Commissioners chose for?—not to make good our losses. What are all the promises of protection and retribution? but to mortify, insult, and disappoint. I have

* This Itinerary does not seem to have survived till the present day. There is no appearance of it.

the best authority to say we are well off if our small pittance is not taken from us. Blessed are ye who expecteth nothing, for ye then will not be disappointed. Enough of this disagreeable subject. I wish never to hear more of it. This is my faith—If this nation does not make the Refugees compensation for the losses they have sustain'd, as far as is in their power, a curse will befall them sooner or later.* I am inclined to think that the curse is already begun.

"I have no business yet, altho' I have posted my name and profession over my door, according to the fashion of the country . . .

"Yr old friend Jon. Jackson has been here and called upon the Judge; and several other of that class of wretches who deserve the halter or the leaden draught. He bragged here of being a member of the Congress.

"Frank Waldo died lately at Tunbridge.

"Mr N. Hatch, about a fortnight since, cut his throat at Pangbourn soon after a cheerful dinner.

"I am sorry the Refugees have begun the English custom of taking leave.

"Ben Pitman has been at London—I met his son—and been here again to take leave, as he intends for America. Mr [blank] of Salem sails in *Callahan* about this time.

"Dr Chandler goes out Bishop of Nova Scotia, where the wise heads here have got a plan formed. His favorite daughter died last spring.

"My old friend Upham I met in London, as cheerful and agreeable as ever, altho' he is Major, and supported by Sr G. Carleton, who has befriended him surprisingly. He goes out under his patronage, and no doubt will be well provided for.

"Cousin Bill Oliver's wife died lately at St. John's.

"Cousin Peter and wife reside at Worcester, with part of the Regiment.

* This last alarming sentence the Doctor has underlined. I leave out the stress on my own responsibility, thinking it strong enough without. The Doctor should not forget the condition in which England found herself at that period—overwhelmed with taxes, and an enormously increasing National Debt, and only just emerging from a long and expensive war with nearly half Europe, besides her American colonies. However willing she might have been, it was hard to satisfy so many claimants.

"Lieut[t] Gov. [Thomas] Oliver and family are going to live in Ireland. His eldest daughter Mary is to be married ere long.

"Bill Jackson has married a smart widow in London, of £6,000; and wonderful to relate, Tom Boylston has given Ward Boylston £12,000, to join with the late Alderman Turner deceas'd, his partner in the sugar baking business; and £12,000 more, if that is not sufficient.

"Andrew Spooner has wrote us since he arrived in America, dated in June, that Sally Seever is going to marry Tommy Russell.

"The widow Borland is married in America, and two of her sons.

"Daniel Bliss's daughter has married a Capt. in the 8th Regiment in Canada.

"Thus you have all the little matters of intelligence, saving that the State of New York are arming themselves to fight the State of Vermont, as they have both confiscated each others estates. Respecting some individuals—tarring and feathering frequent in America, and likewise in Ireland.

"You have not had such a hodge-podge letter a great while.

"My children send their love to all. All join with me in wishing health and happiness to you all.

"Adieu. Y[rs] affectionately

"PETER OLIVER, Jun[r].

"The greatest prospect of hay and corn here in England that has been known for several years."

Thus the father and the son between them, contribute to inform us on the passing events of the day. Fragmentary as the scraps are, they must not be despised if they are so many facts, for facts saved out of the darkness of a past age, are like stars in a dark firmament, and one fact—by which I mean one modicum of truth—is worth more than ten pages of fiction. A fortnight after the preceding, the father took up his pen, and addressing himself on the 9th of August to his former correspondent in France, he shews that though the prevalence of a long war had interrupted industrial pursuits, ruined some, and impoverished many, now that that war was over, those who had suffered so much were looking up their resources and collecting their energies, in order to try and repair their shattered fortunes by a return to the occupations of peace under the Ægis of legal security. English merchants were eager to re-open business with America, and were volunteering large consignments of goods to that country, quite forgetting that at that juncture America was not in a condition to pay for them. The Chief Justice puts the case in the following terms:—

"I am glad that you are content to defer your shipping goods to America untill further advice, for we have accounts from Boston, that the new traders who have been over, write that the country is so overstocked with goods, that they are not able to make speedy remittance. We have also an account from Virginia that their House of Assembly have passed a resolve, that no debt shall be paid to England, untill England hath paid £500,000 for their lost Negroes; and I shall not be surprized to hear that other Provinces adopt the same Resolve; and that Massachusetts insists upon the pay for the destruction of Charlestown, &c.; so that you will have an opportunity on your return, to be satisfied whether you are right or not in your adjournment of adventures. I have not forwarded any one letter which you sent to me.

"Mr Pickman hath sent his son with Mr Mather and his wife to Boulogne to learn French. He was here [at Birmingham] last week on an excursion from London for his health, and seemed to be much out of health and spirits, and a little wasted. He seemed undetermined about his return. I pity him, for he hath heard of the ill health of his wife; and his fears of the sea, and of an ill reception, worry him. Miss Clarke bought a dozen of cotton hose for Mrs Brimmer at 5/6 ℘ pair, and delivered them to Mr Pickman, who promised either to take them with him, or deliver them to some careful hand for Boston.

"So much for business.

"A new Province is made on St. John's river, and called New Brunswick. Genl Carleton's brother, Col. Carleton, is the Governor, and the General to be Govr General of Canada and all. Col. Willard with a thousand Refugees, I hear, is embarking for Nova Scotia, so that they will encrease rapidly, and I suppose that our Province will sink as they rise, for none can return to it without the expense of Naturalization. In the Jersies,* they naturalize their returners by tarring and feathering; and it costs them more in scrubbing and cleaning than an admission is worth, so that you know the fate of treading your *natale solum.*

"Our public affairs go on as swimmingly as your air balloons. Wray and Fox, after 8 or 10,000£ expense, have got as far as to have 25 votes on each side rejected, and with £20,000 more they may finish by the dissolution of this, or the next Parliament.

"Poor Mr Hatch died about 3 weeks since by his own hands; and if the Refugees do not make haste for Nova Scotia, others may be forced to the same.

"I am obliged to your brother for his kind letter. I am loth to put him to the charge of postage: he will have the short detail of news from you. Tell him I rejoice to hear of his and family's welfare. I often think of them, and want to see them. I hope for his return to a good situation in England: my sincere regards await them.

"We have just heard from Mr Startin, in New York. He had been sick—nigh to death, but they were in hopes that he was out of danger. Poor Sally! I feel for her.

"I understand Mr Watson was to be here, and that he was going to America. He hath been in Holland; but where he is to be, must be left to futurity.†

* Jersies is not the correct plural of Jersey, any more than monies is the correct plural of money, though frequently so written. Our Grammars teach us that words ending in *ey*, simply require an *s* for their plural, as Jersey, Jerseys; money, moneys; storey, (of a house), storeys, &c.; but words ending in a *consonant* and a *y*, as *sy*, *ny*, *ry*, *by*, &c., turn the *y* into *ies*; as daisy, daisies; pony, ponies; story, (a narrative), stories; baby, babies; and so on. I mention this little matter because we often see the rule disregarded by some who are accounted writers of fair repute.

† It is not said whether this was a son of Col. Watson, and a brother of Elisha's wife. He seems to have been playing hide-and-seek, judging by the mystery hanging over his movements, and by the hints and innuendoes used in speaking of him: but whether he was suffering disgrace or a reverse of fortune, remains equally unexplained.

"I am glad Polly hath an excuse for not writing again: anything contributing to her ease I rejoice in. My affectionate regards to her and the little ones, which Miss Clarke sincerely joins in.

"Day, day!
"Y^rs,
"P. OLIVER."

"Elisha Hutchinson, Esq."

To his grand-daughter "Dear Polly," on the first of September, 1784, he says:—

"Young Pickman [gone to France], makes one American more; if you increase much more you will all be Bastiled, lest you encourage a revolt in France. His father left Birmingham and embarked for America, but being not well, he disembarqued; but I suppose is sailed by this time." Not at all! for on the 14th of October he wrote—"I understand that Mr Watson is gone to America. Pickman hath made two attempts; but the horrors of the sea, and terrors of tar and feathers keep him back,"

If the facete epistles of the Chief Justice have not palled on the reader's fancy, it may be announced that there are a few more of them bound up in the second volume of the Original Letters, where they are found in a group, arranged in consecutive order according to date. He appears to have been fond of writing, and as all the Hutchinsons were now on the Continent, he became the chief agent in conveying to them such scraps of news, political, domestic, or foreign, as by his industry he was able to pick up. He saw the comic side of most things; and he was not slow to reveal that side, and sometimes he did so in very witty expressions. Alluding to contemplated measures by the Ministry in Parliament, he speaks on the 9th of November, 1784, of a new tax, which in due course was passed, and which has survived to our own time, and which, from its wholesomeness is not likely to be soon abolished. He says:—

"They design a tax upon dogs, down to lap-dogs: I therefore advise you not to return till the tax is expired; for if you have a large breed of the latter, you may find it very heavy upon you."

There was a great outcry in the country against this tax; but that is not to be wondered at, seeing that in our own day every new tax raises a howl—not that it touches everybody, but everybody grumbles lest it should. My late parents were too young at the time to understand, or to trouble their heads about such subjects; but I can well recollect having heard them say that they could remember hearing grown people giving vent to their anger at its having been imposed. There was an immense slaughter of dogs upon the occasion. Those only were saved that had recognised owners, who were willing to pay for them. All the rest were condemned to extinction. The measure was a wise and a wholesome one, in so far that it cleared off a quantity of half-starved mongrels, that prowled about the streets, and infested the alleys, both to the annoyance and the danger of the inhabitants.

Under the head "American Thermometer" he writes:—

"The Congress clipped the guineas down to 17/., but they pour in here by weight. Pennsilvanians and Connecticut men have had a battle on the Susquehanna: several killed, and prisoners in Pennsilvania; and the latter have sent up recruits.

"New York and Massachusetts have quarreled about their lines, and some killed. Trade to America stagnates. They have had a terrible hurricane at Jamaica, and at Hispaniola. Dr S. Gardiner, of 80 years, is married to T. Goldthwait's daughter, of 28.

"I have just heard that Dr Chandler hath lost his only son.

Something has been lost at the end of the following letter, so that it terminates abruptly, and it is without any signature; but the reader will have no difficulty in guessing who was the writer:—

"Birmingham, Decr 6th, 1784.

"Dear Sir!

"Complaints avaunt! I received yours of 23rd October, the day before this, and now answer it.

"I have repeatedly heard from the Doctor at Tenby, where he is pleasantly situated, but fears he shall have no winter. As to us, we have got rid of November, but it was a very clever one.

"Upon the receipt of your last letter, I immediately wrote to M[r] Danforth for the American paquet, but he says that he had orders to convey what came from thence to you, which I suppose he hath done, and that you have rec[d] them. As to the £20, I shall send for it according to your order.

"Your fish is good—we have tried one, and shall reserve most, if not all the rest, for you. You insult us with your lamb, chickens, and grapes:—slunk lamb, and chickens dead with the pip in the egg, are surely very cheap with you: but know, we can buy such here at half your French price: the grapes, I know as well as the fox did, that they are sour, though cousin Jenny says—'No, no, Uncle: for I am sure I eat some when I was fast asleep one night last week, which they had brought over with them, as luscious as I ever ate in all my born days.' But uncle says that if she had been awake, they would have sot her teeth on edge, for they were the grapes of Sodom, and the clusters of Gomorrah.

"You have slipped into your letter a few words from some very uncouth language, that I have no other way to answer you, than by telling you that—*Wannanego huh, yaugahontuaraw menindungo yahhegonauhueconnasseteg weyontorego, huh! huh!*'* Don't forget this excellent maxim, for it sounds with harmony.

"You tell me that you are all Methodists, and expect that I shall be so too:—be it so:—and as I have almost done with you sinners, I will give you a word about the American saints. Their papers tell us of nothing but war and bloodshed in their frontiers: that seven sail of French men-of-war are in the Delaware river—but further says not. The Boston papers

* Having regard to the age and the country wherein the Chief Justice was born and brought up, and from the fact that in his day many remnants of the Indian tribes lingered still in Massachusetts, it is just possible that he may have picked up some knowledge of the native tongues: but whether the specimen above is facetious gibberish of his own coining to amuse the children, or whether it is *bonâ fide* good Massachusetts Indian, I must leave to those who have had a better education than I have. In New York I bought a Prayer Book of the Church of England service, printed in the language of the great Indian tribes; and on comparing what is above with this, there appears to be a strong resemblance between them in the style and character of the words. What strikes me most forcibly in the Prayer Book is, the remarkable length of some of the words. Several are of 26 letters each, and I have found one of 32 letters without break. I presume that these are compound words.

mention the deplorable state of their Province, for want of money—their Collectors being in jail because they cannot collect taxes. One American vessel is taken by the Algerines: another is drove off the African coast by the French: Scotch and Irishmen are sold in America in droves, but Massachusetts will not suffer them to be imported there. They have had bad crops in the northern parts of America for two years past: the manufacturers here have suffered greatly by them, and there is an universal stoppage of exportation to them.

"In England we are in political peace: the window tax shuts up windows, but the weather is so dark that several are opened again, finding candles to be dearer than windows. Dr Jeffries went up last week from Park Lane in a balloon with Blanchard, and in less than an hour and a half sailed twenty-one miles to Dartford, and wrote a letter to a friend, as he says—*far, far above the clouds.* Lunardi, the Italian, went up from London, and made above £2,000 by shewing himself after he came down. We have one a-going up soon from this town from the Five Ways, with two persons, one of whom is a Mr Sadler, a pastry-cook of Oxford, who hath already been up, and was the first Englishman who had made the voyage. Street robberies and burglaries are common in this town; many have been knocked down in the night. Your taylor Herbert had his shop plundered, and all his goods and cloaths; so that I suppose you have lost a pair of old velvet breeches, or so.

"Tell the children we have a pig of knowledge near us, who can tell your thoughts, your name, the year, month, day of the year, hour of the day, &c., and all this by picking out the letter of the alphabet, and the figures. It is a very genteel, well-educated . . . greatest curiosity of the quadruped . . . [paper worn out.]

"Lord Temple is created Marquis of Buckingham, and Lord Shelburne, Marquis of Lansdown—Bishop of Osnaburg, Duke of York. Parliament prorogued to 25th January. Two smugglers hanged, many taken, and the breed pretty well destroyed.

"Lord George G——n hath been at it again, and he takes

so much pains to get hanged, that it is almost a pity he should not be gratified."

The rest is missing.

At last it appears that in the beginning of June 1785, Elisha and his family at all events, returned to England. We owe this piece of information to the same hand that of late has done so much to lay before us the current events of the time, and he welcomes the new arrivals as follows:—

"Birmingham, June 4th 1785.

"Dear Sir!

"I have received yours 23rd May at Paris; and by yours to cozn Daniel, I find you safe arrived in London, but am sorry to hear that my Polly is not well. Tell her it is of great importance to her to nurse her cold. We rejoice at your safe arrivall, and hope to see you all here in health soon; and in the mean time accept of love and friendship. We cannot determine whether your brother and family accompanied you; if so, my love to them.

"I inclose to your care a bill of £50, the property of Miss Clarke, which she asks the favour of you to receive for her. Mr Pim lives in Threadneedle Street, No. 69. If you receive it, she wishes you could get it in to the same fund with the rest of her money; and as they do not take in less than £100, she says she hath a Bank bill by her of £50, which she will pay you on your arrival here, if you will advance that sum to make up the £100.

"As to your house, cozn Daniel says that his lodgings are ready for him in Temple Street, at Mrs Hallowell's and cousin Louisa's also, at Mrs Neal's new house, near to yours. Your rooms are ready—swept, and garnished: strawberries, Indian corn, and other fruits, all flourishing; and the tenement at the further end of the garden, swept and garnished too; so that all things and matters are ready for occupation.

"Further says not,

"P. Oliver.

"P.S.—He further says, that he wishes you would not mention the £50 bills while you are in London: as also, he advises you to buy your stock of candles at Kensington, for he assures you, upon trial, that they are as cheap at 12[d] ꝑ pound, as the best here are at 8[d]. If you buy any tea for yourselves, buy 3[lb] or 4[lb] for me, of the old 12/- sort."

There is however, the transcript of a letter in the handwriting of the elder brother, of June the 9th, which shews that the two brothers, with all their belongings, returned to England together. It emanated from Brompton, and was addressed to Andrew Spooner, who was in America, and is couched in the following terms:—

"Brompton, June 9th 1785.

"Dear Nephew.

"My brother [Elisha] and myself, with our families, arrived here a few days ago from France. Hearing there is a vessel upon sailing for America, I have enquired for some person to whom I might safely trust the note-of-hand of your grandfather Oliver,* but unsuccessfully as yet. However, I send this to let you know of my arrival in England, and that I wrote you in an answer to yours of Dec[r] last, by a M[r] Pickman, which I hope you have received. I have not been here long enough to know the state of my affairs, nor what course I shall take next.

"Your Affectionate Uncle,

"T. HUTCHINSON."

"M[r]. Spooner."

Soon after arriving in England the brothers proceeded to count the cost, and square up their accounts with each other, and in doing this there arose an amicable contention between them, over a balance of £62 3*s*., which Thomas declared was due to Elisha, which the latter could not see, and so he refused to take the money. The statement of accounts was the following:—

* Spooner's mother, Margaret Oliver, was a daughter of the Lieut.-Governor.

Dr. E. H. with T. H.		Expenses Journeying. Cr.	
To Bal. on Cash acc.. . .	145 8 2	1785. June. By the am. expense, Journey to and from Nismes . . .	245 5 9
To cash recd in France, more than half travelling charges	86 17 1	By £70 charged in acc. as settled at Dijon, not taken up by E. H.	70 0 0
To do advanced E. H. en route home	20 17 6		
	253 2 9		
To Bal.	62 3 0		
	£315 3 9		£315 5 9

Brompton, June 13th, 1785.
Errs. Exceptd
T. H.

Writing on the 7th of July, Thomas remarks to his brother —"I send a copy of the acct I meant to have given you had you called, as you promised, and will pay the £62 „ 3 to your Order." But Elisha repudiated the money. Upon this repudiation Thomas wrote to explain, and ended by saying— "You must be mistaken in your calculations somewhere." And so perhaps he was, for he still hesitated; whereupon an *ultimatum* was dispatched, which probably settled the question, for we hear no more of it.

But another and a far more important question now arose to engage their attention. The anxieties attending the uncertain position of the Refugees in England had been great, and their altered circumstances served to keep their anxieties constantly before their eyes. Many there were who desired to return again to America now that the war was over, and in that country to put themselves above want by a resumption of their former occupations. The strong prejudices however that existed in the young Republic against the reappearance of expelled Loyalists amongst them, the necessity for taking the oaths and of becoming naturalised, and the assertion that some who had ventured to return had been imprisoned, or tarred and feathered, were facts that deterred many from taking a decided step. Efforts were at all events being made to recover private debts that had perhaps been contracted before the war began; also to recover rents in arrear from estates that had been temporarily abandoned; but chiefly to take proceedings to try and recover property of various descriptions that had been seized, occupied, or confiscated. Andrew Spooner, who had gone out to America, had acted as a sort of Agent for his relatives now in England. Writing July 4, 1785, to Mr. Daniel Vose of Milton, he said—"I gave my nephew Mr A. Spooner, who went to America in 1782, a list of some debts due to me there, which I took off from my books in a hurry, and among the rest, put yours to me at £106,,3,,6." He found afterwards, that in his hurry, when going to France, he had placed it too high, when he corrected it accordingly.

In the same way he exerted himself on behalf of his sister-in-law Grizel Sanford, who for some time had received no rents from her property at Conanicut, and had suffered much inconvenience in consequence. And in 1785, addressing himself to his nephew on the 17th of August, he says—"I thank you for the account you have given me both of publick and private affairs on your side the Atlantick. I fear you are not yet in that tranquil state as to induce me to take a voyage, and become one of you: you know my penchant for American air." And he applied to a Mr. Taylor, latterly of Quebec, who had had £200 of hers in his hands for more than ten years, and he hoped that Mr. Taylor could make it convenient to return it. One of the farms had been leased to a man called Slocumb: the other was unlet, and he says—"I think the tenants in the old lease, were obliged to plant a certain number of trees annually, as well as to make a certain quantity of stone wall. I sometimes wish myself upon such a farm, where I could inspect the improvements myself; but I must wait till you are more settled and composed."

He was evidently hankering after a return to the American soil.

The claims of the Refugees for compensation for their losses were now being taken up by the English Government. At the commencement of this movement in 1783, he wrote to some "Hon^d^ and Dear Sir," and on the 15th of July he said—"You will see by the papers that Parliament have chosen a Committee for the purpose of investigating the estates of the Loyalists during the recess. May it not be worth your while to forward to England as particular an account of your losses of every kind as you are able?"

Commissioners were in due time appointed. The subjoined original letter mentions an award, taking into account the English laws of descent and primogeniture:—

"Brompton, Aug[t] 31st 1785.

"Dear Brother.

"As they begin paying at the Treasury the grants of 30 and 40 p. c[t], I called to-day to enquire for myself, when they gave me the memorandum as below. As I did not fully understand the distribution, I went immediately to M[r] Forster, who willingly searched the records of their proceedings with me. It seems they consider me as heir to all the real estate by the law of England, and that they had no power to proceed otherwise than by that law, the Will [of the Governor] being deficient to convey real estate. I enclose receipts, which it is necessary you should sign, and I wish to have them as soon as may be.

"I am

"Your Affectionate Brother

"THO[S]. HUTCHINSON.

"Pray let me know
"where I shall lodge y[r] mony.

"Order to pay	Tho[s] Hutchinson	£1860
	Tho[s] and Elisha Hutchinson as Executors .	150
	Elisha Hutchinson	60"

The sum of the above is 2070. The Loyalists were looked upon as people who had fallen between two stools—on the one hand, they had lost everything in America; and on the other, they could not expect much from an impoverished government, exhausted by a long war with various countries, and petitioned by a host of suppliants.

In a subsequent communication of Sep. 15, 1785, he explains the division he had made of the £2070; also, in stating his claims, the value he had put upon the mansion house, and store; and at what sums he had appraised articles of furniture, effects, &c. Thus he says—"Since I have been here I have made out every account due in America to T. and E. H. which, with all the notes of hand, I have lodged in the hands of a friend in the city, that they may be come at if wanted. At present I think there is much less chance than at any time for two years past, of anything being recovered. I shall acquaint you with my situation when fixt, and am, &c.,

"THO^S HUTCHINSON.

I put the Mansion house, which sold for £1200, as I estimate it	1000
My Store I valued at £200, I put at.	100
	1100
Say a payment at 35 p c^t . .	385
E. H. separate grant £60	

Total	2070	
T. H. ded^t . .	385	
	1685	
E. H. ded^t . .	60	
½	1625	
½	812	10
	406	5

T. H. . . .	1197	10
E. H. . . .	466	5
P. O. . . .	406	5
	£2070	0

Such is the memorandum of account appended to the letter. The autumn was approaching, and after some deliberation, he resolved to hybernate again in France. With this intention, about Michaelmas 1785, he crossed the Channel with his family and proceeded to the French capital—then to Blois—then to Mers-sur-Loire. From this place he wrote to his brother on the 19th of October, and amongst other things he said thus:—"Mers is a market town, but is inferior to Blois—about ten English miles nearer Paris, and as great a road as any in France. I found Mr Mather had lately removed from Beaugency, and he now lives about half a mile distance from me on the other side the town, and was instrumental in procuring me my house, having made acquaintance here, during his residence at Beaugency."

Whilst they resided quietly in that country hoping for better times, and chewing the cud of sweet and bitter fancy, Dr. Peter Oliver's Diary shews us that he and his father were applying to the tardy Commissioners for money in England; and it also shews us, that though a man may go forth and make the grand tour of Europe, or of Warwickshire, yet, if he returns back to his house with only one halfpenny in his pocket, he has lived within his means:—

"1786. March 12.—The Judge, Mrs Clarke, Mrs H., and myself, rode to London in the two-days coach, and return'd the 24 Inst. We went before the Commissioners, and soon was rid of them. They boggled about our want of proof, concerning the worth of our works.

"1786. June 26th.—I and the children went to Warwick in a post chaise: breakfasted at Knowle, then went on to Warwick . . .

"27th.— . . . thro' Castle Bromwich, and so home; and when I got to Birmingham I had but one ½ penny left.

"1786. Sepr 9.—A letter from Dowse at Caermarthen, giving me an acc^t of Bill Brown's hanging himself, Ap^l 30, —86: a most worthless character, the son of Govr Brown of Bermudas."

In spite of official delays, cold looks, and postponements, the Doctor persevered, and at last a brighter entry appears in his Diary—

"1787. July 27.—I had an order from the Commissioners to receive 660, as part payment for losses."

The £ is understood. His house in Middleborough, built and given to him by his father, was taken from him but was not burnt, as was the mansion of the Judge, known as "Oliver Hall." As regards the period of this act of incendiarism, the Rev. Doctor Andrew Oliver, writing to me Oct. 5, 1884, says—"I endeavoured in vain this summer, when I was in the neighbourhood of Middleboro', to ascertain the date of the burning of Oliver Hall; but I have no doubt, from all I can learn, that it was sometime during the year 1782, or a little after Mrs Andrew Oliver left it, which was early in that year. She was the Judge's daughter-in-law."

According to some family memorandums, she was Phebe Spooner of Middleborough. Her husband, the said Andrew Oliver, was born Sep. 15, 1746, and died Jan. 21, 1772, so that at the time the house was destroyed, she had been ten years a widow.

A florid account of this event had appeared in some of the

local Journals, founded on a narrative given by an eye-witness. During one of his visits to the neighbourhood, the Rev. Doctor had become acquainted with an old resident in Middleborough, who in his youth had known Mary Norcutt, the housekeeper of Judge Oliver, and she gave him all the particulars of what had occurred. After the fire the ruins gradually fell to decay, and it is difficult now to discover any traces of what once stood there, although several interesting relics have been picked up on the spot.

Besides a sum of money to console him for the loss of his house, Dr. Peter Oliver informs us that the English government granted him a small pension—

"Nov. 15, -88.—I took my oath before Squire Careless for the 1st time, to receive my quarterly Pension at £50 ℘ ann."

The Chief Justice also had to petition and press his suit, and bide his time, and exercise his patience, and the second paragraph of the following letter appears to refer to something of that sort:—

"London, March 18th 1787.

"Dear Sir.

"We are all going to Clapham, to dinner at Mrs Timmins's.

"I have been through the ordeal fire, and was treated with great politeness, and the Doctor also.

"I fully expect to be at home this week, after the ladies have had their frolic out.

"Dr Chauncy is dead.

"My love to the children, to Louisa and Daniel. Tell Polly to take care of home.

"Excuse this writing, having nothing but a rusty straggled nail to write with, and the Dr at the other end of the table, shaking it.

"Yrs P. O——."

It must be allowed that the writing is very bad for the Judge, his caligraphy being usually the very pattern of neatness.

I abhor long foot-notes in other people's books, and have no more love for them in my own, but the disagreables of life are sometimes determined to make themselves felt. The above is the last letter I see written by the Chief Justice; and it seems a pity that the few remaining scraps of information referring to the two branches of the Oliver family that came to England, all the members of which are now died out, should not be preserved. These scraps lie mostly in the Diary of Dr. P. Oliver. His wife Sarah died three weeks after her father the Governor. Their children were Margaret Hutchinson Oliver, born Jan. 7, 1771; Thomas H. Oliver, b. July 15, 1772; Peter, b. Sep. 23, 1774. There were also two infants, each called Daniel, who were born in England, but who both died young; as thus—

Dec. 20, 1778. Daniel born.

Ap. 26, 1779. Daniel died, aged 4 m. 6 days.

May 18, 1780. Daniel born.

Aug. 27, 1780. Daniel the infant died of convulsions.

Aug. 28, 1789. Thomas apprenticed to a Surgeon and Apothecary.

Oct. 14, 1789. Peter sent to sea.

Oct. 13, 1791. The Judge died this morning, aged 78 years, 6 months, and 13 days.

Oct. 19, Wednesday. My father buried under the new church, Mr. Welsh, Mr. Perkins, Mr. Palmer, Mr. Green, Mr. Cope, and J. Freer, Bearers.

Feb. 25, 1792. I put up a Monument in St. Phillip's Church, Birmingham, for the Judge.

July 17, 18, 19, 1794. P. O. [his son] appear'd to be dying slowly.

19th., abt. 9 o'clock P. O. died in the evening, aged 19 years and almost 10 months, wanting 3 days. He was the sickest person in a consumption I ever saw: had lost his voice almost 7 months, and a very bad sore throat most of the time: continual cough and expectoration: high fever: great prostration of strength, and loss of flesh. P. O. was buried in the new Cty, St. Chad's Yard, Wednesday the 23rd.

Sep. 20, 1796. Peggy [his daughter Margaret] died, aged 25 years, 6 months, and 13 days, after being sorely afflicted with a consumption, and the worst symptoms.

June 17, 1799. My birthday: 58 compleat.

Feb. 20, 1805. Gov. Pownall dyed this month at Bath, aged 85.

Jan. 29, 1808. Ld. Gage dyed.

June — 1808. T. Hutchinson, Jun. wife died. [This was Elizabeth Hagen, first wife of the Governor's grandson.]

Aug. 1809. Peter Johannot dyed this month in London, Agd. 79.

Dec. 1809. Sir John Bernard dyed in the West Indies, aged 65.

May 11, 1812. Mr. Perceval shot.

—— 18. Bellingham [who shot him] hanged.

The Diary ends June 28, 1821. Dr. Peter Oliver was buried at Birmingham. His last surviving child Thomas, the only healthy one of the family, reached the age of 92, and died at Great Yarmouth.

He was the last of that branch of the family.

There was however another branch in England. Lieut. Gov. Oliver, by his second wife, had a son named William Sanford, who m. Susannah Honeywell, and had a son also called William Sanford, and another,—"a son, whose death, in infancy, was caused by the rebels in Boston," as a note on the Pedigree informs us. The surviving son was in the navy. He m. Mary, my father's sister. Their eldest d. Mary m. her cousin and went to S. Africa; and Elizabeth Gertrude, the other, died at Sidmouth in 1829; and the son William m. his cousin Rachel H., and had a daughter named Elizabeth Mary, born May 22, 1842. William, the last male representative of this other branch of the Olivers in England, died Jan. 25, 1873, and his daughter, the last survivor of the name, died, May 12, 1876. Thus, as far as I know, they are all extinct in England: but the descendants of the elder branch, by the Lieutenant-Governor's first wife, continue to flourish honourably in America.

The second visit to France had now prolonged itself to the space of nearly three years, when preparations were being made to return. The first intimation of this appears in the Diary of Elisha at Birmingham, where he writes:—

"1788. July 18.—Fair and pleasant. Glass 14, 17. Walked to town after dinner. The Judge and Miss Clarke called, who came from Barr this morning. Cousin Louisa drank tea with us, who has a letter from her brother, [Daniel, or Brinley Sylvester], which mentions Nurse having arrived at Brompton Rowe last Sunday, having left my brother at Paris last week on Wednesday, which he was to leave on Friday, on his way to London where she hourly expected him."

"July 30th.—I wrote to my brother at N°. 83 Tichfield Street, who I heard had arrived from France with his family the 19th of this month."

A little incident occurred on the 20th which enlivened the quiet of Elisha's establishment. It runs as follows, though it is scarcely worthy of extract:—

OLIVER PEDIGREE.

The first five generations by the Chief Justice Peter Oliver in 1780: the remainder by Dr. F. E. Oliver of Boston, Massachusetts.

Owing to limited space, the full particulars are not given.

RICHARD OLIVER = ...
In England.

Thomas O. = Anne.
went to America about 1630. | d. June 3, 1635.

Cap. Peter O. = Sarah Nudigate. b. 1618. — Nathaniel O. d. 1633. — Nathaniel O. d. 1637.

Nathaniel O. . . . — Peter O. — Abigail O. — Daniel O. = Elizabeth Belcher. b. 1663.

Daniel O. d. young. — Daniel O. Ob. cœl. — Mary = Andrew O. = Mary Fitch | b. 1706. Lieut. Gov. of Mass. Bay. | Sanford. — Peter O. d. young. — Peter O. = Mary Clarke. Chief Justice.

Descendants believed to have all died out in the fourth generation.

Descendants believed to have all died out in the third generation.

Daniel O. — Elizabeth O. — Andrew O. = Mary Lynde. b. 1731.

Tho. Fitch O. = Sarah Pynchon. b. 1757. — Ben. Lynde O. Ob. cœl. — Andrew O. Ob. cœl. — Daniel O. Ob. cœl. — Peter O.

Tho. Fitch O. — Mary L. F. O. m. J. Story. — Andrew O. Ob. cœl. — Wm. Pynchon O. Ob. cœl. — Daniel O. = Mary Robinson Pulling. b. 1787. — Ben. Lynde O. Ob. cœl. — Sarah Pynchon O. Ob. cœl. — Eliz. Digby Belcher O. m. Freeman. s. p.

Fitch Edward O. = Susan Laurence Mason. b. 1819. — Peter O. Ob. cœl. — Andrew O. = Adelaide Imlay. b. 1824. — Mary Ellen O. Ob. cœl. — Katherine Seawall O. = Wm. Edw. Coale. — Isabella Louisa O.

Charles Edw. O. b. 1868. — Andrew O. b. 1869. — Others. — Mary P. I. O. — Catherine P. O. — Ethel L. D. O.

"July 20th.—Cloudy: intervals of sunshine: some showers. Glass 13.14.—in the evening fell to 8. About 9 o'clock two shabby looking fellows came and enquired for Mrs H., and when admitted, said they had found a trunk concealed in a barn in this neighbourhood; upon opening of which they had found papers, two of which they had carried to Mr Robbins, to whom they were tenants, one of them being named Grant, and that they were labourers in the Smith's shop, by name of Wallis, adjoining to Mr Robbins, in Snow Hill, where they had left the trunk, having carried it there for making a discovery of the owner, which they had done by applying at Colemore Row, and had come to give us notice, and would bring the trunk, which they accordingly did, Mrs H. not having missed it, although no one could recollect having seen it for a fortnight past. It is a trunk containing all her private letters and papers, none of which seem to be lost, though deranged. The two fellows appearing open and honest, and telling a straight story, I paid them for their trouble, and dismissed them.

"21st.—Fair and pleasant. Glass 13.17. Walked to town, taking George with me to some shops. Called on Mr Robbins, Snow Hill, who gave a fair and open acct, and a good character of the men who found the trunk. We imagine it was taken the night of [blank] having found the window open of a back chamber closet where the trunk was, the next morning, and broke, and the things deranged; but the children having amused themselves there the day before, we did not take much notice of it. They took some other small articles, but of little or no value."

On arriving in London, Thomas communicated with his brother, and in August 1788 he said:—

"As soon as I got to town, and was fixed in a lodging, I called at the American office. Mr Munro told me he was going to write me on the matter of claims made in America, and the value of the estate in Boston, and the farm in Rhode Island Government."

This subject, so closely affecting the interests of the Loyalists in general, is of frequent recurrence; and there are memorandums sufficient among the papers to shew how the family persevered for more than twenty years in their efforts—how they suffered difficulties, delays, and postponements—and how far they eventually succeeded in rescuing and recovering some portions of the value of their estates.

It was at this time that the King's mind visibly felt the strain of the momentous events that had taken place in the kingdom during the course of the last fifteen years: for, as head of the State, and not insensible to the great responsibilities attaching to his high position, from which all other men were free, the considerations bearing on the enormous demands that had been made on his loyal and willing subjects to maintain the dignity, honour, and safety of the nation through the vicissitudes of several long and costly wars, added to the uncertainties of their termination, amounted to an accumulation enough to try the strongest nerves.

Addressing himself to his brother on the 15th of November, 1788, Thomas briefly alluded to the national sympathy in the following sentence :—

"All London, except it be the most profligate part of it, are under the greatest concern for the King, and sincerely praying for his recovery. From what I hear, I fear the event."

Passing by one or two old letters from Grandmamma Phebe Watson, written to Elisha's daughter Mary, acknowledging the receipt of a letter and a Map made in needlework as a present for the Colonel, and explaining that Grandpapa is unable to write himself, or scarcely able to read the names of the places worked on it even with a magnifier, owing to the dimness of his eyesight—and also passing by, as of no great importance, one or two old letters from Roxbury, written by aunt Sarah Brimmer* to the same young lady in England, we will give a little attention to a large and suffering body of people, whose only crime had been that of fidelity to the Mother country. Driven out of the land of their adoption, they had fled back to the land of their ancestors, where most of them were strangers. Some pressed their claims for relief from the English Govern-

* I think Martin Brimmer married Sarah, one of the daughters of Col. Watson.

ment; others applied to the American Courts for recovery of the estates themselves; while others, despairing of success, gave up everything for lost, and sat down resigned to their fate. Sir Francis Bernard lost the valuable Island of Mount Desert, and Sir William Pepperell lost miles of coast line stretching away from Kittery Point to Saco, and extending miles into the interior. These unfortunate people were very difficultly placed —if they had joined the American party, they would have been Rebels to England: but when the war was over and they applied for the restitution of their estates, they were told they were Rebels to America. A Resolution of the Legislature of Virginia in the beginning of 1783, declared that all demands or requests of the British Court for the restitution of confiscated property, unsupported by law, equity, or policy, inadmissible. Adolph. iii. 503. Those who had openly borne arms against the Congress had little or no chance after peace had been established, but civilians stood in a more favourable position. Mr. William Vassell, a Refugee in England, frequently mentioned in Governor Hutchinson's Diary, finding that as the Federal Constitution had been adopted, a State could be sued; and Sabine informs us that he instituted proceedings against Massachusetts in the Court of the United States; and Mr. Hancock, who occupied the Executive Chair, was summoned as defendant in the case. His Excellency declined to appear; and soon after, the eleventh amendment to the Constitution put an end to the right of Loyalists to test the validity of the Confiscation Acts of the Revolution.

The Hutchinsons had very little chance of a favourable hearing in Massachusetts, but their prospects were brighter in Rhode Island on the one side, and in Maine on the other.

"I would observe," writes Thomas to his brother, on the 20th of May, 1789, "that it seems to be pretty generally understood and expected by those concerned, that a provision will be made for such Loyalists as have received no compensation, and who must suffer without it; as also, that where the compensation has not been adequate to the former allowance, a temporary one will be continued. A new list is every day expected at the Treasury, which will render this matter certain."

And in vol. iii. of the Original Letters, on the 27th he writes again:—

"I wrote you last week by M[r] Oliver that a revised list of temporary allowances was expected shortly to be made public at the Treasury. I am now able to acquaint you that you are continued at £100 ℘ annum, and I enclose a blank receipt for the quarter, to April."

Whilst these matters were under discussion, he projected another visit to France, and dating from Boulogne on the 23rd of July, he said to the same—

"Our journey and voyage were both executed very agreeably. We had a very easy five hours passage, tho' were all sea-sick, by reason of the swell of the sea, which we were not sorry for as soon as it was over. In less than a week Mary began to change colour, and to assume her usual spirits, which had for months been greatly changed, and I hope a little time will effect our wishes. This town exceeds the idea I had of it, having only before passed the upper part in the road to Calais: the environs are very pleasant, and the prospects more varied than common in this part of France. The great number of English families here who come to bathe, make it appear an English town. I must be governed by accidents as to the time of our stay, as well as to the course we take at leaving it. I have wrote to London to know whether any or what steps can be taken as to the American debts."

After a pleasant sojourn of three months he prepared to return, and not without being warned to provide for his personal safety, as appears from an expression used in a letter to his brother of October 13, wherein he implies that the ominous thunder clouds of some dire calamity were gathering over France, and that it would be safer to withdraw to England. The horrors of the Revolution manifested themselves in that country not long after. He says:—

"Not without some regret, on the 12th of last month we quitted Boulogne, thinking it imprudent to risque a winter's residence in a country circumstanced as France is at this time. I took the pacquet for the most western port we could make without inconvenience to sea-sick passengers. Southampton proved to be our goal, the wind coming on to blow a gale at west, we ran up the river thro' Spithead, the most beautiful I ever saw, after forty-eight hours very easy sail from our port, and almost without sea-sickness. We did not wish to return to London, and were without any fixed determination where we should stop. Southampton is a pretty place, but very extravagant is the living there. We proceeded on to Pool, which I think must be the cheapest town of its magnitude in the west, but it has a dreary country around it, and from its lonely situation, a kind of peninsula, did not please at all. We stopped at Lyme and Dorchester without meeting anything to induce us to fix. At Axminster Domett would fain have kept us a few days to make a trial of that town. Thinking it too small, tho' very pleasant, we proceeded on to Exeter, and I have taken a house at a mile from the town, but in the neighbourhood, the house furnished, and has every convenience about it, with about six acres of land—mowing, orchard, and garden stocked with fruit trees. I could have had my house and garden without the land, at £45, and am to pay £60 ℘ ann. for the whole. The last year my orchard produced 20 hhds. of cyder, and I begin to build castles in the air, but soon check myself.

"Thus my whole tour, since I left London, appears to me a work of hazard and uncertainty, tho', on reflection, I know not where I could have dropped with more conveniences about me than I imagine to have here.

"A. Spooner refers me to you respecting Eastern Lands. If I had a favorable opportunity I would forward the Bond, without discovering what the advantage can be in so doing; but as you have the date—sum—and know what has been paid, you can make the culculation as well as if in your hands."

He adds the following postscript:—"My landlord is a Mr Cotsford, a two hundred thousand pounder, and Member of Parliament, but I have never but once as yet, had any conversation with him." *

* At the date of their return my father Andrew was a boy of twelve or more, near half of which had been passed in France. He there got well grounded in the French language, and he retained his proficiency in it as long as he lived. He used to make me read 'Gil Blas' and 'Moliere' to him. He told me that when they were in France, some English friend wrote to his father,

Thus the family became settled in a respectable looking old house, built in the Queen Anne style, known as East Wonford House, in the parish of Heavitree, towards the sunrising from Exeter, and at about three quarters of a mile east from Heavitree church, where it still stands. The rent appears to be extraordinarily low. He would not bind himself to a lease, but took it only from year to year, for he still had one eye upon America, and if circumstances should appear encouraging, he cherished the idea that he might yet some day turn his steps, either to Massachusetts or to Rhode Island. This appears from a paragraph in a letter of February the 2nd, 1789, dated at London, and addressed to his nephew Andrew Spooner, who was in America acting as his agent. Thus he says:—

"The receipt of your letters of the 28th and 29th Novr, by Scott, makes it necessary that I should embrace the first opportunity of acquainting you that Mrs Sanford has not the least idea or intention of selling her estate in America, and if it were absolutely necessary for her so to do, I think it probable I should be myself the purchaser, having some views in regard to that country, which may or may not be put in execution, as circumstances occur."

Time went on: some of their friends wrote over to different members of the family, and tried to persuade them to come out at once, and some sent over the gossip of Boston. Aunt Elizabeth Russell—though it is not clear how the relationship was made out—wrote to Elisha's daughter Margaret, and told her the last news from Boston on the 20th of April, 1790.

"You enquire," she said, "after your old friend Miss Harriot Lothrop. You will start perhaps to hear she is going to be married, and for a moment discredit the intelligence; but indeed it is true, and the gentleman of her choice is a son of Parson Robbins's. 'Tis possible you remember him—Mr Chandler Robbins. I am told they are to be married soon:

and through some strange inadvertence, merely addressed the letter, "Thomas Hutchinson, Esq., France," and curiously enough the letter reached him. It arrived at an inn where they had been, but they had gone on. The landlord, at a loss what to do with it, stuck it up in the looking-glass. After a considerable interval they touched at the same inn on their return, when the landlord handed over the letter—rather stale in news.

she is a very fine young lady, possessed of a very good disposition, and very pleasing manners, but is too young to enter into the cares of a family."

The party seem to have been content with their new home. Among the bound-up original letters, there is one from Thomas to his brother, of May 19, 1791, in which he says:—"After eighteen months residence we continue to think this a very agreeable part of England; and perhaps I could not have made a better pitch than I have done."

In another of Nov. 22, 1793, he alludes to the birth of John, Elisha's youngest child, born Sep. 21 of that year, afterwards Canon of Lichfield, and Editor of the third volume of Governor Hutchinson's History, where he says:—"I have been prevented by some necessary occupations from answering your letter of the 30th ultimo sooner. We most sincerely congratulate you and Mrs. Hutchinson on the addition of a son to your family, and wish he may be spared to be a comfort to you both."

December 23, 1796, he writes:—"A few days after you left us M^r and Mrs Sabatier, neither of whom I had any knowledge off [of] before, came into Devonshire and took lodgings about half a mile distance from us. We found them both well informed people and pleasant neighbours. They returned to London the first week in Nov^r, with an intention of spending the next summer here." Mr William Sabatier was the descendant of a Huguenot Refugee, who visited America, and married Margaret, a daughter of Foster Hutchinson, at Halifax, Nova Scotia.

But the American Refugees continued to make their lamentations heard. Many of them were reduced to complete destitution—some tried to earn bread by the most menial occupations—and some broke down in health both bodily and mentally, for the delays were unavoidably prolonged, and he who waits for the corn to grow will starve in the interval. During the course of a long series of years the case of the Loyalists had been occasionally before Parliament, and even for thirty or forty years after the termination of the war was still unsettled in some of its bearings. The 4th Article of the Treaty of Peace stipulated—"That creditors on either side shall meet with no lawful impediment to the recovery of the full value in sterling money of all bona fide debts heretofore contracted."

The 5th Article stipulates that Congress should recommend the restitution of all estates, rights, and properties which had been confiscated, to British subjects, who had not borne arms against the United States; and that persons of any other description should have free liberty to go and remain twelve months in the United States unmolested, in their endeavours to recover their confiscated property.

As regarded the English Government, it was fully admitted that the Loyalists had just claims to compensation at their hands. The King in his Speech said—"I trust that you will agree with me, that a due and generous attention ought to be shewn to those who have relinquished their properties or possessions from motives of loyalty to me, or attachment to the Mother country."

Lord Walsingham, speaking of the Loyalists, observed:- "Their claim upon us is self-evident."

In the Lower House, Mr. Wilberforce declared—"They must be compensated." Mr. Townshend, Secretary of State, said—"This country would feel itself bound in honor to make the Loyalists full compensation for their losses."

The above few facts are taken from a printed "Abstract of the case of the Uncompensated American Loyalists," &c., which I find among the papers. Sabine, to whom I shall have to refer next, though as briefly as possible, gives many particulars relative to their claims, their losses, and the amount of what they recovered. Such were the delays, that even so late as in 1821—thirty-eight years after the war had ended, and forty-three years after the passing of the Confiscation Act—the subject was again mooted in Parliament. In the debates, as reported in the *Globe* newspaper of March 22, that year,—"Mr Courtenay rose to call the attention of the House to the claims of the American Loyalists, who had suffered in the Revolution, for the fulfilment of the engagements and promises made to them by Great Britain, to compensate whatever losses they might have sustained in consequence of their adherence to the Crown of England during that period," &c., and he moved an address for papers on the subject.

Mr. Dickinson seconded, and amongst other things he observed—"These persons were determined to persevere in their claims, for when they went into the Courts of America, they were treated as outlaws, and were told they could get no compensation."

Mr. Wm. Smith lamented the length of time that had been suffered to elapse without meeting their demands. "This," he said, "was one of the greatest hardships they had to complain of. Forty years ago they were entitled to these claims, and the sum would be trebly increased since that time by interest."

The Chancellor of the Exchequer, *inter alia*, admitted—"The lapse of time that has occurred should be no barrier to their claims; they had never been lost sight of," but though the Address was agreed to, he did not hold out much hope that what was demanded could be certainly complied with.

The number of the Loyalists who considered themselves justified in looking to the English Government in their peculiar situation, was extremely great, and it consisted of various classes. As regards the fighting men, Sabine, I. 70, remarks:—

"It may not be possible to ascertain the number of the Loyalists who took up arms, but, from the best evidence which I have been able to obtain, I conclude there were twenty-five thousand at the lowest computation; and unless their killed and wounded in the different battles and affrays in which they were engaged, were unusually large, I have put their aggregate force far too low."

It had been notified that March the 26th, 1784, would be the latest period for presenting claims for the consideration of the Commissioners; and on, or before that day, the number of persons who had preferred their petitions, stood at 2063, and the alleged property lost at £7,046,278. Besides this, there were outstanding debts in America, owing to English creditors, amounting to the sum of £2,354,135.

In 1788 Mr. Pitt submitted a plan for classifying the Claimants, and of classifying and apportioning the nature and amount of consolation to be allotted to each; and to those whose losses had been caused principally by the deprivation of official or professional incomes, he proposed a system of pensions. By the 5th of April this year the Commissioners in England had heard and determined 1680 claims, and had liquidated the same at the sum of £1,887,548.

It appeared finally, that the number of applicants from England, and from the Canadian Provinces, attained to the aggregate of 5072, of whom 954 either withdrew their applications, or failed to press them; and the sum of the losses was stated to have been £8,026,045. Another return however, was made out by Mr. J. E. Wilmot, one of the Commissioners, wherein the amount of the claims is given at £10,358,413, and the amount of the claims allowed at £3,033,091.

The above items will be enough to shadow forth the gigantic dimensions of the work that during forty years had occasionally forced itself upon the attention of the Government. The delays that had occurred were partly owing to the difficulty of investigating the correctness of the claims—the soundness of the evidence—the changes in the Ministry, or in the Departments; and in America the delays were prolonged by hostile or prohibitory Acts that had been enacted during the heat of party fervour, but which, in process of time, and by slow degrees, were either mitigated, or in great part removed. Many of the Loyalists had died in the interval, but in those cases where the efforts at recovery were followed up, the business was continued by their heirs. Though the chances of recovering anything within the limits of Massachusetts were looked upon as hopeless, still, the event proved that other estates—that is to say, the value of them in money—were recovered in Rhode Island, on the south, and also in that large tract stretching away Down East, then under the same government, and mostly unappropriated, but now absorbed in the State of Maine. It will be shewn presently that by perseverance carried on through a long period, the Hutchinsons effected the sale of two farms on the island of Conanicut, opposite Newport, in Narragansett Bay, and received the payment for them, and also disposed of certain tracts, commonly spoken of as the "Eastern Lands," lying near Phillip's Town, at about 100 miles north-by-east from Boston. Surely Sir Francis Bernard and Sir William Pepperell were not more "notorious conspirators," (from the American point of view), than Thomas Hutchinson; and they are to be pitied for not having been able to snatch something out of the wreck, as might have been hoped, considering that their lands were not in Massachusetts proper. It has been remarked, when speaking of the Pepperell family, that their vast possessions extended some thirty miles along the coast, and several miles in width; and the official accounts inform us that when Governor Bernard was in the zenith of his popularity, the admiring colonists presented him with the island of Mount Desert—and a handsome gift it was. From a friend who visited the island in 1879, I have gathered a few personal observations. He went by steamer from Boston down east to the Penobscot river, and then by another of smaller size, twenty or thirty miles further along the coast, calling at intermediate stations, and stopped at the small port of Bar Harbour situated on the western side of the island. There was a small village at that place, but the accommodation was then so limited that he was directed to a farm house three miles off, where he lodged nearly a fortnight. He speaks of the aspect as rocky, with the heights still clothed in the primeval forest, though the low lands had been considerably cleared, and several farms laid out. Towards the western side the island lies very close to the main land, but towards the north-east the coast sweeps round, so that between the two a fine sheltered bay is formed. When the French had Canada, or cruised in American waters at the time of the war, their fleet occasionally resorted to it, where they were secure in all winds but the south-east, and from these visits it obtained the name of Frenchman's Bay. During his stay, my friend amused himself in making excursions and explorations. The island, in shape, is irregularly circular, somewhat prolonged towards the south, with an elevation or mountain in the middle, to the summit of which he ascended, and enjoyed a beautiful view. In size it is near fifteen miles long, by seven or eight wide. The country in this part of America is not very thickly populated: the coast is iron bound, and the climate, though delightful in summer, is severe in the winter months. The steamer that proceeded to Bar Harbour generally carried thither a few summer excursionists; but as the place gets better known, the numbers are year by year on the increase, so that in proportion as it becomes the resort of visitors in the fine season, so its prosperity seems to be advancing.

The following original letter, bearing date November 4, 1801, written by young Thomas Hutchinson, son of the Judge, who had been bred to the law, and who now addressed it to his uncle Elisha, will explain the whole scope of the claims:—

"I take the opportunity of Mr Danl Oliver's return to Birmingham to convey to you the enclosed Power of Attorney for your signature, if it meets with your approbation. You are acquainted with the claims of the Hutchinson and Oliver families to certain lands to the eastward of Boston, and to the Rhode Island estate, heretofore the property of the late Miss Sanford; and you are probably apprised of the defalcation of the Agents in America, whom my father had employed to look after these interests. Till very lately he has not, for some years past, received a line from either Mr Lowell or Mr Spooner, notwithstanding his repeated letters to them on the subject. Mr Sabatier, the gentleman named in the enclosed Power, married a daughter [Margaret] of my great-uncle Foster Hutchinson: he is a man of business and an honest man. Previously to his departure for Nova Scotia, my father, unwilling that the family claims should be entirely given up, and thinking that a longer neglect would weaken them, commissioned Mr Sabatier to obtain what information he could respecting them. Three letters from Mr Sabatier to Mr Spooner have at length produced from the latter a recommendation of a purchaser for the Rhode Island estate. It is apprehended that no considerable difficulty can occur with respect to the title of Miss Sanford's devisees to that estate. It is secured to them by the 9th Article of the Treaty of Commerce with America made in 1794; but what is perhaps a better security, Mr Spooner has been in undisputed possession of it ever since the year 1787. For a year or two previous to Miss Sanford's death he remitted the rents, which were applied to her support: since that period nothing has been received from him. The object of the enclosed Power is, to enable Mr Sabatier to obtain possession, and (if the parties entrusted should think it expedient), to dispose of the family interests in America; and from the present favourable appearances of the title to the Rhode Island estate, it is presumed that the profits therefrom will be sufficient to cover any expenses Mr Sabatier may be at in the recovery of this, or any part of the Eastern Estate. Aware however, of the uncertain issue of claims so distantly preferred, and which have so long lain dormant, Mr S. will be instructed to proceed with such caution as that the heirs may be nothing out of pocket by this experiment.

"P.S. You will, if you think proper, put your signature opposite the second blank seal; the first is intended for my father's. The Power will then be forwarded to Mr Lyde, New York, and from thence to Mr W. S. Oliver, New Brunswick. Mr Danl Oliver will have an opportunity of conveying the Power back to me."

After many delays, it appears by a statement bearing date Jan. 15, 1806, in the Letter Book of young Thomas Hutchinson, the Barister-at-Law, that one portion of the property at Rhode Island, known as the Cotton Farm, had been sold for 5400 dollars. This sum, after a few increments and deductions, that it is not necessary to dally over, eventually produced £858,,5,,11 in sterling money. Grizzel Sanford, by her Will, left her property to be equally divided between the children of her two sisters, one having been married to Lieutenant-Governor Oliver, and the other to Governor Hutchinson.

The other farm, spoken of as the Narhawana Estate, was disposed of by the agency of Mr. Rufus G. Amory towards the latter part of the same year; for in a letter written by him from Boston at that period, he says:—

"Enclosed is Exchange for £1311,,15 sterl., in full for the sale of the Narhawana Estate to H. G. Otis, Esq., being 11/12^ths^ thereof, for 5500 dollars, and one year's interest thereon—say 5830 D. in Exchange at par."

Divested of technicalities, and the provisions which gave

different proportions to different claimants, according to the degree of propinquity in which they stood to the late devisor, and throwing the two sums together, that had been obtained for the two estates, the case stood simply as follows:—

The Cotton Farm	858	5	11
The Narhawana Estate, less T. H.'s costs . .	1308	18	0
To the Heirs of Spooner	166	14	1¾
Total to be divided	£2333	18	0¾

The one-fourteenth for the Heirs of Spooner was at first reserved as a matter of calculation, because it does not seem to have been sent to England at all. The gross sum however, was divided in the following manner:—

Thomas Hutchinson, 1/4th (half of a moiety) .	583	9	6
Ditto, in right of wife, 1/14th (seventh of a moiety)	166	14	1¾
Elisha Hutchinson, 1/4th	583	9	6
Daniel Oliver, 1/14th	166	14	1¾
William Sanford Oliver, do..	166	14	1¾
Mrs. Lyde, (Elizabeth Oliver), do	166	14	1¾
Brinley Sylvester Oliver, do.	166	14	1¾
Mrs. Knight, do..	166	14	1¾
Heirs of Spooner, do.	166	14	1¾
Total, as above	£2333	18	0¼

The next consideration touched the Eastern Lands, but the Governor's eldest son looked at the question with some despair. Writing to Elisha on the 25th of May, 1790, he observed—"Altho', as I have before said, I have not the least expectations from Eastern Lands for myself, yet I am convinced the interest is such as ought to induce those who are concerned for their successors, to endeavour to keep up a family claim. They may increase much in value. By a letter from A. S., [Andrew Spooner], they begin to think so there; and he seems to wish to interest himself therein."

Again, May 19, 1791:—"According to Mr Brimmer's statement of the case, (which I had never heard before), of the Eastern Lands, I have only to join with the other heirs of Peleg Sanford, in appointing some person or Attorney, to appear for us."

From the remark here made, it seems that these lands had

been derived from some early member of the Sanford family, a circumstance that is not mentioned elsewhere.

Concurrently with these transactions, something was done in applications to the Treasury, the American Commissioners, and in endeavours to recover private debts. By the 6th Article of the Treaty of Commerce between the two countries in 1794, a Commission was provided, which sat at Philadelphia, to consider and satisfy demands of British subjects on American subjects, and it was proposed that £600,000 be supplied by America to satisfy these claims. After doing some work, the Commission broke up.

Writing from Brompton August 25, 1785, to Mr. John Lowell at Boston, the Governor's eldest son Thomas says:—"I was possessed of a store or counting House, situate on the south side Town Dock, which with others, was burnt in the time of the Blockade of Boston: but from the situation for trade you are sensible the ground must always be valuable." Three years and a half afterwards, namely, on the 25th of February, 1789, as appears in his Letter Book, he recurs to the subject:—"I mentioned in a former letter an interest my family had in lands to the eastward at Phillip's Town, and also a store which belonged to me, situated on the south side of the Town Dock, neither of which I believe were ever confiscated." Be that as it may, there is nothing to shew that the family ever recovered any thing from the sale of any real property within the limits of Massachusetts proper; and it is not always very clearly explained, in what the sums that occasionally passed, originated in. Young Thomas in London, wrote to his father near Exeter, on the 6th of September, 1808, and said—"The American Commissioners have allowed your claim in respect to the Treas^{y} Note for £500 and Int^{t} to be good to the amount of £994 „ 7 „ 6 Sterl^{g}, upon which they have paid me a Div^{d} of £198 „ 17 „ 6." Other sums passed at other times, but it is not necessary to dwell upon them.

The correspondence entered in the Letter Book of young Thomas, shews that the Eastern Lands were frequently alluded to by him to his Agents in America, or by them to him, thus—

1805, June 2, Mr. Amory writes—"The Eastern Lands remain

as formerly, no settlement being yet made with persons in possession, but I have employed an active Attorney in their neighbourhood, John Holmes Esq., to settle with them."

1805, Oct. 24, he again writes—"I have employed an active Attorney, (John Holmes Esq., of Alfred,) to dispose of the Eastern Lands, and make the best settlement in his power; but as all the *good* land is covered with trespassers, he is obliged to be very moderate, and give great indulgence to all of them."

1807. Jan. 6, Thomas says—"I have written to Mr Amory to expedite the sale of the Eastern Lands."

1808. June 9, again—"You have probably rec^d^ from me of late several parcels, conveying to you various documents relat^g^ to the Eastern Lands, w^h^ have, I trust, been sufficient to enable you to prevail in the suit instituted respecting those lands."

1808. Sep. 26, quoting his uncle W. S. Oliver in New Brunswick, he says—"Perhaps it might forward the business if you were to let Mr H. know that you are apprised of the successful termination of the law suit, and to try to be informed when we may expect a settlem^t^ and a remittance of the money."

According to this the business was not settled by 1808, and I recently applied to my cousin, his daughter, (widow of the Rev. W. H. Oliver,) to know whether she had any later evidence amongst her father's papers, to which application she replied—

"I find letters from my father to Mr Holmes in 1812, acknowledging the undermentioned sums—£330 „ 14 „ 2, £125 „ 0 „ 0 and £124 „ 11 „ 1½.

"Again, in 1818, I find a letter thanking Mr Holmes for his judicious conduct on the conclusion of the claims, and acknowledging a final receipt of £157 „ 10 „ 0, and enquiring whether a sum of £60 had been paid to Edward Lyde. My father would appear to have been trustee to receive for the claimants in England only."

Thus, from 1778, the year in which the Confiscation Act was passed, down to 1818, these claims had remained open, being the space of forty years. The claimants had certainly been very persevering.

I apologise for having dwelt so long upon the subject of the Loyalists—their losses, their sufferings, and their efforts to regain their property—I fear almost to tediousness; but it was an important wind-up to the momentous events of the war: and the matter has still a lingering interest to the many remaining descendants of those who but ill weathered the storm, and who have but an imperfect knowledge of the intricacies of the questions raised between the two nations at the time, or of the obstacles that lay in the way of recovery.

The annexed profile of T. Hutchinson, the Governor's eldest son, was taken from a black silhouette of the same size. It had apparently been done towards the latter years of his life, and from the falling in of the lips, he must have suffered much from the loss of his teeth.

The following heads of Pedigrees, arranged in a Tabular form, will end this Chapter.

PEDIGREE OF MARBURY.

Given to me by the Earl of Donoughmore,
Jan. 15, 1864.

Sir Walter Blunt, Knt. = ...

Sir Thomas Blunt, Knt. = ...

Sir Walter Blunt, Knt. — Thomas Blunt, Second son. = Anne, d. and heir of Sir J. Hawleyt, Kt.

WILLIAM MARBURY = Anne, d. and co-heir of Sir T. Blunt. — Robert Blunt. Ob. s. p. — Sir J. Bruntayne = Margaret. — William Hanford = Elizabeth.

Laurence M. = d. and heir of Williamson. — Robert M. Had a son. — Thomas M. — Humphrey M. — John M. — Jane M. m. Nevell. — Mary M. m. Burton. — Elizabeth M. m. Goldsmith. — Margaret M. A. Nun. — Anne M. — Mary M.

William M. = Anne, d. of J. Leaton.

Edward M. = Mary, d. of J. Welcom. — William M. ob. s. p. — Elizabeth Moore. = Francis M. = 2nd. Bridget, sister of Sir Erasmus Dryden, Bt. — Mary M. m. T. Middleton. — Anne M. m. W. Bloxholme. — Catherine M. m. C. Wentworth.

(by Elizabeth Moore) Susannah. m. Trayford.

(by Bridget) Mary M. m. B. Leyton. — Anne Marbury, co-heiress = William Hutchinson of Lincoln. *See Hutchinson Pedigree.* — Katherine M. m. J. Scott.

See Gov. H.'s mention of her in "Hutchinson in America," page 10–12.

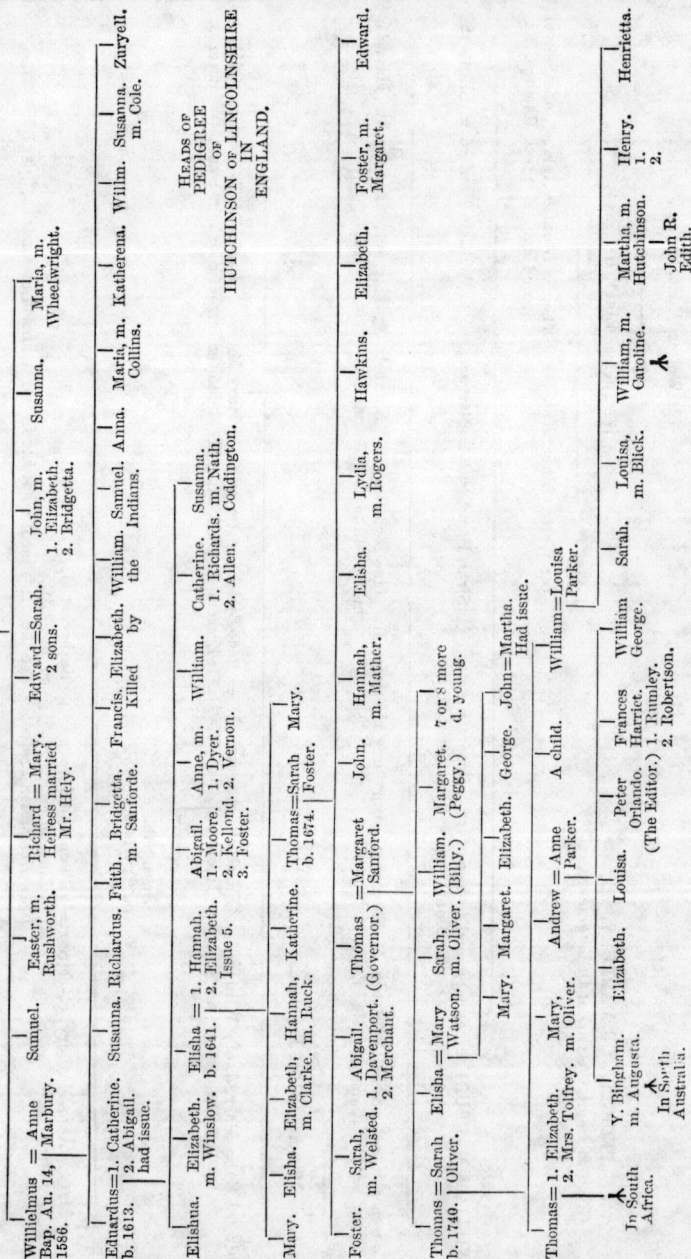

HEADS OF PEDIGREE OF HUTCHINSON OF LINCOLNSHIRE IN ENGLAND.

EDWARD HUTCHINSON = SUSANNE, or SUSANNA.
of Alford, Sepult. 1631.

Willielmus = Anne Marbury. Bap. Au. 14, 1586. | Samuel. | Easter, m. Rushworth. | Richard = Mary. Heiress married Mr. Hely. | Edward=Sarah. 2 sons. | John, m. 1. Elizabeth. 2. Bridgetta. | Susanna. | Maria, m. Wheelwright.

Eduardus=1. Catherine. 2. Abigail. had issue. b. 1613. | Susanna. | Richardus. | Faith. | Bridgetta. m. Sanforde. | Francis. Elizabeth. William. Samuel. Killed by the Indians. | Anna. | Maria, m. Collins. | Katherena. | Willm. | Susanna. m. Cole. | Zuryell.

Elishua. | Elizabeth. m. Winslow. | Elisha = 1. Hannah. 2. Elizabeth. b. 1641. Issue 5. | Abigail. 1. Moore. 2. Kellond. 3. Foster. | Anne, m. 1. Dyer. 2. Vernon. | William. | Catherine. 1. Richards. 2. Allen. | Susanna. m. Nath. Coddington.

Mary. | Elisha. | Elizabeth, m. Clarke. | Hannah, m. Ruck. | Katherine. | Thomas=Sarah Foster. b. 1674. | Mary.

Foster. | Sarah, m. Welsted. | Abigail. 1. Davenport. 2. Merchant. | Thomas (Governor.) =Margaret Sanford. | John. | Hannah, m. Mather. | Elisha. | Lydia, m. Rogers. | Hawkins. | Elizabeth. | Foster, m. Margaret. | Edward.

Thomas = Sarah Oliver. b. 1740. | Elisha = Mary Watson. | Sarah, m. Oliver. | William. (Billy.) | Margaret. (Peggy.) | 7 or 8 more d. young.

(Children of Elisha and Mary Watson:) Mary. | Margaret. | Elizabeth. | George. | John=Martha. Had issue.

Thomas= 1. Elizabeth. 2. Mrs. Tolfrey. | Mary, m. Oliver. | Andrew = Anne Parker. | A child. | William=Louisa Parker.

(Issue of Thomas:) In South Africa.

(Children of Andrew and Anne Parker:) Y. Bingham. m. Augusta. (In South Australia.) | Elizabeth. | Louisa. | Peter Orlando. (The Editor.) | Frances Harriet. 1. Rumley. 2. Robertson. | William George.

(Children of William and Louisa Parker:) Sarah. | Louisa, m. Blick. | William, m. Caroline. | Martha, m. Hutchinson. (John R. Edith.) | Henry. 1. 2. | Henrietta.

PEDIGREE OF HELY-HUTCHINSON OF KNOCKLOFTY, &c., &c.

Edward Hutchinson = Susanne, or Susanna.
Of Alford. Ob. 1631.

William Hutchinson = Anne Marbury. Who went to America.	Samuel. Ob. cœl.	Easter, m. Rushworth.	RICHARD HUTCHINSON = MARY. Favoured by increasing wealth, tho' he lost £60,000 by the fire of London in 1666, he bought lands in Ireland, Norfolk, Lincolnshire, &c.	Edw.	John.	Susanna.	Maria.

Children of Richard Hutchinson and Mary:

Edward = Anne Batty.	Samuel.	Jonathan.	Ezekiel. Major. Buried at Clonmel.	Eliakim. = Sister of Col. Shrimpton. Bap. 1640.	William. D. about 1706 at Jamaica.	Daughter, m. Will. Puckle.	Daughter, m. Bar. Soame.	Elizabeth, m. Peter Gray.	Anne, m. J. Holland.

Children of Edward and Anne Batty:

Richard. = Christian Moore. Ob. s. p. Made his niece his heir.	Thomas. Tombstone at Clonmel.	1st. Dr. Francis Vaughan. Dead before 1699. = Elizabeth = 2nd. Lorenzo Hodson. Married before 1704. (2 daughters.) = 3rd. Abraham Nickson, of Munny, co. Wicklow.	Anne, m. Dr. Lewis Mauzy.	Mary. Died young. Clonmel Tablet.

Children of Elizabeth and Abraham Nickson:

Some authorities say there were 13 children, 4 boys and 9 girls, of whom Christian was the youngest. This appears strange in a woman's third marriage. See the Obs. of the Earl of D. in the larger Pedigree.

Christian Nickson. Created Baroness Donoughmore, Ob. June 24, 1788. = John Hely, Sec. of State, and Keeper of the Privy Seal. On marriage he assumed the name of Hutchinson.

Richard Hely - Hutchinson. Created Viscount Suirdale, Nov. 7, 1797, and Earl of Donoughmore, Dec. 29, 1797. Ob. cœl. Aug. 22, 1825.	John.	Francis.

The remainder is in the Peerage.

Branch of FOSTER HUTCHINSON, communicated by William John Stirling.

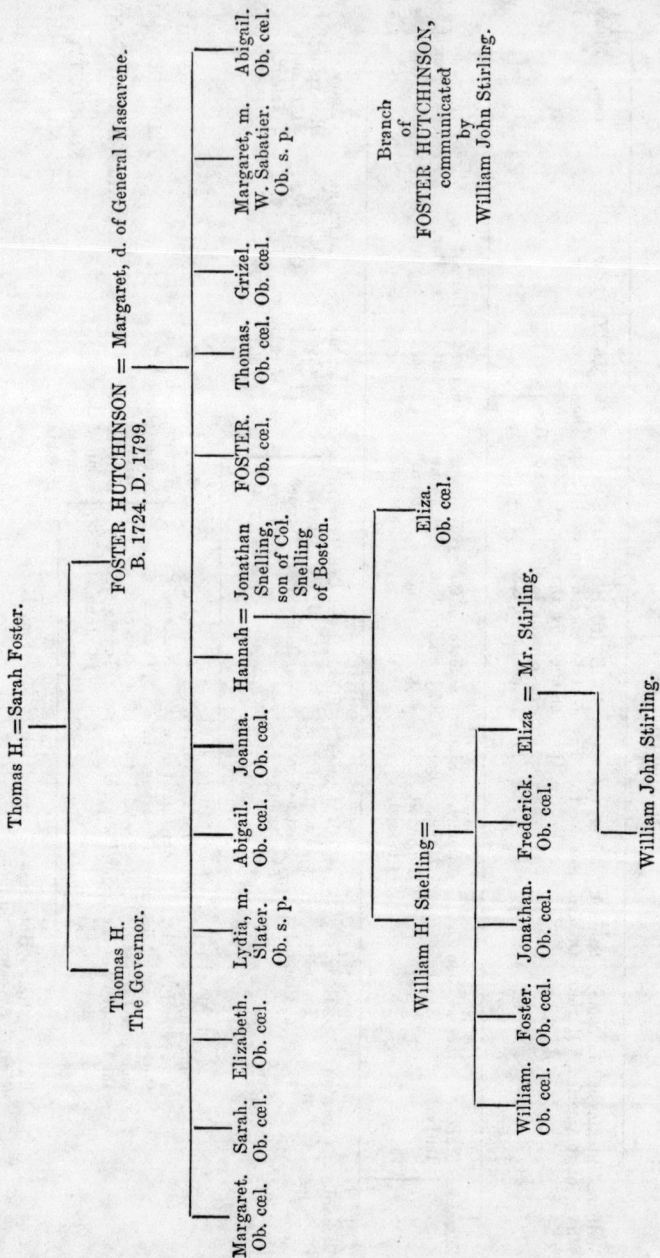

- Thomas H. = Sarah Foster.
  - Thomas H. The Governor.
  - FOSTER HUTCHINSON = Margaret, d. of General Mascarene. B. 1724. D. 1799.
    - Margaret. Ob. cœl.
    - Sarah. Ob. cœl.
    - Elizabeth. Ob. cœl.
    - Lydia, m. Slater. Ob. s. p.
    - Abigail. Ob. cœl.
    - Joanna. Ob. cœl.
    - Hannah = Jonathan Snelling, son of Col. Snelling of Boston.
      - William H. Snelling =
        - William. Ob. cœl.
        - Foster. Ob. cœl.
        - Jonathan. Ob. cœl.
        - Frederick. Ob. cœl.
        - Eliza = Mr. Stirling.
          - William John Stirling.
      - Eliza. Ob. cœl.
    - FOSTER. Ob. cœl.
    - Thomas. Ob. cœl.
    - Grizel. Ob. cœl.
    - Margaret, m. W. Sabatier. Ob. s. p.
    - Abigail. Ob. cœl.

CHAPTER X.

SOME ACCOUNT OF GOVERNOR HUTCHINSON'S FAMILY.

To begin an account with tradition is rather a mythological beginning; and yet, it is just the sort of commencement that most family histories begin with. One consideration at all events is comforting, and that is this—that whatever I may offer as tradition deceives nobody, and the reader may take it for what it is worth and no more. In some of the earlier editions of Burke's Landed Gentry, *in voce* Hutchinson, and perhaps in some of the later, for all I know, it is stated that among the followers of Harold Harfager, King of Norway, who invaded England on the Yorkshire coast shortly before the date of the Battle of Hastings, was one Uitonensis, the reputed founder of the Hutchinson family in this country. The words are these—"The family of Hutchinson is supposed to derive from Uitonensis, who came over from Castle Cronenburg with Harold Harfager, and settled at (or near) Bishop Middleham, then a fortified place." Most of the old coats of arms of our noble families have a legend belonging to their earliest institution; and as to the origin of nations, we know that Rome had its mythical Romulus and Remus, and Carthage had its Dido, with a bull's hide cut into thongs. We graduate somewhat into history when we come to the Annals of the early Chroniclers, where mythistoria stands half way between fable and fact. The King of England had a turbulent and rebellious brother called Tosti, and having collected forces and ships, he joined with the enemy in the invasion. Harfager and his ally, led their united fleet into the Humber—disembarked—had a sharp encounter with the Saxons, led by the Earls Edwin and Morcar—and gained a considerable advantage over them.

Fired with anger and alarm at the intelligence of this disaster, Harold of England hastened with his fighting men to the spot, and meeting the Norwegians at Stamford Bridge, below York, attacked them with great determination. He routed them completely, killing both Harfager and Tosti. "*Haroldus,*" says William of Malmesbury, Lib. ii. fol, 52, "*nuncio accepto, cunctis viribus eo contendit; pugna ingens commissa utrisque gentibus extrema nitentibus. Angli superiorem manum nacti, Noricos in fugam egerunt,*" &c. And the Chronicle of Mailros says:—"*Rex Noreganorum Haroldus Harphagher, frater Sancti Olivi, Regis et Martyris, et Tostius, Comes, apud Strinfordbrige, occiduntur.*" Scarcely, however, was this contest over, and before he had time to complete his arrangements for the final disposal of his invaders, when news arrived that the Normans had made a hostile landing on the south coast; upon which, he was compelled to leave things in Yorkshire as they were, so he collected his forces, and hurried to the field of Hastings, where it is well known he soon lost his own life.

The Norwegians, thus being left to themselves, recovered their equanimity, and taking a survey of the aspect and bearings of the situation, and hearing of the death of the man who had recently chastised them, and conscious now that there was no one near them to be afraid of, deliberated on the next step to be taken. Although some of them resolved to return to their own country, there were many who preferred settling down where they were, and amongst whom Uitonensis. The name of this person as it here stands, wears the appearance of a Latin form, whatever may have been the Norse orthography originally. Of his immediate descendants nothing is positively known, though report places them in the neighbourhood of Bishop Middleham. We do not tread upon firm ground, or arrive at authentic record until the 10th of Edward I., anno 1282, when Barnard Hutchinson heads the regular Pedigree, compiled from authentic sources by Henry St. George, King of Arms, as given in the earlier 4to editions of the Life of Col. John Hutchinson. This was the main stock of the family, from which, at different periods a great number of side branches were at intervals thrown off. And then, there are many trees that have cankered branches, or spurious branches, that cling on to the main stem, bearing the same name, and they keep quiet and bide their time, and hold their tongues, and trust that nobody will discover the secret. Let the Heralds look after them. Some migrated northwards through Durham into Northumberland, into the Lowlands, and by a Scotticism in enunciation, and subsequently in spelling, the name deviated into Hutchison and Hutcheson: some proceeded into Cumberland, and others into Lancashire or Lincolnshire, whilst others crossed over into Ireland. There appears to have been only one head to this family; for on endeavouring to trace back the links of the genealogical chain pertaining to any respectable individual of the name, the results of the search all seem to converge and lead up to the Yorkshire stock. It is with the Lincolnshire branch only that we have to do now.

In the year 1586 Edward Hutchinson, with his wife Susanne or Susanna, was seated at Alford in the county of Lincoln, for on the 14th of August in that year their eldest son William was there baptised, as appears in the Parish Register, which I have carefully examined: and Edward lived there, with occasional intervals, during the long space of 45 years, and having died, he was buried on the 14th of February, 1631. It has been shown that Col. Chester was employed to look up the descent of one branch of the family, and it resulted that whilst he was so occupied, he lighted upon documents containing many particulars relating to other branches. It had been conveyed to me by a mutual friend, that in the prosecution of his researches, he had discovered the name of the said Edward's father, which I did not know, but much wished to know. I had been for more than twenty years trying to discover whether he had left a Will, and where it might be, thinking that I might there ascertain this point, as well as one or two others interesting to me; but I have wholly failed to get any intelligence of such a Will, either in London or Lincoln, or in one or two places where I have made inquiry—not forgetting "Courts of Peculiars." I was told that light was thrown upon this obscurity by the Will of John Hutchinson, Mayor of the city of Lincoln, whose brother was Sheriff, who left real property in half a dozen neighbouring parishes, and amongst whose children was one named Edward, who was the same with Edward of Alford. To satisfy myself in respect to these particulars, I procured an office copy of it at Somerset House. It bears date April 21, 1565, and though there is a son Edward mentioned, to whom the father leaves a tenement, garden, and close, in the parish of St. Peter at Cootes or Coates, and though the dates would tally, still, I see nothing in the Will to prove that the two Edwards were one and the same. But I was further informed that Edward of Alford was appointed Executor, and proved the Will of his cousin Christopher Hutchinson of Mablethorpe, in 1609—so I obtained a copy of this Will at Lincoln. This Christopher made his Will on the last day of August 1592. He leaves to his wife Anne his farm at Mablethorpe, or perhaps Maplethorpe, with great part of the stock: to his eldest son William the third part of his lands in Thedelthorpe and Carleton in the county of Lincoln: to his son Robert a portion of the remainder, with some land and tenements in the city of Lincoln: to his other son Christopher the other portion: to his daughter Marie he gives £100 at full age or on her marriage: and to his other daughter Frances he gives the same. He appoints his brother Thomas Hutchinson of Louth, and Edward Hutchinson of Alford to be his Executors, and Edward of Alford proved the Will at Lincoln on the 16th of February, 1609. But here I was again disappointed. Doubtless the parties herein mentioned were near relatives; but there is no intimation that will show what connection may have existed between Edward of Alford and the testator, and there is not the slightest allusion made to John, the Mayor of Lincoln. Either my informant was not clear in all his facts, or Col. Chester had come upon some piece of evidence which has escaped me,—which indeed might well be, for I have not made it my determined and exclusive business to pursue these researches to their last corners and hiding places. I might have requested him to be so good as to assist me; but considering that he has lost few opportunities of saying unkind and slighting things, both of the descent and of the coat armour of the Loyalist Governor Hutchinson and of his family, and finding that, after looking over his Pedigree of H. of Salem, my confidence was seriously shaken, I preferred keeping my affairs in my own hands. He may have been disappointed that I did not apply to him. He made advances to the Earl of Donoughmore, but the Earl commissioned a gentleman to ascertain all he wished to know, and his services were not required. But although, as yet, I have not been able to prove that the Alford family emanated from the city of Lincoln, it is certain that the connection was very close, and probably very recent, for in the Marbury Pedigree it is stated of Anne Marbury, that she was the wife of William Hutchinson "of Lincoln," though he was baptised at Alford: and what is still more noteable, because a generation farther off, when William's son, young Edward, became a candidate for the married state, from an entry in the Registry of the Bishop of London, "it appears that Richard Hutchinson [his uncle] applied for a licence for the marriage of Edward Hutchinson *of Lincoln* with Catherine Hanbie on the 19th of Octr 1636." The connection with Lincoln was therefore very close.

It is time now to begin the regular Pedigree—but before doing so, this will be a convenient place to make a few remarks on the coat armour. The coloured coat of arms is a facsimile on a reduced scale of an old painting on vellum which came down to my late father, but he knew nothing of its age or history. When I was a child it used to hang in his dressing-room. I can remember it upwards of sixty years, and it looked as old then as it does now; but of course a new print done on new paper is always likely to have a newer appearance than a really old picture. It is one quarter the size of the original, that is to say, one half the height, and one half the width. It exhibits the freedom of a practised hand especially in the mantling. There is no motto. The inscription underneath clearly describes the charges in Heraldic phraseology, and mentions it as pertaining to "Hutchinson of Lincolnshire."

The wood engraving of the shield, but without the Crest, is taken from a silver tankard which is alluded to at page 394 of the former volume. Having been given to the early church in Boston in 1714, it was used for the Communion wine for upwards of 150 years, when the breaking up of the congregation, gave the family an opportunity of buying it back and preserving it in England. It is stamped on the side with EW

over a cross, but there is no Hall mark. The figures 31–17 are incised with a graver on the bottom. The weight is two pounds three ounces avoirdupois. It is in good condition. The arms on the front are but rudely engraved; and the perpendicular lines before the Lion, to indicate red, and the horizontal ones behind him to imply the colour blue, have been forgotten, but nine cross-crosslets are given. There is no motto.

The Governor's oval seal has already been given at the head of the Preface of the first volume. The earliest document that has come under my notice bearing an impress of it, is a letter dated at Milton, near Boston, on the 6th of February, 1774. As contradistinguished from the other two examples, on this there is a motto, which will serve to indicate that it is the most modern of the three. Upon the words—LIBERTATEM COLO, LICENTIAM DETESTOR,

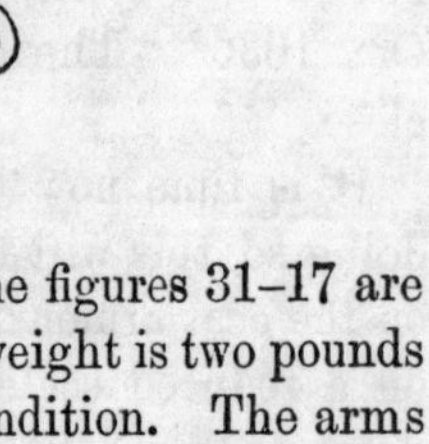

an interesting, and perhaps a profitable discourse might be

He Beareth parted per Pale gules & Azure, A Lyon Rampant Argt Armed & Langued or, ye feild Charged wth Cross Crosslets of ye 4th: for ye Crest a Cockatrice azure Crest: Wattled & Armed Gules, Issuing out of A Ducall Crown or; & is Borne by the name of Hutchinson of Lincolnshire.

written, especially if it could be shown where the one ends and the other begins.

Putting aside John of Lincoln for the present, and keeping him in abeyance until his claim to be admitted will stand the test of scrutiny, we will begin with Edward of Alford. Though John's admission would add another link to the genealogical chain, let us have truth first, and length of chain afterwards. If a doubt hangs over any part of a Pedigree, it is just worth nothing. As this branch is styled "Hutchinson of Lincolnshire" at the end of the inscription on the old coat of arms on vellum, this designation may as well be retained for distinction sake.

In arranging the positions of the junior members of a family and their offspring, I have followed the plan of Burke and Foster, by making them fall back an *m* or an *n* quadrat.

The small tabular Pedigrees will be useful as showing at a glance the positions of the heads or leading members, though there is no room for further detail.

Wishing to give the reader the authorities for statements made, I indicate the references by means of the following abbreviations, e. g.—(A.R.) Alford Register: (H.) Governor Hutchinson's notes and memorandums: (D.) the Earl of Donoughmore's contributions from Wills, Registers, Letters &c.: (F.R.) Family Records of later date.

PEDIGREE OF HUTCHINSON OF LINCOLNSHIRE.

EDWARD HUTCHINSON, or EDVARDUS, as in the Register, m. SUSANNE, or SUSANNA. Sepult. Feb. 14, 1631.

The name of Edward's widow is preserved in America in the List of Admissions to the First Church, Boston, under the following date:—"12th of 4th. moneth, 1636, John Wheelwright, and Marie his wife; Susanne Hutchinson, widdowe." Governor Hutchinson, in his family notes styled "Hutchinson in America," observes—"The first of which I have any memorial was mother to William Hutchinson, and it appears by a minute which he made in one of his books, that she died at York. I have a manuscript book of Edward Hutchinson, son to William, [not forthcoming now], which contains what he says to be his uncle Wheelwright's sermons, and Mr. Hubbard says that the famous Mrs. Hutchinson, with her brother [in law] Wheelwright, his wife and family, took water at Mount Wollaston, (Braintree), to go to Piscataqua, but Mrs. H. changed her mind; and I have no doubt Mrs. Hutchinson's mother [i.e. husband's mother] was one of this family, and was the mother of Mrs. Wheelwright, and that as long as she lived, she shared in Mr. Wheelwright's troubles, who settled at York; but the time of her death I am not able to ascertain." It was before 1640.

The Governor deprecates any of his descendants publishing these family memorandums. I am inclined to look at this as a pretty little piece of misplaced modesty. How am I to write History, if I am forbidden to go to original sources?

Whitmore says she died at Wells. The places were not far from Kittery in Maine.

I. WILLIELMUS, (A.R.) his heir, of whom presently.

II. Samuel, (A.R.) bap. Nov. 1, 1589: ob. cæl. July 14, 1667.

In the Suffolk Deeds at Boston, Liber 1, his name occurs occasionlly, either as principal or as a witness. In "H. in Am.," as above, the Governor writes—"The first notice I find of Samuel is in the votes of the General Court, Nov. 2, 1637. *Mr. Samuel Hutchinson, upon his suit, had leave to stay until the first opportunity after winter.* A law had been made not long before, that no town or person should entertain any stranger more than three weeks without licence from one of the Council, or two Magistrates, on penalty of £100." Again—"A pair of handsome well made tobacco tongs, he being a great smoker, were handed down in the family, by the name of Unkle Samuel's tongs, until they came into my possession. I caused his name, and the year 1660 to be stamped upon them, and laid them by as a memorial; but in the year 1765, the mob carried them off or destroyed them with all the rest of my furniture, papers, and moveables, and I have no memorial left of Unkle Samuel, unless there may be one of his Millenary pamphlets." He wrote on the Millenium. The Governor adds—"He died in Boston, July 14th, 1667, aged 77 years, a batchelor."

III. Easter, (A.R.) or Esther, bap. July 22, 1593, m. Thomas Rushworth, Oct. 7, 1613.

IV. Richard, (H.) not baptised at Alford, m. Mary, as mentioned in his Will. (D.)

In "H. in Am." we read—"Richard was a principal proprietor in Boston, was concerned in the Mills, and part of his estate at the Town Dock remains in his family to this day. His great-grandson Eliakim died since I left Boston in 1774. He died himself in London about the year 1670. He had many children, sons by the names of Edward, Ezekiel, Jonathan, Samuel, Eliakim, and William, and I believe one more, for I think I have heard of seven. He had besides, a daughter, married to Mr. Gray," &c. Richard's increasing wealth, whilst he was a member of the Ironmongers' Company, in spite of his losses by the great fire of London in 1666, enabled him to acquire many estates both in England and Ireland. His will is dated Nov. 4, 1669. He provides for Mary his wife. He leaves her his manor of Albrough in Norfolk, and lands in Boston and Clonbeck, co. Lincoln: settles £100 out of his lands in Ireland on Samuel and Jonathan conditionally: leaves all his real estate to Edward, and his heirs male: if none, to his second son, or third, fourth or fifth. To William his land, saw-mill, &c., in New England. To his daughter Ann 1000 marks, and £1000 if she marry not against her mother's consent. To his three sons-in-law, and their wives 40 shillings apiece: also £10 apiece for mourning. The same to all his sons but Edward. To the Ironmongers' Company a piece of plate of about £14. To the poor 40s. To his brother Edward and wife, each £10 for mourning. The Executors were his wife, and sons Edward and Eliakim. Will proved April 2, 1670. (D.) Richard and Mary were both buried at Hertford, but there is no monument. Their children were—

1. John, bap. 1628. This child does not appear in any of the Pedigrees I have seen; but the Earl of D. gave me some particulars of the researches of Mr. E. Walmisley, made for him, among which are entries of the baptisms of eight of Richard and Mary Hutchinson's children, at St. Mary Magdalen's, Milk Street, London. Perhaps John died an infant, and passed unnoticed.
2. Edward, bap. 1632, Richard's heir. His Will is dated Jan. 19, 1698. He desires that no more than £50 be spent on his funeral. He leaves £50 to his sister Elizabeth, wife of Peter Gray of London, Merchant, if she survives him a year. To his sister Ann, wife of John Holland, £50, or if dead, to her children. To his eldest daughter Elizabeth, wife of Francis Vaughan, of Ballyboe, co. Tipp., M.D., £100, to be paid Nov. 1, 1701: another £100 Nov. 1, 1702: and another £100 Nov. 1, 1703, to which certain arrangements are attached, and conditions specified. His kinsman John Perry of Newcastle, co. Tipp., is continued as manager of his estates, at the same allowance as heretofore; and Edward leaves him a legacy of £100. To his kinswoman Elizabeth, wife of J. Perry 30s. to buy a ring. To his brother-in-law Thomas Batty, of Clonmell £50. To his cousin Mary Long, wife of Robert Long of Graystown, co. Tipp. £20. To his cousin Susanna, wife of Thomas Millet of Priestowne, co. Tipp.

£20. All debts owing to him by his poor tenants at the time of his death, who may not have two cows in the world, he cancels. All his arrangements touching the affairs of his younger daughter Ann H., and his son and heir apparent Richard H. to be settled as soon as possible, and he makes the said Richard residuary legatee. Appoints T. Batty, J. Perry, Dr. F. Vaughan, and R. Long, Executors, and also Guardians of Richard and Ann till they are 24. Apparently by an afterthought, he leaves Hugh Rich £5. Witnessed by N. Lucas, Phin. Ryall, and James Keating. Edward died July 3, 1699, See tombstone at Clonmel. Ann his wife died Nov. 30, 1682. See other stone at Clonmel. (D.)

3. Samuel, bap. 1633.
4. Mary, bap. 1635. Ob. Mar. 24, 1675. See tombstone, Clonmel.
5. Susanna, bap. 1637.
6. Jonathan, bap. 1639.
7. Eliakim, bap. 1640, m. sister of Col. Shrimpton, and had a numerous family. The E. of D. writing to me Dec. 17, 1863 says:—"I have also a letter from Eliakim Hutchinson, dated at Boston, January 1st, 1712–13. He mentions in it that he was 73 years of age: that he had married the sister of Col. Shrimpton, who had borne him 13 children, of whom only three were living: his eldest daughter had married 'one Palmer, a merchant,' and had two sons and one daughter: his son (Christian name not stated), 'one Brinley, of a good family here, and in England,' and had one son and one daughter; his youngest daughter had married 'one Phipps, the heire of Sir William Phipps,' having one son and two daughters. He adds—'If God please, my three daughters (meaning, I suppose, his two daughters and daughter-in-law), may make us a numerous family.'" Governor H. observes (as above quoted), that his grandson Eliakim had died since he, the Governor, had left Boston; and his widow (née Shirley) came to London.
8. Elizabeth, bap. 1642; m. Peter Gray, as stated in Edward's Will, above.
9. William. He was not baptised at St. Mary Magdalen's. Died in Jamaica about 1706.
10. Ann. She m. John Holland, as mentioned in Edward's Will.

Edward, the heir of Richard, succeeded to the Irish and other estates. He died July 3, 1699, and his Will was proved Sep. 29 of the same year. He left issue—

Richard, the said heir of Edward, of whom presently.
Thomas, died Dec. 6, 1682, as on tombstone at Clonmel. (D.)
Elizabeth, mother of the heiress, of whom presently.
Anne, m. Lewis Mauzy, and had Lewis. (D.)
Mary, died young. (D.)

Of Elizabeth the mother of the heiress, it may be observed, that some perplexities appeared to arise out of her three marriages. She married 1st. Dr. Vaughan, M.D.; 2ndly, Lorenzo Hodson, and had two daughters; and 3rdly, she married Abraham Nickson, of Munny, co. Wicklow, by whom she had 13 children, 4 boys, and 9 girls. This seems rather strange in a woman's third marriage—so much so that the Earl of Donoughmore, to whom I had furnished some of the particulars connected with the descent of Governor Hutchinson, replied, Dec. 6, 1859:—"I think I can best repay your kindness by telling you all I know of the branch of the family from which I have inherited the name." At a subsequent period his Lordship sent me sundry extracts from Wills, Leases,

&c., and as bearing on the question of Elizabeth and her children he says—"He [Edward in his Will] speaks of but two daughters, Elizabeth and Anne: another, Mary, died in infancy." In the Marriage Settlement of John Hely-Hutchinson and his wife, dated June 8, 1751, "Anne is spoken of as Anne Mauzy, widow." Again—"In the Will of Richard Hutchinson, 4 August 1757, Anne is here again mentioned as a widow, and mention is made of Lewis her son." His Lordship adds—"From the above it appears evident that Richard, (who died 1757), had but two sisters who lived to a marriageable age,—Elizabeth and Anne. The latter was clearly not the mother of Christian Nickson, my great grandmother: Elizabeth, then, must have been her mother; but if so, she must have been married at least three times—1. To Dr. Francis Vaughan, before 19 January 1698;—2, to Lorenzo Hodson, before 20 January 1704;—and 3rd., to Abraham Nickson who was undoubtedy the father of Christian."

Richard, the grandson of the first Richard, brother of Elizabeth, heir and possessor of the estates while he lived, m. Christian Moore, but having no family, ob. s.p. He made his Will Aug. 4, 1757, and he that day executed a deed, whereby several sums affect his estate, amounting to £10,952 4*s.* 0¼*d.* And whereas Anne Mauzy, and Lewis her son, have agreed to accept £4000 in lieu of all demands. He then directs that John Hely-Hutchinson, Esquire, shall appropriate so much money as shall satisfy this demand. He then bequeaths "the rest and residue of his personal estate and fortune" to his beloved niece Christian Hely-Hutchinson. The only signature is that of Francis Vesey. Upon this performance the Earl remarks—"She was the youngest of nine daughters, and was chosen by her uncle, for what reason I never could understand, to inherit his property."

Thus Christian Nickson became inheritor of her uncle's property. She m. John Hely, Secretary of State and Keeper of the Privy Seal, the Marriage Settlement being dated June 8, 1751, upon which he assumed the name and armorials of Hutchinson, the arms being the same as those of the other branch of the family in America, differenced only in that the Cross-crossletts are silver instead of gold, and quartered with those of Hely. She was created Baroness Donoughmore Oct. 16, 1783, and dying June 24, 1788, left, among other issue—

Richard Hely-Hutchinson, the eldest son, created Viscount Suirdale, Nov. 7, 1797, and Earl of Donoughmore, Dec. 29, 1800.—For the rest, see the Peerage.

V. Edward, fourth son of Edward and Susanne, of Alford. In the Boston Records of Births and Baptisms, 1630 to 1700, there appears the issue of Edward Hutchinson the Elder and his wife Sarah in America.

This Edward returned to England. In "Hutchinson in America" the Governor writes—"Edward returned also from New England, and was alive in England in 1675, of which date I have seen a letter from him at London, to his Nephew Eliakim, then at Boston, complaining of the cruelty of the N. England army in the Indian War, for setting dogs upon a poor Squaw, and worrying her to death, after she had come in and discovered the situation of the Indian Army." He had gone out to America in the same ship with Mr. Cotton, and one or two other noted personages, in the year

1633, his brother William following the year after. One of his sons wrote a History of the Indian War—an interesting book if it could be now procured. He left issue—

1. John, bap. 31 day 6 month, 1634. (Julian Calendar.)
2. Ichabod, bap. 3 day 7 month 1637.

VI. Johannes, (A.R.) or John. His two marriages and his children are entered in the Alford Register. He resided in England. His will is extant. The entries are—

His baptism—" 1598. Joh'es filius Ed'di Hutchinson, bapt. eod' die."—i.e. May 18. First marriage—" 1618. Joannes Hutchinson et Elizabetha Woodthorpe desponsat', Octob. 1." Issue—" 1619. Gulielmus, filius Joannis Hutchinson, bapt. Octobr. 17." Probably died an infant. Secondly, he m. Bridgeta, but not at Alford, though his children were born there, as follows—" 1627. Gulielmus, filius Joannis Hutchinson, bapt. Feb. 1."—2.—" Edvardus, filius Joannis Hutchinson, bapt. Aug. 16." 3.—" 1631. Elizabetha filia Joannis Hutchinson, bapt. July 8." 4.—" 1633. Johannis filius Johannis Hutchinson, bapt. Feb. 6." Among the deaths—" 1633. Johannes filius Johannis Hutchinson, sepult. Febr. 10." 5.—Johannes, filius Johannis Hutchinson, bapt. Jan. 29." 6.—" Susanna, filia Jonannis Hutchinson, et Bridgetæ, uxoris, bapt. Nov. 25." 7.—" 1641. Emme Hutchinson, filia Johannis Hutchinson, et Bridgetæ, ux. b. Febr. 4." 8.—Samuel, bap. Feb. 25, 1643.

VII. Susanna. The entry in the A.R. is this:—" Nov. 1599. Susanna, filia Ed'di Hutchinson, bapt. eod' die"—i.e. Nov. 25. Among the burials—" 1601. Susanna, filia Ed'di Hutchinson, sep. 5 Augusti."

VIII. Marie, or Maria, m. Rev. John Wheelwright, and had issue.

Their names are not in the Alford Register. In the admissions to the Church of Boston, Mass., we read—" 12th. of 4th. moneth 1636, John Wheelwright, and Marie his wife."

WILLIAM, the eldest son of Edward. The entry in the A.R. is this:—" 1586. Will^a^mus filius Ed'di Hutchinson, bap. erat, 14 die" [Aug.].

This is the earliest Hutchinson entry in the Register. He was not married at Alford; but in the one-page Tabular Pedigree, already given, of Blunt and Marbury, from the Visitation of Lincolnshire, it appears that he married Anne, daughter of Rev. Francis Marbury and his wife Bridget, sister of Sir Erasmus Dryden, of Canons Ashby, Bart. William lost his father in 1631; in 1633 his younger brother Edward, (some have thought it was his son,) went to America with the Rev. John Cotton, and the year after he followed with his wife and children. He also took his widowed mother Susanne or Susanna, with him. She died at York or Wells as some say, in the State of Maine, and not far from Kittery. (H.) He was representative, Judge of the Executive Court, and Ruling Elder. The religious zeal of his wife, and the storm that she raised by the dissemination of her opinions, at last brought upon her a sentence of banishment out of the Colony, upon which her husband removed his family in the autumn of 1637 to Rhode Island; and having no other shelter, they lived during the winter in a cave or caves, until the cold weather was passed. Her trial, and the sentence of the Court, are printed at the end of the second volume of Governor Hutchinson's History of Massachussetts. By her influence in Rhode Island, she got William Coddington and other Magistrates displaced, and her husband made Governor, or chief Magistrate. He died in 1642; whereupon she left that place with her family, and settled upon some land near Stamford, in Connecticut, that was in dispute between the Dutch and the Indians, when the latter, either mistaking them for Dutch, or hostile against the whole white race, attacked and murdered her, with most of her children and servants, to the number of sixteen persons, and kidnapped one daughter, who however, was afterwards redeemed, and married to Mr. Cole of Narraganset.

In "H. in Am.," written at the end of the 5th vol. of the Diary, we read—"His wife was a high-spirited woman, of a temper inclining rather to govern than be governed, and he seems to have been entirely under her influence. She could not remain in England when Mr. Cotton and Mr. Wheelwright left it, there being no other Ministers known to her who preached the true doctrine of the Gospel. Before she landed in New England her fame had reached it. She said to Mr. Bartholomew, who soon after came to New England, and was a Deputy there, as they were walking together in St. Paul's Church Yard, that she had never any great thing done about her, but it was revealed to her beforehand. And when she was on ship board, in sight of Boston, and saw the mean appearance it made, she said that if she had not a sure word that England would be destroyed, her heart would shake. She would not allow that this expression was owing to the appearance Boston made. Impressions upon her mind she received as divine revelations, and Mr. Cotton gave too much confidence to her in her opinions."

A little further on he writes—"She had certainly made a great division, not meerly in the churches, but in the state, and the greatest part of Boston seems to have favoured her, and to have sent Deputies to the Court who were in her favour, and Mr. Vane's party in the Government were in general on her side. This caused a vigorous exertion of Mr. Winthrop, Mr. Dudley, and other Magistrates, as well as of Mr. Wilson of Boston, and other Ministers, to leave Mr. Vane out of the Government, and to bring Mr. Winthrop in his stead; and this being effected in May, and Mr. Vane, her chief protector, going to England in August, she was brought upon trial in November [1637] following, and sentenced to banishment. Her husband, with about sixty of the inhabitants of Boston, many of them persons of note, had before been disarmed, but I don't find that he was banished, unless it be said, that by banishing his wife, he must of course be banished himself. They both left the Colony, she being kept in custody at her husband's expense until they could prepare themselves. They tried for liberty to reside in New Plimouth Colony, but could not obtain it. In March (18th) 1638, she went from Boston to his farm at Mount Wollaston, or Braintree, and soon after from thence by land to Providence, most of the way being then very difficult for a woman to travel. Her Husband with Mr. Coddington, and divers others of the same religious opinions, had purchased Aquidnick or Rhode Island, of the natives, [for 40 fathoms of white beads, or whampum, that passed for money.] Thither she and her husband, with some of their children went, and were put to hard shifts. Gorton says they lived in caves the first winter."

Most of the members of the family, after their arrival at Boston, had been duly admitted to the Church. Among the entries in the covenant are the following:—"Ye 10th of 6th moneth 1634. Edward Hutchinson ye younger, a single man."—"26th of 8th moneth 1634. Willm. Hutchinson."—"2nd of 9 moneth 1634, Anne Hutchinson, ye wife of our brother Willm Hutchinson."—"9th of 9th moneth 1634. Richard Hutchinson, Francis Hutchinson, ye sonnes of our brother Willm Hutchinson. Faith Hutchinson, one of his daughters. Anne Freiston, one of his kinswomen."—"28th of 10th moneth 1634. Frances Freiston, one of our brother Willm Hutchinson's kinswomen." I am not informed of the relationship with the Freiston family.

When the father was at Rhode Island, he empowered his son Edward, who was in Boston, to look after his affairs for him. In the Suffolk Deeds, Liber I. folio 22, 7th of 6th mo. 1639, there is a Power of Attorney to collect debts from William Hutchinson "to my sonne Edward, of Boston." It is signed with his initials "W. H.," and styled "of Portsmouth in Aquidnecke Iland, gentln." Witnessed by John Sanford, and Samuell Hutchinson.

William and Anne left issue:—

I. EDWARD, the heir, of whom presently.

II. Susanna. "Sep. 1614. Susanna, filia Willi Hutchinson, bap. 4 die." (A.R.) Her death—"1630. Susanna, filia Gulielmi Hutchinson, sepult. Septemb. 8." (A.R.)

III. Richard. "Dec. 1615. Rich^a^us, filius Willi^a^mi Hutchinson, bap. 8. die." (A.R.)

IV. Faith, b. Aug. 14, 1617. (A.R.)

V. Bridgetta. "Jan. 1618. Bridgetta filia Gulielmi Hutchinson, bapt. Jan. 15." (A.R.)

She married John Sanford of Boston, Linc., whom she had probably known in England. In "H. in Am." the Governor writes—"John Sanford married one of her daughters, I suppose the eldest, named Bridget; and from him descended Peleg Sanford, a principal merchant, and Governor of the Colony, whose son William was father to Margaret Sanford, wife to Thomas Hutchinson [himself], to whose children her blood is conveyed by both their parents." The Gov. says Katherine m. T. Savage, but Whitmore says Faith; and that Bridget m. Willis. The Gov. does not mention Faith. From Richard to Faith are only 8 m. 6 days.

VI. Francis. "1620. Franciscus, filius Gulielmi Hutchinson, bapt. Decemb. 24." (A.R.)

VII. Elizabeth. "1621. Elizabetha, filia Gulielmi Huchinson, [sic] bapt. Febr. 17."—"1630. Elizabetha, filia Gulielmi Hutchinson, sep[ulta], eodem die." [Oct. 4.] (A.R.)

VIII. William. "1623. Gulielmus, filius Gulielmi Huchinson, bapt. June 22." (A.R.)

IX. Samuel. "1624. Samuel filius Gulielmi Hutchinson, bapt. Decemb. 17." (A.R.)

X. Anna. "1626. Anna, filia Gulielmi Huchinson, bapt. Maij 5." (A.R.)

XI. Maria. "1627. Maria, filia Gulielmi Hutchinson, bapt. Feb. 22." (A.R.)

Maria I believe married Mr. Collins, and they were amongst the number of those who were killed.

XII. Katherine. "1629. Katherena, filia Gulielmi Hutchinson, bapt. Febr. 7." (A.R.)

She married Major Thomas Savage.

XIII. William. "1631. Gulielmus, filius Gulielmi Huchinson, bapt. Septemb. 28." (A.R.)

XIV. Susanna. "1633. Susanna, filia Gulielmi Hutchinson, bapt. Novemb. 15." (A.R.)

This was the last child born in England. She was ten years old at the time of the massacre, when her mother and most of her relations were killed by the natives; but she escaped their fate, for in 1651, when she was 18, she was married to a Mr. Cole in Boston. The following is the entry in the record of Births and Baptisms, for which I am indebted to Mr. C. G. Hutchinson—"Hutchinson of Charlestown."—"John Cole, son of Isaac Cole, was married to Susanna Hutchinson, daughter of the late William Hutchinson of Road Island, 30th day, 10th moneth 1651, by Richard Bellingham Esq."

In the same list a daughter born in America is found—"Zuryell, daughter, baptised 13 day 1 month 1636." She is mentioned as of the issue of William Hutchinson. Drake, in his Indian Chronicles, speaks of the murders, and of a child seven or eight years old that was recovered from her captors after she had been four years in captivity, having learnt the Indian language, and had forgotten how to speak English. He is not clear in his dates. The father died in 1642, the mother removed in 1643 to Connecticut, in which latter year the catastrophe took place. I had always been under the impression that the child which was kidnapped was the same that in after years married Mr. Cole; but the tradition in the country where the circumstances took place seems to point to the youngest child, as having been the one.

XV. "Zuryell, daughter, baptised 13 day, 1 month, 1636."

The Governor, in his notes, does not mention the child's name. His version of the story is this:—"The people of New Plimouth claimed Rhode Island, as within their patent. This, it is said, induced her to remove to Stamford, taking her family with her, and her son-in-law Collins, who came from St. Christophers, and seems to have been of some consideration: but here she met with fresh trouble, the land upon which she settled being in controversy between the Dutch and Indians. The latter fell upon her and murdered her, as also her son Francis, and Mr. Collins, and wife, and her whole family, consisting of sixteen, except one daughter which they carried into captivity. When her estate was settled, a sum was deposited for the redemption of this daughter."

He afterwards adds—"This daughter was redeemed, and married Mr. Cole of Narragansett. I have heard Mrs. Hutchinson's descend[ts] speak of her as known to them; and Mrs. Remington, my tenant at Conanicut, who herself lived to be 90, often spoke to me of her, as remembering her well."

This evidence inclines to establish Susanna as the kidnapped child. If so, she was ten at the time, and fourteen when she was recovered.

Having gone through the list of William's children, we now proceed to Edward, his eldest son and heir:—

EDWARD. "May, 1613. Edvardus, filius Willi Hutchinson, bapt. 28 die." (A.R.)

The Governor, in "H. in Am." says of him—"He was born in May 1613, was in England again in 1636, and October 13 that year he was married to Catharine, the daughter of Counsellor Hanby, of Ipswich, and returned with her to New England before 1637, for at a session of the General Court he was then called to appear, for having his name to a seditious Petition, and was fined, disarmed, banished, &c. As his Marriage Licence is dated Oct. 19, he was probably married on the 23rd, and not on the 13th.

"He soon after by some means or other made his peace, and never changed his residence for any length of time." His wife's admission to the Church stands thus—"10th of 12th moneth 1638. Katherine, ye wife of our brother Edward Hutchinson ye Younger."

He was Deputy or Representative, and the same Notes further say—"He was the chief military officer of horse in the Colony, having the command of what was called the Three County Troop. When the Indian war broke out in 1675 he was early employed; was sent with his brother-in-law Major Thomas Savage and others to the Narraganset country, and made a Treaty with those Indians; and soon after was employed upon a like errand to the Nipmug Indians, who he expected to find at Quabaog or Brookfield, [apparently about 17 miles west of Boston], but in his way there, at a place called Meminimisset, about ten miles from Brookfield, August 2nd, 1675, the Indians having the day before promised to meet him at Quabaog, he and his attendants were ambushed by a body of Indians. He was mortally wounded by a bullet in the shoulder, and of 24 men, 8 were shot dead, and many of the rest wounded. He was carried to Marlborough, [eight miles west of Boston], and there languished until the 19th Aug., when he died. In the year 1744, travelling to Albany, in order to treat with the Indians of the Six Nations, I left the company, and with Mr. Welsted, Chaplain to the Comiss[rs], and who married my sister Sarah, turned out of the road to the old burying ground, which then lay open, or not enclosed, and there we discovered his grave stone, with the inscription, about 18 inches above the surface."

This was another member of the same family that perished by the natives, but by this time they had learnt the use of the musket. When the Governor was in England, and being at Ipswich, he made some inquiries after the Hanby family:—Vol. I., p. 253. By his first wife Edward left issue the following, taken from the Boston record of Births and Baptisms:—

I. Elishua, daut[r], baptised . . . 5 day 9 month, 1637.

II. Elizabeth . . . . 10 day 9 month, 1639.

She married Mr. Edward Winslow, and left issue. Whitmore, in his Genealogy of Hutchinson, which is very fragmentary, but very praiseworthy as far as it goes, says she married twice, of which I find no record.

III. ELISHA, the heir, of whom presently.

IV. Abigail. Died March 5, 1710, aged 69. She m. Moore, Kellond, and Foster.

In "H. in Am." he does not mention the name of Abigail, but it is to her apparently that the following remarks belong:—"The other first married Moore, and then Thomas Kellond, a noted merchant in Boston; and after his death, between 1680 and '90, Col. Foster, my mother's father. Mr. Kellond built my dwelling house in Boston, which he gave to his wife, and she gave it to my father her nephew, and he to me, she died in 1710, and left an amiable character as a sincere Christian, as well as what was called in that day, a complete gentlewoman: and I remember to have heard my father say, that Sir Wm. Phips, having married a woman of low condition when he was low himself, after he came to his fortune and title, she was put under Mrs. Foster's instructions, in order to learn polite and decent carriage." The Boston Register says—"John Foster and Abigail Kellond, married by John Richards Esq., Assist., Nov. 28, 1689."

There is some want of clearness in the Pedigrees as to whether Abigail was Elisha's sister or his daughter, but as the Governor, in the preceding extract, calls his father "her nephew," she must have been his father's (Elisha's) sister. This is further supported by their ages, allowing for difference of style.

V. Anne, born 18 day 9 month, baptised 19 day 9 month, 1643.

She m. Dyer, and had issue, 2ndly Daniel Vernon, and had issue.

VI. William, baptised, aged about 1 day, . . . 18 day 11 month 1645.

VII. Catherine, ... 2 days, . . . 14 . . . 3 . . . 1648.

Speaking of Edward's daughters, the Governor says—"One of which married Major Richards, and after his death James Allen." This seems to be the one alluded to.

VIII. Susanna. She m. Nathaniel Coddington. Born June 1649.

In the same notes the Governor says—"Susanna married Nath. Coddington, Esq., of Newport, April 19, 1677." According to Whitmore's Pedigree she married a second time.

Edward m. 2ndly Abigail, widow of Robert Button.

Mr. Whitmore has the following note at the foot of page 9:—"Gov. H. calls his wife Abigail Dudson, but Edward's Will mentions the children she had by her husband, Button, and her dau. Abigail m. Joseph Dudson; hence the mistake. She was the dau. of Widow Alice Vermaies, of Salem." As to her death, the Boston Record has the following entry:—"Abigail, wife of Capt. Edward Hutchinson, died Aug. 10, 1689." By her he had—

I. Edward, b. in Jan. 1652, d. unmarried in Boston, in June 1692.

II. Catherine, b. Feb. 13, 1653. She m. 1st, Henry Bartholomew, of Salem; and 2ndly Mr. Chamberlain, by whom she had at all events, a daughter.

In "H. in Am." the Governor writes—"Before the year 1730 I remember one of his daughters by his second wife, who was then above 70 years old, to whom my father used to send presents at Marblehead, by the name of Aunt Chamberlain, so that she must have been born before 1660. She was poor, and lived near Marblehead with, I think, her daughter's husband, named Blaney. I am not sure whether the Blaneys now there, are descended from her."

III. Benjamin, born June 22, 1656.

IV. Hannah, b. May 16, 1659, m. Peter Walker, of Taunton.

ELISHA, eldest surviving son, born in Boston, Nov. 16, 1641.

Authorities differ ten days in the exact date of his marriage, some making it Nov. 19, and others Nov. 9. In "H. in Am." we read—"He was married to Hannah Hawkins Nov. 9, 1665." And the following mention of his wife's father may be quoted:—"Mr. Hawkins was an Assembly man several years. All that ground where the New North Meeting House stands, and the brick houses opposite, built by my father, and so down to the water, was a pasture belonging to him, called 'Hawkins's Pasture.' Two parts, which belonged to the two daughters, Hutchinson and Foster, came to my father: the other, where Clarke's shipyard is, and the house above, went to Major Richards's heirs."

Elisha was a strong active man, made many voyages at sea, and visited England several times. "In ·88," observes the Governor, "he joined with Mr. Nowell and Mr. Mather, as joint Agents in solliciting favour from King James." This favour, so solicited from the King, was against the high-handed rule of Sir Edmund Andros, against whom the Colonists were rebelling. Just at that time, however, King James was preparing to leave England, for England was rebelling against him.

Again:—"He was early a military man, and rose to be Colonel of Boston Regiment, was once sent out in the eastern war after 1688, having command as Major, but was in no action. There were then no Colonels."

And again:—"He was a very stout man, 6 feet 2 inches high, and large bones; until 60 would lie down and sleep in the open air in the field or upon the deck of a ship; but he had a fever, which then broke his constitution, and left him to be infirm ever after.

"He died December 10th, 1717, and was buried, as the custom then was, with great pomp, the Regiment attending, and marching before the corps [corpse?] from the north part of Boston to the place of burial near the Common. I remember him very well, both at his own house and my father's, particularly when he lay on his death-bed, my father carried me with him to receive (I suppose) his blessing. I was then in my seventh year."

With all his health and activity, he was not successful in life. Being in England in 1693—

"He entered into a contract for supplying masts for the Navy. He seems never to have been successful in business,—apt to involve himself in debt upon plans of payment which did not succeed according to expectation. He suffered greatly by his mast contract. Wm. Partridge, Lt. Gov. of N. Hampshire, being jointly concerned, lived at Portsmouth—procured the masts—had the profits of all the supplies to the workmen, and might raise a fortune out of them, and yet his partner in the contract be impoverished. When the masts came to market, such deductions were made from the prices agreed, on account of defects in the quality, that all the expected profit was sunk. He never recovered his involvement. My father paid some of his debts in England, or he must have been distressed. The last 20 or 15 years of his life he lived upon the rents of his second wife's estate, and what profits he could make from his employments in Government."

"He was a Judge in the Common Pleas for the county of Suffolk, and continued until he died."

Of his marriage the Governor writes—"His first wife was Hannah Hawkins, daughter of Thomas Hawkins, who was a man of property, commander, and part owner of a ship said to be 500 tons. I have had a letter which he wrote, giving an account of an unfortunate voyage made in her." By his first wife he had issue—

I. Mary, b. Oct. 11, 1666, d. July 27, 1667.— Boston Register.

II. Elisha, b. Mar. 16, 1667–8, d. Nov. 18, 1678.—Do.

III. Elizabeth, b. Feb. 24, 1669–70, m. J. Clarke, M.D., d. Dec. 2, 1730.—Do.

In enumerating his children, the Governor in "H. in Am." as before says—"Elizabeth, who, after his [her father's] death, married John Clarke Esq., one of the Council, and a Physician of note, but had no children. She died of a cancer in her breast, about, or soon after the year 1730."

IV. Hannah, b. Jan. 20, 1671–2, m. John Ruck, d. circa. 1740.

The Boston Register says—"John Ruck and Hannah Hutchinson were married Apl. 29, 1697 by Mr. James Allen."

Of her he says—"Hannah, who married John Ruck, a merchant in Boston, and a Justice of Peace. They both lived to old age, dying after 1740." Also he writes—"Three daughters only survived her; the eldest married Benning Wentworth, afterwards Gov. of New Hampshire. Her name was Abigail. She had 3 sons who all died before or soon after her, without issue. Hannah married Joseph Lillie, by whom she had two sons, John, who died, and I think left issue: Theophilus died without issue. The third daughter, Margaret, was living in 1776, not married."

From these mems. the following Tabular arrangement is made out—

1. Abigail Ruck m. Benning Wentworth. 3 sons, ob. s. p.
2. Hannah, m. Joseph Lillie, and had two sons—John, who left issue; and Theophilus, ob. s. p.
3. Margaret, living in 1776 unm.

V. Katherine, b. Feb. 24, 1672–3, d. July 26, 1674.—(H.)

VI. THOMAS, b. Jan. 30, 1674–5, of whom presently.

VII. Mary, b. Sep. 30, 1676, d. Nov. 27, 1676.

The Governor continues—"His [Elisha's] wife Hannah died Oct. 9, 1676, and Sept. 12, 1677, he married Elizabeth Freke, widow of John Freke, merchant, and daughter of Major Thomas Clarke, and by her had—

I. Edward, b. June 18, 1678, who m. Lydia Foster in 1706, and had issue—

1. Elisha, b. Feb. 20, 1708.
2. Lydia, b. July 26, 1710.
3. John, b. Sep. 27, 1711.
4. Elizabeth, b. May 19, 1713.
5. Lydia, b. Sep. 20, 1714.
6. Edward, b. Jan. 24, 1715–6.
7. Elizabeth, b. Mar. 3, 1716–7.
8. Mary, a dau., twins: { both born apparently,
9. Clarke, a son, { Aug. 18, 1718.
10. Sarah, b. May 12, 1722. Ob. cæl.
11. Lydia, b. Feb. 2, 1722–3.
12. Edward, b. Dec. 8, 1729. Ob. cæl.
13. Elizabeth, b. Dec. 1, 1731, m. the Rev. Nathaniel Robbins, whose descendants still survive in honour, and we hope in prosperity.

The above long list of 13 children I have taken from Mr. Whitmore's Genealogies of Hutchinson and Oliver. The Governor's notes do not contain anything like so many. He was in England, writing only from memory, and as the first nine, and the eleventh, all appear to have died in infancy, he had possibly never heard the names of half of them. Perhaps Mr. Whitmore took his list from the Boston Register, for he writes—"See Reg. I, 302." Edward died in March, 1752, and Lydia his wife, July 10, 1748, aged 61.

As the Governor was 41 years old at the time of his uncle's death, of course he knew him well. He speaks of him in the following terms:—"He had what was esteemed a handsome fortune from his mother, and a good position with his wife, but loved ease, and suffered the greatest part of it to moulder away. He travelled when young through Spain and France, and so to England: was Colonel of the Boston Regiment; a Representative of Boston, and of the Council; and a Justice of the Common Pleas many years; and Judge of Probate of County of Suffolk. He was polite in his behaviour; a truly honest man; and scrupulously strict in all the exterior, as well as interior, points of the Christian religion; of not very strong powers of mind, and in his latter years they were much enfeebled; and continuing in his publick posts until his death, which was in 1752, his deficiency began to be matter of complaint. He was also many years Treasurer of Harvard College. I believe his predecessors generally had been persons of academical education, which he was not."

II. Mehetabel, b. Feb. 6, 1679–80, d. Mar. 6, eod. ann.

III. Elisha, b. May, 16, 1681, d. June 23, 1700, at Surinam.

IV. Clarke, b. July 4, 1683, d. Sep. 24, eod. ann.

V. Samuel, b. Oct. 22, 1685, d. Dec. 10, eod. ann.

THOMAS, eldest surviving son of Elisha.

Of him his son the future Governor writes:—"Thomas Hutchinson was born in Boston, January 30, 1674–5. He was intended for the college, but Col. Foster marrying his aunt, [this is another proof that Abigail was Elisha's sister, and Edward's daughter, above discussed,] and being a very noted merchant, it was thought advisable to put him into the Counting house, and he lived with him until he was twenty-one. In 1696 he made a voyage to England, and returning in a large ship, of which Col. Foster and Mr. Lillie were owners, they were drove a shoar in a snow storm in Cape Ann harbour, under the town of Gloucester, and did not know the land until they were informed by the inhabitants, though they had run three or four miles from the mouth of the harbour through a narrow inlet. Before they could get a shoar the water was above the cabin deck, and the things in the drawers at the bottom of a trunk, still in my possession, marked 'T. H. 1696,' were damaged. This deliverance made an impression which never was effaced, and he dated from thence his Christian life."

Of Colonel Foster he says:—"Col. Foster was, as I have reason to believe, born at Ailesbury, [in Buckinghamshire.] His name was John, and his father was of the same name. The son lived with a merchant in London, who made him a factor in a voyage to Barbadoes, soon after 1670. The father also went to Barbadoes. The son went from Barbadoes to Boston, and lodging at the house of Daniel Turell, one of the Selectmen, married his daughter, by whom, besides other children, who died young, he had two daughters, Sarah and Lydia, who survived him. The father came to Boston also, and died there in his son's family. Daniel Turell, is the last named in the Writ of Quo Warranto against the first Charter of Massachusetts Bay. After her death he married the widow of Thomas Kellond, a wealthy merchant, who left no children. She was aunt [another point of evidence] to Thomas Hutchinson, who married the eldest of Col. Foster's daughters, and ten years older than himself—a woman of great sense and great virtue, and was called much of a gentlewoman. She survived her husband about a month, and made her nephew her principle legatee.

"Col. Foster first appeared in public life in 1688–9, being active in the New England Revolution. He was one of the Counsellors named in the new Charter, and was elected every year until his death, which was Febr. 9, 1710–11, being in his 59th year. He was a good grammar scholar; wrote correct English; and was a compleat merchant, and a strictly just and upright man. His widow, Mrs. Abigail Foster, died March 5th following, aged 69."

Continuing his biographical notices of his father, the first Thomas Hutchinson, he remarks:—"After about seven years business, in which he had gained three or four thousand pounds sterling, he married Sarah Foster (December 24, 1703), eldest of two daughters, and of his master Col. Foster, and inherited half his estate. About the year 1706 or 7 he was a Selectman and representative for Boston, and continued so until 1714, when he was elected of the Council, and except one year, was annually elected until his death—about 26 years. When he was left out, Gov. Shute, who heard of it in England, asked what reason they could give for leaving out a man who always spoke his mind without fear, either of the Governor or the people?—That was the only reason of his being left out.

"When he was about 35 years of age, he came into possession of a very handsome fortune. While his estate was small, besides maintaining his family, he added to his estate. When thus enlarged he became less attentive—was generous—charitably disposed—acquired a habit—from year to year his estate lessened, and before he died, had reduced his estate so much as to lessen the income below the necessary expense of a large family, and he lamented at his death his not being able better to provide for his widow and children, and when his eldest son answered, that he had enough, he expressed his satisfaction. His losses were owing to a large concern in ships, and when his son mentioned it to him, he asked—What will become of all the people in my employ, if I should sell all my vessels? I have observed that very few persons in trade in Boston raised fortunes by concerns in shipping, any further than just to make them subservient to some other principal object. Now and then a bold adventure has been fortunate."

If he died a comparatively poor man, he must needs have been rather wealthy at one period of his life; for, comparing his will with that of his son, the

Governor, as we did sundry pages back, the impression then was, that he was in affluent circumstances at the close of his life.

He was born, Jan 30, 1674–5: married Dec. 24, 1703: and died Dec. 3, 1739. His wife Sarah Foster was born about 1664, that is, about ten years before her husband, and died Nov. 6, 1752. They left the following issue:—

I. Foster, b. Sept. 18, 1704, d. in 1721.

"His eldest son, born 18 Sep. 1704, he called Foster, after the surname of his wife's father. He died late in 1721 of the small-pox.—"H. in America."

II. Sarah, b. Mar. 29, 1706, m. Jan. 16, 1728.

"The next child, Sarah, born in 1706, married Mr. Welsted, a minister of Boston, of a most amiable character, who died of a palsie in 1753. She died in 1775."—H.

Mr. Whitmore says she was born in 1708, and calls her husband Welsteed. The H. mem. has 1706, and uniformly Welsted.

III. Abigail, b. Aug. 2, 1709.

"The next, Abigail, married Mr. John Davenport, [Aug. 24, 1732], son of Judge Davenport, by whom she had one daughter. He died soon after, and she married William Merchant, but had no child by him."—H.

IV. Thomas, b. Sep. 9, 1711, the heir, of whom presently.

"Thomas was the next, born September 9, 1711, who is the writer of this in 1778."—H.

He was the Governor of Massachusetts, and there needs no particulars of him here.

V. John.

"John, the next, died an infant."—H.

VI. Hannah, b. Nov. 1, 1714, m. Aug. 23, 1733.

"Hannah, born in 1714, married Mr. Samuel Mather, Minister in Boston."—H.

VII. Elisha, b. Feb. 6, 1715–6, d. Aug. 2, 1739.

"Elisha, born in 1717, died in 1739, Aug. 2."—H. The authorities differ in the year of birth. Elisha died of the fever that almost killed his brother, caught at the Castle when nearly 40 people were infected by it.—See vol. I., p. 50.

VIII. Lydia, b. May 30, 1717, m. May 27, 1736, d. about 1745.

"Lydia married Mr. George Rogers, a merchant in Boston. She died of a consumption about 1745:—left a son Nathaniel, who died about 1770, and a daughter Sarah, who died in 1776."—H.

IX. Hawkins, bapt. Feb. 19, 1720–1.

"Hawkins born, and died of the small pox, an infant, in 1721."—H.

X. Elizabeth, b. May 14, 1723.

"I am not certain," he writes, in speaking of Elizabeth, "whether her birth preceded or followed Hawkins. She outlived him a few years." A comparison of the dates of birth, however, sets this point at rest. Writing from memory in London, and after a very long interval, he was not sure of the date, but this is supplied in Mr. Whitmore's Pedigree.

XI. Foster, b. Sep. 7, 1724.

"Foster, born in 1724, who sustained publick posts, and is now with 9 children an Exile in Halifax, Nova Scotia."—H.

XII. Edward, b. Mar. 27, 1726, d. 1730.

"Edward, born in 1725 or 1726, a sweet tempered delicate boy, died of the small-pox in 1730."—H.

The Governor appends the following remark, speaking of Col. Foster:— "When he married, Col. Foster and his wife, aunt to Mr. Hutchinson, [his father], settled the mansion house, the fee being in Mrs. Foster, on Mr. Hutchinson and his eldest son Foster, the survivor &c." The death of young Foster Hutchinson in 1721, brought the house to the Governor.

Thomas Hutchinson, the Governor, as stated, was born Sep. 9, 1711, married Margaret Sanford May 16, 1734, she died March 12, 1753, and he died, June 3, 1780, at Brompton, and on the 9th of the same month he was interred in a vault in the north transept of Croydon church, Surrey. The unsettled state of the family affairs, owing to the revolutionary scenes through which they had passed, together with the many anxieties consequent on these events, had served to postpone the erection of any memorial. Recently however, a brass, bearing the following inscription, has been affixed against the north wall of the transept. At the upper part there is a shield bearing his armorials, quartered with those of Foster, in right of his mother, who was co-heiress with her sister; and in the centre is placed a shield of pretence charged with those of Sanford, in right of his wife, who was co-heiress with her sisters, whose representatives have all died out.

THOMAS HUTCHINSON Esq., B.A. (HARVARD), DCL. (OXON).
CAPTAIN-GENERAL AND GOVERNOR-IN-CHIEF
OF THE LATE PROVINCE OF MASSACHUSETTS BAY,
IN NORTH AMERICA,
SON OF THOMAS H. AND SARAH (FOSTER,)
SON OF ELISHA H. AND HANNAH (HAWKINS,)
SON OF EDWARD H. AND CATHERINE (HANBY,)
SON OF WILLIAM H. AND ANNE (MARBURY,)
SON OF EDWARD HUTCHINSON AND HIS WIFE SUSANNE,
OF ALFORD IN THE COUNTY OF LINCOLN.
HE WAS BORN SEP[R] 9TH 1711, AND DIED JUNE THE 3RD 1780,
AND WAS INTERRED IN A VAULT UNDER THIS CHURCH.

He had the following issue—

I. THOMAS, the eldest son, of whom presently.

II. Elisha, b. Dec. 24. 1745, o. s. m. Mary, d. of Col. Geo. Watson. She died in 1823, at Birmingham.

He accompanied his father to England in 1774, leaving his wife in America, with the intention of returning in a few months; but owing to the breaking out of open hostilities, his return was prevented, and it was three years before she could join him in England. Having reached his eightieth year, he died at Tutbury June 24, 1824, having had issue—

1. Mary, d. young in America, (F. R.)
2. Margaret, b. 1774, d. 1796.
3. Elizabeth, she died at about the age of 14.
4. George Watson, b. 1782, d. 1818.
5. John, b. Sep. 21, 1793. Perpetual Curate of Blurton, near Trentham, co. Staff. Percentor and Canon of Lichfield, Editor of Vol. 3 of Gov. Hutchinson's Hist. of Massachusetts, in 1828. He m. his cousin, Martha Oliver H., May 10, 1836. He died Ap. 27, and was buried May 2, 1865, at Blurton, having had issue—
   - Judith Rogers, b. Oct. 28, 1838, d. May 4, 1844.
   - Edith Martha, b. Oct. 3, 1845, m. Arthur Bailey, June 15, 1882, and had Arthur John, b. Nov. 28, d. Dec. 4, 1883.
   - John Rogers, b. Mar. 6, 1848, m. Ruth Hombersley, Oct. 19, 1882, at Kirk Ireton, Derbyshire.

III. Sarah, b. about 1745, m. Feb. 1, 1770 to Dr. Peter Oliver, d. June 28, 1780.

It was she who courageously kept by her father when the mob broke into his house at Boston, Aug. 26, 1765, as mentioned in Gov. H.'s Hist. of Mass., III. 124. Dr. P. Oliver writes in his Diary :—

"Feb. 1, 1770. I was married by Dr. Pemberton to Mrs. [abbreviation for Mistress] S. Hutchinson; exceedingly private, of a Thursday Evg., according to the Old Charter. Thus ended the happiest time of my life, as it was freest from cares and solicitudes, which now hastened apace. I was at this time in the latter part of my 29th year, and Mrs. Hutchinson in the 26th year of her age.

"1774. Nothing but mobs and riots all this summer. Wednesday the 14. of Sep. I was mobbed.

"Sep. 23. Mrs. Oliver was brought to bed of another son, a fine hearty boy. My father, the 1st. of this month fled to Boston: my mother the last of Sepr. went to Boston, and never returned.

"Feb. 1, 1775.—I fled to Boston from the mob, abt. the 3rd. or 4th. of Feb. Aunt Welsted died the last of Feb. I sent a coach for Mrs. Oliver and children, and nurse: they came the 1st. of March to Boston." His remarks on the blockade, with the incidents of the voyage to England, have been given in the earlier part of this volume. All his children died young except Thomas. Peter died July 19, 1794, of consumption. The Diary says—" About 9 o'clock P. O. died in the Evg., aged 19 years, and almost 10 months, wanting 3 days. He was the sickest person in a consumption I ever saw: had lost his voice almost 7 months, and a very bad sore throat most of the time: continual cough and expectoration—high fever—great prostration of strength, and loss of flesh. P. O. was buried in the Cty., St. Chad's Yard, Wednesday the 23rd."

"1796, Sep. 20.—Peggy died, aged 25 yrs. 6 months, and 13 days, after being sorely afflicted with a consumption, and the worst symptoms."

His son Thomas was a Surgeon in the Militia. The latter part of his life he resided at Great Yarmouth in Norfolk, and as he did not marry, with him ended the last representative of the Chief Justice Peter Oliver. He survived until Saturday Feb. 4, 1865, having reached his 93rd year.

IV. William, d. unm. Feb. 20, 1780, aged 27. (Billy.)

V. Margaret, d. unm. Sep. 20, 1777, aged 24. (Peggy.)

The other Pedigrees in the family say there were 7 or 8 more who died in infancy.

THOMAS, eldest son of Thomas, the Governor.

He was born in America in 1740, m. Oct. 10, 1771, Sarah, d. of Lieut. Gov. Andrew Oliver, she having been born Sep. 18, 1745. He was Judge of the Court of Probate for the County of Suffolk in Massachusetts. They were shut up in Boston with their two first children during the blockade and bombardment, and got on board ship in March 1776 on the evacuation of the city, when the third child was born [my father] as they were leaving for England. Their career after they had arrived in England has been sufficiently given in the preceding pages. She died May 1, 1802. He died in 1811. They were deposited in a vault in the middle of Heavitree old church. The old church was pulled down, and a new and larger one erected on the same site in 1843 or 4. Being in the church in 1846, and making some enquiries about the vaults, the Sexton told me that when the new church was built, it was judged better, for sanitary reasons, to fill up all the vaults with earth, and it was ordered that all the bones found in the vaults should be collected, and buried in the south-west corner of the churchyard. I was somewhat shocked, but said nothing. They left issue the following:—

I. Thomas, the eldest son, of whom presently.

He was born in America in 1772: brought by his father to England in 1776: he was a Barrister-at-Law, resided during the early years of his career at No. 14 New Boswell Court, Lincoln's Inn, London, and after that in Magdalen Street, Exeter. He married Elizabeth Hagen in 1799: she was born in 1774 or 5, and died in 1808: he m. 2ndly Mrs. Tolfrey, widow, by which latter he had no family. She died before him. He died Nov. 12, 1837, and was interred at the N.W. corner of Heavitree churchyard. A stone, from which I copied the following inscription, marks the spot:—"Underneath | this stone | Lie the mortal remains | of | Thomas Hutchinson Esq., | Barrister-at-Law | who departed this life | the 12th of November, 1837, | aged 65. | Them also which sleep in Jesus | will God bring with him. | I. Thes. 4, 14."

II. Mary Oliver H., b. in America Oct. 14, 1773.

She was brought to England by her father and mother in 1776: m. Cap. W. S. Oliver, R.N., grandson of Lieut. Gov. Andrew Oliver, by his second wife, at Heavitree, in Oct. 1811: she d. at East Teignmouth, Devon, July 11, 1833, at 5 P.M. He was born March 8, 1774, and d. at Truro, in Cornwall, July 26, 1845, having had the following issue:—

1. Mary Hutchinson O., b. Feb. 25, 1813: m. her cousin Frederick Hutchinson, July 1, 1837.—See Frederick H.
2. Elizabeth Gertrude O., b. about 1814, d. at Sidmouth Oct. 14, 1829. She was a pretty girl, and very much admired. She caught a chill at, or coming from, a ball held at the London Hotel: some said it

was eating an ice after being in a hot room. I think her illness did not extend beyond a fortnight. She was buried close outside the north wall of the Parish Church; but when the church was rebuilt in 1860, the more extended wall of the new north transept brought it within side.

3. William Hutchinson O., b. Mar. 26, 1816. Took Holy Orders: m. his cousin, Rachel Hutchinson, Feb. 22, 1841: had a daughter, Elizabeth Mary O., b. May 22, 1842. He died Rector of Stapleford, co. Herts, Jan. 25, 1873. With him, as far as I have been able to ascertain, died the last male representative of the Oliver family in England. His daughter died May 12, 1876, being the last of her race in this country. Thus, as far as I am informed, all the descendants of Mary Sanford, the second wife of Lieut. Governor Andrew Oliver, have passed away; but the offspring of Mary Fitch, his first wife, continue to survive honourably in America.

III. Andrew, b. on board ship, Mar. 24, 1776.

He was brought to England by his father and mother: bapt. at Kensington, Nov. 6, 1777, as in the Governor's Diary: finished his education at Catherine Hall, University of Cambridge: entered the Medical profession: was articled to Mr. Samuel Luscombe, a surgeon of Exeter—the Articles are dated Feb. 20, 1795. In one of his memorandum books is the following entry:—"Entered at Cath. Hall, Apl. 7th, 1796." At the time when he was a student at Exeter Hospital there was no way of obtaining bodies for dissection but by what some would call rather irregular ways. I have a long copy of verses giving an account of an attempt by the students to disinter a body, when they were attacked by a party of soldiers, and driven off. A mem. says—"Written on occasion of an attack made by the Sussex Cavalry on the pupils of the D. and E. Hospital, when disinterring an executed criminal.—Apl. 1796." I have heard my father say that they went out one night with tools to possess themselves of this body, but had not been digging long before they perceived soldiers in the dim glimmer of the night, getting over the fences, and the discharge of sundry horse-pistols among them, made some of the party rather disposed to run for it: they however, held their ground, when the soldiers came up, and handling them pretty roughly, for they were evidently the worse for liquor, and threatening them with instant death, thrust their swords through the coats of some, and then led them all off to the Guard-Room of the Barracks where they were temporarily quartered. When there they loudly demanded to see the officers, but the officers were at the Theatre in Exeter. They were released about midnight, but they laid a strong complaint against the conduct of the men in endangering their lives. The officers made every apology, and had the men drawn out in line, when the complainants passed up and down before them, but they found it impossible to identify or swear to any of their assailants.

I have part of the skin of a Negro, hanged about this period at Heavitree Gallows, and dissected at the Hospital by my father and the other students. It is however, not so much the skin as the cuticle and the colouring matter. It is of a deep brown.

The use of hair powder was at this time general, and frequent mention of it occurs in his cash-book.

"1799, Nov. 15. Powder and pomat .		1	6.
"1800, Ap. 5. Powder Certificate . .	1	1	0.
"1801, Feb. 20. Powder Puff		2	0."

I remember the powder puff. It was an oblate ball of swans' down about as big as a man's fist, with a short handle on the upper side, and kept in a round wooden box (I still have the box) with the hair powder. I have often seen him powder his hair by dabbing this puff against it. When I was a child I one day saw him bathe. He dived into the water with his head white, and he came up with his head black—greatly to my astonishment. The cost of his Degree was this—

" Expenses for Degree, &c.			
"1801, March 26. Gretton's men . .		8	6
" Professor, for Act	7	7	0
" Caution	1	0	0
" University servants	0	10	0
" Registrar	4	5	0
" Proctor	2	10	10
" College fees.	6	19	4
	£23	0	8"

He was elected one of the Physicians of Exeter Hospital in or about Oct. 1801, at the early age of 25, and a Fellow of the Royal Society in May 1804, and an entry referring to it appears thus :—" May 3, Admission fees, &c., to Royal Society . . . £6,,0,,0." He had a brass door plate made, with his name "Dr. Hutchinson" engraved on it, (which I still have,) which is thus recorded—" 1801, June 4, Door plate . . . 0,,9,,0." Further on appears the following—" 1804, Dec. 24, Admiss. and Subs. to London Med[ical] Society . . . £3,,3,,0." He resigned his appointment at Exeter Hospital in Feb. 1804, went to London, lectured on medical subjects, and married, October 29, 1805, Anne, daughter of Vice Admiral Sir William Parker, of Harburn, co. Warwick, Bart., whose widow had a house on Ham Common, in the parish of Kingston-upon-Thames. The following entry—" 1805, Oct. 9, Wg. ring . . . . 0,,7,,6," I doubt not is the Wedding-ring. Though one of the best of mothers has now been 30 years in her grave, I have got this ring, and also the Guard-ring that she wore over it. The other entries are plain—

" 25th.	Marriage Licence	3	3	0
" 29th.	Clergyman	5	0	0
" ——	Clerk	0	10	6
" ——	Ringers and Sexton	1	10	6
" ——	Lady P.'s servants.	2	10	6"

He lived a time at Richmond, in Surrey: was appointed Physician to Winchester Hospital: returned to Devonshire, and eventually died at Sidmouth, Dec 23, 1846. His widow, who was born June 12, 1778, died at Sidmouth, March 5, 1855, having had issue—

1. Young Bingham, (Godfathers, Mr. Young and Admiral Bingham,) b. at Richmond, Surrey, Aug. 14, and bapt. Oct. 14, 1806. He was a good classical scholar, with a quick turn for figures and mathematical studies. He entered the Royal Navy at the usual age, but after some years' service, and having a strong passion for emigration, he joined the first expedition for founding the projected colony of South Australia; and as Cap. Sir John Hindmarsh, the first Governor, had known his uncle the second Sir W. P., he went out in the same ship with him in or about 1835. When there, he joined the exploring parties that searched the country for a good place for the Capital. Influenced by Sir John, who inclined to

think that near the mouth of the great river Murray would be the most advantageous place for the capital city, as opening up a highway to the heart of the country, he bought near 1000 acres at Goolwa, Port Eliot, and the Hindmarsh Valley; but the next Governor decided to place the chief city where Adelaide now stands.

He returned to England; married Augusta Kingdon, of Narracot, June 15, 1852, at Heavitree; sailed again Nov. 5 in the same year, and busied himself on his estates until his death, which occurred Aug. 3, 1870. He left a widow, and the following children:—

Augusta Bingham, b. May 26, 1855.
Parker Oliver, b. Ap. 14, 1857.
Mary Kingdon, b. July 28, 1859, d. Jan. 25, 1864.
Orlando Bingham, b. Ap. 14, 1862.
Jane Collingwood, b. Aug. 6, 1867.

2. Elizabeth Louisa, b. at Richmond, June 2, 1808, bapt. Sep. 10, d. Mar. 11, 1809.
3. Louisa Anne, b. at Richmond, June 26, 1809, bapt. Oct. 8, and d. Mar. 10, buried Mar. 12, 1810, in the parish of St. Laurence, Winchester.
4. Peter Orlando, b. at Winchester, Nov. 10, 1810, bapt. at Heavitree Oct. 22, 1811. (The Editor.)
5. Frances Harriet, b. at Tiverton, Devon, Ap. 24, 1812, bapt. at St. Peter's church, May 21, 1813; m. Charles, eldest son of Gen. Rumley, of Arcot House, Sidmouth, July 18, 1838, at Tiverton. He d. in S. Australia, Mar. 4, 1855, buried at Gawlertown. She m. 2ndly, Mr. John Robertson, widower, of Strowan Grove, near Salisbury, S. A., in 1856. He d. 1870.
6. William George, b. at Tiverton, July 18, and bapt. Aug. 28, 1813. He d. Ap. 6, and buried at St. George's Chapel, Fore Street, Ap. 11, 1822.

IV. A child, whose name is not recorded.

The family papers do not mention such a child, which was probably born between Andrew and William. Its existence is no where alluded to, except by a passing remark in the Governor's Diary, where he speaks of its death, as follows:—"1778, Jan. 10.—At Brompton, at my son's, where I had not been since the death of his child."

V. William, b. June 14, 1778, in England.

From one or two remarks in some of his father's letters, written at the time he was a young man finishing his education and going to College, it appears that his health was not so strong and robust as his father could have wished. He entered the Church, was locum tenens for some time at Heavitree, and Vicar of Colebrook, Devon. In April 1807, he m. Louisa, daughter of Captain Robert Parker, R.N., brother of Sir W. P. of Harburn. In 1797 this Captain Parker was lost at sea in a singular way, and some thought in rather a suspicious way. As he was my mother's uncle, she had often heard the circumstance spoken of in the family, and I have frequently heard her mention it. Captain Parker was in command of a frigate, and was running before the wind in a heavy gale somewhere near the Cape of Good Hope. He was in his cabin at his desk writing, when a heavier lurch of the ship than usual, threw him sideways, desk and all, through the open port into the sea. The man at the helm heard him cry out, "Throw me a rope!" but the pace at which the ship was going, the impossibility of suddenly arresting her course without broaching to, and the certain danger of bringing her broadside to the waves in a heavy sea, together with the suddenness of the event, all combined to paralyse every effort, so that nothing was done. Every sailor will admit the danger of trying to stop a ship under such circumstances; but is every sailor satisfied that a man and his desk could be thrown through the port of a frigate, which, in the small ships of that day was not a very large hole, without his being able to save himself with his arms? This is the point that excited considerable discussion in naval circles. Accident or not, that was his end.

My uncle William died when I was six years old. I remember him once, and only once, when I may have been near five. I was playing with his children at the Vicarage at Heavitree near the bottom of the stairs, when he came out of his room on to the landing above, and calling our attention to a pistol he had in his hand, into which he had put a small charge of powder to amuse us little folks, he fired it high over our heads. The noise of the report, and the sight of the smoke, made a lasting impression on my young mind.

He died early in life, I think of weak lungs, and was buried near his brother Thomas, at the N.W. corner of Heavitree churchyard, where a tombstone bears the following memorials of himself, his wife, and his youngest child:—"To the Memory | of the Rev[d]. | William Hutchinson | who departed this life | on the 3rd day of May | 1816, Æt. 37. | Also of Henrietta Jane Hutchinson | his youngest daughter, who died | the 28th of August 1816, | Aged 1 year & 7 months. | Also of | Louisa Collingwood | Hutchinson | his widow, who departed this life | on the 7th day of August, 1829." They left issue—

1. Sarah Louisa, b. Ap. 8, 1808, d. Dec. 2, 1876. Buried at Normacot.
2. Louisa Augusta, b. July 3, 1809, m. Rev. Edward Blick, M.A., Rector of Rotherhithe, b. 1791, Inducted 1835, d. June 25, 1867.
3. William Pyke Hargood, b. Aug. 25, 1810, Vicar of Blurton, co. Staff., and Prebendary of Curborough, in Lichfield Cathedral: m. Caroline Allen, b. Jan. 5, 1825, m. Sep. 19, 1850, and have issue—
   Florence Caroline, b. May 9, 1852.
   Sanford William, b. Oct. 26, 1853. In Holy Orders.
   Allen, b. Jan. 8, 1855.
   Edward Oliver, b. Dec. 9, 1856; m. Josephine Hickson.
   Anne Whitacre, b. May 30, 1859.
   Katharine, b. Dec. 27, 1861.
4. Martha Oliver, b. Ap. 1, 1812, m. her cousin John Hutchinson May 10, 1836, as above, and d. Aug. 2, 1863.
5. Henry Sanford, b. July 15, 1813, m. Georgina Catherine Willis, circa 1833, 2ndly, Sarah Munn, June 2, 1863, and has had—Henry Munn, b. Mar. 2, 1864. 2, William Robert, b. Aug. 3, 1865. 3, Edith Sarah Henrietta, b. June 18, 1867. 4, Arthur Edward, b. Nov. 5, 1868. 5, Lizzie Catherine Georgina, b. Jan. 22, 1871. 6, Frederick Parker, b. Mar. 14, d. Ap. 7, 1872.
6. Henrietta Jane, b. Jan. 1815, and d. in Aug. 1816. She was buried at the N.W. part of Heavitree churchyard, where a separate stone, erected to her memory, bears the following inscription:—"Henrietta Jane | Hutchinson | died 26th August, | 1816." Upon this inscription it may be observed, that the day of her death is said to have been August 26, whereas, on the stone erected to her father and mother, above, it is stated to have been August 28. There is an oversight somewhere.

THOMAS, eldest grandson of the Governor.

It has been observed above that he was born in America in 1772, being the first child of Thomas, the Judge of the Court of Probate for the county of Suffolk, and his wife Sarah, daughter of Lieut. Gov. Andrew Oliver. He was in Boston during the siege; and on the evacuation of the city, in March 1776, he was brought to England by his parents. He married twice: by his second wife Mrs. Tolfrey, he had no family; but by Elizabeth Hagen, his first, he had issue:—

I. THOMAS, of whom presently.

II. William, d. unm.

III. Frederick Oliver, eventual heir.

He was born Jan. 20, 1804, m. 1stly, his cousin Mary H. Oliver, July 1, 1837. Removed to south Africa. She was born Feb. 25, 1813, and died June 4, 1852, having had issue by her husband the following—

1. Leslie, b. Sep. 30, 1838, d. June 30, 1840.
2. Mary, b. Ap. 20, 1840.
3. Thomas Sylvester, b. Oct. 20, 1841.
4. Frederick, b. Ap. 9, 1844.
5. Lucy, b. Feb. 24, 1846.
6. John Copley, b. July 11, 1850.

He m. 2ndly, Dorothea Lange, Mar. 13, 1853, and dying Mar. 31, 1873, had issue—

1. Arthur, b. Jan. 2, 1854.
2. A girl, stillborn, 1855.
3. Herbert Waldo, b. May 11, 1856.
4. Edward, b. Jan. 5, 1858.

IV. Rachel, b. May 2, 1806.

She m. her cousin the Rev. W. H. Oliver, Feb. 22, 1841, at Rotherhithe, and had offspring, a daughter named Elizabeth Mary, b. May 22, 1842. He d. Jan. 25, 1873, being, as before observed, the last male representative of the Olivers in England. Elizabeth Mary died May 12, 1876.

THOMAS, the eldest son of Thomas and Elizabeth Hagen.

He was born July 29, 1800. Entered the navy of the Hon. East India Company. In 1823 he m. Gertrude Tolfrey, daughter of his father's second wife, by her first husband. After he retired from the service, he lived at Antwerp and at Bruges; and being of an ingenious turn of mind, he undertook and successfully accomplished the difficult task of building at the former city a steamer called the "Antwerpen," assisted only by the natives, of whose language he knew little. This turned out to be a very good sea boat, and she used to run between Antwerp and London. Afterwards, in 1838, he built another for the Government. She was called the "Bruges d'Anvers," and was built at Bruges. He died in London Aug. 5, 1842, and was interred at Rotherhithe. His wife, whose health had been much impaired by ague in the low countries, died Sep. 16, in the same year, aged 49. As he died without offspring, his brother Frederick became the heir.

COLOPHON.

All those who may have turned their attention to genealogies, have found out how easy it is to make mistakes, and how hard it is to avoid oversights. Where a multitude of dates have to be carefully recorded, and where the same names recur at irregular intervals in different generations, extreme caution is necessary to prevent straying from the path of accuracy. The preceding Pedigree of Governor Hutchinson's branch of the great stock has been compiled from all available materials, both English and American. A thing of this sort, from its very nature, can never be complete, because something more may always be added. Though short, compared with some Pedigrees, it is at all events respectable. I can say with truth I have no where discovered the presence of a scamp, a spendthrift, or a black sheep: neither have I met with any immoral connection; and the rigidity of the Puritan laws and customs in America, may be accepted as an assurance that no irregularities occurred during the 150 years that they were in that country. Of all things in this world I hold sham, false, and cooked-up Pedigrees in the greatest contempt. Stop!—there is one thing I hold still more contemptible—and that is, the person who can make them.

If, in these volumes, I have anywhere said anything of my American friends that is untrue, or too harsh for the occasion, I regret it should have been so, and I willingly withdraw it altogether. I need not apologise for any unkind remarks that may have been made by the Governor, though most concerned, for he made none: and when they have made reparation for all the slander and misrepresentation which they have persistently heaped upon him during the last 120 years, then—we shall be quits.

It is time to bury the hatchet. Farewell.

INDEX TO VOL. II.

ACT to proscribe Loyalists, 230–2–6, 268, 337.
Adams, Ch. Justice, 14; pamphlet by J. Adams, 32; he and Lord Howe, 119, 122; on board ship, 202; anecdote, 220–9, 324; leaves France, 246; Ambassador, 312, 314–5; S. Adams, 404.
Admiralty Court for Rhode Island, 241–4, 255.
Allen, Ethan, 288.
Americans and Representation, 183.
Amherst, Sir Jeffery, 31; Lord Amherst, 78.
Apathy in public affairs, 209, 212, 213, 273, 291.
Apple tree on Rumsey tower, 265.
Apthorpe's Petition, 22; at Croydon, 97; at Bow church, 204; William, 269, 284; death, 298, 364.
Arbuthnot, Admiral, 256, 288.
Ardent, man-of-war, taken, 272–3.
Armorial Bearings, 380–2–4, 453, 471.
Army in America, 70.
Arnold taken prisoner at Quebec, 19; wounded, 20; betrayed, 23; false reports, 161.
Ashburton and the French prisoners, 267.
Auchmuty's twins, 18.
Aurora borealis, 159.
Aylesbury, 76.

BALLOONS, 396, 416.
Bancroft, Dr. 141, 144.
Bankes, Sir Joseph, 320.
Banks, Commodore, 48.
Barré, Col., 207.
Barrington, Lord, 195; retires, 228; Admiral, 280.
Battles, Naval, off Cape Fear, 91; at sea, 156, 205, 328; Byron and D'Estaigne, 280; Paul Jones and Cap. Pierson, 286; Rodney, 328, 339; East Indies, 398; on the Lakes, 116.
Battles, Military, of Brooklyn, or Long Island, 102, 122; Kingsbridge, 116, 120, 160; Fort Washington, 123–4; S. Carolina, 254; Stamford Bridge, Yorkshire, 450.
Bed of Justice—what it is, 27.
Beggar's Opera, 123.
Belcher, Ch. Justice, 61.
Berkenhout, Dr., 239.
Bernard, Sir Francis,—his son drowned, 27; at dinner, 72; taken ill, 76; in London, 141, 195; Lady Bernard's death, 208; his death, 262; anecdote, 318; portrait, 322, 438.
Black girl at Lord Mansfield's, 276.
Blackburne, Mr., 59, 71.
Blaquiere, Sir John, 258.
Bolingbroke, Lord, 118.
Bolton, Duke and Duchess of, 122, 124.
Boston evacuated, 27, 41–2–6, 253; quarrel at, 222.
Boucher, Mr., 93; his opinion of Washington, 164.
Boutineau, Mr., 205.
Boylstone family, 410.
Brattle, General, 221; Thomas, 305.
Bread at Pompeii, 307.
Bristol on fire, 129; visited, 148.
Bromley, Sir Charles, 138.
Browne, Col., 41; Judge, 249; Bill Brown, 423.

Browne, the Planner of gardens, 133.
Bruce, the Traveller, 31; Lord Bruce, 59; Col. Bruce, 89; Cap. Bruce, and the tea, 310.
Brunswick troops, 30-1-2, 74.
Buckinghamshire, Lord, appointed Lord Lieutenant of Ireland, 114.
Budget, 244.
Bull, Lieut. Governor, 163.
Burch, W., 107.
Burgoyne, General, 16, 31, 55; arrives at Quebec, 65, 73; on the Lakes, 112; dissatisfied, 117; in England, 142; at Quebec, 151; Ticonderoga, 154; his Address, 155; surrender, 169, 170–3; in England, 205–7, 210, 270.
Burial, Reflections on, 240.
Burke's Conciliatory Bill, 28; on fasting, 111; pamphlet, 118; he questions Galloway, 261; "the St. Omer's Hero," 407.
Bute, Lord, 262.
Byng, Mr., refused the Chiltern Hundreds, 307.
Byron, Admiral Lord, 219, 228, 245, 311.

CAMBRIDGE Concordance, 267.
Camden, Lord, 199.
Caner, Dr., 72–4; £100 for him, 130–1-4.
Carleton, General, in Canada, 65, 73, 112, 116; in England, 217, 411.
Carlisle, Lord, 191, 197.
Castle William destroyed, 47.
Candle Room, 224.
Celts, or palstaves, 164.
Chandler, Dr., 72; Colonel, 85–7, 121, 409, 414, 433.
Charleston, S. C., summoned, 88; attacked, 92–5.
Chatham, Lord, Inflammatory speech of, 149; views towards the Colonies, 171, 183; his illness, 198; inconsistency, 199; death, 200; funeral, 204; his wax figure, 368.
Chauncey, Dr., 424.
Chester, Colonel, 380, 451.
Chudleigh, Miss, Duchess of Kingston, 33, 34.
Church, Old North, Boston, 17.
Clarendon House in Piccadilly, 181.
Clarke family, 3, 7.
Clinton, General, 31, 84, 90, 103, 135, 177; and Howe, 180; battle, 214; returned, 225.
Coat Armour, 380-2-4, 453; Earl of Donoughmore's, 459; Col. J. Hutchinson's, 385.
Coddington, William, 461; Nathaniel, 446, 465.
Coffin, Nathaniel, 4, 90.
Cold weather, 7, 12, 14, 15, 245, 330.
Collier, Sir G., 103, 285, 298.
Commissioners at Halifax, 83, 89; to go out, 185, 191; named, 197; sailed, 202.
Commons, House of, 111, 182–5; Bills introduced, 186–8–9; confusion in, 190, 206; motion, 226; Palliser and Keppel debates, 228; Americans disloyal, 258; Lord George Gordon in, 330.
Compton, Earl of Wilmington, 3.
Conanicut Island, 17, 134, 145; Blackpoint Farm, 146, 180, 420; Cotton Farm sold, 440; Narhawana Estate, *ib.*
Conciliation tried, 181, 185.
Confiscation Acts, 230–2–6, 268, 337.
Congress and Lord Howe, 119, 122; removed to Reading, 139; debate in, 178.
Conway, General, 26, 256.
Cooke, Captain, his life and death, 319.
Cooper, Dr., of New York, 31–4, 77, 156, 337; death, 404.
Copley, the Painter, 200, 307, 407.
Cornwall, Mr., 55.
Cornwallis, Lord, at sea, 24, 72, 124; in England, 178; gone out, 201; in Council, 257; capitulates, 372.
Court, Levée, Drawing-Room, 60, 113, 141–4, 158, 160, 176–9, 202–5, 216, 222, 230-9, 247, 269, 291, 316.
Coventry, The Earl of, foretells the loss of the Colonies, 29.
Cranborne, Lord, 325.
Cranley, Lord, 60.
Crown Point, 116, 120.
Croydon, 97, 159, 284.
Cruger, Mr., 45.

Cumberland, Duke of, 200.
Czar of Russia, 114.

DALRYMPLE, Col., 16, 139.
Danbury attacked, 149, 151.
Danforth, Mr., 253.
Dartmouth, Lord, and troops in Boston, 22, 44; sends admission tickets, 34.
D. C. L. conferred, 75.
Deane, one of the Congress, 25, 140; Silas Deane and John-the-Painter, 141, 143; in Paris, 163; letter intercepted, 246.
Debates in Parliament, 25–8, 135–7, 165–6, 182, 198, 229, 262–4, 306; Mr. Byng, 307.
Deblois, Gilbert, 121.
Degrees of D.C.L., 75.
De Grey, Mr., 132; visit to, 161, 206.
De Lancey, Brigadier General, 402.
Delegates, 89, 122.
Desert, Mount, 321–3.
Deshon hanged, 311.
Deskau, Princess, at Court, 114.
D'Estaigne, Adm. Count, 214, 217; in Carolina, 313.
Dignum, the Convict, 150.
Dillon, Mr., his claims for Lord Chamberlain, 367.
Dissenters, and the Revolt, 239.
Dod, Dr., and his forgery, 134; convicted, 138; executed, 151.
Dog tax proposed, 413.
Dominica attacked, 221; surrendered, 222.
Donoughmore, Earl of, Pedigree, 457–8–9; in Tabular form, 447.
Douglas, Sir C., 129.
Douglas, Captain, and the £500, 313, 316.
Down, Jonathan, 111.
D'Oyly, Mr., 23, 55, 56, 102, 184; raving, 186.
Duels,—Lee and Laurence or Laurens, 242, 248; Fox and Adams, 298–9.
Duke of Richmond, 28; of Grafton, 258; of Newcastle, 35; of Dorset, 36; of Northumberland, 43; of Norfolk, 164; of Bolton, 124.
Dunmore, Lord, 23, 87, 93, 120.
Dutch convoying, 317.

EARTHQUAKE, 399.
Eclipse of the Moon, 85.
Eden, Governor, 87, 93.
Eden, Captain, R.N., 244.
Effingham, Lord, 29.
Eliot, Dr., 63; death, 223-4.
Ellis, Mr. Welbore, 1, 43, 57; Treasurer of the Navy, 149; opinion on affairs, 175.
Encænia at Oxford, 74, 77.

FANEUIL, Benjamin, 90.
Farmer's Letters, 229.
Fast Day, 120.
Fight on the ice, which broke, 401.
Fireship at Quebec, 73.
Fitch, Mr., King's Advocate, 94, 119, 130.
Fleet on the Lakes, 112.
Fleets in the British Channel, 271–4–8.
Flucker, Mr., 71, 82, 328; death, 391.
Forces in America, 70.
Fort Penobscot, 216, 217, 285.
Fort Washington, 123, 124.
Fortiter gerit Crucem, 385.
Foster, Colonel John, 469, 471.
Fothergill, Dr., Vice Chancellor, 75.
Fox, Charles, 137, 182, 244, 251; duel with Adams, 298; speech, 344, 347; coalition with Lord North, 397–8; lost election, 407–8, 412.
France intriguing with America, 32, 186, 210; sinks an English ship, 140; her fleet at sea, 145; war expected, 175; declared, 192–3, 222; alarm in England, 279.
Franklin, Dr. Benjamin, 66, 116, 118, 119, 122, 127; and Hume, 195; and Galloway, 237; in France, 246; writes to the papers, 248; takes lodgings, 274; his grandson, 276; he and Hutchinson, 279; correspondence, 337; his wax model, 368.
Franklin, William, 88–9, 258.
Francklin, Lieut. Governor of Nova Scotia, 132.
French opinions on the war, 209; take St. Vincent, 269.

G. G. and his misfortune, 7.
Gage, Lord, 117, 180, 227; at Furle,

214; came in warm, 317; Lady Gage's rout, 31.
Gage, General, 25.
Galloway, Lord, 225.
Galloway, Mr., 226-8; his opinion of Gen. Howe, 233; and Franklin, 237; conversation, 247, 254-9; at the Bar of the House, 261; and Lord Howe, 264; in London, 370.
Gambier, Admiral, 188, 273.
Garnier, Monsieur, with French news, 26, 92.
Garrick, David, 32; at Court, 144; death, 240; burial, 241.
Gates, General, and Lord Loudoun, 182.
Gay, the Poet, 123.
Gayton, Admiral, 220.
George the Second, 3; George the Third, 18, 20, 27, 59.
Germaine, Lord George, his character, 11; Levée, 119; house damaged by the mob, 242.
Giant at Birmingham, 352.
Gibraltar, Siege of, 335.
Goldthwaite, T., 300, 341, 414.
Goose at Michaelmas, 218.
Gordon, Lord George, 330; his ill-judged zeal, 356, 416.
Grafton, Duke of, 25; joins the Whigs, 28; at home, 116.
Grant's horse's head shot off, 152.
Graves, Admiral, 19.
Gray, Treasurer, 155.
Greene, Mr., 87, 221.
Groote, De, his death, 242.
Grotius, 242.

Habeas corpus Act, 133, 137.
Hackman shoots Miss Ray, 249; trial and execution, 251.
Haldiman, General, 159.
Halifax, Nova Scotia, 49.
Halloway, Mr., 90.
Halsell, Mr., Clerk of the House of Commons, 117.
Hancock, John, 230.
Handel Jubilee, 407.
Hardy, Admiral Sir C., 261, 279.
Harcourt, Col., captures Gen. Lee, 136.
Hardwicke, Lord, 19, 24, 31; sends tickets for Duchess of Kingston's trial, 32, 34, 38; note to Gov. H., 39; present of venison, 73; of books, 117; visit, 131, 218; chimney blown down, 238.
Harold, King of England, 449.
Harrowby, Lord, 57, 60.
Hartley's attempt at pacification, 28.
Hatch, Mr. N., 409, 412.
Heavitree, near Exeter, 432.
Heberden, Dr., 15, 43, 463.
Hely-Hutchinson—see Hutchinson.
Henry, Patrick, 98.
Hessian troops, 25-8, 30-3-4-9, 69, 73, 85, 90, 113, 136-9.
Highlanders, 70, 88-9, 90.
Hillsborough, Lord, 25, 35-6, 84, 182-6; his letter to Gov. H., 192; his political life, 201-5, 269, 277, 294-6, 325.
Holderness, Lord, 59.
Hood, Sir Samuel, 295.
Hopkins, attacks Bahama, 45-6; at Rhode Island, 130.
Hotham, Commodore, 44, 72, 90, 102.
Houghton, Sir H., 59, 241.
Howe, Lord, 33-4-9, 83, 98, 119; and Washington, 121; as Commissioner, 201; at New York, 213-4; his fleet, 217-19; returned, 220; his conduct, 222; toasted by Col. Parker, 268.
Howe, General Sir W., 63; Mrs. Howe, 69; Gen. H., 70; at Staten Island, 88, 102-5; takes Philadelphia, 162-3; his march south condemned, 169; clamour against, 172; recalled, 184; French opinion of him, 209; arrives, 211; anecdote, 247; asks enquiry, 255-6, 311, 336.
Huck, Dr., 115.
Hume, David, and Franklin, 195.
Huntingdon, Lord, 136, 171; condemns Gen. Howe, 175-7; dinner party, 179; opinion of Clinton, 296.
Hutchinson, Hely, 10, 247, 293; tabular Pedigree, 447; enlarged Pedigree, 457-8-9.
Hutchinson, Thomas, Governor; his opinion on taxing, 58; D. C. L. Degree, 74; at his History, 78, 172, 218; his house seized, 85; changes houses in London, 90; letter to the King, 112; dines at the Duke of

Bolton's, 124-6; at the temple, 141; Peggy dies, 159; goes to Sackville Street, 160; gives his Hist. to the Bp. of Rochester, 165; dined with the Archbishop, 178, 317; dinner at home, 188; nurse maid, 190; journey—recovers ring, loses wig, 210; his losses, 216; finishes his History, 218; lent it, 329; buys *Reliquæ Romanæ*, 223; Wilkins hopes H. is hanged, 228; visits Governor Johnstone, 242; letter imputed to him, 254; longs to return, 257; his father at Plymouth, 267; footman run over, 277; H. and Franklin, 279; diet, 283; his Milton estate sold, 287; his son's £500, 313; Billy's death, 342; his letters, 337; his death, 353; his burial, 356, 364; his Will, 364-5; accounts, 361; three heads of families, 377, 386, 388; prospects of returning, 420, 433; Pedigree, 446, 449; Brass to his memory, 471.

Hutchinson, Foster, 208, Note; Pedigree, 448, 470-1.

Hutchinson, Richard, of Knocklofty, 447, 457.

Hutchinson, Thomas, leaves America, 42; arrives in London, 46; visits France; 394; settles near Exeter, 432; Pedigree, 473.

Hutchinson, Elisha, 147; wife arrives, 159; writing up hill, 137.

Hutchinson, Edward (who m. Lydia Foster), 467; another Edward, 154, 375.

Hutchinson, Eliakim, and family, 22, 85, 97; Kate buried, 130; William, 158; at dinner, 172.

Hutchinson of Salem, 377.

Hutchinson of Charlestown, 386, 463.

Hutchinson, Mr., Gov. of St. Helena, 130.

Icebergs, 51.

Independence, 58, 137; voted, 229.

Indian language, 415.

Ingram, Duncan, 96.

Ireland, Lords Lieutenant of, 114; insurrection, 257; Union, 296; measures for, 306.

Jackson, Mr., 26, 76.

Jefferds, Dr., 30, 75.

Jenkinson, Mr., 187, 228.

Jersey attacked, 256-7.

Jenyns, Soame, 43, 62, 182; Mrs. Jenyns' party, 31.

Johannot family, 66, 85, 253, 292.

John-the-Painter, and fire at Portsmouth, 119, 128-9; trial, 140; account of, 141; execution, 142; his remains recently found, 143.

Johnson, Mrs., and Petition for relief, 271.

Johnstone, Governor, goes out Commissioner, 197; resigns, 219; returns, 220; his inconsistency, 225, 235; Gov. H. visits him, 242.

Jones, Paul, 259, 286, 291, 314.

Kellond, Thomas, 464, 469.

Keppel, Admiral, takes two French frigates, 210, 222; quarrel with Palliser, 228; alleged duel, 236; court-martial and acquittal, 242-3; and the Ministry, 299; his portrait, 309; his enemies, 311.

King inquisitive at Court, 20, 82.—See Court.

King's Declaration to the Irish Parliament, 18; to the Common Council, 27; Levée, 59; Royal Speech, 108-9. King in Council, 136; in conversation, 160, 262; his statue decapitated, 103-4; 167; his policy, 187; in Cheapside, 219; his portrait by West, 309; his courage, 339; his illness, 429.

King's Chapel, Service at, 18.

Kingsbridge, Battle at, 116, 120.

Kingston, Duchess of—her trial, 32-5.

Knox, Mr., 45, 66, 217, 326.

Lamb, Serjeant, his Journal, 116.

Lambert, Sir John, 401.

Learned pig, 416.

Lechmere family, 61, 71, 227.

Lee, Mr., from Philadelphia, 55.

Lee, General, in N. Carolina, 60, 177; Lee and Fort Washington, 123; taken prisoner, 136; Lee and Laurence, or Laurens, duel, 242, 248.

Lee—*Junius Americanus.*
Lee, Sir William, at Hartwell, 76.
Legge, Governor, 51, 86, 245.
Leonard, Colonel, 90, 212.
Lethieulier, Mr., 150.
Letters—abstracted, 337.
Levée, 59.—See Court.
Lexington, Affair at, 118.
Lillie, Mr., his death, 84.
Lisburne, Lord, 298, 316.
Littelton, Lord, 297.
Livingstone, Gov., nearly captured, 254.
Livius, Mr., of Quebec, 310, 318.
Lords, House of, 108–9, 198, 201, 227.
Loring, Captain, 44, 71, 155.
Lothrop, Mr., 85, 433.
Loyalists, 372, 389; estates lost, 391; Conanicut, and Eastern Lands, 392, 437; compensation, 402, 408, 421–2, 430; claims, 435; their numbers, 436.
Lyde, Mr., at Halifax, 49; Dr. Lyde, in prison, 82; at New York, 440.
Lyme, and the Duke of Monmouth, 265.

Maclean, Colonel, 93.
Mahon, Lord, in Copley's painting, 200.
Malcombe, John, 100.
Manchester, Duke of, and French Treaty, 175.
Mansfield, Lord, 116; receptions, 181; dinner, 274; house burnt, 357.
Manuscripts found, 26.
Markham, Bishop, 78.
Mason, Mr., and his claim to Laconia, 131.
Massachusetts Resolves, 204.
Mather, Mr., 90, 422.
Mauduit, Mr., 72; changes his views, 196; ship *Trident*, 202; his pamphlet, 203–4, 293.
Mauditicus, 99.
Meeting House, Old North, pulled down for fuel, 9, 17; Dr. Cooper's, and Howard's, 10.
Montagu, Admiral, 114.
Montgomery killed at Quebec, 19, 73.
Moody, Lieutenant, his career, 81.
Moon eclipsed, 86.
Morland, and Bernard, 322.
Mount Desert, 323, 438.
Mure, Hutchinson, 223.

Negroes emancipated, 274, 276.
New Brunswick constituted, 411.
Newcastle, Duke of, 35, 51.
Newport, Rhode Island, 132.
New York, threatened, 24, 98, 103; taken, 105; fired, 111.
Norfolk, Duke of, 164.
North church, 17.
North, Lord, 21; defends his measures, 29, 112; illness, and anecdote, 141; perplexities, 181; his character, 182; plan of accommodation, 185; censured, 193; resigned, 374; coalition with Fox, 397–8; censured by Mr. Macdonald, 306.
Northern Light, 159.
Northumberland, Duke of, 43; Northumberland House, 54.
Norton, Sir Fletcher, attacks Lord North, 206.

Odisse quem læseris, 272.
Oliver, Chief Justice Peter, and his Diary, 46; leaves Boston for Halifax, 48; voyage to England, 51; Falmouth, 52; journey to London, 67; at Court, 88; at the House of Lords, 109; at Oxford, 77; at Lord North's Levée, 133; at Birmingham, 203; his letters, 395, 408; house burnt, 423; his death and his descendants, 425; Peter O., 337; Daniel, 88; Brinley Sylvester, 41; Louisa, 290; Dr. Peter, 9, 42; marriage, 472; wife died, 360.
Oliver, Captain W. S., R.N., 473.
Oliver Pedigree, 427.
Oliver, Thomas, Lieut. Gov., 17, 61, 66; his salary, 83.
Ormesby, Dr., 75.
Ormond, Duke of, 181.
Otis, Mr., 232, 440.
Oxford, and D.C.L., 74, 77.

Paintings, 39.
Palliser, Admiral Sir H., 222, 228, 236 house assaulted, 242–3; court-martial, 251; acquitted, 256, 279.

Paoli, General, 179, 192, 285.
Parker, Adm. Sir Peter, 69, 74, 91, 99; at Charleston, 177.
Parker, Adm. Sir Hyde, 254, 267, 313, 319.
Parker, Adm. Sir. William, of Harburn, 475; and Lord Hood, 295, Note.
Parker, Captain Robert, drowned, 476.
Parliament, Debates in, 25, 197; opening, 109, 225; meets, 405–7.—See Debates.
Parsons, Nancy, and the Duke of G., 35.
Parrot died, 208.
Paul Jones, 259, 286, 291, 314.
Paxton, Mr., 240.
Peace with America, 372, 390.
Pedigree of the Earl of Donoughmore, 447, 458.
Pedigrees, 301, 378, 425, 449.
Pedigrees, Tabular, 381, 387, 427, 445-6-7-8.
Penobscot, 217, 290.
Penn, Governor, at Philadelphia, 56.
Pepperell, Sir William, 9, 19, 20-1-2, 44, 270; Pedigree, 301, 364, 390.
Percy, Lord, 103; arrives in England, 149; called, 180.
Perkins, Dr. Nathaniel, 94.
Perreau, Brothers, Execution of, 6.
Philadelphia taken, 163, 169.
Phips, Colonel, 129; Sir William, 465.
Pickman, Col. Ben., 392, 406–8, 411, 413.
Pitt, William, 403, 407.
Plymouth, Visit to, 267.
Polly Pecham, Actress, 123.
Pondicherry taken, 246.
Porter and sixpence, 213.
Portsmouth Dockyard fired, 119, 128.
Pownall, Governor, joins the Tories, 28, 99, 127, 170; loses wife, 134; visit of condolence, 144; correspondence, 337; death, 425.
Pownall, John, 45, 55, 230.
Pownall, Captain, R.N., 241.
Poynton, Captain, 252.
Prescot, General, captured, 156.
Press-gangs, 264.
Prevost, General, 273.
Price, Dr., and his Pamphlet, 35, 38.
Prince of Wales, 59, 76, 408.
Princess born, 36; christened, 56.
Privateers, 86-7, 131; under false colours, 262-3; captures, 316.
Putnam, Mr., Salary for, 187, 208; Colonel, 331.
Pynchon, Mr., 14.

QUAKERS hanged, 233.
Quebec, 10; assaulted, 18; assertion questioned, 24, 26; confirmed, 39, 56, 65, 85, 87, 89, 151.
Queen and Princess, 36, 114; Queen's Caudle, 162; Queen's apartments, 163.

RANDOLPH, Mr., 402.
Ranelagh, 34, 57.
Rashleigh, Mr., 196, 219; Rev. Mr. 264.
Ray, Miss, shot by Hackman, 249.
Rebel: use of the term, 20.
Rebellion, Cause of the, 53, 79, 81, 165.
Reeve, Mr., 92, 95.
Refugees, 59, 61, 83-5, 90; estates advertised, 271; propose to return, 419; losses, 429.
Representation in Parliament, 183, 332.
Reynolds, Sir Joshua, 308.
Rhode Island, 221, 225, 297; evacuated, 300.
Richmond, Duke of, 28, 198, 199, 332.
Riots and mob law, 242.
Rivington, the Printer, from New York, 26.
Robbins, Rev. Chandler, 375, 433; Nathaniel, 468.
Robertson, General, 176; R. said H. "deserves to be hanged," 177; Gov. of N. York, 248; examined before the House, 260–1.
Robertson, Dr., the Historian, 194.
Robie, Mr., from Halifax, 16.
Robinson, Mr., of the Treasury, 118.
Rockingham Ministry, 31; his Lordship's death, 289.
Rodney, Adm. Sir G., 248; sailed, 314; his captures, 328, 339, 343.
Ross, Dr., new Bishop of Exeter, 176.
Royall, Mr., 95.
Rumford, Count, 337, 344, 404.
Russian Lady at Court, 113.

SABATIER, Mr. and Mrs., 434, 439.
Sandwich, Lord, and Miss Ray, 249.
Sanford, Grizel, her American estates, 143; lodging, 363.
Sanford, Peleg, 441.
Saratoga, 173, 198; Convention of, 202.
Saye, Lady, and her head-dress, 276.
Scotch and Irish sold for slaves, 416.
Servants' fees, 218.
Sewall family, 66, 224, 264, 266.
Sheep on the Downs, 68, 107.
Shelburne, Lord and Lady, 294.
Shuldham, Admiral, 14, 16, 47, 48, 85, 136; Lord Shuldham, 139; at Plymouth, 267.
Sidmouth, 265.
Silvester, Richard, 228.
Slavery, 416.
Slaves emancipated, 274.
Sloane, Sir Hans, 327.
Solander, Dr., 320.
South Carolina expedition, 95.
Spain and America, 196; declares war with England, 260, 329.
Sparhawk family, 44, 61.
Spartan, at Oxford, 76.
Stamp Act, MS. referring to, 26, 58.
Stamp Master, and Franklin, 116.
Stanley, Mr., 325-6-9.
Startin, Mrs., 403, 406, 412.
Statue of the King at New York, 104; head of 167.
Sterling, Lord (so called), 102; decapitated the King's Statue, 104, 167.
Stewart, the Architect, &c., 244.
Stormont, Lord, 97, 193, 292.
Strachey, Mr., M.P., 33, 39.
Strahan, M.P., the Printer, 118, 246, 324-5.
Suffolk, Lord, 245.
Suffrage, Universal, 332.
Sullivan, General, 122, 180.
Sutton, Sir R., 259; and Keppel, 299.

TABULAR Pedigrees, 381, 387, 445-6-7-8.
Talbot, Lord, 114.
Tankard, 453.
Tarpley, Dr., 73.
Tarring and feathering, 410, 412.
Taxing America, 58, 246.
Tea destroyed, 228, 310; price of, 362, 364, 418.
Temperature, 86-7, 245.
Temple, Lord, 29, 190; death of, by accident, 283, 416.
Temple, John, 238, 269, 270, 273, 293, 399.
Thereabouts—abouts there, 316.
Thompson, Benjamin, Count Rumford, 337, 344, 404.
Thurlow, Lord Chancellor, 208.
Ticonderoga, 115, 117, 120; taken, 154, 157.
Timmins, Mrs., 424.
Townshend, Lord, 116, 119; at Raynham, 161; in London, and shews head of the King's statue, 167; called, 179; angry, 186; in a frenzy, 188.
Treason explained, 20.
Trial of the Duchess of Kingston, 33.
Troops blockading Boston, 1; in Boston, 22; proposal to remove troops, 23; going to America, 6, 8, 70; foreign troops, 28-9, 113, 231, 249.
Troutbeck, Mr., 17, 72.
Tryon, Gov. of N. York, 55; promoted, 151.
Tucker, Dean, 18.
Tylney Hall, Mr. Ellis's residence, 1, 122.

VAN SCHAACK, Peter, 293.
Vane, Mr., 207, 461.
Vardell, Mr., 45.
Vassall family, 61, 66, 129, 248, 430.
Vaughan, General, 152, 169; at Charleston, 177; at dinner, 298, 305; leaves, 311.
Venison, 172, 213.
Vessel and cargo taken, 32.
Vindication printed, 7.

WALDO, Frank, death, 409.
Wallace, Sir James, 318, 340.
Walpole, Sir R., 2; tired of books, 178; quoted, 250, 356.
Walsingham, Lord, 435.
Walter, Mr., 85.
Wanton, Governor, 134, 145.

Water-works, London-bridge, burnt, 292.
Washington, General, 98, 102-3; at New York, 105; at Kingsbridge, 111, 116; and Lord Howe, 121; promoted, 145; reported dead, 148.
Watson, Mr. Brook, Garlick Hill, 15, 32, 120, 160, 412.
Wedderburne, Mr., 206, 208.
Weekes, Mr., 229, 232.
Welsted, Rev. Mr., 369.
Wentworth, Paul, 129, 163; Sir Charles, 130; Governor, 192.
West, the Painter, 309.
Westminster Abbey, 368.
Weymouth, Lord, 161.
Whately, and the Letters, 118.
Wilkes loses his Election for Chamberlain, 21.
Willard, Abel, 85, 232, 270, 372, 412.
William, Prince, and King, 260.
Willingham, Sir Clifford, 93.
Wills and Administrations, 365.
Winchendon, and Sir F. Bernard, 321.
Winslow, General, 57; Isaac, 82, 134; Joshua, 298; Pelham, 372.
Winthrop leaves England, 148, 195, 461.
Wool, English and American, 68.
Woolridge, Alderman, 93, 327.
Wright, Sir James, 72, 170.
Wright, Mrs., the Modeller in wax, 368.

Yorke, Charles, 179.

THE END.